Beginning Visual C#®

Karli Watson
David Espinosa
Zach Greenvoss
Christian Nagel
Jacob Hammer Pedersen
Jon D. Reid
Matthew Reynolds
Morgan Skinner
Eric White

wrox
Programmer to Programmer

Beginning Visual C#®

Published by
Wiley Publishing, Inc.
10475 Crosspoint Boulevard
Indianapolis, IN 46256
www.wiley.com

Copyright © 2003 by Wiley Publishing, Inc., Indianapolis, Indiana

Published simultaneously in Canada

Library of Congress Card Number: 2003107071

ISBN: 0-7645-4382-2

Manufactured in the United States of America

10 9 8 7 6 5 4 3 2 1

1M/RQ/QW/QT/IN

Trademark Acknowledgments

Wrox has endeavored to provide trademark information about all the companies and products mentioned in this book by the appropriate use of capitals. However, Wrox cannot guarantee the accuracy of this information.

Credits

Authors
Karli Watson
David Espinosa
Zach Greenvoss
Christian Nagel
Jacob Hammer Pedersen
Jon D. Reid
Matthew Reynolds
Morgan Skinner
Eric White

Authors (1st Edition)
Marco Bellinaso
Ollie Cornes

Commissioning Editor (1st Edition)
Julian Skinner

Managing Editor
Louay Fatoohi

Technical Editors
Mankee Cheng
Matthew Cumberlidge
Douglas Paterson

Project Manager
Claire Robinson

Author Agent
Charlotte Smith

Production Coordinator
Sarah Hall

Cover
Natalie O'Donnell

Indexers
Andrew Criddle
Michael Brinkman(1st Edition)
Fiona Murray (1st Edition)

Technical Reviewers
Cristian Darie
Karli Watson

Technical Reviewers (1st Edition)
Kenneth Avellino
Ramesh Balaji
Christopher Blexrud
Brandon Bohling
Richard Bonneau
Paul Brazdzionis
Beth Breidenbach
Andreas Christiansen
Steve Danielson
Scott Hanselman
Ben Hickman
Mark Horner
Deepak Kumer
Ron Landers
Don Lee
Shaun Mcaravey
Angela Mallet
Jason Montgomery
Johan Normén
Aruna Panangipally
Phil Powers-DeGeorge
Jawaharlal Puvvala
Matthew Reynolds
Scott Robertson
Kristy Saunders
Keyur Shah
Helmut Watson
Donald Xie

Proofreaders
Fiona Berryman
Chris Smith

About the Authors

Karli Watson

Karli Watson is an in-house author for Wrox Press with a penchant for multicolored clothing. He started out with the intention of becoming a world famous nanotechnologist, so perhaps one day you might recognize his name as he receives a Nobel Prize. For now, though, Karli's computing interests include all things mobile, and upcoming technologies such as C#. He can often be found preaching about these technologies at conferences, as well as after hours in drinking establishments. Karli is also a snowboarding enthusiast, and wishes he had a cat.

> *Thanks go to the Wrox team, both for helping me get into writing, and then dealing with the results when I started. Finally, and most importantly, thanks to my wife, Donna, for continuing to put up with me.*

David Espinosa

David Espinosa is a Senior Programmer and owner of Espinosa Consulting. Born in Barcelona, Spain, David moved to the United States at an early age. He attended the University of Nevada and received a Bachelor of Arts degree in Political Science.

David concentrates on Microsoft technologies and tools. In 1999, he worked with Microsoft as a Lead Author for the Desktop Visual FoxPro Certification Exam. Recently, David has been focusing on e-commerce and data integration solutions and works for the a manufacturing company based out of Reno, Nevada.

> *I would like to dedicate my work to Mom and Dad, who sacrificed so much so I could have a better chance.*
>
> *I would also like to dedicate my work to my three favorite girls in the world: Cynthia, Jayme, and Emily. Thank you for all your support.*

Zach Greenvoss

Zach Greenvoss, MCSD is a Senior Consultant with Magenic Technologies, a Microsoft Gold Certified consulting firm in Northern California. He specializes in middle-tier architecture and implementation, utilizing various technologies including COM+, MSMQ, BizTalk, and XML. Before Magenic, Zach worked at the Defense Manpower Data Center in Monterey California, where he developed client-server applications for the Department of Defense. Zach and his wife Amanda enjoy globetrotting, caving, gaming, and playing with their two cats. He can be reached at zachg@magenic.com.

> *I would like to thank my wife Amanda for all her patience, love, and understanding of the time required to both work and write. I would also like to thank Kay Rigg for his mentorship and guidance: without you I would not be where I am today. Finally, I am proud to say that I am a CSU Monterey Bay graduate – Go Otters!*

Christian Nagel

Christian Nagel works as a trainer and consultant for Global Knowledge, the largest independent information technology training provider. Christian started his computing career with PDP 11 and VAX/VMS platforms. Since then he has used a variety of languages and platforms, including Pascal, C, X-Windows, Motif, C++, Java, COM/ATL, COM+, and currently C# and .NET. With his profound knowledge of Microsoft technologies – he's certified as Microsoft Certified Trainer (MCT), Solution Developer (MCSD), and Systems Engineer (MCSE) – he enjoys teaching others programming and architecting distributed solutions. As founder of the .NET User Group Austria and as MSDN Regional Director he is speaker at European conferences (TechEd, VCDC), and is contacted by many developers for coaching, consulting, and teaching customized courses and boot camps. You will find Christian's web site at http://christian.nagel.net/.

I would like to thank the people at Wrox who got me started writing books, and Christian Seidler who supports my activities at Global Knowledge. Special thanks are also sent to the people at Microsoft, primarily to Alex Holy in Vienna for his organization of Visual Studio events and for his support of the .NET user community. Finally, and most importantly, I would like to thank my wife Elisabeth for her love and support.

Jacob Hammer Pedersen

Jacob Hammer Pedersen is a systems developer at ICL Invia – a member of the Fujitsu Group.

He pretty much started programming when he was able to spell the word 'BASIC', which, incidentally is the language he's primarily using today. He started programming the PC in the early 90s, using Pascal, but soon changed his focus to C++, which still holds his interest. In the mid 90s his focus changed again, this time to Visual Basic. In the summer of 2000 he discovered C# and has been happily exploring it ever since.

Primarily working on the Microsoft platforms, other expertise includes MS Office development, COM, COM+ and Visual Basic .Net.

A Danish citizen, he works and lives in Aarhus, Denmark.

Jon D. Reid

Jon is the Chief Technology Officer for Micro Data Base Systems, Inc. (www.mdbs.com), maker of the TITANIUM Database Engine and GURU Expert System tool. His primary current activity is developing database tools for the Microsoft .NET environment. He was editor for the C++ and Object Query Language (OQL) components of the Object Data Management Group (ODMG) standard, and has co-authored other Wrox titles including *ADO.NET Programmer's Reference* and *Professional SQL Server 2000 XML*. When not working, writing, or bicycling, he enjoys spending time with his wife and two young sons. Jon would like to thank his family and the team at Wrox for their support and encouragement.

Matthew Reynolds

After working with Wrox Press on a number of projects since 1999, Matthew is now an in-house author for Wrox Press writing about and working with virtually all aspects of Microsoft .NET. He's also a regular contributor to Wrox's ASPToday, C#Today and Web Services Architect. He lives and works in North London and can be reached on matthewr@wrox.com.

Thanks very much to the following in their support and assistance in writing this book: Len, Edward, Darren, Alex, Jo, Tim, Clare, Martin, Niahm, Tom, Ollie, Amir, Gretchen, Ben, Brandon, Denise, Rob, Waggy, Mark, Elaine, James, Zoe, Faye, and Sarah. And, also thanks to my new friends at Wrox, which include Charlotte, Laura, Karli, Dom S, Dom L, Ian, Kate, Joy, Pete, Helen, John, Dave, Adam, Craig, Jake, Julian, and Paul.

Morgan Skinner

I started my computing at a tender age on a ZX80 at school, where I was underwhelmed by some code my teacher had put together and decided I could do better in assembly language. After getting hooked on Z80 (much better than those paltry three registers in 6502 land!) I graduated through the school ZX81s to my own ZX Spectrum.

Since then I've used all sorts of languages and platforms, including VAX Macro Assembler (way cool!), Pascal, Modula2, Smalltalk, x86 assembly language, PowerBuilder, C/C++, Visual Basic, and currently C#. I've managed to stay in the same company for nearly 12 years, largely down to the diversity of the job and a good working environment.

In my spare time I'm a bit of a DIY nut, I spend lots of money on bicycles, and 'relax' by fighting weeds on my allotment.

I can be reached by e-mail at morgan.skinner@totalise.co.uk.

Eric White

Eric White is an independent consultant, specializing in managing offshore development with some hotshot developers in India. Having written well over a million lines of code, Eric has over 20 years experience in building Management Information Systems, accounting systems, and other types of fat-client and n-tier database applications. Eric has particular interest in Object-Oriented design methodologies, including use case analysis, UML, and design patterns. After years of working with too many varieties of technologies to list, he is currently specializing in C#, VB.NET, ASP.NET, ADO.NET, XML, COM+, GDI+, SQL Server, and other Microsoft technologies.

He loves meeting new people and traveling to far-flung places, and is equally at ease wandering around the streets of Bangalore, London, and San Francisco. When he is not in front of a computer, he loves hiking in the mountains of Colorado and India. He can be reached at eric@ericwhite.com.

Table of Contents

Table of Contents

Table of Contents

Table of Contents

Table of Contents

Table of Contents

Table of Contents

Table of Contents

Introduction

Why should I learn C#? If you've bought this book, you've probably answered that question for yourself anyway, but it's worth reiterating. C# is Microsoft's brand new language, designed for its brand new platform, the .NET Framework. As such, C# is likely to be the language of choice for developing applications in the Microsoft world. That alone would make C# a great choice as a first language to learn. But, perhaps more importantly, C# is a very elegantly designed language, which encourages good programming practice (in particular with regard to object-oriented programming). C# is descended directly from the powerful but complex C++ language, and inherits most of the power without the complexity. C# has also been deeply influenced by other languages, including Java and Delphi, and its fans believe that it has been able to take the best of these languages – while avoiding their mistakes.

This book has been designed to teach you C# from first principles, without assuming any prior programming experience. We'll give you a thorough grounding in the syntax of the C# language itself, and then we'll look at the most common different types of applications you can build with C# – Windows applications, ASP.NET web applications, and web services. It's important to stress from the outset that C# programming cannot be separated from .NET programming (in fact, the C# compiler comes as part of the .NET Framework), and everything you do in C# will rely very heavily on the .NET Framework. Therefore, this book goes beyond the mere syntax of the C# language and shows you how to use the .NET classes from within C# to build real applications. As a result, once you've learned C#, you won't have too much difficulty picking up other .NET languages, such as Visual Basic .NET or Managed C++.

Who Is This Book For?

This book is aimed at relatively inexperienced programmers who want to learn how to build applications using C#. Developers who have a little experience with earlier languages such as Visual Basic will also find this book helpful as a hands-on tutorial to C#. This book is for everyone who's tired of C# books that assume you've got ten-plus years' experience of writing C++ programs!

> This is a Wrox *Beginning...* series book, so we will aim to teach you everything you need to know from scratch. If you already have experience of programming in C++, VB, or Java, you may be more comfortable starting at a somewhat quicker pace with the natural follow-up title *Professional C# 2nd Edition* (Wrox Press, ISBN 1-86100-704-3).

This book will be ideal for two types of beginner:

❑ You're a **beginner to programming** and you've chosen C# as your first language. As we said earlier, C# is an excellent language to learn programming through, and this book will help you through the challenge of learning some strange new concepts!

❑ You have some experience programming in another language, but you're a **beginner to .NET programming**. .NET represents a revolution in programming concepts, and the fundamental importance of object-oriented programming (OOP) to .NET can be confusing if you're not familiar with this technique. If you're coming to C# from a language which doesn't support (or only partially supports) OOP, you will appreciate the entire section dedicated to OOP in this book.

What Does This Book Cover?

This book was written using Version 1.0 of the .NET Framework, released in January 2002, and Version 1.0 of Visual Studio .NET, released in February 2002. These versions are the release versions of these products, and no major changes are expected in the near future.

The book is divided into seven main sections:

Getting Started

In the first two chapters we quickly introduce the major concepts you need to understand before writing a C# application, and then go on to create a very simple C# program using Visual Studio .NET to do most of the hard work for us.

C# Language Basics

Chapters 3 through 7 introduce the basic building blocks of the C# language. This section looks at how we store data in C# variables, how we control the flow of our program with conditional branches and loops, and how we structure code with functions.

Programming with Objects

Objects and the principles of object-oriented programming (OOP) play a fundamental role in C#, so Chapters 8 through 12 will introduce the notion of OOP and the philosophy behind it, and look at how we use objects within our C# code.

Working with Windows Forms

The first sections concentrate mostly on creating simple console applications in order to give you a thorough grounding in the C# language itself. In this section, we go beyond those to look in detail at how we create real Windows applications in C#.

Programming on the .NET Framework

As already mentioned, almost everything we do in C# is totally dependent on the .NET Framework. This section looks at some important topics where we need to use classes from the .NET Framework, including accessing databases and working with files on the local machine or network. We also take a more detailed look at two features specific to .NET programming – assemblies (the actual unit of deployment of a .NET program), and attributes (a feature of .NET that allows us to provide additional information about parts of our program).

C# and the Web

Once we've come so far, we'll take a quick look at a whole new topic, but one that's integral to the whole idea of the .NET Framework – programming for the Internet. In this last section of the book we look at ASP.NET and web services. ASP.NET allows us to write dynamic web pages in C#, and web services enable applications to exchange information across the Internet.

> Most of the chapters in the book have a series of exercises at the end, to help you as you learn C#. The answers to these exercises can be found on the P2P web site at http://p2p.wrox.com. We'll tell you how to register for P2P at the end of this introduction.

What Do I Need to Use This Book?

Obviously, the most important thing you need to write C# programs is the C# compiler itself. This comes with the .NET Framework SDK, which can be downloaded from Microsoft's site the following URL:

```
http://msdn.microsoft.com/downloads/default.asp?URL=/code
          /sample.asp?url=/MSDN-FILES/027/000/976/msdncompositedoc.xml
```

This is the current link, but may be subject to change. (We've broken the link up in two lines here for formatting purposes – the URL should be entered as one continuous string). Be warned that this currently weighs in at a hefty 131 MB, so it will take a while to download! This runs on Windows 2000, Windows XP, and Windows NT4, and contains all you need to write all types of C# applications. A minimal version of the .NET Framework can be installed on Windows 95, 98, and ME, but this installation does not include many of the tools you will need.

However, in this book we will be making heavy use of the Visual Studio .NET development environment, which simplifies writing C# code in many ways, but is particularly useful for writing Windows applications because it contains a visual form designer. If you are not using Visual Studio .NET, then you will not be able to get full value from this book.

Version 1.0 of Visual Studio .NET is available in three editions (Professional, Enterprise Developer, and Enterprise Architect), any of which will do for the code in this book. Full information is available at http://msdn.microsoft.com/vstudio/, including the system requirements. Like the .NET Framework SDK, Visual Studio.NET also runs on Windows 2000, XP, and NT4.

Alternatively, and if you are on a tighter budget, you might like to check out Microsoft Visual C# .NET Standard Edition, a C# only developer environment has many of the features of Visual Studio .NET – but not all of them. Because of the feature limitations of Visual C# .NET Standard Edition compared to Visual Studio .NET, not every aspect of the book can be used from Visual C# .NET Standard Edition, and we've highlighted these areas. If you are using Visual C# .NET Standard Edition, remember that the C# compiler has not been restricted – this is separate from the development environment – it is only features of the development environment that are limited.

> This book is intended for users of Visual Studio .NET or Visual C# .NET Standard Edition.

Conventions

We've used a number of different styles of text and layout in this book to help differentiate between the different kinds of information. Here are examples of the styles we used and an explanation of what they mean.

Code has several styles. If it's a word that we're talking about in the text – for example, when discussing a `for (...)` loop, it's in this font. If it's a block of code that can be typed as a program and run, then it's also in a gray box:

```
for (int i=0; i<10; i++)
{
    Console.WriteLine(i);
}
```

Sometimes we'll see code in a mixture of styles, like this:

```
for (int i=0; i<10; i++)
{
    Console.Write("The next number is: ");
    Console.WriteLine(i);
}
```

In cases like this, the code with a white background is code we are already familiar with; the line highlighted in gray is a new addition to the code since we last looked at it.

Advice, hints, and background information comes in this type of font.

> **Important pieces of information come in boxes like this.**

Bullets appear indented, with each new bullet marked as follows:

❑ **Important words** are in a bold type font.

❑ Words that appear on the screen, or in menus like the File or Window, are in a similar font to the one you would see on a Windows desktop.

❑ Keys that you press on the keyboard like *Ctrl* and *Enter*, are in italics.

Customer Support

We always value hearing from our readers, and we want to know what you think about this book: what you liked, what you didn't like, and what you think we can do better next time. You can send us your comments, either by returning the reply card in the back of the book, or by e-mail to feedback@wrox.com. Please be sure to mention the book title in your message.

How to Download the Sample Code for the Book

When you visit the Wrox site, http://www.wrox.com/, simply locate the title through our Search facility or by using one of the title lists. Click on Download in the Code column, or on Download Code on the book's detail page.

When you click to download the code for this book, you are presented with a page with three options:

- ❑ If you are already a member of the Wrox Developer Community (if you have already registered on ASPToday, C#Today, or Wroxbase), you can log in with your usual username and password combination to receive your code.

- ❑ If you are not already a member, you are asked if you would like to register for free code downloads. In addition you will also be able to download several free articles from Wrox Press. Registering will allow us to keep you informed about updates and new editions of this book.

- ❑ The third option is to bypass registration completely and simply download the code.

Registration for code download is not mandatory for this book, but should you wish to register for your code download, your details will not be passed to any third party. For more details, you may wish to view our terms and conditions, which are linked from the download page.

Once you reach the code download section, you will find that the files that are available for download from our site have been archived using WinZip. When you have saved the files to a folder on your hard drive, you will need to extract the files using a de-compression program such as WinZip or PKUnzip. When you extract the files, the code is usually extracted into chapter folders. When you start the extraction process, ensure your software (WinZip, PKUnzip, etc.) is set to use folder names.

Errata

We've made every effort to make sure that there are no errors in the text or in the code. However, no one is perfect and mistakes do occur. If you find an error in one of our books, like a spelling mistake or a faulty piece of code, we would be very grateful for feedback. By sending in errata you may save another reader hours of frustration, and of course, you will be helping us provide even higher quality information. Simply e-mail the information to support@wrox.com, where your information will be checked and, if correct, posted to the errata page for that title, or used in subsequent editions of the book.

To find errata on the web site, go to http://www.wrox.com/, and simply locate the title through our Advanced Search or title list. Click on the Book Errata link, which is below the cover graphic on the book's detail page.

E-mail Support

If you wish to directly query a problem in the book with an expert who knows the book in detail then e-mail support@wrox.com, with the title of the book and the last four numbers of the ISBN in the subject field of the e-mail. A typical e-mail should include the following things:

- ❑ The **title of the book, last four digits of the ISBN (7582),** and **page number** of the problem in the Subject field

❑ Your **name**, **contact information**, and the **problem** in the body of the message

We **won't** send you junk mail. We need the details to save your time and ours. When you send an e-mail message, it will go through the following chain of support:

❑ Customer Support – Your message is delivered to our customer support staff, who are the first people to read it. They have files on most frequently asked questions and will answer anything general about the book or the web site immediately.

❑ Editorial – Deeper queries are forwarded to the technical editor responsible for that book. They have experience with the programming language or particular product, and are able to answer detailed technical questions on the subject.

❑ The Authors – Finally, in the unlikely event that the editor cannot answer your problem, they will forward the request to the author. We do try to protect the author from any distractions to their writing; however, we are quite happy to forward specific requests to them. All Wrox authors help with the support on their books. They will e-mail the customer and the editor with their response, and again all readers should benefit.

The Wrox Support process can only offer support to issues that are directly pertinent to the content of our published title. Support for questions that fall outside the scope of normal book support, is provided via the community lists of our http://p2p.wrox.com/ forum.

p2p.wrox.com

For author and peer discussion join the P2P mailing lists. Our unique system provides **programmer to programmer™** contact on mailing lists, forums, and newsgroups, all in addition to our one-to-one e-mail support system. If you post a query to P2P, you can be confident that it is being examined by the many Wrox authors and other industry experts who are present on our mailing lists. At p2p.wrox.com you will find a number of different lists that will help you, not only while you read this book, but also as you develop your own applications. Particularly appropriate to this book are the beginning_c_sharp and c_sharp (for more advanced discussion) lists in the .NET category of the web site.

To subscribe to a mailing list just follow these steps:

1. Go to http://p2p.wrox.com/

2. Choose the appropriate category from the left menu bar

3. Click on the mailing list you wish to join

4. Follow the instructions to subscribe and fill in your e-mail address and password

5. Reply to the confirmation e-mail you receive

6. Use the subscription manager to join more lists and set your e-mail preferences

Why This System Offers the Best Support

You can choose to join the mailing lists or you can receive them as a weekly digest. If you don't have the time, or facilities, to receive the mailing list, then you can search our online archives. Junk and spam mails are deleted, and your own e-mail address is protected by the unique Lyris system. Queries about joining or leaving lists, and any other general queries about lists, should be sent to listsupport@p2p.wrox.com.

Exercise Answers

The answers to the exercises in this book can also be found on the P2P web site. To view these, you will need to register for the **Beginning C#** exercises discussion list. Once you've registered with P2P follow these steps:

1. Click on the Exercises link on the P2P home page (in the list of Categories on the left-hand side)

2. Enter your e-mail address to log in to P2P.

3. Select Beginning C# (csharp_beginners_exercises) from the Subscribe to an exercises discussion list textbox, and click the Subscribe button next to it.

4. Enter and confirm a password to use for this list (or leave these boxes blank if you don't want to use a password) and select the subscription type you want (message by message, daily digest, etc.), and click on Subscribe.

5. You will now be sent a confirmation e-mail; reply to this e-mail to confirm your subscription, and P2P will now send another e-mail to confirm that you are subscribed to the list.

6. Return to the Exercises page (you may need to log in again), and click on the csharp_beginners_exercises link.

7. You will now be presented with a list of all the chapters with exercises, and you can click on any of the chapter names to view the exercises for that chapter. For each exercise, there is a link that will take you straight to the answer!

Introducing C#

Welcome to the first chapter of the first section of this book. Over the course of this section we'll be taking a look at the basic knowledge required to get up and running. In this first chapter we'll be looking at an overview of C# and the .NET Framework, and we'll consider what these technologies are, the motivation behind using them, and how they relate to each other.

We'll start with a general discussion of the .NET Framework. This is a new technology, and contains many concepts that are tricky to get to grips with at first (mainly because the Framework introduces a "new way of doing things" to application development). This means that the discussion will, by necessity, cover many new concepts in a short space of time. However, a quick look at the basics is essential to understand how to program in C#, so this is a necessary evil. Later on in the book we'll revisit many of the topics covered here in more detail.

After this discussion, we'll move on to a simple description of C# itself, including its origins and similarities to C++.

Finally, we'll look at the main tool that will be used throughout this book: Visual Studio .NET (VS).

What is the .NET Framework?

The .NET Framework is a new and revolutionary platform created by Microsoft for developing applications.

The most interesting thing about this statement is how vague I've been – but there are good reasons for this. For a start, note that I didn't say "developing applications on the Windows operating system". Although the first release of the .NET Framework runs on the Windows operating system, future plans include versions that will work on others, such as FreeBSD, Linux, Macintosh, and even personal digital assistant (PDA) class devices. One of the key motivational forces behind this technology is its intention as a means of integrating disparate operating systems.

In addition, the definition of the .NET Framework given above includes no restriction on the type of applications that are possible. This is because there is no restriction – the .NET Framework allows the creation of Windows applications, web applications, web services, and pretty much anything else you can think of.

The .NET Framework has been designed such that it can be used from any language. This includes the subject of this book, C#, as well as C++, Visual Basic, JScript, and even older languages such as COBOL. In order for this to work, .NET-specific versions of these languages have also appeared: Managed C++, Visual Basic .NET, JScript .NET, J#, and so on – and more are being released all the time. Not only do all of these have access to the .NET Framework, they can also communicate with each other. It is perfectly possible for C# developers to make use of code written by Visual Basic .NET programmers, and vice versa.

All of this provides a hitherto unthinkable level of versatility, and is part of what makes using the .NET Framework such an attractive prospect.

What's in the .NET Framework?

The .NET Framework consists primarily of a gigantic library of code that we use from our client languages (such as C#) using object-oriented programming (OOP) techniques. This library is categorized into different modules – we use portions of it depending on the results we want to achieve. For example, one module contains the building blocks for Windows applications, another for network programming, and another for web development. Some modules are divided into more specific sub-modules, such as a module for building web services within the module for web development.

The intention here is that different operating systems may support some or all of these modules, depending on their characteristics. A PDA, for example, would include support for all the core .NET functionality, but is unlikely to require some of the more esoteric modules.

Part of the .NET Framework library defines some basic **types**. A type is a representation of data, and specifying some of the most fundamental of these (such as "a 32-bit signed integer") facilitates interoperability between languages using the .NET Framework. This is called the **Common Type System** (**CTS**).

As well as supplying this library, the framework also includes the .NET **Common Language Runtime** (**CLR**), which is responsible for maintaining the execution of all applications developed using the .NET library.

How do I Write Applications using the .NET Framework?

Writing an application using the .NET Framework means writing code (using any of the languages that support the framework) using the .NET code library. In this book we'll be using VS for our development, which is a powerful integrated development environment that supports C# (as well as managed and unmanaged C++, Visual Basic .NET, and some others). The advantage of this environment is the ease with which .NET features may be integrated into our code. The code that we will create will be entirely C#, but will use the .NET Framework throughout, and we'll make use of the additional tools in VS where necessary.

In order for C# code to execute it must be converted into a language that the target operating system understands, known as **native** code. This conversion is called **compiling** code, an act that is performed by a **compiler**. Under the .NET Framework, however, this is a two-stage process.

MSIL and JIT

When we compile code that uses the .NET Framework library, we don't immediately create operating system-specific native code. Instead, we compile our code into **Microsoft Intermediate Language** (**MSIL**) code. This code isn't specific to any operating system, and isn't specific to C#. Other .NET languages – for example, Visual Basic .NET – also compile to this language as a first stage. This compilation step is carried out by VS when we use it to develop C# applications.

Obviously, in order to execute an application more work is necessary. This is the job of a **Just-In-Time** (**JIT**) compiler, which compiles MSIL into native code that is specific to the OS and machine architecture being targeted. Only at this point can the OS execute the application. The "just-in-time" part of the name here reflects the fact that MSIL code is only compiled as and when it is needed.

In the past it has often been necessary to compile your code into several applications, each of which targets a specific operating system and CPU architecture. Often, this was a form of optimization (in order to get code to run faster on an AMD chipset, for example), but at times it was critical (for applications to work on both Win9x and WinNT/2000 environments, for example). This is now unnecessary, as JIT compilers (as their name suggests) use MSIL code, which is independent of the machine, operating system, and CPU. Several JIT compilers exist, each targeting a different architecture, and the appropriate one will be used to create the native code required.

The beauty of all this is that it requires a lot less work on our part – in fact we can just forget about system-dependent details, and concentrate on the more interesting functionality of our code.

Assemblies

When we compile an application, the MSIL code created is stored in an **assembly**. Assemblies include both executable application files that we can run directly from Windows without the need for any other programs (these have a .exe file extension), and libraries for use by other applications (which have a .dll extension).

As well as containing MSIL, assemblies also contain **meta** information (that is, information about the information contained in the assembly, also known as **metadata**) and optional **resources** (additional data used by the MSIL, such as sound files and pictures). The meta information allows assemblies to be fully self-descriptive. We need no other information in order to use an assembly, meaning that we avoid situations such as failing to add required data to the system registry and so on, which was often a problem when developing using other platforms.

This means that deploying applications is often as simple as copying the files into a directory on a remote computer. Since no additional information is required on the target systems, we can just run an executable file from this directory and (assuming the .NET CLR is installed) away we go.

Of course, we won't necessarily want to include everything required to run an application in one place. We might write some code that performs tasks required by multiple applications. In situations like this, it is often useful to place this reusable code in a place accessible to all applications. In the .NET Framework, this is the **Global Assembly Cache** (**GAC**). Placing code in this cache is simple – we just place the assembly containing the code in the directory containing this cache.

Managed Code

The role of the CLR doesn't end once we have compiled our code to MSIL and a JIT compiler has compiled this to native code. Code written using the .NET Framework is **managed** when it is executed (this stage is usually referred to as being at "**runtime**"). This means that the CLR looks after our applications, by managing memory, handling security, allowing cross-language debugging, and so on. By contrast, applications that do not run under the control of the CLR are said to be **unmanaged** and certain languages such as C++ can be used to write such applications, that, for example, access low-level functions of the operating system. However, in C# we can only write code that runs in a managed environment. We will make use of the managed features of the CLR and allow .NET itself to handle any interaction with the operating system.

Garbage Collection

One of the most important features of managed code is the concept of **garbage collection**. This is the .NET method of making sure that the memory used by an application is freed up completely when the application is no longer in use. Prior to .NET this has mostly been the responsibility of programmers, and a few simple errors in code could result in large blocks of memory mysteriously disappearing as a result of being allocated to the wrong place in memory. This usually meant a progressive slowdown of your computer followed by a system crash.

.NET garbage collection works by inspecting the memory of your computer every so often, and removing anything from it that is no longer needed. There is no set timeframe for this, it might happen thousands of times a second, once every few seconds, or whenever, but you can rest assured that it will happen.

There are some implications for programmers here. Since this work is done for you at an unpredictable time applications have to be designed with this in mind. Code that requires a lot of memory to run should tidy itself up rather than waiting for garbage collection to happen, but this isn't anything like as tricky as it sounds.

Fitting it Together

Before moving on, let's summarize the steps required to create a .NET application as discussed above:

1. Application code is written using a .NET-compatible language such as C#:

2. This code is compiled into MSIL, which is stored in an assembly:

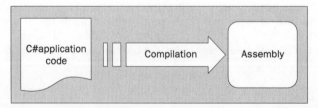

3. When this code is executed (either in its own right if it is an executable, or when it is used from other code) it must first be compiled into native code using a JIT compiler:

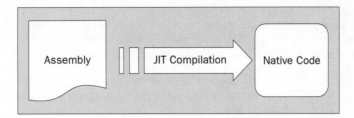

4. The native code is executed in the context of the managed CLR, along with any other running applications or processes:

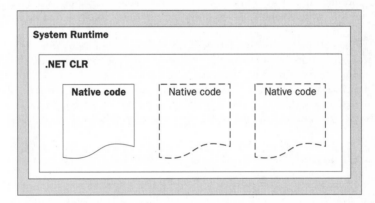

Linking

There is one additional point to note concerning the above process. The C# code that compiles into MSIL in step 2 needn't be contained in a single file. It is possible to split application code across multiple source code files, which are then compiled together into a single assembly. This process is known as **linking**, and is extremely useful. The reason for this is that it is far easier to work with several smaller files that one enormous one. You can separate out logically related code into an individual file, so that it can be worked on independently, and then practically forgotten about when completed. This also makes it much easier to locate specific pieces of code when you need them, and enables teams of developers to divide up the programming burden into manageable chunks, where individuals can "check out" pieces of code to work on without risking damage to otherwise satisfactory sections, or sections that other people are working on.

What is C#?

C#, as mentioned above, is one of the languages that can be used to create applications that will run in the .NET CLR. It is an evolution of the C and C++ languages and has been created by Microsoft specifically to work with the .NET platform. As it is a recent development, the C# language has been designed with hindsight, taking into account many of the best features from other languages while clearing up their problems.

Developing applications using C# is simpler than using C++, as the language syntax is simpler. However, C# is a powerful language and there is little we might want to do in C++ that we can't do in C#. Having said that, those features of C# which parallel the more advanced features of C++, such as directly accessing and manipulating system memory, can only be carried out using code marked as **unsafe**. This advanced programmatic technique is potentially dangerous (hence its name), as it is possible to overwrite system-critical blocks of memory with potentially catastrophic results. For this reason, and others, we are not going to cover this topic in this book.

At times, C# code is slightly more verbose than C++. This is a consequence of C# being a **type-safe** language (unlike C++). In layman's terms, this means that once some data has been assigned to a type, it cannot subsequently transform itself into another unrelated type. Consequently, there are strict rules that must be adhered to when converting between types, which means that we will often need to write more code to carry out the same task in C# as we might do in C++, but we get the benefit that code is more robust and debugging is simpler – .NET can always track what type a piece of data is at any time. In C# we therefore may not be able to do things such as "take the region of memory 4 bytes into this data and 10 bytes long and interpret it as X", but that's not necessarily a bad thing.

C# is just one of the languages available for .NET development, but in my opinion it is certainly the best. It has the advantage of being the only language designed from the ground-up for the .NET Framework and may be the principal language used in versions of .NET that are ported to other operating systems. To keep languages such as Visual Basic .NET as similar as possible to their predecessors yet compliant with the CLR, certain features of the .NET code library are not fully supported. By contrast C# is able to make use of every feature that the .NET Framework code library has to offer.

What Kind of Applications Can I Write with C#?

The .NET Framework has no restrictions on the types of application possible, as we discussed above. C# uses the framework, and so also has no restrictions on possible applications. However, let's look at a few of the more common application types:

❑   **Windows Applications** – These are applications such as Microsoft Office, which have a familiar Windows look and feel about them. This is made simple using the **Windows Forms** module of the .NET Framework, which is a library of **controls** (such as buttons, toolbars, menus, and so on) that we can use to build a Windows user interface (UI).

❑   **Web Applications** – These are web pages such as might be viewed through any web browser. The .NET Framework includes a powerful system of generating web content dynamically, allowing personalization, security, and much more. This system is called **Active Server Pages.NET** (**ASP.NET**), and we can use C# to create ASP.NET applications using **Web Forms**.

❑   **Web Services** – These are a new and exciting way of creating versatile distributed applications. Using web services we can exchange virtually any data over the Internet, using the same simple syntax regardless of the language used to create a web service, or the system that it resides on.

Any of these types may also require some form of database access, which can be achieved using the **Active Data Objects.NET** (**ADO.NET**) section of the .NET Framework. Many other resources can be drawn on, such as tools for creating networking components, outputting graphics, performing complex mathematical tasks, and so on.

C# in This Book

The second and third sections of this book deal with the syntax and usage of the C# language without too much emphasis on the .NET Framework. This is necessary, as we won't be able to use the .NET Framework at all without a firm grounding in C# programming. We'll start off even simpler, in fact, and leave the more involved topic of Object-Oriented Programming (OOP) until we've covered the basics. These will be taught from first principles, assuming no programming knowledge at all.

Once we have done this, we will be ready to move on to developing the types of application listed in the last section. Section four of this book will look at Windows Forms programming, section five will look at some other .NET topics of interest (such as accessing databases), and section six will look at web application and web service programming. Finally, we'll have a look at some more involved case studies that make use of what we have learned in the earlier parts of the book.

Visual Studio .NET

In this book we'll use Visual Studio .NET (VS) for all of our C# development, from simple command line applications, to the more complex project types considered. VS isn't essential for developing C# applications, but it makes things much easier for us. We can (if we wish to) manipulate C# source code files in a basic text editor, such as the ubiquitous Notepad application, and compile code into assemblies using the command line compiler that is part of the .NET Framework. However, why do this when we have the full power of VS to help us?

The following is a quick list of some of the features of VS that make it an appealing choice for .NET development:

❑ VS automates the steps required to compile source code, but at the same time gives us complete control over any options used should we wish to override them.

❑ The VS text editor is tailored to the languages VS supports (including C#), such that it can intelligently detect errors and suggest code where appropriate as we are typing.

❑ VS includes designers for Windows Forms and Web Forms applications, allowing simple drag-and-drop design of UI elements.

❑ Many of the types of project possible in C# may be created with "boilerplate" code already in place. Instead of starting from scratch, we will often find that various code files are started off for us, reducing the amount of time spent getting started on a project.

❑ VS includes several wizards that automate common tasks, many of which can add appropriate code to existing files without us having to worry about (or even, in some cases, remember) the correct syntax.

❑ VS contains many powerful tools for visualizing and navigating through elements of our projects, whether they are C# source code files, or other resources such as bitmap images or sound files.

❑ As well as simply writing applications in VS, it is possible to create deployment projects, making it easy to supply code to clients and for them to install it without much trouble.

❑ VS enables us to use advanced debugging techniques when developing projects, such as the ability to step through code one instruction at a time while keeping an eye on the state of our application.

There is much more than this, but hopefully you've got the idea!

Visual C# .NET Standard Edition

Visual C# .NET Standard Edition is a cut-down version of Visual Studio .NET Professional, and at a cut-down price too. While it offers many of the same features as Visual Studio .NET Professional, there are some notable feature absences, although not so many that they will prevent you from using the Standard Edition to work through this book.

Throughout the book, unless stated otherwise, the term "Visual Studio .NET" (or simply "VS") will refer to either version – Visual Studio .NET or the Visual C# .NET Standard Edition. There will be some occasions where we mean one version or the other in particular, and we shall mark these carefully, so that if you are an owner of the version not being discussed, you will not get confused!

VS Solutions

When we use VS to develop applications, we do so by creating **solutions**. A solution, in VS terms, is more than just an application. Solutions contain **projects**, which might be "Windows Forms projects", "Web Form projects", and so on. However, solutions can contain *multiple* projects, so that we can group together related code in one place, even if it will eventually compile to multiple assemblies in various places on our hard disk.

This is very useful, as it allows us to work on "shared" code (which might be placed in the Global Assembly Cache) at the same time as applications that use this code. Debugging code is a lot easier when only one development environment is used, as we can step through instructions in multiple code modules.

Summary

In this chapter we've looked at the .NET Framework in general terms, and discussed how it makes it easy for us to create powerful and versatile applications. We've seen what is necessary to turn code in languages such as C# into working applications, and what benefits we gain from using managed code running in the .NET Common Language Runtime.

We've also seen what C# actually is, and how it relates to the .NET Framework, and described the tool that we'll be using for C# development – Visual Studio .NET.

In the next chapter we'll get some C# code running using VS, which will give us enough knowledge to sit back and concentrate on the C# language itself, rather than worrying too much about how VS works.

Writing a C# Program

Now we've spent some time discussing what C# is, and how it fits into the .NET Framework, it's time to get our hands dirty and write some code. We'll be using Visual Studio .NET (VS) throughout this book, so the first thing to do is to have a look at some of the basics of this development environment. VS is an enormous and complicated product, and can be daunting to first time users, but using it to create simple applications can be surprisingly simple. As we start to use VS in this chapter, we will see that we don't need to know a huge amount about it in order to start playing with C# code. Later on in the book we will see some of the more complicated operations that VS can perform, but for now a basic working knowledge is all that is required.

Once we've had a look at VS, we'll put together two simple applications. We won't worry too much about the code in these for now, we'll just prove that things work and run through the application creation procedures that will become second nature before too long.

The first application we'll create will be a simple **console application**. Console applications are those that don't make use of the graphical windows environment, so we won't have to worry about buttons, menus, interaction with the mouse pointer, and so on. Instead, we will run our application in a command prompt window, and interact with it in a much simpler way.

The second application will be a **Windows Forms application**. The look and feel of this will be very familiar to Windows users, and (surprisingly) the application doesn't require much more effort to create. However, the syntax of the code required is more complicated, even though in many cases we don't actually have to worry about details.

We'll be using both types of application over the next two sections of the book, with slightly more emphasis on console applications to start with. The additional flexibility of windows applications isn't necessary when we are learning the C# language, while the simplicity of console applications allows us to concentrate on learning the syntax and not worrying about the look and feel of the application.

So, without further ado, it's time to get started!

The Visual Studio .NET Development Environment

When VS is first loaded, it immediately presents us with a host of windows, most of which are empty, along with an array of menu items and toolbar icons. We will be using most of these in the course of this book, and you can rest assured that they will look far more familiar before too long.

If this is the first time you have run VS you will be presented with a list of preferences intended for users with experience of previous releases of this development environment. The default settings for these are fine, so just accept them for now – there is nothing here that can't be changed later.

The VS environment layout is completely customizable, but again the default is fine for us. It is arranged as follows:

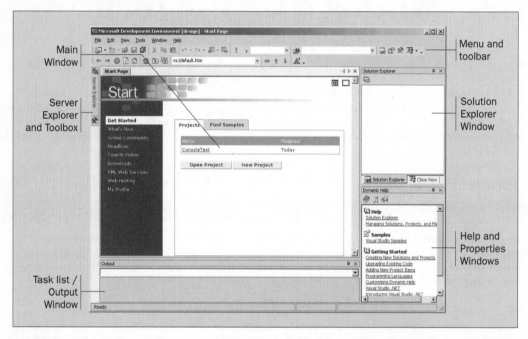

The main window, which displays an introductory "start page" when VS is started, is the one where all our code will be displayed. This window is tabbed so that we can switch between several files with ease by clicking on their filenames. It also has other functions: it can display graphical user interfaces that we are designing for our projects, plain text files, HTML, and various tools that are built into VS. We'll describe all of these as we come across them in the course of this book.

Above the main window, we have toolbars and the VS menu. There are several different toolbars that can be placed here, with functionality ranging from saving and loading files, to building and running projects, to debugging controls. Again, we'll discuss these as and when we need to use them.

Here are brief descriptions of each of the main features of VS that you will use the most:

- ❑ The Server Explorer and toolbox toolbars pop up when the mouse moves over them, and provide various additional capabilities, such as providing access to server settings and services, and access to the user interface building blocks for Windows applications.

- ❑ The Solution Explorer window displays information about the currently loaded **solution**. A solution is VS terminology for one or more projects along with their configuration. The Solution Explorer window displays various views of the projects in a solution, such as what files they contain, and what is contained in those files.

- ❑ The Properties window allows a more detailed view of the contents of a project, allowing us to perform additional configuration of individual elements. For example, we can use this window to change the appearance of a button in a Windows form. The same window is also used to display dynamic help information.

- ❑ The Task List and Output window displays information when projects are compiled, along with tasks to be completed (in a similar kind of display as is found in the task list in Microsoft Outlook). These tasks might be entered manually, or may be automatically generated by VS.

This may seem like a lot to take in, but don't worry, it doesn't take long to get used to. Let's start building the first of our example projects, which will involve the use of many of the VS elements described above.

Console Applications

We will be using console applications regularly in this book, particularly to start off with, so let's step through the creation of a simple one.

Try it Out – Creating a Simple Console Application

1. Create a new console application project by selecting the File | New | Project... menu item:

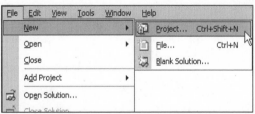

2. Select the Visual C# Projects folder from the Project Types: pane of the window that appears, and the Console Application project type in the Templates: pane (you'll have to scroll down a bit). Change the Location: text box to C:\BegVCSharp\Chapter2 (this directory will be created automatically if it doesn't already exist), and leave the default text in the Name: text box as it is:

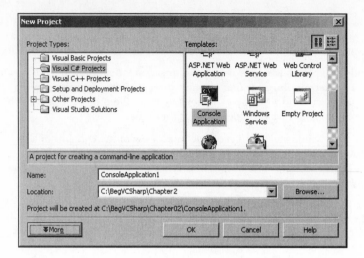

3. Click the OK button.

4. Once the project is initialized, add the following line of code to the file displayed in the main window:

```
using System;

namespace ConsoleApplication1
{
/// <summary>
    /// Summary description for Class1.
    /// </summary>
    class Class1
    {
        /// <summary>
        /// The main entry point for the application.
        /// </summary>
        [STAThread]
        static void Main(string[] args)
        {
            //
            // TODO: Add code to start application here
            //
            Console.WriteLine("The first app in Beginning C# Programming!");
        }
    }
}
```

5. Select the Debug | Start Without Debugging menu item. After a few moments you should see the following:

6. Press a key to exit the application.

How it Works

For now, we won't dissect the code we have used in this project, as we're more concerned with how to use VS to get code up and running. As you can see, VS does an awful lot for us, and makes the process of compiling and executing code very simple. In fact, there are multiple ways of performing even these simple steps. For example, creating a new project can be achieved using the File | New | Project... menu item as above, or by pressing *Ctrl+Shift+N*, or by clicking on the corresponding icon in the toolbar.

Similarly, our code can be compiled and executed in several ways. The process we used above, selecting the Debug | Start Without Debugging menu item, also has a keyboard shortcut (*Ctrl+F5*) and a toolbar icon. We can also run code in debug mode using the Debug | Start menu item (also possible by pressing *F5* or clicking on the corresponding toolbar icon), or compile our project without running it (with debugging on or off) using Build | Build, *Ctrl+Shift+B*, or another toolbar icon. Once we have compiled our code, we can also execute it simply by running the .exe file produced in Windows Explorer, or from the command prompt. To do this, we'd open a command prompt window, change the directory to `C:\BegVCSharp\Chapter2\ConsoleApplication1\bin\Debug\`, type `ConsoleApplication1` and hit return.

In future examples, I'll just say "create a new console project" or "execute the code", and you can choose whichever method you wish to perform these steps. Unless otherwise stated, all code should be run with debugging enabled.

One point to note here is that the "Press any key to continue" prompt that we saw in the example only appears if you execute code without debugging. If we run our project in debug mode, then the console window it runs in will close as soon as the code has executed. In general this is fine, but for the last example it was helpful to have this prompt so that the window didn't disappear as soon as it popped up, which would have made it difficult to see the results.

Now we've created a project we can take a more detailed look at some of the regions of the development environment.

The Solution Explorer

The first window to look at is the Solution Explorer / Class View window in the top right of the screen, shown below in both modes of operation (you can toggle between them by clicking on the tabs at the bottom of the window):

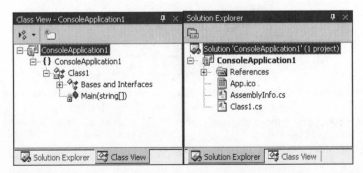

This **Solution Explorer** view shows the files that make up our `ConsoleApplication1` project. The file we added code to, `Class1.cs`, is shown along with another code file, `AssemblyInfo.cs`. (All C# code files have a `.cs` file extension.) This other code file isn't one we have to worry about for the moment; it contains extra information about our project that doesn't concern us yet. An icon, `App1.ico`, is also included, which initially contains a default icon for use with our application (since we are using a console application, however, this icon will not be used in the rendering of the start bar tab – the default console application icon will be used instead).

We can use this window to change what code is displayed in the main window by double-clicking on `.cs` files, right-clicking on them and selecting **View Code**, or selecting them and clicking on the toolbar button that appears at the top of the window. We can also perform other operations on files here, such as renaming them or deleting them from our project. Other types of files can appear here as well, such as project resources (resources are files used by the project that might not be C# files, such as bitmap images and sound files, as well as the icon file `App1.ico`). Again, we can manipulate them through the same interface.

The **References** entry contains a list of the .NET libraries we are using in our project. Again, this is something we'll look at later, as the standard references are fine for us to get started with.

The other view, **Class View**, presents an alternative view of our project by looking at the structure of the code we have created. We'll come back to this later in the book, so for now the **Solution Explorer** display is our display of choice.

As you click on files or other icons in these windows, you may notice that the contents of the window below changes. This is another window that has multiple views, but the most important of these is the **Properties** view.

The Properties Window

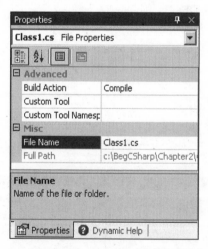

This window shows additional information about whatever we select in the window above it. For example, the above view is displayed when the `Class1.cs` file from our project is selected. This window will also display information about other things that might be selected, such as user interface components as we will see in the windows application section of this chapter.

Often, changes we make to entries in the Properties window will affect our code directly, adding lines of code or changing what we have in our files. With some projects, we'll spend as much time manipulating things through this window as making manual code changes.

Next, lets take a look at the Output window. When we executed our example code you probably noticed that a section of text appeared here before the console window created by our application appeared. On my computer this appeared:

```
------ Build started: Project: ConsoleApplication1, Configuration: Debug .NET ----
--

Preparing resources...
Updating references...
Performing main compilation...

Build complete -- 0 errors, 0 warnings
Building satellite assemblies...




-------------------- Done --------------------

     Build: 1 succeeded, 0 failed, 0 skipped
     Deploy: 0 succeeded, 0 failed, 0 skipped
```

As you can probably guess, this is showing us a status report as our files are compiled. This is also where we will get reports of any errors that occur during compilation. As an example, try removing the semicolon from the line of code we added in the last section and recompiling. This time you should see:

```
------ Build started: Project: ConsoleApplication1, Configuration: Debug .NET ----
--

Preparing resources...
Updating references...
Performing main compilation...
c:\begvcsharp\chapter2\consoleapplication1\class1.cs(19,67): error CS1002: ;
expected

Build complete -- 1 errors, 0 warnings
Building satellite assemblies...




-------------------- Done --------------------

     Build: 0 succeeded, 1 failed, 0 skipped
     Deploy: 0 succeeded, 0 failed, 0 skipped
```

This time the project won't run.

In the next chapter, when we start looking at C# syntax, we will see how semicolons are expected throughout our code – at the end of most lines in actual fact.

25

Since we have something to do now in order to get the code working, VS automatically adds a task to the task list that shares space with the Output window:

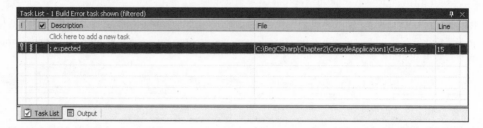

This window will help us eradicate bugs in our code, as it keeps track of what we have to do in order to compile projects. If we double click on the error shown here, the cursor will jump to the position of the error in our source code (the source file containing the error will be opened if it isn't already open), so we can fix it quickly. We will also see red wavy lines at the positions of errors in the code, so we can quickly scan source code to see where problems lie.

Note that the error location was specified as a line number. By default line numbers aren't displayed in the VS text editor, but this is something that is well worth turning on. To do this, we need to tick the relevant check box in the Options dialog, obtained through the Tools I Options... menu item. The check box is called Line Numbers, and is found in the Text Editor I C# I General category, as shown below:

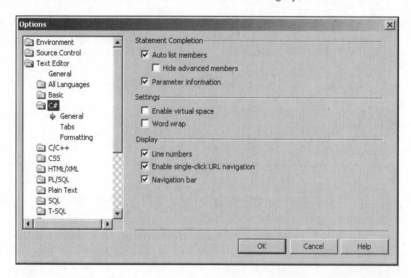

There are many useful options that can be found through this dialog, and we will use several of them throughout this book.

Windows Forms Applications

It is often easier to demonstrate code by running it as part of a Windows application rather than through a console window or via a command prompt. We can do this using user interface building blocks to piece together a user interface.

For now, we'll just see the basics of doing this and show you how to get a Windows application up and running, though we will not go into too much detail about what the application is actually doing. Later on in the book, we will take a detailed look at Windows applications.

Try it Out – Creating a Simple Windows Application

1. Create a new project of type **Windows Application** in the same location as before (C:\BegVCSharp\Chapter2) with the default name **WindowsApplication1**. If the first project is still open, then make sure the **Close Solution** option is selected in order to start a new solution:

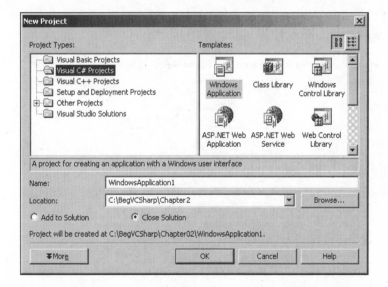

2. Move the mouse pointer to the **Toolbox** bar on the left of the screen, then to the **Button** entry of the **Windows Forms** tab, and double-click the left mouse button on the entry to add a button to the main form of the application (Form1):

3. Double-click on the button that has been added to the form.

4. The C# code in `Form1.cs` should now be displayed. Modify it as follows (only part of the code in the file is shown here for brevity):

```
private void button1_Click(object sender, System.EventArgs e)
{
    MessageBox.Show("The first windows app in the book!");
}
```

5. Run the application.

6. Click on the button presented to open a message dialog box:

How It Works

Again, it is plain that VS has done a lot of work for us, and made it simple to create functional Windows applications with little effort. The application we have created behaves just like other windows – we can move it around, resize it, minimize it, and so on. We don't have to write the code to do that – it just works. The same goes for the button we added. Simply by double clicking on it, VS knew that we wanted to write code to execute when a user clicked on the button in the running application. All we had to do was to provide that code, getting full button-clicking functionality for free.

Of course, Windows applications aren't limited to plain forms with buttons. If you have a look at the toolbar where we found the Button option you will see a whole host of user interface building blocks, some of which may be familiar, and some not. We'll get to use most of these at some point in the book, and you'll find that they are all just as easy to use, saving us a lot of time and effort.

The code for our application, in `Form1.cs`, may look a fair bit more complicated than the code in the last section, but in actual fact, the main reason it looks more complicated is that there's more of it. Much of the code in this file is concerned with the layout of **controls** on the form, which is why we can view the code in **design view** in the main window, which is a visual translation of this layout code. A button is an example of a **control** that we can use, as are the rest of the UI building blocks found in the **Windows Forms** section of the **Toolbox** bar.

Let's take a closer look at the button as a control example. Switch back to the Design View of the form using the tab on the main window, and click once on the button to select it. When we do this, the **Properties** window in the bottom right of the screen will show the properties of the button control (controls have properties much like the files we saw in the last example). Scroll down to the `Text` property, which is currently set to button1, and change the value to **Click Me**:

The text written on the button in `Form1` should also change to reflect this.

There are many properties for this button, ranging from simple formatting of the color and size of the button, to more obscure settings such as data binding settings, which allow links to databases. As briefly mentioned in the last example, changing properties often results in direct changes to code, and this is no exception. Switch back to the code view of `Form1.cs`, and we'll take a little peek at the change we just made.

At a cursory glance, you might not notice anything different in the code at all. This is because the sections of C# code that deal with the layout and formatting of controls on a form are hidden from us (after all, we hardly need to look at the code if we have a graphical display of the results).

VS uses a system of **code outlining** to achieve this subterfuge. We can see this in the following screenshot:

```
Start Page | Form1.cs [Design]* | Form1.cs*                                    ◁ ▷ ×
WindowsApplication1.Form1                    ▼   Main()                         ▼
   39|       {
   40|              if (components != null)
   41|              {
   42|                  components.Dispose();
   43|              }
   44|       }
   45|       base.Dispose( disposing );
   46|   }
   47|
   48|⊞  Windows Form Designer generated code
   77|
   78|⊟  /// <summary>
   79|   /// The main entry point for the application.
   80|   /// </summary>
   81|   [STAThread]
   82|⊟  static void Main()
   83|   {
   84|          Application.Run(new Form1());
   85|   }
   86|
   87|⊟  private void button1_Click(object sender, System.EventArgs
   88|   {
```

Looking down the left hand side of the code (just next to the line numbers if you've turned them on), you may notice some gray lines and boxes with + and - symbols in them. These boxes are used to expand and contract regions of code. Around the middle of the file (line 48 in mine, although this may vary) is a box with a + in it and a box in the main body of the code reading **Windows Form Designer generated code**. This label basically is saying "here is some code generated by VS that you don't need to know about". We can look at it if we want, however, and see what we have done by changing the button properties. Simply click on the box with the + in it and the code will become visible, and somewhere in there you should see the following line:

```
this.button1.Text = "Click Me";
```

Without worrying too much about the syntax used here, we can see that the text we typed in to the **Properties** window has popped up directly in our code.

This outlining method can be very handy when we are writing code, as we can expand and contract many other regions, not just those that are normally hidden from us. Just as looking at the table of contents of a book can help us by giving us a quick summary of the contents, looking at a series of collapsed regions of code can make it much easier for us to navigate through what can be vast amounts of C# code.

Summary

In this chapter, we've introduced some of the tools that we'll be using throughout the rest of this book. We have had a quick tour around the Visual Studio .NET development environment, and used it to build two types of applications. The simpler of these, the console application, is quite enough for most of our needs, and allows us to focus on the basics of C# programming. Windows applications are more complicated, but are visually more impressive and intuitive to use to anyone accustomed to a Windows environment (and let's face it, that's most of us).

Now we know how we can create simple applications, we can get down to the real task of learning C#. The next section of this book will deal with basic C# syntax and program structure, before we move on to more advanced object-oriented methods later. Once we've covered all that, we can start to look at how we use C# to gain access to the power available in the .NET Framework.

Variables and Expressions

Perhaps the most fundamental description of a computer program is that it is a series of operations that manipulate data. This is true even of the most complicated examples, such as vast, multi-featured Windows applications like the Microsoft Office Suite. Although this is often completely hidden from the users of applications, it is always going on behind the scenes.

To illustrate this further, consider the display unit of your computer. What you see on screen is often so familiar that it is difficult to imagine it as anything other than a 'moving picture'. In actual fact, however, what you see is only a representation of some data, which in its raw form is merely a stream of zeros and ones stashed away somewhere in the memory of your computer. Anything you do on screen, then, whether it is moving a mouse pointer, clicking on an icon, or typing text into a word processor, will result in the shunting around of data in memory.

Of course, there are less abstract situations that show this just as well. If you use a calculator application, you are supplying data in the form of numbers and performing operations on these numbers in much the same way as you would do with piece of paper and a pencil – although a lot quicker!

If computer programs are fundamentally performing operations on data, then this implies that we need some way of storing that data, and some methods of manipulating it. These two functions are provided by **variables** and **expressions** respectively, and in this chapter we will explore what this means both in general and specific terms.

Before we start with that, though, we should take a look at the basic syntax involved in C# programming.

Basic C# Syntax

The look and feel of C# code is similar to that of C++ and Java. At first this syntax can look quite confusing, and is a lot less like written English than some other languages. However, you will find as you immerse yourself in the world of C# programming that the style used is a sensible one, and it is possible to write very readable code without too much trouble.

Unlike the compilers of some other languages, C# compilers take no notice of additional spacing in code, whether made up of spaces, carriage return, or tab characters (these characters are known collectively as **white space** characters). This means that we have a lot of freedom in the way that we format our code, although conforming to certain rules can help to make things easier to read.

C# code is made up of a series of **statements**, each of which is terminated with a semicolon. Since white space is ignored therefore, we can have multiple statements on one line, but for readability's sake it is usual to add carriage return statements after semicolons, so we don't have multiple statements on one line. It is perfectly acceptable (and quite normal), however, to use statements that span several lines of code.

C# is a **block-structured** language, meaning that all statements are part of a **block** of code. These blocks, which are delimited with "curly brackets" ("{" and "}"), may contain any number of statements, or none at all. Note that the curly bracket characters do not need accompanying semicolons.

So, a simple block of C# code could take the following form:

```
{
    <code line 1, statement 1>;
    <code line 2, statement 2>
        <code line 3, statement 2>;
}
```

Here the `<code line x, statement y>` sections are not actual pieces of C# code, I've just used this text as a placeholder for where C# statements would go. Note that in this case, the second and third lines of code are part of the same statement, as there is no semicolon after the second line.

In this simple section of code, I have also used **indentation** to clarify the C# itself. This isn't some random invention of mine, it is standard practice, and in fact VS will automatically do this for you by default. In general, each block of code has its own **level** of indentation, meaning how far to the right it is. Blocks of code may be **nested** inside each other (that is, blocks may contain other blocks), in which case nested blocks will be indented further:

```
{
    <code line 1>;
    {
        <code line 2>;
        <code line 3>;
    }
    <code line 4>;
}
```

Also, lines of code that are continuations of previous lines are usually indented further as well, as in the third line of code in the first example above.

Remember, this kind of style is by no means mandatory. If you don't use it, however, you will quickly find that things can get very confusing as we move through this book!

Another thing you will often see in C# code is **comments**. A comment is not strictly speaking C# code at all, but happily cohabits with it. Comments do exactly what it says on the tin; they allow you to add descriptive text to your code – in plain English (or French, German, Outer Mongolian, and so on) – that will be ignored by the compiler. When we start dealing with lengthy sections of code, it can be useful to add reminders about exactly what we are doing, like "this line of code asks the user for a number" or "this section of code was written by Bob". C# has two ways of doing this. We can either place markers at the beginning and end of a comment, or we can use a marker that means "everything on the rest of this line is a comment". This latter method is an exception to the rule mentioned above about C# compilers ignoring carriage returns, but it is a special case.

To mark out comments using the first method, we use "/*" characters at the start of the comment and "*/" characters at the end. These may occur on a single line, or on different lines, in which case all lines in between are part of the comment. The only thing we can't type in the body of a comment is "*/", as this is interpreted as the end marker. So the following are OK:

```
/* This is a comment */

/* And so...

              ... is this! */
```

But the following will cause problems:

```
/* Comments often end with "*/" characters */
```

Here the end of the comment (the characters after "*/") will be interpreted as C# code, and errors will occur.

The other commenting approach involves starting a comment with "//". Next we can write whatever we like... as long as we keep to one line! The following is OK:

```
// This is a different sort of comment.
```

But the following will fail however, as the second line will be interpreted as C# code:

```
// So is this,
   but this bit isn't.
```

This sort of commenting is useful to document statements, as both can be placed on a single line:

```
<A statement>;          // Explanation of statement
```

There is a third type of comment in C# which allows you to document your code. They are single line comments that start with three "/" symbols instead of two like this.

```
/// A special comment
```

Under normal circumstances, they are ignored by the compiler – just like other comments, but you can configure VS to extract the text after these comments and create a specially formatted text file when a project is compiled, which we can then use to create documentation. We'll look at this in detail in Chapter 18.

A *very* important point to note about C# code is that it is **case-sensitive**. Unlike some other languages, we must enter code using exactly the right case, as simply using an upper case letter instead of a lower case one will prevent a project compiling.

Basic C# Console Application Structure

Let's take another look at the console application example from the last chapter (ConsoleApplication1), and break down the structure a bit. The code was as follows:

```
using System;

namespace ConsoleApplication1
{
    /// <summary>
    /// Summary description for Class1.
    /// </summary>
    class Class1
    {
        /// <summary>
        /// The main entry point for the application.
        /// </summary>
        [STAThread]
        static void Main(string[] args)
        {
            //
            // TODO: Add code to start application here
            //
            Console.WriteLine("The first app in Beginning Visual C#!");
        }
    }
}
```

We can immediately see that all the syntactic elements discussed in the last section are present here. We see semicolons, curly braces, and comments, along with appropriate indentation.

The most important section of code as far as we're concerned at the moment is the following:

```
static void Main(string[] args)
{
    //
    // TODO: Add code to start application here
    //
    Console.WriteLine("The first app in Beginning Visual C#!");
}
```

This is the code that is executed when we run our console application, or to be more precise, the code block enclosed in curly braces is what is executed. The only line of code that will actually do anything here is the one we added to the automatically generated code, which is the only line in the code block that isn't a comment. This code simply outputs some text to the console window, though the exact mechanisms of this shouldn't concern us for now.

For now we won't worry about the other code in the example, as the purpose of these first few chapters is to explain basic C# syntax, so the exact method of how the application execution gets to the point where `Console.WriteLine()` is called is not our concern. Later on, the significance of this additional code will be made clear.

Variables

As discussed in the introduction to this chapter, variables are concerned with the storage of data. Essentially, we can think of variables in computer memory as boxes sitting on a shelf. With boxes we can put things in and take them out again, or we can just look inside a box to see if anything is there. The same goes for variables; we place data in them and can take it out or look at it, as required.

Although all data in a computer is effectively the same thing (a series of zeros and ones), variables come in different flavors, known as **types**. Again, using our box analogy we can imagine that our boxes come in different shapes and sizes, and some things will only fit in certain boxes. The reasoning behind this type system is that different types of data may require different methods of manipulation, and by restricting variables into individual types we can avoid getting mixed up. It wouldn't, for example, make much sense to treat the series of zeros and ones that make up a digital picture as an audio file.

In order to use variables, we have to **declare** them. This means that we have to assign them a **name** and a **type**. Once we have declared variables we can use them as storage units for the type of data that we declared them to hold.

The C# syntax for declaring variables simply involves specifying the type and variable name as follows:

```
<type> <name>;
```

If we try to use a variable that hasn't been declared, then our code won't compile, but in this case the compiler will tell us exactly what the problem was, so this isn't really a disastrous error. In addition, trying to use a variable without assigning it a value will also cause an error, but again, the compiler will detect this.

So, what are the types that we can use?

Well, in actual fact there are an infinite number of types that we can use. The reason for this is that we can define our own types to hold whatever convoluted data we like.

Having said this, there are certain types of data that just about everyone will want to use at some point or another, such as a variable that stores a number, for example. Because of this there are a number of simple, pre-defined types that we should be aware of.

Simple Types

Simple types are those types such as numbers and Boolean (true or false) values that make up the fundamental building blocks for our applications, and for other, more complex types. Most of the simple types available are numeric, which at first glance seems a bit strange – surely we only need one type to store a number?

The reason for the plethora of numeric types is down to the mechanics of storing numbers as a series of zeros and ones in the memory of a computer. For integer values, we simply take a number of **bits** (individual digits that can be zero or one) and represent our number in binary format. A variable storing N bits will allow us to represent any number between 0 and $(2^N - 1)$. Any numbers above this value will be too big to fit into this variable.

As an example, let's say we have a variable that can store 2 bits. The mapping between integers and the bits representing those integers is therefore as follows:

```
0 = 00
1 = 01
2 = 10
3 = 11
```

If we want to be able to store more numbers, we need more bits (3 bits will let us store the numbers from 0 to 7, for example).

The inevitable conclusion of this argument is that we would need an infinite number of bits to be able to store every imaginable number, which isn't going to fit in our trusty PC. Even if there were an amount of bits we could use for every number, it surely wouldn't be efficient to use all these bits for a variable that, for example, was only required to store the numbers between 0 and 10 (as storage would be wasted). 4 bits would do the job fine here, allowing us to store many more values in this range in the same space of memory.

Instead, we have a number of different integer types that can be used to store various ranges of numbers, and take up differing amounts of memory (up to 64 bits). The list of these is as follows:

> *Note that each of these types makes use of one of the standard types defined in the .NET Framework. As discussed in Chapter 1, this use of standard types is what allows interoperability between languages. The names we use for these types in C# are aliases for the types defined in the framework. The table lists the names of these types as they are referred to in the .NET Framework library.*

Type	Alias for	Allowed Values
sbyte	System.SByte	Integer between –128 and 127.
byte	System.Byte	Integer between 0 and 255.
short	System.Int16	Integer between –32768 and 32767.
ushort	System.UInt16	Integer between 0 and 65535.
int	System.Int32	Integer between –2147483648 and 2147483647.
uint	System.UInt32	Integer between 0 and 4294967295.
long	System.Int64	Integer between – 9223372036854775808 and 9223372036854775807.
ulong	System.UInt64	Integer between 0 and 18446744073709551615.

The "u"s before some variable names are shorthand for "unsigned", meaning that we can't store negative numbers in variables of those types, as can be seen in the Allowed Values column of the table.

Of course, as well as integers we also need to store **floating point** values, which are those that aren't whole numbers. There are three floating point variable types that we can use: float, double, and decimal. The first two of these store floating points in the form $+/- m \times 2^e$, where the allowed values for m and e differ for each type. decimal uses the alternative form $+/- m \times 10^e$. These three types are shown below, along with their allowed values of m and e, and these limits in real numeric terms:

Type	Alias for	Minm	Maxm	Mine	Maxe	Approx Min Value	Approx Max Value
float	System.Single	0	224	-149	104	1.5×10^{-45}	3.4×10^{38}
double	System.Double	0	253	-1075	970	5.0×10^{-324}	1.7×10^{308}
decimal	System.Decimal	0	296	-28	0	1.0×10^{-28}	7.9×10^{28}

In addition to numeric types there are three other simple types available:

Type	Alias for	Allowed Values
char	System.Char	Single Unicode character, stored as an integer between 0 and 65535.
bool	System.Boolean	Boolean value, true or false.
string	System.String	A sequence of characters.

Note that there is no upper limit on the amount of characters making up a string, as it can use varying amounts of memory.

The Boolean type bool is one of the most commonly used variable types in C#, and indeed similar types are equally prolific in code in other languages. Having a variable that can be either true or false has important ramifications when it comes to the flow of logic in an application. As a simple example, consider how many questions there are that can be answered with true or false (or yes and no). Performing comparisons between variable values or validating input are just two of the programmatic uses of Boolean variables that we'll be examining very soon.

Now we've seen these types, let's have a quick example of declaring and using them.

Try it Out – Using Simple Type Variables

1. Create a new console application called Ch03Ex01 in the directory C:\BegVCSharp\Chapter3.

2. Add the following code to Class1.cs (and delete the comment lines):

```
static void Main(string[] args)
{
    int myInteger;
    string myString;
    myInteger = 17;
    myString = "\"myInteger\" is";
    Console.WriteLine("{0} {1}.", myString, myInteger);
}
```

3. Execute the code (remember that running in debug mode will cause the console application window to close before you can see what has happened!):

How It Works

The code we have added does three things:

- ❑ It declares two variables
- ❑ It assigns values to those two variables
- ❑ It outputs the values of the two variables to the console

Variable declaration occurs in the following code:

```
int myInteger;
string myString;
```

The first line declares a variable of type int with a name of myInteger, and the second line declares a variable of type string called myString.

Note that variable naming is restricted and we can't just use any sequence of characters. We'll look at this in the section on naming variables below.

The next two lines of code assign values:

```
myInteger = 17;
myString = "\"myInteger\" is";
```

Here we assign two fixed values (known as **literal** values in code) to our variables using the = **assignment operator** (we will cover more on operators in the *Expressions* section of this chapter). We assign the integer value 17 to myInteger, and the string "myInteger" is (including the quotes) to myString. When we assign string literal values in this way, note that double quotes are required to enclose the string. Due to this, there are certain characters that may cause problems if they are included in the string itself, such as the double quote characters, and we must **escape** some characters by substituting a sequence of characters (an **escape sequence**) that represents the character we want to use. In this example, we use the sequence \ " to escape a double quote:

```
myString = "\"myInteger\" is";
```

If we didn't use these escape sequences and tried coding this:

```
myString = ""myInteger" is";
```

We would get a compiler error.

Note that assigning string literals is another situation where we must be careful with line breaks – the C# compiler will reject string literals that span more than one line. If we want to add a line break we can use the escape sequence for a carriage return in our string, which is \n. For example, the following assignment:

```
myString = "This string has a\nline break.";
```

would be displayed on two lines in the console view as follows:

```
This string has a
line break.
```

All escape sequences consist of the backslash symbol followed by one of a small set of characters (we'll look at the full set a little later). Because this symbol is used for this purpose there is also an escape sequence for the backslash symbol itself, which is simply two consecutive backslashes, \\.

Getting back to the code, there is one more line that we haven't looked at:

```
Console.WriteLine("{0} {1}.", myString, myInteger);
```

This looks similar to the simple method of writing out text to the console that we saw in our first example, but now we are specifying our variables. Now, we don't want to get ahead of ourselves here, so I'm not going to go into too much detail about this line of code at this point. Suffice to say that it is the technique we will be using in the first part of this book to output text to the console window. Within the brackets we have two things:

❑   A string

❑   A list of variables whose values we want to insert into the output string, separated by commas

The string we are outputting, "{0} {1}.", doesn't seem to contain much useful text. As you will have seen, however, this is not what you actually see when you run the code. The reason for this is that the string is actually a template into which we insert the contents of our variable. Each set of curly brackets in the string is a placeholder that will contain the contents of each of the variables in the list. Each placeholder (or format string) is represented as an integer enclosed in curly brackets. The integers start at 0 and increment by 1, and the total number of placeholders should match the number of variables specified in the comma-separated list following the string. When the text is output to the console, each placeholder is replaced by the corresponding value for each variable. In this above example, the {0} is replaced with the actual value of the first variable, myString, and {1} is replaced with the contents of myInteger.

This method of outputting text to the console is what we will use to display output from our code in the examples that follow.

Variable Naming

As mentioned in the last section, we can't just choose any sequence of characters as a variable name. This isn't as worrying as it might sound at first, however, as we are still left with a very flexible naming system.

The basic variable naming rules are as follows:

❑   The first character of a variable name must be either a letter, an underscore character ("_"), or "@"

❑   Subsequent characters may be letters, underscore characters, or numbers

In addition, there are certain keywords that have a specialized meaning to the C# compiler, such as the `using` and `namespace` keywords we saw earlier. If you should use one of these by mistake the compiler will complain and you'll soon know you've done something wrong, so don't worry about this too much.

For example, the following variable names are fine:

```
myBigVar
VAR1
_test
```

These aren't however:

```
99BottlesOfBeer
namespace
It's-All-Over
```

And remember, C# is case sensitive, so we have to be careful not to forget the exact casing used when we declare our variables. References to them made later in the program with even so much as a single letter in the wrong case will prevent compilation.

A further consequence of this is the fact that we can have multiple variables whose names differ only in casing, for example the following are all separate names:

```
myVariable
MyVariable
MYVARIABLE
```

Naming Conventions

Variable names are something you will use *a lot*. Because of this, it's worth spending a bit of time discussing the sort of names that you should use. Before we get started, though, it is worth bearing in mind that this is controversial ground. Over the years, different systems have come and gone, and some developers will fight tooth and nail to justify their personal system.

Up until recently the most popular system was what is known as **Hungarian notation**. This system involves placing a lower case prefix on all variable names that identifies the type. For example, if a variable was of type `int` then we might place an i (or n) in front of it, for example iAge. Using this system it is easy to see at a glance what types different variables are.

More modern languages, however, such as C# make this system tricky to implement. OK, so with the types we've seen so far we could probably come up with one or two letter prefixes signifying each type. However, since we can create our own types, and there are many hundreds of these more complex types in the basic .NET framework, this quickly becomes unworkable. With several people working on a project it can be easy for different people to come up with different and confusing prefixes, with potentially disastrous consequences.

Developers have now realized, that it is far better to name variables appropriately to their purpose. If any doubt arises it is easy enough to work out what the type of a variable is. In VS, we just have to hover the mouse pointer over a variable name and a pop-up box will tell us what the type is soon enough.

There are currently two naming conventions in use in the .NET framework namespaces, known as **PascalCase** and **camelCase**. The casing used in the names is indicative of their usage. They both apply to names that are made up of multiple words, and specify that each word in a name should be in lower case except for its first letter, which should be upper case. In camelCasing, there is an additional rule: that the first word should start with a lower case letter.

The following are camelCase variable names:

```
age
firstName
timeOfDeath
```

Then the following are PascalCase:

```
Age
LastName
WinterOfDiscontent
```

For our simple variables we shall stick to camelCase, and use PascalCase for certain more advanced naming, which is the Microsoft recommendation.

Finally, it is worth noting that many past naming systems involved frequent use of the underscore character, usually as separators between words of variable names, such as `my_first_variable`. This usage is now discouraged (one thing I'm happy about – I always thought it looked ugly!).

Literal Values

In the earlier example, we saw two examples of literal values, integer and string. The other variable types also have associated literal values, as shown in the table below. Many of these involve **suffixes**, where we add a sequence of characters to the end of the literal value in order to specify the type desired. Some literals have multiple types, determined at compile time by the compiler based on their context:

Type(s)	Category	Suffix	Example / Allowed Values
`bool`	Boolean	None	`true` or `false`
`int, uint, long, ulong`	Integer	None	`100`
`uint, ulong`	Integer	u or U	`100U`

Table continued on following page

Type(s)	Category	Suffix	Example / Allowed Values
`long, ulong`	Integer	l or L	100L
`ulong`	Integer	ul, uL, Ul, UL, lu, lU, Lu, or LU	100UL
`float`	Real	f or F	1.5F
`double`	Real	None, d or D	1.5
`decimal`	Real	m or M	1.5M
`char`	Character	None	'a', or escape sequence
`string`	String	None	"a...a", may include escape sequences

String Literals

Earlier on in this chapter, we saw a few of the escape sequences that we can use in string literals. It is worth presenting a full table of these here for reference purposes:

Escape Sequence	Character Produced	Unicode Value of Character
`\'`	Single quote	0x0027
`\"`	Double quote	0x0022
`\\`	Backslash	0x005C
`\0`	Null	0x0000
`\a`	Alert (causes a beep)	0x0007
`\b`	Backspace	0x0008
`\f`	Form feed	0x000C
`\n`	New line	0x000A
`\r`	Carriage return	0x000D
`\t`	Horizontal tab	0x0009
`\v`	Vertical tab	0x000B

The Unicode value column of the above table shows the hexadecimal values of the characters as they are found in the Unicode character set.

As well as the above, we can specify any Unicode character using a Unicode escape sequence. These consist of the standard \ character followed by a u and a four digit hexadecimal value (for example, the four digits after the x in the above table).

This means that the following strings are equivalent:

```
"Karli\'s string."
"Karli\u0027s string"
```

Obviously, we have more versatility using Unicode escape sequences.

We can also specify strings **verbatim**. This means that all characters contained between two double quotes are included in the string, including end of line characters and characters that would otherwise need escaping. The only exception to this is the escape sequence for the double quote character, which must be specified in order to avoid ending the string. To do this, we place a @ character before the string:

```
@"Verbatim string literal."
```

This string could just as easily be specified in the normal way, but the following requires this method:

```
@"A short list:
item 1
item 2"
```

Verbatim strings are particularly useful in filenames, since these use plenty of backslash characters. Using normal strings we have to use double backslashes all the way along the string, for example:

```
"C:\\Temp\\MyDir\\MyFile.doc"
```

With verbatim string literals we can make this more readable. The following verbatim string is equivalent to the above:

```
@"C:\Temp\MyDir\MyFile.doc"
```

> *Note that, as we will see later in the book, strings are **reference** types, unlike the other types we've seen in this chapter which are **value** types. One consequence of this is that strings can also be assigned the value null, which means that the string variable doesn't reference a string. This will be explained in more detail later on in this book.*

Variable Declaration and Assignment

As a quick recap, recall that we declare variables simply using their type and name, for example:

```
int age;
```

We then assign values to variables using the = assignment operator:

```
age = 25;
```

Remember that variables must be initialized before we use them. The above assignment could be used as an initialization.

There are a couple of other things we can do here that you are likely to see in C# code. The first, is declaring multiple variables of the same type at the same time, which we can do by separating their names with commas after the type, for example:

```
int xSize, ySize;
```

Here xSize and ySize are both declared as integer types.

The second technique you are likely to see, is assigning values to variables at the same time as declaring them, which basically means combining two lines of code:

```
int age = 25;
```

We can use both these techniques together:

```
int xSize = 4, ySize = 5;
```

Here both xSize and ySize are assigned different values.

Note that the following:

```
int xSize, ySize = 5;
```

will result in only ySize being initialized – xSize is just declared.

Expressions

Now that we've seen how to declare and initialize variables, it's time to look at manipulating them. C# contains a number of **operators** for this purpose, including the = assignment operator we've used already. By combining operators with variables and literal values (together referred to as **operands** when used with operators) we can create **expressions**, which are the basic building blocks of computation.

The operators available range from the simple to highly complex ones, some of which you might never encounter outside of mathematical applications. The simple ones include all the basic mathematical operations, such as the + operator to add two operands, and the complex ones include manipulations of variable content via the binary representation of this content. There are also logical operators specifically for dealing with Boolean values, and assignment operators like =.

In this chapter, we'll concentrate on the mathematical and assignment operators, leaving the logical ones to the next chapter, where we will examine Boolean logic in the context of controlling program flow.

Operators can be roughly classified into three categories:

❑ **Unary** operators, which act on single operands

❑ **Binary** operators, which act on two operands

❑ **Ternary** operators, which act on three operands

Most operators fall into the binary category, with a few unary ones, and a single ternary one called the **conditional** operator (the conditional operator is a logical one, that is it returns a Boolean value, and we'll discuss it in the next chapter).

Let's start by looking at the mathematical operators, which span both unary and binary categories.

Mathematical Operators

There are five simple mathematical operators, two of which have binary and unary forms. In the table below I've listed each of these operators, along with a quick example of their use and results when used with simple numeric types (integer and floating point):

Operator	Category	Example Expression	Result
+	binary	`var1 = var2 + var3;`	`var1` is assigned the value that is the sum of `var2` and `var3`.
-	binary	`var1 = var2 - var3;`	`var1` is assigned the value that is the value of `var3` subtracted from the value of `var2`.
*	binary	`var1 = var2 * var3;`	`var1` is assigned the value that is the product of `var2` and `var3`.
/	binary	`var1 = var2 / var3;`	`var1` is assigned the value that is the result of dividing `var2` by `var3`.
%	binary	`var1 = var2 % var3;`	`var1` is assigned the value that is the remainder when `var2` is divided by `var3`.
+	unary	`var1 = +var2;`	`var1` is assigned the value of `var2`.
-	unary	`var1 = -var2;`	`var1` is assigned the value of `var2` multiplied by -1.

I've shown examples using simple numeric types, since the result can be unclear when using the other simple types. What would you expect if you add two Boolean values together, for example? In this case, nothing, as the compiler will complain if you try to use + (or any of the other mathematical operators) with `bool` variables. Adding `char` variables is also slightly confusing. Remember, `char` variables are actually stored as numbers, so adding two `char` variables together will also give you a number (of type `int`, to be precise). This is an example of **implicit conversion**, and I'll have a lot more to say about this subject, and **explicit conversion** shortly, as it also applies to cases where `var1`, `var2`, and `var3` are of mixed types.

Having said all this, the binary + operator *does* make sense when used with string type variables. In this case, the table entry should read:

Operator	Category	Example Expression	Result
+	binary	var1 = var2 + var3;	var1 is assigned the value that is the concatenation of the two strings stored in var2 and var3.

None of the other mathematical operators, however, will work with strings.

The other two operators we should look at here are the increment and decrement operators, both of which are unary operators that can be used in two ways: either immediately before or immediately after the operand. Let's take a quick look at the results obtained in simple expressions and then discuss them.

Operator	Category	Example Expression	Result
++	unary	var1 = ++var2;	var1 is assigned the value of var2 + 1. var2 is incremented by 1.
--	unary	var1 = --var2;	var1 is assigned the value of var2 - 1. var2 is decremented by 1.
++	unary	var1 = var2++;	var1 is assigned the value of var2. var2 is incremented by 1.
--	unary	var1 = var2--;	var1 is assigned the value of var2. var2 is decremented by 1.

The key factor here is that these operators always result in a change to the value stored in their operand:

❑ ++ always results in its operand being incremented by one

❑ -- always results in its operand being decremented by one

The difference between the results stored in var1 are a consequence of the fact that the placement of the operator determines when it takes effect. Placing one of these operators before its operand means that the operand is affected before any other computation takes place. Placing it after the operand means that the operand is affected after all other computation of the expression is completed.

This merits another example! Consider this code:

```
int var1, var2 = 5, var3 = 6;
var1 = var2++ * --var3;
```

The question is, what value will be assigned to var1? Before the expression is evaluated, the -- operator preceding var3 will take effect, changing its value from 6 to 5. We can ignore the ++ operator that follows var2, as it won't take effect until after the calculation is completed, so var1 will be the product of 5 and 5, or 25.

These simple unary operators come in very handy in a surprising amount of situations. OK, so they are really just a shorthand for expressions such as:

```
var1 = var1 + 1;
```

This sort of expression has many uses, however, particularly where **looping** is concerned, as we'll see in the next chapter.

Let's look at an example of how to use the mathematical operators, and introduce a couple of other useful concepts as well.

Try it Out – Manipulating Variables with Mathematical Operators

1. Create a new console application called `Ch03Ex02` in the directory `C:\BegVCSharp\Chapter3`.

2. Add the following code to `Class1.cs`:

```
static void Main(string[] args)
{
    double firstNumber, secondNumber;
    string userName;
    Console.WriteLine("Enter your name:");
    userName = Console.ReadLine();
    Console.WriteLine("Welcome {0}!", userName);
    Console.WriteLine("Now give me a number:");
    firstNumber = Convert.ToDouble(Console.ReadLine());
    Console.WriteLine("Now give me another number:");
    secondNumber = Convert.ToDouble(Console.ReadLine());
    Console.WriteLine("The sum of {0} and {1} is {2}.", firstNumber,
            secondNumber, firstNumber + secondNumber);
    Console.WriteLine("The result of subtracting {0} from {1} is {2}.",
            secondNumber, firstNumber, firstNumber - secondNumber);
    Console.WriteLine("The product of {0} and {1} is {2}.", firstNumber,
            secondNumber, firstNumber * secondNumber);
    Console.WriteLine("The result of dividing {0} by {1} is {2}.",
            firstNumber, secondNumber, firstNumber / secondNumber);
    Console.WriteLine("The remainder after dividing {0} by {1} is {2}.",
            firstNumber, secondNumber, firstNumber % secondNumber);
}
```

3. Execute the code:

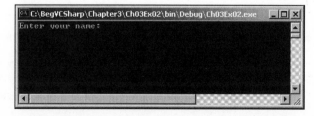

4. Enter your name and press enter:

5. Enter a number, press enter, then another number, then enter again:

How it Works

As well as demonstrating the mathematical operators, this code introduces two important concepts, which we will come across many times in our worked examples:

❏   User input

❏   Type conversion

User input uses a similar syntax to the `Console.WriteLine()` command we've already seen – we use `Console.ReadLine()`. This command prompts the user for input, which is stored in a `string` variable:

```
string userName;
Console.WriteLine("Enter your name:");
userName = Console.ReadLine();
Console.WriteLine("Welcome {0}!", userName);
```

This code writes the contents of the assigned variable, `userName`, straight to the screen.

We also read in two numbers in this example. This is slightly more involved, as the `Console.ReadLine()` command generates a string, and we want a number. This introduces the topic of **type conversion**. We'll look at this in more detail in Chapter 5, but let's have a look at the code used in this example first.

First, we declare the variables we want to store the number input in:

```
double firstNumber, secondNumber;
```

Next, we supply a prompt and use the command `Convert.ToDouble()` on a string obtained by `Console.ReadLine()` to convert the string into a `double` type. We assign this number to the `firstNumber` variable we have declared:

```
Console.WriteLine("Now give me a number:");
firstNumber = Convert.ToDouble(Console.ReadLine());
```

This syntax is remarkably simple, and you may not be surprised to learn that many other conversions can be performed in a similar way.

The remainder of the code obtains a second number in the same way:

```
Console.WriteLine("Now give me another number:");
secondNumber = Convert.ToDouble(Console.ReadLine());
```

Next we output the results of adding, subtracting, multiplying, and dividing the two numbers, in addition to displaying the remainder after division, using the remainder (%) operator:

```
Console.WriteLine("The sum of {0} and {1} is {2}.", firstNumber,
          secondNumber, firstNumber + secondNumber);
Console.WriteLine("The result of subtracting {0} from {1} is {2}.",
          secondNumber, firstNumber, firstNumber - secondNumber);
Console.WriteLine("The product of {0} and {1} is {2}.", firstNumber,
          secondNumber, firstNumber * secondNumber);
Console.WriteLine("The result of dividing {0} by {1} is {2}.",
          firstNumber, secondNumber, firstNumber / secondNumber);
Console.WriteLine("The remainder after dividing {0} by {1} is {2}.",
          firstNumber, secondNumber, firstNumber % secondNumber);
```

Note that we are supplying the expressions, `firstNumber + secondNumber` and so on, as a parameter to the `Console.WriteLine()` statement, without going via an intermediate variable:

```
Console.WriteLine("The sum of {0} and {1} is {2}.", firstNumber,
          secondNumber, firstNumber + secondNumber);
```

This kind of syntax can make our code very readable, and cut down on the amount of lines of code we need to write.

Assignment Operators

Up till now, we've been using the simple = assignment operator, and it may come as a surprise that any other assignment operators exist at all. There are more, however, and the biggest surprise is probably that they're quite useful!

All of the assignment operators other than = work in a similar way. As with = they all result in a value being assigned to the variable on their left hand side based on the operands and operators on their right hand side.

As we did before, let's look at the operators and their explanations in tabular form:

Operator	Category	Example Expression	Result
=	Binary	var1 = var2;	var1 is assigned the value of var2
+=	Binary	var1 += var2;	var1 is assigned the value that is the sum of var1 and var2
-=	Binary	var1 -= var2;	var1 is assigned the value that is the value of var2 subtracted from the value of var1
*=	Binary	var1 *= var2;	var1 is assigned the value that is the product of var1 and var2
/=	Binary	var1 /= var2;	var1 is assigned the value that is the result of dividing var1 by var2
%=	Binary	var1 %= var2;	var1 is assigned the value that is the remainder when var1 is divided by var2

As you can see, the additional operators result in var1 being included in the calculation so, code like:

```
var1 += var2;
```

gives exactly the same result as:

```
var1 = var1 + var2;
```

Note that the += operator can also be used with strings, just like +.

Using these operators, especially when employing long variable names, can make code much easier to read.

Operator Precedence

When an expression is evaluated each operator is processed in sequence. However, this doesn't necessarily mean evaluating these operators from left to right.

As a trivial example, consider the following:

```
var1 = var2 + var3;
```

Here, the + operator acts before the = operator.

There are other situations where operator precedence isn't so obvious, for example:

```
var1 = var2 + var3 * var4;
```

Here the * operator acts first, followed by the + operator, and finally the = operator. This is the standard mathematical order of doing things, and gives the same result as you would expect from working out the equivalent algebraic calculation on paper.

Like such calculations, we can gain control over operator precedence by using parentheses, for example:

```
var1 = (var2 + var3) * var4;
```

Here the content of the parentheses is evaluated first, meaning that the + operator acts before the * operator.

Of the operators we've encountered so far the order of precedence is as follows, where operators of equal precedence (such as * and /) are evaluated in a left to right manner:

Precedence	Operators
Highest	++, -- (used as prefixes); +, - (unary)
	*, /, %
	+, -
	=, *=, /=, %=, +=, -=
Lowest	++, -- (used as suffixes)

Note that parentheses can be used to override this precedence order, as described above.

Namespaces

Before we move on, it's worth spending some time on one more important subject – **namespaces**. These are the .NET way of providing containers for application code, such that code and its contents may be uniquely identified. Namespaces are also used as a means of categorizing items in the .NET Framework. Most of these items are type definitions, such as the simple types detailed in this chapter (System.Int32 and so on).

C# code, by default, is contained in the **global namespace**. This means that items contained in this code are accessible from other code in the global namespace simply by referring to them by name. We can use the namespace keyword, however, to explicitly define the namespace for a block of code enclosed in curly brackets. Names in such a namespace must be **qualified** if they are to be used from code outside of this namespace.

A qualified name is one that contains all of its hierarchical information. In basic terms, this means that if we have code in one namespace that needs to use a name defined in a different namespace, we must include a reference to this namespace. Qualified names use period characters (".") between namespace levels.

For example:

```
namespace LevelOne
{
    // code in LevelOne namespace

    // name "NameOne" defined
}

// code in global namespace
```

This code defines one namespace, LevelOne, and a name in this namespace, NameOne (note that I haven't shown any actual code here in order to keep the discussion general, instead I've placed a comment where this definition would go). Code written inside the LevelOne namespace can simply refer to this name using "NameOne" – no classification is necessary. Code in the global namespace, however, must refer to this name using the classified name "LevelOne.NameOne".

Within a namespace, we can define nested namespaces, also using the namespace keyword. Nested namespaces are referred to via their hierarchy, again using periods to classify each level of the hierarchy. This is best illustrated with an example. Consider the following namespaces:

```
namespace LevelOne
{
    // code in LevelOne namespace

    namespace LevelTwo
    {
        // code in LevelOne.LevelTwo namespace

        // name "NameTwo" defined
    }
}

// code in global namespace
```

Here, NameTwo must be referred to as LevelOne.LevelTwo.NameTwo from the global namespace, LevelTwo.NameTwo from the LevelOne namespace, and NameTwo from the LevelOne.LevelTwo namespace.

The important point to note here is that names are uniquely defined by their namespace. We could define the name NameThree in the LevelOne and LevelTwo namespaces:

```
namespace LevelOne
{
    // name "NameThree" defined

    namespace LevelTwo
    {
        // name "NameThree" defined
    }
}
```

This defines two separate names, LevelOne.NameThree and LevelOne.LevelTwo.NameThree, that can be used independently of each other.

Once namespaces are set up, we can use the `using` statement to simplify access to the names they contain. In effect, the `using` statement says "OK, we'll be needing names from this namespace, so don't bother asking me to classify them every time". For example, in the following code we are saying that code in the `LevelOne` namespace should have access to names in the `LevelOne.LevelTwo` namespace without classification:

```
namespace LevelOne
{
    using LevelTwo;

    namespace LevelTwo
    {
        // name "NameTwo" defined
    }
}
```

Code in the `LevelOne` namespace can now refer to `LevelTwo.NameTwo` by simply using `NameTwo`.

There are times, as with our `NameThree` example above, when this can lead to problems with clashes between identical names in different namespaces (in which case code is unlikely to compile). In cases such as these, we can provide an **alias** for a namespace as part of the `using` statement:

```
namespace LevelOne
{
    using LT = LevelTwo;

    // name "NameThree" defined

    namespace LevelTwo
    {
        // name "NameThree" defined
    }
}
```

Here, code in the `LevelOne` namespace can refer to `LevelOne.NameThree` as `NameThree` and `LevelOne.LevelTwo.NameThree` as `LT.NameThree`.

`using` statements apply to the namespace they are contained in, and any nested namespaces that might also be contained in this namespace. In the above code, the global namespace can't use `LT.NameThree`. However, if this `using` statement were declared as follows:

```
using LT = LevelOne.LevelTwo;

namespace LevelOne
{
    // name "NameThree" defined

    namespace LevelTwo
    {
        // name "NameThree" defined
    }
}
```

Then code in the global namespace and the `LevelOne` namespace can use `LT.NameThree`.

There is one more important point to note here. The `using` statement doesn't in itself give you access to names in another namespace. Unless the code in a namespace is in some way linked to your project, by being defined in a source file in the project, or being defined in some other code linked to the project, we won't have access to the names contained. Also, if code containing a namespace is linked to our project, we have access to the names contained, regardless of whether we use `using`. `using` simply makes it easier for us to access these names, and can shorten otherwise lengthy code to make it more readable.

Going back to the code in `ConsoleApplication1` we saw at the start of this chapter, we see the following lines that apply to namespaces:

```
using System;

namespace ConsoleApplication1
{
    ...
}
```

The first line uses `using` to declare that the `System` namespace will be used in this C# code, and should be accessible from all namespaces in this file without classification. The `System` namespace is the root namespace for .NET Framework application, and contains all the basic functionality we need for console applications.

Next, a namespace is declared for the application code itself, `ConsoleApplication1`.

Summary

In this chapter, we've covered a fair amount of ground on the way to creating usable (if basic) C# applications. We've looked at the basic C# syntax and analyzed the basic console application code that VS generated for us when we create a console application project.

The major part of this chapter concerned the use of variables. We have seen what variables are, how we create them, how we assign values in them, and how we manipulate them and the values that they contain. Along the way, we've also looked at some basic user interaction, by showing how we can output text to a console application and read user input back in. This involved some very basic type conversion, a complex subject that we'll be covering in more depth in Chapter 5.

We have also seen how we can assemble operators and operands into expressions, and looked at the way these are executed, and the order in which this takes place.

Finally, we looked at namespaces, which will become more and more important as the book progresses. By introducing this topic in a fairly abstract way here, the groundwork is completed for later discussions.

So far all of our programming has taken the form of line-by-line execution. In the next chapter, we will see how we can make our code more efficient by controlling the flow of execution using looping techniques and conditional branching.

Exercises

1. In the following code, how would we refer to the name `great` from code in the namespace `fabulous`?

```
namespace fabulous
{
   // code in fabulous namespace
}

namespace super
{
   namespace smashing
   {
      // great name defined
   }
}
```

2. Which of the following are not legal variable names:

a   myVariableIsGood

b   99Flake

c   _floor

d   time2GetJiggyWidIt

e   wrox.com

3. Is the string "supercalifragilisticexpialidocious" too big to fit in a `string` variable? Why?

4. By considering operator precedence, list the steps involved in the computation of the following expression:

```
resultVar += var1 * var2 + var3 % var4 / var5;
```

5. Write a console application that obtains four `int` values from the user and displays the product. Hint: you may recall that the `Convert.ToDouble()` command was used to covert the input from the console to a `double`; the equivalent command to convert from a `string` to an `int` is `Convert.ToInt32()`.

Flow Control

All of the C# code we've seen so far has had one thing in common. In each case, program execution has proceeded from one line to the next in top-to-bottom order, missing nothing. If all applications worked like this then we would be very limited in what we could do.

In this chapter we will look at two methods of controlling program flow, that is, the order of execution of lines of C# code. These two methods are:

❑ Branching – where we execute code conditionally, depending on the outcome of an evaluation, such as "only execute this code if myVal is less than 10".

❑ Looping – repeatedly executing the same statements (for a certain number of times or until a test condition has been reached).

Both of these techniques involve the use of **Boolean logic**. In the last chapter we saw the bool type, but didn't actually do much with it. In this chapter we'll be using it a lot, and so we will start by discussing what we mean by Boolean logic so that we can use it in flow control scenarios.

Boolean Logic

The bool type introduced in the last chapter can hold one of only two values, true or false. This type is often used to record the result of some operation, such that we can act on this result. In particular, bool types are used to store the result of a **comparison**.

> *As an historical aside, it is worth remembering (and respecting) the English mathematician George Boole, whose work in the mid-nineteenth century forms the basis of Boolean logic.*

As an example, consider the situation (as mentioned in the introduction to this chapter) that we want to execute code based on whether a variable, myVal, is less than 10. In order to do this we need some indication of whether the statement "myVal is less than 10" is true or false, that is, we need to know the Boolean result of a comparison.

Boolean comparisons require the use of Boolean **comparison** operators (also known as **relational** operators), which are shown in the table below. In all cases here `var1` is a `bool` type variable, while the types of `var2` and `var3` may vary.

Operator	Category	Example Expression	Result
==	binary	`var1 = var2 == var3;`	`var1` is assigned the value `true` if `var2` is equal to `var3`, or `false` otherwise.
!=	binary	`var1 = var2 != var3;`	`var1` is assigned the value `true` if `var2` is not equal to `var3`, or `false` otherwise.
<	binary	`var1 = var2 < var3;`	`var1` is assigned the value `true` if `var2` is less than `var3`, or `false` otherwise.
>	binary	`var1 = var2 > var3;`	`var1` is assigned the value `true` if `var2` is greater than `var3`, or `false` otherwise.
<=	binary	`var1 = var2 <= var3;`	`var1` is assigned the value `true` if `var2` is less than or equal to `var3`, or `false` otherwise.
>=	binary	`var1 = var2 >= var3;`	`var1` is assigned the value `true` if `var2` is greater than or equal to `var3`, or `false` otherwise.

We might use operators such as these on numeric values in code such as:

```
bool isLessThan10;
isLessThan10 = myVal < 10;
```

This code will result in `isLessThan10` being assigned the value `true` if `myVal` stores a value less than 10, or `false` otherwise.

We can also use these comparison operators on other types, such as strings:

```
bool isKarli;
isKarli = myString == "Karli";
```

Here `isKarli` will only be true if `myString` stores the string `"Karli"`.

We can also focus on Boolean values:

```
bool isTrue;
isTrue = myBool == true;
```

Although here we are limited to the use of == and != operators.

> *Note that a common code error occurs if you unintentionally assume that because val1 < val2 is false, then val1 > val2 is true. If val1 == val2 then both these statements will be false. I'm mentioning this here as it's a mistake I've made in the past!*

There are some other Boolean operators that are intended specifically for working with Boolean values:

Operator	Category	Example Expression	Result
!	unary	var1 = ! var2;	var1 is assigned the value true if var2 is false, or false if var2 is true. (Logical NOT.)
&	binary	var1 = var2 & var3;	var1 is assigned the value true if var2 and var3 are both true, or false otherwise. (Logical AND.)
|	binary	var1 = var2 | var3;	var1 is assigned the value true if either var2 or var3 (or both) are true, or false otherwise. (Logical OR.)
^	binary	var1 = var2 ^ var3;	var1 is assigned the value true if either var2 or var3, but not both, are true, or false otherwise. (Logical XOR, or exclusive OR.)

So the last code snippet above could also be expressed as:

```
bool isTrue;
isTrue = myBool & true;
```

The & and | operators also have two similar operators:

Operator	Category	Example Expression	Result
&&	binary	var1 = var2 && var3;	var1 is assigned the value true if var2 and var3 are both true, or false otherwise. (Logical AND.)
||	binary	var1 = var2 || var3;	var1 is assigned the value true if either var2 or var3 (or both) are true, or false otherwise. (Logical OR.)

The result of these operators is exactly the same as & and |, but there is an important difference in the way this result is obtained, which can result in better performance. Both of these look at the value of their first operand (var2 in the table above), and based on the value of this operand may not need to process the second operator (var3 above) at all.

If the value of the first operand of the && operator is `false` then there is no need to consider the value of the second operand, as the result will be `false` regardless. Similarly, the || operator will return `true` if its first operand is `true`, regardless of the value of the second operand.

This isn't the case for the & and | operators we saw above. With these, both operands will always be evaluated.

Because of this conditional evaluation of operands we will see a small performance increase if we use && and || instead of & and |. This will be particularly apparent in applications that use these operators a lot. As a rule of thumb, *always* use && and || where possible.

Bitwise Operators

In the light of the discussion in the last section, you may be asking why the & and | operators exist at all. The reason is that these operators may be used to perform operations on numeric values. In fact, they operate on the series of bits stored in a variable rather than the value of the variable.

Let's consider these in turn, starting with &. Each bit in the first operand is compared with the bit in the same position in the second operand, resulting in the bit in the same position in the resultant value being assigned a value as follows:

Operand 1 bit	Operand 2 bit	& Result bit
1	1	1
1	0	0
0	1	0
0	0	0

| is similar, but the result bits are different, as follows:

Operand 1 bit	Operand 2 bit	| Result bit
1	1	1
1	0	1
0	1	1
0	0	0

For example, consider the operation shown in the following code:

```
int result, op1, op2;
op1 = 4;
op2 = 5;
result = op1 & op2;
```

Here we must consider the binary representations of op1 and op2, which are 100 and 101 respectively. The result is obtained by comparing the binary digits in equivalent positions in these two representations as follows:

❑ The leftmost bit of result is 1 if the leftmost bit of op1 and op2 are both 1, or 0 otherwise.

❑ The next bit of result is 1 if the next bit of op1 and op2 are both 1, or 0 otherwise.

❑ Continue for all remaining bits.

In this example the leftmost bits of op1 and op2 are both 1, so the leftmost bit of result will be 1, too. The next bits are both 0, and the third bits are 1 and 0 respectively, so the second and third bits of result will be 0. The final value of result in binary representation is therefore 100, so result is assigned the value 4.

The following illustrates this:

	1	0	0		
	1	0	0		4
&	1	0	1	&	5
	1	0	0		4

The same process occurs if we use the | operator, except that in this case each result bit is 1 if either of the operand bits in the same position is 1:

	1	0	0		
	1	0	0		4
|	1	0	1	|	5
	1	0	1		5

We can also use the ^ operator in the same way, where each result bit is 1 if one or other of the operand bits in the same position is one, but not both:

Operand 1 bit	Operand 2 bit	^ Result bit
1	1	0
1	0	1
0	1	1
0	0	0

C# also allows the use of a unary bitwise operator "~", which acts on its operand by inverting each of its bits, such that the result is a variable having values of 1 for each bit in the operand that is 0, and vice versa:

Operand bit	~ Result bit
1	0
0	1

These bitwise operations are quite useful in certain situations, as they allow a simple method of making use of individual variable bits to store information. Consider a simple representation of a color using three bits to specify red, green, and blue content. We can set these bits independently to change the three bits to one of the following configurations:

Bits	Decimal Representation	Meaning
000	0	black
100	4	red
010	2	green
001	1	blue
101	5	magenta
110	6	yellow
011	3	cyan
111	7	white

Let's say we store these values in a variable of type int. Starting from a black color, that is, an int variable with the value of 0, we can perform operations like:

```
int myColor = 0;
bool containsRed;
myColor = myColor | 2;           // Add green bit, myColor now stores 010
myColor = myColor | 4;           // Add red bit, myColor now stores 110
containsRed = (myColor & 4) == 4; // Check value of red bit
```

The final line of code assigns a value of true to containsRed, as the 'red bit' of myColor is 1.

This technique can be quite useful for making efficient use of information, particularly as the operations involved can be used to check the values of multiple bits simultaneously (32 in the case of int values). However, there are better ways of storing extra information in single variables, making use of the advanced variable types discussed in the next chapter.

In addition to these four bitwise operators there are two others that I'd like to look at in this section. These are as follows:

Operator	Category	Example Expression	Result
>>	binary	var1 = var2 >> var3;	var1 is assigned the value obtained when the binary content of var2 is shifted var3 bits to the right.
<<	binary	var1 = var2 << var3;	var1 is assigned the value obtained when the binary content of var2 is shifted var3 bits to the left.

These operators, commonly called **bitwise shift operators**, are best illustrated with a quick example:

```
int var1, var2 = 10, var3 = 2;
var1 = var2 << var3;
```

Here, `var1` is assigned the value 40. This can be explained by considering that the binary representation of 10 is "1010", which shifted to the left by two places is "101000" – the binary representation of 40. In effect what we have done is carried out a multiplication operation. Each bit shifted to the left multiplies the value by 2, so two bit-shifts to the left results in multiplication by 4. Conversely each bit shifted to the right has the effect of dividing the operand by 2 with any integer remainder being lost:

```
int var1, var2 = 10;
var1 = var2 >> 1;
```

In this example, `var1` contains the value 5, whereas the following code gives a value of 2:

```
int var1, var2 = 10;
var1 = var2 >> 2;
```

You are unlikely to use these operators in most code, but it is worth being aware of their existence. Their primary use is in highly optimized code, where the overhead of other mathematical operations just won't do. For this reason they are often used in, for example, device drivers or system code.

Boolean Assignment Operators

The last operators to look at in this section are those that combine some of the operators we've seen above with assignment, much like the mathematical assignment operators in the last chapter (+=, *=, etc.). These are as follows:

Operator	Category	Example Expression	Result
&=	binary	var1 &= var2;	var1 is assigned the value that is the result of var1 & var2.
|=	binary	var1 |= var2;	var1 is assigned the value that is the result of var1 | var2.
^=	binary	var1 ^= var2;	var1 is assigned the value that is the result of var1 ^ var2.

These work with both Boolean and numeric values in the same way as &, |, and ^.

Note that &= and |= use & and |, not && and ||, and get the overhead associated with these simpler operators.

The bitwise shift operators also have assignment operators as follows:

Operator	Category	Example Expression	Result
>>=	unary	var1 >>= var2;	var1 is assigned the value obtained when the binary content of var1 is shifted var2 bits to the right.
<<=	unary	var1 <<= var2;	var1 is assigned the value obtained when the binary content of var1 is shifted var2 bits to the left.

Try it Out – Using the Boolean and Bitwise Operators

1. Create a new console application called Ch04Ex01 in the directory C:\BegVCSharp\Chapter4.

2. Add the following code to Class1.cs:

```
static void Main(string[] args)
{
    Console.WriteLine("Enter an integer:");
    int myInt = Convert.ToInt32 (Console.ReadLine());
    Console.WriteLine("Integer less than 10? {0}", myInt < 10);
    Console.WriteLine("Integer between 0 and 5? {0}",
                      (0 <= myInt) && (myInt <= 5));
    Console.WriteLine("Bitwise AND of Integer and 10 = {0}", myInt & 10);
}
```

3. Execute the application and enter an integer when prompted.

How it Works

The first two lines of code prompt for and accept an integer value using techniques we've already seen:

```
Console.WriteLine("Enter an integer:");
int myInt = Convert.ToInt32(Console.ReadLine());
```

We use Convert.ToInt32() to obtain an integer from the string input, which is simply another conversion command in the same family as the Convert.ToDouble() command we used previously.

The remaining three lines of code perform various operations on the number obtained and display results. We'll work through this code assuming that the user enters 6, as shown in the screenshot.

The first output is the result of the operation `myInt < 10`. If `myInt` is 6, which is less than 10, then the result will be true, which is what we see displayed. Values of `myInt` of 10 or above will result in `false`.

The second output is a more involved calculation: `(0 <= myInt) && (myInt <= 5)`. This involves two comparison operations, to see whether `myInt` is greater than or equal to 0 and less than or equal to 5, and a Boolean AND operation on the results obtained. With a value of 6 `(0 <= myInt)` returns `true`, and `(myInt <= 5)` returns `false`. The end result is then `(true) && (false)`, which is `false` as we can see from the display.

Finally, we perform a bitwise AND on the value of `myInt`. The other operand is 10, which has the binary representation 1010. If `myInt` is 6, which has the binary representation 110, then the result of this operation is 10, or 2 in decimal:

	0	1	1	0		6
&	1	0	1	0	&	10
	0	0	1	0		2

Operator Precedence Updated

Now we have a few more operators to consider we should update our operator precedence table from the last chapter to include them:

Precedence	Operators
Highest	++, -- (used as prefixes); ( ), +, - (unary), !, ~
	*, /, %
	+, -
	<<, >>
	<, >, <=, >=
	==, !=
	&
	^
	&&
	=, *=, /=, %=, +=, -=, <<=, >>=, &=, ^=, |=
Lowest	++, -- (used as suffixes)

This adds quite a few more levels, but explicitly defines how expressions such as the following will be evaluated:

```
var1 = var2 <= 4 && var2 >= 2;
```

Where the && operator is processed after the <= and >= operators.

One point to note here is that it doesn't hurt to add parentheses to make expressions such as this one clearer. The compiler knows what order to process operators in, but we humans are prone to forget such things (and we might want to change the order). Writing the above expression as:

```
var1 = (var2 <= 4) && (var2 >= 2);
```

Solves this problem by being explicit about the order of computation.

The goto Statement

C# allows us to label lines of code and then jump straight to them using the goto statement. This has its benefits and problems. The main benefit is that it is a very simple way of controlling what code is executed when. The main problem is that excessive use of this technique can result in difficult to understand "spaghetti" code.

Let's look at how we use this technique to clarify this.

The goto statement is used as follows:

```
goto <labelName>;
```

And labels are defined in the following way:

```
<labelName>:
```

For example, consider the following:

```
int myInteger = 5;
goto myLabel;
myInteger += 10;
myLabel:
Console.WriteLine("myInteger = {0}", myInteger);
```

Execution proceeds as follows:

❑   myInteger is declared as an int type and assigned the value 5

❑   The goto statement interrupts normal execution and transfers control to the line marked myLabel:

❑   The value of myInteger is written to the console

The line of code highlighted below is *never* executed:

```
int myInteger = 5;
goto myLabel;
myInteger += 10;
myLabel:
Console.WriteLine("myInteger = {0}", myInteger);
```

In fact, if you try this out in an application you will see that this is noted in the task list as a warning when you try to compile the code, labeled "Unreachable code detected" along with a line number.

goto statements have their uses, but they can make things very confusing indeed.

As an example of some "spaghetti" code arising from the use of goto, consider the following:

```
start:
int myInteger = 5;
goto addVal;
writeResult:
Console.WriteLine("myInteger = {0}", myInteger);
goto start;
addVal:
myInteger += 10;
goto writeResult;
```

This is perfectly valid code, but very difficult to read! You might like to try this out for yourself and see what happens. Before doing that, though, try and work out what this code will do by looking at it, so you can give yourself a pat on the back if you're right.

We'll come back to this statement a little later, as it has implications for use with some of the other structures in this chapter (although, to be honest, I don't advocate its use).

Branching

Branching is the act of controlling which line of code should be executed next. The line to jump to is controlled by some kind of conditional statement. This conditional statement will be based on a comparison between a test value and one or more possible values using Boolean logic.

In this section we will look at the three branching techniques available in C#:

- ❑ The ternary operator
- ❑ The if statement
- ❑ The switch statement

The Ternary Operator

The simplest way of performing a comparison is to use the **ternary** (or **conditional**) operator mentioned in the last chapter. We've already seen unary operators that work on one operand, and binary operators that work on two operands, so it may come as no surprise that this operator works on three operands. The syntax is as follows:

```
<test> ? <resultIfTrue> : <resultIfFalse>
```

Here, `<test>` is evaluated to obtain a Boolean value, and the result of the operator is either `<resultIfTrue>` or `<resultIfFalse>` based on this value.

We might use this as follows:

```
string resultString = (myInteger < 10) ? "Less than 10"
                                        : "Greater than or equal to 10";
```

Here the result of the ternary operator is one of two strings, both of which may be assigned to `resultString`. The choice of which string to assign is made by comparing the value of `myInteger` to 10, where a value of less than 10 results in the first string being assigned, and a value of greater than or equal to 10 the second string. For example, if `myInteger` is 4 then `resultString` will be assigned the string `"Less than 10"`.

This operator is fine for simple assignments such as this, but isn't really suitable for executing larger amounts of code based on a comparison. A much better way of doing this is to use the `if` statement.

The if Statement

The `if` statement is a far more versatile and useful way of making decisions. Unlike `?:` statements, `if` statements don't have a result (so we can't use them in assignments); instead we use the statement to conditionally execute other statements.

The simplest use of an `if` statement is as follows:

```
if (<test>)
   <code executed if <test> is true>;
```

Where `<test>` is evaluated (it *must* evaluate to a Boolean value for the code to compile) and the line of code shown below the statement is executed if `<test>` evaluates to `true`. After this code is executed, or if it isn't executed due to `<test>` evaluating to `false`, program execution resumes at the next line of code.

We can also specify additional code using the `else` statement in combination with an `if` statement. This statement will be executed if `<test>` evaluate to `false`:

```
if (<test>)
   <code executed if <test> is true>;
else
   <code executed if <test> is false>;
```

Both sections of code can span multiple lines using blocks in braces:

```
if (<test>)
{
    <code executed if <test> is true>;
}
else
{
    <code executed if <test> is false>;
}
```

As a quick example, let's rewrite the code from the last section that used the ternary operator:

```
string resultString = (myInteger < 10) ? "Less than 10" : "Greater than 10";
```

Since the result of the if statement cannot be assigned to a variable we have to assign a value to the variable in a separate step:

```
string resultString;
if (myInteger < 10)
    resultString = "Less than 10";
else
    resultString = "Greater than or equal to 10";
```

Code such as this, although more verbose, is far easier to read and understand than the equivalent ternary form, and allows far more flexibility.

Let's look at an example.

Try it Out – Using the if Statement

1. Create a new console application called Ch04Ex02 in the directory C:\BegVCSharp\Chapter4.

2. Add the following code to Class1.cs:

```
static void Main(string[] args)
{
    string comparison;
    Console.WriteLine("Enter a number:");
    double var1 = Convert.ToDouble(Console.ReadLine());
    Console.WriteLine("Enter another number:");
    double var2 = Convert.ToDouble(Console.ReadLine());
    if (var1 < var2)
        comparison = "less than";
    else
    {
        if (var1 == var2)
            comparison = "equal to";
        else
            comparison = "greater than";
    }
    Console.WriteLine("The first number is {0} the second number.",
                      comparison);
}
```

3. Execute the code, and enter two numbers at the prompts:

```
C:\BegVCSharp\Chapter4\Ch04Ex02\bin\Debug\Ch04Ex02.exe
Enter a number:
7.9
Enter another number:
8.0
The first number is less than the second number.
Press any key to continue
```

How it Works

The first section of code is familiar, and simply obtains two `double` values from user input:

```
string comparison;
Console.WriteLine("Enter a number:");
double var1 = Convert.ToDouble(Console.ReadLine());
Console.WriteLine("Enter another number:");
double var2 = Convert.ToDouble(Console.ReadLine());
```

Next we assign a string to the `string` variable `comparison` based on the values obtained for `var1` and `var2`. First we check to see if `var1` is less than `var2`:

```
if (var1 < var2)
    comparison = "less than";
```

If this isn't the case then `var1` is either greater than or equal to `var2`. In the `else` section of the first comparison we need to nest a second comparison:

```
else
{
    if (var1 == var2)
        comparison = "equal to";
```

The else section of this second comparison will only be reached if `var1` is greater than `var2`:

```
    else
        comparison = "greater than";
}
```

Finally we write the value of comparison to the console:

```
Console.WriteLine("The first number is {0} the second number.",
                  comparison);
```

The nesting we have used here is just one way of doing things. We could equally have written:

```
if (var1 < var2)
    comparison = "less than";
if (var1 == var2)
    comparison = "equal to";
if (var1 > var2)
    comparison = "greater than";
```

The disadvantage with this method is that we are performing three comparisons regardless of the values of var1 and var2. With the first method we only perform one comparison if var1 < var2 is true and two comparisons otherwise (we also perform the var1 == var2 comparison), resulting in fewer lines of code being executed. The difference in performance here will be slight, but would be significant in applications where speed of execution is crucial.

Checking More Conditions Using if Statements

In the above example we checked for three conditions involving the value of var1. This covered all possible values for this variable. At other times we might want to check for specific values, say if var1 is equal to 1, 2, 3 or 4, and so on. Using code such as that above can result in annoyingly nested code, for example:

```
if (var1 == 1)
{
    // do something
}
else
{
    if (var1 == 2)
    {
        // do something else
    }
    else
    {
        if (var1 == 3 || var1 == 4)
        {
            // do something else
        }
        else
        {
            // do something else
        }
    }
}
```

Note that it is a common mistake to write conditions such as the third condition as
if (var1 == 3 || 4). Here, owing to operator precedence, the == operator is processed first, leaving
the || operator to operate on a Boolean and a numeric operand. This will cause an error.

In these situations it can be worth using a slightly different indentation scheme and contracting the block of code for the else blocks (that is, using a single line of code after the else blocks rather than a block of code). When we do this we end up with a structure involving else if statements:

```
if (var1 == 1)
{
    // do something
}
else if (var1 == 2)
{
    // do something else
}
else if (var1 == 3 || var1 == 4)
{
    // do something else
}
else
{
    // do something else
}
```

These `else if` statements are really two separate statements, and the code is functionally identical to the above code. However, this code is much easier to read.

When making multiple comparisons such as this, it can be worth considering the `switch` statement as an alternative branching structure.

The switch Statement

The `switch` statement is very similar to the `if` statement in that it executes code conditionally based on the value of a test. However, `switch` allows us to test for multiple values of a test variable in one go, rather than just a single condition. This test is limited to discrete values, rather than clauses such as "greater than X", so its use is slightly different, but it can be a powerful technique.

The basic structure of a `switch` statement is as follows:

```
switch (<testVar>)
{
    case <comparisonVal1>:
        <code to execute if <testVar> == <comparisonVal1> >
        break;
    case <comparisonVal2>:
        <code to execute if <testVar> == <comparisonVal2> >
        break;
    ...
    case <comparisonValN>:
        <code to execute if <testVar> == <comparisonValN> >
        break;
    default:
        <code to execute if <testVar> != comparisonVals>
        break;
}
```

The value in `<testVar>` is compared to each of the `<comparisonValX>` values (specified with `case` statements), and if there is a match then the code supplied for this match is executed. If there is no match then the code in the `default` section is executed if this block exists.

On completion of the code in each section, we have an additional command, `break`. It is illegal for the flow of execution to reach a second `case` statement after processing one `case` block.

> *Note that this behavior is one area where C# differs from C++, where the processing of case statements is allowed to run from one to another.*

The `break` statement here simply terminates the `switch` statement, and processing continues on the statement following the structure.

There are alternative methods of preventing flow from one case statement to the next in C# code. We can use the `return` statement, which results in termination of the current function rather than just the `switch` structure (see Chapter 6 for more details about this), or a `goto` statement. `goto` statements (as detailed earlier) work here, since `case` statements in effect define labels in C# code. For example:

```
switch (<testVar>)
{
   case <comparisonVal1>:
      <code to execute if <testVar> == <comparisonVal1> >
      goto case <comparisonVal2>;
   case <comparisonVal2>:
      <code to execute if <testVar> == <comparisonVal2> >
      break;
   ...
```

There is one exception to the rule that the processing of one `case` statement can't run freely into the next. If we place multiple `case` statements together (**stack** them) before a single block of code, we are in effect checking for multiple conditions at once. If any of these conditions is met the code is executed, for example:

```
switch (<testVar>)
{
   case <comparisonVal1>:
   case <comparisonVal2>:
      <code to execute if <testVar> == <comparisonVal1> or
                           <testVar> == <comparisonVal2> >
      break;
   ...
```

Note that these conditions also apply to the `default` statement. There is no rule saying that this statement must be the last in the list of comparisons, and we can stack it with case statements if we wish. Adding a break point with `break`, `goto`, or `return` ensures that a valid execution path exists through the structure in all cases.

Each of the `<comparisonValX>` comparisons must be a constant value. One way of doing this is to provide literal values, for example:

```
switch (myInteger)
{
   case 1:
      <code to execute if myInteger == 1 >
      break;
   case -1:
      <code to execute if myInteger == -1 >
      break;
   default:
      <code to execute if myInteger != comparisons>
      break;
}
```

Another way is to use **constant variables**. Constant variables are just like any other variable, except for one key factor: the value they contain *never* changes. Once we assign a value to a constant variable that is the value it will have for the duration of code execution. Constant variables can come in handy here, as it is often easier to read code where the actual values being compared are hidden from us at the time of comparison.

We declare constant variables using the `const` keyword in addition to the variable type, and *must* assign them values at this time, for example:

```
const int intTwo = 2;
```

This code is perfectly valid, but if we try:

```
const int intTwo;
intTwo = 2;
```

we will get a compile error. This also happens if we try and change the value of a constant variable through any other means after initial assignment.

Let's look at an example of a `switch` statement that uses constant variables.

Try it Out – Using the switch Statement

1. Create a new console application called `Ch04Ex03` in the directory `C:\BegVCSharp\Chapter4`.

2. Add the following code to `Class1.cs`:

```
static void Main(string[] args)
{
    const string myName = "karli";
    const string sexyName = "angelina";
    const string sillyName = "ploppy";
    string name;
    Console.WriteLine("What is your name?");
    name = Console.ReadLine();
    switch (name.ToLower ())
    {
        case myName:
            Console.WriteLine("You have the same name as me!");
            break;
        case sexyName:
            Console.WriteLine("My, what a sexy name you have!");
            break;
        case sillyName:
            Console.WriteLine("That's a very silly name.");
            break;
    }
    Console.WriteLine("Hello {0}!", name);
}
```

3. Execute the code and enter a name:

How It Works

Our code sets up three constant strings, accepts a string from the user, and then writes out text to the console based on the string entered. In this case the strings are names.

When we compare the name entered (in the variable `name`) to our constant values we first force it into lower case with `name.ToLower()`. This is a standard command that will work with all string variables, and comes in handy when you're not sure what has been entered by the user. Using this technique the strings `"Karli"`, `"kArLi"`, `"karli"`, and so on will all match the test string `"karli"`.

The `switch` statement itself attempts to match the string entered with the constant values we have defined, and writes out a personalized message, if successful, to greet the user. If no match is made we simply greet the user.

`switch` statements have no limit on the amount of `case:` sections they contain, so you could extend this code to cover every name you can think of should you wish... but it might take a while!

Looping

Looping is where statements are executed repeatedly. This technique can come in very handy, as it means we can repeat operations as many times as we want (thousands, even millions, of times) without having to write the same code each time.

As a simple example, consider the following code for calculating the amount of money in a bank account after 10 years, assuming that interest is paid each year and no other money flows into or out of the account:

```
double balance = 1000;
double interestRate = 1.05; // 5% interest/year
balance *= interestRate;
balance *= interestRate;
balance *= interestRate;
balance *= interestRate;
balance *= interestRate;
balance *= interestRate;
balance *= interestRate;
balance *= interestRate;
balance *= interestRate;
balance *= interestRate;
```

Writing the same code out 10 times seems a bit wasteful, and what if we want to change the duration from 10 years to some other value? We'd have to manually copy the line of code the required amount of times, which would be a bit of a pain!

Luckily we don't have to do this. Instead we can just have a loop that executes the instruction we want the required number of times.

Another important type of loop is one where we loop until a certain condition is fulfilled. These loops are slightly simpler than the situation detailed above (although no less useful), so we'll start with them.

do Loops

do loops operate in the following way. The code we have marked out for looping is executed, then a Boolean test is performed, and the code executes again if this test evaluates to `true`, and so on. When the test evaluates to `false` the loop exits.

The structure of a do loop is as follows:

```
do
{
    <code to be looped>
} while (<Test>);
```

Where `<Test>` evaluates to a Boolean value.

The semicolon after the `while` statement is required, and it's a common error to miss this out.

For example, we could use this to write out the numbers from 1 to 10 in a column:

```
int i = 1;
do
{
    Console.WriteLine("{0}", i++);
} while (i <= 10);
```

Here we use the suffix version of the ++ operator to increment the value of i after it is written to the screen, so we need to check for i <= 10 in order to include ten in the numbers written to the console.

Let's use this for a slightly modified version of the code in the introduction to this section, where we calculated the balance in an account after 10 years. Here we will use a loop to calculate how many years it will take to get a specified amount of money in your account based on a starting amount and an interest rate.

Try it Out – Using do Loops

1. Create a new console application called `Ch04Ex04` in the directory `C:\BegVCSharp\Chapter4`.

2. Add the following code to `Class1.cs`:

```
static void Main(string[] args)
{
    double balance, interestRate, targetBalance;
    Console.WriteLine("What is your current balance?");
    balance = Convert.ToDouble(Console.ReadLine());
    Console.WriteLine("What is your current annual interest rate (in %)?");
    interestRate = 1 + Convert.ToDouble(Console.ReadLine()) / 100.0;
    Console.WriteLine("What balance would you like to have?");
```

```
        targetBalance = Convert.ToDouble(Console.ReadLine());

        int totalYears = 0;
        do
        {
            balance *= interestRate;
            ++totalYears;
        }
        while (balance < targetBalance);
        Console.WriteLine("In {0} year{1} you'll have a balance of {2}.",
                        totalYears, totalYears == 1 ? "" : "s", balance);
    }
```

3. Execute the code and enter some values:

```
C:\BegVCSharp\Chapter4\Ch04Ex04\bin\Debug\Ch04Ex04.exe
What is your current balance?
1000
What is your current annual interest rate (in %)?
4.2
What balance would you like to have?
10000
In 56 years you'll have a balance of 10013.6466385922.
Press any key to continue
```

How It Works

This code simply repeats the simple annual calculation of balance with a fixed interest rate as many times as is necessary for the balance to satisfy the terminating condition. We keep a count of how many years have been accounted for by incrementing a counter variable with each loop cycle:

```
        int totalYears = 0;
        do
        {
            balance *= interestRate;
            ++totalYears;
        }
        while (balance < targetBalance);
```

We can then use this counter variable as part of the result output:

```
        Console.WriteLine("In {0} year{1} you'll have a balance of {2}.",
                        totalYears, totalYears == 1 ? "" : "s", balance);
```

Note that this is perhaps the most common usage of the ? : (ternary) operator – to conditionally format text with the minimum of code. Here we output an 's' after 'year' if totalYears isn't equal to 1.

Unfortunately this code isn't perfect. Consider the situation where the target balance is less than the current balance. Here the output will be along the lines of:

```
C:\BegVCSharp\Chapter4\Ch04Ex04\bin\Debug\Ch04Ex04.exe
What is your current balance?
10000
What is your current annual interest rate (in %)?
4.2
What balance would you like to have?
1000
In 1 year you'll have a balance of 10420.
Press any key to continue
```

do loops *always* execute at least once. Sometimes, as in this situation, this isn't ideal. Of course, we could add an if statement:

```
int totalYears = 0;
if (balance < targetBalance)
{
    do
    {
        balance *= interestRate;
        ++totalYears;
    }
    while (balance < targetBalance);
}
Console.WriteLine("In {0} year{1} you'll have a balance of {2}.",
                  totalYears, totalYears == 1 ? "" : "s", balance);
```

But this does seem like we're adding unnecessary complexity. A far better solution is to use a while loop.

while Loops

while loops are very similar to do loops, but have one important difference. The Boolean test in a while loop takes place at the start of the loop cycle, not the end. If the test evaluates to false then the loop cycle is *never* executed. Instead, program execution jumps straight to the code following the loop.

while loops are specified in the following way:

```
while (<Test>)
{
    <code to be looped>
}
```

And can be used in almost the same way as do loops, for example:

```
int i = 1;
while (i <= 10)
{
    Console.WriteLine("{0}", i++);
}
```

This code gives the same result as the do loop we saw earlier, as it outputs the numbers 1 to 10 in a column.

So, let's modify the last example to use a `while` loop.

1. Create a new console application called `Ch04Ex05` in the directory `C:\BegVCSharp\Chapter4`.

2. Modify the code as follows (use the code from `Ch04Ex04` as a starting point, and remember to delete the `while` statement at the end of the original `do` loop):

```
static void Main(string[] args)
{
    double balance, interestRate, targetBalance;
    Console.WriteLine("What is your current balance?");
    balance = Convert.ToDouble(Console.ReadLine());
    Console.WriteLine("What is your current annual interest rate (in %)?");
    interestRate = 1 + Convert.ToDouble(Console.ReadLine()) / 100.0;
    Console.WriteLine("What balance would you like to have?");
    targetBalance = Convert.ToDouble(Console.ReadLine());

    int totalYears = 0;
    while (balance < targetBalance)
    {
        balance *= interestRate;
        ++totalYears;
    }
    Console.WriteLine("In {0} year{1} you'll have a balance of {2}.",
                      totalYears, totalYears == 1 ? "" : "s", balance);
}
```

3. Execute the code again, but this time use a target balance that is less than the starting balance:

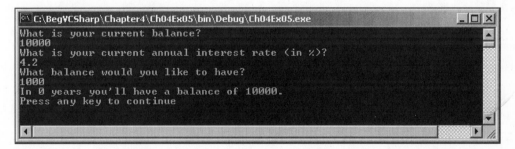

```
C:\BegVCSharp\Chapter4\Ch04Ex05\bin\Debug\Ch04Ex05.exe
What is your current balance?
10000
What is your current annual interest rate (in %)?
4.2
What balance would you like to have?
1000
In 0 years you'll have a balance of 10000.
Press any key to continue
```

How it Works

This simple change from a `do` loop to a `while` loop has solved the problem in the last example. By moving the Boolean test to the start we provide for the circumstance where no looping is required, and we can jump straight to the result.

There are, of course, other alternatives in this situation. For example, we could check the user input to ensure that the target balance is greater than the starting balance. In situations like this we can place the user input section in a loop as follows:

```
Console.WriteLine("What balance would you like to have?");
do
{
    targetBalance = Convert.ToDouble(Console.ReadLine());
    if (targetBalance <= balance)
        Console.WriteLine("You must enter an amount greater than " +
                    "your current balance!\nPlease enter another value.");
}
while (targetBalance <= balance);
```

This will reject values that don't make sense, so we'll get output as follows:

This **validation** of user input is an important topic when it comes to application design, and we'll see many examples of it over the course of this book.

for Loops

The last type of loop we'll look at in this chapter is the `for` loop. This type of loop is one that executes a set number of times, and maintains its own counter. To define a `for` loop we need the following information:

- ❑ A starting value to initialize the counter variable
- ❑ A condition for continuing the loop, involving the counter variable
- ❑ An operation to perform on the counter variable at the end of each loop cycle

For example, if we want a loop with a counter that increments from 1 to 10 in steps of one then the starting value is 1, the condition is that the counter is less that or equal to 10, and the operation to perform at the end of each cycle is to add one to the counter.

This information must be placed into the structure of a `for` loop as follows:

```
for (<initialization>; <condition>; <operation>)
{
    <code to loop>
}
```

This works in exactly the same way as the following `while` loop:

```
<initialization>
while (<condition>)
{
    <code to loop>
    <operation>
}
```

But the format of the `for` loop makes the code easier to read, as the syntax involves the complete specification of the loop in one place, rather than being divided over several statements in different areas of the code.

Earlier we used `do` and `while` loops to write out the numbers from 1 to 10. Let's look at the code required to do this using a `for` loop:

```
int i;
for (i = 1; i <= 10; ++i)
{
    Console.WriteLine("{0}", i);
}
```

The counter variable, an integer called `i`, starts with a value of 1, and is incremented by 1 at the end of each cycle. During each cycle the value of `i` is written to the console.

Note that when code resumes after the loop `i` has a value of 11. This is because at the end of the cycle where `i` was equal to 10, `i` gets incremented to 11. This happens before the condition that `i <= 10` is processed, at which point the loop ends.

As with `while` loops, `for` loops only execute if the condition evaluates to `true` before the first cycle, so the code in the loop doesn't necessarily run at all.

As a final note, we can declare the counter variable as part of the `for` statement, rewriting the above code as:

```
for (int i = 1; i <= 10; ++i)
{
    Console.WriteLine("{0}", i);
}
```

If we do this, though, the variable `i` won't be accessible from code outside this loop (see the section on **variable scope** in the next chapter).

Let's look at an example using `for` loops. Since we have used loops quite a bit now I'll make this example a bit more interesting: it will display a Mandelbrot set (using plain text characters, so it won't look that spectacular!).

1. Create a new console application called `Ch04Ex06` in the directory `C:\BegVCSharp\Chapter4`.

2. Add the following code to `Class1.cs`:

```
static void Main(string[] args)
{
    double realCoord, imagCoord;
    double realTemp, imagTemp, realTemp2, arg;
    int iterations;
    for (imagCoord = 1.2; imagCoord >= -1.2; imagCoord -= 0.05)
    {
        for (realCoord = -0.6; realCoord <= 1.77; realCoord += 0.03)
        {
            iterations = 0;
            realTemp = realCoord;
            imagTemp = imagCoord;
            arg = (realCoord * realCoord) + (imagCoord * imagCoord);
            while ((arg < 4) && (iterations < 40))
            {
                realTemp2 = (realTemp * realTemp) - (imagTemp * imagTemp)
                        - realCoord;
                imagTemp = (2 * realTemp * imagTemp) - imagCoord;
                realTemp = realTemp2;
                arg = (realTemp * realTemp) + (imagTemp * imagTemp);
                iterations += 1;
            }
            switch (iterations % 4)
            {
            case 0:
                Console.Write(".");
                break;
            case 1:
                Console.Write("o");
                break;
            case 2:
                Console.Write("O");
                break;
            case 3:
                Console.Write("@");
                break;
            }
        }
        Console.Write("\n");
    }
}
```

3. Execute the code:

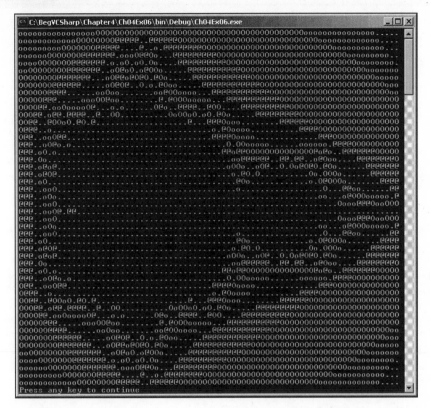

How It Works

Now, I don't want to get into too much detail about how to calculate Mandelbrot sets, but I will go through the basics to explain why we need the loops that we have used in this code. Feel free to skim through the following two paragraphs if the mathematics doesn't interest you, as it's an understanding of the code that is important here.

Each position in a Mandelbrot image corresponds to an imaginary number of the form $N = x + y*i$, where the real part is x, the imaginary part is y, and i is the square root of -1. The x and y coordinates of the position in the image correspond to the x and y parts of the imaginary number.

For each position on the image we look at the argument of N, which is the square root of $x*x + y*y$. If this value is greater than or equal to 2 we say that the position corresponding to this number has a value of 0. If the argument of N is less than 2 we change N to a value of $N*N - N$ (giving us $N = (x*x-y*y-x) + (2*x*y-y)*i$), and check the argument of this new value of N again. If this value is greater than or equal to 2 we say that the position corresponding to this number has a value of 1. This process continues until we either assign a value to the position on the image or perform more than a certain number of iterations.

Based on the values assigned to each point in the image we would, in a graphical environment, place a pixel of a certain color on the screen. However, as we are using a text display we simply place characters on screen instead.

Let's look at the code, and the loops contained in it.

We start by declaring the variables we will need for our calculation:

```
double realCoord, imagCoord;
double realTemp, imagTemp, realTemp2, arg;
int iterations;
```

Here, `realCoord` and `imagCoord` are the real and imaginary parts of N, and the other `double` variables are for temporary information during computation. `iterations` records how many iterations it takes before the argument of N (`arg`) is 2 or greater.

Next we start two `for` loops to cycle through coordinates covering the whole of the image (using slightly more complex syntax for modifying our counters than `++` or `--`, a common and powerful technique):

```
for (imagCoord = 1.2; imagCoord >= -1.2; imagCoord -= 0.05)
{
    for (realCoord = -0.6; realCoord <= 1.77; realCoord += 0.03)
    {
```

I've chosen appropriate limits to show the main section of the Mandelbrot set. Feel free to play around with these if you want to try 'zooming in' on the image.

Within these two loops we have code that pertains to a single point in the Mandelbrot set, giving us a value for N to play with. This is where we perform our calculation of iteration required, giving us a value to plot for the current point.

First we initialize some variables:

```
iterations = 0;
realTemp = realCoord;
imagTemp = imagCoord;
arg = (realCoord * realCoord) + (imagCoord * imagCoord);
```

Next we have a `while` loop to perform our iterating. We use a `while` loop rather than a `do` loop, in case the initial value of N has an argument greater than 2 already, in which case `iterations = 0` is the answer we are looking for and no further calculations are necessary.

Note that I'm not quite calculating the argument fully here, I'm just getting the value of $x*x + y*y$ and checking to see if that value is less than 4. This simplifies the calculation, as we know that 2 is the square root of 4 and don't have to calculate any square roots ourselves:

```
while ((arg < 4) && (iterations < 40))
{
    realTemp2 = (realTemp * realTemp) - (imagTemp * imagTemp)
                    - realCoord;
    imagTemp = (2 * realTemp * imagTemp) - imagCoord;
    realTemp = realTemp2;
    arg = (realTemp * realTemp) + (imagTemp * imagTemp);
    iterations += 1;
}
```

The maximum number of iterations of this loop, which calculates values as detailed above, is 40.

Once we have a value for the current point stored in `iterations` we use a switch statement to choose a character to output. We just use four different characters here, instead of the 40 possible values, and use the modulus operator (%) such that values of 0, 4, 8, and so on give one character, values of 1, 5, 9, and so on give another character, etc.:

```
switch (iterations % 4)
{
   case 0:
      Console.Write(".");
      break;
   case 1:
      Console.Write("o");
      break;
   case 2:
      Console.Write("O");
      break;
   case 3:
      Console.Write("@");
      break;
}
```

Note that we use `Console.Write()` here rather than `Console.WriteLine()`, as we don't want to start a new line every time we output a character.

At the end of one of the innermost `for` loops, we do want to end a line, so we simply output an end of line character using the escape sequence we saw earlier:

```
   }
   Console.Write("\n");
}
```

This results in each row being separated from the next and lining up appropriately.

The final result of this application, though not spectacular, is fairly impressive, and certainly shows how useful looping and branching can be.

Interrupting Loops

There are times when we want finer grained control over the processing of looping code. C# provides four commands that help us here, three of which we've seen before in other situations:

❑   `break` – causes the loop to end immediately

❑   `continue` – causes the current loop cycle to end immediately (execution continues with the next loop cycle)

❑   `goto` – allows jumping out of a loop to a labeled position (not recommended if you want your code to be easy to read and understand)

❑   `return` – jumps out of the loop and its containing function (see Chapter 6)

The `break` command simply exits the loop, and execution continues at the first line of code after the loop, for example:

```
int i = 1;
while (i <= 10)
{
   if (i == 6)
      break;
   Console.WriteLine("{0}", i++);
}
```

This code will write out the numbers from 1 to 5, as the `break` command causes the loop to exit when i reaches 6.

`continue` only stops the current cycle, not the whole loop, for example:

```
int i;
for (i = 1; i <= 10; i++)
{
   if ((i % 2) == 0)
      continue;
   Console.WriteLine(i);
}
```

In the above example, whenever the remainder of i divided by 2 is zero, the `continue` statement stops the execution of the current cycle, and so only the numbers 1,3,5,7,9 are displayed.

The third method of interrupting a loop is to use `goto` as we saw earlier, for example:

```
int i = 1;
while (i <= 10)
{
   if (i == 6)
      goto exitPoint;
   Console.WriteLine("{0}", i++);
}
Console.WriteLine("This code will never be reached.");
exitPoint:
Console.WriteLine("This code is run when the loop is exited using goto.");
```

Note that exiting a loop with `goto` is legal (if slightly messy), but it is illegal to use `goto` to jump into a loop from outside.

Infinite Loops

It is possible, through both coding errors or design, to define loops that never end, so-called **infinite** loops. As a very simple example, consider the following:

```
while (true)
{
   // code in loop
}
```

This situation can be useful at times, and we can always exit such loops using code such as `break` statements.

However, when this occurs by accident it can be annoying. Consider the following loop, which is similar to the `for` loop in the last section:

```
int i = 1;
while (i <= 10)
{
    if ((i % 2) == 0)
        continue;
    Console.WriteLine("{0}", i++);
}
```

Here, `i` doesn't get incremented until the last line of code in the loop, which occurs after the `continue` statement. If this `continue` statement is reached (which it will be when `i` is 2,) the next loop cycle will be using the same value of `i`, continuing the loop, testing the same value of `i`, continuing the loop and so on. This will cause the application to freeze. Note that it's still possible to quit the frozen application in the normal way, so you won't have to reboot your computer if this happens.

Summary

In this chapter we have developed our programming knowledge by considering various structures that we can use in our code. The proper use of these structures is essential when we start making more complex applications, and we will see them time and again throughout this book.

First we spent some time looking at Boolean logic, with a bit of bitwise logic thrown in for good measure. Looking back on this after working through the rest of the chapter confirms the starting assumption that we made, which is that this topic is very important when it comes to implementing branching and looping code in our programs. It is essential to become very familiar with the operators and techniques detailed in this section.

Branching enables us to conditionally execute code, which, when combined with looping, allows us to create convoluted structures in our C# code. When you have loops inside loops inside `if` structures inside loops, you start to see why code indentation is so useful! If we shift all our code to the left of the screen it instantly becomes difficult to parse by eye, and even more difficult to debug. It is well worth making sure you've got the hang of indentation at this stage – you'll appreciate it later on! OK, so VS does a lot of this for us, but it's a good idea to indent code as you type it anyway.

Exercises

1. If we have two integers stored in variables `var1` and `var2`, what Boolean test can we perform to see if one or the other (but not both) is greater than 10?

2. Write an application that includes the logic from Exercise 1, that obtains two numbers from the user and displays them, but rejects any input where both numbers are greater than 10 and asks for two new numbers.

3. What is wrong with the following code?

```
int i;
for (i = 1; i <= 10; i++)
{
   if ((i % 2) = 0)
      continue;
   Console.WriteLine(i);
}
```

4. Modify the Mandelbrot set application to request image limits from the user and display the chosen section of the image. The current code outputs as many characters as will fit on a single line of a console application; consider making every image chosen fit in the same amount of space to maximize the viewable area.

More About Variables

Now we've seen a bit more of the C# language it's time to go back and tackle some of the more involved topics concerning variables.

The first topic we'll look at is **type conversion**, where we convert values from one type into another. We've already seen a bit of this, but we'll look at it formally here. A grasp of this topic gives us a greater understanding of what happens when we mix types in expressions (intentionally or unintentionally), and tighter control over the way in which data is manipulated. This helps us to streamline our code, and avoid nasty surprises.

Once we've covered this we'll look at a few more types of variable that you can use:

- ❑ **Enumerations** – variable types that have a user defined discrete set of possible values that can be used in a human-readable way.

- ❑ **Structs** – composite variable types made up of a user-defined set of other variable types.

- ❑ **Arrays** – types that hold multiple variables of one type, allowing index access to the individual values.

These are slightly more complex than the simple types we've been using up to now, but can make our lives much easier.

Once we've covered these topics we'll look at another useful subject concerning strings – basic string manipulation.

Type Conversion

Earlier in this book we discussed the fact that all data, regardless of type, is simply a sequence of bits, that is, a sequence of zeros and ones. The meaning of the variable comes through the way in which this data is interpreted. The simplest example of this is the char type. This type represents a character in the Unicode character set using a number. In fact, this number is stored in exactly the same way as a ushort – both of them store a number between 0 and 65535.

However, in general you will find that the different types of variable use varying schemes to represent data. This implies that even if it is possible to place the sequence of bits from one variable into a variable of a different type (perhaps they use the same amount of storage, or perhaps the target type has enough storage space to include all the source bits), the results might not be what you expect!

Instead of this one-to-one mapping of bits from one variable into another, we need to use **type conversion** on the data.

Type conversion takes two forms:

❑   **Implicit conversion** – where conversion from type A to type B is possible in all circumstances and the rules for performing the conversion are simple enough for us to trust in the compiler.

❑   **Explicit conversion** – where conversion from type A to type B is only possible in certain circumstances, or where the rules for conversion are complicated enough to merit additional processing of some kind.

Let's look at these in turn.

Implicit Conversions

Implicit conversion requires no work on our part, and no additional code. Consider the code shown below:

```
var1 = var2;
```

This assignment may involve an implicit conversion, if the type of var2 can be implicitly converted into the type of var1, but it could just as easily involve two variables with the same type, and no implicit conversion is necessary.

Let's look at an example.

The values of ushort and char are effectively interchangeable, as both store a number between 0 and 65535. We can convert values between these types implicitly, as illustrated by the following code:

```
ushort destinationVar;
char sourceVar = 'a';
destinationVar = sourceVar;
Console.WriteLine("sourceVar val: {0}", sourceVar);
Console.WriteLine("destinationVar val: {0}", destinationVar);
```

Here the value stored in sourceVar is placed in destinationVar. When we output the variables with the two Console.WriteLine() commands we get the following output:

```
sourceVar val: a
destinationVar val: 97
```

Even though the two variables store the same information, they are interpreted in different ways using their type.

There are many implicit conversions of simple types; `bool` and `string` have no implicit conversions, but the numeric types have a few. For reference, the following table shows the numeric conversions which the compiler can perform implicitly (remember that `char`s are stored as numbers, so `char` counts as a numeric type):

Type	Can safely be converted to
byte	short, ushort, int, uint, long, ulong, float, double, decimal
sbyte	short, int, long, float, double, decimal
short	int, long, float, double, decimal
ushort	int, uint, long, ulong, float, double, decimal
int	long, float, double, decimal
uint	long, ulong, float, double, decimal
long	float, double, decimal
ulong	float, double, decimal
float	double
char	ushort, int, uint, long, ulong, float, double, decimal

Don't worry – you don't need to learn this table off by heart, as it's actually quite easy to work out which conversions the compiler can do implicitly. Back in Chapter 3 we saw a table showing the range of possible values for every simple numeric type. The implicit conversion rule for these types is this: any type A whose range of possible values completely fits inside the range of possible values of type B can be implicitly converted into that type.

The reasoning for this is simple. If you try to fit a value into a variable and that value is outside of the range of values that the variable can take, then there will be a problem. For example, a `short` type variable is capable of storing values up to 32767, and the maximum value allowed into a `byte` is 255, so there could be problems if we try to convert a `short` value into a `byte` value. If the `short` holds a value between 256 and 32767, it simply won't fit into a byte.

However, if you *know* that the value in your `short` type variable is less than 255 then surely you should be able to convert the value, right?

The simple answer is that of course you can. The slightly more complex answer is that of course you can, but you must use an **explicit** conversion. Performing an explicit conversion is a bit like saying "OK, I know you've warned me about doing this, but I'll take responsibility for what happens".

Explicit Conversions

As their name suggests, explicit conversions occur when we explicitly ask the compiler to convert a value from one data type to another. Because of this, they require extra code, and the format of this code may vary depending on the exact conversion method. Before we look at any of this explicit conversion code, let's look at what happens if we *don't* add any.

For example, the following modification to the code from the last section attempts to convert a short value into a byte:

```
byte destinationVar;
short sourceVar = 7;
destinationVar = sourceVar;
Console.WriteLine("sourceVar val: {0}", sourceVar);
Console.WriteLine("destinationVar val: {0}", destinationVar);
```

If you attempt to compile this code you will receive the following error:

```
Cannot implicitly convert type 'short' to 'byte'
```

Luckily for us, the C# compiler can detect missing explicit conversions!

In order to get this code to compile, we need to add the code to perform an explicit conversion. The easiest way to do this in this context is to **cast** the short variable into a byte. Casting basically means forcing data from one type into another, and involves the following simple syntax:

```
(destinationType)sourceVar
```

This will convert the value in *sourceVar* into *destinationType*.

> *Note that this is only possible in some situations. Types that bear little or no relation to each other are likely not to have casting conversions defined.*

We can therefore modify our example using this syntax to force the conversion from a short to a byte:

```
byte destinationVar;
short sourceVar = 7;
destinationVar = (byte)sourceVar;
Console.WriteLine("sourceVar val: {0}", sourceVar);
Console.WriteLine("destinationVar val: {0}", destinationVar);
```

Resulting in the following output:

```
sourceVar val: 7
destinationVar val: 7
```

So, what happens when we try to force a value into a variable that won't fit? Modifying our code as follows illustrates this:

```
byte destinationVar;
short sourceVar = 281;
destinationVar = (byte)sourceVar;
Console.WriteLine("sourceVar val: {0}", sourceVar);
Console.WriteLine("destinationVar val: {0}", destinationVar);
```

This results in:

```
sourceVar val: 281
destinationVar val: 25
```

What happened? Well, if we look at the binary representations of these two numbers, along with the maximum value that can be stored in a byte, which is 255:

```
281 = 100011001
 25 = 000011001
255 = 011111111
```

We can see that the leftmost bit of the source data has been lost. This immediately raises a question: how we can tell when this happens? Obviously there will be times where we will need to explicitly cast one type into another, and it would be nice to know if any data has been lost along the way. If we didn't detect this, it could cause serious errors, for example in an accounting application, or an application determining the trajectory of a rocket to the moon.

One way of doing this is simply to check the value of the source variable and compare it with the known limits of the destination variable. We also have another technique, which is to force the system to pay special attention to the conversion at run-time. Attempting to fit a value into a variable when that value is too big for the type of that variable results in an **overflow**, and this is the situation we want to check for.

Two keywords exist for setting what is called the **overflow checking context** for an expression: checked and unchecked. We use these in the following way:

```
checked(expression)
unchecked(expression)
```

Let's force overflow checking in our last example:

```
byte destinationVar;
short sourceVar = 281;
destinationVar = checked((byte)sourceVar);
Console.WriteLine("sourceVar val: {0}", sourceVar);
Console.WriteLine("destinationVar val: {0}", destinationVar);
```

When this code is executed it will crash with the following error message (I've compiled this in a project called OverflowCheck):

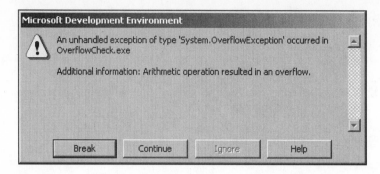

However, if we replace checked with unchecked in this code we will get the result we saw earlier, and no error will occur. This is identical to the default behavior we saw earlier.

As well as these two keywords, we can configure our application to behave as if every expression of this type includes the checked keyword, unless that expression explicitly uses the unchecked keyword (in other words, we can change the default setting for overflow checking). To do this, we modify the properties for our project in VS by right-clicking on the project in the **Solution Explorer** window and selecting the **Properties** option. Click on the **Configuration Properties** folder on the left-hand side of the window, and this will bring up a list of three sub-items (**Build**, **Debugging**, and **Advanced**). The property we want to change is one of the compiler settings, so make sure that the **Build** sub-item is selected. In the top group of properties (**Code Generation**), there is an option called **Check for Arithmetic Overflow/Underflow**. By default, this setting is **False**, but changing it to **True** gives the checked behavior detailed above:

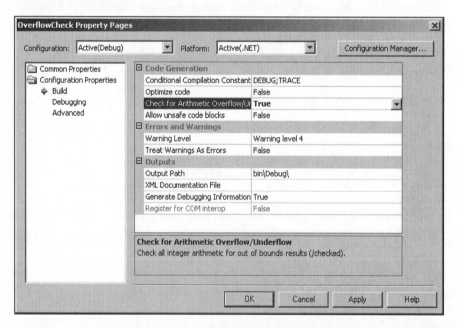

Explicit Conversions Using the Convert Commands

The type of explicit conversion we have been using in many of the Try it Out examples in this book is a bit different to those we have seen so far in this chapter. We have been converting string values into numbers using commands such as `Convert.ToDouble()`, which is obviously something that won't work for every possible string.

If, for example, we try to convert a string like "Number" into a double value using `Convert.ToDouble()`, we will see the following dialog when we execute the code:

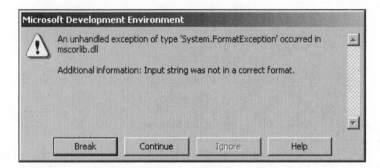

As you can see, the operation fails. In order for this type of conversion to work, the string supplied *must* be a valid representation of a number, and that number must be one that won't cause an overflow. A valid representation of a number is one that contains an optional sign (that is, plus or minus), zero or more digits, an optional period followed by one or more digits, and an optional "e" or "E" followed by an optional sign and one or more digits and *nothing else except spaces* (before or after this sequence). Using all of these optional extras we can recognize strings as complex as -1.2451e-24 as being a number.

There are many such explicit conversions that we can specify in this way, for example:

Command	Result
`Convert.ToBoolean(val)`	*val* converted to `bool`.
`Convert.ToByte(val)`	*val* converted to `byte`.
`Convert.ToChar(val)`	*val* converted to `char`.
`Convert.ToDecimal(val)`	*val* converted to `decimal`.
`Convert.ToDouble(val)`	*val* converted to `double`.
`Convert.ToInt16(val)`	*val* converted to `short`.
`Convert.ToInt32(val)`	*val* converted to `int`.
`Convert.ToInt64(val)`	*val* converted to `long`.
`Convert.ToSByte(val)`	*val* converted to `sbyte`.

Table continued on following page

Command	Result
`Convert.ToSingle(val)`	*val* converted to `float`.
`Convert.ToString(val)`	*val* converted to `string`.
`Convert.ToUInt16(val)`	*val* converted to `ushort`.
`Convert.ToUInt32(val)`	*val* converted to `uint`.
`Convert.ToUInt64(val)`	*val* converted to `ulong`.

Here `val` can be most types of variable (if it's a type that can't be handled by these commands the compiler will tell you).

Unfortunately, as the table above shows, the names of these conversions are slightly different to the C# type names; for example, to convert to an `int` we use `Convert.ToInt32()`. This is because these commands come from the .NET Framework `System` namespace, rather than being native C#. This allows them to be used from other .NET-compatible languages besides C#.

The important thing to note about these conversions is that they are *always* overflow-checked, and the `checked` and `unchecked` keywords and project property settings have no effect.

Let's look at an example that covers many of the conversion types from this section.

Try it Out – Type Conversions in Practice

1. Create a new console application called `Ch05Ex01` in the directory `C:\BegVCSharp\Chapter5`.

2. Add the following code to `Class1.cs`:

```
static void Main(string[] args)
{
    short  shortResult, shortVal = 4;
    int    integerVal = 67;
    long   longResult;
    float  floatVal = 10.5F;
    double doubleResult, doubleVal = 99.999;
    string stringResult, stringVal = "17";
    bool   boolVal = true;

    Console.WriteLine("Variable Conversion Examples\n");

    doubleResult = floatVal * shortVal;
    Console.WriteLine("Implicit, -> double: {0} * {1} -> {2}", floatVal,
        shortVal, doubleResult);

    shortResult = (short)floatVal;
    Console.WriteLine("Explicit, -> short: {0} -> {1}", floatVal,
        shortResult);
```

```
        stringResult = Convert.ToString(boolVal) +
           Convert.ToString(doubleVal);
        Console.WriteLine("Explicit, -> string: \"{0}\" + \"{1}\" -> {2}",
           boolVal, doubleVal, stringResult);

        longResult = integerVal + Convert.ToInt64(stringVal);
        Console.WriteLine("Mixed,    -> long:   {0} + {1} -> {2}",
           integerVal, stringVal, longResult);
     }
```

3. Execute the code:

```
C:\BegVCSharp\Chapter5\Ch05Ex01\bin\Debug\Ch05Ex01.exe
Variable Conversion Examples

Implicit, -> double: 10.5 * 4 -> 42
Explicit, -> short:  10.5 -> 10
Explicit, -> string: "True" + "99.999" -> True99.999
Mixed,    -> long:   67 + 17 -> 84
Press any key to continue
```

How it Works

This example contains all of the conversion types we've seen so far, both in simple assignments as in the short code examples in the discussion above, and in expressions. We need to consider both cases, as the processing of *every* non-unary operator may result in type conversions, not just assignment operators. For example:

```
    shortVal * floatVal
```

Here we are multiplying a short value by a float value. In situations such as these, where no explicit conversion is specified, implicit conversion will be used if possible. In this example the only implicit conversion that makes sense is to convert the short into a float (as converting a float into a short requires explicit conversion), so this is the one that will be used.

However, we can override this behavior should we wish, using:

```
    shortVal * (short)floatVal
```

This doesn't mean a short will be returned from this operation. Since the result of multiplying two shorts is quite likely to exceed 32767 (the maximum value a short can hold), this operation actually returns an int.

Explicit conversions performed using this casting syntax take the same operator precedence as other unary operators (such as ++ used as a prefix), that is, the highest level of precedence.

When we have statements involving mixed types, conversions occur as each operator is processed, according to the operator precedence. This means that "intermediate" conversions may occur, for example:

```
doubleResult = floatVal + (shortVal * floatVal);
```

The first operator to be processed here is *, which, as discussed above, will result in shortVal being converted to a float. Next we process the + operator, which won't require any conversion, as it acts on two float values (floatVal and the float type result of shortVal * floatVal). Finally, the float result of this calculation is converted into a double when the = operator is processed.

This conversion process can seem complex at first glance, but as long as you break expressions down into parts by taking the operator precedence order into account you should be able to work things out.

Complex Variable Types

So far we've looked at all the simple variable types that C# has to offer. There are three slightly more complex (but very useful) sorts of variable that we will look at here:

❑ Enumerations

❑ Structures

❑ Arrays

Enumerations

Each of the types we've seen so far (with the exception of string) has a clearly defined set of allowed values. Admittedly this set is so large in types such as double that it can practically be considered a continuum, but it *is* a fixed set nevertheless. The simplest example of this is the bool type, which can only take one of two values: true or false.

There are many other situations where you might want to have a variable that can take one of a fixed set of results. For example, you might want to have an orientation type that can store one of the values north, south, east, or west.

In situations like this, **enumerations** can be very useful. Enumerations do exactly what we want for this orientation type: they allow the definition of a type that can take one of a finite set of values that we supply.

What we need to do, then, is create our own enumeration type called orientation that can take one of the four possible values shown above.

Note that there is an additional step involved here – we don't just declare a variable of a given type, we declare and detail a user-defined type and then we declare a variable of this new type.

Defining Enumerations

Enumerations can be defined using the enum keyword as follows:

```
enum typeName
{
    value1,
    value2,
    value3,
    ...
    valueN
}
```

Next we can declare variables of this new type with:

```
typeName varName;
```

And assign values using:

```
varName = typeName.value;
```

Enumerations have an **underlying type** used for storage. Each of the values that an enumeration type can take is stored as a value of this underlying type, which by default is int. We can specify a different underlying type by adding the type to the enumeration declaration:

```
enum typeName : underlyingType
{
    value1,
    value2,
    value3,
    ...
    valueN
}
```

Enumerations can have underlying types of byte, sbyte, short, ushort, int, uint, long and ulong.

By default, each value is assigned a corresponding underlying type value automatically according to the order in which it is defined, starting from zero. This means that *value1* will get the value 0, *value2* will get 1, *value3* will get 2, and so on. We can override this assignment by using the = operator and specifying actual values for each enumeration value:

```
enum typeName : underlyingType
{
    value1 = actualVal1,
    value2 = actualVal2,
    value3 = actualVal3,
    ...
    valueN = actualValN
}
```

In addition, we can specify identical values for multiple enumeration values by using one value as the underlying value of another:

```
enum typeName : underlyingType
{
    value1 = actualVal1,
    value2 = value1,
    value3,
    ...
    valueN = actualValN
}
```

Any values left unassigned will be given an underlying value automatically, where the values used are in a sequence starting from 1 greater that the last explicitly declared one. In the above code, for example, `value3` will get the value `value1 + 1`.

Note that this can cause unpredicted problems, where values specified after a definition such as `value2 = value1` will be identical to other values. For example, in the following code `value4` will have the same value as `value2`:

```
enum typeName : underlyingType
{
    value1 = actualVal1,
    value2,
    value3 = value1,
    value4,
    ...
    valueN = actualValN
}
```

Of course, if this is the behavior you want then this code is fine.

Note also that assigning values in a circular fashion will cause an error, for example:

```
enum typeName : underlyingType
{
    value1 = value2,
    value2 = value1
}
```

Let's look at an example of all of this.

Try it Out – Using an Enumeration

1. Create a new console application called Ch05Ex02 in the directory C:\BegVCSharp\Chapter5.

2. Add the following code to Class1.cs:

```
namespace Ch05Ex02
{
    enum orientation : byte
    {
        north = 1,
        south = 2,
        east  = 3,
        west  = 4
    }

    /// <summary>
    /// Summary description for Class1.
    /// </summary>
    class Class1
    {
        /// <summary>
        /// The main entry point for the application.
        /// </summary>
        [STAThread]
        static void Main(string[] args)
        {
            orientation myDirection = orientation.north;
            Console.WriteLine("myDirection = {0}", myDirection);

        }
    }
}
```

3. Execute the application. You should see the following output to the console:

4. Quit the application and modify the code as follows:

```
byte directionByte;
string directionString;
orientation myDirection = orientation.north;
Console.WriteLine("myDirection = {0}", myDirection);
directionByte = (byte)myDirection;
directionString = Convert.ToString(myDirection);
Console.WriteLine("byte equivalent = {0}", directionByte);
Console.WriteLine("string equivalent = {0}", directionString);
```

5. Execute the application again:

```
C:\BegVCSharp\Chapter5\Ch05Ex02\bin\Debug\Ch05Ex02.exe          _ □ ×
myDirection = north
byte equivalent = 1
string equivalent = north
Press any key to continue
```

How It Works

This code defines and uses an enumeration type called `orientation`. The first thing to notice is that the type definition code is placed in our namespace, `Ch05Ex02`, but not in the same place as the rest of our code. This is because definitions are not executed as such; that is, at run-time we don't step through the code in a definition as we do the lines of code in our application. Application execution starts in the place we're used to, and has access to our new type as it belongs to the same namespace.

The first iteration of the example demonstrates the basic method of creating a variable of our new type, assigning it a value, and outputting it to the screen.

Next we modified our code to show the conversion of enumeration values into other types. Note that we *must* use explicit conversions here. Even though the underlying type of `orientation` is `byte`, we still have to use the `(byte)` cast to convert the value of `myDirection` into a `byte` type:

```
directionByte = (byte)myDirection;
```

The same explicit casting is necessary in the other direction too, if we want to convert a `byte` into an `orientation`. For example, we could use the following code to convert a `byte` variable called `myByte` into an orientation and assign this value to `myDirection`:

```
myDirection = (orientation)myByte;
```

Of course, care must be taken here as not all permissible values of `byte` type variables map to defined `orientation` values. The `orientation` type can store other byte values, so we won't get an error straight away, but this may break logic later in the application.

To get the string value of an enumeration value we can use `Convert.ToString()`:

```
directionString = Convert.ToString(myDirection);
```

Using a `(string)` cast won't work, as the processing required is more complicated than just placing the data stored in the enumeration variable into a `string` variable.

Alternatively, we can use the `ToString()` command of the variable itself. The following code gives us the same result as using `Convert.ToString()`:

```
directionString = myDirection.ToString();
```

Converting a `string` to an enumeration value is also possible, except that here the syntax required is slightly more complex. A special command exists for this sort of conversion, `Enum.Parse()`, which is used in the following way:

```
(enumerationType)Enum.Parse(typeof(enumerationType), enumerationValueString);
```

This uses another operator, `typeof`, which obtains the type of its operand. We could use this for our `orientation` type as follows:

```
string myString = "north";
orientation myDirection = (orientation)Enum.Parse(typeof(orientation),
                                                  myString);
```

Of course, not all string values will map to an `orientation` value! If we pass in a value that doesn't map to one of our enumeration values, we will get an error. Like everything else in C#, these values are case-sensitive, so we'll still get an error if our string agrees with a value in everything but case (for example, if `myString` is set to `"North"` rather than `"north"`).

Structs

The next sort of variable that we will look at is the **struct** (short for "structure"). Structs are just that – data structures are composed of several pieces of data, possibly of different types. They allow us to define our own types of variable based on this structure. For example, suppose we want to store the route to a location from a starting point, where the route consists of a direction and a distance in miles. For simplicity we'll assume that the direction is one of the compass points (such that it can be represented using the `orientation` enumeration from the last section), and that distance in miles can be represented as a `double` type.

Now, we could use two separate variables for this using code we've seen already:

```
orientation myDirection;
double      myDistance;
```

There is nothing wrong with using two variables like this, but it is would be far simpler (especially where multiple routes are required) to store this information in one place.

Defining Structs

Structs are defined using the `struct` keyword as follows:

```
struct <typeName>
{
   <memberDeclarations>
}
```

The `<memberDeclarations>` section contains declarations of variables (called the **data members** of the struct) in almost the same format as usual. Each member declaration takes the form:

```
<accessibility> <type> <name>;
```

To allow the code that calls the struct to access the struct's data members, we use the keyword `public` for `<accessibility>`. For example:

```
struct route
{
   public orientation direction;
   public double        distance;
}
```

Once we have a struct type defined, we use it by defining variables of the new type:

```
route myRoute;
```

And have access to the data members of this composite variable via the period character:

```
myRoute.direction = orientation.north;
myRoute.distance = 2.5;
```

Let's put this type into an example.

Try it Out – Using a Struct

1. Create a new console application called `Ch05Ex03` in the directory `C:\BegVCSharp\Chapter5`.

2. Add the following code to `Class1.cs`:

```
namespace Ch05Ex03
{
    enum orientation : byte
    {
       north = 1,
       south = 2,
       east  = 3,
       west  = 4
    }
    struct route
    {
       public orientation direction;
       public double        distance;
    }
    /// <summary>
    /// Summary description for Class1.
    /// </summary>
    class Class1
    {
       /// <summary>
       /// The main entry point for the application.
       /// </summary>
       [STAThread]
       static void Main(string[] args)
       {
```

```
        route myRoute;
        int myDirection = -1;
        double myDistance;
        Console.WriteLine("1) North\n2) South\n3) East\n4) West");
        do
        {
           Console.WriteLine("Select a direction:");
           myDirection = Convert.ToInt32(Console.ReadLine());
        }
        while ((myDirection < 1) || (myDirection > 4));
        Console.WriteLine("Input a distance:");
        myDistance = Convert.ToDouble(Console.ReadLine());
        myRoute.direction = (orientation)myDirection;
        myRoute.distance = myDistance;
        Console.WriteLine("myRoute specifies a direction of {0} and a " +
           "distance of {1}", myRoute.direction, myRoute.distance);
     }
  }
}
```

3. Execute the code, select a direction, and then enter a distance:

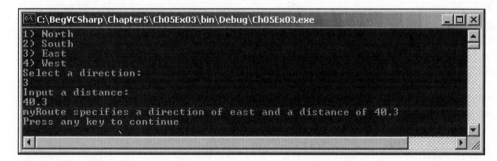

How it Works

Structs, like enumerations, are declared outside of the main body of the code. We declare our `route` struct just inside the namespace declaration, along with the `orientation` enumeration that it uses:

```
enum orientation : byte
{
   north = 1,
   south = 2,
   east  = 3,
   west  = 4
}
struct route
{
   public orientation direction;
   public double      distance;
}
```

The main body of the code follows a similar structure to some of the example code we've already seen, requesting input from the user and displaying it. We perform some simple validation of user input by placing the direction selection in a do loop, rejecting any input that isn't an integer between 1 and 4 (with values chosen such that they map onto the enumeration members for easy assignment).

The interesting point to note is that when we refer to the members of route they are treated in exactly the same way as variables of the same type as the member would be. The assignment is as follows:

```
myRoute.direction = (orientation)myDirection;
myRoute.distance = myDistance;
```

We could simply take the input value directly into myRoute.distance with no ill effects as follows:

```
myRoute.distance = Convert.ToDouble(Console.ReadLine());
```

The extra step allows for more validation, although none is performed in this code.

Any access to members of a structure is treated in the same way. Expressions of the form structVar.memberVar can be said to evaluate to a variable of the type of memberVar.

Arrays

All the types we've seen so far have one thing in common: each of them stores a single value (or a single set of values in the case of structs). Sometimes, in situations where we want to store a lot of data, this isn't very convenient. Sometimes we want to store several values of the same type at the same time, without having to use a different variable for each value.

For example, let's say you want to perform some processing that involves the names of all of your friends. You could use simple string variables such as:

```
string friendName1 = "Robert Barwell";
string friendName2 = "Mike Parry";
string friendName3 = "Jeremy Beacock";
```

But this looks like it will need a lot of effort, especially as we'll need to write different code to process each variable. We couldn't, for example, iterate through this list of strings in a loop.

The alternative is to use an **array**. Arrays are indexed lists of variables stored in a single array type variable. For example, let's say we have an array that stores the three names shown above, called friendNames. We can access individual members of this array by specifying their index in square brackets as shown below:

```
friendNames[<index>]
```

This index is simply an integer, starting with 0 for the first entry, 1 for the second, and so on. This means that we can go through the entries using a loop, for example:

```
int i;
for (i = 0; i < 3; i++)
{
```

```
        Console.WriteLine("Name with index of {0}: {1}", i, friendNames[i]);
    }
```

Arrays have a single **base type**, that is, individual entries in an array are all of the same type. This `friendNames` array has a base type of string, as it is intended for storing `string` variables.

Array entries are often referred to as **elements**.

Declaring Arrays

Arrays are declared in the following way:

```
<baseType>[] <name>;
```

Here, *<baseType>* may be any variable type, including the enumeration and struct types we've seen in this chapter.

Arrays must be initialized before we have access to them. We can't just access or assign values to the array elements like this:

```
int[] myIntArray;
myIntArray[10] = 5;
```

Arrays can be initialized in two ways. We can either specify the complete contents of the array in a literal form, or we can specify the size of the array and use the new keyword to initialize all array elements.

Specifying an array using literal values simply involves providing a comma-separated list of element values enclosed in curly braces, for example:

```
int[] myIntArray = {5, 9, 10, 2, 99};
```

Here `myIntArray` has five elements, each with an assigned integer value.

The other method requires syntax as follows:

```
int[] myIntArray = new int[5];
```

Here we use the new keyword to explicitly initialize the array, and a constant value to define the size. This method results in all the array members being assigned a default value, which is 0 for numeric types. We can also use non-constant variables for this initialization, for example:

```
int[] myIntArray = new int[arraySize];
```

We can also combine these two methods of initialization if we wish:

```
int[] myIntArray = new int[5] {5, 9, 10, 2, 99};
```

With this method the sizes *must* match. We can't, for example, write:

```
int[] myIntArray = new int[10] {5, 9, 10, 2, 99};
```

Here the array is defined as having 10 members, but only 5 are defined, so compilation will fail. A side effect of this is that if we define the size using a variable that variable must be a constant, for example:

```
const int arraySize = 5;
int[] myIntArray = new int[arraySize] {5, 9, 10, 2, 99};
```

If we omit the `const` keyword this code will fail.

As with other variable types, there is no need to initialize an array on the same line that we declare it. The following is perfectly legal:

```
int[] myIntArray;
myIntArray = new int[5];
```

We've done enough to look at an example, so let's try out some code.

Try it Out – Using an Array

1. Create a new console application called `Ch05Ex04` in the directory `C:\BegVCSharp\Chapter5`.

2. Add the following code to `Class1.cs`:

```
static void Main(string[] args)
{
    string[] friendNames = {"Robert Barwell", "Mike Parry",
                            "Jeremy Beacock"};
    int i;
    Console.WriteLine("Here are {0} of my friends:",
                      friendNames.Length);
    for (i = 0; i < friendNames.Length; i++)
    {
        Console.WriteLine(friendNames[i]);
    }
}
```

3. Execute the code:

How It Works

This code sets up a `string` array with three values, and lists them in the console in a `for` loop. Note that we have access to the number of elements in the array using `friendNames.Length`:

```
Console.WriteLine("Here are {0} of my friends:", friendNames.Length);
```

This is a handy way to get the size of an array.

Outputting values in a `for` loop is easy to get wrong. For example, try changing < to <= as follows:

```
for (i = 0; i <= friendNames.Length; i++)
{
    Console.WriteLine(friendNames[i]);
}
```

Compiling this results in the following dialog popping up:

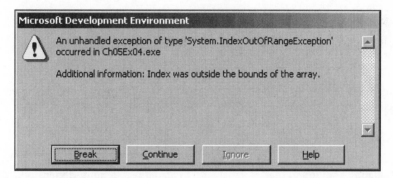

Here we have attempted to access `friendNames[3]`. Remember, array indices start from 0, so the last element is `friendNames[2]`. If we attempt to access elements outside of the array size the code will fail.

It just so happens that there is a more resilient method of accessing all the members of an array, using `foreach` loops.

foreach Loops

A `foreach` loop allows us to address each element in an array using the simple syntax:

```
foreach (<baseType> <name> in <array>)
{
    // can use <name> for each element
}
```

This loop will cycle through each element, placing each one in the variable *<name>* in turn, without danger of accessing illegal elements. We don't have to worry about how many elements there are in the array, and we can be sure that we'll get to use each one in the loop. Using this, we can modify the code in the last example as follows:

```
static void Main(string[] args)
{
    string[] friendNames = {"Robert Barwell", "Mike Parry",
                            "Jeremy Beacock"};
    Console.WriteLine("Here are {0} of my friends:", friendNames.Length);
    foreach (string friendName in friendNames)
    {
        Console.WriteLine(friendName);
    }
}
```

The output of this code will be exactly the same as the previous example.

The main difference between using this method and a standard `for` loop is that `foreach` gives us *read-only* access to the array contents, so we can't change the values of any of the elements. We couldn't, for example, do the following:

```
foreach (string friendName in friendNames)
{
    friendName = "Rupert the bear";
}
```

If we try this, compilation will fail. If we use a simple `for` loop, however, we can assign values to array elements.

Multi-dimensional Arrays

From the title of this section you would be forgiven for thinking that we are about to discuss some low-budget science fiction addition to the C# language. In actual fact, a multi-dimensional array is simply one that uses multiple indices to access its elements.

For example, consider the situation where you want to plot the height of a hill against the position measured. We might specify a position using two coordinates, x and y. We want to use these two coordinates as indices, such that an array called `hillHeight` would store the height at each pair of coordinates. This involves using multi-dimensional arrays.

A two-dimensional array such as this is declared as follows:

```
<baseType>[,] <name>;
```

Arrays of more dimensions simply require more commas; for example:

```
<baseType>[,,,] <name>;
```

This would declare a four-dimensional array.

Assigning values also uses a similar syntax, with commas separating sizes. To declare and initialize the two-dimensional array `hillHeight` discussed above with a base type of `double`, an x size of 3, and a y size of 4 requires the following:

```
double[,] hillHeight = new double[3,4];
```

Alternatively, we can use literal values for initial assignment. Here we use nested blocks of curly braces, separated by commas; for example:

```
double[,] hillHeight = {{1, 2, 3, 4}, {2, 3, 4, 5}, {3, 4, 5, 6}};
```

This array has the same dimension sizes as the previous one, but has values explicitly defined.

To access individual elements of a multidimensional array, we simply specify the indices separated by commas; for example:

```
hillHeight[2,1]
```

We can then manipulate this element just as with other elements.

This expression will access the second element of the third nested array as defined above (the value will be 4). Remember that we start counting from 0, and that the first number is the nested array. In other words, the first number specifies the pair of curly braces, and the second number the element within that pair of braces. We can represent this array visually like this:

hillHeight [0,0]	hillHeight [0,1]	hillHeight [0,2]	hillHeight [0,3]
1	2	3	4

hillHeight[1,0]	hillHeight[1,1]	hillHeight[1,2]	hillHeight[1,3]
2	3	4	5

hillHeight[2,0]	hillHeight[2,1]	hillHeight[2,2]	hillHeight[2,3]
3	4	5	6

The `foreach` loop allows us access to all elements in a multi-dimensional way just as with single-dimensional arrays; for example:

```
double[,] hillHeight = {{1, 2, 3, 4}, {2, 3, 4, 5}, {3, 4, 5, 6}};
foreach (double height in hillHeight)
{
    Console.WriteLine("{0}", height);
}
```

The order in which the elements are output is the same as the order used to assign literal values:

```
hillHeight[0,0]
hillHeight[0,1]
hillHeight[0,2]
hillHeight[0,3]
```

```
hillHeight[1,0]
hillHeight[1,1]
hillHeight[1,2]
```

... and so on.

Arrays of Arrays

Multidimensional arrays as discussed in the last section are said to be **rectangular**. This is because each "row" is the same size. Using the last example, we can have a y coordinate of 0 to 3 for any of the possible x coordinates.

It is also possible to have **jagged** arrays, where "rows" may be different sizes. To do this we need to have an array where each element is another array. We could also have arrays of arrays of arrays if we want, or even more complex situations. However, note that all this is only possible if the arrays have the same base type.

The syntax for declaring arrays of arrays involves specifying multiple sets of square brackets in the declaration of the array, for example:

```
int[][] jaggedIntArray;
```

Unfortunately, initializing arrays such as this isn't as simple as initializing multi-dimensional arrays. We can't, for example, follow this declaration with:

```
jaggedIntArray = new int[3][4];
```

Even if we could do this, it wouldn't be that useful, as we can achieve the same effect with simple multi-dimensional arrays with less effort. We also can't use code such as:

```
jaggedIntArray = {{1, 2, 3}, {1}, {1, 2}};
```

We have two options. We can initialize the array that contains other arrays (I'll call these sub-arrays for clarity) and then initialize the sub-arrays in turn:

```
jaggedIntArray = new int[2][];
jaggedIntArray[0] = new int[3];
jaggedIntArray[1] = new int[4];
```

Or we can use a modified form of the above literal assignment:

```
jaggedIntArray = {new int[] {1, 2, 3}, new int[] {1}, new int[] {1, 2}};
```

We can use foreach loops with jagged arrays, but we'll often need to nest these to get to the actual data. For example, let's say we have the following jagged array that contains ten arrays, each of which contains an array of integers that are divisors of an integer between one and ten:

```
int[][] divisors1To10 = {new int[] {1},
                         new int[] {1, 2},
                         new int[] {1, 3},
                         new int[] {1, 2, 4},
                         new int[] {1, 5},
                         new int[] {1, 2, 3, 6},
                         new int[] {1, 7},
                         new int[] {1, 2, 4, 8},
                         new int[] {1, 3, 9},
                         new int[] {1, 2, 5, 10}};
```

The following code will fail:

```
foreach (int divisor in divisors1To10)
{
    Console.WriteLine(divisor);
}
```

This is because the array `divisors1To10` contains `int[]` elements, not `int` elements. Instead we have to loop through every sub-array as well as through the array itself:

```
foreach (int[] divisorsOfInt in divisors1To10)
{
    foreach(int divisor in divisorsOfInt)
    {
        Console.WriteLine(divisor);
    }
}
```

As you can see, the syntax for using jagged arrays can quickly become complex! In most cases it is easier to use rectangular arrays, or a simpler storage method. However, there may well be situations where we are forced to use this method, and a working knowledge can't hurt!

String Manipulation

Our use of strings so far has consisted of writing strings to the console, reading strings from the console, and concatenating strings using the + operator. In the course of programming more interesting applications you will soon discover that the manipulation of strings is something that we end up doing *a lot*. Because of this it is worth us spending a few pages looking at some of the more common string manipulation techniques available in C#.

To start with, it is well worth noting that a `string` type variable can be treated as a read-only array of `char` variables. This means that we can access individual characters using syntax like:

```
string myString = "A string";
char myChar = myString[1];
```

However, we can't assign individual characters in this way.

To get a `char` array that we can write to, we can use the following code. This uses the `ToCharArray()` command of the array variable:

```
string myString = "A string";
char[] myChars = myString.ToCharArray();
```

And then we can manipulate the `char` array in the standard way.

We can also use strings in `foreach` loops, for example:

```
foreach (char character in myString)
{
    Console.WriteLine("{0}", character);
}
```

As with arrays we can also get the number of elements using `myString.Length`. This gives us the number of characters in the string, for example:

```
string myString = Console.ReadLine();
Console.WriteLine("You typed {0} characters.", myString.Length);
```

Other basic string manipulation techniques use commands with a similar format to this `<string>.ToCharArray()` command. Two simple, but useful, ones are `<string>.ToLower()` and `<string>.ToUpper()`. These enable strings to be converted into lower and upper case respectively. To see why this is useful, consider the situation where you want to check for a specific response from a user, for example the string `"yes"`. If we convert the string entered by the user into lower case then we can also check for the strings `"YES"`, `"Yes"`, `"yeS"`, and so on – we saw an example of this in the previous chapter if you recall:

```
string userResponse = Console.ReadLine();
if (userResponse.ToLower() == "yes")
{
    // act on response
}
```

Note that this command, like the others in this section, doesn't actually change the string to which it is applied. Instead, combining this command with a string results in a new string being created, which we can compare to another string (as shown above), or assign to another variable. This other variable may be the same one that is being operated on, for example:

```
userResponse = userResponse.ToLower();
```

This is an important point to remember, as just writing:

```
userResponse.ToLower();
```

doesn't actually achieve very much!

Let's see what else we can do to ease the interpretation of user input. What if the user accidentally put an extra space at the beginning or end of their input? In this case the above code won't work. We need to trim the string entered, which we can do using the `<string>.Trim()` command:

```
string userResponse = Console.ReadLine();
userResponse = userResponse.Trim();
if (userResponse.ToLower() == "yes")
{
    // act on response
}
```

Using this, we will also be able detect strings like:

```
"  YES"
"Yes "
```

We can also use these commands to remove any other characters, by specifying them in a `char` array, for example:

```
char[] trimChars = {' ', 'e', 's'};
string userResponse = Console.ReadLine();
userResponse = userResponse.ToLower();
userResponse = userResponse.Trim(trimChars);
if (userResponse == "y")
{
    // act on response
}
```

This gets rid of any occurrences of spaces, the letter "e", and the letter "s" from the beginning or end of our string. Providing there isn't any other character in the string, this will result in the detection of strings such as:

```
"Yeeeees"
"  y"
```

And so on.

We can also use the `<string>.TrimStart()` and `<string>.TrimEnd()` command, which will trim spaces from the beginning and end of a string respectively. These can also have `char` arrays specified.

There are two other string commands that we can use to manipulate the spacing of strings: `<string>.PadLeft()` and `<string>.PadRight()`. These allow us to add spaces to the left or right of a string in order to force it to the desired length. We use these as follows:

```
<string>.PadX(<desiredLength>);
```

For example:

```
myString = "Aligned";
myString = myString.PadLeft(10);
```

This would result in three spaces being added to the left of the word "Aligned" in myString. These methods can be useful for aligning strings in columns, which is particularly useful for placing number strings below others.

As with the trimming commands, we can also use these commands in a second way, by supplying the character to pad the string with. This involves a single char, not an array of chars as with trimming. For example:

```
myString = "Aligned";
myString = myString.PadLeft(10, '-');
```

This would add three dashes to the start of myString.

There are many more of these string manipulation commands, many of which are only useful in very specific situations. I'll discuss these as and when we use them in the forthcoming chapters. Before moving on, though, it is worth looking at one of the features of VS that you may have noticed over the course of the last few chapters, and especially this one.

Try it Out – Statement Auto-completion in VS

1. Create a new console application called Ch05Ex05 in the directory C:\BegVCSharp\Chapter5.

2. Type the following code to Class1.cs, exactly as written:

```
static void Main(string[] args)
{
    string myString = "This is a test.";
    char[] separator = {' '};
    string[] myWords;
    myWords = myString.
}
```

3. As you type the final period, note the following window that pops up:

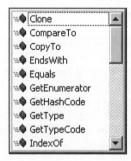

4. Without moving the cursor, type "s". The pop-up window changes, and a yellow tooltip pop-up appears:

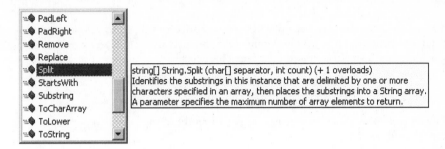

5. Type the following characters: "(separator);". The code should look as follows, and the pop-up windows should disappear:

```
static void Main(string[] args)
{
    string myString = "This is a test.";
    char[] separator = {' '};
    string[] myWords;
    myWords = myString.Split(separator);
}
```

6. Add the following code, noting the windows as they pop up:

```
static void Main(string[] args)
{
    string myString = "This is a test.";
    char[] separator = {' '};
    string[] myWords;
    myWords = myString.Split(separator);
    foreach (string word in myWords)
    {
        Console.WriteLine("{0}", word);
    }
}
```

7. Execute the code:

```
C:\BegVCSharp\Chapter5\Ch05Ex05\bin\Debug\Ch05Ex05.exe
This
is
a
test.
Press any key to continue
```

How It Works

There are two main points to note in this code. The first is the new string command we have used, and the second is the use of the auto-completion function in VS. We'll tackle these one at a time.

The command we have used, `<string>.Split()`, converts a `string` into a `string` array by splitting it at the points specified. These points take the form of a `char` array, which in this case is simply populated by a single element, the space character:

```
char[] separator = {' '};
```

The following code obtains the sub-strings we get when the string is split at each space, that is, we get an array of individual words:

```
string[] myWords;
myWords = myString.Split(separator);
```

Next we loop through the words in this array using `foreach`, and write each one to the console:

```
foreach (string word in myWords)
{
    Console.WriteLine("{0}", word);
}
```

Note that each word obtained will have no spaces, neither embedded in the word nor at either end. The separators are removed when we use `Split()`.

Next, let's look at the auto-completion. VS is a very intelligent package, and works out a lot of information about your code as you type it in. By the time you type the period after `myString`, it knows that `myString` is a string, detects that you want to specify a string command, and presents the available options. At this point you can stop typing should you wish, and select the command you want using the up and down arrow keys. As you move through what is available, VS tells you what the currently selected command means, and what the syntax for using it is.

When we start typing more characters VS moves the selected command to the top of the commands you might mean automatically. Once it shows the command you want, you can simply carry on typing as if you'd typed the whole name, so typing "(" takes us straight to the point where we specify the additional information that some commands require – and VS even tells us the format this extra information must be in, presenting options for those commands that accept varying amounts of information.

This feature of VS can come in very handy, and allows us to find out information about strange types with ease. You may find it interesting to look at all the commands that the `string` type exposes and experiment – nothing you do is going to break the computer, so play away!

Summary

In this chapter we've spent some time expanding our current knowledge of variables and filling in some of the blanks from earlier on. Perhaps the most important topic covered in this chapter is type conversion, as this is one that will come back and haunt you throughout this book. Getting a sound grasp of the concepts involved now will make things a lot easier later!

We've also seen a few more variable types that we can use to help us to store data in a more developer-friendly way. We've seen how enumerations can make our code much more readable with easily discernable values, how structs can be used to combine multiple related data elements in one place, and how we can group similar data together in arrays. We'll see all of these types used many times throughout the rest of this book.

Finally, we turned our attention to string manipulation, discussing some of the basic techniques and principles involved. There are many individual string commands available here, and we only looked at a few, but we also saw how we can look at the available commands in VS. Using this technique you can have some fun trying things out. At least one of the examples below can be solved using one or more string commands we haven't discussed yet, but I'm not telling you which!

Exercises

1. Which of the following conversions can't be performed implicitly:

    a. `int` to `short`

    b. `short` to `int`

    c. `bool` to `string`

    d. `byte` to `float`

2. Give the code for a `color` enumeration based on the `short` type containing the colors of the rainbow plus black and white. Can this enumeration be based on the `byte` type?

3. Modify the Mandelbrot set generator example from the last chapter to use the following struct for complex numbers:

```
struct imagNum
{
    public double real, imag;
}
```

4. Will the following code compile? If not, why not?

```
string[] blab = new string[5]
blab[5] = 5th string.
```

5. Write a console application that accepts a string from the user and outputs a string with the characters in reverse order.

6. Write a console application that accepts a string and replaces all occurrences of the string "no" with "yes".

7. Write a console application that places double quotes around each word in a string.

Functions

All the code we have seen so far has taken the form of a single block, perhaps with some looping to repeat lines of code and branching to execute statements conditionally. If we've needed to perform an operation on our data then this has meant placing the code required right where we want it to work.

This kind of code structure is limited. We will often find that some tasks, for example finding the highest value in an array, may need to be performed at several points in a program. We can just place identical (or near identical) sections of code in our application whenever necessary, but this has its own problems. Changing even one minor detail concerning a common task (to correct a code error, for example) may require changes to multiple sections of code, which may be spread throughout the application. Missing one of these could have dramatic consequences, and cause the whole application to fail. In addition, the application could get very lengthy.

The solution to this problem is to use **functions**. Functions in C# are a means of providing blocks of code that can be executed at any point in an application.

> *Functions of the specific type we are considering in this chapter are known as* **methods**. *However, this term has a very specific meaning in .NET programming that will only become clear later in the book, so for now we'll avoid the use of this term.*

For example, we could have a function that calculates the maximum value in an array. We can use this function from any point in our code, and use the same lines of code in each case. Since we only need to supply this code once any changes we make to it will affect this calculation wherever it is used. This function can be thought of as containing **reusable** code.

Functions also have the advantage of making our code more readable, as we can use them to group related code together. If we do this, then our application body itself can be made very short, as the inner workings of the code are separated out. This is similar to the way in which we can collapse regions of code together in VS using the outline view, and gives a more logical structure to our application.

Functions can also be used to create **multi-purpose** code, allowing them to perform the same operations on varying data. We can supply a function with information to work with in the form of **parameters**, and we can obtain results from functions in the form of **return values**. In the above example, we could supply an array to search as a parameter and obtain the maximum value in the array as a return value. This means that we can use the same function to work with a different array each time. The parameters and return value of a function collectively define the **signature** of a function.

In this chapter, we'll start by looking at the way in which we can define and use simple functions that don't accept or return any data. After this, we'll move on to look at the way in which we can achieve transfer of data to and from functions.

Next we'll take a look at the issue of **variable scope**. This concerns the way in which data in a C# application is localized to specific regions of code, an issue that becomes especially important when we are separating our code into multiple functions.

After this, we'll take an in depth look at an important function in C# applications: Main(). We'll see how we can use the built in behavior of this function to make use of **command line arguments**, which enable us to transfer information into applications when we run them.

Next, we'll take a look at an additional feature of the struct types that we saw in the last chapter, the fact that you can supply functions as members of struct types.

Finally we'll turn our attention to two more advanced topics: **function overloading** and **delegates**. Function overloading is a technique that allows us to provide multiple functions with the same name, but different signatures. A delegate is a variable type that allows us to use functions indirectly. The same delegate can be used to call any function that matches a specific signature, giving us the ability to choose between several functions at run time.

Defining and Using Functions

In this section, we'll look at how we can add functions to our applications and then use (**call**) them from our code. We'll start with the basic, looking at simple functions that don't exchange any data with code that calls them, and then move on to look at more advanced function usage.

To get things moving, let's look at an example.

Try it Out – Defining and Using a Basic Function

1. Create a new console application called Ch06Ex01 in the directory C:\BegVCSharp\Chapter6.

2. Add the following code to Class1.cs:

```
class Class1
{
    static void Write()
    {
        Console.WriteLine("Text output from function.");
    }

    /// <summary>
    /// The main entry point for the application.
    /// </summary>
    [STAThread]
    static void Main(string[] args)
```

```
    {
        Write();
    }
}
```

3. Execute the code:

How It Works

The following four lines of our code define a function called `Write()`:

```
static void Write()
{
    Console.WriteLine("Text output from function.");
}
```

The code contained here simply outputs some text to the console window. However, this behavior isn't that important to us at the moment, as we're more concerned with the mechanisms behind function definition and use.

The function definition here consists of the following:

❑ Two keywords, `static` and `void`.

❑ A function name followed by parentheses, `Write()`.

❑ A block of code to execute enclosed in curly braces.

The code that defines the `Write()` function looks very similar to some of the other code in our application:

```
static void Main(string[] args)
{
    ...
}
```

This is because all the code we have written so far (apart from type definitions) has been part of a function. This function, `Main()`, is (as suggested by the comment in the auto-generated code) the **entry point** function for a console application. When a C# application is executed, the entry point function it contains is called, and when this function completes the application terminates. All C# executable code must have an entry point.

The only difference between the `Main()` function and our `Write()` function (apart from the lines of code they contain), is that there is some code inside the parentheses after the function name `Main`. This is how we specify parameters, which we'll discuss in more detail shortly.

As mentioned above, both `Main()` and `Write()` are defined using `static` and `void` keywords. The `static` keyword relates to object-oriented concepts, which we'll come back to later in the book. For now you only need to remember that all the functions we'll use in our applications in this section of the book *must* use this keyword.

`void`, on the other hand, is much simpler to explain. This keyword is to indicate the function does not return a value. Later on in this chapter, we'll see what we need to write when a function has a return value.

Moving on, the code that calls our function is as follows:

```
Write();
```

We simply type the name of the function followed by empty parentheses. When program execution reaches this point the code in the `Write()` function will run.

Note that the parentheses used, both in the function definition and where the function is called, are mandatory. Try removing them if you like – the code won't compile.

Return Values

The simplest way of exchanging data with a function is to make use of a return value. Functions that have return values *evaluate* to that value, in exactly the same way as variables evaluate to the value they contain when we use them in expressions. Just like variables, return values have a type.

For example, we might have a function called `getString()` whose return value is a string. We could use this in code, such as:

```
string myString;
myString = getString();
```

Alternatively, we might have a function called `getVal()` that returns a `double` value, which we could use in a mathematical expression:

```
double myVal;
double multipler = 5.3;
myVal = getVal() * multiplier;
```

When a function returns a value, we have to modify your function in two ways:

❑ Specify the type of the return value in the function declaration instead of using the `void` keyword

❑ Use the `return` keyword to end the function execution and transfer the return value to the calling code

In code terms, this looks like the following in a console application function of the type we've been looking at:

```
static <returnType> <functionName>()
{
   ...
   return <returnValue>;
}
```

The only limitation here is that *<returnValue>* must be a value that is either of type *<returnType>*, or can be implicitly converted to that type. However, *<returnType>* can be any type we want, including the more complicated types we've seen.

This might be as simple as:

```
static double getVal()
{
   return 3.2;
}
```

However, return values are usually the result of some processing carried out by the function, as the above could be achieved just as easily by using a const variable.

When the return statement is reached, program execution returns to the calling code immediately. No lines of code after this statement will be executed. However, this doesn't mean that return statements can only be placed on the last line of a function body. We can use return earlier in the code, perhaps after performing some branching logic. Placing return in a for loop, an if block, or any other structure causes the structure to terminate immediately and the function to terminate. For example:

```
static double getVal()
{
   double checkVal;
   // checkVal assigned a value through some logic.
   if (checkVal < 5)
      return 4.7;
   return 3.2;
}
```

Here one of two values may be returned depending on the value of checkVal.

The only restriction here is that a return statement must be processed before reaching the closing } of the function. The following is illegal:

```
static double getVal()
{
   double checkVal;
   // checkVal assigned a value through some logic.
   if (checkVal < 5)
      return 4.7;
}
```

If checkVal is >= 5, then no return statement is met, which isn't allowed. All processing paths must reach a return statement.

As a final note, return can be used in functions declared using the void keyword (that don't have a return value). If we do so, then the function will simply terminate. When we use return in this way, it is an error to provide a return value in between the return keyword and the semicolon that follows.

Parameters

When a function is to accept parameters, we must specify the following:

❑ A list of the parameters accepted by a function in its definition, along with the types of those parameters

❑ A matching list of parameters in each function call

This involves the following code:

```
static <returnType> <functionName>(<paramType> <paramName>, ...)
{
   ...
   return <returnValue>;
}
```

Where we can have any number of parameters, each with a type and a name. The parameters are separated using commas. Each of these parameters is accessible from code within the function as a variable.

For example, a simple function might take two double parameters and return their product:

```
static double product(double param1, double param2)
{
   return param1 * param2;
}
```

Let's look at a more complex example.

Try it Out – Exchanging Data with a Function

1. Create a new console application called Ch06Ex02 in the directory C:\BegVCSharp\Chapter6.

2. Add the following code to Class1.cs (comments, etc. have been removed for clarity):

```
class Class1
{
   static int MaxValue(int[] intArray)
   {
      int maxVal = intArray[0];
      for (int i = 1; i < intArray.Length; i++)
```

```
        {
            if (intArray[i] > maxVal)
                maxVal = intArray[i];
        }
        return maxVal;
    }

    static void Main(string[] args)
    {
        int[] myArray = {1, 8, 3, 6, 2, 5, 9, 3, 0, 2};
        int maxVal = MaxValue(myArray);
        Console.WriteLine("The maximum value in myArray is {0}", maxVal);
    }
}
```

3. Execute the code:

How It Works

This code contains a function that does what the example function discussed in the introduction to this chapter hoped to do. It accepts an array of integers as a parameter and returns the highest number in the array. The function definition is as follows:

```
static int MaxValue(int[] intArray)
{
    int maxVal = intArray[0];
    for (int i = 1; i < intArray.Length; i++)
    {
        if (intArray[i] > maxVal)
            maxVal = intArray[i];
    }
    return maxVal;
}
```

The function, MaxValue(), has a single parameter defined, an int array called intArray. It also has a return type of int. The calculation of the maximum value is simple. A local integer variable called maxVal is initialized to the first value in the array, and then this value is compared with each of the subsequent elements in the array. If an element contains a higher value than maxVal, then this value replaces the current value of maxVal. When the loop finishes, maxVal contains the highest value in the array, and is returned using the return statement.

The code in Main() declares and initializes a simple integer array to use with the MaxValue() function:

```
int[] myArray = {1, 8, 3, 6, 2, 5, 9, 3, 0, 2};
```

The call to `MaxValue()` is used to assign a value to the `int` variable `maxVal`:

```
int maxVal = MaxValue(myArray);
```

Next, we write this value to the screen using `Console.WriteLine()`:

```
Console.WriteLine("The maximum value in myArray is {0}", maxVal);
```

Parameter Matching

When we call a function, we must match the parameters as specified in the function definition exactly. This means matching the parameter types, the number of parameters, and the order of the parameters. This means, for example, that the following function:

```
static void myFunction(string myString, double myDouble)
{
   ...
}
```

can't be called using:

```
myFunction (2.6, "Hello");
```

Here we are attempting to pass a `double` value as the first parameter and a `string` value as the second parameter, which is not the order in which the parameters are defined in the function definition.

We also can't use:

```
myFunction("Hello");
```

Here we are only passing a single `string` parameter, where two parameters are required.

Attempting to use either of the two function calls above will result in a compiler error, as the compiler forces us to match the signatures of the functions we use.

Going back to our example, this means that `MaxValue()` can only be used to obtain the maximum `int` in an array of `int` values. If we replace the code in `Main()` with the following code:

```
static void Main(string[] args)
{
    double[] myArray = {1.3, 8.9, 3.3, 6.5, 2.7, 5.3};
    double maxVal = MaxValue(myArray);
    Console.WriteLine("The maximum value in myArray is {0}", maxVal);
}
```

then the code won't compile, as the parameter type is wrong.

Later on in this chapter, in the *Overloading Functions* section, we'll see a useful technique for getting round this problem.

Parameter Arrays

C# allows us to specify one (and only one) special parameter for a function. This parameter, which must be the last parameter in the function definition, is known as a **parameter array**. Parameter arrays allow us to call functions using a variable amount of parameters, and are defined using the params keyword.

Parameter arrays can be a useful way to simplify our code, as we don't have to pass arrays from our calling code. Instead, we pass several parameters of the same type that are placed in an array that we can use from within our function.

The following code is required to define a function that uses a parameter array:

```
static <returnType> <functionName>(<p1Type> <p1Name>, ... ,
                                    params <type>[] <name>)
{
   ...
   return <returnValue>;
}
```

We can call this function using code like:

```
<functionName>(<p1>, ... , <val1>, <val2>, ...)
```

Here *<val1>*, *<val2>*, and so on are values of type *<type>* that are used to initialize the *<name>* array. There is no limit on the amount of parameters that we can specify here; the only restriction is that they are all of type *<type>*. We can even specify no parameters at all.

This final point makes parameter arrays particularly useful for specifying additional information for functions to use in their processing. For example, let's say we have a function called getWord() that takes a string value as its first parameter and returns the first word in the string:

```
string firstWord = getWord("This is a sentence.");
```

Here firstWord will be assigned the string "This".

We might add a params parameter to getWord() allowing us to optionally select an alternative word to return by its index:

```
string firstWord = getWord("This is a sentence.", 2);
```

Assuming that we start counting at 1 for the first word, this would result in firstWord being assigned the string "is".

We might also add the capability to limit the amount of characters returned in a third parameter, also accessible through the params parameter:

```
string firstWord = getWord("This is a sentence.", 4, 3);
```

Here firstWord would be assigned the string "sen".

Let's see a full example.

Try it Out – Exchanging Data with a Function Part 2

1. Create a new console application called `Ch06Ex03` in the directory `C:\BegVCSharp\Chapter6`.

2. Add the following code to `Class1.cs`:

```
class Class1
{
    static int sumVals(params int[] vals)
    {
        int sum = 0;
        foreach (int val in vals)
        {
            sum += val;
        }
        return sum;
    }

    static void Main(string[] args)
    {
        int sum = sumVals(1, 5, 2, 9, 8);
        Console.WriteLine("Summed Values = {0}", sum);
    }
}
```

3. Execute the code:

How It Works

In this example, the function `sumVals()` is defined using the `params` keyword to accept any number of `int` parameters (and no others):

```
static int sumVals(params int[] vals)
{
    ...
}
```

The code in this function simply iterates through the value in the `vals` array, and adds the values together, returning the result.

In `Main()` we call this function with five integer parameters:

```
int sum = sumVals (1, 5, 2, 9, 8);
```

However, we could just as easily have called this function with none, one, two, or a hundred integer parameters – there is no limit to the amount we can specify.

Reference and Value Parameters

All the functions we have defined so far in this chapter have had **value** parameters. What I mean by this is that when we have used parameters we have passed a value into a variable used by the function. Any changes made to this variable in the function have *no effect* on the parameter specified in the function call. For example, consider a function that doubles and displays the value of a passed parameter:

```
static void showDouble(int val)
{
    val *= 2;
    Console.WriteLine("val doubled = {0}", val);
}
```

Here the parameter, val, is doubled in this function. If we call it in the following way:

```
int myNumber = 5;
Console.WriteLine("myNumber = {0}", myNumber);
showDouble(myNumber);
Console.WriteLine("myNumber = {0}", myNumber);
```

The text output to the console is as follows:

```
myNumber = 5
val doubled = 10
myNumber = 5
```

Calling showDouble() with myNumber as a parameter doesn't affect the value of myNumber in Main(), even though the parameter it is assigned to, val, is doubled.

This is all very well, but if we *want* the value of myNumber to change we have a problem. We could use a function that returns a new value for myNumber, and call it using:

```
int myNumber = 5;
Console.WriteLine("myNumber = {0}", myNumber);
myNumber = showDouble(myNumber);
Console.WriteLine("myNumber = {0}", myNumber);
```

But this code is hardly intuitive, and won't cope with changing the values of multiple variables used as parameters (as functions have only one return value).

Instead, we want to pass the parameter by **reference**. This means that the function will work with exactly the same variable as the one used in the function call, not just a variable that has the same value. Any changes made to this variable will, therefore, be reflected in the value of the variable used as a parameter. To do this we simply have to use the ref keyword to specify the parameter:

```
static void showDouble(ref int val)
{
    val *= 2;
    Console.WriteLine("val doubled = {0}", val);
}
```

And again in the function call (this is mandatory, as the fact that the parameter is a `ref` parameter is part of the function signature):

```
int myNumber = 5;
Console.WriteLine("myNumber = {0}", myNumber);
showDouble(ref myNumber);
Console.WriteLine("myNumber = {0}", myNumber);
```

The text output to the console is now follows:

```
myNumber = 5
val doubled = 10
myNumber = 10
```

This time `myNumber` has been modified by `showDouble()`.

There are two limitations on the variable used as a `ref` parameter. First, the function *may* result in a change to the value of a reference parameter, so we must use a *non-constant* variable in the function call. The following is therefore illegal:

```
const int myNumber = 5;
Console.WriteLine("myNumber = {0}", myNumber);
showDouble(ref myNumber);
Console.WriteLine("myNumber = {0}", myNumber);
```

Second, we must use an initialized variable. C# doesn't allow us to assume that a `ref` parameter will be initialized in the function that uses it. The following code is also illegal:

```
int myNumber;
showDouble(ref myNumber);
Console.WriteLine("myNumber = {0}", myNumber);
```

Out Parameters

In addition to passing values by reference, we can also specify that a given parameter is an **out** parameter using the `out` keyword, which is used in the same way as the `ref` keyword (as a modifier to the parameter in the function definition and in the function call). In effect, this gives us almost exactly the same behavior as a reference parameter in that the value of the parameter at the end of the function execution is returned to the variable used in the function call. However, there are important differences:

❑ Whereas it is illegal to use an unassigned variable as a `ref` parameter, we can use an unassigned variable as an `out` parameter

❑ In addition, an `out` parameter must be treated as an unassigned value by the function that uses it

This means that while it is permissible for calling code to use an assigned variable as an `out` parameter, the value stored in this variable will be lost when the function executes.

As an example, consider an extension to the `MaxValue()` function we saw earlier that returns the maximum value of an array. We'll modify the function slightly such that we obtain the index of the element with the maximum value within the array. To keep things simple, we'll just obtain the index of the first occurrence of this value where there are multiple elements with the maximum value. To do this, we add an out parameter by modifying the function as follows:

```
static int MaxValue(int[] intArray, out int maxIndex)
{
    int maxVal = intArray[0];
    maxIndex = 0;
    for (int i = 1; i < intArray.Length; i++)
    {
        if (intArray[i] > maxVal)
        {
            maxVal = intArray[i];
            maxIndex = i;
        }
    }
    return maxVal;
}
```

We might use this function as follows:

```
int[] myArray = {1, 8, 3, 6, 2, 5, 9, 3, 0, 2};
int maxIndex;
Console.WriteLine("The maximum value in myArray is {0}",
                  MaxValue(myArray, out maxIndex));
Console.WriteLine("The first occurrence of this value is at element {0}",
                  maxIndex + 1);
```

This results in:

```
The maximum value in myArray is 9
The first occurrence of this value is at element 7
```

An important point to note here is that we must use the `out` keyword in the function call, just as with the `ref` keyword.

> *Note that I've added one to the value of* maxIndex *returned here when it is displayed on screen. This is to translate the index to a more readable form, such that the first element in the array is referred to element 1 rather than element 0.*

Variable Scope

Throughout the last section, you may have been wondering why exchanging data with functions is necessary. The reason is that variables in C# are only accessible from localized regions of code. A given variable is said to have a **scope** from where it is accessible.

Variable scope is an important subject, and one best introduced with an example.

Try it Out – Defining and Using a Basic Function

1. Make the following changes to Ch06Ex01 in Class1.cs:

```
class Class1
{
    static void Write()
    {
        Console.WriteLine("myString = {0}", myString);
    }

    static void Main(string[] args)
    {
        string myString = "String defined in Main()";
        Write();
    }
}
```

2. Compile the code, and note the error and warning that appear in the task list:

```
The name 'myString' does not exist in the class or namespace 'Ch06Ex01.Class1'
The variable 'myString' is assigned but its value is never used
```

How It Works

So, what went wrong? Well, the variable myString defined in the main body of our application (the Main() function) isn't accessible from the Write() function.

The reason for this inaccessibility is that variables have a scope within which they are valid. This scope encompasses the code block that they are defined in and any directly nested code blocks. The blocks of code in functions are separate from the blocks of code from which they are called. Inside Write() the name myString is undefined, and the myString variable defined in Main() is **out of scope** – it can only be used from within Main().

In fact, we can have a completely separate variable in Write() called myString. Try modifying the code as follows:

```
class Class1
{
    static void Write()
    {
        string myString = "String defined in Write()";
        Console.WriteLine("Now in Write()");
        Console.WriteLine("myString = {0}", myString);
    }
```

```
        static void Main(string[] args)
        {
            string myString = "String defined in Main()";
            Write();
            Console.WriteLine("\nNow in Main()");
            Console.WriteLine("myString = {0}", myString);
        }
    }
```

This code does compile, and results in the following:

The operations performed by this code are as follows:

❑   Main() defines and initializes a string variable called myString

❑   Main() transfers control to Write()

❑   Write() defines and initializes a string variable called myString, which is a different variable to the myString defined in Main()

❑   Write() outputs a string to the console containing the value of myString as defined in Write()

❑   Write() transfers control back to Main()

❑   Main() outputs a string to the console containing the value of myString as defined in Main()

Variables whose scope covers a single function in this way are known as **local** variables. It is also possible to have **global** variables, whose scope covers multiple functions. Modify the code as follows:

```
    class Class1
    {
        static string myString;

        static void Write()
        {
            string myString = "String defined in Write()";
            Console.WriteLine("Now in Write()");
            Console.WriteLine("Local myString = {0}", myString);
            Console.WriteLine("Global myString = {0}", Class1.myString);
        }

        static void Main(string[] args)
        {
            string myString = "String defined in Main()";
```

```
        Class1.myString = "Global string";
        Write();
        Console.WriteLine("\nNow in Main()");
        Console.WriteLine("Local myString = {0}", myString);
        Console.WriteLine("Global myString = {0}", Class1.myString);
    }
}
```

The result is now:

Here we have added another variable called myString, this time further up the hierarchy of names in the code. This variable is defined as follows:

```
    static string myString;
```

Note that again we require the static keyword here. Again, I'm not going to say any more about this at this point other than that in console applications of this form we *must* use either the static or const keyword for global variables of this form. If we want to modify the value of the global variable we need to use static, as const prohibits the value of the variable changing.

In order to differentiate between this variable and the local variables in Main() and Write() with the same names, we have to classify the variable name using a fully qualified name, as introduced in Chapter 3. Here we refer to the global version as Class1.myString. Note that this is only necessary when we have global and local variables with the same name, if there was no local myString variable, we could simply use myString to refer to the global variable, rather than Class1.myString. When we have a local variable with the same name as a global variable the global variable is said to be **hidden**.

The value of the global variable is set in Main() with:

```
        Class1.myString = "Global string";
```

and accessed in Write() with:

```
        Console.WriteLine("Global myString = {0}", Class1.myString);
```

Now, you may be wondering why we shouldn't just use this technique to exchange data with functions, rather than the parameter passing we saw earlier; there are indeed situations where this is the preferable way to exchange data, but there are just as many (if not more) where it isn't. The choice of whether to use global variables depends on the intended use of the function in question. The problem with using global variables is that they are generally unsuitable for "general purpose" functions, which are capable of working with whatever data we supply, not just limited to data in a specific global variable. We'll look at this in more depth a little later.

Variable Scope in Other Structures

Before we move on, it is worth noting that one of the points made in the last section has consequences above and beyond variable scope between functions. I stated that the scope of variables encompasses the code block that they are defined in and any directly nested code blocks. This also applies to other code blocks, such as those in branching and looping structures. Consider the following code:

```
int i;
for (i = 0; i < 10; i++)
{
    string text = "Line " + Convert.ToString(i);
    Console.WriteLine("{0}", text);
}
Console.WriteLine("Last text output in loop: {0}", text);
```

Here the string variable `text` is local to the `for` loop. This code won't compile, as the call to `Console.WriteLine()` that occurs outside of this loop attempts to use the variable `text`, which is out of scope outside of the loop. Try modifying the code as follows:

```
int i;
string text;
for (i = 0; i < 10; i++)
{
    text = "Line " + Convert.ToString(i);
    Console.WriteLine("{0}", text);
}
Console.WriteLine("Last text output in loop: {0}", text);
```

This code will also fail. The reason for this is that variables must be declared and be initialized before use, and `text` is only initialized in the `for` loop. The value assigned to text is lost when the loop block is exited. However, we can also make the following change:

```
int i;
string text = "";
for (i = 0; i < 10; i++)
{
    text = "Line " + Convert.ToString(i);
    Console.WriteLine("{0}", text);
}
Console.WriteLine("Last text output in loop: {0}", text);
```

This time `text` is initialized outside of the loop, and we have access to its value. The result of this simple code is shown in the following screenshot:

Here the last value assigned to `text` in the loop is accessible from outside the loop.

As you can see, this topic requires a bit of work to get to grips with. It is not immediately obvious why, in the light of the earlier example, `text` doesn't retain the empty string it is assigned before the loop in the code after the loop.

The explanation for this behavior concerns the memory allocation for the `text` variable, and indeed any variable. Simply declaring a simple variable type doesn't result in very much happening. It is only when values are assigned to the variable that values are allocated a place in memory to be stored. When this allocation takes place inside a loop, the value is essentially defined as a local value, and goes out of scope outside of the loop.

Even though the variable itself isn't localized to the loop, the value it contains is. However, assigning a value outside of the loop ensures that the value is local to the main code, and is still in scope inside the loop. This means that the variable doesn't go out of scope before the main code block is exited, so we have access to its value outside of the loop.

Luckily for us, the C# compiler will detect variable scope problems, and responding to the error messages it generates certainly helps us to understand the topic of variable scope.

As a final note, we should turn to "best practice". In general, it is worth declaring and initializing all variables before using them in any code blocks. An exception to this is where we declare looping variables as part of a loop block, for example:

```
for (int i = 0; i < 10; i++)
{
    ...
}
```

Here `i` is localized to the looping code block, but this is fine as we will rarely require access to this counter from external code.

Parameters and Return Values versus Global Data

In this section, we'll take a closer look at exchanging data with functions via global data and via parameters and return values. To recap, consider the following code:

```
class Class1
{
    static void showDouble(ref int val)
    {
        val *= 2;
        Console.WriteLine("val doubled = {0}", val);
    }

    static void Main(string[] args)
    {
        int val = 5;
        Console.WriteLine("val = {0}", val);
        showDouble(ref val);
        Console.WriteLine("val = {0}", val);
    }
}
```

Note that this code is slightly different to the code we saw earlier in this chapter, where we used the variable name myNumber *in* Main()*. This illustrates the fact that local variables can have identical names and yet not interfere with each other. It also means that the two code samples shown here are more similar, allowing us to focus more on the specific differences without worrying about variable names.*

And compare it with this code:

```
class Class1
{
    static int val;

    static void showDouble()
    {
        val *= 2;
        Console.WriteLine("val doubled = {0}", val);
    }

    static void Main(string[] args)
    {
        val = 5;
        Console.WriteLine("val = {0}", val);
        showDouble();
        Console.WriteLine("val = {0}", val);
    }
}
```

The result of both of these showDouble() functions is identical.

Now, there are no hard and fast rules for using one method rather than another, and both techniques are perfectly valid. However, there are some guidelines you might like to consider.

To start with, as we mentioned when we first introduced this topic, the `showDouble()` version that uses the global value will only ever use the global variable `val`. In order to use this version, we *must* use this global variable. This limits the versatility of the function slightly, and means that we must continuously copy the global variable value into other variables if we intend on storing results. In addition, global data might be modified by code elsewhere in our application, which could cause unpredicted results (values might change without us realizing until too late).

However, this loss of versatility can often be a bonus. There are times when we only ever want to use a function for one purpose, and using a global data store reduces the possibility that we will make an error in a function call, perhaps passing it the wrong variable.

Of course, it could also be argued that this simplicity actually makes our code more difficult to understand. Explicitly specifying parameters allows us to see at a glance what is changing. If we see a call that reads `myFunction(val1, out val2)`, we instantly know that `val1` and `val2` are the important variables to consider, and that `val2` will be assigned a new value when the function completes. Conversely, if this function took no parameters we would be unable to make any assumptions as to what data it manipulated.

Finally, it should be remembered that using global data isn't always possible. Later on in the book, we will see code written in different files and/or belonging to different namespaces communicating with each other via functions. In cases such as this, the code is often separated to such a degree that there is no obvious choice for a global storage location.

So, to summarize, feel free to use either technique to exchange data. I would, in general, urge you to use parameters rather than global data, but there are certainly cases where global data might be more suitable, and it certainly isn't an error to use this technique.

The Main() Function

Now we've covered most of the simple techniques used in the creation and use of functions, let's go back and take a closer look at the `Main()` function.

Earlier on, we said that `Main()` is the entry point for a C# application and that the execution of this function encompasses the execution of the application. We also saw that this function has a parameter, `string[] args`, but we haven't as yet seen what this parameter represents. In this section, we'll see what this parameter is, and how we use it.

Note that there are four possible signatures that we can use for the Main() function:

- ❑   `static void Main()`
- ❑   `static void Main(string[] args)`
- ❑   `static int Main()`
- ❑   `static int Main(string[] args)`

We can, if we wish, omit the `args` *argument discussed here. The reason we've used the version with this argument up till now, is that it is the version that is generated automatically for us when we create a console application in VS.*

The third and fourth versions shown above return an `int` *value, which can be used to signify how the application terminates, often used as an indication of an error (although this is by no means mandatory). In general, returning a value of 0 reflects "normal" termination (that is, the application has completed and can terminate safely).*

The `args` parameter of `Main()` is a method for accepting information from outside the application, specified at runtime. This information takes the form of **command-line parameters**.

You may well have come across command-line parameters already. When we execute an application from the command-line, we are often able to specify information directly, such as a file to load on application execution. As an example, consider the Notepad application in Windows. We can run this application simply by typing Notepad in a command prompt window, or in the window that appears when we select the Run option from the Windows Start Menu. We can also type something like notepad "myfile.txt" in these locations. The result of this is that Notepad will load the file `myfile.txt` when it runs, or offer to create this file if it doesn't already exist. Here, "myfile.txt" is a command-line argument. We can write console applications that work in much the same way by making use of the `args` parameter.

When a console application is executed, any command line parameters that are specified are placed in this `args` array. We can then use these parameters in our application as required.

Let's look at an example of this in action.

Try it Out – Command Line Arguments

1. Create a new console application called `Ch06Ex04` in the directory `C:\BegVCSharp\Chapter6`.

2. Add the following code to `Class1.cs`:

```
class Class1
{
    static void Main(string[] args)
    {
        Console.WriteLine("{0} command line arguments were specified:",
                          args.Length);
        foreach (string arg in args)
            Console.WriteLine(arg);
    }
}
```

3. Open up the property pages for the project (right-click on the **Ch06Ex04** project name in the Solution Explorer window and select **Properties**).

4. Select the **Configuration Properties | Debugging** page and add whatever command line arguments you want to the **Command Line Arguments** setting:

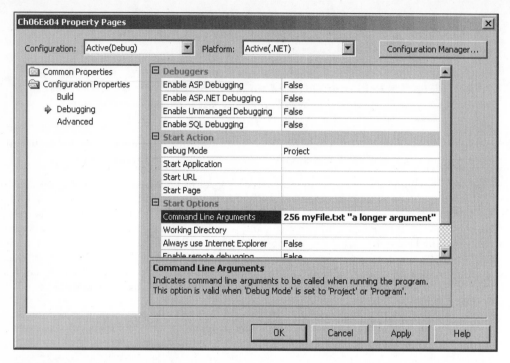

5. Run the application:

```
C:\BegVCSharp\Chapter6\Ch06Ex04\bin\Debug\Ch06Ex04.exe 256 myFile.txt "a longer argument"
3 command line arguments were specified:
256
myFile.txt
a longer argument
Press any key to continue
```

How it Works

The code used here is very simple:

```
Console.WriteLine("{0} command line arguments were specified:",
                  args.Length);
foreach (string arg in args)
   Console.WriteLine(arg);
```

We're just using the args parameter like we would any other string array. We're not doing anything fancy with the arguments, we're just writing whatever is specified to the screen.

In this example, we supplied the arguments via the Project Properties dialog in VS. This is a handy way of using the same command line arguments whenever you run the application from VS, rather than having to type them at a command-line prompt every time. The same result as above could be obtained by opening a command prompt window in the same directory as the project output (C:\BegCSharp\Chapter6\Ch06Ex04\bin\Debug) and typing the following:

```
Ch06Ex04 256 myFile.txt "a longer argument"
```

Note that each argument is separated from the next by spaces, but we can also enclose arguments in double quotes should we want a longer argument (this is necessary if the argument includes spaces, so as not to be interpreted as multiple arguments).

Struct Functions

In the last chapter we looked at struct types for storing multiple data elements in one place. Structs are actually capable of a lot more than this. One important extra capability they offer is the ability to contain functions as well as data. This is something that may seem a little strange at first, but is in fact very useful indeed.

As a simple example, consider the following struct:

```
struct customerName
{
    public string firstName, lastName;
}
```

If we have variables of type `customerName`, and we want to output a full name to the console, we are forced to build the name from its component parts. We might use the following syntax for a `customerName` variable called `myCustomer`, for example:

```
customerName myCustomer;
myCustomer.firstName = "John";
myCustomer.lastName = "Franklin";
Console.WriteLine("{0} {1}", myCustomer.firstName, myCustomer.lastName);
```

By adding functions to structs, we can simplify this by centralizing the processing of common tasks such as this. We can add a suitable function to the struct type as follows:

```
struct customerName
{
    public string firstName, lastName;

    public string Name ()
    {
        return firstName + " " + lastName;
    }
}
```

This looks much like any other function we've looked at in this chapter, except that we haven't used the `static` modifier. The reasons for this will become clear later in the book, for now it is enough to know that this keyword isn't required for struct functions. We can use this function as follows:

```
customerName myCustomer;
myCustomer.firstName = "John";
myCustomer.lastName = "Franklin";
Console.WriteLine(myCustomer.Name());
```

This syntax is much simpler, and much easier to understand, than the earlier one.

An important point to note here is that the `Name()` function has direct access to the `firstName` and `lastName` struct members. Within the `customerName` struct they can be thought of as global.

Overloading Functions

Earlier on in this chapter, we saw how we must match the signature of a function when we call it. This implied that we would need to have separate functions to operate on different types of variable. Function overloading provides us with the ability to create multiple functions with the same name, but each working with different parameter types.

For example, we used the following code earlier, that contained a function called `MaxValue()`:

```
class Class1
{
    static int MaxValue(int[] intArray)
    {
        int maxVal = intArray[0];
        for (int i = 1; i < intArray.Length; i++)
        {
            if (intArray[i] > maxVal)
                maxVal = intArray[i];
        }
        return maxVal;
    }

    static void Main(string[] args)
    {
        int[] myArray = {1, 8, 3, 6, 2, 5, 9, 3, 0, 2};
        int maxVal = MaxValue(myArray);
        Console.WriteLine("The maximum value in myArray is {0}", maxVal);
    }
}
```

This function can only be used with arrays of `int` values. Now, we could provide different named functions for different parameter types, perhaps renaming the above function as `IntArrayMaxValue()` and adding functions such as `DoubleArrayMaxValue()` to work with other types. Alternatively, we could just add the following function to our code:

```
...
static double MaxValue(double[] doubleArray)
{
    double maxVal = doubleArray[0];
```

```
        for (int i = 1; i < doubleArray.Length; i++)
        {
            if (doubleArray[i] > maxVal)
                maxVal = doubleArray[i];
        }
        return maxVal;
    }
    ...
```

The difference here is that we are using `double` values. The function name, `MaxValue()`, is the same, but (crucially) it's *signature* is different. It would be an error to define two functions with the same name and signature, but since these two functions have different signatures, this is fine.

Now we have two versions of `MaxValue()`, which accept `int` and `double` arrays, and return an `int` or `double` maximum respectively.

The beauty of this type of code is that we don't have to explicitly specify which of these two functions we wish to use. We simply provide an array parameter and the correct function will be executed depending on the type of the parameter used.

At this point, it is worth noting another feature of the IntelliSense feature in VS. If we have the two functions shown above in an application, and then proceed to type the name of the function in (for example) `Main()`, VS will show us the available overloads for the function. If we type the following:

```
double result = MaxValue(
```

VS gives us information about both versions of `MaxValue()`, which we can scroll between using the up and down arrow keys:

```
▲1 of 2▼  int Class1.MaxValue (int[] intArray)
```

```
▲2 of 2▼  double Class1.MaxValue (double[] doubleArray)
```

All aspects of the function signature are included when overloading functions. We might, for example, have two different functions that take parameters by value and by reference respectively:

```
static void showDouble(ref int val)
{
    ...
}
```

```
static void showDouble(int val)
{
    ...
}
```

The choice as to which of these versions to use is based purely on whether the function call contains the `ref` keyword. The following would call the reference version:

```
showDouble(ref val);
```

And the following would call the value version:

```
showDouble(val);
```

Alternatively, we could have functions that differ in the number of parameters they require, and so on.

Delegates

A **delegate** is a type that enables us to store references to functions. Although this sounds quite involved, the mechanism is surprisingly simple. The most important purpose of delegates won't become clear until later in this book when we look at events and event handling, but we can get a fair amount of mileage by looking at delegates here. When we come to use them later on they'll look familiar, which will make some more complicated topics a lot easier to comprehend.

Delegates are declared much like functions, but with no function body and using the `delegate` keyword. The delegate declaration specifies a function signature consisting of a return type and the parameter list. After defining a delegate we can declare a variable with the type of that delegate. We can then initialize this variable to be a reference to any function that has the same signature as that delegate. Once we have done this we can call that function by using the delegate variable as if it were a function.

We have a variable that refers to a function we can also perform other operations that would be impossible by any other means. For example, we can pass a delegate variable to a function as a parameter, then that function can use the delegate to call whatever function it refers to, without having knowledge as to what function will be called until runtime.

Let's look at an example.

Try it Out – Using a Delegate to Call a Function

1. Create a new console application called `Ch06Ex05` in the directory `C:\BegVCSharp\Chapter6`.

2. Add the following code to `Class1.cs`:

```
class Class1
{
    delegate double processDelegate(double param1, double param2);

    static double Multiply(double param1, double param2)
    {
        return param1 * param2;
    }

    static double Divide(double param1, double param2)
    {
        return param1 / param2;
    }
```

```
static void Main(string[] args)
{
    processDelegate process;
    Console.WriteLine("Enter 2 numbers separated with a comma:");
    string input = Console.ReadLine();
    int commaPos = input.IndexOf(',');
    double param1 = Convert.ToDouble(input.Substring(0, commaPos));
    double param2 = Convert.ToDouble(input.Substring(commaPos + 1,
                                            input.Length - commaPos - 1));
    Console.WriteLine("Enter M to multiply or D to divide:");
    input = Console.ReadLine();
    if (input == "M")
        process = new processDelegate(Multiply);
    else
        process = new processDelegate(Divide);
    Console.WriteLine("Result: {0}", process(param1, param2));
}
}
```

3. Execute the code:

How It Works

This code defines a delegate (`processDelegate`) whose signature matches that of the two functions (`Multiply()` and `Divide()`). The delegate definition is as follows:

```
delegate double processDelegate(double param1, double param2);
```

The `delegate` keyword specifies that the definition is for a delegate, rather than a function (the definition appears in the same place as a function definition might). Next, we have a signature that specifies a `double` return value and two `double` parameters. The actual names used are arbitrary, so we can call the delegate type and parameter name whatever we like. Here, we've used a delegate name of `processDelegate` and double parameters called `param1` and `param2`.

The code in `Main()` starts by declaring a variable using our new delegate type:

```
static void Main(string[] args)
{
    processDelegate process;
```

Next, we have some fairly standard C# code that requests two numbers separated by a comma and places these numbers in two `double` variables:

```
Console.WriteLine("Enter 2 numbers separated with a comma:");
string input = Console.ReadLine();
int commaPos = input.IndexOf(',');
double param1 = Convert.ToDouble(input.Substring(0, commaPos));
double param2 = Convert.ToDouble(input.Substring(commaPos + 1,
                                    input.Length - commaPos - 1));
```

Note that, for demonstration purposes, I've included no user input validation here. If this were "real" code, we'd spend much more time ensuring that we got valid values in the local param1 *and* param2 *variables.*

Next we ask the user whether to multiply or divide these numbers:

```
Console.WriteLine("Enter M to multiply or D to divide:");
input = Console.ReadLine();
```

Based on the user choice we initialize the process delegate variable:

```
if (input == "M")
    process = new processDelegate(Multiply);
else
    process = new processDelegate(Divide);
```

To assign a function reference to a delegate variable, we use slightly odd looking syntax. Much like assigning array values, we must use the new keyword to create a new delegate. After this keyword we specify the delegate type and supply a parameter referring to function we want to use, namely the Multiply() or Divide() function. Note that this parameter doesn't match the parameters of the delegate type or the target function, it is a syntax unique to delegate assignment. The parameter is simply the name of the function to use, without any parentheses.

Finally, we call the chosen function using the delegate. The same syntax works here, regardless of which function the delegate refers to:

```
Console.WriteLine("Result: {0}", process(param1, param2));
    }
```

Here, we treat the delegate variable just as if it were a function name. Unlike functions, however, we can also perform additional operations on this variable, such as passing it to a function via a parameter. A simple example of such a function might be:

```
static void executeFunction(processDelegate process)
{
    process(2.2, 3.3);
}
```

This means that we can control the behavior of functions by passing them function delegates, much like choosing a "snap-in" to use. For example, we might have a function that sorts a string array alphabetically. There are several methods of sorting lists with varying performance depending on the characteristics of the list being sorted. By using delegates, we could specify the method to use by passing a sorting algorithm function delegate to a sorting function.

There are many such uses for delegates, but, as mentioned earlier, their most prolific use is in event handling. We'll come to this subject in Chapter 12.

Summary

In this chapter, we've seen a fairly complete overview of the use of functions in C# code. Much of the additional features that functions offer (delegates in particular) are more abstract, and we'll only need to discuss them in the light of object-oriented programming, which is a subject that we'll be discussing very soon.

To summarize what has been covered in this chapter:

- ❑ Defining and using functions in console applications
- ❑ Exchanging data with functions via return values and parameters
- ❑ Parameter arrays
- ❑ Passing values by reference or by value
- ❑ Specifying out parameters for additional return values
- ❑ The concept of variable scope
- ❑ Details of the Main() function, including command line parameter usage
- ❑ Using functions in struct types
- ❑ Function overloading
- ❑ Delegates

Exercises

1. The following two functions have errors. What are they?

```
static bool Write()
{
   Console.WriteLine("Text output from function.");
}
```

```
static void myFunction(string label, params int[] args, bool showLabel)
{
   if (showLabel)
      Console.WriteLine(label);
   foreach (int i in args)
      Console.WriteLine("{0}", i);
}
```

2. Write an application that uses two command line arguments to place values into a string and an integer variable respectively. Then display these values.

2. Create a delegate and use it to impersonate the `Console.ReadLine()` function when asking for user input.

3. Modify the following struct to include a function that returns the total price of an order:

```
struct order
{
    public string itemName;
    public int    unitCount;
    public double unitCost;
}
```

4. Add another function to the `order` struct that returns a formatted string as follows, where italic entries enclosed in angle brackets are replaced by appropriate values:

```
Order Information: <unit count> <item name> items at $<unit cost> each, total cost
$<total cost>
```

Debugging and Error Handling

So far in this book, we have covered all the basics of simple programming in C#. Before we move on to look at object-oriented programming in the next section of the book, it's time to look at debugging and error handling in C# code.

Errors in code are something that will always be with us. No matter how good a programmer is, there will always be problems that slip through, and part of being a good programmer is realizing that this is the case and being prepared to deal with it. Of course, these may be minor problems that don't affect the execution of an application, perhaps a spelling mistake on a button or such like. They may also be glaring errors that cause applications to fail completely (usually known as **fatal** errors). Fatal errors include both simple errors in code that will prevent compilation (**syntax** errors), but may be more involved and only occur at runtime. Alternatively, errors may be subtler. Perhaps your application will fail to add a record to a database if a requested field is missing, or adds a record with the wrong data in other restricted circumstances. Errors such as these, where application logic is in some way flawed, are known as **semantic** errors (also known as **logic** errors).

Often the first that you might hear about the more subtle errors will be when a user of your application complains that something isn't working properly. This then leaves you with the task of tracing through your code to try to find out what *is* happening, and how you can change your code so that it does what it was intended to do.

In situations like this, you will find that the debugging capabilities of VS are a fantastic help. In the first part of this chapter, we'll look at some of the techniques on offer and apply them to some common problems.

In addition to this, we will also look at the **error handling** techniques available in C#. These enable us to take precautions in cases where errors are likely, and write code that is resilient enough to cope with errors that might otherwise be fatal. These techniques are part of the C# language rather than a debugging feature of VS, but VS does provide some tools to help us here too.

Debugging in Visual Studio

When programs are run in debug mode, there is more going on than simply the code you have written being executed. Debug builds maintain **symbolic information** about your application, such that VS is capable of knowing exactly what is happening as each line of code is executed. Symbolic information means keeping track of, for example, the names of variables used in uncompiled code, such that they can be matched up to the values that exist in the compiled machine code application, which won't contain such human-readable information. This information is contained in .pdb files, which you may have seen appearing in Debug directories on your computer. This enables us to perform many useful operations, which include:

❑ Outputting debugging information to VS

❑ Looking at (and editing) the values of variables in scope during application execution

❑ Pausing and restarting program execution

❑ Automatically halting execution at certain points in the code

❑ Stepping through program execution a line at a time

❑ Monitoring changes in variable content during application execution

❑ Modifying variable content at runtime

❑ Performing test calls of functions

In this section, we'll take a look at these techniques and how we can use them to identify and fix those areas of code which do not work as expected, a process more commonly known as debugging.

We'll divide up the techniques into two sections by the way in which they are used. In general, debugging is performed either by interrupting program execution or by making notes for later analysis. In VS terms, an application is either running or is in **break mode**, that is, normal execution is halted. We'll look at the non-break mode (runtime or normal) techniques first.

Debugging in Non-Break (Normal) Mode

One of the commands we've been using throughout this book is the Console.WriteLine() function that outputs text to the console. When we are developing applications this function can come in handy for getting extra feedback on operations, for example:

```
Console.WriteLine("MyFunc() Function about to be called.");
MyFunc ("Do something.");
Console.WriteLine("MyFunc() Function execution completed.");
```

This code snippet shows how we can give extra information concerning a function called MyFunc().

Doing this is all very well, but can make our console output a bit cluttered. As an alternative, we can output text to a separate location – the Output window in VS.

Back in Chapter 2 we took a quick look at the Output window, which is (by default) located at the bottom of the VS development environment, sharing space with the Task List window. We saw how this window displays information relating to the compilation and execution of code, including errors encountered during compilation and so forth. We can also use this window to display custom diagnostic information by writing to it directly. We can see this window in the screenshot below:

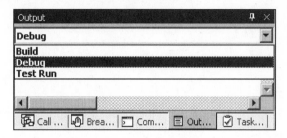

Note that this window has three modes that can be selected using the drop-down box it contains. We can toggle between Build, Debug, and Test Run modes. The Build and Debug modes show us compilation and run time information respectively. When I refer to "writing to the Output window" in this section I actually mean "writing to the Debug mode view of the Output window".

Alternatively, we might want to create a **logging** file, which would have information appended to it when our application is executed. The techniques for doing this are much the same as for writing text to the Output window, although it requires an understanding of how to access the file system from C# applications. For now, we'll leave this functionality on the back burner, as there is plenty we can do without getting bogged down by file access techniques.

Outputting Debugging Information

Writing text to the Output window at run time is a very simple thing to do. We simply need to replace calls to `Console.WriteLine()` with the required call to write text where we want it. There are two commands we can use to do this:

- ❑   `Debug.WriteLine()`
- ❑   `Trace.WriteLine()`

These commands function in almost exactly the same way – with one key difference. The first of these two commands only works in debug builds, the latter will work for release builds as well. In fact, the `Debug.WriteLine()` command won't even be compiled into a release build; it'll just disappear, which certainly has its advantages (the compiled code will be smaller in size for a start). We can in effect have two versions of our application created from a single source file. The debug version displays all kinds of extra diagnostic information whereas the release version won't have this overhead, and won't display messages to users that might otherwise be annoying!

Note that these functions don't work exactly like `Console.WriteLine()`. They only work with a single string parameter for the message to output, rather than letting us insert variable values using `{X}` syntax. This means that we must use the + operator to insert variable values in strings. However, we can (optionally) supply a second string parameter, which is used to display a **category** for the output text. This allows us to see at a glance what output messages are displayed in the Output window, useful for when similar messages are output from different places in the application.

161

The general output of these functions is as follows:

```
<category>: <message>
```

For example, the following statement, which has `"MyFunc"` as the optional category parameter:

```
Debug.WriteLine("Added 1 to i", "MyFunc");
```

would result in:

```
MyFunc: Added 1 to i
```

Let's look at an example.

Try it Out – Writing Text to the Output Window

1. Create a new console application called `Ch07Ex01` in the directory `C:\BegVCSharp\Chapter7`.

2. Modify the code as follows:

```
using System;
using System.Diagnostics;

namespace Ch07Ex01
{
    class Class1
    {
        static void Main(string[] args)
        {
            int[] testArray = {4, 7, 4, 2, 7, 3, 7, 8, 3, 9, 1, 9};
            int[] maxValIndices;
            int maxVal = Maxima(testArray, out maxValIndices);
            Console.WriteLine("Maximum value {0} found at element indices:",
                              maxVal);
            foreach (int index in maxValIndices)
            {
                Console.WriteLine(index);
            }
        }

        static int Maxima(int[] integers, out int[] indices)
        {
            Debug.WriteLine("Maximum value search started.");
            indices = new int[1];
            int maxVal = integers[0];
            indices[0] = 0;
            int count = 1;
            Debug.WriteLine("Maximum value initialized to " + maxVal +
```

```
                              ", at element index 0.");
         for (int i = 1; i < integers.Length; i++)
         {
            Debug.WriteLine("Now looking at element at index " + i + ".");
            if (integers[i] > maxVal)
            {
               maxVal = integers[i];
               count = 1;
               indices = new int[1];
               indices[0] = i;
               Debug.WriteLine("New maximum found. New value is " + maxVal +
                               ", at element index " + i + ".");
            }
            else
            {
               if (integers[i] == maxVal)
               {
                  count++;
                  int[] oldIndices = indices;
                  indices = new int[count];
                  oldIndices.CopyTo(indices, 0);
                  indices[count - 1] = i;
                  Debug.WriteLine("Duplicate maximum found at element index " +
                                  i + ".");
               }
            }
         }
         Trace.WriteLine("Maximum value " + maxVal + " found, with " + count +
                         " occurrences.");
         Debug.WriteLine("Maximum value search completed.");
         return maxVal;
      }
   }
}
```

3. Execute the code in debug mode:

4. Terminate the application, and look at the contents of the Output window (in **Debug** mode):

```
'DefaultDomain': Loaded 'c:\winnt\microsoft.net\framework\v1.0.3705\mscorlib.dll',
No symbols loaded.
'Ch07Ex01': Loaded 'C:\BegVCSharp\Chapter7\Ch07Ex01\bin\Debug\Ch07Ex01.exe',
Symbols loaded.
'Ch07Ex01.exe': Loaded
'c:\winnt\assembly\gac\system\1.0.3300.0__b77a5c561934e089\system.dll', No symbols
loaded.
'Ch07Ex01.exe': Loaded
'c:\winnt\assembly\gac\system.xml\1.0.3300.0__b77a5c561934e089\system.xml.dll', No
```

```
symbols loaded.
Maximum value search started.
Maximum value initialized to 4, at element index 0.
Now looking at element at index 1.
New maximum found. New value is 7, at element index 1.
Now looking at element at index 2.
Now looking at element at index 3.
Now looking at element at index 4.
Duplicate maximum found at element index 4.
Now looking at element at index 5.
Now looking at element at index 6.
Duplicate maximum found at element index 6.
Now looking at element at index 7.
New maximum found. New value is 8, at element index 7.
Now looking at element at index 8.
Now looking at element at index 9.
New maximum found. New value is 9, at element index 9.
Now looking at element at index 10.
Now looking at element at index 11.
Duplicate maximum found at element index 11.
Maximum value 9 found, with 2 occurrences.
Maximum value search completed.
The program '[1840] Ch07Ex01.exe' has exited with code 0 (0x0).
```

5. Change to **Release** mode using the drop-down menu on the **Standard** toolbar:

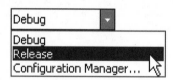

6. Run the program again, this time in **Release** mode, and take another look at the Output window when execution terminates:

```
'DefaultDomain': Loaded 'c:\winnt\microsoft.net\framework\v1.0.3705\mscorlib.dll',
No symbols loaded.
'Ch07Ex01': Loaded 'C:\BegVCSharp\Chapter7\Ch07Ex01\bin\Release\Ch07Ex01.exe', No
symbols loaded.
'Ch07Ex01.exe': Loaded
'c:\winnt\assembly\gac\system\1.0.3300.0__b77a5c561934e089\system.dll', No symbols
loaded.
'Ch07Ex01.exe': Loaded
'c:\winnt\assembly\gac\system.xml\1.0.3300.0__b77a5c561934e089\system.xml.dll', No
symbols loaded.
Maximum value 9 found, with 2 occurrences.
The program '[1840] Ch07Ex01.exe' has exited with code 0 (0x0).
```

How It Works

This application is an expanded version of one that we saw in the last chapter, using a function to calculate the maximum value in an integer array. This version also returns an array of the indices where maximum values are found in an array, so that the calling code can manipulate these elements. Let's look through the code.

To start with, note that an additional `using` directive appears at the start of the code:

```
using System.Diagnostics;
```

This simplifies access to the functions discussed above this example, as they are contained in the `System.Diagnostics` namespace. Without this `using` directive, code such as:

```
Debug.WriteLine("Bananas");
```

Would need further qualification, and would need to be rewritten as:

```
System.Diagnostics.Debug.WriteLine("Bananas");
```

The `using` directive keeps our code simple and reduces verbosity.

The code in `Main()` simply initializes a test array of integers called `testArray`; it also declares another integer array called `maxValIndices` to store the index output of `Maxima()` (the function that performs the calculation), then calls this function. Once the function returns, the code simply outputs the results.

`Maxima()` is slightly more complicated, but doesn't use much code that we haven't already seen. The search through the array is performed in a similar way to the `MaxVal()` function in the last chapter, except that a record is kept of the indices of maximum values.

Perhaps the key point to note in the code (other than those lines that output debugging information) is the function used to keep track of the indices. Rather than returning an array that would be large enough to store every index in the source array (needing the same dimensions as the source array), `Maxima()` returns an array just large enough to hold the indices found. It does this by continually recreating arrays of different sizes as the search progresses. This is necessary as arrays can't be resized once created.

To start with, the search is initialized by assuming that the first element in the source array (called `integers` locally) is the maximum value, and that there is only one maximum value in the array. Values can, therefore, be set for `maxVal` (the return value of the function, and the maximum value found) and `indices`, the `out` parameter array that stores the indices of the maximum values found. `maxVal` is assigned the value of the first element in `integers`, and `indices` is assigned a single value, simply 0, which is the index of the first element in the array. We also store the number of maximum values found in a variable called `count`, which allows us to keep track of the `indices` array.

The main body of the function is a loop that cycles through the values in the `integers` array, omitting the first one as this has already been processed. Each value is compared to the current value of `maxVal`, and ignored if `maxVal` is greater. If the currently inspected array value is greater than `maxVal` then `maxVal` and `indices` are changed to reflect this. If the value is equal to `maxVal` then `count` is incremented and a new array is substituted for `indices`. This new array is one element bigger than the old `indices` array, containing the new index found.

The code for this last piece of functionality is as follows:

```
if (integers[i] == maxVal)
{
   count++;
   int[] oldIndices = indices;
   indices = new int[count];
   oldIndices.CopyTo(indices, 0);
   indices[count - 1] = i;
   Debug.WriteLine("Duplicate maximum found at element index " +
                   i + ".");
}
```

Note that this works by "backing up" the old `indices` array into `oldIndices`, an integer array local to this `if` code block. Note also that the values in `oldIndices` are copied into the new `indices` array using the `<array>.CopyTo()` function. This function simply takes a target array and an index to use for the first element to copy to, and pastes all values into the target array.

Throughout the code, various pieces of text are output using the `Debug.WriteLine()` and `Trace.WriteLine()` functions. The end result of this when run in debug mode is a complete record of the steps taken in the loop that give us our result. In release mode, we just see the end result of the calculation, as no `Debug.WriteLine()` functions work.

As well as these `WriteLine()` functions there are a few more we should be aware of. To start with, there are equivalents to `Console.Write()`:

❑   `Debug.Write()`

❑   `Trace.Write()`

Both these functions use the same syntax as the `WriteLine()` functions (one or two parameters, with a message and an optional category), but differ in that they don't add end of line characters.

There are also the following commands:

❑   `Debug.WriteLineIf()`

❑   `Trace.WriteLineIf()`

❑   `Debug.WriteIf()`

❑   `Trace.WriteIf()`

Each of these has the same parameters as the non-`If` counterparts, with the addition of an extra mandatory parameter that precedes them in the parameter list. This parameter takes a Boolean value (or an expression that evaluates to a Boolean value), and will result in the function only writing text if this value evaluates to `true`. We can use these functions to conditionally output text to the Output window.

For example, we might only require debugging information to be output in certain situations, so we can have a great many `Debug.WriteLineIf()` statements in our code that all depend on a certain condition being met. If this condition doesn't occur, then they won't be displayed, which will stop the Output window getting cluttered up with superfluous information.

Debugging in Break Mode

The rest of the debugging techniques we'll look at in this chapter work in break mode. This mode can be entered in several ways, all of which result in the program pausing in some way. The first thing we will look at in this section is how we go about this, and then we'll look at what we can achieve once break mode is entered.

Entering Break Mode

The simplest way of entering break mode is to hit the pause button in VS while an application is running. This pause button is found on the Debug toolbar, which we should add to the toolbars that appear by default in VS. To do this, right-click in the toolbar area and select the Debug toolbar:

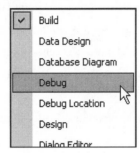

The toolbar that appears looks like this:

The first four buttons on this toolbar allow manual control of breaking. In the screenshot above, three of these are grayed out, as they won't work with a program that isn't currently being executed. The one that is enabled, Start, is identical to the button that exists on the standard toolbar. In the following sections we'll look at the rest of the buttons when needed.

When an application is running, the toolbar changes to look like the following:

Now the three buttons that were grayed out before are enabled, and let us:

❑ Pause the application and enter break mode

❑ Stop the application completely (this doesn't enter break mode, it just quits)

❑ Restart the application

Pausing the application is perhaps the simplest way of entering break mode, but it doesn't give us fine-grained control over exactly where to stop. We are likely to stop in a natural pause in the application, perhaps where we request user input. We might also be able to enter break mode during a lengthy operation, or a long loop, but the exact point we stop at is likely to be fairly random.

In general, it is far better to use **breakpoints**.

Breakpoints

A breakpoint is a marker in your source code that triggers automatic entry into break mode. They may be configured to:

- ❑ Enter break mode immediately when the breakpoint is reached

- ❑ Enter break mode when the breakpoint is reached if a Boolean expression evaluates to `true`

- ❑ Enter break mode once the breakpoint is reached a set number of times

- ❑ Enter break mode once the breakpoint is reached and a variable value has changed since the last time the breakpoint was reached

Note that the above is only available in debug builds. If you compile a release build then all breakpoints will be ignored.

There are three ways of adding breakpoints. To add simple breakpoints that break when a line is reached we simply left-click on the gray area to the left of the line of code, or right-click on the line, and select the Insert Breakpoint menu option:

The breakpoint will appear as a red circle next to the line of code, and a highlight on the line of code:

```
11   static void Main(string[] args)
12   {
13       int[] testArray = {4, 7, 4, 2, 7, 3, 7, 8, 3, 9, 1, 9};
14       int[] maxValIndices;
15       int maxVal = Maxima(testArray, out maxValIndices);
16       Console.WriteLine("Maximum value {0} found at element indices:", maxVal);
17       foreach (int index in maxValIndices)
18       {
19           Console.WriteLine(index);
20       }
21   }
```

We can also see information about the breakpoints in a file using the **Breakpoints** window. We need to enable this window first, by selecting the **Debug | Windows | Breakpoints** menu option. The following window will then appear at the bottom of the screen, in the same place as the **Task List** and **Output** windows:

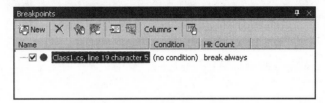

Here, we can disable breakpoints (by removing the tick to the left of a description; a disabled breakpoint shows up as an unfilled red circle), delete breakpoints, and edit the properties of breakpoints.

The properties shown in this window, **Condition** and **Hit Count**, are only two of the available ones, but they are the most useful. We can edit these by right-clicking on a breakpoint (in code or in this window) and selecting the **Properties** menu option. We can then use the three tabs, **Function**, **File**, and **Address**, to change the location of the breakpoint (**Address** lets us specify an absolute memory address for a breakpoint, an involved subject that we won't cover here), and the **Condition...** and **Hit Count...** buttons to change the two properties mentioned above.

Selecting the **Condition** button pops up the following dialog:

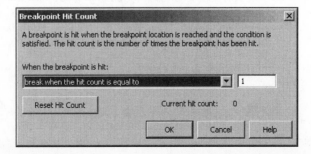

Here, we can type any Boolean expression, which may involve any variables that are in scope at the breakpoint. The above screenshot shows a breakpoint that will trigger when it is reached and the value of `maxVal` is greater than 4. We can also check to see if this expression has changed, and only trigger the breakpoint then (in the above case, we might trigger if `maxVal` had changed from 2 to 6 between breakpoint encounters).

Selecting the **Hit Count** button pops up the following dialog:

Here we can specify how many times a breakpoint needs to be hit before it is triggered. The drop-down list offers the following options:

```
break always
break when the hit count is equal to
break when the hit count is a multiple of
break when the hit count is greater than or equal to
```

The option chosen, combined with the value entered in the text box next to the list, determines the behavior of the breakpoint.

This hit count is useful in long loops, when we might want to break after, say, the first 5000 cycles. It would be a pain to break and restart 5000 times if we couldn't do this!

Other Ways of Entering Break Mode

There are two additional ways to get into break mode. One is to choose to enter it when an **unhandled exception** is thrown. This subject is covered later in this chapter, when we look at error handling. The other way is to break when an **assertion** is generated.

Assertions are instructions that can interrupt application execution with a user-defined message. They are often used in the development of an application as a means to test that things are going smoothly. For example, we might at some point in our application require a given variable to have a value less than 10. We can use an assertion to check that this is true and interrupt the program if this isn't the case. When the assertion occurs we have the option to Abort, which will terminate the application; Retry, causing break mode to be entered; or Ignore, and the application will continue as normal.

As with the debug output functions we saw earlier, there are two versions of the assertion function:

❑   `Debug.Assert()`

❑   `Trace.Assert()`

Again, the debug version will only be compiled into debug builds.

These functions take three parameters. The first is a Boolean value, where a value of `false` will cause the assertion to trigger. The second and third are two string parameters to write information both to a pop-up dialog and the Output window. The above example would need a function call such as:

```
Debug.Assert(myVar < 10, "myVar is 10 or greater.",
             "Assertion occurred in Main().");
```

Assertions are often useful in the early stages of user adoption of an application. We can distribute release builds of our application containing `Trace.Assert()` functions to keep tabs on things. Should an assertion be triggered, the user will be informed, and they can pass this information on to us developers. We'll then be able to work out what has gone wrong even if we don't know *how* it went wrong.

We might, for example, provide a brief description of the error in the first string with instructions as to what to do next as the second string:

```
Trace.Assert(myVar < 10, "Variable out of bounds.",
             "Please contact vendor with the error code KCW001.");
```

Should this assertion occur, the user will see the following:

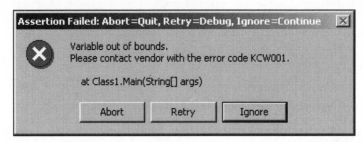

If the user has VS installed and hits the **Retry** button for a release build they won't see our code, they'll see the assembly language instructions for our application, which aren't nearly as revealing. The following is an example section of assembly code from the example in the last section:

```
00000196  nop
00000197  pop    ebx
00000198  pop    esi
00000199  pop    edi
0000019a  mov    esp,ebp
0000019c  pop    ebp
0000019d  ret    4
```

This isn't the easiest thing to understand, and only people who have assembly language experience will have a hope. This means that our code is safe from (most) prying eyes!

The next topics to cover concern what we can actually do once application execution is halted and we find ourselves in break mode. In general, we will be entering break mode in order to track down an error in our code (or just to reassure ourselves that things are working properly). Once we are in break mode there are various techniques that we can draw on, all of which enable us to analyze our code and the exact state of our application at the point in its execution where it is paused.

Monitoring Variable Content

Monitoring variable content is just one example of an area where VS helps us a great deal by making things simple. The easiest way of checking the value of a variable is to hover the mouse over its name in the source code while in break mode. A yellow tooltip showing information about the variable will appear, including the current value of the variable.

We can also highlight whole expressions to get information about their results in the same way. This technique is limited however, and won't, for example, show us the contents of an array.

Now, you may have noticed that when we run an application through VS, the layout of the various windows in the environment changes. By default, the following occurs at runtime:

❑ The **Properties** window disappears

❑ A **Running Documents** tab is added to the **Solution Explorer** window, showing us what documents in the project are in use, if any

❑ The size of the **Output** window changes, as half the bottom of the screen is replaced by a new window

171

The new window that appears is a particularly useful one for debugging. It allows us to keep tabs on the values of variables in our application when in break mode. It has three tabs, which have the following uses:

❑ **Autos** – variables in use in the current and previous statements

❑ **Locals** – all variables in scope

❑ **Watch *N*** – customizable variable and expression display (where *N* is 1 to 4)

The new screen layout can be seen in the screenshot below:

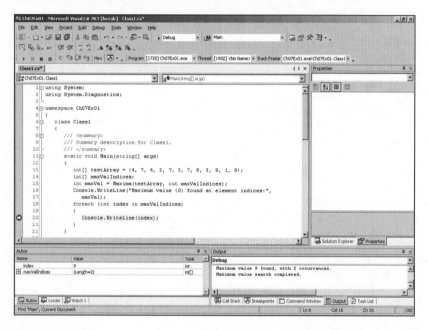

All these windows work in more or less the same way, with various additional features depending on their specific function. In general, each window will contain a list of variables, with information on variable name, value, and type. More complex variables, such as arrays, may be further interrogated using the + and – tree expansion/contraction symbols to the left of their names, allowing a tree view of their content. For example, this is a display obtained by placing a breakpoint in the code for the earlier example, just after the call to Maxima():

Locals		
Name	Value	Type
args	{Length=0}	string[]
index	0	int
⊞ testArray	{Length=12}	int[]
⊟ maxValIndices	{Length=2}	int[]
[0]	9	int
[1]	11	int
maxVal	9	int

Here, I've expanded the view for one of the array variables, maxValIndices.

We can also edit the content of variables from this view. This effectively bypasses any other variable assignment that might have happened in earlier code. To do this, we simply type a new value into the Value column for the variable we want to edit. We might do this to try out some scenarios that might otherwise require code changes, for example.

The Watch windows, of which there may be up to 4, allow us to monitor specific variables or expressions involving specific variables. To use this window, we simply type the name of a variable or expression into the Name column and observe the results. Note that not all variables in an application will be in scope all the time, and will be labeled as such in a Watch window. For example, the following screenshot shows a Watch window with a few sample variables and expressions in it. Again, the code from the last example is used here, paused in the execution of the Maxima() function:

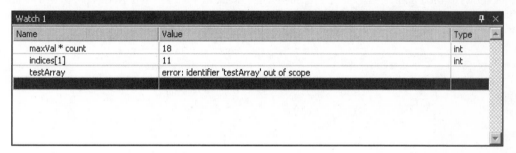

The testArray array is local to Main(), so we don't see a value here. Instead, we get a message informing us that the variable isn't in scope.

We can also add variables to a Watch window by dragging them from the source code into the widow.

To add more windows, we can use the Debug | Windows | Watch | Watch *N* menu options to toggle the four possible windows on or off. Each window may contain an individual set of watches on variables and expressions, so we can group related variables together for easy access.

As well as these watch windows, there is also a QuickWatch window that can give us detailed information about a variable in the source code quickly. To use this, we simply right-click on the variable we want to interrogate and select the QuickWatch menu option. In most cases, though, it is just as easy to use the standard Watch windows.

An important point to note about watches is that they are maintained between application executions. If we terminate an application then re-run it we don't have to add watches again – VS will remember what we were looking at the last time.

Stepping Through Code

So far, we've seen how to discover what is going on in our applications at the point where break mode is entered. Next, we will look at how we can use VS to "step through" code while remaining in break mode, allowing us to see exactly the results of the code being executed. This is an extremely valuable technique for those of us who can't think as fast as computers can.

When break mode is entered, a cursor appears to the left of the code view (which may initially appear inside the red circle of a breakpoint if a breakpoint has been used to enter break mode), by the line of code that is about to be executed:

```
11    static void Main(string[] args)
12    {
13        int[] testArray = {4, 7, 4, 2, 7, 3, 7, 8, 3, 9, 1, 9};
14        int[] maxValIndices;
15        int maxVal = Maxima(testArray, out maxValIndices);
16        Console.WriteLine("Maximum value {0} found at element indices:", maxVal);
17        foreach (int index in maxValIndices)
18        {
19            Console.WriteLine(index);
20        }
21    }
```

This shows us what point execution has reached when break mode is entered. At this point, we can choose to have execution proceed on a line-by-line basis. To do this, we use some more of the **Debug** toolbar buttons we saw earlier:

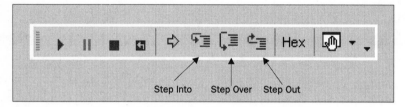

The sixth, seventh, and eighth icons control program flow in break mode. In order, they are:

- ❑ **Step Into** – execute and move to the next statement to execute
- ❑ **Step Over** – as above, but won't enter nested blocks of code
- ❑ **Step Out** – run to end of code block, and resume break mode at the statement that follows

If we want to look at every single operation carried out by the application then we can use **Step Into** to follow the instructions sequentially. This includes moving inside functions, such as `Maxima()` in the above example. Clicking on this icon when the cursor reaches line 15, the call to `Maxima()`, will result in the cursor moving to the first line inside the `Maxima()` function. Alternatively, clicking on **Step Over** when we reach line 15, will move the cursor straight to line 16, without having to go through the code in `Maxima()` (although this code is still executed). If we do step into a function that we aren't interested in we can hit **Step Out** to return to the code that called the function.

As we step through code, the values of variables are likely to change. By keeping an eye on the monitoring windows discussed in the last section, we can see this happening with ease.

In code that has semantic errors, this technique is perhaps the most useful one at our disposal. We can step through code right up to the point where we expect problems to occur and the errors will be generated as if we were running the program normally. Along the way, we can keep an eye on data and see just what is going wrong. Later on in this chapter we will use this technique to find out what is happening in an example application.

There are a couple of other windows left to cover: two more tabs appear on the **Task List / Output** window during debugging – **Command Window** and **Call Stack**.

Immediate Commands

The Command Window has two modes: Command and Immediate. Command mode allows us to perform VS operations manually (such as menu and toolbar operations), and Immediate mode allows us to execute additional code in addition to the source code lines being executed and to evaluate expressions.

In Command mode the window contains a right angle bracket (>) symbol at the start of each line. We can swap to immediate mode by typing "immed" in this window and hitting return, and back by typing ">cmd" and hitting return.

We'll concentrate on the Immediate mode here, as the Command mode is only really useful for complex operations.

The simplest use of this window is simply to evaluate expressions, a bit like a "one shot" use of the Watch windows. To do this, we simply type an expression and hit return. The information requested will then be displayed. For example:

```
Command Window - Immediate
>immed
testArray[3] * 10
20
```

We can also change variable content here, for example:

```
Command Window - Immediate
>immed
testArray[3] * 10
20
testArray[3] += 7
9
```

In most cases, we can get the effects we want more easily using the variable monitoring windows we saw earlier, but this technique can still be handy for tweaking values, and is good for testing expressions where we are unlikely to be interested in the results at a later date.

The Call Stack Window

The final window we'll look at here shows us the way in which the current location was reached. In simple terms, this means showing the current function along with the function that called it, the function that called that, and so on (that is, a list of nested function calls). The exact points where calls are made are also recorded.

175

In our earlier example, entering break mode when in `Maxima()`, or moving into this function using code stepping, reveals the following:

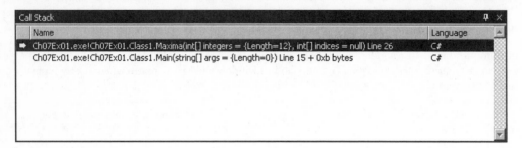

This window is particularly useful when errors are first detected, as they allow us to see what has happened immediately before the error. Where errors occur in commonly used functions, this will help us to see the source of the error.

Note that sometimes this window will show some very confusing information. Sometimes, for example, errors occur outside of our applications due to using external functions in the wrong way. At times like this, there could be a long list of entries in this window, but only one or two look familiar.

Error Handling

The first part of this chapter has dealt with finding and correcting errors during application development so that they won't occur in release level code. There are times, however, when we know that errors are likely to occur and there is no way of being 100% sure that they won't. In these situations it may be preferable to anticipate problems and write code that is robust enough to deal with these errors gracefully, without interrupting execution.

Error handling is the name for all techniques of this nature, and here we'll look at exceptions and how we can deal with them.

Exceptions

An exception is an error generated either in our code or in a function called by our code that occurs at runtime. The definition of "error" here is more vague than it has been up until now, as exceptions may be generated manually in functions and so on. For example, we might generate an exception in a function if one of its string parameters doesn't start with the letter "a" This isn't strictly speaking an error outside of the context of this function, although it is treated as one by the code that calls the function.

We've come across exceptions a few times already in this book. Perhaps the simplest example is attempting to address an array element that is out of range, for example:

```
int[] myArray = {1, 2, 3, 4};
int myElem = myArray[4];
```

This generates the following exception message, and then terminates the application:

```
An unhandled exception of type 'System.IndexOutOfRangeException' occurred in
<file>.exe
```

Where `<file>` is the name of the file containing the exception.

Exceptions are defined in namespaces, and most have names that make it clear what they are intended for. In this example, the exception generated is called `System.IndexOutOfRangeException`, which makes sense as we have supplied an index that is not in the range of indices permissible in `myArray`.

This message only appears and the application only terminates when the exception is unhandled. So, what exactly do we have to do to "handle" an exception?

try...catch...finally

The C# language includes syntax for **Structured Exception Handling** (**SEH**). Keywords exist to mark code out as being able to handle exceptions, along with instructions as to what to do if an exception occurs. The three keywords we use for this are `try`, `catch`, and `finally`. Each of these has an associated code block, and must be used in consecutive lines of code. The basic structure is as follows:

```
try
{
    ...
}
catch (<exceptionType> e)
{
    ...
}
finally
{
    ...
}
```

It is also possible, however, to have a `try` block and a `finally` block with no `catch` block, or a `try` block with multiple `catch` blocks. If one or more `catch` blocks exist then the `finally` block is optional, else it is mandatory.

The usage of the blocks is as follows:

❑   `try` – contains code that might **throw** exceptions ("throw" is the C# way of saying "generate" or "cause" when talking about exceptions).

❑   `catch` – contains code to execute when exceptions are thrown. `catch` blocks may be set to respond only to specific exception types (such as `System.IndexOutOfRangeException`) using `<exceptionType>`, hence the ability to provide multiple `catch` blocks. It is also possible to omit this parameter entirely, to get a **general** `catch` block that will respond to all exceptions.

❑   `finally` – contains code that is always executed, either after the `try` block if no exception occurs, after a `catch` block if an exception is handled, or just before an unhandled exception terminates the application (the fact that this block is processed at this time is the reason for its existence, otherwise we might just as well place code after the block).

177

The sequence of events that occurs after an exception occurs in code in a `try` block is as follows:

- ❑ The `try` block terminates at the point where the exception occurred.

- ❑ If a `catch` block exists then a check is made to see if the block matches the type of exception that has been thrown. If no `catch` block exists, then the `finally` block (which must be present if there are no `catch` blocks) executes.

- ❑ If a `catch` block exists, but there is no match, then a check is made for other `catch` blocks.

- ❑ If a `catch` block matches the exception type, then the code it contains executes, and then the `finally` block executes if it is present.

- ❑ If no `catch` blocks match the exception type then the `finally` block of code executes if it is present.

Let's look at an example to demonstrate handling exceptions.

Try it Out – Writing Exception Text to the Output Window

1. Create a new console application called `Ch07Ex02` in the directory `C:\BegVCSharp\Chapter7`.

2. Modify the code as follows:

```
class Class1
{
    static string[] eTypes = {"none", "simple", "index", "nested index"};

    static void Main(string[] args)
    {
        foreach (string eType in eTypes)
        {
            try
            {
                Console.WriteLine("Main() try block reached.");          // Line 18
                Console.WriteLine("ThrowException(\"{0}\") called.", eType);
                                                                          // Line 19
                ThrowException(eType);
                Console.WriteLine("Main() try block continues.");        // Line 21
            }
            catch (System.IndexOutOfRangeException e)                    // Line 23
            {
                Console.WriteLine("Main() System.IndexOutOfRangeException catch"
                            + " block reached. Message:\n\"{0}\"",
                            e.Message);
            }
            catch                                                         // Line 29
            {
```

```
                Console.WriteLine("Main() general catch block reached.");
            }
            finally
            {
                Console.WriteLine("Main() finally block reached.");
            }
            Console.WriteLine();
        }
    }

    static void ThrowException(string exceptionType)
    {
                                                              // Line 43
        Console.WriteLine("ThrowException(\"{0}\") reached.", exceptionType);
        switch (exceptionType)
        {
            case "none" :
                Console.WriteLine("Not throwing an exception.");
                break;                                        // Line 48
            case "simple" :
                Console.WriteLine("Throwing System.Exception.");
                throw (new System.Exception());               // Line 51
                break;
            case "index" :
                Console.WriteLine("Throwing System.IndexOutOfRangeException.");
                eTypes[4] = "error";                          // Line 55
                break;
            case "nested index" :
                try                                           // Line 58
                {
                    Console.WriteLine("ThrowException(\"nested index\") " +
                                    "try block reached.");
                    Console.WriteLine("ThrowException(\"index\") called.");
                    ThrowException("index");                  // Line 63
                }
                catch                                         // Line 65
                {
                    Console.WriteLine("ThrowException(\"nested index\") general"
                                    + " catch block reached.");
                }
                finally
                {
                    Console.WriteLine("ThrowException(\"nested index\") finally"
                                    + " block reached.");
                }
                break;
        }
    }
}
```

3. Run the application:

How it Works

This application has a `try` block in `Main()` that calls a function called `ThrowException()`. This function may throw exceptions, depending on the parameter it is called with:

❑ `ThrowException("none")` – doesn't throw an exception

❑ `ThrowException("simple")` – generates a general exception

❑ `ThrowException("index")` – generates a `System.IndexOutOfRangeException` exception

❑ `ThrowException("nested index")` – contains its own `try` block, which contains code that calls `ThrowException("index")` to generate a `System.IndexOutOfRangeException` exception

Each of these `string` parameters is held in the global `eTypes` array, which is iterated through in the `Main()` function to call `ThrowException()` once with each possible parameter. During this iteration various messages are written to the console to indicate what is happening.

This code gives us an excellent opportunity to use the code stepping techniques we saw earlier in this chapter. By working our way through the code a line at a time you can see exactly how code execution progresses.

Add a new breakpoint (with the default properties) to line 18 of the code, which reads:

```
Console.WriteLine("Main() try block reached.");
```

Note that I'll refer to code by line numbers as they appear in the downloadable version of this code. If you have line numbers turned off, remember that you can turn them back on through the Tools | Options... menu item and the Text Editor | C# | General option section. Comments are included in the code shown above so that you can follow the text without having the file open in front of you.

Run the application in debug mode.

Almost immediately, the program will enter break mode, with the cursor on line 18. If you select the **Locals** tab in the variable monitoring window, you should see that eType is currently "none". Use the **Step Into** button to process lines 18 and 19, and check that the first line of text has been written to the console. Next, use the **Step Into** button to step into the ThrowException() function on line 20.

Once in the ThrowException() function (on line 43), the **Locals** window changes. eType and args are no longer in scope (they are local to Main()); instead, we see the local exceptionType argument, which is of course "none". Keep pressing **Step Into** and you'll reach the switch statement that checks the value of exceptionType and execute the code that writes out the string "Not throwing an exception" to the screen. When we execute the break statement (on line 48) we exit the function and resume processing in Main() at line 21. As no exception was thrown the try block continues.

Next, processing continues with the finally block. Click **Step Into** a few more times to complete the finally block and the first cycle of the foreach loop. The next time we reach line 20, ThrowException() is called using a different parameter, "simple".

Continue using **Step Into** through ThrowException() and you'll eventually reach line 51:

```
throw (new System.Exception());
```

Here we use the C# throw keyword to generate an exception. This keyword simply needs to be provided with a new-initialized exception as a parameter, and it will throw that exception. Here we are using another exception from the System namespace, System.Exception.

When we process this statement with **Step Into** we find ourselves at the general catch block starting on line 29. There was no match with the earlier catch block starting on line 23, so this one is processed instead. Stepping through this code takes us through this block, through the finally block, and back into another loop cycle that calls ThrowException() with a new parameter on line 20. This time the parameter is "index".

This time, ThrowException() generates an exception on line 55:

```
eTypes[4] = "error";
```

The eTypes array is global, so we have access to it here. However, here we are attempting to access the 5th element in the array (remember counting starts at 0), which generates a System.IndexOutOfRangeException exception.

This time there is a matched catch block in Main(), and stepping into the code takes us to this block, starting at line 23.

The Console.WriteLine() call in this block writes out the message stored in the exception using e.Message (we have access to the exception through the parameter of the catch block). Again, stepping through takes us through the finally block (but not the second catch block, as the exception is already handled) and back into the loop cycle, again calling ThrowException() on line 20.

When we reach the `switch` structure in `ThrowException()` this time we enter a new `try` block, starting on line 58. When we reach line 63, we perform a nested call to `ThrowException()`, this time with the parameter `"index"`. If you like, use the **Step Over** button to skip the lines of code that are executed here, as we've been through them already. As before, this call generates a `System.IndexOutOfRangeException` exception. However, this time the exception is handled in the nested `try...catch...finally` structure, the one in `ThrowException()`. This structure has no explicit match for this type of exception, so the general `catch` block (starting on line 65) deals with it.

As with the earlier exception handling, we now step through this `catch` block, and the associated `finally` block, and reach the end of the function call. However, there is one crucial difference. Although an exception has been thrown, it has also been handled – by the code in `ThrowException()`. This means that there is no exception left to handle in `Main()`, so we go straight to the `finally` block, and after that the application terminates.

Listing and Configuring Exceptions

The .NET Framework contains a whole host of exception types, and we are free to throw and handle any of these in our own code, or even throw them from our code so that they may be caught in more complex applications. VS supplies a dialog for examining and editing the available exceptions, which can be called up with the **Debug | Exceptions...** menu item (or pressing *Ctrl+Alt+E*):

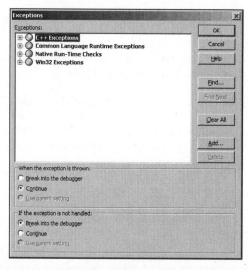

Exceptions are listed by category and .NET library namespace. We can see the exceptions in the `System` namespace by expanding the **Common Language Runtime Exceptions** tab, and then the **System** tab. This list includes the `System.IndexOutOfRangeException` exception we used above.

Each exception may be configured using the radio buttons at the bottom of the dialog. Most are set to **Use parent setting** by default, which means that they use the category level options (which are all as shown in the above screenshot). We can use the first option, **When the exception is thrown**, to cause a break into the debugger even for exceptions that are handled. The second option allows us to ignore unhandled exceptions, and suffer the consequences.

In most cases the default settings here are fine for us.

Notes on Exception Handling

Note that we must always supply `catch` blocks for more specific exceptions before more general catching. If we get this the wrong way round the application will fail to compile.

Note also that we can throw exceptions from within `catch` blocks, either in the ways used in the last example or by simply using the expression:

```
throw;
```

This expression results in the exception handled by the `catch` block being re-thrown.

If we throw an exception in this way, it will not be handled by the current `try...catch...finally` block, but by parent code (although the `finally` block in the nested structure will still execute).

For example, if we changed the `try...catch...finally` block in `ThrowException()` as follows:

```
try
{
   Console.WriteLine("ThrowException(\"nested index\") " +
                     "try block reached.");
   Console.WriteLine("ThrowException(\"index\") called.");
   ThrowException("index");
}
catch
{
   Console.WriteLine("ThrowException(\"nested index\") general"
      + " catch block reached.");
   throw;
}
finally
{
   Console.WriteLine("ThrowException(\"nested index\") finally"
      + " block reached.");
}
```

then execution would proceed first to the `finally` block shown here, then with the matching `catch` block in `Main()`. The resulting console output changes as follows:

In this screenshot, we see extra lines of output from the `Main()` function, as the `System.IndexOutOfRangeException` is caught in this function.

Summary

This chapter has concentrated on techniques that you can use to debug your applications. There are a variety of techniques available here, most of which are available for whatever type of project you are creating, not just console applications.

We have looked at:

❑ Using `Debug.WriteLine()` and `Trace.WriteLine()` to write text to the Output window

❑ Break mode and how to enter it, including the versatile breakpoints

❑ Debugging information windows in VS

❑ Stepping through code

❑ Exception handling using `try...catch...finally`

We have now covered everything that we need to produce simple console applications, along with the methods of debugging them. In the next section of this book, we will look at the powerful technique of object-oriented programming.

Exercises

1. "Using `Trace.WriteLine()` is preferable to using `Debug.WriteLine()` as the Debug version only works in debug builds." Do you agree with this statement? Why?

2. Provide code for a simple application containing a loop that generates an error after 5000 cycles. Use a breakpoint to enter break mode just before the error is caused on the 5000th cycle (note: a simple way to generate an error is to attempt to access a non existent array element, such as `myArray[1000]` in an array with a hundred elements).

3. "`finally` code blocks only execute if a `catch` block isn't executed." True or false?

4. Given the enumeration data type `orientation` defined below, write an application that uses Structured Exception Handling (SEH) to cast a byte type variable into an `orientation` type variable in a safe way. Note that you can force exceptions to be thrown using the `checked` keyword, an example of which is shown below. This code should be used in your application:

```
enum orientation : byte
{
   north = 1,
   south = 2,
   east  = 3,
   west  = 4
}
```

```
myDirection = checked((orientation)myByte);
```

Introduction to Object-Oriented Programming

At this point in the book we've covered all the basics of C# syntax and programming, and seen how to debug our applications. Already, we can assemble usable console applications. However, to get access to the real power of the C# language and the .NET Framework we need to make use of **object-oriented programming** (**OOP**) techniques. In actual fact, as we will soon see, we've been using these techniques already, although, to keep things simple, we have not focused on this when presenting the code examples.

In this chapter we will steer away from code temporarily and focus instead on the principles behind OOP. This will soon lead us back into the C# language, as it has a symbiotic relationship with OOP. All of the concepts introduced in this chapter will be returned to in later chapters, with illustrative code – so don't panic if you don't grasp everything in the first read-through of this material.

To start with, we'll look at the basics of OOP, which will include answering that most fundamental of questions "What is an Object?". We will quickly find that there is a lot of terminology related to OOP that can be quite confusing at first, and there will be plenty of explanation of the language used. We will also see that using OOP requires us to look at programming in a different way.

As well as discussing the general principles of OOP, we will also take a look at one area where a thorough understanding of OOP is essential: in Windows Forms applications. This type of application (which makes use of the Windows environment with features such as menus, buttons, etc.) provides plenty of scope for description, and we will be able to illustrate OOP points effectively in the Windows Forms environment.

> *Note that OOP as presented in this chapter is really .NET OOP, and that some of the techniques presented here don't apply to other OOP environments. Since when programming in C#, we use .NET-specific OOP, it makes good sense to concentrate on these aspects.*

So, let's start from the beginning.

What is Object-Oriented Programming?

Object-oriented programming is a relatively new approach to creating computer applications that seeks to address many of the problems with so-called "traditional" programming techniques. The type of programming we have seen so far is known as **functional** (or **procedural**) programming, often resulting in so-called **monolithic** applications, meaning that all functionality is contained in a few modules of code (often just one). With OOP techniques we often use many more modules of code, each offering specific functionality, and where each module may be isolated or even completely independent of others. This **modular** method of programming gives us much more versatility, and provides more opportunity for code-reuse.

To illustrate this further, imagine that a high performance application on your computer is a top-of-the-range racing car. If written with traditional programming techniques this sports car is basically a single unit. If we want to improve this car we have to replace the whole unit, by sending it back to the manufacturer and getting their expert mechanics to upgrade it, or by buying a new one. If OOP techniques are used then we could simply buy a new engine from the manufacturer and follow their instructions to replace it ourselves.

In a more "traditional" application the flow of execution is often simple and linear. Applications are loaded into memory, start executing at point A, end at point B, and are then unloaded from memory. Along the way various other entities might be used, such as files on storage media, or the capabilities of a video card, but the main body of the processing goes on in one place. The code along the way is generally concerned with manipulating data through various mathematical and logical means. The methods of manipulation are usually quite simple, using basic types such as integers and Boolean values to build up more complex representations of data.

With OOP things are rarely so linear. Although the same results are achieved, the way of getting there is often very different. OOP techniques are firmly rooted in the structure and meaning of data, and the interaction between that data and other data. This usually means putting more effort into the design stages of a project, but has the benefit of extensibility. Once an agreement is made as to the representation of a specific type of data, that agreement can be worked into later versions of an application, and even entirely new applications. The fact that an agreement exists can reduce development time dramatically. This explains how the above racing car example works. The agreement here is how the code for the "engine" is structured, such that new code (for a new engine) can be substituted with ease, rather than requiring a trip back to the manufacturers.

As well as agreeing on data representation, OOP programming often simplifies things by agreeing on the structure and usage of more abstract entities. For example, an agreement can be made not just on the format of data that should be used to send output to a device such as a printer, but also on the methods of data exchange with that device. This would include what instructions it understands, and so on.

As the name of the technology suggests, this is achieved using **objects**. So, what is an object?

What is an Object?

An **object** is a building block of an OOP application. This building block encapsulates part of the application, which may be a process, a chunk of data, or some more abstract entity.

In the simplest sense an object may be very similar to a struct type such as we have seen earlier in the book, containing members of variable and function types. The variables contained make up the data stored in the object, and the functions contained give access to the functionality of the object. Slightly more complex objects might not maintain any data; instead they can represent a process by containing only functions. For example, an object representing a printer might be used, which would have functions enabling control over a printer (allowing you to print a document, print a test page, and so on).

Objects in C# are created from types, just like the variables we've seen already. The type of an object is known by a special name in OOP, its **class**. We can use class definitions to **instantiate** objects, which means to create a real, named **instance** of a class. The phrases "instance of a class" and "object" mean the same thing here; be sure to note at this point that "class" and "object" mean fundamentally different things.

In this chapter we'll picture classes and objects using **Universal Modeling Language** (**UML**) syntax. UML is a language designed for modeling applications, from the objects that build them up, to the operations they perform, and to the use cases that are expected. Here we'll only be using the basics of this language, explaining these as we go along, and won't worry about the more complex aspects.

> *The diagrams in this chapter have been created using Microsoft Visio, which ships with the Enterprise Architect edition of VS.*

The following is a UML representation of our printer class, called `Printer`:

The class name is shown in the top section of this box (we'll worry about the bottom two sections a little later).

The following is a UML representation of an instance of this `Printer` class called `myPrinter`:

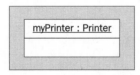

Here the instance name is shown first in the top section, followed by the name of its class. These two names are separated by a colon.

Properties and Fields

Properties and fields provide access to the data contained in an object. This object data is what differentiates separate objects, as it is possible for different objects of the same class to have different values stored in properties and fields.

At this point it is worth introducing another term – the various pieces of data contained in an object together make up the **state** of that object.

Imagine an object class that represents a cup of coffee, called `CupOfCoffee`. When we instantiate this class (that is, we create an object of this class) we must provide it with state for it to be meaningful. Here we might use properties and fields to enable code using this object to set the type of coffee used, whether the coffee contains milk or sugar, whether the coffee is instant, and so on. A given coffee cup object would then have a given state, such as "Columbian filter coffee with milk and two sugars".

Both fields and properties are typed, so we can store information in them as `string` variables, as `int` variables, and so on. However, properties differ from fields in that they don't provide *direct* access to data. Objects are capable of shielding users from the nitty-gritty details of their data, which needn't be represented on a 1-to-1 basis in the properties that exist. If we used a field for the number of sugars in a `CupOfCoffee` instance then users could place whatever value they liked in the field, but if we used a property then we could limit this value to, say, a number between 0 and 2.

In general, it is better to provide properties rather than fields for state access, as we have more control over what goes on. This choice doesn't affect code that uses object instances, as the syntax for using properties and fields is the same.

Read/write access to properties may also be clearly defined by an object. Certain properties may be read-only, allowing us to see what they are but not change them (at least not directly). This is often a useful technique for reading several pieces of state simultaneously. We might have a read-only property of our `CupOfCoffee` class called `Description`, returning a string representing the state of an instance of this class (such as the string given earlier) when requested. We might be able to assemble the same data by interrogating several properties, but a property such as this one may save us time and effort. We might also have write-only properties operating in a similar way.

As well as this read/write access for properties, it is also possible to specify a different sort of access permission for both fields and properties, known as **accessibility**. Accessibility determines what code can access these members, that is, whether they are available to all code (**public**), only to code within the class (**private**), or a more complex scheme (we'll cover this in more detail later on in the chapter, as it becomes pertinent). One very common practice is to make fields private and provide access to them via public properties. This means that code within the class can have direct access to the data stored in the field, while the public property shields external users from this data and prevents them from placing invalid content here. Public members are said to be **exposed** by the class.

One way of visualizing this is to equate it with variable scope. Private fields and properties, for example, can be thought of as local to the object that possesses them, whereas the scope of public fields and properties also encompasses code external to the object.

In the UML representation of a class we use the second section to display properties and fields, for example:

This is a representation of our `CupOfCoffee` class, with five members (properties or fields, as no distinction is made in UML) defined as discussed earlier. Each of the entries contains the following information:

❏   Accessibility: a + symbol is used for a public member, a - symbol is used for a private member. In general, though, I won't show private members in the diagrams in this chapter, as this information is internal to the class. No information is provided as to read/write access.

❏   The member name.

❏   The type of the member.

A colon is used to separate the member names and types.

Methods

"Method" is the term used to refer to functions exposed by objects. These may be called in the same way as any other function, and may use return values and parameters in the same way – we looked at functions in detail in Chapter 6.

Methods are used to give access to the functionality of objects. Like fields and properties they can be public or private, restricting access to external code as necessary. They will often make use of object state to affect their operation, and have access to private members such as private fields if required. For example, our `CupOfCoffee` class might define a method called `AddSugar()`, which would provide a more readable syntax for incrementing the sugar property than setting the corresponding `Sugar` property.

In UML, class boxes show methods in the third section:

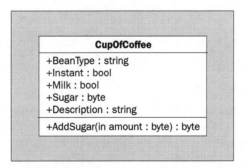

The syntax here is similar to that for fields and properties, except that the type shown at the end is the return type and method parameters are shown. Each parameter is displayed in UML with one of the following identifiers: in, out, or inout. These are used to signify the direction of data flow, where out and inout roughly correspond to the use of the C# keywords `out` and `ref` described in Chapter 6. in roughly corresponds to the C# behavior where neither of these keywords is used.

Everything's an Object

At this point it's time for me to come clean – we have been using objects, properties, and methods throughout this book. In fact, everything in C# and the .NET Framework is an object! The `Main()` function in a console application is a method of a class. Every variable type we've looked at is a class. Every command we have used has been a property or a method, such as `<String>.Length` and `<String>.ToUpper()` and so on. The period character here separates the object instance name from the property or method name.

Objects really are everywhere, and the syntax to use them is often very simple. It has certainly been simple enough for us to concentrate on some of the more fundamental aspects of C# up until now.

From here on in, we'll start to look at objects in more detail. Bear in mind that the concepts introduced here have far-reaching consequences – applying even to that simple little `int` variable you've been happily playing around with.

The Lifecycle of an Object

Every object has a clearly defined lifecycle. Apart from the normal state of "being in use", this lifecycle includes two important stages:

❑ **Construction** – when an object is first instantiated it needs to be initialized. This initialization is known as construction, and is carried out by a **constructor** function.

❑ **Destruction** – when an object is destroyed there will often be some clean up tasks to perform, such as freeing up memory. This is the job of a **destructor** function.

Constructors

Basic initialization of an object is automatic. For example, we don't have to worry about finding the memory to fit a new object into. However, there are times where we will want to perform additional tasks during an object's initialization stage. For example, we will often need to initialize the data stored by an object. A constructor function is what we use to do this.

All objects have a **default constructor**, which is a parameterless method with the same name as the class itself. In addition, a class definition might include several constructor methods with parameters, known as **non-default constructors**. These enable code that instantiates an object to do so in many ways, perhaps providing initial values for data stored in the object.

In C#, constructors are called using the new keyword. For example, we could instantiate a `CupOfCoffee` object using its default constructor in the following way:

```
CupOfCoffee myCup = new CupOfCoffee();
```

Objects may also be instantiated using non-default constructors. For example, our `CupOfCoffee` class might have a non-default constructor that uses a parameter to set the bean type at instantiation:

```
CupOfCoffee myCup = new CupOfCoffee("Blue Mountain");
```

Constructors, like fields, properties, and methods, may be public or private. Code external to a class can't instantiate an object using a private constructor; it must use a public constructor. In this way we can, for example, force users of our classes to use a non-default constructor.

Some classes have no public constructors, meaning that it is impossible for external code to instantiate them. However, this doesn't make them completely useless, as we will see shortly.

Destructors

Destructors are used by the .NET Framework to clean up after objects. In general, we don't have to provide code for a destructor method; instead the default operation works for us. However, we can provide specific instructions if anything important needs to be done before the object instance is deleted.

> **It is important to remember that the destructor method of an object doesn't get called as soon as we stop using that object.**

When a variable goes out of scope, for example, it may not be accessible from our code, but it may still exist somewhere in your computer's memory. It is only when the .NET runtime performs its garbage collection clean up that the instance is completely destroyed.

This means that we shouldn't rely on the destructor to free up resources that are used by an object instance, as this may be a long time after the object is of no further use to us. If the resources in use are critical this can cause problems. However, there is a solution to this – see the Disposable Objects section later in this chapter.

Static and Instance Class Members

As well as having members such as properties, methods, and fields that are specific to object instances, it is also possible to have **static** (also known as **shared**) members, which may be methods, properties, or fields. Static members are shared between instances of a class, so they can be thought of as global for objects of a given class. Static properties and fields allow us access to data that is independent of any object instances, and static methods allow us to execute commands related to the class type but not specific to object instances. When using static members, in fact, we don't even need to instantiate an object.

For example, the `Console.WriteLine()` and `Convert.ToString()` methods we have been using are static. At no point do we need to instantiate the `Console` or `Convert` classes (indeed, if we try it we'll find that we can't, as the constructors of these classes aren't publicly accessible, as discussed earlier).

There are many situations such as these where static properties and methods can be used to good effect. For example, we might use a static property to keep track of how many instances of a class have been created.

In UML syntax, static members of classes are shown underlined:

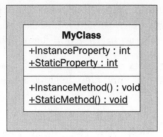

OOP Techniques

Now we've covered the basics and know what objects are and how they work, we should spend some time looking at some of the other features of objects. We'll look at:

❑ Interfaces

❑ Inheritance

❑ Polymorphism

❑ Relationships between objects

❑ Operator overloading

❑ Events

Interfaces

An interface is a collection of implicitly public methods and properties that are grouped together to encapsulate specific functionality. Once an interface has been defined, we can implement it in a class. This means that the class will then support all of the properties and members specified by the interface.

Note that interfaces cannot exist on their own. We can't "instantiate an interface" as we can a class. In addition, interfaces cannot contain any code that implements its members; it just defines the members themselves. The implementation must come from classes that implement the interface.

In our earlier coffee example, we might group together many of the more general purpose properties and methods into an interface, such as AddSugar(), Milk, Sugar, and Instant. We could call this interface something like IHotDrink (interface names are normally prefixed with a capital I). We could use this interface on other objects, perhaps those of a CupOfTea class. We could therefore treat these objects in a similar way, and they may still have their own individual properties (BeanType for CupOfCoffee and LeafType for CupOfTea, for example).

Interfaces implemented on objects in UML are shown using a "lollipop" syntax. In the diagram below I've split the members of IHotDrink into a separate box using class-like syntax (unfortunately the current version of Visio doesn't allow interfaces to possess fields or properties):

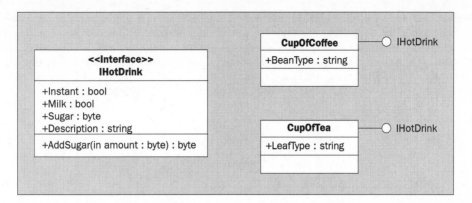

A class can support multiple interfaces, and multiple classes can support the same interface. The concept of an interface, therefore, makes life easier for users and other developers. For example, you might have some code that uses an object with a certain interface. Provided you don't use other properties and methods of this object it is possible to replace one object with another (code using the `IHotDrink` interface shown above could work with both `CupOfCoffee` and `CupOfTea` instances, for example). In addition, the developer of the object itself could supply you with an updated version of an object, and as long as it supports an interface that is already in use it becomes easy to use this new version in your code.

Disposable Objects

One interface of particular interest is `IDisposable`. An object that supports the `IDisposable` interface must implement the `Dispose()` method, that is, they must provide code for this method. This method can be called when an object is no longer needed (just before it goes out of scope, for example), and should be used to free up any critical resources which might otherwise linger until the destructor method is called on garbage collection. This gives you more control over the resources used by your objects.

C# allows us to use a structure that makes excellent use of this method. The `using` keyword allows us to initialize an object that uses critical resources in a code block, where `Dispose()` is automatically called at the end of this code block. The usage is as follows:

```
using (<ClassName> <VariableName> = new <ClassName>())
{
   ...
}
```

Here the variable `<VariableName>` will be usable within this code block, and will be disposed of automatically at the end (that is, `Dispose()` is called when the code block finishes executing).

Inheritance

Inheritance is one of the most important features of OOP. Any class may **inherit** from another, which means that it will have all the members that the class it **inherits** from has. In OOP terminology, the class being inherited (also known as **derived**) from is the **parent** class (also known as the **base** class). Note that objects in C# may only descend from a single base class.

Inheritance allows us to extend or create more specific classes from a single, more generic base class. For example, consider a class that represents a farm animal (as used by ace octogenarian developer Old MacDonald in his livestock application). This class might be called `Animal`, and possess methods such as `EatFood()` or `Breed()`. We could create a derived class called `Cow`, which would support all of these methods, but might also supply its own, such as `Moo()` and `SupplyMilk()`. We could also create another derived class, `Chicken`, with `Cluck()` and `LayEgg()` methods.

In UML we indicate inheritance using arrows, for example:

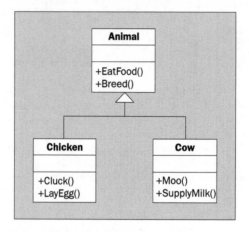

Here I've omitted the member return types for clarity.

When inheriting from a base class the question of member accessibility becomes an important one. Private members of the base class will not be accessible from a derived class, but public members will. However, public members are accessible to both the derived class and external code. This means that if we could only use these two levels of accessibility we couldn't have a member that was accessible by the base class and the derived class but not external code.

To get round this, there is a third type of accessibility, **protected**, where only derived classes have access to a member. As far as external code is aware, this is identical to a private member – it doesn't have access in either case.

As well as the protection level of a member, we can also define an inheritance behavior for it. Members of a base class may be **virtual**, which means that the member can be **overridden** by the class that inherits it. What this means is that the derived class *may* provide an alternative implementation for the member. This alternative implementation doesn't delete the original code, which is still accessible from within the class, but it does shield it from external code. If no alternative is supplied the external code has access to the base class implementation of the member.

Note that virtual members cannot be private, as this would cause a paradox – it is impossible to say that a member can be overridden by a derived class at the same time as saying that it is inaccessible from the derived class.

In our animals example, we could make `EatFood()` virtual, and provide a new implementation for it on any derived class, for example just on the `Cow` class:

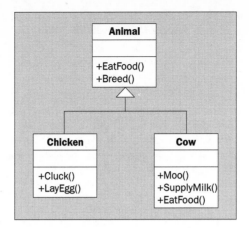

Here I've displayed the `EatFood()` method on the `Animal` and `Cow` classes to signify that they have their own implementations.

Base classes may also be defined as **abstract** classes. An abstract class can't be instantiated directly; to use it you need to inherit from it. Abstract classes may have abstract members, which have no implementation in the base class, so an implementation *must* be supplied in the derived class.

If `Animal` were an abstract class then the UML would be as follows:

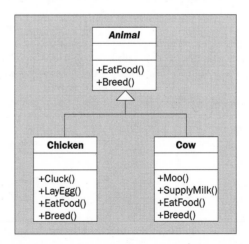

Abstract classes are shown with their name in italics (or sometimes with a dashed line for their box).

Finally, a class may be **sealed**. A sealed class may not be used as a base class, so no derived classes are possible.

In C# there is a common base class for all objects called `object` (which is an alias for the `System.Object` class in the .NET Framework). We'll take a closer look at this class in the next chapter.

Interfaces, described earlier in this chapter, may also inherit from other interfaces. Unlike classes, interfaces may inherit from multiple base interfaces (in the same way that classes can support multiple interfaces).

Polymorphism

One consequence of inheritance is that classes deriving from a base class have an overlap in the methods and properties that they expose. Because of this, it is often possible to treat objects instantiated from classes with a base type in common using identical syntax. For example, if a base class called Animal has a method called EatFood() then the syntax for calling this method from the derived classes Cow and Chicken will be similar:

```
Cow myCow = new Cow();
Chicken myChicken = new Chicken();
myCow.EatFood();
myChicken.EatFood();
```

Polymorphism takes this a step further. We can assign a variable that is of the base type to a variable of one of the derived types, for example:

```
Animal myAnimal = myCow;
```

No casting is required for this. We can then call methods of the base class through this variable:

```
myAnimal.EatFood();
```

This will result in the implementation of EatFood() in the derived class being called. Note that we can't call methods defined on the derived class in the same way. The following code won't work:

```
myAnimal.Moo();
```

However, we can cast a base type variable into a derived class variable and call the method of the derived class that way:

```
Cow myNewCow = (Cow)myAnimal;
myNewCow.Moo();
```

This casting will cause an exception to be raised if the type of the original variable was anything other than Cow or a class derived from Cow. There are ways of telling what type an object is, but we'll leave that until the next chapter.

Polymorphism is an extremely useful technique for performing tasks on different objects descending from a single class with the minimum of code.

Note that it isn't just classes sharing the same parent class that can make use of polymorphism. It is also possible to treat, say, a child and a grandchild class in the same way, as long as there is a common class in their inheritance hierarchy.

As a further note here, remember that in C# all classes derive from the base class object at the root of their inheritance hierarchy. It is therefore possible to treat *all* objects as instances of the class object. This is how Console.WriteLine() is able to process an infinite number of parameter combinations when building up strings. Every parameter after the first is treated as an object instance, allowing output from any object to be written to the screen. To do this the method ToString() (a member of object) is called. We can override this method to provide an implementation suitable for our class, or simply use the default, which returns the class name (qualified according to any namespaces it is in).

Interface Polymorphism

Earlier on we introduced the concept of interfaces for grouping together related methods and properties. Although we cannot instantiate interfaces in the same way as objects, it is possible to have a variable of an interface type. We can then use this variable to get access to methods and properties exposed by this interface on objects that support it.

For example, let's say that instead of an Animal base class being used to supply the EatFood() method we place this EatFood() method on an interface called IConsume. The Cow and Chicken classes could both support this interface; the only difference being that they are forced to provide an implementation for EatFood() (as interfaces contain no implementation). We can then access this method using code such as:

```
Cow myCow = new Cow();
Chicken myChicken = new Chicken();
IConsume consumeInterface;
consumeInterface = myCow;
consumeInterface.EatFood();
consumeInterface = myChicken;
consumeInterface.EatFood();
```

This provides a simple way for multiple objects to be called in the same way, and doesn't rely on a common base class. In this code, calling consumeInterface.EatFood() results in the EatFood() method of the Cow or Chicken class being called, depending on which instance has been assigned to the interface type variable.

Relationships Between Objects

Inheritance is a simple relationship between objects that results in a base class being completely exposed by a derived class, where the derived class may also have some access to the inner working of its base class (through protected members). There are other situations where relationships between objects become important.

In this section we'll take a brief look at:

❑ Containment – where one class contains another. This is similar to inheritance but allows the containing class to control access to the members of the contained class, and even perform additional processing before using members of a contained class.

❑ Collections – where one class acts as a container for multiple instances of another class. This is similar to having arrays of objects, but has additional scope, including indexing, sorting, resizing, and more.

Containment

Containment is simple to achieve by using a member field to hold an object instance. This member field might be public, in which case users of the container object will have access to its exposed methods and properties much like inheritance. However, we won't have access to the internals of the class via the derived class as we would with inheritance.

Alternatively, we can make the contained member object a private member. If we do this, none of its members will be accessible directly by users, even if they are public. Instead, we can provide access to these members using members of the containing class. This means we have complete control over what members of the contained class to expose, if any, and can also perform additional processing in the containing class members before accessing the contained class members.

For example, a Cow class might contain an Udder class with the public method Milk(). The Cow object could call this method as required, perhaps as part of its SupplyMilk() method, but these details will not be apparent (or important) to users of the Cow object.

Contained classes may be visualized in UML using an association line. For simple containment we label the ends of the lines with 1s, showing a one-to-one relationship (one Cow instance will contain one Udder instance). We can also show the contained Udder class instance as a private field of the Cow class for clarity:

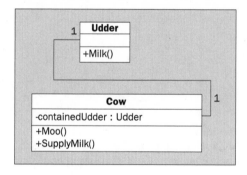

Collections

Back in Chapter 5 we saw how we can use arrays to store multiple variables of the same type. This also works for objects (remember, the variable types we have been using are really objects, so this is no real surprise). For example:

```
Animal[] animals = new Animal[5];
```

A collection is basically an array with bells and whistles. Collections are implemented as classes in much the same way as other objects. They are often named in the plural form of the objects they store, for example a class called Animals might contain a collection of Animal objects.

The main difference from arrays is that collections usually implement additional functionality, such as Add() and Remove() methods to add and remove items from the collection. There is also usually an Item property that returns an object based on its index. More often than not this property is implemented in such a way as to allow more sophisticated access. For example, it would be possible to design Animals such that a given Animal object could be accessed by its name.

In UML we can visualize this as follows:

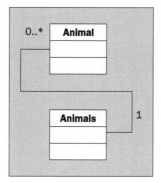

I've left off the members here, as it's the relationship that is being illustrated. The numbers on the ends of the connecting lines here show that one `Animals` object will contain zero or more `Animal` objects

We'll be taking a more detailed look at collections in Chapter 11.

Operator Overloading

Earlier on in the book we saw how operators can be used to manipulate simple variable types. There are times when it would be logical to use operators with objects instantiated from our own classes. This is possible because classes can contain instructions as to how operators should be treated.

For example, we might add a new property to our `Animal` class called `Weight`. We could then compare animal weights using:

```
if (cowA.Weight > cowB.Weight)
{
   ...
}
```

Using operator overloading we could provide logic that used the `Weight` property implicitly in our code, such that we could write code such as:

```
if (cowA > cowB)
{
   ...
}
```

Here the greater than operator > has been **overloaded**. An overloaded operator is one for which we have written the code to perform the operation involved – this code is added to the class definition of one of the classes that it operates on. In the above example we are using two `Cow` objects, so the operator overload definition is contained in the `Cow` class. We can also overload operators to work with different classes in the same way, where one (or both) of the class definitions contains the code to achieve this.

Note that we can only overload existing C# operators in this way; we can't create new ones. However, we can provide implementations for both unary and binary usages of operators such as +.

We'll see how to do this in C# in Chapter 11.

Events

Objects may raise (and consume) **events** as part of their processing. Events are important occurrences that we can act on in other parts of code, similar to (but more powerful than) exceptions. We might, for example, want some specific code to execute when an `Animal` object is added to an `Animals` collection, where that code isn't part of either the `Animals` class or the code that calls the `Add()` method. To do this we need to add an **event handler** to our code, which is a special kind of function that is called when the event occurs. We also need to configure this handler to listen for the event we are interested in.

Using events, we can create **event-driven** applications, which are far more prolific than you might think at this stage. As an example, it is worth bearing in mind that Windows-based applications are entirely dependent on events. Every button click or scrollbar drag you perform is achieved through event handling, where the events are triggered by the mouse or keyboard.

Later on in this chapter we'll see how this works in Windows applications, and we'll have a more in-depth discussion of events in Chapter 12.

Reference versus. Value Types

Data in C# is stored in a variable in one of two ways depending on the type of the variable. This type will fall into one of two categories; it is either a **reference** type or a **value** type. The difference is as follows:

❑   Value types store themselves and their content in one place in memory

❑   Reference types hold a reference to somewhere else in memory (called the heap) where content is stored

In actual fact we don't have to worry about this too much when using C#. So far we've used `string` variables (which are reference types) and other simple variables (most of which are value types, such as `int`) in pretty much the same way.

The only simple types that are reference types are `string` and `object`, although arrays are implicitly reference types as well. Every class we create will be a reference type, which is why I'm making this point now.

Structs

At this point there is an important point to note. The key difference between struct types and classes is that struct types are value types.

The fact that struct types and classes are similar may have occurred to you, particularly as we saw in Chapter 6 how we can use functions in struct types. We'll see more details about this in the next chapter.

OOP in Windows Applications

Back in Chapter 2 we saw how to create a simple Windows application in C#. Windows applications are heavily dependent on OOP techniques, and in this section we'll take a look at this to illustrate some of the points made in this chapter. To do this we'll work through a simple example.

Try it Out – Objects in Action

1. Create a new Windows application in the directory `C:\BegVCSharp\Chapter8` called `Ch08Ex01`.

2. Add a new `Button` control using the **Toolbox** bar, and position it in the center of `Form1`:

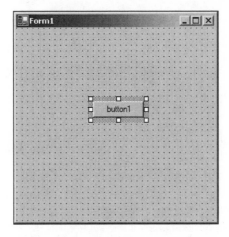

3. Double-click on the button to add code for a mouse click. Modify the code that appears as follows:

```
private void button1_Click(object sender, System.EventArgs e)
{
    ((Button)sender).Text = "Clicked!";
    Button newButton = new Button();
    newButton.Text = "New Button!";
    newButton.Click += new EventHandler(newButton_Click);
    Controls.Add(newButton);
}

private void newButton_Click(object sender, System.EventArgs e)
{
    ((Button)sender).Text = "Clicked!!";
}
}
```

4. Run the application:

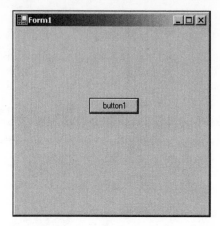

5. Click on the button marked button1:

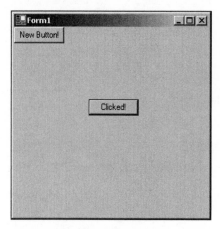

6. Click on the button marked New Button!:

How it Works

By adding just a few lines of code we've created a Windows application that does something, while at the same time illustrating some OOP techniques in C#. The phrase "Everything's an object" is even more true when it comes to Windows applications. From the form that runs, to the controls on the form, we need to make use of OOP techniques all the time. Throughout this example description I've highlighted some of the concepts that we've looked at earlier in this chapter to show how everything fits together.

The first thing we did in our application was to add a new button to the Form1 form. This button is an **object**, called Button. Next, by double-clicking on the button we added an **event handler** to listen out for the Click **event** that the Button object generates. This event handler is added into the code for the Form object that encapsulates our application, as a **private method**:

```
private void button1_Click(object sender, System.EventArgs e)
{
}
```

This uses the C# keyword private as a qualifier. Don't worry too much about this for now; in the next chapter we'll be looking at the C# code required for the OOP techniques we've seen in this chapter.

The first line of code we added changes the text on the button that is clicked. This makes use of **polymorphism** as seen earlier in this chapter. The Button object representing the button that we click is sent to the event handler as an object parameter, which we cast into a Button type (this is possible as the Button object **inherits** from System.Object, which is the .NET class that object is an alias for). We then change the Text **property** of the object to change the text displayed:

```
((Button)sender).Text = "Clicked!";
```

Next, we create a new Button object with the new keyword (note that namespaces are set up in this project to enable this simple syntax, otherwise we'd need to use the fully qualified name of this object, System.Windows.Forms.Button):

```
Button newButton = new Button();
newButton.Text = "New Button!";
```

Elsewhere in the code a new **event handler** is added, which we'll use to respond to the Click event generated by our new button:

```
private void newButton_Click(object sender, System.EventArgs e)
{
    ((Button)sender).Text = "Clicked!!";
}
```

We then register this event handler as a listener for the Click event using some **overloaded operator** syntax. Along the way we create a new EventHandler object using a **non-default constructor**, using the name of the new event handler function:

```
newButton.Click += new EventHandler(newButton_Click);
```

Finally, we make use of the `Controls` property. This property is an object that is a collection of all the controls on our form, and we use its `Add()` method to add our new button to the form:

```
Controls.Add(newButton);
```

The `Controls` property illustrates that properties need not necessarily be simple types such as strings or integers, but can be any kind of object.

This short example has used almost all the techniques introduced in this chapter. As you can see, OOP programming needn't be complicated – it just requires a different point of view to get right.

Summary

This chapter has presented us with a full description of object-oriented techniques. We have gone through this in the context of C# programming, but this has mainly been illustrative. The vast majority of this chapter is relevant to OOP in any language.

We started by covering the basics, such as what is meant by the term **object**, and how an object is an **instance** of a **class**. Next we saw how objects can have various **members**, such as **fields**, **properties**, and **methods**. These members can have restricted accessibility, and we looked at what we mean by **public** and **private** members. Later on, we saw that members can also be **protected**, as well as being able to be **virtual** and **abstract** (where abstract methods are only permissible on abstract classes). We also looked at the difference between **static** (**shared**) and **instance** members.

Next we took a quick look at the lifecycle of an object, including how **constructors** are used in object creation, and **destructors** in object deletion. Later on, after examining groups of members in **interfaces**, we looked at more advanced object destruction with **disposable** objects supporting the `IDisposable` interface.

Most of the remainder of the chapter looked at features of OOP, many of which we'll be seeing in more depth in the chapters that follow. We looked at **inheritance**, where classes **inherit** from **base classes**, two versions of **polymorphism**, through base classes and shared interfaces, and saw how objects can be used to contain one or more other objects (through **containment** and **collections**). Finally, we saw how **operator overloading** can be used to simplify the syntax of object usage, and how objects often raise **events**.

The last part of this chapter demonstrated much of the theory in this chapter using a Windows application as an example.

In the next chapter we'll look at defining classes using C#.

Exercises

1. Which of the following are real levels of accessibility in OOP?

- ❏ Friend
- ❏ Public
- ❏ Secure
- ❏ Private
- ❏ Protected
- ❏ Loose
- ❏ Wildcard

2. "We must call the destructor of an object manually, or it will waste memory." True or False?

3. Do you need to create an object in order to call a static method of its class?

4. Draw a UML diagram similar to the ones shown in this chapter for the following classes and interface:

- ❏ An abstract class called HotDrink that has the methods Drink(), AddMilk(), and AddSugar(), and the properties Milk, and Sugar.
- ❏ An interface called ICup that has the methods Refill() and Wash(), and the properties Color and Volume.
- ❏ A class called CupOfCoffee that derives from HotDrink, supports the ICup interface, and has the additional property BeanType.
- ❏ A class called CupOfTea that derives from HotDrink, supports the ICup interface, and has the additional property LeafType.

5. Write some code for a function that would accept either of the two cup objects in the above example as a parameter. The function should call the AddMilk(), Drink(), and Wash() methods for any cup object it is passed.

Defining Classes

In the last chapter we looked at the features of object-oriented programming (OOP). In this chapter we'll put theory into practice and look at defining classes in C#.

We won't go so far as to define class members in this chapter, as we'll concentrate on the class definitions themselves for now. This may sound a little limiting, but don't worry, there's plenty here to get your teeth into!

To start off with, we'll look at the basic class definition syntax, the keywords we can use to determine class accessibility and so on, and the way in which we can specify inheritance. We'll also look at interface definitions, as they are similar to class definitions in many ways.

The rest of the chapter will look at various topics that apply when defining classes in C#, including:

- ❑ The `System.Object` class
- ❑ Helpful tools provided by Visual Studio .NET (VS)
- ❑ Class libraries
- ❑ A comparison between interfaces and abstract classes
- ❑ Struct types
- ❑ Copying objects

So, to start with let's dive into the basics.

Class Definitions in C#

C# uses the `class` keyword to define classes. The basic structure required is as follows:

```
class MyClass
{
    // class members
}
```

This code defines a class called `MyClass`. Once we have defined a class we are free to instantiate it anywhere else in our project that has access to the definition. By default, classes are declared as **internal**, meaning that only code in the current project will have access to it. We can specify this explicitly using the `internal` access modifier keyword as follows (although we don't have to):

```
internal class MyClass
{
   // class members
}
```

Alternatively, we can specify that the class is public, and should also be accessible to code in other projects. To do this we use the `public` keyword:

```
public class MyClass
{
   // class members
}
```

> *Note that classes declared in their own right in this way cannot be private or protected. However, it is possible to use these modifiers for declaring classes as class members, which we'll look at in the next chapter.*

As well as these two access modifier keywords, we can also specify that the class is either **abstract** (cannot be instantiated, only inherited, and can have abstract members) or **sealed** (cannot be inherited). To do this we use one of the two mutually exclusive keywords `abstract` or `sealed`. An abstract class must therefore be declared in the following way:

```
public abstract class MyClass
{
   // class members, may be abstract
}
```

Here `MyClass` is a public abstract class, while internal abstract classes are also possible.

Sealed classes are declared as follows:

```
public sealed class MyClass
{
   // class members
}
```

As with abstract classes, sealed classes may be public or internal.

Inheritance can also be specified in the class definition. To do this we simply put a colon after the class name, followed by the base class name. For example:

```
public class MyClass : MyBase
{
   // class members
}
```

Note that *only one* base class is permitted in C# class definitions, and that if we inherit from an abstract class we *must* implement all the abstract members inherited (unless the derived class is also abstract).

The compiler will not allow a derived class to be more accessible than its base class. This means that an internal class *can* inherit from a public base, but a public class *can't* inherit from an internal base. This means that the following code is legal:

```
public class MyBase
{
    // class members
}

internal class MyClass : MyBase
{
    // class members
}
```

But the following code won't compile:

```
internal class MyBase
{
    // class members
}

public class MyClass : MyBase
{
    // class members
}
```

If no base class is used then the class will inherit only from the base class `System.Object` (which has the alias `object` in C#). Ultimately *all* classes have `System.Object` at the root of their inheritance hierarchy. We'll take a closer look at this fundamental class a little later.

As well as specifying base classes in this way, we can also specify interfaces supported after the colon character. If a base class is specified it must be the first thing after the colon, with interfaces specified afterwards. If there is no base class specified we specify the interfaces straight after the colon. Commas must be used to separate the base class name (if there is one) and the interface names from one another.

For example, we could add an interface to `MyClass` as follows:

```
public class MyClass : IMyInterface
{
    // class members
}
```

All interface members *must* be implemented in any class that supports the interface, although we can provide an "empty" implementation (with no functional code) if we don't want to do anything with a given interface member.

The following declaration is invalid, as the base class `MyBase` isn't the first entry in the inheritance list:

```
public class MyClass : IMyInterface, MyBase
{
    // class members
}
```

The correct way to specify a base class and an interface is as follows:

```
public class MyClass : MyBase, IMyInterface
{
    // class members
}
```

And remember that multiple interfaces are possible, so the following is also valid:

```
public class MyClass : MyBase, IMyInterface, IMySecondInterface
{
    // class members
}
```

As a quick recap, here is a table of allowed access modifier combinations for class definitions:

Modifier	Meaning
none or internal	Class accessible only from within the current project.
public	Class accessible from anywhere.
abstract or internal abstract	Class accessible only from within the current project, cannot be instantiated, only derived from.
public abstract	Class accessible from anywhere, cannot be instantiated, only derived from.
sealed or internal sealed	Class accessible only from within the current project, cannot be derived from, only instantiated.
public sealed	Class accessible from anywhere, cannot be derived from, only instantiated.

Interface Definitions

Interfaces are declared in a similar way to classes, but using the interface keyword rather than class. For example:

```
interface IMyInterface
{
    // interface members
}
```

The access modifier keywords `public` and `internal` are used in the same way, so to make an interface publicly accessible we must use the `public` keyword:

```
public interface IMyInterface
{
    // interface members
}
```

The keywords `abstract` and `sealed` are not allowed in interfaces because neither modifier makes sense in the context of interfaces (they contain no implementation, so can't be instantiated directly, and they must be inheritable to be useful).

Interface inheritance is also specified in a similar way to class inheritance. The main difference here is that multiple base interfaces can be used, for example:

```
public interface IMyInterface : IMyBaseInterface, IMyBaseInterface2
{
    // interface members
}
```

Interfaces inherit from `System.Object` in the same way as classes. This is the mechanism through which interface polymorphism is possible. However, as already discussed, it is impossible to instantiate an interface in the same way as a class. Let's look at an example of some class definitions, along with some code that uses them.

Try it Out – Defining Classes

1. Create a new console application called `Ch09Ex01` in the directory `C:\BegVCSharp\Chapter9`.

2. Modify the code in `Class1.cs` as follows:

```
namespace Ch09Ex01
{
    public abstract class MyBase
    {
    }

    internal class MyClass : MyBase
    {
    }

    public interface IMyBaseInterface
    {
    }

    internal interface IMyBaseInterface2
    {
    }

    internal interface IMyInterface : IMyBaseInterface, IMyBaseInterface2
    {
    }

    internal sealed class MyComplexClass : MyClass, IMyInterface
    {
```

```
        }

    class Class1
    {
        static void Main(string[] args)
        {
            MyComplexClass myObj = new MyComplexClass();
            Console.WriteLine(myObj.ToString());
        }
    }
}
```

3. Execute the project:

How It Works

This project defines classes and interfaces in the following inheritance hierarchy:

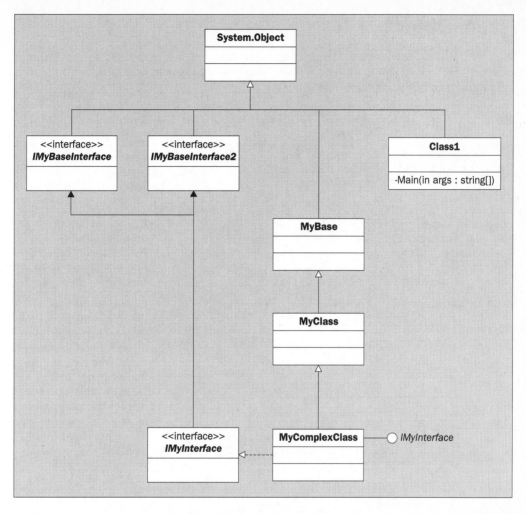

I've included Class1 here as it is a class defined in the same way as our other classes, even though it isn't part of the main class hierarchy. The Main() method possessed by this class is the entry point for our application as discussed earlier in the book.

MyBase and IMyBaseInterface are public definitions, so they are available from other projects. The other classes and interfaces are internal, and are only available in this project.

The code in Main() calls the ToString() method of myObj, an instance of MyComplexClass:

```
MyComplexClass myObj = new MyComplexClass();
Console.WriteLine(myObj.ToString());
```

This is one of the methods inherited from System.Object (not shown in the diagram as I've omitted the members of this class for clarity), and simply returns the class name of the object as a string, qualified by any relevant namespaces.

System.Object

Since all classes inherit from System.Object, all classes will have access to the protected and public members of this class. This means that it is well worth taking a look at what is available there. System.Object contains the following methods:

Method	Return Type	Virtual	Static	Description
Object()	N/A	No	No	Constructor for the System.Object type. Automatically called by constructors of derived types.
~Object() (also known as Finalize() – see next section)	N/A	No	No	Destructor for the System.Object type. Automatically called by destructors of derived types, cannot be called manually.
Equals(object)	bool	Yes	No	Compares the object for which this method is called with another object, and returns true if they are equal. The default implementation checks to see if the object parameter *refers* to the same object (as objects are reference types). This method can be overridden if you wish to compare objects in a different way, such as if they hold equivalent data.
Equals(object, object)	bool	No	Yes	This method compares the two objects passed to it and checks to see if they are equal This check is performed using the Equals(object) method. Note that if both objects are null references this method returns true.
ReferenceEquals (object, object)	bool	No	Yes	This method compares the two objects passed to it and checks to see if they are references to the same instance.

Method	Return Type	Virtual	Static	Description
ToString()	string	Yes	No	Returns a string corresponding to the object instance. By default this is the qualified name of the class type (see earlier example), but this can be overridden to provide an implementation appropriate to the class type.
MemberwiseClone()	object	No	No	Copies the object by creating a new object instance and copying members. Note that this member copying will *not* result in new instances of these members. Any reference type members of the new object will refer to the same objects as the original class. This method is protected, and so can only be used from within the class or from derived classes.
GetType()	System. Type	No	No	Returns the type of the object in the form of a System.Type object.
GetHashCode()	int	Yes	No	Used as a **hash function** for objects where this is required. A hash function is one that returns a value identifying the object state in some compressed form.

These methods are the basic ones that must be supported by object types in the .NET Framework, although we might never use some of them (or use them only in special circumstances, such as GetHashCode()).

GetType() is a useful method when we are using polymorphism, as it allows us to perform different operations with objects depending on their type, rather than the same operation for all objects as is often the case. For example, if we have a function that accepts an object type parameter (meaning that we can pass it just about anything) we might perform additional tasks if certain objects are encountered. Using a combination of GetType() and typeof() (a C# operator that converts a class name into a System.Type object) we can perform comparisons such as:

```
if (myObj.GetType() == typeof(MyComplexClass))
{
    // myObj is an instance of the class MyComplexClass
}
```

The `System.Type` object returned is capable of a lot more than this, but we won't cover this here. This topic is covered in more detail in Chapter 22.

It can also be very useful to override the `ToString()` method, particularly in situations where the contents of an object can be easily represented with a single human-readable string.

We'll be seeing these `System.Object` methods repeatedly over the coming chapters, so we'll end this discussion for now, and go into more detail as necessary.

Constructors and Destructors

When we define a class in C# there is often no need to define associated constructors and destructors, as the base class `System.Object` provides a default implementation for us. However, we can provide our own if required, enabling us to initialize and clean up after our objects respectively.

A simple constructor can be added to a class using the following syntax:

```
class MyClass
{
    public MyClass()
    {
        // Constructor code
    }
}
```

This constructor has the same name as the class that contains it, has no parameters (making it the default constructor for the class), and is public so that objects of the class may be instantiated using this constructor (check back to the discussion in the last chapter for more information on this).

We can also use a private default constructor, meaning that object instances of this class cannot be created using this constructor (see discussion in the last chapter):

```
class MyClass
{
    private MyClass()
    {
        // Constructor code
    }
}
```

Finally, we can add non-default constructors to our class in a similar way, simply by providing parameters. For example:

```
class MyClass
{
    public MyClass()
    {
        // Default constructor code
    }

    public MyClass(int myint)
    {
        // Non-default constructor code (uses myInt)
    }
}
```

There is no limit to the amount of constructors we can supply.

Destructors are declared using a slightly different syntax. The destructor used in .NET (and supplied by the System.Object class) is called Finalize(), but this isn't the name we use to declare a destructor. Instead of overriding Finalize() we use the following:

```
class MyClass
{
    ~MyClass()
    {
        // destructor body
    }
}
```

Thus the destructor of a class is declared by the class name (like the constructor is), with the ~ prefix. The code in the destructor will be executed when garbage collection occurs, allowing us to free resources. After this destructor is called, implicit calls to the destructors of base classes also occur, including a call to Finalize() in the System.Object root class. This technique allows the .NET Framework to ensure that this occurs, as overriding Finalize() would mean that base class calls would need to be explicitly performed, which is potentially dangerous (we'll see how to call base class methods in the next chapter).

Constructor Execution Sequence

If we perform multiple tasks in the constructors of a class it can be handy to have this code in one place, which has the same benefits as splitting code into functions as we saw earlier in the book. We could do this using a method (see next chapter), but C# provides a nice alternative. Any constructor can be configured to call any other constructor before it executes it's own code.

Before looking at this, though, we need to take a closer look at what happens by default when we instantiate a class instance.

In order for a derived class to be instantiated its base class must be instantiated. In order for this base class to be instantiated the base class of this base class must be instantiated, right the way back to System.Object. The result of this is that whatever constructor we use to instantiate a class, System.Object.Object() is always called first.

If we use a non-default constructor of a class then the default behavior is to use a constructor on the base class that matches the signature of this constructor. If none is found then the default constructor for the base class is used (which will always happen for the ultimate root System.Object, as this class has no non-default constructors). Let's look at a quick example of this to illustrate the sequence of events. Consider the following object hierarchy:

```
public class MyBaseClass
{
    public MyBaseClass()
    {
    }

    public MyBaseClass(int i)
    {
    }
}

public class MyDerivedClass : MyBaseClass
{
    public MyDerivedClass()
    {
    }

    public MyDerivedClass(int i)
    {
    }

    public MyDerivedClass(int i, int j)
    {
    }
}
```

We could instantiate MyDerivedClass in the following way:

```
MyDerivedClass myObj = new MyDerivedClass();
```

In this case the following sequence of events will occur:

❑   The System.Object.Object() constructor will execute.

❑   The MyBaseClass.MyBaseClass() constructor will execute.

❑   The MyDerivedClass.MyDerivedClass() constructor will execute.

Alternatively, we could use the following:

```
MyDerivedClass myObj = new MyDerivedClass(4);
```

Here the sequence will be as follows:

❑   The System.Object.Object() constructor will execute.

❑   The MyBaseClass.MyBaseClass(int i) constructor will execute.

❑   The MyDerivedClass.MyDerivedClass(int i) constructor will execute.

Finally, we could use the following:

```
MyDerivedClass myObj = new MyDerivedClass(4, 8);
```

This results in the following sequence:

❑   The `System.Object.Object()` constructor will execute.

❑   The `MyBaseClass.MyBaseClass()` constructor will execute.

❑   The `MyDerivedClass.MyDerivedClass(int i, int j)` constructor will execute.

This system works fine, and ensures that any inherited members are accessible to constructors in our derived classes. However, there are times when a little more control over the events that take place is required, or just desirable. For example, in the last instantiation example we might want to have the following sequence:

❑   The `System.Object.Object()` constructor will execute.

❑   The `MyBaseClass.MyBaseClass(int i)` constructor will execute.

❑   The `MyDerivedClass.MyDerivedClass(int i, int j)` constructor will execute.

Using this we could place the code that uses the `int i` parameter in `MyBaseClass(int i)`, meaning that the `MyDerivedClass(int i, int j)` constructor would have less work to do – it would only need to process the `int j` parameter. (This assumes that the `int i` parameter has an identical meaning in both cases, which might not always be the case, but in practice with this kind of arrangement it usually is.) C# allows us to specify this kind of behavior should we wish.

To do this we simply specify the base class constructor to use in the definition of the constructor in our derived class as follows:

```
public class MyDerivedClass : MyBaseClass
{
   ...

   public MyDerivedClass(int i, int j) : base(i)
   {
   }
}
```

The `base` keyword directs the .NET instantiation process to use the base class constructor matching the signature specified. Here we are using a single `int` parameter, so `MyBaseClass(int i)` will be used. Doing this means that `MyBaseClass()` will not be called, giving us the sequence of events listed prior to this example – exactly what we wanted here.

We can also use this keyword to specify literal values for base class constructors, perhaps using the default constructor of `MyDerivedClass` to call a non-default constructor of `MyBaseClass`:

```
public class MyDerivedClass : MyBaseClass
{
```

```
    public MyDerivedClass() : base(5)
  {
  }


    ...

}
```

This gives us the following sequence:

❑ The `System.Object.Object()` constructor will execute.

❑ The `MyBaseClass.MyBaseClass(int i)` constructor will execute.

❑ The `MyDerivedClass.MyDerivedClass()` constructor will execute.

As well as this `base` keyword, there is one more keyword that we can use here: `this`. This keyword instructs the .NET instantiation process to use a non-default constructor on the *current* class before the specified constructor is called. For example:

```
public class MyDerivedClass : MyBaseClass
  {
    public MyDerivedClass() : this(5, 6)
    {
    }

    ...

    public MyDerivedClass(int i, int j) : base(i)
    {
    }
}
```

Here we will have the following sequence:

❑ The `System.Object.Object()` constructor will execute.

❑ The `MyBaseClass.MyBaseClass(int i)` constructor will execute.

❑ The `MyDerivedClass.MyDerivedClass(int i, int j)` constructor will execute.

❑ The `MyDerivedClass.MyDerivedClass()` constructor will execute.

The only limitation to all this is that we can only specify a single constructor using the `this` or `base` keywords. However, as demonstrated in the last example above, this isn't much of a limitation, as we can still construct fairly sophisticated execution sequences.

We'll see this technique in action a little later in the book.

OOP Tools in Visual Studio .NET

Since OOP is such a fundamental subject in the .NET Framework there are several tools provided by VS to aid development of OOP applications. In this section we'll look at some of these.

The Class View Window

Back in Chapter 2 we saw that the Solution Explorer window shares space with a window called Class View. This window shows us the class hierarchy of our application, and enables us to see at a glance the characteristics of the classes we use. There are a few different modes for viewing this information, the default of which is Sort By Type. For the example project in the earlier section the view is as follows:

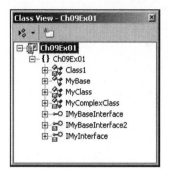

There are many symbols that may be used here, including:

- ❑   📇 – Project
- ❑   { } – Namespace
- ❑   ◆ – Class
- ❑   ⊸○ – Interface
- ❑   ◆ – Method
- ❑   📑 – Property
- ❑   ◈ – Field
- ❑   ◈ – Struct
- ❑   📇 – Enumeration
- ❑   📇 – Enumeration item
- ❑   ⚡ – Event

Note that some of these are used for type definitions other than classes, such as enumerations and struct types.

Some of the entries may have other symbols placed below them signifying their access level (no symbol appears for public entries):

- ❑   🔒 – Private
- ❑   ⚷ – Protected
- ❑   ✉ – Internal

No symbols are used to denote abstract, sealed, or virtual entries.

All the available modes work in basically the same way, and allow us to expand the definitions of classes using the standard tree view controls. Expanding our classes and interfaces down to the System.Object level reveals the following:

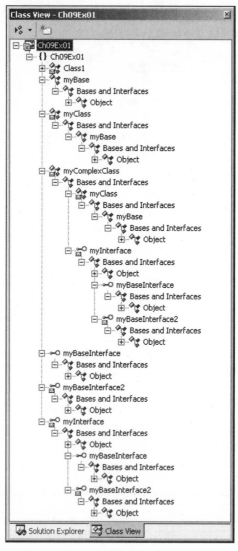

Here we can see all the class information in a project.

As well as being able to look at this information here, we can also get access to the relevant code for many of these items. Double-clicking on an item, or right-clicking and selecting Go to Definition, takes us straight to the code in our project that defines the item, if it is available. If the code isn't available, such as code in an inaccessible base type like System.Object, we will instead be taken into the Object Browser view.

The Object Browser

The Object Browser is an expanded version of the Class View window, allowing us to view other classes available to our project, and even completely external classes. It is entered either automatically (for example in the situation noted in the last section), or manually via View | Other Windows | Object Browser. The view appears in the main window, and we can browse it in the same way as the Class View window:

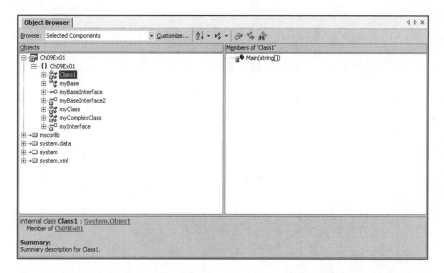

This window shows classes and members of classes in different places, unlike Class View, and includes all the .NET modules referenced by our project. We can browse through, for example, entries in the System namespace using this tool.

When an item is selected we also get information about it below the window. Here we can see the access level, base class, and namespace for Class1. We can use this information to navigate as well – clicking on System.Object will take us straight to the information pertaining to this class, for example. We can also see some Summary information here. This is generated by the XML documentation comments in the code (which begin with ///):

```
/// <summary>
/// Summary description for Class1.
/// </summary>
class Class1
{
    static void Main(string[] args)
    {
        MyComplexClass myObj = new MyComplexClass();
        Console.WriteLine(myObj.ToString());
    }
}
```

We'll look at XML documentation comments in more depth in Chapter 18.

Adding Classes

VS contains tools that can speed up some common tasks, and some of these are applicable to OOP. One of these tools allows us to add new classes to our project with the minimum of typing.

This tool is accessible through the File | Add New Item... menu item, or by right-clicking on our project in the Solution Explorer window and selecting the appropriate item. Either way, a dialog appears, allowing us to choose the type of item to add. To add a class we select the Class entry in the window on the right, provide a filename for the file that will contain the class, then click Open. The class created will be named according to the filename chosen.

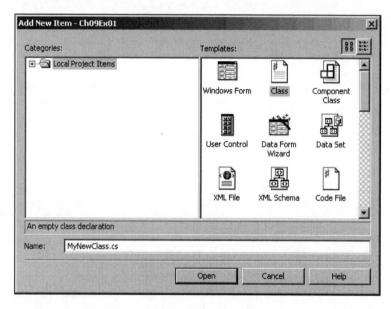

In the example earlier in this chapter we added class definitions manually to our Class1.cs file. It is often the case that keeping classes in separate files makes it easier to keep track of our classes.

Entering the information in the dialog above when the Ch09Ex01 project is open results in the following code being generated in MyNewClass.cs:

```
using System;

namespace Ch09Ex01
{
    /// <summary>
    /// Summary description for MyNewClass.
    /// </summary>
    public class MyNewClass
    {
        public MyNewClass()
        {
            //
```

```
            // TODO: Add constructor logic here
            //
        }
    }
}
```

This class, `MyNewClass`, is defined in the same namespace as our entry point class, `Class1`, so we can use it from code just as if it were defined in the same file.

As you can see from the code (or, more specifically, the comment in the code) the class that is generated for us contains a default constructor.

Class Library Projects

As well as placing classes in separate files within our project, we can also place them in completely separate projects. A project that contains nothing but classes (along with other relevant type definitions, but no entry point) is called a **class library**.

Class library projects compile into `.dll` assemblies, and we can gain access to their contents by adding references to them from other projects (which might be part of the same solution, but don't have to be). This extends the encapsulation that objects provide, as class libraries may be revised and updated without touching the projects that use them, allowing you to upgrade services provided by classes easily (which might affect multiple consumer applications).

> There is a minor problem with creating class libraries in Visual C# Standard Edition
> – it doesn't allow you to create them directly. However, it is possible to get round this,
> and for users of the Standard Edition, you can see how to create a class library after
> the *How it Works* section for the next example. I recommend that you skip ahead to
> read about that now, and once you have created your class library in the Standard
> Edition, you return to work through this example.

Let's look at an example of a class library project and a separate project that makes use of the classes that it contains.

Try it Out – Using a Class Library

1. Create a new project of type **Class Library** called `Ch09ClassLib` in the directory `C:\BegVCSharp\Chapter9`:

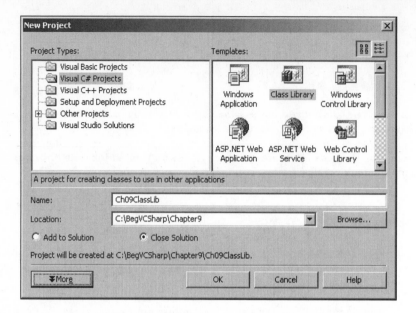

2. Rename the file `Class1.cs` as `MyExternalClass.cs` (you can do this by right-clicking on the file in the **Solution Explorer** window and selecting **Rename**).

3. Modify the code in `MyExternalClass.cs` to reflect this class name change:

```
public class MyExternalClass
{
    public MyExternalClass()
    {
        //
        // TODO: Add constructor logic here
        //
    }
}
```

4. Add a new class to the project, using the filename `MyInternalClass.cs`.

5. Modify the code to make the class `MyInternalClass` internal:

```
internal class MyInternalClass
{
    public MyInternalClass()
    {
        //
        // TODO: Add constructor logic here
        //
    }
}
```

6. Compile the project (note that this project has no entry point, so you can't run it as normal – instead you can build it by selecting the Build | Build menu option).

7. Create a new console application project called Ch09Ex02 in the directory C:\BegVCSharp\Chapter9.

8. Select the Project | Add Reference... menu item, or select the same option after right-clicking on References in the Solution Explorer window.

9. Click on the Browse... button, navigate to C:\BegVCSharp\Chapter9\Ch09ClassLib\bin\Debug\, and double-click on Ch09ClassLib.dll.

10. Click OK.

11. When the operation completes, check that a reference has been added in the Solution Explorer window:

12. Open the Object Browser window and examine the new reference to see what objects it contains:

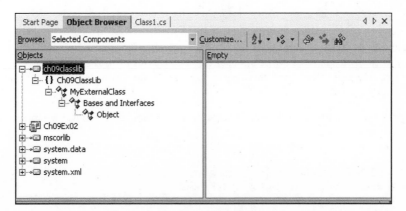

13. Modify the code in `Class1.cs` as follows:

```
using System;
using Ch09ClassLib;

namespace Ch09Ex02
{
    class Class1
    {
        static void Main(string[] args)
        {
            MyExternalClass myObj = new MyExternalClass();
            Console.WriteLine(myObj.ToString());
        }
    }
}
```

14. Run the application:

How it Works

In this example we have created two projects, one class library project and one console application project. The class library project, `Ch09ClassLib`, contains two classes: `MyExternalClass` – which is publicly accessible – and `MyInternalClass` – which is internally accessible. The console application, `Ch09Ex02`, contains simple code that makes use of the class library project.

In order to use the classes in `Ch09ClassLib` we added a reference to `Ch09ClassLib.dll` to the console application. For the purposes of this example we simply pointed at the output file for the class library, although it would have been just as easy to copy this file to a location local to `Ch09Ex02`, allowing us to continue development of the class library without affecting the console application. To replace the old version of the assembly with the new one, we would simply copy the newly generated DLL file over the old one.

After adding the reference we took a look at the available classes using the object browser. Since one of the two classes (`MyInternalClass`) is internal we can't see it in this display – it isn't accessible to external projects. However, the other class (`MyExternalClass`) is accessible, and this is the one we use in the console application.

We could replace the code in the console application with code attempting to use the internal class as follows:

```
        static void Main(string[] args)
        {
            MyInternalClass myObj = new MyInternalClass();
            Console.WriteLine(myObj.ToString());
        }
```

If we attempt to compile this code we will receive the following compilation error:

```
C:\BegVCSharp\Chapter9\Ch09Ex02\Class1.cs(13): 'Ch09ClassLib.MyInternalClass' is
inaccessible due to its protection level
```

This technique of making use of classes in external assemblies is key to programming with C# and the .NET Framework. It is in fact exactly what we are doing when we make use of any of the classes in the .NET Framework, as they are treated in the same way.

Creating a Class Library with C# Standard Edition

As we have already mentioned, Visual C# .NET Standard Edition does not have the ability to create a class library project. However, there is a simple process for creating a class library that will work in the Standard Edition – this section need only be read by users of the Standard Edition, so if that's not you, skip ahead to the next section, *Interfaces versus Abstract Classes*.

The following process will create a class library project called Ch09ClassLib:

1. Create a new console application project (or add a new one to the current solution), giving it the name that you want for your class library (in our case Ch09ClassLib). Remember where it is being created (in our case we will still be in C:\BegVCSharp\Chapter9).

2. Right-click on the auto-generated Class1.cs source code file in the Solution Explorer, and select Delete.

3. Select File | Close Solution, and save any changes.

4. Run Notepad, and open the .csproj file that was created in the location of your console application project.

5. The .csproj file is an XML file that describes your project (you can read more about XML in Chapter 18, but it is not important right now). In the <Settings> element, find the line with OutputType = "Exe" – and change the value from "Exe" to "Library":

```
<VisualStudioProject>
    <CSHARP
        ProjectType = "Local"
        ProductVersion = "7.0.9466"
        SchemaVersion = "1.0"
        ProjectGuid = "{16EB2B73-60D5-4C18-BC46-956DF31D58BD}"
    >
        <Build>
            <Settings
                ApplicationIcon = "App.ico"
                AssemblyKeyContainerName = ""
                AssemblyName = "DataLayer"
                AssemblyOriginatorKeyFile = ""
                DefaultClientScript = "JScript"
                DefaultHTMLPageLayout = "Grid"
```

```
            DefaultTargetSchema = "IE50"
            DelaySign = "false"
            OutputType = "Library"
            RootNamespace = "Ch09ClassLib"
            StartupObject = ""
      >
  . . .
```

6. Save the file.

7. Now return to Visual C# .NET, and re-open the solution. It should be the first item in the File | Recent Files menu.

Your console application will now have become a class library. It will now build to a .dll file, and you will be able to reference it from other projects, as you will see when you return to the previous *Try It Out* example.

This project is currently empty, and for it to be useful you will need to add some classes, as we saw in the *Adding Classes* section earlier. Before you can return to the previous *Try it Out* example that I advised you to skip, we need to add a class called MyExternalClass.cs. You can do this, for example, by right-clicking on the project in Solution Explorer, selecting Add | Add New Item and choosing Class from the Add New Item dialog.

Now that your class library has been created and you've added a class to it, you can return to the previous *Try it Out* example, and start from step 3. (The first two steps simply create the class library and add the class MyExternalClass – but we've already done this!)

Interfaces versus Abstract Classes

In this chapter we've seen how we can create both interfaces and abstract classes (without members for now – we'll be getting to them in the next chapter). The two types are similar in a number of ways, and it is worth taking a look at this and seeing the situation where we would want to use one technique or the other.

First, the similarities: both abstract classes and interfaces may contain members that can be inherited by a derived class. Neither interfaces nor abstract classes may be directly instantiated, but we can declare variables of these types. If we do so, we can use polymorphism to assign objects that inherit from these types to variables of these types. In both cases we can then use the members of these types through these variables, although we don't have direct access to the other members of the derived object.

And now, the differences: derived classes may only inherit from a single base class, which means that only a single abstract class may be inherited directly (although it is possible for a chain of inheritance to include multiple abstract classes). Conversely, classes may use as many interfaces as they wish. However, this doesn't make a massive difference – similar results can be achieved in either case. It's just that the interface way of doing things is slightly different.

Abstract classes may possess both abstract members (these have no code body and *must* be implemented in the derived class unless the derived class is itself abstract) and non-abstract members (these possess a code body, and can be virtual so that they *may* be overridden in the derived class). Interface members, on the other hand, must *all* be implemented on the class that uses the interface – they do not possess code bodies. Also, interface members are by definition public (as they are intended for external use), but members of abstract classes may also be private (as long as they aren't abstract), protected, internal, or protected internal (where protected internal members are accessible only from code within the application or from a derived class). In addition, interfaces can't contain fields, constructors, destructors, static members, or constants.

This indicates that the two types are intended for different purposes. Abstract classes are intended for use as the base class for families of objects that share certain central characteristics, such as a common purpose and structure. Interfaces are intended for use by classes that might differ on a far more fundamental level, but can still do some of the same things.

As an example, consider a family of objects representing trains. The base class, `Train`, contains the core definition of a train, such as wheel gauge and engine type (which could be steam, diesel, and so on). However, this class is abstract, as there is no such thing as a "generic" train. In order to create an "actual" train we need to add characteristics specific to that train. To do this we derive classes such as `PassengerTrain`, `FreightTrain` and `424DoubleBogey`:

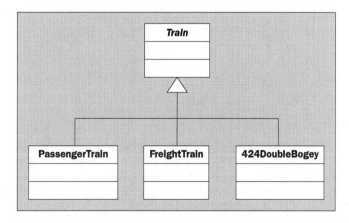

A family of car objects might be defined in the same way, with an abstract base class of `Car`, and derived classes such as `Compact`, `SUV`, and `PickUp`. `Car` and `Train` might even derive from a common base class, such as `Vehicle`:

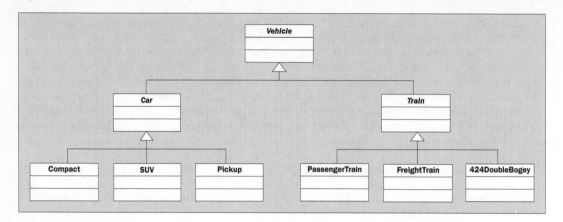

Now, some of the classes further down the hierarchy may share characteristics because of their purpose, not just because of what they derive from. For example, PassengerTrain, Compact, SUV, and Pickup are all capable of carrying passengers, so they might possess an IPassengerCarrier interface. FreightTrain and PickUp can carry heavy loads so they might both have an IHeavyLoadCarrier interface as well.

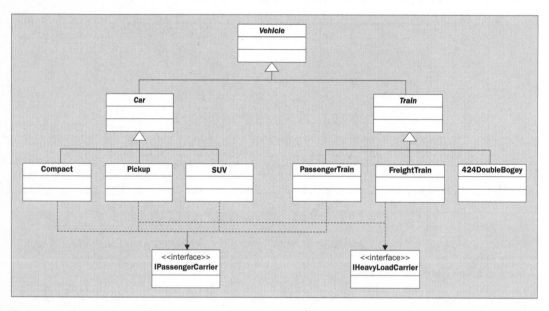

By breaking down an object system in this way before going about assigning specifics, we can clearly see which situations should use abstract classes rather than interfaces, and vice versa. The result of this example couldn't have been achieved using only interfaces or only abstract inheritance.

Struct Types

In the last chapter we noted that structs and classes are very similar, but that structs are value types and classes are reference types. So what does this actually mean to us? Well, the simplest way of looking at this is to look at an example.

Try it Out – Classes versus Structs

1. Create a new console application project called Ch09Ex03 in the directory C:\BegVCSharp\Chapter9.

2. Modify the code as follows:

```
namespace Ch09Ex03
{
    class MyClass
    {
        public int val;
    }

    struct myStruct
    {
        public int val;
    }

    class Class1
    {
        static void Main(string[] args)
        {
            MyClass objectA = new MyClass();
            MyClass objectB = objectA;
            objectA.val = 10;
            objectB.val = 20;
            myStruct structA = new myStruct();
            myStruct structB = structA;
            structA.val = 30;
            structB.val = 40;
            Console.WriteLine("objectA.val = {0}", objectA.val);
            Console.WriteLine("objectB.val = {0}", objectB.val);
            Console.WriteLine("structA.val = {0}", structA.val);
            Console.WriteLine("structB.val = {0}", structB.val);
        }
    }
}
```

3. Run the application:

```
objectA.val = 20
objectB.val = 20
structA.val = 30
structB.val = 40
Press any key to continue
```

How It Works

This application contains two type definitions, one for a struct called `myStruct`, which has a single public `int` field called `val`, and one for a class called `MyClass` that contains an identical field (we'll be looking at class members such as fields in the next chapter, for now it's enough just to point out that the syntax is the same here). Next we perform the same operations on instances of both of these types:

- ❏ Declare a variable of the type.
- ❏ Create a new instance of the type in this variable.
- ❏ Declare a second variable of the type.
- ❏ Assign the first variable to the second variable.
- ❏ Assign a value to the `val` field in the instance in the first variable.
- ❏ Assign a value to the `val` field in the instance in the second variable.
- ❏ Display the values of the `val` fields for both variables.

Although we are performing the same operations on variables of both types the outcome is different. When we display the values of the `val` field we find that both `object` types have the same value, while the struct types have different values.

So, what has happened?

Objects are *reference* types. When we assign an object to a variable we are actually assigning that variable with a **pointer** to the object it refers to. A pointer, in real code terms, is an address in memory. In this case the address is the point in memory where the object is found. When we assign the first object reference to the second variable of type `MyClass` with the following line, we are actually copying this address.

```
MyClass objectB = objectA;
```

This means that both variables contain pointers to the *same object*.

Structs are *value* types. Instead of the variable holding a pointer to the struct, the variable contains the struct itself. When we assign the first struct to the second variable of type `myStruct` with the following line, we are actually copying all the information from one struct to the other.

```
myStruct structB = structA;
```

This behavior is identical to that we have observed earlier in this book for simple variable types such as `int`. The end result is that the two struct type variables contain *different* structs.

This whole technique of using pointers is hidden from us in managed C# code, making our code much simpler. It is possible to get access to lower level operations such as pointer manipulation in C# using unsafe code, but that is an advanced topic that we won't cover here.

Shallow versus Deep Copying

Copying objects from one variable to another by value instead of by reference (that is, copying them in the same way as structs) can be quite complex. Because a single object may contain references to many other objects, as field members and so on, there may be an awful lot of processing involved. Simply copying each member from one object to another might not work, as some of these members might be reference types in their own right.

The .NET Framework takes this into account. Simple object copying by members is achievable through the method `MemberwiseClone()`, inherited from `System.Object`. This is a protected method, but it would be easy to define a public method on an object that called this method. The copying supplied by this method is known as **shallow** copying, in that it doesn't take reference type members into account. This means that reference members in the new object will refer to the same objects as the equivalent members in the source object, which isn't ideal in many cases. If we want to create new instances of the members in question, copying the values across rather than the references, then we need to perform a **deep** copy.

There is an interface we can implement that allows us to do this in a standard way: `ICloneable`. If we use this interface we must implement the single method it contains, `Clone()`. This method returns a value of type `System.Object`. We can use whatever processing we wish to obtain this object, by implementing the method body however we choose. This means that we can implement a deep copy if we wish to (although the exact behavior isn't mandatory, so we could perform a shallow copy if we want).

We'll take a closer look at this in Chapter 11.

Summary

In this chapter we've seen how we can define classes and interfaces in C#, which has put the theory from the last chapter into a more concrete form. We've seen the C# syntax required for basic declarations as well as the accessibility keywords we can use, the way in which we can inherit from interfaces and other classes, how to define abstract and sealed classes to control this inheritance, and how to define constructors and destructors.

We took a look at `System.Object`, which is the root base class of *any* class that we define. This class supplies several methods for us to use, some of which are `virtual` such that we can override their implementation. This class also allows us to treat any object instance as an instance of this type, enabling polymorphism with any object.

We also took a look at some of the tools supplied by VS.NET for OOP development, including the **Class View** window, the **Object Browser** window, and a quick way to add new classes to a project. As an extension of this multi-file concept, we also saw how we can create assemblies that we can't execute, but that contain class definitions that we can use in other projects.

Next we drilled down into abstract classes and interfaces, looking at the similarities and differences between them and the situations where we might use one or the other.

Finally, we resumed our discussion of reference and value types, looking at structs (the value type equivalent of objects) in slightly more detail. This led to a discussion on shallow and deep copying of objects, a subject we'll be returning to later on in the book.

In the next chapter we'll look at defining class members, such as properties and methods, which will allow us to take OOP in C# to the level required to create real applications.

Exercises

1. What is wrong with the following code?

```
public sealed class MyClass
{
    // class members
}

public class myDerivedClass : MyClass
{
    // class members
}
```

2. How would you define a non-creatable class?

3. Why are non-creatable classes still useful? How do we make use of their capabilities?

4. Write code in a class library project called `Vehicles` that implements the `Vehicle` family of objects discussed earlier in this chapter, in the section on interfaces versus abstract classes. There are nine objects and two interfaces that require implementation.

5. Create a console application project, `Traffic`, which references `Vehicles.dll` (created in Q4 above). Include a function called `AddPassenger()` that accepts any object with the `IPassengerCarrier` interface. To prove that the code works, call this function using instances of each object that supports the interface, calling the `ToString()` method inherited from `System.Object` on each one and writing the result to the screen.

Defining Class Members

In this chapter we'll continue our discussion of class definitions in C# by looking at how we define field, property, and method class members.

We'll start by looking at the code required for each of these types, and also look at how to generate the structure of this code using VS wizards. We'll also see how we can modify members quickly by editing their properties.

When we've covered the basics of member definition we'll take a look at some more advanced techniques involving members: hiding base class members, calling overridden base class members, and nested type definitions.

Finally, we'll put theory into practice and create a class library that we can build on and use in later chapters.

Member Definitions

Within a class definition we provide definitions for all members of the class, including fields, methods, and properties. All members have their own accessibility level, defined in all cases by one of the following keywords:

❑ `public` – member accessible from any code

❑ `private` – member accessible only from code that is part of the class (the default if no keyword is used)

❑ `internal` – member accessible only from code within the project (assembly) where it is defined

❑ `protected` – member accessible only from code that is part of either the class or a derived class

The last two of these can be combined, such that `protected internal` members are also possible. These are only accessible from code-derived classes within the project (more accurately, the assembly – we will cover assemblies in Chapter 21).

Fields, methods, and properties can also be declared using the keyword `static`, which means that they will be static members owned by the class rather than by object instances, as discussed in Chapter 8.

Defining Fields

Fields are defined using standard variable declaration format (with optional initialization), along with the modifiers discussed above. For example:

```
class MyClass
{
    public int MyInt;
}
```

> *Public fields in the .NET Framework are named using PascalCasing rather than camelCasing, and I'll use this casing methodology here. This is why the field above is called* MyInt *instead of* myInt. *This is only a suggested casing scheme, but it makes a lot of sense to me. There is no recommendation for private fields, which are usually named using camelCasing.*

Fields can also use the keyword `readonly`, meaning that the field may only be assigned a value during constructor execution or by initial assignment. For example:

```
class MyClass
{
    public readonly int MyInt = 17;
}
```

As noted in the introduction to this chapter, fields may be declared as static using the `static` keyword, for example:

```
class MyClass
{
    public static int MyInt;
}
```

Static fields may be accessed via the class that defines them (`MyClass.MyInt` in the above example), not through object instances of that class.

In addition, we can use the keyword `const` to create a constant value. `const` members are static by definition, so there is no need to use the `static` modifier (indeed, it is an error to do so).

Defining Methods

Methods use standard function format, along with accessibility and optional `static` modifiers. For example:

```
class MyClass
{
    public string GetString()
    {
        return "Here is a string.";
    }
}
```

Public methods in the .NET framework, like fields, are named using PascalCasing rather than camelCasing.

Note that if we use the `static` keyword this method will only be accessible through the class, not the object instance.

We can also use the following keywords with method definitions:

- ❏ `virtual` – method may be overridden
- ❏ `abstract` – method must be overridden (only permitted in abstract classes)
- ❏ `override` – method overrides a base class method (must be used if a method is being overridden)
- ❏ `extern` – method definition is found elsewhere

The following code shows an example of a method override:

```
public class MyBaseClass
{
    public virtual void DoSomething()
    {
        // Base implementation
    }
}

public class MyDerivedClass : MyBaseClass
{
    public override void DoSomething()
    {
        // Derived class implementation, overrides base implementation
    }
}
```

If `override` is used then `sealed` may also be used to specify that no further modifications can be made to this method in derived classes, that is, this method can't be overridden by derived classes. For example:

```
public class MyDerivedClass : MyBaseClass
{
    public override sealed void DoSomething()
    {
        // Derived class implementation, overrides base implementation
    }
}
```

Using `extern` allows us to provide the implementation of a method externally to the project. This is an advanced topic and I won't go into any more detail here.

Defining Properties

Properties are defined in a similar way to fields, but there's more to them. Properties, as already discussed, are more involved than fields in that they can perform additional processing before modifying state – and, indeed, might not modify state at all. They achieve this by possessing two function-like blocks, one for getting the value of the property and one for setting the value of the property.

These blocks, also known as **accessors**, defined using get and set keywords respectively, may be used to control the access level of the property. It is possible to omit one or the other of these blocks to create read-only or write-only properties (where omitting the get block gives us write-only access, and omitting the set block gives us read-only access). Of course, this only applies to external code, as code elsewhere within the class will have access to the same data that these code blocks have. We must include at least one of these blocks to obtain a valid property (and, let's face it, a property you can neither read nor change wouldn't be that useful).

The basic structure of a property consists of the standard access modifying keyword (public, private, and so on), followed by a type name, the property name, and one or both of the get and set blocks that contain the property processing, for example:

```
public int MyIntProp
{
    get
    {
        // Property get code
    }
    set
    {
        // Property set code
    }
}
```

> *Public properties in the .NET Framework are also named using PascalCasing rather than camelCasing, and as with fields and methods, I'll use this casing here.*

The first line of the definition is the bit that is very similar to a field definition. The difference is that there is no semicolon at the end of the line; instead we have a code block containing nested get and set blocks.

get blocks must have a return value of the type of the property. Simple properties are often associated with a single private field controlling access to that field, in which case the get block may return the value of that field directly, for example:

```
// Field used by property
private int myInt;

// Property
public int MyIntProp
{
    get
    {
        return myInt;
    }
    set
    {
        // Property set code
    }
}
```

Note that code external to the class *cannot* access this `myInt` field directly due to its accessibility level (it's private). Instead it *must* use the property to get access to the field.

The `set` function assigns a value to the field in a similar way. Here we can use the keyword `value` to refer to the value received from the user of the property:

```
// Field used by property
private int myInt;

// Property
public int MyIntProp
{
    get
    {
        return myInt;
    }
    set
    {
        myInt = value;
    }
}
```

`value` equates to a value of the same type as the property, so if the property uses the same type as the field we never have to worry about casting in situations like this.

This simple property does little more than shield direct access to the `myInt` field. The real power of properties comes when we exert a little more control over the proceedings. For example, we might implement our `set` block using:

```
set
{
    if (value >= 0 && value <= 10)
        myInt = value;
}
```

Here we only modify `myInt` if the value assigned to the property is between 0 and 10. In situations like this we have an important design choice to make: what should we do if an invalid value is used? We have four options:

❑   Do nothing (as in the code above).

❑   Assign a default value to the field.

❑   Continue as if nothing had gone wrong but log the event for future analysis.

❑   Throw an exception.

In general, the last two options are the preferable ones. The choice between these two options depends on how the class will be used, and how much control should be assigned to the users of the class. Exception throwing gives users a fair amount of control, and lets them know what is going on so that they can respond appropriately. We can use a standard `System` exception for this, for example:

245

```
set
{
    if (value >= 0 && value <= 10)
        myInt = value;
    else
        throw (new ArgumentOutOfRangeException("MyIntProp", value,
                "MyIntProp must be assigned a value between 0 and 10."));
}
```

This can be handled using `try...catch...finally` logic in the code that uses the property, as we saw in Chapter 7.

Logging data, perhaps to a text file, can be useful in (for example) production code where problems really shouldn't occur. They allow developers to check up on performance, and perhaps debug existing code if necessary.

Properties can use the `virtual`, `override`, and `abstract` keywords just like methods, something that isn't possible with fields.

Try it Out – Using Fields, Methods, and Properties

1. Create a new console application project called `Ch10Ex01` in the directory `C:\BegVCSharp\Chapter10`.

2. Add a new class called `MyClass` using the VS shortcut, in the file `MyClass.cs`.

3. Modify the code in `MyClass.cs` as follows:

```
public class MyClass
{
    public readonly string Name;
    private int intVal;

    public int Val
    {
        get
        {
            return intVal;
        }
        set
        {
            if (value >= 0 && value <= 10)
                intVal = value;
            else
                throw (new ArgumentOutOfRangeException("Val", value,
                    "Val must be assigned a value between 0 and 10."));
        }
    }
    public override string ToString()
    {
        return "Name: " + Name + "\nVal: " + Val;
```

```
   }

   private MyClass() : this("Default Name")
   {
   }

   public MyClass(string newName)
   {
      Name = newName;
      intVal = 0;
   }
}
```

4. Modify the code in `Class1.cs` as follows:

```
static void Main(string[] args)
{
   Console.WriteLine("Creating object myObj...");
   MyClass myObj = new MyClass("My Object");
   Console.WriteLine("myObj created.");
   for (int i = -1; i <= 0; i++)
   {
      try
      {
         Console.WriteLine("\nAttempting to assign {0} to myObj.Val...",
                           i);
         myObj.Val = i;
         Console.WriteLine("Value {0} assigned to myObj.Val.", myObj.Val);
      }
      catch (Exception e)
      {
         Console.WriteLine("Exception {0} thrown.", e.GetType().FullName);
         Console.WriteLine("Message:\n\"{0}\"", e.Message);
      }
   }
   Console.WriteLine("\nOutputting myObj.ToString()...");
   Console.WriteLine(myObj.ToString());
   Console.WriteLine("myObj.ToString() Output.");
}
```

5. Run the application:

How It Works

The code in `Main()` creates and uses an instance of the `MyClass` class defined in `MyClass.cs`. Instantiating this class must be performed using a non-default constructor, as the default constructor of `MyClass` is private:

```
private MyClass() : this("Default Name")
{
}
```

Note that I've used `this("Default Name")` to ensure that `Name` gets a value if this constructor ever gets called, which is possible if this class is used to derive a new class. This is necessary as not assigning a value to the `Name` field could be a source of errors later.

The non-default constructor used assigns values to the `readonly` field `name` (we can only do this by assignment in the field declaration or in a constructor), and the private field `intVal`.

Next, `Main()` attempts two assignments to the `Val` property of `myObj` (the instance of `MyClass`). A `for` loop is used to assign the values `-1` and `0` in two cycles, and a `try...catch` structure is used to check for any exception thrown. When `-1` is assigned to the property an exception of type `System.ArgumentOutOfRangeException` is thrown, and code in the `catch` block outputs information about the exception to the console window. In the next loop cycle, the value `0` is successfully assigned to the `Val` property, and through that property to the private `intVal` field.

Finally, we use the overridden `ToString()` method to output a formatted string representing the contents of the object:

```
public override string ToString()
{
    return "Name: " + Name + "\nVal: " + Val;
}
```

This method must be declared using the `override` keyword, as it is overriding the virtual `ToString()` method of the base `System.Object` class. The code here uses the property `Val` directly rather than the private field `intVal`. There is no reason why we shouldn't use properties from within classes in this way, although there may be a small performance hit (so small that we are unlikely to notice it). Of course, using the property also gives us the validation inherent in property use, which may be beneficial for code within the class as well.

VS Member Wizards

In the last chapter we saw how we can use a shortcut in VS to create a new class, complete with its own `.cs` file. There are a few more of these shortcuts (known as wizards) that we can use to modify our classes. Specifically, there are wizards to add properties, methods, and fields to classes. In this section we'll take a quick look at these.

All the member wizards are accessed in the same way. In the **Class View** window, which displays the classes defined in our projects along with their members, we right-click on a class and select an option from the **Add** submenu:

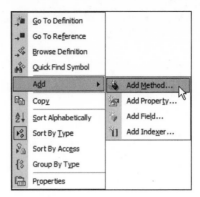

There are four options here, but we will only discuss three of them in this section, as we will be covering indexers in the next chapter.

The Add Method Wizard

This wizard allows us, surprisingly enough, to add a method to a class. This is achieved through the following dialog (I've filled in a few fields already here):

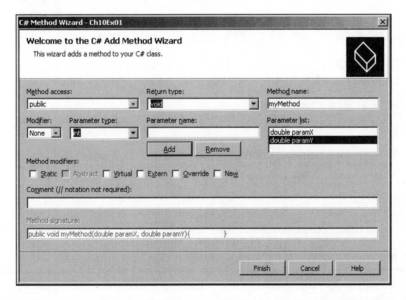

This dialog provides access to all the method features we've looked at. We can change the accessibility level through the **Method access** drop-down, a return type with the **Return type** drop-down (or we can type our own type into this field), a name with **Method name**, and other modifiers with **Method modifiers**. These modifier check boxes only permit valid combinations, and only allow abstract methods in abstract classes. We can also add parameters using the series of text and listboxes on the second row of the dialog in the **Parameter type** and **Parameter name** fields. The **Modifier** box allows us to specify the type of parameter: ordinary (**None**), `ref` or `out`. Added parameters appear in the **Parameter** list view when we click the **Add** button, and we can remove parameters from this list using the **Remove** button.

This dialog also allows us to provide a comment to place before the method definition with the Comment field, and shows us a preview of the code that will be generated in the Method signature box.

With the settings as shown above, clicking on Finish will add the following code to our class:

```
public double myMethod(double paramX, double paramY)
{
    return 0;
}
```

Obviously, this wizard can't provide the method implementation for us, but it does provide the basic structure, and certainly cuts down on typing errors!

The Add Property Wizard

The Add Property wizard uses the following dialog (again, I've filled in some values):

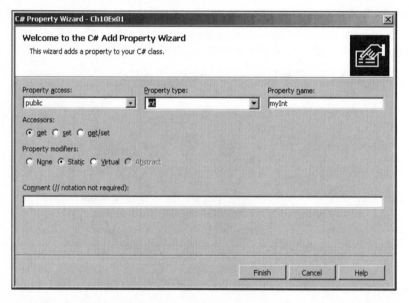

We select an accessibility type in the Property access drop-down, a type in the Property type drop-down, enter a name in the Property name field, choose whether we want get, set, or both get and set blocks, and optionally add modifiers and a comment. Clicking on Finish with the above choices generates the following code:

```
public static int myInt
{
    get
    {
        return 0;
    }
}
```

Note that we are left to provide the complete implementation ourselves, which includes matching up the property with a field for simple properties. However, the basic structure is provided for us.

The Add Field Wizard

Finally, the Add Field wizard. This dialog is even simpler:

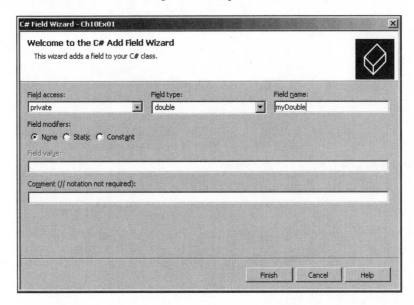

This is basically the same as adding a property, except that we don't have the choice of `get` or `set` blocks, and we can't use the `virtual` or `abstract` keywords. However, we can define a field as being constant, in which case we can use the Field value field to provide the value of the field.

The code generated is simple and self-explanatory:

```
private double myDouble;
```

Member Properties

The last basic topic to look at here is modifying member properties using the Properties window. If we select a member from the Class View window we will see the properties of the member in the Properties window:

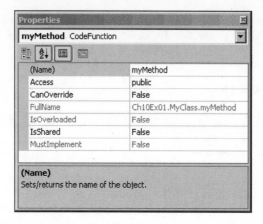

We can change many of these properties directly from this window, such as accessibility level through the Access property (shown highlighted above). If we do this, the code will be modified automatically, without us having to do any typing ourselves.

Note that CanOverride defines whether the member is `virtual`, and IsShared whether the member is `static`.

Additional Class Member Topics

Now we've covered the basics of member definition, it's time to look at some more advanced member topics. In this section we'll look at:

❑ Hiding base class methods

❑ Calling overridden or hidden base class methods

❑ Nested type definitions

Hiding Base Class Methods

When we inherit a (non-abstract) member from a base class we also inherit an implementation. If the inherited member is virtual we can override this implementation with the `override` keyword. Regardless of whether the inherited member is virtual we can, if we want to, **hide** the implementation. This is useful when, for example, a public inherited member doesn't work quite as we would want it to.

We can do this simply by using code such as:

```
public class MyBaseClass
{
    public void DoSomething()
    {
        // Base implementation
    }
}
```

```
public class MyDerivedClass : MyBaseClass
{
   public void DoSomething()
   {
      // Derived class implementation, hides base implementation
   }
}
```

Although this code works fine, it will generate a warning that we are hiding a base class member. This gives us the chance to correct things if we have accidentally hidden a member that we actually want to use. If we really do want to hide the member, we can say explicitly that this is what we want to do using the new keyword:

```
public class MyDerivedClass : MyBaseClass
{
   new public void DoSomething()
   {
      // Derived class implementation, hides base implementation
   }
}
```

This will work in exactly the same way, but won't show a warning.

At this point it is worth pointing out the difference between hiding and overriding base class members. Consider the following code:

```
public class MyBaseClass
{
   public virtual void DoSomething()
   {
      Console.WriteLine("Base imp");
   }
}

public class MyDerivedClass : MyBaseClass
{
   public override void DoSomething()
   {
      Console.WriteLine("Derived imp");
   }
}
```

Here the overriding method replaces the implementation in the base class, such that the following code will use the new version, even though it does so through the base class type (using polymorphism):

```
MyDerivedClass myObj = new MyDerivedClass();
MyBaseClass myBaseObj;
myBaseObj = myObj;
myBaseObj.DoSomething();
```

This gives the output:

```
Derived imp
```

Alternatively, we could hide the base class method instead, using:

```
public class MyBaseClass
{
    public virtual void DoSomething()
    {
        Console.WriteLine("Base imp");
    }
}

public class MyDerivedClass : MyBaseClass
{
    new public void DoSomething()
    {
        Console.WriteLine("Derived imp");
    }
}
```

The base class method needn't be virtual for this to work, but the effect is exactly the same and the above code only requires changes to one line of code. The result, for a virtual or non-virtual base class method, is the following:

```
Base imp
```

Although the base implementation is hidden we still have access to it through the base class.

Calling Overridden or Hidden Base Class Methods

Whether we override or hide a member we still have access to the base class member from the derived class. There are many situations when this can be useful, for example:

- ❑ When we want to hide an inherited public member from users of a derived class, but still want access to its functionality from within the class.

- ❑ When we want to add to the implementation of an inherited virtual member rather than simply replacing it with a new overridden implementation.

To achieve this, we can use the base keyword, which refers to the implementation of the base class that is contained within a derived class (in a similar way to its use in controlling constructors as we saw in the last chapter), for example:

```
public class MyBaseClass
{
    public virtual void DoSomething()
    {
        // Base implementation
    }
}
```

```
public class MyDerivedClass : MyBaseClass
{
    public override void DoSomething()
    {
        // Derived class implementation, extends base class implementation
        base.DoSomething();
        // More derived class implementation
    }
}
```

This code executes the version of DoSomething() contained in MyBaseClass, the base class of MyDerivedClass, from within the version of DoSomething() contained in MyDerivedClass.

As base works using object instances it is an error to use it from within a static member.

The this Keyword

As well as using base in the last chapter we also used the this keyword. As with base, this can also be used from within class members, and, like base, this keyword refers to an object instance. The object instance referred to by this is the current object instance (which means that we can't use this keyword in static members, as static members are not part of an object instance).

The most useful function of the this keyword is the ability to pass a reference to the current object instance to a method, for example:

```
public void doSomething()
{
    MyTargetClass myObj = new MyTargetClass();
    myObj.DoSomethingWith(this);
}
```

Here, the MyTargetClass that is instantiated has a method called DoSomethingWith() that takes a single parameter of a type compatible with the class that contains the above method. This parameter type might be of this class type, a class type that is inherited by this class, an interface implemented by the class, or (of course) System.Object.

Nested Type Definitions

As well as defining types such as classes in namespaces, we can also define them inside other classes. If we do this then we can use the full range of accessibility modifiers for the definition, rather than just public and internal, and may also use the new keyword to hide a type definition inherited from a base class.

For example, the following code defining MyClass also defines a nested class called myNestedClass:

```
public class MyClass
{
    public class myNestedClass
    {
        public int nestedClassField;
    }
}
```

If we want to instantiate `myNestedClass` from outside `MyClass` we must qualify the name, for example:

```
MyClass.myNestedClass myObj = new MyClass.myNestedClass();
```

However, we may not be able to do this at all if the nested class is declared as private, or another accessibility level that is incompatible with the code at the point at which this instantiation is performed.

The main reason for the existence of this feature is to define classes that are private to the containing class, such that no other code in the namespace has access to it.

Interface Implementation

Before moving on, it's worth taking a closer look at how we go about defining and implementing interfaces. In the last chapter we saw that interfaces are defined in a similar way to classes, using code such as:

```
interface IMyInterface
{
    // interface members
}
```

Interface members are defined like class members except for a few important differences:

- ❑ No access modifiers (`public`, `private`, `protected`, or `internal`) are allowed – all interface members are implicitly public

- ❑ Interface members can't contain code bodies

- ❑ Interfaces can't define field members

- ❑ Interface members can't be defined using the keywords `static`, `virtual`, `abstract`, or `sealed`

- ❑ Type definition members are forbidden

We can, however, define members using the `new` keyword if we wish to hide members inherited from base interfaces, for example:

```
interface IMyBaseInterface
{
    void DoSomething();
}

interface IMyDerivedInterface : IMyBaseInterface
{
    new void DoSomething();
}
```

This works in exactly the same way as hiding inherited class members.

Properties defined in interfaces define the access blocks, `get` and/or `set`, that are permitted for the property, for example:

```
interface IMyInterface
{
    int MyInt
    {
        get;
        set;
    }
}
```

Here the `int` property `MyInt` has both `get` and `set` accessors. Either of these may be omitted for a property with more restricted access.

Note, though, that interfaces do not specify how the property should be stored. Interfaces cannot specify fields, for example, which might be used to store property data.

Finally, interfaces, like classes, may be defined as members of classes (but not as members of other interfaces, since interfaces cannot contain type definitions).

Implementing Interfaces in Classes

A class that implements an interface *must* contain implementations for all members of that interface, which must match the signatures specified (including matching the specified `get` and `set` blocks), and must be public. It is possible to implement interface members using the keywords `virtual` or `abstract`, but not `static` or `const`. For example:

```
public interface IMyInterface
{
    void DoSomething();
    void DoSomethingElse();
}

public class MyClass : IMyInterface
{
    public void DoSomething()
    {
    }

    public void DoSomethingElse()
    {
    }
}
```

Interface members may also be implemented on base classes, for example:

```
public interface IMyInterface
{
    void DoSomething();
    void DoSomethingElse();
}
```

```
public class MyBaseClass
{
   public void DoSomething()
   {
   }
}

public class MyDerivedClass : MyBaseClass, IMyInterface
{
   public void DoSomethingElse()
   {
   }
}
```

Inheriting from a base class that implements a given interface means that the interface is implicitly supported by the derived class, for example:

```
public interface IMyInterface
{
   void DoSomething();
   void DoSomethingElse();
}
```

```
public class MyBaseClass : IMyInterface
{
   public virtual void DoSomething()
   {
   }

   public virtual void DoSomethingElse()
   {
   }
}

public class MyDerivedClass : MyBaseClass
{
   public override void DoSomething()
   {
   }
}
```

As shown above, it is useful to define implementations in base classes as virtual, such that derived classes can replace the implementation rather than hiding it. If we were to hide a base class member using the new keyword rather than overriding it in this way then the method IMyInterface.DoSomething() would always refer to the base class version, even if the derived class were being accessed via this interface.

Explicit Interface Member Implementation

Interface members can also be implemented **explicitly** by a class. If we do this then the member can only be accessed through the interface, not through the class. **Implicit** members, which are what we used in the code in the last section, can be accessed either way.

For example, if the class MyClass implemented the DoSomething() method of IMyInterface implicitly, as shown above, then the following code is valid:

```
    MyClass myObj = new MyClass();
    myObj.DoSomething();
```

As is:

```
    MyClass myObj = new MyClass();
    IMyInterface myInt = myObj;
    myInt.DoSomething();
```

Alternatively, if `MyDerivedClass` implements `DoSomething()` explicitly then only the latter technique is permitted. The code for doing this is as follows:

```
    public class MyClass : IMyInterface
    {
        void IMyInterface.DoSomething()
        {
        }

        public void DoSomethingElse()
        {
        }
    }
```

Here `DoSomething()` is implemented explicitly and `DoSomethingElse()` implicitly. Only the latter is accessible directly through an object instance of `MyClass`.

Example Application

To illustrate some of the techniques we've been using so far we'll develop a class module that we'll be able to build on and make use of in subsequent chapters. This class module will contain two classes:

- ❑ `Card` – represents a standard playing card, with a suit of club, diamond, heart, or spade, and a rank that lies between Ace and King

- ❑ `Deck` – represents a full deck of 52 cards, with access to cards by position in the deck and the ability to shuffle the deck

We'll also develop a simple client to make sure things are working, but we won't use the deck in a full card game application – yet!

Planning the Application

The class library for this application, `Ch10CardLib`, will contain our classes. Before we get down to any code, though, we should plan out the required structure and functionality of our classes.

The Card Class

The `Card` class is basically a container for two read-only fields: `suit` and `rank`. The reason for making the fields read-only is that it doesn't make sense to have a "blank" card, and cards shouldn't be able to change once they have been created. To facilitate this we'll make the default constructor private, and provide an alternative constructor that builds a card from a supplied suit and rank.

Other than this, the Card class will override the ToString() method of System.Object, so that we can easily obtain a human-readable string representing the card. To make things a little simpler we'll provide enumerations for the two fields suit and rank.

The Card class looks like this:

The Deck Class

The Deck class will maintain 52 Card objects. We'll just use a simple array type for this. This array won't be directly accessible, as access to the Card objects will be achieved through a GetCard() method, which will return the Card object with the given index.

This class should also expose a Shuffle() method to rearrange the cards in the array, so it looks like this:

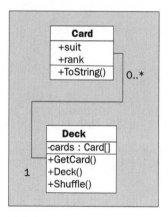

Writing the Class Library

For the purposes of this example I'll assume that you are familiar enough with VS to move away from the standard "Try it Out" way of doing things, so I won't list the steps explicitly.

Both our classes and our enumerations will be contained in a class library project called Ch10CardLib. This project will contain two .cs files, Card.cs that contains the Card class definition along with Suit and Rank enumerations, and Deck.cs that contains the Deck class definition.

Card.cs

In this section we'll break down and work through the code for Card.cs. To start with we have the usual using directive and namespace declaration:

```
using System;

namespace Ch10CardLib
{
```

Next we have the `Suit` enumeration definition:

```
public enum Suit
{
    Club,
    Diamond,
    Heart,
    Spade
}
```

Next we have the `Rank` enumeration definition, which will start with a base type representation of 1 for Ace for simplicity:

```
public enum Rank
{
    Ace = 1,
    Deuce,
    Three,
    Four,
    Five,
    Six,
    Seven,
    Eight,
    Nine,
    Ten,
    Jack,
    Queen,
    King
}
```

Both these enumeration types are public, as we can expect to use them from outside of this class library.

Now we move on to the main section of this file, the `Card` class definition:

```
public class Card
{
```

The first section of code in the `Card` definition defines the two read-only fields, which use the enumeration types defined at the beginning of the file:

```
public readonly Suit suit;
public readonly Rank rank;
```

The overridden `ToString()` method is made very simple due to the enumeration types used:

```
        public override string ToString()
        {
            return "The " + rank + " of " + suit + "s";
        }
```

Placing the field names in a string in this way simply writes the string representation of the enumeration value stored to the returned string.

Next we have our constructors. First the private default constructor:

```
        private Card()
        {
        }
```

And next the constructor that must be used to create `Card` instances, which simply takes `Suit` and `Rank` parameters and initializes the read-only fields:

```
        public Card(Suit newSuit, Rank newRank)
        {
            suit = newSuit;
            rank = newRank;
        }
    }
}
```

And that completes the code for this file.

Deck.cs

This file starts in the same way as `Card.cs`, with the standard code:

```
using System;

namespace Ch10CardLib
{
```

There are no types other than the `Deck` class to define here, so we dive straight into the class definition:

```
    public class Deck
    {
```

The first member we'll define is the private array of `Card` objects, which we'll call `cards`.

```
        private Card[] cards;
```

Next we have the constructor, which simply creates and assigns 52 cards in the `cards` field. We'll iterate through all combinations of the two enumerations, using each to create a card. This results in `cards` initially containing an ordered list of cards:

```
public Deck()
{
    cards = new Card[52];
    for (int suitVal = 0; suitVal < 4; suitVal++)
    {
        for (int rankVal = 1; rankVal < 14; rankVal++)
        {
            cards[suitVal * 13 + rankVal -1] = new Card((Suit)suitVal,
                                                        (Rank)rankVal);
        }
    }
}
```

Next we implement the `GetCard()` method, which either returns the `Card` object with the requested index or throws an exception in the same way we saw earlier:

```
public Card GetCard(int cardNum)
{
    if (cardNum >= 0 && cardNum <= 51)
        return cards[cardNum];
    else
        throw (new System.ArgumentOutOfRangeException("cardNum", cardNum,
                "Value must be between 0 and 51."));
}
```

Finally, we implement the `Shuffle()` method. This method works by creating a temporary card array and copying cards from the existing `cards` array into this array at random. The main body of this function is a loop that counts from 0 to 51. On each cycle we generate a random number between 0 and 51 using an instance of the `System.Random` class from the .NET Framework. Once instantiated, an object of this class will generate a random number between 0 and X using the method `Next(X)`. When we have a random number we simply use that as the index of the `Card` object in our temporary array in which to copy a card from the `cards` array.

To keep a record of assigned cards we also have an array of `bool` variables, and assign these to `true` as each card is copied. When we are generating random numbers we check against this array to see if we have already copied a card to the location in the temporary array specified by the random number, and if we have we simply generate another.

This isn't the most efficient way of doing things, as many random numbers may be generated before a vacant slot to copy a card into is found. However, it works, and because C# code executes so quickly we will hardly notice a delay.

The code is as follows:

```
public void Shuffle()
{
    Card[] newDeck = new Card[52];
    bool[] assigned = new bool[52];
    Random sourceGen = new Random();
    for (int i = 0; i < 52; i++)
    {
```

```
            int destCard = 0;
            bool foundCard = false;
            while (foundCard == false)
            {
                destCard = sourceGen.Next(52);
                if (assigned[destCard] == false)
                    foundCard = true;
            }
            assigned[destCard] = true;
            newDeck[destCard] = cards[i];
        }
        newDeck.CopyTo(cards, 0);
    }
  }
}
```

The last line of this method uses the CopyTo() method of the System.Array class (used whenever we create an array) to copy each of the cards in newDeck back into cards. This means that we are using the same set of Card objects in the same cards object rather than creating any new instances. If we had instead used cards = newDeck then we would be replacing the object instance referred to by cards with another. This could cause problems if code elsewhere was retaining a reference to the original cards instance – which wouldn't be shuffled!

That completes our class library code.

A Client Application for the Class Library

To keep things simple here we can add a client console application to the solution containing the class library. To do this we simply need to ensure that the **Add to Solution** option is selected when we create the project, which we'll call Ch10CardClient.

In order to use the class library we have created from this new console application project we simply need to add a reference to our Ch10CardLib class library project. Once the project has been created we can do this though the **Projects** tab of the **Add Reference** dialog:

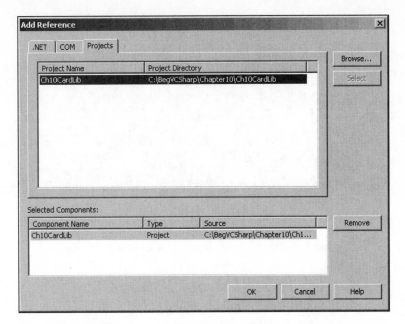

Select the project, click on **Select**, then on **OK**, and the reference is added.

As this new project was the second one to be created we also need to specify that it is the startup project for the solution, meaning that it is the one that will be executed when we hit the run button. To do this we simply right-click on the project name in the **Solution Explorer** window and select the **Set as StartUp Project** menu option.

Next we need to add the code that uses our new classes. This doesn't require anything particularly special, so the following code will do:

```csharp
using System;
using Ch10CardLib;

namespace Ch10CardClient
{
   class Class1
   {
      static void Main(string[] args)
      {
         Deck myDeck = new Deck();
         myDeck.Shuffle();
         for (int i = 0; i < 52; i++)
         {
            Card tempCard = myDeck.GetCard(i);
            Console.Write(tempCard.ToString());
            if (i != 51)
               Console.Write(", ");
            else
               Console.WriteLine();
         }
      }
   }
}
```

The result is as follows:

```
C:\BegVCSharp\Chapter10\Ch10CardClient\bin\Debug\Ch10CardClient.exe                        _ □ ×
The Seven of Hearts, The Deuce of Diamonds, The Ten of Hearts, The Ace of Clubs,
 The Jack of Diamonds, The Six of Clubs, The Queen of Diamonds, The Deuce of Hea
rts, The Ace of Hearts, The Nine of Diamonds, The Queen of Hearts, The Deuce of
Spades, The Ten of Diamonds, The Seven of Spades, The Three of Diamonds, The Sev
en of Clubs, The Five of Hearts, The Ten of Spades, The King of Spades, The Seve
n of Diamonds, The Three of Hearts, The Nine of Clubs, The Eight of Spades, The
Jack of Clubs, The Eight of Diamonds, The King of Diamonds, The Six of Hearts, T
he Queen of Spades, The Ten of Clubs, The Queen of Clubs, The Nine of Hearts, Th
e King of Hearts, The Five of Diamonds, The Four of Spades, The Eight of Clubs,
The Five of Spades, The Four of Clubs, The Deuce of Clubs, The Three of Spades,
The Five of Clubs, The Six of Spades, The Three of Clubs, The Ace of Spades, The
 King of Clubs, The Eight of Hearts, The Six of Diamonds, The Nine of Spades, Th
e Jack of Hearts, The Ace of Diamonds, The Jack of Spades, The Four of Diamonds,
 The Four of Hearts
Press any key to continue
```

This is a random arrangement of the 52 playing cards in the deck.

We'll continue to develop and use this class library in later chapters.

Summary

In this chapter we have completed our discussion on how to define basic classes. There's plenty still to cover, but the techniques covered so far enable us to create quite complicated applications already.

We looked at how to define fields, methods, and properties, discussing the various access levels and modifier keywords as we went along. To cap this off we looked at the VS wizards and tools that can be used to get the outline of a class together in double-quick time.

Once we had covered these basic subjects we looked in greater detail at inheritance behavior, by seeing how we can hide unwanted inherited members with the new keyword, and extend base class members rather than replacing their implementation using the base keyword. We also looked at nested class definitions.

After this, we took a more detailed look at interface definition and implementation, including the concepts of explicit and implicit implementation.

Finally, we developed and used a simple class library representing a deck of playing cards. We'll make further use of this library in later chapters.

In the next chapter we'll look at some of the more advanced possibilities of class generation, such as collections, operator overloading, and deep copying.

Exercises

1. Write code that defines a base class, MyClass, with the virtual method GetString(). This method should return the string stored in the protected field myString, accessible through the write-only public property ContainedString.

2. Derive a class, `MyDerivedClass`, from `MyClass`. Override the `GetString()` method to return the string from the base class using the base implementation of the method, but add the text " (output from derived class)" to the returned string.

3. Write a class called `MyCopyableClass` that is capable of returning a copy of itself using the method `GetCopy()`. This method should use the `MemberwiseClone()` method inherited from `System.Object`. Add a simple property to the class, and write client code that uses the class to check that everything is working.

4. Write a console client for the `Ch10CardLib` library that "draws" five cards at a time from a shuffled `Deck` object. If all five cards are the same suit then the client should display the card names on screen along with the text "Flush!", else it should quit after 50 cards with the text "No flush".

More About Classes

We've covered all the basic OOP techniques in C# now, but there are some more advanced techniques that are worth becoming familiar with. In this chapter we'll look at the following:

❑ **Collections** – objects that can contain arrays of other objects, and which contain functionality that controls access to these objects

❑ **Operator overloading** – configuring classes such that we can use operators such as + with instances of the class

❑ **Advanced conversion** – some of the more advanced C# type-conversion capabilities

❑ **Deep copying** – ensuring that cloned objects don't contain references to data stored in their source object

❑ **Custom exceptions** – creating your own exceptions in order to provide additional information to code that catches the exception

Collections

In Chapter 5, we saw how we can use arrays to create variable types that contain a number of objects or values. Arrays, however, have their limitations. The biggest of these is that once they have been created, they have a fixed size, so we can't add new items to the end of an existing array without creating a new one. This often means that the syntax used to manipulate arrays can become overly complicated. OOP techniques allow us to create classes that perform much of this manipulation internally, thus simplifying the code that uses lists of items or arrays.

Arrays in C# are implemented as instances of the System.Array class, and are just one type of what are known as **collection** classes. Collection classes in general are used for maintaining lists of objects, and may expose additional functionality above that of simple arrays. This functionality comes through implementing interfaces from the System.Collections namespace, thus standardizing collection syntax. This namespace also contains some other interesting things, such as classes that implement these interfaces in ways other than System.Array.

As the collection functionality (including basic functions such as accessing collection items using [`index`] syntax) is available through interfaces we aren't limited to using basic collection classes such as `System.Array`. Instead, we can create our own customized collection classes. These can be made more specific to the objects we wish to enumerate (that is, the objects we want to maintain collections of). One advantage of doing this, as we will see, is that custom collection classes can be **strongly typed**. This means that when we extract items from the collection we don't need to cast them into the correct type.

There are a number of interfaces in the `System.Collections` namespace that provide basic collection functionality:

❑ `IEnumerable` – provides the capability to loop through items in a collection

❑ `ICollection` – provides the ability to obtain the number of items in a collection, and to copy items into a simple array type (inherits from `IEnumerable`)

❑ `IList` – provides a list of items for a collection along with the capabilities for accessing these items, and some other basic capabilities related to lists of items (inherits from `IEnumerable` and `ICollection`)

❑ `IDictionary` – similar to `IList`, but provides a list of items accessible via a key value rather than an index (inherits from `IEnumerable` and `ICollection`)

The `System.Array` class implements `IList`, `ICollection`, and `IEnumerable`, but doesn't support some of the more advanced features of `IList`, and represents a list of items with a fixed size.

Using Collections

One of the classes in the `Systems.Collections` namespace, `System.Collections.ArrayList`, also implements `IList`, `ICollection`, and `IEnumerable`, but does so in a more sophisticated way than `System.Array`. Whereas arrays are fixed in size (we can't add or remove elements), this class may be used to represent lists of items with a variable size. To get more of a feel for what is possible with such a more advanced collection, let's look at an example that uses this class, as well as a simple array.

Try it Out – Arrays versus More Advanced Collections

1. Create a new console application called `Ch11Ex01` in the directory `C:\BegVCSharp\Chapter11`.

2. Add a new class, `Animal`, to the project in the file `Animal.cs` using the **Add Class** wizard.

3. Modify the code in `Animal.cs` as follows:

```
namespace Ch11Ex01
{
    public abstract class Animal
    {
        protected string name;

        public string Name
        {
            get
```

```
            {
                return name;
            }
            set
            {
                name = value;
            }
        }

        public Animal()
        {
            name = "The animal with no name";
        }

        public Animal(string newName)
        {
            name = newName;
        }

        public void Feed()
        {
            Console.WriteLine("{0} has been fed.", name);
        }
    }
    public class Cow : Animal
    {
        public void Milk()
        {
            Console.WriteLine("{0} has been milked.", name);
        }

        public Cow(string newName) : base(newName)
        {
        }
    }

    public class Chicken : Animal
    {
        public void LayEgg()
        {
            Console.WriteLine("{0} has laid an egg.", name);
        }

        public Chicken(string newName) : base(newName)
        {
        }
    }
}
```

4. Modify the code in `Class1.cs` as follows:

```
using System;
using System.Collections;

namespace Ch11Ex01

{
    class Class1
    {
        static void Main(string[] args)
        {

            Console.WriteLine("Create an Array type collection of Animal " +
                            "objects and use it:");
```

```
            Animal[] animalArray = new Animal[2];
            Cow myCow1 = new Cow("Deirdre");
            animalArray[0] = myCow1;
            animalArray[1] = new Chicken("Ken");

            foreach (Animal myAnimal in animalArray)
            {
                Console.WriteLine("New {0} object added to Array collection, " +
                                "Name = {1}", myAnimal.ToString(), myAnimal.Name);
            }

            Console.WriteLine("Array collection contains {0} objects.",
                            animalArray.Length);
            animalArray[0].Feed();
            ((Chicken)animalArray[1]).LayEgg();
            Console.WriteLine();

            Console.WriteLine("Create an ArrayList type collection of Animal " +
                            "objects and use it:");
            ArrayList animalArrayList = new ArrayList();
            Cow myCow2 = new Cow("Hayley");
            animalArrayList.Add(myCow2);
            animalArrayList.Add(new Chicken("Roy"));

            foreach (Animal myAnimal in animalArrayList)
            {
                Console.WriteLine("New {0} object added to ArrayList collection," +
                                " Name = {1}", myAnimal.ToString(), myAnimal.Name);
            }
            Console.WriteLine("ArrayList collection contains {0} objects.",
                    animalArrayList.Count);
            ((Animal)animalArrayList[0]).Feed();
            ((Chicken)animalArrayList[1]).LayEgg();
            Console.WriteLine();

            Console.WriteLine("Additional manipulation of ArrayList:");
            animalArrayList.RemoveAt(0);
            ((Animal)animalArrayList[0]).Feed();
            animalArrayList.AddRange(animalArray);
            ((Chicken)animalArrayList[2]).LayEgg();
            Console.WriteLine("The animal called {0} is at index {1}.",
                            myCow1.Name, animalArrayList.IndexOf(myCow1));
            myCow1.Name = "Janice";
            Console.WriteLine("The animal is now called {0}.",
                            ((Animal)animalArrayList[1]).Name);
        }
    }
}
```

5. Run the application:

```
C:\BegVCSharp\Chapter11\Ch11Ex01\bin\Debug\Ch11Ex01.exe                    _ □ X
Create an Array type collection of Animal objects and use it:
New Ch11Ex01.Cow object added to Array collection, Name = Deirdre
New Ch11Ex01.Chicken object added to Array collection, Name = Ken
Array collection contains 2 objects.
Deirdre has been fed.
Ken has laid an egg.

Create an ArrayList type collection of Animal objects and use it:
New Ch11Ex01.Cow object added to ArrayList collection, Name = Hayley
New Ch11Ex01.Chicken object added to ArrayList collection, Name = Roy
ArrayList collection contains 2 objects.
Hayley has been fed.
Roy has laid an egg.

Additional manipulation of ArrayList:
Roy has been fed.
Ken has laid an egg.
The animal called Deirdre is at index 1.
The animal is now called Janice.
Press any key to continue
```

How it Works

This example creates two collections of objects, the first using the `System.Array` class (that is, a simple array), and the second using the `System.Collections.ArrayList` class. Both collections are of `Animal` objects, which are defined in `Animal.cs`. The `Animal` class is abstract so it can't be instantiated, although we can (through polymorphism) have items in our collection that are instances of the `Cow` and `Chicken` classes, which are derived from `Animal`.

Once created in the `Main()` method in `Class1.cs`, these arrays are manipulated to show their characteristics and capabilities. Several of the operations performed apply to both `Array` and `ArrayList` collections, although their syntax differs slightly. There are some, however, that are only possible using the more advanced `ArrayList` type.

Let's look at the similar operations first, comparing the code and results for both types of collection.

First, collection creation. With simple arrays we must initialize the array with a fixed size in order to use it. We do this to an array called `animalArray` using the standard syntax we saw in Chapter 5:

```
Animal[] animalArray = new Animal[2];
```

`ArrayList` collections, on the other hand, don't need a size to be initialized, so we can create our list (called `animalArrayList`) simply using:

```
ArrayList animalArrayList = new ArrayList();
```

There are two other constructors we can use with this class. The first copies the contents of an existing collection to the new instance by specifying the existing collection as a parameter; the other sets the **capacity** of the collection, also via a parameter. This capacity, specified as an `int` value, sets the initial number of items that can be contained in the collection. This is not an absolute capacity, however, as it will be doubled automatically if the number of items in the collection ever exceeds this value.

With arrays of reference types (such as our `Animal` and `Animal`-derived objects), simply initializing the array with a size doesn't initialize the items it contains. In order to use a given entry that entry needs initializing, which means we need to assign initialized objects to the items:

```
Cow myCow1 = new Cow("Deirdre");
animalArray[0] = myCow1;
animalArray[1] = new Chicken("Ken");
```

This code does this in two ways, once by assignment using an existing Cow object, and once by assignment through the creation of a new Chicken object. The main difference here is that the former method leaves us with a reference to the object in the array – a fact that we make use of later in the code.

With our ArrayList collection there are no existing items, not even null-referenced ones. This means that we can't assign new instances to indices in the same way. Instead, we use the Add() method of the ArrayList object to add new items:

```
Cow myCow2 = new Cow("Hayley");
animalArrayList.Add(myCow2);
animalArrayList.Add(new Chicken("Roy"));
```

Apart from the slightly different syntax, we can add new or existing objects to the collection in the same way.

Once we have added items in this way, we can overwrite them using syntax identical to that for arrays, for example:

```
animalArrayList[0] = new Cow("Alma");
```

We won't do this in this example though.

In Chapter 5, we saw how the foreach structure can be used to iterate through an array. This is possible as the System.Array class implements the IEnumerable interface, and the only method on this interface, GetEnumerator(), allows us to loop through items in the collection. We'll look at this in more depth a little later. In our code, we write out information about each Animal object in the array:

```
foreach (Animal myAnimal in animalArray)
{
   Console.WriteLine("New {0} object added to Array collection, " +
                     "Name = {1}", myAnimal.ToString(), myAnimal.Name);
}
```

The ArrayList object we use also supports the IEnumerable interface, and can also be used with foreach. In this case, the syntax is identical:

```
foreach (Animal myAnimal in animalArrayList)
{
   Console.WriteLine("New {0} object added to ArrayList collection, " +
                     "Name = {1}", myAnimal.ToString(), myAnimal.Name);
}
```

Next, we use the Length property of the array to output the number of items in the array to the screen:

```
Console.WriteLine("Array collection contains {0} objects.",
                  animalArray.Length);
```

We can achieve the same thing with our `ArrayList` collection, except that we use the `Count` property that is part of the `ICollection` interface:

```
Console.WriteLine("ArrayList collection contains {0} objects.",
                  animalArrayList.Count);
```

Collections – whether simple arrays or more complex collections – wouldn't be much use unless they provided access to the items that belong to them. Simple arrays are strongly typed – that is, they allow direct access to the type of the items they contain. This means that we can call the methods of the item directly:

```
animalArray[0].Feed();
```

The type of the array is the abstract type `Animal`, therefore we can't call methods supplied by derived classes directly. Instead we must use casting:

```
((Chicken)animalArray[1]).LayEgg();
```

The `ArrayList` collection is a collection of `System.Object` objects (we have assigned `Animal` objects via polymorphism). This means that we must use casting for all items:

```
((Animal)animalArrayList[0]).Feed();
((Chicken)animalArrayList[1]).LayEgg();
```

The remainder of the code looks at some of the capabilities of the `ArrayList` collection that go beyond those of the `Array` collection.

First, we can remove items using the `Remove()` and `RemoveAt()` methods, part of the `IList` interface implementation in the `ArrayList` class. These remove items from an array based on an item reference or index respectively. In our example, we use the latter method to remove the first item added to the list, the `Cow` object with a `Name` property of "Hayley":

```
animalArrayList.RemoveAt(0);
```

Alternatively, we could use:

```
animalArrayList.Remove(myCow2);
```

as we already have a local reference to this object – we added an existing reference to the array via `Add()`, rather than creating a new object.

Either way, the only item left in the collection is the `Chicken` object, which we access in the following way:

```
((Animal)animalArrayList[0]).Feed();
```

Any modifications to the items in the `ArrayList` object resulting in N items being left in the array will be executed in such a way as to maintain indices from 0 to N-1. For example, removing the item with the index 0 results in all other items being shifted one place in the array, so we access the `Chicken` object with the index 0, not 1. There is no longer an item with an index of 1 (because we only had two items in the first place), so an exception would be thrown if we tried the following:

```
    ((Animal)animalArrayList[1]).Feed();
```

ArrayList collections allow us to add several items at once with the `AddRange()` method. This method accepts any object with the `ICollection` interface, which includes the `animalArray` array we created earlier in the code:

```
    animalArrayList.AddRange(animalArray);
```

To check that this works, we can attempt to access the third item in the collection, which will be the second item in `animalArray`:

```
    ((Chicken)animalArrayList[2]).LayEgg();
```

The `AddRange()` method isn't part of any of the interfaces exposed by `ArrayList`. This method is specific to the `ArrayList` class, and demonstrates the fact that we can exhibit customized behavior in our collection classes, above and beyond what is required by the interfaces we have looked at. This class exposes other interesting methods too, such as `InsertRange()`, for inserting an array of objects at any point in the list, and methods for tasks such as sorting and reordering the array.

Finally, we come back to the fact that we can have multiple references to the same object. Using the `IndexOf()` method (part of the `IList` interface) we can see not only that `myCow1` (an object originally added to `animalArray`) is now part of the `animalArrayList` collection, but also what its index is:

```
Console.WriteLine("The animal called {0} is at index {1}.",
                  myCow1.Name, animalArrayList.IndexOf(myCow1));
```

As an extension of this, the next two lines of code rename the object via the object reference and display the new name via the collection reference:

```
myCow1.Name = "Janice";
Console.WriteLine("The animal is now called {0}.",
                  ((Animal)animalArrayList[1]).Name);
```

Defining Collections

Now we've seen what is possible using more advanced collection classes, it's time to look at how we can create our own, strongly typed collection. One way of doing this is to implement the required methods manually, but this can be quite time consuming, and in some cases quite complex. Alternatively, we can derive our collection from a class, such as `System.Collections.CollectionBase`, an abstract class that supplies much of the implementation of a collection for us. This is the recommended option.

The `CollectionBase` class exposes the interfaces `IEnumerable`, `ICollection`, and `IList`, but only provides some of the required implementation, notably the `Clear()` and `RemoveAt()` methods of `IList`, and the `Count` property of `ICollection`. We need to implement everything else ourselves if we want the functionality provided.

To facilitate this, `CollectionBase` provides two protected properties that give access to the stored objects themselves. We can use `List`, which gives us access to the items through an `IList` interface, and `InnerList`, which is the `ArrayList` object used to store items.

For example, the basics of a collection class to store `Animal` objects could be defined as follows (we'll see a fuller implementation shortly):

```
public class Animals : CollectionBase
{
    public void Add(Animal newAnimal)
    {
        List.Add(newAnimal);
    }

    public void Remove(Animal oldAnimal)
    {
        List.Remove(oldAnimal);
    }

    public Animals()
    {
    }
}
```

Here, `Add()` and `Remove()` have been implemented as strongly typed methods that use the standard `Add()` method of the `IList` interface used to access the items. The methods exposed will now only work with `Animal` classes or classes derived from `Animal`, unlike the `ArrayList` implementations we saw earlier that work with any object.

The `CollectionBase` class allows us to use the `foreach` syntax with our derived collections. We can, for example, use code, such as:

```
Console.WriteLine("Using custom collection class Animals:");
Animals animalCollection = new Animals();
animalCollection.Add(new Cow("Sarah"));
foreach (Animal myAnimal in animalCollection)
{
    Console.WriteLine("New {0} object added to custom collection, " +
                    "Name = {1}", myAnimal.ToString(), myAnimal.Name);
}
```

We can't however, do the following:

```
animalCollection[0].Feed();
```

In order to access items via their indices in this way, we need to use an **indexer**.

Indexers

An **indexer** is a special kind of property that we can add to a class to provide array-like access. In actual fact we can provide more complex access via an indexer, as we can define and use complex parameter types with the square bracket syntax as we wish. Implementing a simple numeric index for items, however, is the most common usage.

We can add an indexer to our `Animals` collection of `Animal` objects as follows:

```
public class Animals : CollectionBase
{
    ...
    public Animal this[int animalIndex]
    {
        get
        {
            return (Animal)List[animalIndex];
        }
        set
        {
            List[animalIndex] = value;
        }
    }
}
```

The `this` keyword is used along with parameters in square brackets, but otherwise this looks much like any other property. This syntax is logical, because we'll access the indexer using the name of the object followed by the index parameter(s) in square brackets (for example, `MyAnimals[0]`).

This code uses an indexer on the `List` property (that is, on the `IList` interface that gives us access to the `ArrayList` in `CollectionBase` that stores our items):

```
return (Animal)List[animalIndex];
```

Explicit casting *is* necessary here, as the `IList.List` property returns a `System.Object` object.

The important thing to note here is that we define a type for this indexer. This is the type that will be obtained when accessing an item using this indexer. This means that we can write code such as:

```
animalCollection[0].Feed();
```

Rather than:

```
((Animal)animalCollection[0]).Feed();
```

This is another handy feature of strongly typed custom collections. Let's expand the last example properly to put this into action.

Try it Out – Implementing an Animals Collection

1. Create a new console application called `Ch11Ex02` in the directory `C:\BegVCSharp\Chapter11`.

2. Right-click on the project name in the Solution Explorer window, and select the Add | Add Existing Item... option:

3. Select the `Animal.cs` file from the `C:\BegVCSharp\Chapter11\Ch11Ex01` directory, and click on **Open**:

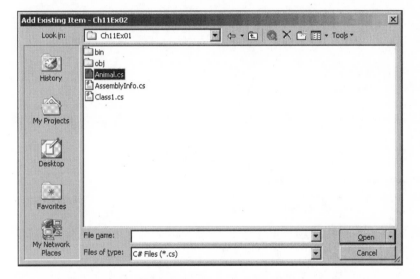

4. Modify the namespace declaration in `Animal.cs` to be as follows:

```
namespace Ch11Ex02
```

5. Add a new class using the **Add Class** wizard, called `Animals`, and store it in `Animals.cs`.

6. Modify the code in `Animals.cs` as follows:

```
using System;
using System.Collections;

namespace Ch11Ex02
{
    public class Animals : CollectionBase
    {
```

```csharp
      public void Add(Animal newAnimal)
      {
         List.Add(newAnimal);
      }

      public void Remove(Animal newAnimal)
      {
         List.Remove(newAnimal);
      }

      public Animals()
      {
      }

      public Animal this[int animalIndex]
      {
         get
         {
            return (Animal)List[animalIndex];
         }
         set
         {
            List[animalIndex] = value;
         }
      }
   }
}
```

7. Modify `Class1.cs` as follows:

```csharp
static void Main(string[] args)
{
   Animals animalCollection = new Animals();
   animalCollection.Add(new Cow("Jack"));
   animalCollection.Add(new Chicken("Vera"));
   foreach (Animal myAnimal in animalCollection)
   {
      myAnimal.Feed();
   }
}
```

8. Execute the application:

How It Works

This example uses code detailed in the last section to implement a strongly typed collection of `Animal` objects in a class called `Animals`. The code in `Main()` simply instantiates an `Animals` object called `animalCollection`, adds two items (an instance each of `Cow` and `Chicken`), and uses a `foreach` loop to call the `Feed()` method that both these objects inherit from their base class `Animal`.

The Add Indexer Wizard

VS contains another wizard for use in C# OOP, the **Add Indexer** wizard. This is found in the same place as the wizards for adding properties, methods, and fields (right-click on the class name in the **Class View** window and select **Add | Add Indexer...**) The wizard presents us with the following dialog:

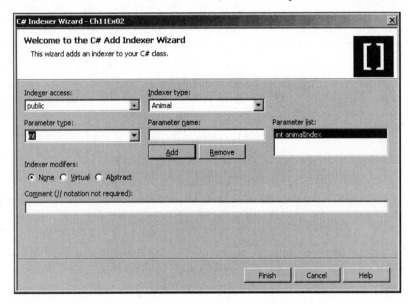

The wizard allows us to specify the protection level (`public`, as we want the indexer to be available from outside the collection), and type of our indexer (here `Animal`, because we want the indexer to be strongly typed and return items of the `Animal` class). We can also specify the types and names of the parameters; for our example, we just want the typical one `int` parameter, with the name `animalIndex`. Finally, we can specify whether we want any modifiers for the indexer – we can specify that we want our indexer to be virtual, or (for an abstract class) abstract. If an indexer is declared as `virtual`, then we allow the indexer to be overridden in any classes derived from the indexed class – just like the virtual methods we saw in the last chapter. Abstract indexers are like virtual indexers, but we don't provide any code to implement them – that's up to the classes that derive from our abstract class.

The above entries would give us the structure for the `Animals` class indexer shown earlier:

```
public Animal this[int animalIndex]
{
    get
    {
        return null;
    }
}
```

```
        set
        {
        }
    }
```

Note that we have to provide the workings ourselves, by filling in the get and set code blocks.

Keyed Collections and IDictionary

Instead of the IList interface, it is also possible for collections to implement the similar IDictionary interface, which allows items to be indexed via a key value (such as a string name), rather than by an index.

This is also achieved by using an indexer, although this time the indexer parameter used is a key associated with a stored item, rather than an int index, which can make the collection a lot more user friendly.

As with indexed collections, there is a base class that we can use to simplify implementation of the IDictionary interface: DictionaryBase. This class also implements IEnumerable and ICollection, providing the basic collection manipulation capabilities that are the same for any collection.

DictionaryBase, like CollectionBase, implements some (but not all) of the members obtained through its supported interfaces. Like CollectionBase the Clear() and Count members are implemented, although RemoveAt() isn't. This is because RemoveAt() is a method on the IList interface and doesn't appear on the IDictionary interface. IDictionary does, however, have a Remove() method, which is one of the methods we should implement in a custom collection class based on DictionaryBase.

The following code shows an alternative version of the Animals class from the last section, this time derived from DictionaryBase. Implementations are included for Add(), Remove(), and a key-accessed indexer:

```
public class Animals : DictionaryBase
{
    public void Add(string newID, Animal newAnimal)
    {
        Dictionary.Add(newID, newAnimal);
    }

    public void Remove(string animalID)
    {
        Dictionary.Remove(animalID);
    }

    public Animals()
    {
    }

    public Animal this[string animalID]
    {
        get
```

```
            {
                return (Animal)Dictionary[animalID];
            }
            set
            {
                Dictionary[animalID] = value;
            }
        }
    }
```

The differences in these members are:

❑ Add() – takes two parameters, a key and a value, to store together. Our dictionary collection has a member called Dictionary inherited from DictionaryBase, which is an IDictionary interface. This interface has its own Add() method, which takes two object parameters. Our implementation takes a string value as a key, and an Animal object as the data to store alongside this key.

❑ Remove() – takes a key parameter rather than an object reference. The item with the key value specified is removed.

❑ Indexer – uses a string key value rather than an index, which is used to access the stored item via the Dictionary inherited member. Again, casting is necessary here.

One other difference between collections based on DictionaryBase and collections based on CollectionBase is that foreach works slightly differently. The collection from the last section allowed us to extract Animal objects directly from the collection. Using foreach with the DictionaryBase derived class gives us DictionaryEntry structs, another type defined in the System.Collections namespace. To get to the Animal objects themselves we must use the Value member of this struct, or we can use the Key member of the struct to get the associated key. To get code equivalent to the earlier:

```
foreach (Animal myAnimal in animalCollection)
{
    Console.WriteLine("New {0} object added to custom collection, " +
                    "Name = {1}", myAnimal.ToString(), myAnimal.Name());
}
```

We need the following:

```
foreach (DictionaryEntry myEntry in animalCollection)
{
    Console.WriteLine("New {0} object added to custom collection, " +
                    "Name = {1}", myEntry.Value.ToString(),
                    ((Animal)myEntry.Value).Name);
}
```

It is possible to override this behavior such that we can get at Animal objects directly through foreach, but this topic is quite complex and we won't go into it in this book.

Upgrading CardLib Part 1

In the last chapter, we created a class library project called Ch10CardLib that contained a Card class representing a playing card, and a Deck class representing a deck of cards, that is, a collection of Card classes. This collection was implemented as a simple array.

In this chapter, we'll add a new class to this library, which we'll rename as Ch11CardLib. This new class, Cards, will be a custom collection of Card objects, giving us all the benefits described earlier in this chapter. You may find it easier to create a new class library called Ch11CardLib in the C:\BegVCSharp\Chapter11 directory, and from File | Add Existing Item, select the Card.cs and Deck.cs files from the C:\BegVCSharp\Chapter10\Ch10CardLib directory and add them to your project.

> *Don't forget that when copying the source files from Ch10CardLib to Ch11CardLib, we must change the namespace declarations to refer to Ch11CardLib. This also applies to the Ch10CardClient console application that we will use for testing.*

The code for our new class, in Cards.cs, is as follows (where code that is modified from that generated by the wizard is highlighted):

```csharp
using System;
using System.Collections;

namespace Ch11CardLib
{
    public class Cards : CollectionBase
    {
        public void Add(Card newCard)
        {
            List.Add(newCard);
        }

        public void Remove(Card oldCard)
        {
            List.Remove(oldCard);
        }

        public Cards()
        {
        }

        public Card this[int cardIndex]
        {
            get
            {
                return (Card)List[cardIndex];
            }
            set
            {
                List[cardIndex] = value;
            }
        }
    }
```

```
            // Utility method for copying card instances into another Cards
            // instance - used in Deck.Shuffle(). This implementation assumes that
            // source and target collections are the same size.
            public void CopyTo(Cards targetCards)
            {
                for (int index = 0; index < this.Count; index++)
                {
                    targetCards[index] = this[index];
                }
            }

            // Check to see if the Cards collection contains a particular card.
            // This calls the Contains method of the ArrayList for the collection,
            // which we access through the InnerList property.
            public bool Contains(Card card)
            {
                return InnerList.Contains(card);
            }
        }
    }
```

Next, we need to modify Deck.cs to make use of this new collection, rather than an array:

```
using System;

namespace Ch11CardLib
{
    public class Deck
    {
        private Cards cards = new Cards();

        public Deck()
        {
            // line of code removed here.
            for (int suitVal = 0; suitVal < 4; suitVal++)
            {
                for (int rankVal = 1; rankVal < 14; rankVal++)
                {
                    cards.Add(new Card((Suit)suitVal, (Rank)rankVal));
                }
            }
        }

        public Card GetCard(int cardNum)
        {
            if (cardNum >= 0 && cardNum <= 51)
                return cards[cardNum];
            else
                throw (new System.ArgumentOutOfRangeException("cardNum", cardNum,
                        "Value must be between 0 and 51."));
        }
```

```
        public void Shuffle()
        {
            Cards newDeck = new Cards();
            bool[] assigned = new bool[52];
            Random sourceGen = new Random();
            for (int i = 0; i < 52; i++)
            {
                int sourceCard = 0;
                bool foundCard = false;
                while (foundCard == false)
                {
                    sourceCard = sourceGen.Next(52);
                    if (assigned[sourceCard] == false)
                        foundCard = true;
                }
                assigned[sourceCard] = true;
                newDeck.Add(cards[sourceCard]);
            }
            newDeck.CopyTo(cards);
        }
    }
}
```

There aren't that many changes necessary here. Most of those involve changing the shuffling logic to cater for the fact that cards are added to the beginning of the new `Cards` collection `newDeck` from a random index in cards, rather than to a random index in `newDeck` from a sequential position in `cards`.

The client console application for the `Ch10CardLib` solution, `Ch10CardClient`, may be used with this new library with the same result as before, as the method signatures of `Deck` are unchanged. Clients of this class library can now make use of the `Cards` collection class, however, rather than relying on arrays of `Card` objects, for example in defining hands of cards in a card game application.

Operator Overloading

The next subject we will cover in this chapter is that of **operator overloading**. This enables us to use standard operators, such as +, >, and so on, with classes that we design. This is called overloading, because we are supplying our own implementations for these operators when used with specific parameter types, in much the same way that we overload methods by supplying different parameters for methods with the same name.

Operator overloading is useful as we can perform whatever processing we want in the implementation of the operator overload, which might not be as simple as, say, + meaning "add these two operands together". In a little while, we'll see a good example of this in a further upgrade of the `CardLib` library. We'll provide implementations for comparison operators that compare two cards to see which would beat the other in a "trick" (one round of card game play). As a trick in many card games depends on the suits of the cards involved, this isn't as straightforward as comparing the numbers on the cards. If the second card laid down is a different suit to the first, then the first card will win regardless of its rank. We can implement this by considering the order of the two operands. We can also take a "trump" suit into account, where trumps beat other suits, even if that isn't the first suit laid down. This means that calculating that card1 > card2 is `true` (that is, card1 will beat card2, if card1 is laid down first), doesn't necessarily imply that card2 > card1 is `false`. If neither card1 nor card2 are trumps and they belong to different suits, then both these comparisons will be `true`.

To start with, though, let's look at the basic syntax for operator overloading.

Operators may be overloaded by adding operator type members (which must be `static`) to a class. Some operators have multiple uses (such as -, which has unary and binary capabilities), therefore we also specify how many operands we are dealing with, and what the types of these operands are. In general, we will have operands that are the same type as the class where the operator is defined, although it is possible to define operators that work on mixed types, as we will see shortly.

As an example, consider the simple type `AddClass1`, defined as follows:

```
public class AddClass1
{
    public int val;
}
```

This is just a wrapper around an `int` value, but will serve to illustrate the principles.

With this class, code, such as the following, will fail to compile:

```
AddClass1 op1 = new AddClass1();
op1.val = 5;
AddClass1 op2 = new AddClass1();
op2.val = 5;
AddClass1 op3 = op1 + op2;
```

The error you get informs you that the + operator cannot be applied to operands of the `AddClass1` type, as we haven't defined an operation to perform yet.

Code such as the following, will work, although it won't give you the result you might want:

```
AddClass1 op1 = new AddClass1();
op1.val = 5;
AddClass1 op2 = new AddClass1();
op2.val = 5;
bool op3 = op1 == op2;
```

Here, op1 and op2 are compared using the == binary operator to see if they refer to the same object, and *not* to verify whether their values are equal. op3 will be `false` in the above code, even though op1.val and op2.val are identical.

To overload the + operator, we use the following code:

```
public class AddClass1
{
    public int val;

    public static AddClass1 operator +(AddClass1 op1, AddClass1 op2)
    {
        AddClass1 returnVal = new AddClass1();
        returnVal.val = op1.val + op2.val;
        return returnVal;
    }
}
```

As you can see, operator overloads look much like standard static method declarations, except that they use the keyword `operator` and the operator itself rather than a method name.

We can now successfully use the + operator with this class, as in the previous example:

```
AddClass1 op3 = op1 + op2;
```

Overloading all binary operators fits the same pattern. Unary operators look similar, but only have one parameter:

```
public class AddClass1
{
    public int val;

    public static AddClass1 operator +(AddClass1 op1, AddClass1 op2)
    {
        AddClass1 returnVal = new AddClass1();
        returnVal.val = op1.val + op2.val;
        return returnVal;
    }

    public static AddClass1 operator -(AddClass1 op1)
    {
        AddClass1 returnVal = new AddClass1();
        returnVal.val = -op1.val;
        return returnVal;
    }
}
```

Both these operators work on operands of the same type as the class, and have return values that are also of that type. Consider, however, the following class definitions:

```
public class AddClass1
{
    public int val;

    public static AddClass3 operator +(AddClass1 op1, AddClass2 op2)
    {
        AddClass3 returnVal = new AddClass3();
        returnVal.val = op1.val + op2.val;
        return returnVal;
    }
}

public class AddClass2
{
    public int val;
}

public class AddClass3
{
    public int val;
}
```

This will allow the following code:

```
AddClass1 op1 = new AddClass1();
op1.val = 5;
AddClass2 op2 = new AddClass2();
op2.val = 5;
AddClass3 op3 = op1 + op2;
```

Where appropriate, we can mix types in this way. Note, however, that if we added the same operator to `AddClass2`, the above code would fail, as it would be ambiguous as to which operator to use. We should, therefore, take care not to add operators with the same signature to more than one class.

Also note, that if we mix types, the operands *must* be supplied in the same order as the parameters to the operator overload. If we attempt to use our overloaded operator with the operands in the "wrong" order, the operation will fail. So we can't use the operator like this:

```
AddClass3 op3 = op2 + op1;
```

Unless, of course, we supply another overload with the parameters reversed:

```
public static AddClass3 operator +(AddClass2 op1, AddClass1 op2)
{
   AddClass3 returnVal = new AddClass3();
   returnVal.val = op1.val + op2.val;
   return returnVal;
}
```

The following operators can be overloaded:

❑   Unary operators: +, -, !, ~, ++, --, `true`, `false`

❑   Binary operators: +, -, *, /, %, &, |, ^, <<, >>

❑   Comparison operators: ==, !=, <, >, <=, >=

> *If we overload the `true` and `false` operators then we can use classes in Boolean expressions, such as `if (op1) {}`.*

We can't overload assignment operators, such as +=, but these operators use their simple counterparts, such as +, so we don't have to worry about that. Overloading + will mean that += will function as expected. The = operator is included in this – it would make little sense to overload this operator, since it has such a fundamental usage. This operator, however, is related to the user-defined conversion operators, which we talk about in the next section.

We also can't overload && and ||, but these operators use the & and | operators to perform their calculations, so overloading these is enough.

Some operators, such as < and >, must be overloaded in pairs. That is to say, we can't overload < unless we also overload >. In many cases, we can simply call other operators from these to reduce the code required (and the errors that might occur), for example:

```
public class AddClass1
{
    public int val;

    public static bool operator >=(AddClass1 op1, AddClass1 op2)
    {
        return (op1.val >= op2.val);
    }

    public static bool operator <(AddClass1 op1, AddClass1 op2)
    {
        return !(op1 >= op2);
    }

    // Also need implementations for <= and > operators
}
```

In more complex operator definitions this can save on lines of code, and it also means that we have less code to change should we wish to change the implementation of these operators.

The same applies to == and !=, but with these operators it is often worth overriding `Object.Equals()` and `Object.GetHashCode()`, as both of these functions may also be used to compare objects. By overriding these methods, we ensure that whatever technique users of the class use, they get the same result. This isn't essential, but is worth adding for completeness. It requires the following non-static override methods:

```
public class AddClass1
{
    public int val;

    public static bool operator ==(AddClass1 op1, AddClass1 op2)
    {
        return (op1.val == op2.val);
    }

    public static bool operator !=(AddClass1 op1, AddClass1 op2)
    {
        return !(op1 == op2);
    }

    public override bool Equals(object op1)
    {
        return val == ((AddClass1)op1).val;
    }

    public override int GetHashCode()
    {
        return val;
    }
}
```

Note that `Equals()` uses an `object` type parameter. We need to use this signature or we will be overloading this method rather than overriding it, and the default implementation will still be accessible to users of the class. This means that we must use casting to get the result we require (although more code might be added here to make this more robust than the above example, which will fail unless the `op1` parameter is an `AddClass1` instance, or an instance of a class derived from this class).

`GetHashCode()` is used to obtain a unique `int` value for an object instance based on its state. Here, using `val` is fine, as it is also an `int` value.

Conversion Operators

As well as overloading the mathematical operators as shown above, we can also define both implicit and explicit conversions between types. This is necessary if we want to convert between types that aren't related, if there is no inheritance relationship between them and no shared interfaces, for example.

Let's say we define an implicit conversion between `ConvClass1` and `ConvClass2`. This means that we can write code, such as:

```
ConvClass1 op1 = new ConvClass1();
ConvClass2 op2 = op1;
```

Alternatively, we can define an explicit conversion, called in the following code:

```
ConvClass1 op1 = new ConvClass1();
ConvClass2 op2 = (ConvClass2)op1;
```

As an example, consider the following code:

```
public class ConvClass1
{
    public int val;

    public static implicit operator ConvClass2(ConvClass1 op1)
    {
        ConvClass2 returnVal = new ConvClass2();
        returnVal.val = op1.val;
        return returnVal;
    }
}

public class ConvClass2
{
    public double val;

    public static explicit operator ConvClass1(ConvClass2 op1)
    {
        ConvClass1 returnVal = new ConvClass1();
        checked {returnVal.val = (int)op1.val;};
        return returnVal;
    }
}
```

Here, `ConvClass1` contains an int value and `ConvClass2` contains a double value. Since int values may be converted into double values implicitly, we can define an implicit conversion between `ConvClass1` and `ConvClass2`. The reverse is not true, however, and we should define the conversion operator between `ConvClass2` and `ConvClass1` as explicit.

In the code, we specify this using the `implicit` and `explicit` keywords as shown.

With these classes the following code is fine:

```
ConvClass1 op1 = new ConvClass1();
op1.val = 3;
ConvClass2 op2 = op1;
```

A conversion in the other direction, however, requires the following explicit casting conversion:

```
ConvClass2 op1 = new ConvClass2();
op1.val = 3e15;
ConvClass1 op2 = (ConvClass1)op1;
```

Note that as we have used the `checked` keyword in our explicit conversion, we will get an exception in the above code, since the val property of op1 is too large to fit into the val property of op2.

Upgrading CardLib Part 2

Let's upgrade our `Ch11CardLib` project again, adding operator overloading to the card class. First, though, we'll add the extra fields to the `Card` class that allow for trump suits and a choice to place Aces high. We make these static, since when they are set, they apply to all `Card` objects:

```
public class Card
{
    // Flag for trump usage. If true, trumps are valued higher
    // than cards of other suits.
    public static bool useTrumps = false;

    // Trump suit to use if useTrumps is true.
    public static Suit trump = Suit.Club;

    // Flag that determines whether Aces are higher than Kings or lower
    // than deuces.
    public static bool isAceHigh = true;
```

As we have done this, it is worth adding a few more constructors to the `Deck` class, in order to initialize decks with different characteristics:

```
public Deck()
{
    for (int suitVal = 0; suitVal < 4; suitVal++)
    {
        for (int rankVal = 1; rankVal < 14; rankVal++)
        {
            cards.Add(new Card((Suit)suitVal, (Rank)rankVal));
```

```
            }
        }
    }
```

```
    // Non-default constructor. Allows aces to be set high.
    public Deck(bool isAceHigh) : this()
    {
        Card.isAceHigh = isAceHigh;
    }
```

```
    // Non-default constructor. Allows a trump suit to be used.
    public Deck(bool useTrumps, Suit trump) : this()
    {
        Card.useTrumps = useTrumps;
        Card.trump = trump;
    }
```

```
    // Non-default constructor. Allows aces to be set high and a trump suit
    // to be used.
    public Deck(bool isAceHigh, bool useTrumps, Suit trump) : this()
    {
        Card.isAceHigh = isAceHigh;
        Card.useTrumps = useTrumps;
        Card.trump = trump;
    }
```

Each of these constructors is defined using the : this() syntax we saw in Chapter 9, so that in all cases, the default constructor is called before the non-default one, initializing the deck.

Next, we add our operator overloads (and suggested overrides) to the Card class:

```
    public Card(Suit newSuit, Rank newRank)
    {
        suit = newSuit;
        rank = newRank;
    }
```

```
    public static bool operator ==(Card card1, Card card2)
    {
        return (card1.suit == card2.suit) && (card1.rank == card2.rank);
    }
```

```
    public static bool operator !=(Card card1, Card card2)
    {
        return !(card1 == card2);
    }
```

```
    public override bool Equals(object card)
    {
        return this == (Card)card;
    }
```

```csharp
public override int GetHashCode()
{
   return 13*(int)rank + (int)suit;
}

public static bool operator >(Card card1, Card card2)
{
   if (card1.suit == card2.suit)
   {
      if (isAceHigh)
      {
         if (card1.rank == Rank.Ace)
         {
            if (card2.rank == Rank.Ace)
               return false;
            else
               return true;
         }
         else
         {
            if (card2.rank == Rank.Ace)
               return false;
            else
               return (card1.rank > card2.rank);
         }
      }
      else
      {
         return (card1.rank > card2.rank);
      }
   }
   else
   {
      if (useTrumps && (card2.suit == Card.trump))
         return false;
      else
         return true;
   }
}

public static bool operator <(Card card1, Card card2)
{
   return !(card1 >= card2);
}

public static bool operator >=(Card card1, Card card2)
{
   if (card1.suit == card2.suit)
   {
      if (isAceHigh)
      {
         if (card1.rank == Rank.Ace)
         {
```

```
                    return true;
                }
                else
                {
                    if (card2.rank == Rank.Ace)
                        return false;
                    else
                        return (card1.rank >= card2.rank);
                }
            }
            else
            {
                return (card1.rank >= card2.rank);
            }
        }
        else
        {
            if (useTrumps && (card2.suit == Card.trump))
                return false;
            else
                return true;
        }
    }
```

```
    public static bool operator <=(Card card1, Card card2)
    {
        return !(card1 > card2);
    }
```

There's not much to note about this code, except perhaps the slightly lengthy code for the > and >= overloaded operators. If we step through the code for > we can see how it works, and why these steps are necessary.

We are comparing two cards, card1 and card2, where card1 is assumed to be the first one laid down on the table. As discussed earlier, this becomes important when we are using trump cards, as a trump will beat a non-trump, even if the non-trump has a higher rank. Of course, if the suits of the two cards are identical then whether the suit is the trump suit or not is irrelevant, so this is the first comparison we make:

```
    public static bool operator >(Card card1, Card card2)
    {
        if (card1.suit == card2.suit)
        {
```

If the static isAceHigh flag is true, then we can't compare the card ranks directly via their value in the Rank enumeration, as the rank of Ace has a value of 1 in this enumeration, which is less than that of all other ranks. Instead, we need the following steps:

❑   If the first card is an Ace we check to see if the second card is also an Ace. If it is then the first card won't beat the second. If the second card isn't an Ace then the first card will win:

```
            if (isAceHigh)
            {
               if (card1.rank == Rank.Ace)
               {
                  if (card2.rank == Rank.Ace)
                     return false;
                  else
                     return true;
               }
```

❑   If the first card isn't an Ace we also need to check to see if the second one is. If it is, then the second card wins, otherwise we can compare the rank values as we know that Aces aren't an issue:

```
               else
               {
                  if (card2.rank == Rank.Ace)
                     return false;
                  else
                     return (card1.rank > card2.rank);
               }
            }
```

❑   Alternatively, if Aces aren't high, we can just compare the rank values:

```
            else
            {
               return (card1.rank > card2.rank);
            }
```

The remainder of the code concerns the case where the suits of card1 and card2 are different. Here the static useTrumps flag is important. If this flag is true and card2 is of the trump suit, then we can say definitively that card1 isn't a trump (because the two cards have different suits), and trumps always win, so card2 is the higher card:

```
      else
      {
         if (useTrumps && (card2.suit == Card.trump))
            return false;
```

If card2 isn't a trump (or useTrumps is false) then card1 wins, as it was the first card laid down:

```
         else
            return true;
      }
   }
```

Only one other operator (>=) uses similar code to this, and the other operators are very simple, so I needn't go into any more detail about them.

The following simple client code tests out these operators (place it in the Main() function of a client project to test it out, like the client code we've seen earlier in the earlier CardLib examples):

```
Card.isAceHigh = true;
Console.WriteLine("Aces are high.");
Card.useTrumps = true;
Card.trump = Suit.Club;
Console.WriteLine("Clubs are trumps.");

Card card1, card2, card3, card4, card5;
card1 = new Card(Suit.Club, Rank.Five);
card2 = new Card(Suit.Club, Rank.Five);
card3 = new Card(Suit.Club, Rank.Ace);
card4 = new Card(Suit.Heart, Rank.Ten);
card5 = new Card(Suit.Diamond, Rank.Ace);
Console.WriteLine("{0} == {1} ? {2}",
    card1.ToString(), card2.ToString(), card1 == card2);
Console.WriteLine("{0} != {1} ? {2}",       card1.ToString(), card3.ToString(),
card1 != card3);
Console.WriteLine("{0}.Equals({1}) ? {2}",
    card1.ToString(), card4.ToString(), card1.Equals(card4));
Console.WriteLine("Card.Equals({0}, {1}) ? {2}",
    card3.ToString(), card4.ToString(), Card.Equals(card3, card4));
Console.WriteLine("{0} > {1} ? {2}",
    card1.ToString(), card2.ToString(), card1 > card2);
Console.WriteLine("{0} <= {1} ? {2}",
    card1.ToString(), card3.ToString(), card1 <= card3);
Console.WriteLine("{0} > {1} ? {2}",
    card1.ToString(), card4.ToString(), card1 > card4);
Console.WriteLine("{0} > {1} ? {2}",
    card4.ToString(), card1.ToString(), card4 > card1);
Console.WriteLine("{0} > {1} ? {2}",
    card5.ToString(), card4.ToString(), card5 > card4);
Console.WriteLine("{0} > {1} ? {2}",
    card4.ToString(), card5.ToString(), card4 > card5);
```

The results are as follows:

```
C:\BegVCSharp\Chapter11\Ch11CardClient\bin\Debug\Ch11CardClient.exe
Aces are high.
Clubs are trumps.
The Five of Clubs == The Five of Clubs ? True
The Five of Clubs != The Ace of Clubs ? True
The Five of Clubs.Equals(The Ten of Hearts) ? False
Card.Equals(The Ace of Clubs, The Ten of Hearts) ? False
The Five of Clubs > The Five of Clubs ? False
The Five of Clubs <= The Ace of Clubs ? True
The Five of Clubs > The Ten of Hearts ? True
The Ten of Hearts > The Five of Clubs ? False
The Ace of Diamonds > The Ten of Hearts ? True
The Ten of Hearts > The Ace of Diamonds ? True
Press any key to continue
```

In each case, the operators are applied taking the specified rules into account. This is particularly apparent in the last four lines of output, demonstrating how trump cards always beat non-trumps.

Advanced Conversions

Now that we know how to define conversion operators we are in a position to round off our knowledge of type conversion by looking at a few more features of the C# language. In this section, we'll look at:

- ❑ Boxing and unboxing – conversion between reference and value types
- ❑ The `is` operator – used to check a variable to see if it is of a given type, or if it is compatible with that type
- ❑ The `as` operator – used to convert a variable into a given type, in a slightly different way to casting

Boxing and Unboxing

In Chapter 8, we discussed the difference between reference and value types, which was illustrated in Chapter 9 by comparing structs (which are value types) with classes (which are reference types). **Boxing** is the act of converting a value type into the `System.Object` type, or to an interface type that is implemented by the value type. **Unboxing** is the opposite conversion.

For example, suppose we have the following struct type:

```
struct MyStruct
{
    public int Val;
}
```

We can box a struct of this type by placing it into an `object`-type variable:

```
MyStruct valType1 = new MyStruct();
valType1.Val = 5;
object refType = valType1;
```

Here we create a new variable (`valType1`) of type `MyStruct`, assign a value to the `Val` member of this `struct`, then box it into an `object`-type variable (`refType`).

The object created by boxing a variable in this way contains a reference to a copy of the value-type variable, not a reference to the original value-type variable. We can verify this by modifying the contents of the original struct, then unboxing the struct contained in the object into a new variable and examining its contents:

```
valType1.Val = 6;
MyStruct valType2 = (MyStruct)refType;
Console.WriteLine("valType2.Val = {0}", valType2.Val);
```

This code would give us the following output:

```
valType2.Val = 5
```

When we assign a reference type to an object, however, we get a different behavior. We can illustrate this by changing `MyStruct` into a class (ignoring the fact that the name of this class isn't appropriate any more):

```
class MyStruct
{
    public int Val;
}
```

With no changes to the client code shown above (again ignoring the misnamed variables), we get the following output:

```
valType2.Val = 6
```

We can also box value types into interface types, so long as they implement that interface. For example, suppose our `MyStruct` type implements the `IMyInterface` interface as follows:

```
interface IMyInterface
{
}
```

```
struct MyStruct : IMyInterface
{
    public int Val;
}
```

We can then box the struct into an `IMyInterface` type as follows:

```
MyStruct valType1 = new MyStruct();
IMyInterface refType = valType1;
```

and we can unbox it using the normal casting syntax:

```
MyStruct ValType2 = (MyStruct)refType;
```

As you can see from these examples, boxing is performed without our intervention (that is, we don't have to write any code to make this possible). Unboxing a value requires an explicit conversion, however, and requires us to make a cast (boxing is implicit and doesn't have this requirement).

You might be wondering why we would actually want to do this. There are actually two very good reasons why boxing is extremely useful. Firstly, it allows us to use value types in collections (such as `ArrayList`), where the items are of type `object`. Secondly, it's the internal mechanism that allows us to call `object` methods on value types, such as `int`s and structs.

As a final note, it is worth remarking that unboxing is necessary before access to the value type contents is possible.

The is Operator

The is operator allows us to check whether an unknown variable (perhaps one passed as an object parameter to a method) can be converted into a given type, evaluating to true if a conversion is possible. We can use this before calling methods on the object to check that the object is of a type that implements that method.

> The is operator does *not* check whether two types are identical, but whether they are compatible.

The is operator has the syntax:

```
<operand> is <type>
```

The possible results of this expression are as follows:

- ❑ If `<type>` is a class type then the result is true if `<operand>` is of that type, if it inherits from that type, or if it can be boxed into that type.

- ❑ If `<type>` is an interface type then the result is true if `<operand>` is of that type, or if it is a type that implements the interface.

- ❑ If `<type>` is a value type then the result is true if `<operand>` is of that type, or if it is a type that can be unboxed into that type.

Let's look at a few examples to see how this works in practice.

Try it Out – Using the is Operator

1. Create a new console application called Ch11Ex03 in the directory C:\BegVCSharp\Chapter11.

2. Modify the code in Class1.cs as follows:

```
namespace Ch11Ex03
{
    class Checker
    {
        public void Check(object param1)
        {
            if (param1 is ClassA)
                Console.WriteLine("Variable can be converted to ClassA.");
            else
                Console.WriteLine("Variable can't be converted to ClassA.");
```

```
        if (param1 is IMyInterface)
            Console.WriteLine("Variable can be converted to IMyInterface.");
        else
            Console.WriteLine("Variable can't be converted to IMyInterface.");

        if (param1 is MyStruct)
            Console.WriteLine("Variable can be converted to MyStruct.");
        else
            Console.WriteLine("Variable can't be converted to MyStruct.");
    }
}

interface IMyInterface
{
}

class ClassA : IMyInterface
{
}

class ClassB : IMyInterface
{
}
class ClassC
{
}

class ClassD : ClassA
{
}

struct MyStruct : IMyInterface
{
}

class Class1
{
    static void Main(string[] args)
    {
        Checker check = new Checker();
        ClassA try1 = new ClassA();
        ClassB try2 = new ClassB();
        ClassC try3 = new ClassC();
        ClassD try4 = new ClassD();
        MyStruct try5 = new MyStruct();
        object try6 = try5;
        Console.WriteLine("Analyzing ClassA type variable:");
        check.Check(try1);

        Console.WriteLine("\nAnalyzing ClassB type variable:");
        check.Check(try2);
        Console.WriteLine("\nAnalyzing ClassC type variable:");
        check.Check(try3);
```

```
            Console.WriteLine("\nAnalyzing ClassD type variable:");
            check.Check(try4);
            Console.WriteLine("\nAnalyzing MyStruct type variable:");
            check.Check(try5);
            Console.WriteLine("\nAnalyzing boxed MyStruct type variable:");
            check.Check(try6);
        }
    }
}
```

3. Execute the code:

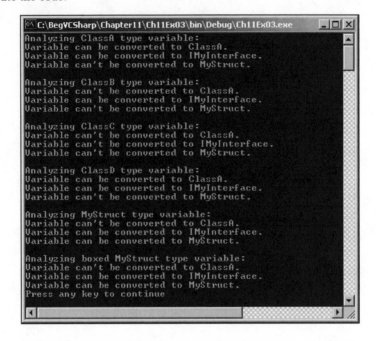

How It Works

This example illustrates the various results possible when using the is operator. Three classes, an interface, and a structure are defined and used as parameters to a method of a class that uses the is operator to see if they can be converted into the ClassA type, the interface type, and the struct type.

Only ClassA and ClassD (which inherits from ClassA) types are compatible with ClassA. Types that don't inherit from a class are not compatible with that class.

The ClassA, ClassB, and MyStruct types all implement IMyInterface, so these are all compatible with the IMyInterface type. ClassD inherits from ClassA, so that it too is compatible. Therefore, only ClassC is incompatible.

Finally, only variables of type MyStruct itself and boxed variables of that type are compatible with MyStruct, as we can't convert reference types to value types (except, of course, that we can unbox previously boxed variables).

The as Operator

The as operator converts a type into a specified reference type using the following syntax:

```
<operand> as <type>
```

This is only possible in certain circumstances:

❑ If *<operand>* is of type *<type>*

❑ If *<operand>* can be implicitly converted to type *<type>*

❑ If *<operand>* can be boxed into type *<type>*

If no conversion from *<operand>* to *<type>* is possible then the result of the expression will be null.

Note that conversion from a base class to a derived class is possible using an explicit conversion, but won't always work. Consider the two classes ClassA and ClassD from our last example, where ClassD inherits from ClassA. The following code uses the as operator to convert from a ClassA instance stored in obj1 into the ClassD type:

```
ClassA obj1 = new ClassA();
ClassD obj2 = obj1 as ClassD;
```

This will result in obj2 being null.

However, it is possible to store ClassD instances in ClassA-type variables using polymorphism. The following code illustrates this, and uses the as operator to convert from a ClassA-type variable containing a ClassD-type instance into the ClassD type:

```
ClassD obj1 = new ClassD();
ClassA obj2 = obj1;
ClassD obj3 = obj2 as ClassD;
```

This time the result is that obj3 ends up containing a reference to the same object as obj1, not null.

This functionality makes the as operator very useful, as the following code using simple casting results in an exception being thrown:

```
ClassA obj1 = new ClassA();
ClassD obj2 = (ClassD)obj1;
```

The as equivalent of this code results in a null value being assigned to obj2 – no exception is thrown. This means that code such as the following (using two of the classes developed earlier in this chapter, Animal and a class derived from Animal called Cow) is very common in C# applications:

```
public void MilkCow(Animal myAnimal)
{
    Cow myCow = myAnimal as Cow;
    if (myCow != null)
    {
        myCow.Milk();
    }
    else
    {
        Console.WriteLine("{0} isn't a cow, and so can't be milked.",
            myAnimal.Name);
    }
}
```

This is much simpler than checking for exceptions!

Deep Copying

In Chapter 9, we saw how we can perform shallow copying using the
`System.Object.MemberwiseClone()` protected method, using a method like the `GetCopy()` one
shown below:

```
public class Cloner
{
    public int Val;

    public Cloner(int newVal)
    {
        Val = newVal;
    }

    public object GetCopy()
    {
        return MemberwiseClone();
    }
}
```

Suppose we have fields that are reference types rather than value types (for example, objects):

```
public class Content
{
    public int Val;
}

public class Cloner
{
    public Content MyContent = new Content();

    public Cloner(int newVal)
    {
        MyContent.Val = newVal;
    }
```

```
    public object GetCopy()
    {
        return MemberwiseClone();
    }
}
```

In this case, the shallow copy obtained though `GetCopy()` will have a field that refers to the same object as the original object.

The following code demonstrates this using this class:

```
Cloner mySource = new Cloner(5);
Cloner myTarget = (Cloner)mySource.GetCopy();
Console.WriteLine("myTarget.MyContent.Val = {0}", myTarget.MyContent.Val);
mySource.MyContent.Val = 2;
Console.WriteLine("myTarget.MyContent.Val = {0}", myTarget.MyContent.Val);
```

The fourth line, which assigns a value to `mySource.MyContent.Val`, the `Val` public field of the `MyContent` public field of the original object, also changes the value of `myTarget.MyContent.Val`. This is because `mySource.MyContent` refers to the same object instance as `myTarget.MyContent`. The output of the above code is as follows:

```
myTarget.MyContent.Val = 5
myTarget.MyContent.Val = 2
```

To get round this we need to perform a deep copy. We could just modify the `GetCopy()` method used above to do this, but it is preferable to use the standard .NET Framework way of doing things. To do this, we implement the `ICloneable` interface, which has the single method `Clone()`. This method takes no parameters, and returns an `object` type result, giving it a signature identical to the `GetCopy()` method used above.

Modifying the classes used above, we might use the following deep copy code:

```
public class Content
{
    public int Val;
}

public class Cloner : ICloneable
{
    public Content MyContent = new Content();

    public Cloner(int newVal)
    {
        MyContent.Val = newVal;
    }

    public object Clone()
    {
        Cloner clonedCloner = new Cloner(MyContent.Val);
        return clonedCloner;
    }
}
```

Here we create a new `Cloner` object using the `Val` field of the `Content` object contained in the original `Cloner` object (`MyContent`). This field is a value type, so no deeper copying is necessary.

Using code similar to that shown above to test the shallow copy, but using `Clone()` instead of `GetCopy()`, gives us the following result:

```
myTarget.MyContent.Val = 5
myTarget.MyContent.Val = 5
```

This time the contained objects are independent.

Note that there are times where calls to `Clone()` will be made recursively, in more complex object systems. For example, if the `MyContent` field of the `Cloner` class also required deep copying, we might need the following:

```
public class Cloner : ICloneable
{
    public Content MyContent = new Content();

    ...

    public object Clone()
    {
        Cloner clonedCloner = new Cloner();
        clonedCloner.MyContent = MyContent.Clone();
        return clonedCloner;
    }
}
```

We're calling the default constructor here to simplify the syntax of creating a new `Cloner` object. In order for this code to work we would also need to implement `ICloneable` on the `Content` class.

Upgrading CardLib Part 3

Let's put this into practice by implementing the ability to copy `Card`, `Cards`, and `Deck` objects using the `ICloneable` interface. This might be useful in some card games, where we might not necessarily want two decks with references to the same set of `Card` objects, although we might conceivably want to set up one deck to have the same card order as another.

Implementing cloning functionality for the `Card` class in `Ch11CardLib` is simple, as shallow copying is sufficient (`Card` only contains value-type data, in the form of fields). We just need to make the following changes to the class definition:

```
public class Card : ICloneable
{
    public object Clone()
    {
        return MemberwiseClone();
    }
```

Note that this implementation of ICloneable is just a shallow copy. There is no rule determining what should happen in the Clone() method, and this is sufficient for our purposes.

Next we need to implement ICloneable on the Cards collection class. This is slightly more complicated as it involves cloning every Card object in the original collection – so we need to make a deep copy:

```
public class Cards : CollectionBase, ICloneable
{
   public object Clone()
   {
      Cards newCards = new Cards();
      foreach (Card sourceCard in List)
      {
         newCards.Add(sourceCard.Clone() as Card);
      }
      return newCards;
   }
```

Finally, we need to implement ICloneable on the Deck class. There is a slight problem here: the Deck class has no way of modifying the cards it contains, short of shuffling them. There is no way, for example, to modify a Deck instance to have a given card order. To get round this we define a new private constructor for the Deck class that allows a specific Cards collection to be passed in when the Deck object is instantiated. The code to implement cloning in this class is therefore:

```
public class Deck : ICloneable
{
   public object Clone()
   {
      Deck newDeck = new Deck(cards.Clone() as Cards);
      return newDeck;
   }

   private Deck(Cards newCards)
   {
      cards = newCards;
   }
}
```

Again, we can test this out with some simple client code (as before, this should be placed within the Main() method of a client project to test this out):

```
Deck deck1 = new Deck();
Deck deck2 = (Deck)deck1.Clone();
Console.WriteLine("The first card in the original deck is: {0}",
               deck1.GetCard(0));
Console.WriteLine("The first card in the cloned deck is: {0}",
               deck2.GetCard(0));
deck1.Shuffle();
Console.WriteLine("Original deck shuffled.");
Console.WriteLine("The first card in the original deck is: {0}",
               deck1.GetCard(0));
Console.WriteLine("The first card in the cloned deck is: {0}",
               deck2.GetCard(0));
```

The output will be something like this:

```
C:\BegVCSharp\Chapter11\Ch11CardClient\bin\Debug\Ch11CardClient.exe
The first card in the original deck is: The Ace of Clubs
The first card in the cloned deck is: The Ace of Clubs
Original deck shuffled.
The first card in the original deck is: The Five of Clubs
The first card in the cloned deck is: The Ace of Clubs
Press any key to continue
```

One point to note here is that the current card rules, which are defined in static members of the Card class, apply to all Card objects in every Deck. It is not possible to have two decks of cards with cards contained in each that obey different rules. This is fine for this class library, however, as we can safely assume that if a single application wants to use separate rules then it could maintain these itself, perhaps setting the static members of Card whenever decks are switched.

Custom Exceptions

Earlier in the book, we discussed exceptions and how we can use try...catch...finally blocks to act on them. We also saw several standard .NET exceptions, including the base class for exceptions System.Exception. Sometimes it can be useful to derive your own exception classes from this base class and use them in your applications, instead of using the standard exceptions. This allows you to be more specific about the information you send to whatever code catches the exception, and allows catching code to be more specific about which exceptions it handles. You might, for example, add a new property to your exception class that permits access to some underlying information, making it possible for the receiver of the exception to make the required changes, or just giving more information as to the exception cause.

Once we have defined an exception class we can add it to the list of exceptions recognized by VS using the Debug | Exceptions... menu item. Through this dialog we can control how VS responds when an unhandled exception of that type is thrown. The dialog allows us to get VS to stop execution and start the debugger or to continue executing. We can choose to do this either as soon as an exception of this type is thrown or only if the exception is not handled:

Upgrading CardLib Part 4

The use of custom exceptions is, once again, best illustrated by upgrading the `Ch11CardLib` project. The `Deck.GetCard()` method currently throws a standard .NET exception if an attempt is made to access a card with an index less than 0 or greater than 51, but we'll modify this to use a custom exception.

First, we need to define the exception. We do this with a new class defined in a new class file called `Exceptions.cs`, which we can add to the `Ch11CardLib` project with **File | Add New Item**:

```
public class CardOutOfRangeException : Exception
{
   private Cards deckContents;

   public Cards DeckContents
   {
      get
      {
         return deckContents;
      }
   }

   public CardOutOfRangeException(Cards sourceDeckContents) :
         base("There are only 52 cards in the deck.")
   {
      deckContents = sourceDeckContents;
   }
}
```

An instance of the `Cards` class is required for this classes's constructor. It allows access to this `Cards` object through a `DeckContents` property, and supplies a suitable error message to the base `Exception` constructor, so that it is available through the `Message` property of the class.

Next we add code to throw this exception to `Deck.cs` (replacing the old standard exception):

```
public Card GetCard(int cardNum)
{
    if (cardNum >= 0 && cardNum <= 51)
        return cards[cardNum];
    else
        throw new CardOutOfRangeException(cards.Clone() as Cards);
}
```

The `DeckContents` property is initialized with a deep copy of the current contents of the `Deck` object, in the form of a `Cards` object. This means that we see what the contents were at the point where the exception was thrown, so subsequent modification to the deck contents won't "lose" this information.

To test this out, we can use the following client code:

```
Deck deck1 = new Deck();
try
{
    Card myCard = deck1.GetCard(60);
}
catch (CardOutOfRangeException e)
{
    Console.WriteLine(e.Message);
    Console.WriteLine(e.DeckContents[0]);
}
```

resulting in:

Here the catching code has written the exception `Message` property to the screen. We also displayed the first card in the `Cards` object obtained through `DeckContents`, just to prove that we can access the `Cards` collection through our custom exception object.

Summary

In this chapter we have covered many of the techniques that we can use to make our OOP applications far more powerful, and more interesting. Although these techniques take a little effort to accomplish they can make our classes much easier to work with, and therefore simplify the task of writing the rest of the code.

Each of the topics covered has many uses. You're likely to come across collections of one form or another in almost any application, and creating strongly typed collections can make our life much easier if we need to work with a group of objects of the same type. Once we have our collection, we saw how we can add indexers to get easy access to objects within the collection.

We also looked at operator overloading, which allows us to define how operators such as + and – work with our classes, and at deep copying, which can be fundamentally important to avoid one of the most common errors in OOP – accidentally passing a reference to internal data to a user. Finally, we saw how to implement our own exception objects, and pass more detailed information to the exception handler.

In the next chapter we'll look at one last, and very important, aspect of OOP in .NET – events.

Exercises

1. Create a collection class called `People` that is a collection of the `Person` class shown below. The items in the collection should be accessible via a string indexer that is the name of the person, identical to the `Person.Name` property:

```
public class Person
{
    private string name;
    private int age;

    public string Name
    {
        get
        {
            return name;
        }
        set
        {
            name = value;
        }
    }

    public int Age
    {
        get
        {
            return age;
        }
        set
        {
            age = value;
        }
    }
}
```

2. Extend the `Person` class from the above exercise so that the >, <, >=, and <= operators are overloaded, and compare the `Age` properties of `Person` instances.

3. Add a `GetOldest()` method to the `People` class that returns an array of `Person` objects with the greatest `Age` property (1 or more objects, as multiple items may have the same value for this property), using the overloaded operators defined above.

4. Implement the `ICloneable` interface on the `People` class to provide deep copying capability.

Events

This is the last chapter in the OOP section of this book, and completes our discussion by looking at one of the most frequently used OOP techniques in .NET: **events**.

We'll start, as usual, with the basics – looking at what events actually are. After this we'll move on to see some simple events in action and look at what we can do with them. Once this is described, we'll move on to look at how we can create and use events of our own.

In the second part of this chapter we'll polish off our CardLib class library by adding an event. In addition, and since this is the last port of call before hitting some more advanced topics, we'll have a bit of fun. We'll create a card game application that uses this class library.

To start with, then, let's look at what events are.

What is an Event?

Events are similar to exceptions in that they are **raised** (thrown) by objects and we can supply code that acts on them. However, there are several important differences. The most important of these is that there is no equivalent to the try...catch structure for handling events. Instead we must **subscribe** to them. Subscribing to an event means supplying code that will be executed when an event is raised, in the form of an **event handler**.

An event can have many handlers subscribed to it, which will all be called when the event is raised. This may include event handlers that are part of the class of the object that raises the event, but event handlers are just as likely to be found in other classes.

Event handlers themselves are simply functions. The only restriction on an event handler function is that it must match the signature (return type and parameters) required by the event. This signature is part of the definition of an event, and is specified by a **delegate**.

The fact that delegates are used in events is what makes delegates such useful things. This is the reason we devoted some time to them back in Chapter 6, and you may wish to re-read that section to refresh your memory as to what delegates are and how we use them.

The sequence of processing goes something like this.

First, an application creates an object that can raise an event. As an example, let's say that the application is an instant messaging application, and that the object it creates represents a connection to a remote user. This connection object might raise an event, say, when a message arrives through the connection from the remote user.

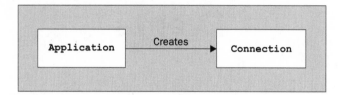

Next, the application subscribes to the event. Our instant messaging application would do this by defining a function that could be used with the delegate type specified by the event, and passing a reference to this function to the event. This event handler function might be a method on another object, let's say an object representing a display device to display instant messages on when they arrive.

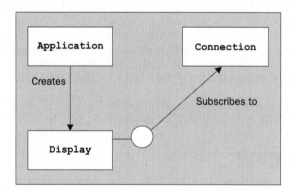

When the event is raised, the subscriber is notified. When an instant message arrives through the connection object, the event handler method on the display device object is called. As we are using a standard method, the object that raises the event may pass any relevant information via parameters, making events very versatile. In our example case, one parameter might be the text of the instant message, which the event handler could display on the display device object.

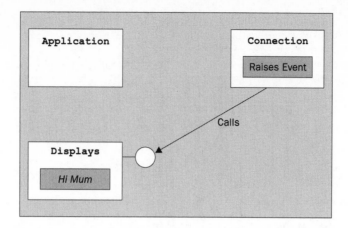

Using Events

In this section we'll look at the code required for handling events, then move on to look at how we can define and use our own.

Handling Events

As we have discussed, to handle an event we need to subscribe to the event by providing an event handler function whose signature matches that of the delegate specified for use with the event. Let's look at an example that uses a simple timer object to raise events, which will result in a handler function being called.

Try it Out – Handling Events

1. Create a new console application called `Ch12Ex01` in the directory `C:\BegVCSharp\Chapter12`.

2. Modify the code in `Class1.cs` as follows:

```
using System;
using System.Timers;

namespace Ch12Ex01
{
   class Class1
   {
      static int counter = 0;

      static string displayString =
                      "This string will appear one letter at a time. ";

      static void Main(string[] args)
      {
```

```
        Timer myTimer = new Timer(100);
        myTimer.Elapsed += new ElapsedEventHandler(WriteChar);
        myTimer.Start();
        Console.ReadLine();
    }

    static void WriteChar(object source, ElapsedEventArgs e)
    {
        Console.Write(displayString[counter++ % displayString.Length]);
    }
  }
}
```

3. Run the application (once running, hitting enter will terminate the application):

```
C:\BegVCSharp\Chapter12\Ch12Ex01\bin\Debug\Ch12Ex01.exe                    _ □ X
This string will appear one letter at a time. This string will ap▲
at a time. This string will appear one letter at a time. This st
r one letter at a time. This string will appear one letter at a t
g will appear one letter at a time. This string will appear one l
. This string will appear one letter at a time. This string will ▼
◄                                                                  ► //
```

How it Works

The object we are using to raise events is an instance of the `System.Timers.Timer` class. This object
is initialized with a time period (in milliseconds). When the `Timer` object is started using its `Start()`
method a stream of events will be raised, spaced out in time according to the specified time period.
`Main()` initializes a `Timer` object with a timer period of 100 milliseconds, so it will raise events 10
times a second when started:

```
        static void Main(string[] args)
        {
            Timer myTimer = new Timer(100);
```

The `Timer` object possesses an event called `Elapsed`, and the event handler signature required by this
event is that of the `System.Timers.ElapsedEventHandler` delegate type, which is one of the
standard delegates defined in the .NET Framework. This delegate is used for functions that match the
following signature:

```
   void functionName(object source, ElapsedEventArgs e);
```

The `Timer` object sends a reference to itself in the first parameter, and an instance of an
`ElapsedEventArgs` object in its second parameter. It is safe to ignore these parameters for now, but
we'll take a look at them a little later.

In our code we have a method that matches this signature:

```
        static void WriteChar(object source, ElapsedEventArgs e)
        {
            Console.Write(displayString[counter++ % displayString.Length]);
        }
```

This method uses the two static fields of `Class1`, `counter` and `displayString`, to display a single character. Every time the method is called the character displayed will be different.

The next task is to hook this handler up to the event – to subscribe to it. To do this we use the `+=` operator to add a handler to the event in the form of a new delegate instance initialized with our event handler method:

```
static void Main(string[] args)
{
    Timer myTimer = new Timer(100);
    myTimer.Elapsed += new ElapsedEventHandler(WriteChar);
```

This command (which uses slightly strange looking syntax, specific to delegates) adds a handler to the list that will be called when the `Elapsed` event is raised. We can add as many handlers as we like to this list, as long as they all meet the criteria required. Each handler will be called in turn when the event is raised.

All that is left for `Main()` is to start the timer running:

```
    myTimer.Start();
```

Since we don't want the application terminating before we have handled any events, we then put the `Main()` function on hold. The simplest way of doing this is to request user input, since this command won't finish processing until the user has entered a line of text and/or pressed enter.

```
    Console.ReadLine();
```

Although processing in `Main()` effectively ceases here, processing in the `Timer` object continues. When it raises events it calls our `WriteChar()` method, which runs concurrently with the `Console.ReadLine()` statement.

Defining Events

Next, let's look at defining and using our own events. We'll implement an example version of the instant messaging case set out in the introduction to events in this chapter, and create a `Connection` object that raises events that are handled by a `Display` object.

Try it Out – Defining Events

1. Create a new console application called `Ch12Ex02` in the directory `C:\BegVCSharp\Chapter12`.

2. Add a new class, `Connection`, stored in `Connection.cs`:

```
using System;
using System.Timers;

namespace Ch12Ex02
{
public delegate void MessageHandler(string messageText);
```

```csharp
public class Connection
{
    public event MessageHandler MessageArrived;

    private Timer pollTimer;

    public Connection()
    {
        pollTimer = new Timer(100);
        pollTimer.Elapsed += new ElapsedEventHandler(CheckForMessage);
    }

    public void Connect()
    {
        pollTimer.Start();
    }

    public void Disconnect()
    {
        pollTimer.Stop();
    }

    private void CheckForMessage(object source, ElapsedEventArgs e)
    {
        Console.WriteLine("Checking for new messages.");
        Random random = new Random();
        if ((random.Next(9) == 0) && (MessageArrived != null))
        {
            MessageArrived("Hello Mum!");
        }
    }
}
```

3. Add a new class, `Display`, stored in `Display.cs`:

```csharp
using System;

namespace Ch12Ex02
{
    public class Display
    {
        public void DisplayMessage(string message)
        {
            Console.WriteLine("Message arrived: {0}", message);
        }
    }
}
```

4. Modify the code in `Class1.cs` as follows:

```csharp
using System;

namespace Ch12Ex02
{
    class Class1
```

```
{
    static void Main(string[] args)
    {
        Connection myConnection = new Connection();
        Display myDisplay = new Display();
        myConnection.MessageArrived +=
                new MessageHandler (myDisplay.DisplayMessage);
        myConnection.Connect();
        Console.ReadLine();
    }
}
}
```

5. Run the application:

How it Works

The class that does most of the work in this application is the `Connection` class. Instances of this class make use of a `Timer` object much like the one we saw in the first example of this chapter, initializing it in the class constructor and giving access to its state (enabled or disabled) via `Connect()` and `Disconnect()`:

```
public class Connection
{
    private Timer pollTimer;

    public Connection()
    {
        pollTimer = new Timer(100);
        pollTimer.Elapsed += new ElapsedEventHandler(CheckForMessage);
    }

    public void Connect()
    {
        pollTimer.Start();
    }
```

```
        public void Disconnect()
        {
            pollTimer.Stop();
        }

        ...

    }
```

Also in the constructor, we register an event handler for the `Elapsed` event in the same way as we did in the first example. The handler method, `CheckForMessage()`, will raise an event on average once every ten times it is called. Before we look at the code for this, though, let's look at the event definition itself.

Before we define an event we must define a delegate type to use with the event, that is, a delegate type that specifies the signature that an event handling method must conform to. We do this using standard delegate syntax, defining it as public inside the `Ch11Ex02` namespace in order to make the type available to external code:

```
namespace Ch12Ex02
{
    public delegate void MessageHandler(string messageText);
```

This delegate type, which we've called `MessageHandler` here, is a signature for a `void` function that has a single `string` parameter. We can use this parameter to pass an instant message received by the `Connection` object to the `Display` object.

Once a delegate has been defined (or a suitable existing delegate has been located) we can define the event itself, as a member of the `Connection` class:

```
    public class Connection
    {
        public event MessageHandler MessageArrived;
```

We simply name the event (here we have used the name `MessageArrived`), and declare it using the `event` keyword and the delegate type to use (the `MessageHandler` delegate type defined earlier).

Once we have declared an event in this way we can raise it simply by calling it by its name as if it were a method with the signature specified by the delegate. For example, we could raise this event using:

```
    MessageArrived("This is a message.");
```

If the delegate had been defined without any parameters we could use simply:

```
    MessageArrived();
```

Alternatively we could have defined more parameters, which would have required more code to raise the event.

Our `CheckForMessage()` method looks like this:

```
private void CheckForMessage(object source, ElapsedEventArgs e)
{
    Console.WriteLine("Checking for new messages.");
    Random random = new Random();
    if ((random.Next(9) == 0) && (MessageArrived != null))
    {
        MessageArrived("Hello Mum!");
    }
}
```

We use an instance of the `Random` class that we have seen in earlier chapters to generate a random number between 0 and 9, and raise an event if the number generated is 0, which should happen 10% of the time. This simulates polling the connection to see if a message has arrived, which won't be the case every time we check.

Note that we supply additional logic. We only raise an event if the expression `MessageArrived !=` `null` evaluates to `true`. This expression, which again uses the delegate syntax in a slightly unusual way, means: "Does the event have any subscribers?" If there are no subscribers, `MessageArrived` will evaluate to `null`, and there would be no point in raising the event.

The class that will subscribe to the event is called `Display`, and contains the single method `DisplayMessage()` defined as follows:

```
public class Display
{
    public void DisplayMessage(string message)
    {
        Console.WriteLine("Message arrived: {0}", message);
    }
}
```

This method matches the delegate type method signature (and is public, which is a requirement of event handlers in classes other than the class that generates the event), so we can use it to respond to the `MessageArrived` event.

All that is left now is for the code in `Main()` to initialize instances of the `Connection` and `Display` classes, hook them up, and start things going. The code required here is similar to that from the first example:

```
static void Main(string[] args)
{
    Connection myConnection = new Connection();
    Display myDisplay = new Display();
    myConnection.MessageArrived +=
            new MessageHandler(myDisplay.DisplayMessage);
    myConnection.Connect();
    Console.ReadLine();
}
```

Again, we call `Console.ReadLine()` to pause the processing of `Main()` once we have started things moving with the `Connect()` method of the `Connection` object.

Multi-Purpose Event Handlers

The signature we saw earlier, for the `Timer.Elapsed` event, contained two parameters that are of a type often seen in event handlers. These parameters are:

- ❑   `object source` – a reference to the object that raised the event
- ❑   `ElapsedEventArgs e` – parameters sent by the event

The reason that the `object` type parameter is used in this event, and indeed in many other events, is that we will often want to use a single event handler for several identical events generated by different objects and still tell which object generated the event.

To explain and illustrate this, let's extend our last example a little.

Try it Out – Using a Multi-Purpose Event Handler

1.   Create a new console application called `Ch12Ex03` in the directory `C:\BegVCSharp\Chapter12`.

2.   Copy the code across for `Class1.cs`, `Connection.cs`, and `Display.cs` from `Ch12Ex02`, making sure you change the namespaces in each file from `Ch12Ex02` to `Ch12Ex03`.

3.   Add a new class, `MessageArrivedEventArgs`, stored in `MessageArrivedEventArgs.cs`:

```
using System;

namespace Ch12Ex03
{
    public class MessageArrivedEventArgs : EventArgs
    {
        private string message;

        public string Message
        {
            get
            {
                return message;
            }
        }

        public MessageArrivedEventArgs()
        {
            message = "No message sent.";
        }

        public MessageArrivedEventArgs(string newMessage)
        {
            message = newMessage;
        }
    }
}
```

4. Modify `Connection.cs` as follows:

```
namespace Ch12Ex03
{
    public delegate void MessageHandler(Connection source,
                                        MessageArrivedEventArgs e);

    public class Connection
    {
        public event MessageHandler MessageArrived;

        private string name;

        public string Name
        {
            get
            {
                return name;
            }
            set
            {
                name = value;
            }
        }

        ...

        private void CheckForMessage(object source, EventArgs e)
        {
            Console.WriteLine("Checking for new messages.");
            Random random = new Random();
            if ((random.Next(9) == 0) && (MessageArrived != null))
            {
                MessageArrived(this, new MessageArrivedEventArgs("Hello Mum!"));
            }
        }

        ...

    }
}
```

5. Modify `Display.cs` as follows:

```
        public void DisplayMessage(Connection source, MessageArrivedEventArgs e)
        {
            Console.WriteLine("Message arrived from: {0}", source.Name);
            Console.WriteLine("Message Text: {0}", e.Message);
        }
```

6. Modify `Class1.cs` as follows:

```
static void Main(string[] args)
{
    Connection myConnection1 = new Connection();
    myConnection1.Name = "First connection.";
    Connection myConnection2 = new Connection();
    myConnection2.Name = "Second connection.";
    Display myDisplay = new Display();
    myConnection1.MessageArrived +=
                    new MessageHandler(myDisplay.DisplayMessage);
    myConnection2.MessageArrived +=
                    new MessageHandler(myDisplay.DisplayMessage);
    myConnection1.Connect();
    myConnection2.Connect();
    Console.ReadLine();
}
```

7. Run the application:

How it Works

By sending a reference to the object that raises an event as one of the event handler parameters we can customize the response of the handler to individual objects. The reference gives us access to the source object, including its properties.

By sending parameters that are contained in a class that inherits from `System.EventArgs` (as `ElapsedEventArgs` does) we can supply whatever additional information necessary as parameters (such as the `Message` parameter on our `MessageArrivedEventArgs` class).

In addition, these parameters will benefit from polymorphism. We could define a handler for the `MessageArrived` event such as:

```
        public void DisplayMessage(object source, EventArgs e)
    {
        Console.WriteLine("Message arrived from: {0}",
                          ((Connection)source).Name);
        Console.WriteLine("Message Text: {0}",
                          ((MessageArrivedEventArgs)e).Message);
    }
```

and modify the delegate definition in `Connection.cs` as follows:

```
    public delegate void MessageHandler(object source, EventArgs e);
```

The application will execute exactly as it did before, but we have made the `DisplayMessage()` function more versatile (in theory at least – more implementation would be needed to make this production quality). This same handler could work with other events, such as the `Timer.Elapsed`, although we'd have to modify the internals of the handler a bit more such that the parameters sent when this event is raised are handled properly (casting them to `Connection` and `MessageArrivedEventArgs` objects in this way will cause an exception; we should use the `as` operator instead).

Return Values and Event Handlers

All the event handlers we've seen so far have had a return type of `void`. It is possible to provide a return type for an event, but this can lead to problems. This is because a given event may result in several event handlers being called. If all of these handlers return a value it leaves us in some doubt as to which value was actually returned.

The system deals with this by only allowing us access to the last value returned by an event handler. This will be the value returned by the last event handler to subscribe to an event.

Perhaps this functionality might be of use in some situations, although I can't think of one off the top of my head. I'd recommend using `void` type event handlers, as well as avoiding `out` type parameters.

Expanding and Using CardLib

Now we've had a look at defining and using events, let's add to the class library developed in the last chapter, `Ch11CardLib`. As before, we'll use a class library project called `Ch12CardLib` which will initially have code identical to that in `Ch11CardLib` (apart from the namespace names used being `Ch12CardLib` instead of `Ch11CardLib`).

The event we'll add to our library will be generated when the last `Card` object in a `Deck` object is obtained using `GetCard`, and will be called `LastCardDrawn`. This event will allow subscribers to reshuffle the deck automatically, cutting down on the processing necessary by a client. The delegate defined for this event (`LastCardDrawnHandler`) needs to supply a reference to the `Deck` object such that the `Shuffle()` method will be accessible from wherever the handler is. Add the following code to `Deck.cs`:

```
    namespace Ch12CardLib
    {
        public delegate void LastCardDrawnHandler(Deck currentDeck);
```

The code to define the event and raise it is simply:

```
public event LastCardDrawnHandler LastCardDrawn;

public Card GetCard(int cardNum)
{
    if (cardNum >= 0 && cardNum <= 51)
    {
        if ((cardNum == 51) && (LastCardDrawn != null))
            LastCardDrawn(this);
        return cards[cardNum];
    }
    else
        throw new CardOutOfRangeException((Cards)cards.Clone());
}
```

This is all the code required to add the event to our Deck class definition. Now we just need to use it.

A Card Game Client for CardLib

After spending all this time developing the CardLib library it would be a shame not to use it. Before finishing this section on OOP in C# and the .NET Framework, it's time to have a little fun, and write the basics of a card game application that uses our familiar playing card classes.

As in previous chapters, we'll add a client console application to the Ch12CardLib solution, add a reference to the Ch12CardLib project, and make it the startup project. This application will be called Ch12CardClient.

To start with we'll create a new class called Player in a new file in Ch12CardClient, Player.cs. This class will contain a private Cards field called hand, a private string field called name, and two read-only properties: Name and PlayHand. These properties simply expose the private fields. Note that even though the PlayHand property is read-only we will have write access to the reference to the hand field returned, allowing us to modify the cards in the player's hand.

We'll also hide the default constructor by making it private, and supply a public non-default constructor that accepts an initial value for the Name property of Player instances.

Finally, we'll provide a bool type method called HasWon(). This will return true if all the cards in the player's hand are of the same suit (a simple winning condition, but that doesn't matter too much).

The code for Player.cs is as follows:

```
using System;
using Ch12CardLib;

namespace Ch12CardClient
{
    public class Player
    {
        private Cards hand;
        private string name;
```

```
        public string Name
        {
            get
            {
                return name;
            }
        }

        public Cards PlayHand
        {
            get
            {
                return hand;
            }
        }

        private Player()
        {
        }

        public Player(string newName)
        {
            name = newName;
            hand = new Cards();
        }

        public bool HasWon()
        {
            bool won = true;
            Suit match = hand[0].suit;
            for (int i = 1; i < hand.Count; i++)
            {
                won &= hand[i].suit == match;
            }
            return won;
        }
    }
}
```

Next we define a class that will handle the card game itself, called Game. This class is found in the file Game.cs of the Ch12CardClient project.

This class has four private member fields:

- ❏ playDeck – a Deck type variable containing the deck of cards to use
- ❏ currentCard – an int value used as a pointer to the next card in the deck to draw
- ❏ players – an array of Player objects representing the players of the game
- ❏ discardedCards – a Cards collection for the cards that have been discarded by players but not shuffled back into the deck

The default constructor for the class initializes and shuffles the Deck stored in playDeck, sets the currentCard pointer variable to 0 (the first card in playDeck), and wires up an event handler called Reshuffle() to the playDeck.LastCardDrawn event. This handler simply shuffles the deck, including the cards in discardedCards, and resets currentCard to 0, ready to read cards from the new deck.

The Game class also contains two utility methods, SetPlayers() for setting the players for the game (as an array of Player objects), and DealHands() for dealing hands to the players (7 cards each). The number of players allowed is restricted from 2 to 7 in order to make sure that there are enough cards to go round.

Finally, there is a PlayGame() method that contains the game logic itself. We'll come back to this function shortly, after we've looked at the code in Class1.cs. The rest of the code in Game.cs is as follows:

```csharp
using System;
using Ch12CardLib;

namespace Ch12CardClient
{
    public class Game
    {
        private int currentCard;
        private Deck playDeck;
        private Player[] players;
        private Cards discardedCards;

        public Game()
        {
            currentCard = 0;
            playDeck = new Deck(true);
            playDeck.LastCardDrawn += new LastCardDrawnHandler(Reshuffle);
            playDeck.Shuffle();
        }

        private void Reshuffle(Deck currentDeck)
        {
            currentDeck.Shuffle();
            discardedCards = new Cards();
            currentCard = 0;
        }

        public void SetPlayers(Player[] newPlayers)
        {
            if (newPlayers.Length > 7)
                throw new ArgumentException("A maximum of 7 players may play this" +
                                            " game.");

            if (newPlayers.Length < 2)
                throw new ArgumentException("A minimum of 2 players may play this" +
                                            " game.");

            players = newPlayers;
```

```
        }

        private void DealHands()
        {
            for (int p = 0; p < players.Length; p++)
            {
                for (int c = 0; c < 7; c++)
                {
                    players[p].PlayHand.Add(playDeck.GetCard(currentCard++));
                }
            }
        }

        public int PlayGame()
        {
            // Code to follow.
        }
    }
}
```

Class1.cs contains our Main() function, which will initialize and run the game. This function performs the following steps:

❑   An introduction is displayed.

❑   The user is prompted for a number of players between 2 and 7.

❑   An array of Player objects is set up accordingly.

❑   Each player is prompted for a name, used to initialize one Player object in the array.

❑   A Game object is created, and players assigned using the SetPlayers() method.

❑   The game is started using the PlayGame() method.

❑   The int return value of PlayGame() is used to display a winning message (the value returned is the index of the winning player in the array of Player objects).

The code for this (commented for clarity) is shown below:

```
static void Main(string[] args)
{
    // Display introduction.
    Console.WriteLine("KarliCards: a new and exciting card game.");
    Console.WriteLine("To win you must have 7 cards of the same suit in" +
                      " your hand.");
    Console.WriteLine();

    // Prompt for number of players.
    bool inputOK = false;
    int choice = -1;
    do
    {
        Console.WriteLine("How many players (2-7)?");
```

```
                string input = Console.ReadLine();
                try
                {
                    // Attempt to convert input into a valid number of players.
                    choice = Convert.ToInt32(input);
                    if ((choice >= 2) && (choice <= 7))
                        inputOK = true;
                }
                catch
                {
                    // Ignore failed conversions, just continue prompting.
                }
            } while (inputOK == false);

            // Initialize array of Player objects.
            Player[] players = new Player[choice];

            // Get player names.
            for (int p = 0; p < players.Length; p++)
            {
                Console.WriteLine("Player {0}, enter your name:", p + 1);
                string playerName = Console.ReadLine();
                players[p] = new Player(playerName);
            }

            // Start game.
            Game newGame = new Game();
            newGame.SetPlayers(players);
            int whoWon = newGame.PlayGame();

            // Display winning player.
            Console.WriteLine("{0} has won the game!", players[whoWon].Name);
        }
```

Next we come to `PlayGame()`, the main body of the application. Now, I'm not going to go into a huge amount of detail about this method, but I have filled it with comments to make it a bit more comprehensible. In actual fact, none of the code is that complicated, there's just quite a bit of it.

Play proceeds with each player viewing their cards and an upturned card on the table. They may either pick up this card or draw a new one from the deck. After drawing a card they must discard one, replacing the card on the table with another one if it has been picked up, or placing the discarded card on top of the one on the table (adding the previous card on the table to the `discardedCards` collection.

One key point to bear in mind when digesting this code is the way in which the `Card` objects are manipulated. The reason why these objects are defined as reference types rather than as value types (using a struct) should now become clear. A given `Card` object may appear to exist in several places at once, as references can be held by the `Deck` object, the hand fields of the `Player` objects, the `discardedCards` collection, and the `playCard` object (the card currently on the table). This makes it easy to keep track of the cards, and is used in particular in the code that draws a new card from the deck. The card is only accepted if it isn't in any player hand, on the table, or in the `discardedCards` collection.

The code is as follows:

```
public int PlayGame()
{
    // Only play if players exist.
    if (players == null)
        return -1;

    // Deal initial hands.
    DealHands();

    // Initialize game vars, including an initial card to place on the
    // table: playCard.
    bool GameWon = false;
    int currentPlayer;
    Card playCard = playDeck.GetCard(currentCard++);

    // Main game loop, continues until GameWon == true.
    do
    {
        // Loop through players in each game round.
        for (currentPlayer = 0; currentPlayer < players.Length;
            currentPlayer++)
        {
            // Write out current player, player hand, and the card on the
            // table.
            Console.WriteLine("{0}'s turn.", players[currentPlayer].Name);
            Console.WriteLine("Current hand:");
            foreach (Card card in players[currentPlayer].PlayHand)
            {
                Console.WriteLine(card);
            }
            Console.WriteLine("Card in play: {0}", playCard);

            // Prompt player to pick up card on table or draw a new one.
            bool inputOK = false;
            do
            {
                Console.WriteLine("Press T to take card in play or D to " +
                                  "draw:");
                string input = Console.ReadLine();
                if (input.ToLower() == "t")
                {
                    // Add card from table to player hand.
                    Console.WriteLine("Drawn: {0}", playCard);
                    players[currentPlayer].PlayHand.Add(playCard);
                    inputOK = true;
                }
                if (input.ToLower() == "d")
                {
                    // Add new card from deck to player hand.
                    Card newCard;
```

```
            // Only add card if it isn't already in a player hand.
            bool cardIsInPlayerHand;
            do
            {
                newCard = playDeck.GetCard(currentCard++);
                cardIsInPlayerHand = false;
                // Loop through all player hands to see if newCard is
                // already in a hand.
                foreach (Player testPlayer in players)
                {
                    cardIsInPlayerHand |=
                        testPlayer.PlayHand.Contains(newCard);
                }
            } while (cardIsInPlayerHand);
            // Add the card found to player hand.
            Console.WriteLine("Drawn: {0}", newCard);
            players[currentPlayer].PlayHand.Add(newCard);
            inputOK = true;
        }
} while (inputOK == false);

// Display new hand with cards numbered.
Console.WriteLine("New hand:");
for (int i = 0; i < players[currentPlayer].PlayHand.Count; i++)
{
    Console.WriteLine("{0}: {1}", i + 1,
                        players[currentPlayer].PlayHand[i]);
}

// Prompt player for a card to discard.
inputOK = false;
int choice = -1;
do
{
    Console.WriteLine("Choose card to discard:");
    string input = Console.ReadLine();
    try
    {
        // Attempt to convert input into a valid card number.
        choice = Convert.ToInt32(input);
        if ((choice > 0) && (choice <= 8))
            inputOK = true;
    }
    catch
    {
        // Ignore failed conversions, just continue prompting.
    }
} while (inputOK == false);

// Place reference to removed card in playCard (place the card
// on the table), then remove card from player hand.
playCard = players[currentPlayer].PlayHand[choice - 1];
players[currentPlayer].PlayHand.RemoveAt(choice - 1);
```

```
                  Console.WriteLine("Discarding: {0}", playCard);

                  // Space out text for players
                  Console.WriteLine();

                  // Check to see if player has won the game, and exit the player
                  // loop if so.
                  GameWon = players[currentPlayer].HasWon();
                  if (GameWon == true)
                     break;
               }
            } while (GameWon == false);

            // End game, noting the winning player.
            return currentPlayer;
         }
```

Have fun playing the game – and make sure you spend some time going through it in detail. One thing to try is to put a breakpoint in the Reshuffle() method and play the game with 7 players. If you keep drawing cards and discarding the cards drawn it won't take long for reshuffles to occur, as with 7 players there are only three cards spare. This way you can prove to yourself that things are working properly by noting the three cards when they reappear.

Summary

In this chapter we have looked at the important topic of events and event handling. Although quite subtle, and initially difficult to get your head around, the code involved is quite simple – and you'll certainly be using event handlers a lot in the rest of the book.

As well as looking at some simple illustrative examples of events and how to handle them, we also made one final addition to the CardLib library we've been building up over the last few chapters. Once complete, we used this library to create a simple card game application. This application should serve as a demonstration of pretty much all the techniques we've looked at in the first part of this book.

With this chapter we have completed not only a complete description of OOP as applied to C# programming, but also a complete description of the C# language. From this point on we will be applying this knowledge to more complex scenarios, such as creating Windows and Web applications, as well as making more use of the .NET Framework.

Exercises

1. Show the code for an event handler that uses the general-purpose (object sender, EventArgs e) syntax that will accept either the Timer.Elapsed event or the Connection.MessageArrived event from the code earlier in this chapter. The handler should output a string specifying which type of event has been received, along with the Message property of the MessageArrivedEventArgs parameter or the SignalTime property of the ElapsedEventArgs parameter, depending on which event occurs.

2. Modify the card game example to check for the more interesting winning condition of the popular card game rummy. This means that a player wins the game if their hand contains two "sets" of cards, one of which consists of three cards, and one of which consists of four cards. A set is defined as either a sequence of cards of the same suit (such as 3H, 4H, 5H, 6H) or several cards of the same rank (such as 2H, 2D, 2S).

Using Windows Form Controls

In recent years Visual Basic has won great acclaim for granting programmers the tools for creating highly detailed user interfaces via an intuitive form designer, along with an easy to learn programming language that together produced probably the best environment for rapid application development out there. One of the advantages offered by Rapid Application Development (RAD) tool such as Visual Basic is that it provided access to a number of prefabricated controls that could be used to quickly build the user interface for an application.

At the heart of the development of most Visual Basic Windows applications is the form designer. You create a user interface by dragging and dropping controls from a toolbox to your form, placing them where you want them to be when you run the program, double-clicking the control adds a handler for that control. The controls provided by Microsoft along with further custom controls that could be bought at reasonable prices have supplied programmers with an unprecedented pool of reusable, thoroughly tested code that is no more than a mouse-click away. Such application development is now available to C# developers through Visual Studio .NET.

In this chapter, we'll look at working with Windows forms, and use some of the many controls that ship with the .NET Framework. These controls cover a wide range of functionality, and through the design capabilities of Visual Studio .NET, developing user interfaces and handling user interaction is very straightforward – and fun! Presenting all of the controls present in Visual Studio .NET would be impossible within the scope of this book, and so in this chapter we'll look at some of the most commonly used controls, ranging from labels and text boxes to list views and status bars.

First, let's have a look at the form itself.

Working with Windows Forms

Let's start straight away – create a new Windows application called FormTest in the C:\BegVCSharp\Chapter13 folder. You will see the Windows Form Designer, the main surface for the design of your user interface:

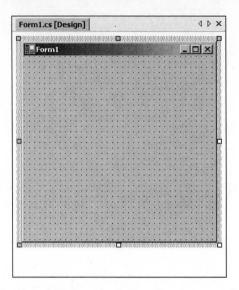

From the design view, we can drag and drop controls onto our form, adjust their size, position and a great many more properties that range from determining the text displayed on the control to specifying a data source from which to populate the control. Before we look at the controls available, let's take a look at the form itself – right-click on the form, select **View Code** from the menu that appears, and you'll be taken to the code editor. Here's the top portion of the code that you'll see:

```
using System;
using System.Drawing;
using System.Collections;
using System.ComponentModel;
using System.Windows.Forms;
using System.Data;

namespace FormTest
{
    /// <summary>
    /// Summary description for Form1.
    /// </summary>
    public class Form1 : System.Windows.Forms.Form
    {
```

As you can see, there is a number of using directives at the top of the code for importing a number of namespaces that are commonly used in writing a Windows applications – we've highlighted the System.Windows.Forms namespace. The functionality for creating Windows applications such as interface display, and user interaction is provided by the classes in this namespace. The other line highlighted above is the class definition for the Form1 class – the : System.Windows.Forms.Form syntax indicates that this class derives from the Form class of the System.Windows.Forms namespace. The form that is displayed to the user with all its controls making up your carefully crafted user interface is in fact an instance of a class that derives from System.Windows.Forms.Form (in this case it would be our Form1 class). This means we have access to all the basic functionality of the System.Windows.Forms.Form class. We'll see in a moment where the instance of the class is actually created in the code.

Click on the Form1.cs [Design] tab to return to the design view, click on the form to select it, and then set its Name property to MyForm in the Properties window. Now if you return to the code view, you will find the class has been renamed:

```
public class MyForm : System.Windows.Forms.Form
```

However, if you attempt to run the application at this point you will receive the error The type or namespace name 'Form1' could not be found – it seems that not all references to Form1 have been changed to MyForm. The culprit is found in the Main() method:

```
static void Main()
{
    Application.Run(new Form1());
}
```

Application is a class of the System.Windows.Forms namespace, providing the functionality that take cares of the behind the scenes activities for the execution of Windows applications. Here a new instance of our Form1 class is passed to the Run() method, which starts our application and displays the form. This is code we don't have to worry about, except when we change the name of the form in the form designer – in Visual Studio .NET, if you change the name of the form in the form designer, you have to manually change its name in the Run() parameter in the Main() method as well. Thus, our Main() method needs to become:

```
static void Main()
{
    Application.Run(new MyForm());
}
```

We'll keep reminding you of this point when we change the name of forms in our examples; it's easy to forget!

The Toolbox

Let's have a closer look at the Toolbox. If you haven't already, move your mouse pointer over the toolbox on the left of the screen, and pin it to the foreground by clicking the pin at the top right of the panel that unfolds.

> *If you accidentally remove the toolbox by clicking the X instead, you can make it reappear by selecting Toolbox from the View menu, or by pressing Ctrl-Alt-X.*

The Toolbox contains a selection of all the controls available to you as a .NET developer. The controls available from the Windows Forms section of the Toolbox are the ones of interest to us in this chapter, and as you can see, there's quite a few of them (we only show some of them here!):

The Toolbox consists of the controls that ship with the .NET Framework – you are not limited to use this selection, and it is possible to customize the Toolbox by adding your own custom built or bought controls. Building custom controls is something we'll look at in the next chapter, but for now we'll concentrate on a subset of the controls that are found in the picture above.

Now that your Toolbox is open, double-click on the Button control, and an instance will appear on your form. Drag the Button to the middle of your form:

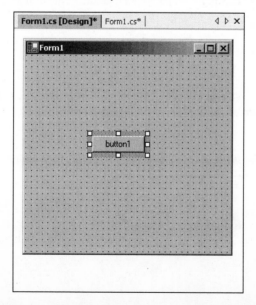

Well, we've not written Microsoft Word just yet, but it's a start! Double-click on the `Button` and you'll be taken back to the code editor with the following method signature provided for you:

```
private void button1_Click(object sender, System.EventArgs e)
{

}
```

The code generated by Visual Studio .NET is the event handler for the `Button` control's `Click` event – we'll take a closer look at the events available to controls in a moment, but for now we'll just mention the `Click` event is the event raised when the `Button` is clicked with the left mouse button. Each control has a default event, and when you double-click on the control in the design view of Visual Studio .NET, code will be added to your file that allows the control to subscribe to the event, and the method signature for handling the event will also be added, and you will be taken to this code. We've seen the event handler, but where is the code for subscribing to the event?

If you look through the file you will find a region labeled **Windows Form Designer generated code** that you can expand – we looked briefly at this region in Chapter 2. When you expand this region, you will see the following code:

```
#region Windows Form Designer generated code
/// <summary>
/// Required method for Designer support - do not modify
/// the contents of this method with the code editor.
/// </summary>
private void InitializeComponent()
{
    this.button1 = new System.Windows.Forms.Button();
    this.SuspendLayout();
    //
    // button1
    //
    this.button1.Location = new System.Drawing.Point(96, 112);
    this.button1.Name = "button1";
    this.button1.TabIndex = 0;
    this.button1.Text = "button1";
    this.button1.Click += new System.EventHandler(this.button1_Click);
    //
    // MyForm
    //
    this.AutoScaleBaseSize = new System.Drawing.Size(5, 13);
    this.ClientSize = new System.Drawing.Size(292, 273);
    this.Controls.AddRange(new System.Windows.Forms.Control[] {
                                             this.button1});
    this.Name = "MyForm";
    this.Text = "Form1";
    this.ResumeLayout(false);
}
```

The `InitializeComponent()` method contains the code automatically generated by Visual Studio .NET.

Be very careful if you modify the code in this method, (the comment before the method advises you against it!) since it is possible to introduce errors that prevent your form from being displayed in the designer until you have corrected the error.

The highlighted lines above show the Button control's (button1) contribution to this method, including the line that subscribes the Button to the Click event:

```
this.button1.Click += new System.EventHandler(this.button1_Click);
```

You should take a minute to look over the statements in this section. You will see exactly why it is possible to create a Windows Application without using Visual Studio .NET. Everything in this section could simply be entered in Notepad or a similar text editor and compiled. You will also see why that is not advisable. Keeping track of everything in here is difficult at the best of times; it is easy to introduce errors and, because you cannot see the effects of what you are doing, arranging the controls on the form to look right is a cumbersome task. This does, however, open the door for third-party software producers to write their own programming environments to rival Visual Studio .NET because the compilers used to create the actual applications are included with the .NET Framework rather than being dedicated to Visual Studio .NET.

Now that we know where we'll be doing our work, and we've had a quick peek behind the scenes, let's look at controls in general.

Controls

Most controls in .NET derive from the System.Windows.Forms.Control class. This class defines the basic functionality of the controls, which is why many properties and events in the controls we'll see are identical. Many of these classes are themselves base classes for other controls, as is the case with the Label and TextBoxBase classes in the diagram below.

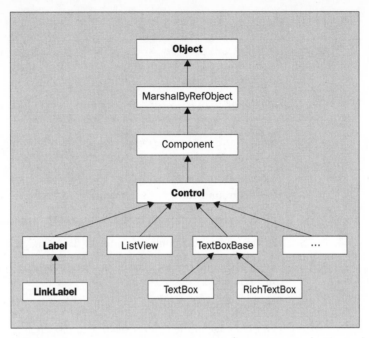

Some controls, named custom or user controls, derive from another class:
System.Windows.Forms.UserControl. This class is itself derived from the Control
class and provides the functionality we need to create controls ourselves. We'll cover this class in
Chapter 14. Incidentally, controls used for designing Web user interfaces derive from yet another
class, System.Web.UI.Control.

Properties

All controls have a number of properties that are used to manipulate the behavior of the control. The base class of most controls, System.Windows.Forms.Control, has a number of properties that other controls either inherit directly or override to provide some kind of custom behavior.

The table below shows some of the most common properties of the Control class. These properties will be present in most of the controls we'll visit in this chapter, and they will therefore not be explained in detail again, unless the behavior of the properties is changed for the control in question. Note that this table is not meant to be exhaustive; if you want to see all of the properties in the class, please refer to the .NET Framework SDK Documentation.

Name	Description
Anchor	Using this property, you can specify how the control behaves when its container is resized. See below for a detailed explanation of this property.
BackColor	The background color of a control.

Table continued on following page

Name	Description
Bottom	By setting this property, you specify the distance from the top of the window to the bottom of the control. This is not the same as specifying the height of the control.
Dock	Allows you to make a control dock to the edges of a window. See below for a more detailed explanation of this property.
Enabled	Setting Enabled to true usually means that the control can receive input from the user. Setting Enabled to false usually means that it cannot.
ForeColor	The foreground color of the control.
Height	The distance from the top to the bottom of the control.
Left	The left edge of the control relative to the left edge of the window.
Name	The name of the control. This name can be used to reference the control in code.
Parent	The parent of the control.
Right	The right edge of the control relative to the left edge of the window.
TabIndex	The number the control has in the tab order of its container.
TabStop	Specifies whether the control can be accessed by the *Tab* key.
Tag	This value is usually not used by the control itself and is there for you to store information about the control on the control itself. When this property is assigned a value through the Windows Form designer, you can only assign a string to it.
Text	Holds the text that is associated with this control.
Top	The top edge of the control relative to the top of the window.
Visible	Specifies whether or not the control is visible at runtime.
Width	The width of the control.

If you have experience with Visual Basic you may notice that in .NET, the Text *property is used to set the text that is displayed, rather than a* Caption *property. You will find that all intrinsic .NET controls use the name* Text *to describe the main text for a control. Before .NET,* Caption *and* Text *were used interchangeably between different controls.*

Anchor and Dock Properties

These two properties are especially useful when you are designing your form. Ensuring that a window doesn't become a mess to look at if the user decides to resize the window is far from trivial, and numerous lines of code have been written to achieve this. Many programs solve the problem by simply disallowing the window from being resized, which is clearly the easiest way around the problem, but not always the best. The Anchor and Dock properties that have been introduced with .NET let you solve this problem without writing a single line of code.

The Anchor property is used to specify how the control behaves when a user resizes the window. You can specify if the control should resize itself, anchoring itself in proportion to its own edges, or stay the same size, anchoring its position relative to the window's edges.

The Dock property is used to specify that a control should dock to an edge of its container. If a user resizes the window, the control will continue to be docked to the edge of the window. If, for instance, you specify that a control should dock with the bottom of its container, the control will resize and/or move itself to always occupy the bottom part of the window, no matter how the window is resized.

See the text box example later in this chapter for the exact use of the Anchor property.

Events

In the last chapter, we saw what events are, and how we can use them. Here we will talk about a particular kind of events, specifically the events generated by Windows Forms controls. These events are usually associated with actions of the user. For example, when the user clicks or presses a button, that button generates an event in which it says what just happened to it. Handling the event is the means by which the programmer can provide some functionality for that button.

The Control class defines a number of events that are common to the controls we'll use in this chapter. The table below describes a number of these events. Once again, this is just a selection of the most common events; if you need to see the entire list, please refer to the .NET Framework SDK Documentation.

Name	Description
Click	Occurs when a control is clicked. In some cases, this event will also occur when a user presses *Enter*.
DoubleClick	Occurs when a control is double-clicked. Handling the Click event on some controls, such as the Button control will mean that the DoubleClick event can never be called.
DragDrop	Occurs when a drag-and-drop operation is completed, in other words, when an object has been dragged over the control, and the user releases the mouse button.
DragEnter	Occurs when an object being dragged enters the bounds of the control.
DragLeave	Occurs when an object being dragged leaves the bounds of the control.
DragOver	Occurs when an object has been dragged over the control.

Table continued on following page

Name	Description
KeyDown	Occurs when a key becomes pressed while the control has focus. This event always occurs before KeyPress and KeyUp.
KeyPress	Occurs when a key becomes pressed while a control has focus. This event always occurs after KeyDown and before KeyUp. The difference between KeyDown and KeyPress is that KeyDown passes the keyboard code of the key that has been pressed, while KeyPress passes the corresponding char value for the key.
KeyUp	Occurs when a key is released while a control has focus. This event always occurs after KeyDown and KeyPress.
GotFocus	Occurs when a control receives focus. Do not use this event to perform validation of controls. Use Validating and Validated instead.
LostFocus	Occurs when a control loses focus. Do not use this event to perform validation of controls. Use Validating and Validated instead.
MouseDown	Occurs when the mouse pointer is over a control and a mouse button is pressed. This is not the same as a Click event because MouseDown occurs as soon as the button is pressed and *before* it is released.
MouseMove	Occurs continually as the mouse travels over the control.
MouseUp	Occurs when the mouse pointer is over a control and a mouse button is released.
Paint	Occurs when the control is drawn.
Validated	This event is fired when a control with the CausesValidation property set to true is about to receive focus. It fires after the Validating event finishes and indicates that validation is complete.
Validating	Fires when a control with the CausesValidation property set to true is about to receive focus. Note that the control which is to be validated is the control which is losing focus, not the one that is receiving it.

We will see many of these events in the examples in the rest of the chapter. All our examples will follow the same format, where we first create the form's visual appearance, choosing and positioning controls, etc., before we then move onto adding the event handlers – this is where the main work of our examples takes places.

To handle a particular event, there are three basic ways of going about it. The first is to double-click on the control in question, and you will be taken to the event-handler for the control's default event – this event is different for different controls. If that's the event you want, then you're fine. If you want an event different from the default one of the control, there are two possible ways of proceeding.

One way is to use the Events list in the Properties window:

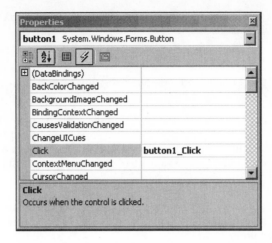

The grayed event is that control's default event. To add a handler for a particular event, double-click on that event in the Events list, and the code to subscribe the control to the event will be generated, along with the method signature to handle the event. Alternatively, you can type a name for the method to handle the particular event next to that event in the Events list, and when you press enter the event handler will be generated with your chosen name.

Another option is to add the code to subscribe to the event yourself – we'll do this often in this and the next chapter by adding the code to the form's constructor after the InitializeComponent() call. Of course, we still have to add the method signature to handle the event ourselves as well, and this method has the drawback that you need to know the exact method signature for that event.

Note that each of these two options require two steps – subscription to the event and the correct signature for the method handler. If you double-click on a control and try to handle another event by editing the method signature of the default event for the event that you actually want handled, you will fail – you also need to alter the event subscription code in InitializeComponent(), and so this "cheating" method is not really a quick way to handle particular events.

We are now ready to start looking at the controls themselves, and we'll start with one that we've seen in previous chapters, the Button control.

The Button Control

When you think of a button, you are probably thinking of a rectangular button that can be clicked to perform some task. However, the .NET Framework provides a class derived from Control – System.Windows.Forms.ButtonBase – that implements the basic functionality needed in button controls, so any programmer can derive from this class and create his or hers custom button controls.

The System.Windows.Forms namespace provides us with three controls that derive from ButtonBase – Button, CheckBox and RadioButton. In this section we will focus on the Button control (which is the standard, well known rectangular button), and we'll cover the other two later in this chapter.

The `Button` control exists on just about any Windows dialog you can think of. A button is primarily used to perform three kinds of tasks:

❑ To close a dialog with a state (for example, OK and Cancel buttons)

❑ To perform an action on data entered on a dialog (for example clicking Search after entering some search criteria)

❑ To open another dialog or application (for example, Help buttons)

Working with the button control is very straightforward. It usually consists of adding the control to your form and double-clicking it to add the code to the `Click` event, which will probably be enough for most applications you'll work on.

Let's look at some of the commonly used properties and events of the control. This will give you an idea what can be done with it. After that, we'll create a small example that demonstrates some of the basic properties and events of a button.

Button Properties

We'll list the most commonly used properties of the `Button` class, even if technically they are defined in the `ButtonBase` base class. Only the most commonly used properties are explained here. Please refer to the .NET Framework SDK Documentation for a complete listing.

Name	Description
FlatStyle	The style of the button can be changed with this property. If you set the style to `Popup`, the button will appear flat until the user moves the mouse pointer over it. When that happens, the button pops up to its normal 3D look.
Enabled	We'll mention this here even though it is derived from `Control`, because it's a very important property for a button. Setting the `Enabled` property to `false` means that the button becomes grayed out and nothing happens when you click it.
Image	Allows you to specify an image (bitmap, icon, etc.), which will be displayed on the button.
ImageAlign	With this property, you can set where the image on the button should appear.

Button Events

By far the most used event of a button is the `Click` event. This happens whenever a user clicks the button, by which we mean pressing the left mouse button and releasing it again while over the button. This means that if you left-click on the button and then draw the mouse away from the button before releasing it the `Click` event will not be raised. Also, the `Click` event is raised when the button has focus and the user presses *Enter*. If you have a button on a form, you should always handle this event.

Let's move to the example. We'll create a dialog with three buttons. Two of the buttons will change the language used from English to Danish and back. (Feel free to use whatever language you prefer.) The last button closes the dialog.

Try it Out – Button Test

1. Create a new Windows application called `ButtonTest` in the directory `C:\BegVCSharp\Chapter13`.

2. Pin the Toolbox down, and double-click the `Button` control three times. Then move the buttons and resize the form as shown in the picture below.

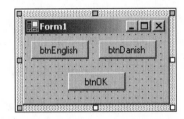

3. Right-click a button and select **Properties**. Then change the name of each button as indicated in the picture above by selecting the **(Name)** edit field in the **Properties** window and typing the relevant text.

4. Change the `Text` property of each button the be the same as the name, but omit the `btn` prefix for the `Text` property value.

5. We want to display a flag in front of the text to make it clear what we are talking about. Select the **English** button and find the `Image` property. Click (...) to the right of it to bring up a dialog where you can select an image. The flag icons we want to display come with Visual Studio .NET. If you installed to the default location (on an English language installation) they should be located in `C:\Program Files\Microsoft Visual Studio .NET\Common7\Graphics\icons\Flags`. Select the icon `flguk.ico`. Repeat this process with the **Danish** button, selecting the `flgden.ico` file instead. (If you want to use a different flag here, then this directory will have other flags to choose from.)

6. You'll notice at this point that the button text and icon are placed on top of each other, so we need to change the alignment of the icon. For both the English and Danish buttons, change the `ImageAlign` property to `MiddleLeft`.

7. At this point you may want to adjust the width of the buttons so that the text doesn't start right where the images end. Do this by selecting each of the buttons and pulling the notch on the right-hand edge of the button.

8. Finally, click on the form and change the `Text` property to Do you speak English?

That's it for the user interface of our dialog. You should now have something that looks like this:

Now we are ready to add the event handlers to the dialog. Double-click the **English** button. This will take you directly to the event handler for the control's default event – the `Click` event is the default event for the button and so that is the handler created.

Adding the Event Handlers

Double-click on the `Button` and add the following code to the event handler:

```
private void btnEnglish_Click(object sender, System.EventArgs e)
{
    this.Text = "Do you speak English?";
}
```

When Visual Studio .NET creates a method to handle such an event, the method name is a concatenation of the name of the control, followed by an underscore and the name of the event that is handled.

For the `Click` event, the first parameter, `object sender`, will hold the control that was clicked. In this example, this will always be the control indicated by the name of the method, but in other cases many controls may use the same method to handle an event, and in that case you can find out exactly which control is calling by checking this value. The text box example later in this chapter demonstrates how to use a single method for multiple controls. The other parameter, `System.EventArgs e`, holds information about what actually happened. In this case, we'll not be needing any of this information.

Return to the design view and double-click the **Danish** button and you will be taken to the event handler for that button. Here is the code:

```
private void btnDanish_Click(object sender, System.EventArgs e)
{
    this.Text = "Taler du dansk?";
}
```

This method is identical to the `btnEnglish_Click`, except that the text is in Danish. Finally, we add the event handler for the **OK** button in the same way as we've done twice now. The code is a little different though:

```
private void btnOK_Click(object sender, System.EventArgs e)
{
    Application.Exit();
}
```

With this we exit the application and, with it, this first example. Compile it, run it and press a few of the buttons. You will get output similar to this:

The Label and LinkLabel Controls

The `Label` control is probably the most used control of them all. Look at any Windows application and you'll see a `Label` on just about any dialog you can find. The `Label` is a simple control with one purpose only – to display text on the form.

The .NET Framework includes two label controls that present themselves to the user in two distinct ways:

❑ `Label`, the standard Windows label

❑ `LinkLabel`, a label similar to the standard one (and derived from it), but presents itself as an Internet link (a hyperlink)

In the picture below, one of each of the two types of `Label` has been dragged to a form to illustrate the difference in appearance between the two:

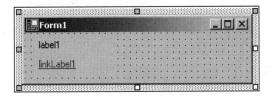

And that's it for most uses of the `Label` control. Usually you need to add no event handling code for a standard `Label`, although it does support events like all controls. In the case of the `LinkLabel`, however, some extra code is needed if you want to allow the user to click it and take him or her to the web page shown in the text.

The `Label` control has a surprising number of properties that can be set. Most of these are derived from `Control`, but some are new. The following table lists the most common ones. Unless stated otherwise, the properties are common to both the `Label` and `LinkLabel` controls.

Name	Description
BorderStyle	Allows you to specify the style of the border around the `Label`. The default is no border.
DisabledLinkColor	(`LinkLabel` only) The color of the `LinkLabel` after the user has clicked it.

Table continued on following page

Name	Description
FlatStyle	Controls how the control is displayed. Setting this property to Popup will make the control appear flat until the user moves the mouse pointer over the control. At that time, the control will appear raised.
Image	This property allows you to specify a single image (bitmap, icon, etc.) to be displayed in the label.
ImageAlign	(Read/Write) Where in the Label the image is shown.
LinkArea	(LinkLabel only) The range in the text that should be displayed as a link.
LinkColor	(LinkLabel only) The color of the link.
Links	(LinkLabel only) It is possible for a LinkLabel to contain more than one link. This property allows you to find the link you want. The control keeps track of the links displayed in the text. Not available at design time.
LinkVisited	(LinkLabel only) Returns whether a link has been visited or not.
TextAlign	Where in the control the text is shown.

The TextBox Control

Text boxes should be used when you want the user to enter text that you have no knowledge of at design time (for example the name of the user). The primary function of a text box is for the user to enter text, but any characters can be entered, and it is quite possible to force the user to enter numeric values only.

The .NET Framework comes with two basic controls to take text input from the user: TextBox and RichTextBox. Both controls are derived from a base class called TextBoxBase which itself is derived from Control.

TextBoxBase provides the base functionality for text manipulation in a text box, such as selecting text, cutting to and pasting from the Clipboard, and a wide range of events. We'll not focus so much now on what is derived from where, but instead look at the simpler of the two controls first – TextBox. We'll build one example that demonstrates the TextBox properties and build on that to demonstrate the RichTextBox control later.

TextBox Properties

As has been stated earlier in this chapter, there are simply too many properties for us to describe them all, and so this listing includes only the most common ones.

Name	Description
CausesValidation	When a control that has this property set to true is about to receive focus, two events are fired: Validating and Validated. You can handle these events in order to validate data in the control that is losing focus. This may cause the control never to receive focus. The related events are discussed below.
CharacterCasing	A value indicating if the TextBox changes the case of the text entered. The possible values are: ❑ Lower: All text entered is converted lower case. ❑ Normal: No changes are made to the text. ❑ Upper: All text entered is converted to upper case.
MaxLength	A value that specifies the maximum length in characters of any text, entered into the TextBox. Set this value to zero if the maximum limit is limited only by available memory.
Multiline	Indicates if this is a multiline control, which means it is able to show multiple lines of text. When Multiline property is set to true, you'll usually want to set WordWrap to true as well.
PasswordChar	Specifies if a password character should replace the actual characters entered into a single line TextBox. If the Multiline property is true then this has no effect.
ReadOnly	A Boolean indicating if the text is read only.
ScrollBars	Specifies if a multiline TextBox should display scrollbars.
SelectedText	The text that is selected in the TextBox.
SelectionLength	The number of characters selected in the text. If this value is set to be larger than the total number of characters in the text, it is reset by the control to be the total number of characters minus the value of SelectionStart.
SelectionStart	The start of the selected text in a TextBox.
WordWrap	Specifies if a multiline TextBox should automatically wrap words if a line exceeds the width of the control.

TextBox Events

Careful validation of the text in the TextBox controls on a form can make the difference between happy users and angry ones.

You have probably experienced how annoying it is when a dialog only validates its contents when you click OK. This approach to validating the data usually results in a message box being displayed informing you that the data in "TextBox number three" is incorrect. You can then continue to click OK until all the data is correct. Clearly this is not a good approach to validating data, so what can we do instead?

The answer lies in handling the validation events a `TextBox` control provides. If you want to make sure that invalid characters are not entered in the text box or only values within a certain range are allowed, then you will want to indicate to the user of the control whether the value entered is valid or not.

The `TextBox` control provides these events (all of which are inherited from `Control`):

Name	Description
Enter GotFocus Leave Validating Validated LostFocus	These six events occur in the order they are listed here. They are known as "Focus Events" and are fired whenever a control's focus changes, with two exceptions. `Validating` and `Validated` are only fired if the control that receives focus has the `CausesValidation` property set to `true`. The reason why it's the receiving control that fires the event is that there are times where you do not want to validate the control, even if focus changes. An example of this is if the user clicks a Help button.
KeyDown KeyPress KeyUp	These three events are known as "Key Events". They allow you to monitor and change what is entered into your controls. `KeyDown` and `KeyUp` receive the key code corresponding to the key that was pressed. This allows you to determine if special keys such as *Shift* or *Control* and *F1* were pressed. `KeyPress`, on the otherhand, receives the character corresponding to a keyboard key. This means that the value for the letter "a" is not the same as the letter "A". It is useful if you want to exclude a range of characters, for example, only allowing numeric values to be entered.
TextChanged	Occurs whenever the text in the `TextBox` is changed, no matter what the change.

Try it Out – TextBoxTest

We'll create a dialog on which you can enter your name, address, occupation, and age. The purpose of this example is to give you a good grounding in manipulating properties and using events, not to create something that is incredibly useful.

We'll build the user interface first.

1. Create a new Windows application called `TextBoxTest` in the directory `C:\BegVCSharp\Chapter13`.

2. Create the form shown below by dragging some `Label`, `TextBox`, and `Button` controls onto the design surface. Before you can resize the two `TextBox` controls txtAddress and txtOutput as shown you must set their `Multiline` property to true. Do this by right-clicking the controls and select **Properties**.

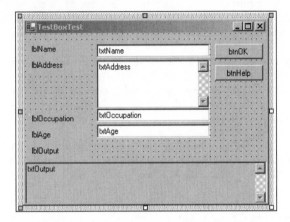

3. Name the controls as indicated in the picture above.

4. Set the `Text` property of each `TextBox` to an empty string, which means that they will contain nothing when the application is first run.

5. Set the `Text` property of all the other controls to the same as the name of the control, except for the first three letters. Set the `Text` property to **TextBoxTest**.

6. Set the `Scrollbars` property of the two controls txtOutput and txtAddress to **Vertical**.

7. Set the `ReadOnly` property of the txtOutput control to true.

8. Set the `CausesValidation` property of the btnHelp `Button` to false. Remember from the discussion of the `Validating` and `Validated` events that setting this to false will allow the user to click this `Button` without having to be concerned about entering invalid data.

9. When you have sized the form to fit snugly around the controls, it is time to anchor the controls so they behave properly when the form is resized. Let's set the `Anchor` property for each type of control in one go – first of all, select all the `Label` controls by holding down the *Ctrl* key while you select each `Label` in turn. Once you've selected them all, set the `Anchor` property to **Top**, **Left** from the Properties window, and the `Anchor` property for each of the selected `Label` controls will be set as well. Repeat this procedure to set the `Anchor` property for each `TextBox` to **Top**, **Left**, **Right**, and additionally set the `Anchor` property for the txtOutput `TextBox` to **Top**, **Bottom**, **Left**, **Right**. Now set the `Anchor` property for both `Button` controls to **Top**, **Right**.

The reason why `txtOutput` is anchored rather than docked to the bottom of the form is that we want the output text area to be resized as we pull the form. If we had docked the control to the bottom of the form, it would be moved to stay at the bottom, but it would not be resized.

10. One final thing should be set. On the form, find the `Size` and `MinimumSize` properties. Our form has little meaning if it is sized to something smaller than it is now, therefore you should set the `MinimumSize` property to the same as the `Size` property.

The job of setting up the visual part of the form is now complete. If you run it nothing happens when you click the buttons or enter text, but if you maximize or pull in the dialog, the controls behave exactly as you want them to in a proper user interface, staying put and resizing to fill the whole of the dialog.

Adding the Event Handlers

From the design view, double-click the **btnOK** button. Repeat this with the other button. As we saw in the button example earlier in this chapter this causes event handlers for the `Click` event of the buttons to be created. When the **OK** button is clicked, we want to transfer the text in the input text boxes to the read-only output box.

Here is the code for the two `Click` event-handlers.

```
private void btnOK_Click(object sender, System.EventArgs e)
{
    // No testing for invalid values are made, as that should
    // not be necessary

    string output;

    // Concatenate the text values of the four TextBoxes
    output = "Name: " + this.txtName.Text + "\r\n";
    output += "Address: " + this.txtAddress.Text + "\r\n";
    output += "Occupation: " + this.txtOccupation.Text + "\r\n";
    output += "Age: " + this.txtAge.Text;

    // Insert the new text
    this.txtOutput.Text = output;
}

private void btnHelp_Click(object sender, System.EventArgs e)
{
    // Write a short description of each TextBox in the Output TextBox
    string output;

    output = "Name = Your name\r\n";
    output += "Address = Your address\r\n";
    output += "Occupation = Only allowed value is 'Programmer'\r\n";
    output += "Age = Your age";

    // Insert the new text
    this.txtOutput.Text = output;
}
```

In both functions the `Text` property of each `TextBox` is used, either retrieved, set in the `btnOK_Click()` function, or simply set as in the `btnHelp_Click()` function.

We insert the information the user has entered without bothering to check if it is correct. This means that we must do the checking elsewhere. In this example, there are a number of criteria that we wish to enforce in order for the values to be correct:

❑   The name of the user cannot be empty

❑   The age of the user must be a number greater than or equal to zero

❑   The occupation of the user must be "Programmer" or be left empty

❑   The address of the user cannot be empty

From this we can see that the check that must be done for two of the text boxes (`txtName` and `txtAddress`) is the same. We also see that we should prevent the user from entering anything invalid into the `Age` box, and finally we must check if the user claims to be a programmer.

To prevent the user from clicking **OK** before anything is entered we start by setting the **OK** button's `Enabled` property to `false` – this time we'll do it in the constructor of our form rather than from the Properties window. If you do set properties in the constructor, make sure not to set them until after the generated code in `InitializeComponent()` has been called.

```
public Form1()
{
    //
    // Required for Windows Form Designer support
    //
    InitializeComponent();
    this.btnOK.Enabled = false;
}
```

Now we'll create the handler for the two text boxes that must be checked to see if they are empty. We do this by subscribing to the `Validating` event of the text boxes. We inform the control that the event should be handled by a method named `txtBoxEmpty_Validating()`, so that's a single event-handling method for two different controls.

We also need a way to know the state of our controls. For this purpose, we use the `Tag` property of the `TextBox` control. If you recall the discussion of this property from earlier in the chapter, we said that only strings can be assigned to the `Tag` property from the Forms Designer. However, as we are setting the `Tag` value from code, we can do pretty much what we want with it, since the `Tag` property takes an `object`, and it is more appropriate to enter a Boolean value here.

To the constructor we add the following statements:

```
this.btnOK.Enabled = false;

// Tag values for testing if the data is valid
this.txtAddress.Tag = false;
this.txtAge.Tag = false;
this.txtName.Tag = false;
this.txtOccupation.Tag = false;
```

```
// Subscriptions to events
this.txtName.Validating += new
System.ComponentModel.CancelEventHandler(this.txtBoxEmpty_Validating);
this.txtAddress.Validating += new
        System.ComponentModel.CancelEventHandler(this.txtBoxEmpty_Validating);
```

Unlike the button event handler we've seen previously, the event handler for the `Validating` event is a specialized version of the standard handler `System.EventHandler`. The reason this event needs a special handler is that should the validation fail, there must be a way to prevent any further processing. If we were to cancel further processing, that would effectively mean that it would be impossible to leave a text box until the data entered is valid.

The `Validating` and `Validated` events combined with the `CausesValidation` property fix a nasty problem that occurred when using the `GotFocus` and `LostFocus` events to perform validation of controls. The problem occurred when the `GotFocus` and `LostFocus` events were continually fired because validation code was attempting to shift the focus between control, which created an infinite loop.

We add the event handler as follows:

```
private void txtBoxEmpty_Validating(object sender,
                                    System.ComponentModel.CancelEventArgs e)
{
    // We know the sender is a TextBox, so we cast the sender object to that
    TextBox tb = (TextBox)sender;

    // If the text is empty we set the background color of the
    // Textbox to red to indicate a problem. We use the tag value
    // of the control to indicate if the control contains valid
    // information.
    if (tb.Text.Length == 0)
    {
        tb.BackColor = Color.Red;
        tb.Tag = false;

        // In this case we do not want to cancel further processing,
        // but if we had wanted to do this, we would have added this line:
        // e.Cancel = true;
    }
    else
    {
        tb.BackColor = System.Drawing.SystemColors.Window;
        tb.Tag = true;
    }

    // Finally, we call ValidateAll which will set the value of
    // the OK button.
    ValidateAll();
}
```

Because more than one text box is using this method to handle the event, we cannot be sure which is calling the function. We do know, however, that the effect of calling the method should be the same no matter who is calling, so we can simply cast the `sender` parameter to a `TextBox` and work on that:

```
TextBox tb = (TextBox)sender;
```

If the length of the text in the text box is zero, we set the background color to red and the `Tag` to `false`. If it is not, we set the background color to the standard Windows color for a window.

You should always use the colors found in the `System.Drawing.SystemColors` enumeration when you want to set a standard color in a control. If you simply set the color to white, your application will look strange if the user has changed the default color settings.

We'll postpone our description of the `ValidateAll()` function until the end of this example.

Keeping with the `Validating` event, the next handler we'll add is for the `Occupation` text box. The procedure is exactly the same as for the two previous handlers, but the validation code is different because occupation must be Programmer or an empty string to be valid. We therefore add a new line to the constructor.

```
this.txtOccupation.Validating += new
    System.ComponentModel.CancelEventHandler(this.txtOccupation_Validating);
```

And then the handler itself:

```
private void txtOccupation_Validating(object sender,
                                      System.ComponentModel.CancelEventArgs e)
{
    // Cast the sender object to a textbox
    TextBox tb = (TextBox)sender;

    // Check if the values are correct
    if (tb.Text.CompareTo("Programmer") == 0 || tb.Text.Length == 0)
    {
        tb.Tag = true;
        tb.BackColor = System.Drawing.SystemColors.Window;
    }
    else
    {
        tb.Tag = false;
        tb.BackColor = Color.Red;
    }

    // Set the state of the OK button
    ValidateAll();
}
```

Our second to last challenge is the age text box. We don't want the user to type anything but positive numbers (including 0 to make the test simpler). To achieve this we'll use the `KeyPress` event to remove any unwanted characters before they are shown in the text box.

First, we subscribe to the `KeyPress` event. Select the `txtAge` text box and double-click on the **KeyPress** event in the Events list of the Properties window. The `KeyPress` event handler is specialized as well. The `System.Windows.Forms.KeyPressEventHandler` is supplied because the event needs information about the key that was pressed.

Add the following code to the event handler itself:

```
private void txtAge_KeyPress(object sender,
                            System.Windows.Forms.KeyPressEventArgs e)
{
    if ((e.KeyChar < 48 || e.KeyChar > 57) && e.KeyChar != 8)
        e.Handled = true; // Remove the character
}
```

The ASCII values for the characters between 0 and 9 lie between 48 and 57, so we make sure that the character is within this range. We make one exception though. The ASCII value 8 is the *Backspace* key, and for editing reasons, we allow this to slip through.

Setting the Handled property of KeyPressEventArgs to true tells the control that it shouldn't do anything else with the character, and so if the key pressed isn't a digit or a backspace, it is not shown.

As it is now, the control is not marked as invalid or valid. This is because we need another check to see if anything was entered at all. This is a simple thing as we've already written the method to perform this check and we simply subscribe to the Validating event for the Age control as well by adding this line to the constructor:

```
this.txtAge.Validating += new
        System.ComponentModel.CancelEventHandler(this.txtBoxEmpty_Validating);
```

One last case must be handled for all the controls. If the user has entered valid text in all the textboxes and then changes something, making the text invalid, the **OK** button remains enabled. So we have to handle one last event handler for all of the text boxes: the Change event which will disable the **OK** button should any text field contain invalid data.

The TextChanged event is fired whenever the text in the control changes. We subscribe to the event by adding the following lines to the constructor:

```
this.txtName.TextChanged += new System.EventHandler(this.txtBox_TextChanged);
this.txtAddress.TextChanged += new
                            System.EventHandler(this.txtBox_TextChanged);
this.txtAge.TextChanged += new System.EventHandler(this.txtBox_TextChanged);
this.txtOccupation.TextChanged += new
                            System.EventHandler(this.txtBox_TextChanged);
```

The TextChanged event uses the standard event handler we know from the Click event. Finally, we add the event itself.

```
private void txtBox_TextChanged(object sender, System.EventArgs e)
{
    // Cast the sender object to a Textbox
    TextBox tb = (TextBox)sender;

    // Test if the data is valid and set the tag and background
    // color accordingly.
    if (tb.Text.Length == 0 && tb != txtOccupation)
    {
```

```
        tb.Tag = false;
        tb.BackColor = Color.Red;
    }
    else if (tb == txtOccupation &&
                (tb.Text.Length != 0 && tb.Text.CompareTo("Programmer") != 0))
    {
        // Don't set the color here, as it will color change while the user
        // is typing
        tb.Tag = false;
    }
    else
    {
        tb.Tag = true;
        tb.BackColor = SystemColors.Window;
    }

    // Call ValidateAll to set the OK button
    ValidateAll();
}
```

This time we must find out exactly which control is calling the event handler, because we don't want the background color of the Occupation text box to change to red when the user starts typing. We do this by checking the Name property of the text box that was passed to us in the sender parameter.

Only one thing remains: the ValidateAll method that enables or disables the OK button.

```
private void ValidateAll()
{
    // Set the OK button to enabled if all the Tags are true
    this.btnOK.Enabled = ((bool)(this.txtAddress.Tag) &&
                          (bool)(this.txtAge.Tag) &&
                          (bool)(this.txtName.Tag) &&
                          (bool)(this.txtOccupation.Tag));
}
```

The method simply sets the value of the Enabled property of the OK button to true if all of the Tag properties are true. We need to cast the value of the Tag properties to a Boolean because it is stored as an object type.

If you test the program now, you should see something like this:

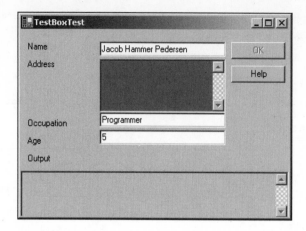

Notice that you can click the **Help** button while you are in a text box with invalid data without the background color changing to red.

The example we've just completed is quite long compared to the others you will see in this chapter – this is because we'll build on this example rather than starting from scratch with each example.

Remember you can download the source code for all the examples in this book from www.wrox.com.

The RadioButton and CheckBox Controls

As mentioned earlier, the RadioButton and CheckBox controls share their base class with the Button control, although their appearance and use differs substantially from the button.

Radio buttons traditionally display themselves as a label with a dot to the left of it, which can be either selected or not. You should use the radio buttons when you want to give the user a choice between several mutually exclusive options. An example of this could be, if you want to ask for the gender of the user.

To group radio boxes together so that they create one logical unit you must use a GroupBox control. By first placing a GroupBox onto a form, and then placing the RadioButton controls you need within the borders of the GroupBox, the RadioButton controls will know to change their state to reflect that only one within the group box can be selected. If you do not place them within a GroupBox, only one RadioButton on the form can be selected at any given time.

A CheckBox traditionally displays itself as a label with a small box with a checkmark to the left of it. You should use the check box when you want to allow the user to choose one or more options. An example could be a questionnaire asking which operating systems the user has tried (for example, Windows 95, Windows 98, Linux, etc.).

We'll look at the important properties and events of the two controls, starting with the RadioButton, and then move on to a quick example of their use.

RadioButton Properties

As the control derives from `ButtonBase` and we've already seen in our example that used the button earlier, there are only a few properties to describe. As always, should you need a complete list, please refer to the .NET Framework SDK Documentation.

Name	Description
Appearance	A `RadioButton` can be displayed either as a label with a circular check to the left, middle or right of it, or as a standard button. When it is displayed as a button, the control will appear pressed when selected and not pressed otherwise.
AutoCheck	When this property is `true`, a check mark is displayed when the user clicks the radio button. When it is `false` the radio button must be manually checked in code from the `Click` event handler.
CheckAlign	By using this property, you can change the alignment of the check box portion of the radio button. The default is `ContentAlignment.MiddleLeft`.
Checked	Indicates the status of the control. It is `true` if the control has a check mark, and `false` otherwise.

RadioButton Events

You will commonly only use one event when working with `RadioButton` controls, but as always there are many others that can be subscribed to. We'll only cover two in this chapter, and the only reason the second event is mentioned is that there is a subtle difference between the two that should be noted.

Name	Description
CheckedChanged	This event is sent when the check of the `RadioButton` changes.
Click	This event is sent every time the `RadioButton` is clicked. This is not the same as the `CheckedChange` event, because clicking a `RadioButton` two or more times in succession only changes the `Checked` property once – and only if it wasn't checked already. Moreover, if the `AutoCheck` property of the button being clicked is `false`, the button will not get checked at all, and again only the `Click` event will be sent.

CheckBox Properties

As you would imagine, the properties and events of this control are very similar to those of the `RadioButton`, but there are two new ones.

Name	Description
CheckState	Unlike the RadioButton, a CheckBox can have three states: Checked, Indeterminate, and Unchecked. When the state of the check box is Indeterminate, the control check next to the label is usually grayed, indicating that the current value of the check is not valid or has no meaning under the current circumstances.
ThreeState	When this property is false, the user will not be able to change the CheckState state to Indeterminate. You can, however, still change the CheckState property to Indeterminate from code.

CheckBox Events

You will normally use only one or two events on this control. Note that, even though the CheckChanged event exists on both the RadioButton and the CheckBox controls, the effects of the events differ.

Name	Description
CheckedChanged	Occurs whenever the Checked property of the check box changes. Note that in a CheckBox where the ThreeState property is true, it is possible to click the check box without changing the Checked property. This happens when the check box changes from checked to indeterminate state.
CheckedStateChanged	Occurs whenever the CheckedState property changes. As Checked and Unchecked are both possible values of the CheckedState property, this event will be sent whenever the Checked property changes. In addition to that, it will also be sent when the state changes from Checked to Indeterminate.

This concludes the events and properties of the RadioButton and CheckBox controls. But before we look at an example using these, let's take a look at the GroupBox control which we mentioned earlier.

The GroupBox Control

The GroupBox control is often used to logically group a set of controls such as the RadioButton and CheckBox, and provide a caption and a frame around this set.

Using the group box is as simple as dragging it onto a form, and then dragging the controls it should contain onto it (but not the other way round – you can't lay a group box over some pre-existing controls). The effect of this is that the parent of the controls becomes the group box, rather than the form, and it is therefore possible to have more than one RadioButton selected at any given time. Within the group box, however, only one RadioButton can be selected.

The relationship between parent and child probably needs to be explained a bit more. When a control is placed on a form, the form is said to become the parent of the control, and hence the control is the child of the form. When you place a GroupBox on a form, it becomes a child of a form. As a group box can itself contain controls, it becomes the parent of these controls. The effect of this is that moving the GroupBox will move all of the controls placed on it.

Another effect of placing controls on a group box is that it allows you to affect the contained controls by setting the corresponding property on the group box. For instance, if you want to disable all the controls within a group box, you can simply set the Enabled property of the GroupBox to false.

We will demonstrate the use of the GroupBox in the following example.

Try it Out – RadioButton and CheckBox Example

We'll modify the TextBoxTest example we created earlier when we demonstrated the use of text boxes. In that example, the only possible occupation was Programmer. Instead of forcing the user to type this out in full, we'll change this text box to a check box.

To demonstrate the use of the RadioButton, we'll ask the user to provide one more piece of information: their gender.

Change the text box example like this:

1. Remove the label named lblOccupation and the text box named txtOccupation.

2. Add a CheckBox, a GroupBox and two RadioButton controls, and name the new controls as shown in the picture below.

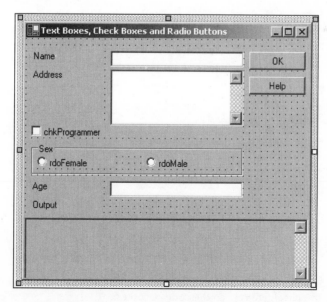

3. The Text property of the RadioButton and CheckBox controls should be the same as the names of the controls without the first three letters, and for the GroupBox the Text property should be Sex.

4. Set the Checked property of the chkProgrammer check box to true.

5. Set the Checked property of either rdoMale or rdoFemale to true. Note that you cannot set both to true. If you try to, the value of the other RadioButton is automatically changed to false.

No more needs to be done on the visual part of the example, but there are a number of changes in the code. First, we need to remove all the references to the text box that we've removed. Go to the code and complete the following steps.

6. In the constructor of the form, remove the three lines which refer to txtOccupation. This includes subscriptions to the Validating and TextChanged events and the line which sets the Tag property to false.

7. Remove the txtOccupation_Validating() method entirely.

Adding the Event Handlers

The txtBox_TextChanged method included tests to see if the calling control was the txtOccupation TextBox. We now know for sure that it will not be (since we removed it), and so we change the method by removing the else if block and modify the if test as follows:

```
private void txtBox_TextChanged(object sender, System.EventArgs e)
{
    // Cast the sender object to a Textbox
    TextBox tb = (TextBox)sender;

    // Test if the data is valid and set the tag background
    // color accordingly.
    if (tb.Text.Length == 0)
    {
        tb.Tag = false;
        tb.BackColor = Color.Red;
    }
    else
    {
        tb.Tag = true;
        tb.BackColor = SystemColors.Window;
    }

    // Call ValidateAll to set the OK button
    ValidateAll();
}
```

Another place in which we check the value of the text box we've removed is in the ValidateAll() method. Remove the check entirely so the code becomes:

```
private void ValidateAll()
{
    // Set the OK button to enabled if all the Tags are true
    this.btnOK.Enabled = ((bool)(this.txtAddress.Tag) &&
        (bool)(this.txtAge.Tag) &&
        (bool)(this.txtName.Tag));
}
```

Since we are using a check box rather than a text box we know that the user cannot enter any invalid information, as he or she will always be either a programmer or not.

We also know that the user is either male or female, and because we set the property of one of the RadioButtons to true, the user is prevented from choosing an invalid value. Therefore, the only thing left to do is change the help text and the output. We do this in the button event handlers:

```
private void btnHelp_Click(object sender, System.EventArgs e)
{
    // Write a short descrption of each TextBox in the Output TextBox
    string output;

    output = "Name = Your name\r\n";
    output += "Address = Your address\r\n";
    output += "Programmer = Check 'Programmer' if you are a programmer\r\n";
    output += "Sex = Choose your sex\r\n";
    output += "Age = Your age";

    // Insert the new text
    this.txtOutput.Text = output;
}
```

Only the help text is changed, so nothing surprising in the help method. It gets slightly more interesting in the OK method:

```
private void btnOK_Click(object sender, System.EventArgs e)
{
    // No testing for invalid values are made, as that should
    // not be neccessary

    string output;

    // Concatenate the text values of the four TextBoxes
    output = "Name: " + this.txtName.Text + "\r\n";
    output += "Address: " + this.txtAddress.Text + "\r\n";
    output += "Occupation: " + (string)(this.chkProgrammer.Checked ?
            "Programmer" : "Not a programmer") + "\r\n";
    output += "Sex: " + (string)(this.rdoFemale.Checked ? "Female" :
                                                "Male") + "\r\n";
    output += "Age: " + this.txtAge.Text;

    // Insert the new text
    this.txtOutput.Text = output;
}
```

The first of the highlighted lines is the line in which the occupation of the user is printed. We investigate the Checked property of the CheckBox, and if it is true, we write the string **Programmer**. If it is false, we write **Not a programmer**.

The second line examines only the radio button rdoFemale. If the Checked property is true on that control, we know that the user claims to be female. If it is false we know that the user claims to be male. It is possible to have radio buttons without any of them being checked when we start the program – but because we checked one of the radio buttons at design time, we know for sure that one of the two radio buttons will always be checked.

When you run the example now, you should get a result similar to this:

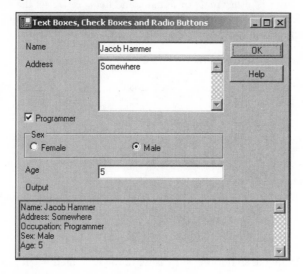

The RichTextBox Control

Like the normal TextBox, the RichTextBox control is derived from TextBoxBase. Because of this, it shares a number of features with the TextBox, but is much more diverse. Where a TextBox is commonly used with the purpose of obtaining short text strings from the user, the RichTextBox is used to display and enter formatted text (for example **bold**, underline and *italic*). It does so using a standard for formatted text called Rich Text Format or RTF.

In the previous example, we used a standard TextBox. We could just as well have used a RichTextBox to do the job. In fact, as we'll see in the example later, you can remove the TextBox name txtOutput and insert a RichTextBox in its place with the same name, and the example behaves exactly as it did before.

RichTextBox Properties

If this kind of text box is more advanced than the one we explored in the previous section, you'd expect there are new properties that can be used, and you'd be correct. Here are descriptions of the most commonly used properties of the RichTextBox:

Name	Description
CanRedo	This property is true when the last undone operation can be reapplied using Redo.
CanUndo	This property is true if it is possible to undo the last action on the RichTextBox. Note that CanUndo is defined in TextBoxBase, so it is available to TextBox controls as well.
RedoActionName	This property holds the name of an action that would be performed by the Redo method.
DetectUrls	Set this property to true to make the control detect URLs and format them (underline as in a browser).
Rtf	This corresponds to the Text property, except that this holds the text in RTF.
SelectedRtf	Use this property to get or set the selected text in the control, in RTF. If you copy this text to another application, for example, Word, it will retain all formatting.
SelectedText	Like SelectedRtf you can use this property to get or set the selected text. However, unlike the RTF version of the property, all formatting is lost.
SelectionAlignment	This represents the alignment of the selected text. It can be Center, Left, or Right.
SelectionBullet	Use this property to find out if the selection is formatted with a bullet in front of it, or use it to insert or remove bullets.
BulletIndent	Use this property to specify the number of pixels a bullet should be indented.
SelectionColor	Allows you to change the color of the text in the selection.
SelectionFont	Allows you to change the font of the text in the selection.
SelectionLength	Using this property, you either set or retrieve the length of a selection.
SelectionType	This property holds information about the selection. It will tell you if one or more OLE objects are selected or if only text is selected.
ShowSelectionMargin	If you set this property to true, a margin will be shown at the left of the RichTextBox. This will make it easier for the user to select text.
UndoActionName	Gets the name of the action that will be used if the user chooses to undo something.
SelectionProtected	You can specify that certain parts of the text should not be changed by setting this property to true.

As you can see from the listing above, most of the new properties have to do with a selection. This is because, any formatting you will be applying when a user is working on his or her text will probably be done on a selection made by that user. In case no selection is made, the formatting will start from the point in the text where the cursor is located, called the insertion point.

RichTextBox Events

Most of the events used by the `RichTextBox` are the same as those used by the `TextBox`. There are a few new ones of interest though:

Name	Description
LinkedClick	This event is sent when a user clicks on a link within the text.
Protected	This event is sent when a user attempts to modify text that has been marked as protected.
SelectionChanged	This event is sent when the selection changes. If for some reason you don't want the user to change the selection, you can prevent the change here.

Try it Out – RichTextBox Example

We'll create a very basic text editor in this example. It demonstrates how to change basic formatting of text and how to load and save the text from the `RichTextBox`. For the sake of simplicity, the example loads from and saves to a fixed file.

As always, we'll start by designing the form:

1. Create a new C# Windows application called `RichTextBoxTest` in the `C:\BegVCSharp\Chapter13` directory.

2. Create the form as shown in the picture below. The text box named `txtSize` should be a `TextBox` control. The text box named `rtfText` should be a `RichTextBox` control.

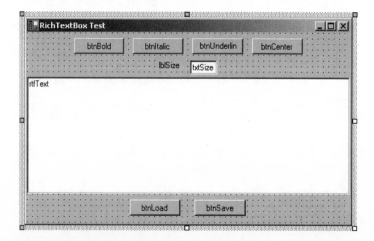

3. Name the controls as indicated in the picture above and clear the `Text` property of both `rtfText` and `txtSize`.

4. Apart from the text boxes, set the `Text` of all controls to the same as the names except for the first three letters.

5. Change the `Text` property of the `txtSize` text box to 10.

6. Anchor the controls as in the following table.

Control name	Anchor value
`btnLoad` and `btnSave`	Bottom
`RtfText`	Top, Left, Bottom, Right
All others	Top

7. Set the `MinimumSize` property of the form to the same as the `Size` property.

Adding the Event Handlers

That concludes the visual part of the example and we'll move straight to the code. Double-click the Bold button to add the `Click` event handler to the code. Here is the code for the event:

```
private void btnBold_Click(object sender, System.EventArgs e)
{
    Font oldFont;
    Font newFont;

    // Get the font that is being used in the selected text
    oldFont = this.rtfText.SelectionFont;

    // If the font is using bold style now, we should remove the
    // Formatting
    if (oldFont.Bold)
        newFont = new Font(oldFont, oldFont.Style & ~FontStyle.Bold);
    else
        newFont = new Font(oldFont, oldFont.Style | FontStyle.Bold);

    // Insert the new font and return focus to the RichTextBox
    this.rtfText.SelectionFont = newFont;
    this.rtfText.Focus();
}
```

We start by getting the font that is being used in the current selection and assigning it to a local variable `oldFont`. Then we check if this selection is already bold. If it is, we want to remove the bold setting; otherwise we want to set it. We create a new font using `oldFont` as the prototype but add or remove the bold style as needed.

Finally, we assign the new font to the selection and return focus to the `RichTextBox` – we'll look more at the `Font` object in Chapters 15 and 16.

The event handlers for `btnItalic` and `btnUnderline` are the same as the one above, except we are checking the appropriate styles. Double-click the two buttons **Italic** and **Underline** and add this code:

```
private void btnItalic_Click(object sender, System.EventArgs e)
{
    Font oldFont;
    Font newFont;

    // Get the font that is being used in the selected text
    oldFont = this.rtfText.SelectionFont;

    // If the font is using Italic style now, we should remove it
    if (oldFont.Italic)
        newFont = new Font(oldFont, oldFont.Style & ~FontStyle.Italic);
    else
        newFont = new Font(oldFont, oldFont.Style | FontStyle.Italic);

    // Insert the new font
    this.rtfText.SelectionFont = newFont;
    this.rtfText.Focus();
}

private void btnUnderline_Click(object sender, System.EventArgs e)
{
    Font oldFont;
    Font newFont;

    // Get the font that is being used in the selected text
    oldFont = this.rtfText.SelectionFont;

    // If the font is using Underline style now, we should remove it
    if (oldFont.Underline)
        newFont = new Font(oldFont, oldFont.Style & ~FontStyle.Underline);
    else
        newFont = new Font(oldFont, oldFont.Style | FontStyle.Underline);

    // Insert the new font
    this.rtfText.SelectionFont = newFont;
    this.rtfText.Focus();
}
```

Double-click the last of the formatting buttons, `Center`, and add the following code:

```
private void btnCenter_Click(object sender, System.EventArgs e)
{
    if (this.rtfText.SelectionAlignment == HorizontalAlignment.Center)
        this.rtfText.SelectionAlignment = HorizontalAlignment.Left;
    else
        this.rtfText.SelectionAlignment = HorizontalAlignment.Center;
    this.rtfText.Focus();
}
```

Here we must check another property, `SelectionAlignment`, to see if the text in the selection is already centered. `HorizontalAlignment` is an enumeration with values `Left`, `Right`, `Center`, `Justify`, and `NotSet`. In this case we simply check if `Center` is set, and if it is, we set the alignment to left. If it isn't we set it to `Center`.

The final formatting our little text editor will be able to perform is setting the size of text. We'll add two event handlers for the text box `Size`, one for controlling the input, and one to detect when the user has finished entering a value.

Add the following lines to the constructor of the form:

```
public Form1()
{
    InitializeComponent();

    // Event Subscription
    this.txtSize.KeyPress += new
        System.Windows.Forms.KeyPressEventHandler(this.txtSize_KeyPress);
    this.txtSize.Validating += new
        System.ComponentModel.CancelEventHandler(this.txtSize_Validating);
}
```

We saw these two event handlers in the previous example. Both of the events use a helper method called `ApplyTextSize` that takes a string with the size of the text.

```
private void txtSize_KeyPress(object sender,
                            System.Windows.Forms.KeyPressEventArgs e)
{
    // Remove all characters that are not numbers, backspace and enter
    if ((e.KeyChar < 48 || e.KeyChar > 57) &&
                                        e.KeyChar != 8 && e.KeyChar != 13)
    {
        e.Handled = true;
    }
    else if (e.KeyChar == 13)
    {
        // Apply size if the user hits enter
        TextBox txt = (TextBox)sender;

        if (txt.Text.Length > 0)
            ApplyTextSize(txt.Text);
        e.Handled = true;
        this.rtfText.Focus();
    }
}

private void txtSize_Validating(object sender,
                            System.ComponentModel.CancelEventArgs e)
{
    TextBox txt = (TextBox)sender;
```

```
      ApplyTextSize(txt.Text);
      this.rtfText.Focus();
}

private void ApplyTextSize(string textSize)
{
    // Convert the text to a float because we'll be needing a float shortly
    float newSize = Convert.ToSingle(textSize);
    FontFamily currentFontFamily;
    Font newFont;

    // Create a new font of the same family but with the new size
    currentFontFamily = this.rtfText.SelectionFont.FontFamily;
    newFont = new Font(currentFontFamily, newSize);

    // Set the font of the selected text to the new font
    this.rtfText.SelectionFont = newFont;
}
```

The work we are interested in takes place in the helper method `ApplyTextSize()`. It starts by converting the size from a string to a float. We've prevented the user from entering anything but integers, but when we create the new font, we need a `float`, so convert it to the correct type.

After that, we get the family to which the font belongs and we create a new font from that family with the new size. Finally, we set the font of the selection to the new font.

That's all the formatting we can do, but some is handled by the `RichTextBox` itself. If you try to run the example now, you will be able to set the text to bold, italic, and underline, and you can center the text. That is what you expect, but there is something else that is interesting – try to type a web address, for example www.wrox.com in the text. The text is recognized by the control as an Internet address, is underlined, and the mouse pointer changes to a hand when you move it over the text. If that leads you to believe that you can click it and be brought to the page, you are almost correct. We need to handle the event that is sent when the user clicks a link: `LinkClicked`.

We do this by subscribing to the event in the constructor:

```
this.rtfText.LinkClicked += new
        System.Windows.Forms.LinkClickedEventHandler(this.rtfText_LinkedClick);
```

We haven't seen this event handler before – it is used to provide the text of the link that was clicked. The handler is surprisingly simple and looks like this:

```
private void rtfText_LinkedClick(object sender,
                                 System.Windows.Forms.LinkClickedEventArgs e)
{
    System.Diagnostics.Process.Start(e.LinkText);
}
```

This code opens the default browser if it isn't open already and navigates to the site to which the link that was clicked is pointing.

The editing part of the application is now done. All that remains is to load and save the contents of the control. We'll use a fixed file to do this.

Double-click the Load button, and add the following code:

```
private void btnLoad_Click(object sender, System.EventArgs e)
{
   // Load the file into the RichTextBox
   try
   {
      rtfText.LoadFile("../../Test.rtf");
   }
   catch (System.IO.FileNotFoundException)
   {
      MessageBox.Show("No file to load yet");
   }
}
```

That's it! Nothing else has to be done. Because we are dealing with files, there is always a chance that we might encounter exceptions, and we have to handle these. In the Load method we handle the exception that is thrown if the file doesn't exist. It is equally simple to save the file. Double-click the Save button and add this:

```
private void btnSave_Click(object sender, System.EventArgs e)
{
   // Save the text
   try
   {
      rtfText.SaveFile("../../Test.rtf");
   }
   catch (System.Exception err)
   {
      MessageBox.Show(err.Message);
   }
}
```

Run the example now, format some text and click Save. Clear the text box and click Load and the text you just saved should reappear.

This concludes the RichTextBox example. When you run it, you should be able to produce something like this:

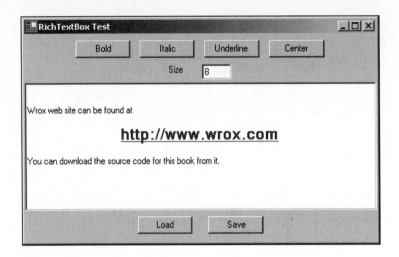

The ListBox and CheckedListBox Controls

List boxes are used to show a list of strings from which one or more can be selected at a time. Just like check boxes and radio buttons, the list box provides a means of asking the user to make one or more selections. You should use a list box when at design time you don't know the actual number of values the user can choose from (an example could be a list of co-workers). Even if you know all the possible values at design time, you should consider using a list box if there are a great number of values.

The ListBox class is derived from the ListControl class, which provides the basic functionality for list-type controls that ship with the .NET Framework.

Another kind of list box available is called CheckedListBox and is derived from the ListBox class. It provides a list just like the ListBox, but in addition to the text strings it provides a check for each item in the list.

ListBox Properties

In the list below all the properties exist in both the ListBox class and CheckedListBox class unless explicitly stated.

Name	Description
SelectedIndex	This value indicates the zero-based index of the selected item in the list box. If the list box can contain multiple selections at the same time, this property holds the index of the first item in the selected list.
ColumnWidth	In a list box with multiple columns, this property specifies the width of the columns.

Name	Description
Items	The `Items` collection contains all of the items in the list box. You use the properties of this collection to add and remove items.
MultiColumn	A list box can have more than one column. Use this property to get or set the number of columns in the list box.
SelectedIndices	This property is a collection, which holds all of the zero-based indices of the selected items in the list box.
SelectedItem	In a list box where only one item can be selected, this property contains the selected item if any. In a list box where more than one selection can be made, it will contain the first of the selected items.
SelectedItems	This property is a collection, which contains all of the items currently selected.
SelectionMode	You can choose between four different modes of selection from the `ListSelectionMode` enumeration in a list box: ❑ None: No items can be selected ❑ One: Only one item can be selected at any time ❑ MultiSimple: Multiple items can be selected ❑ MultiExtended: Multiple items can be selected and the user can use the *Ctrl*, *Shift* and arrows keys to make selections
Sorted	Setting this property to `true` will cause the `ListBox` to sort the items it contains alphabetically.
Text	We've seen `Text` properties on a number of controls, but this one works differently from any we've seen so far. If you set the `Text` property of the list box control, it searches for an item that matches the text, and selects it. If you get the `Text` property, the value returned is the first selected item in the list. This property cannot be used if the `SelectionMode` is None.
CheckedIndices	(`CheckedListBox` only) This property is a collection which contains indexes of all the items in the `CheckedListBox` that have a checked or indeterminate state.
CheckedItems	(`CheckedListBox` only) This is a collection of all the items in a `CheckedListBox` that are in a checked or indeterminate state.
CheckOnClick	(`CheckedListBox` only) If this property is `true`, an item will change its state whenever the user clicks it.
ThreeDCheckBoxes	(`CheckedListBox` only) You can choose between `CheckBoxes` that are flat or normal by setting this property.

ListBox Methods

In order to work efficiently with a list box, you should know a number of methods that can be called. The following table lists the most common methods. Unless indicated, the methods belong to both the `ListBox` and `CheckedListBox` classes:

Name	Description
ClearSelected()	Clears all selections in the `ListBox`.
FindString()	Finds the first string in the `ListBox` beginning with a string you specify (for example `FindString("a")` will find the first string in the `ListBox` beginning with a.
FindStringExact()	Like `FindString` but the entire string must be matched.
GetSelected()	Returns a value that indicates whether an item is selected.
SetSelected()	Sets or clears the selection of an item.
ToString()	Returns the currently selected item.
GetItemChecked()	(`CheckedListBox` only) Returns a value indicating if an item is checked or not.
GetItemCheckState()	(`CheckedListBox` only) Returns a value indicating the check state of an item.
SetItemChecked()	(`CheckedListBox` only) Sets the item specified to a checked state.
SetItemCheckState()	(`CheckedListBox` only) Sets the check state of an item.

ListBox Events

Normally the events you will want to be aware of when working with a `ListBox` or `CheckedListBox` are those that have to do with the selections that are being made by the user:

Name	Description
ItemCheck	(`CheckedListBox` only) Occurs when the check state of one of the list items changes.
SelectedIndexChanged	Occurs when the index of the selected item changes.

Try it Out – ListBox Example

We will create a small example with both a `ListBox` and a `CheckedListBox`. The user can check items in the `CheckedListBox` and then click a button which will move the checked items to the normal `ListBox`. We create the dialog as follows:

1. Create a new Windows application called `Lists` in directory `C:\BegVCSharp\Chapter13`.

2. Add a `ListBox`, a `CheckedListBox` and a button to the form and change the names as shown in the picture below.

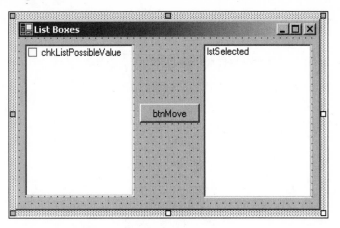

3. Change the `Text` property of the button to **Move**.

4. Change the `CheckOnClick` property of the `CheckedListBox` to **true**.

Adding the Event Handlers

Now we are ready to add some code. When the user clicks the **Move** button, we want to find the items that are checked, and copy those into the right-hand list box.

Double-click the button and enter this code:

```
private void btnMove_Click(object sender, System.EventArgs e)
{
    // Check if there are any checked items in the CheckedListBox
    if (this.chkListPossibleValues.CheckedItems.Count > 0)
    {
        // Clear the ListBox we'll move the selections to
        this.lstSelected.Items.Clear();

        // Loop through the CheckedItems collection of the CheckedListBox
        // and add the items in the Selected ListBox
        foreach (string item in this.chkListPossibleValues.CheckedItems)
        {
            this.lstSelected.Items.Add(item.ToString());
        }

        // Clear all the checks in the CheckedListBox
        for (int i = 0; i < this.chkListPossibleValues.Items.Count; i++)
            this.chkListPossibleValues.SetItemChecked(i, false);
    }
}
```

We start by checking the `Count` property of the `CheckedItems` collection. This will be greater than zero if any items in the collection are checked. We then clear all items in the `lstSelected` list box, and loop through the `CheckedItems` collection, adding each item to the `lstSelected` list box. Finally, we remove all the checks in the `CheckedListBox`.

Now we just need something in the `CheckedListBox` to move. We can add the items while in design mode, by selecting the `Items` property in the Properties window and adding the items there:

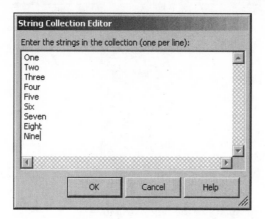

Also we can add items in code, for example in the constructor of our form:

```
public Form1()
{
    //
    // Required for Windows Form Designer support
    //
    InitializeComponent();

    // Add a tenth element to the CheckedListBox
    this.chkListPossibleValues.Items.Add("Ten");
}
```

Here we add a tenth element to the `CheckedListBox`, since we already have entered nine from the designer.

This concludes the list box example, and if you run it now, you will get something like this:

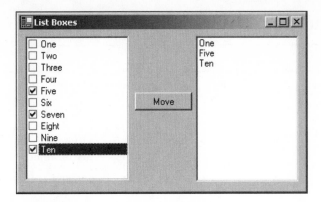

The ListView Control

The list from which you select files to open in the standard dialog boxes in Windows is a `ListView` control. Everything you can do to the view in the standard list view dialog (Large icons, details view, etc.), you can do with the `ListView` control provided with the .NET Framework.

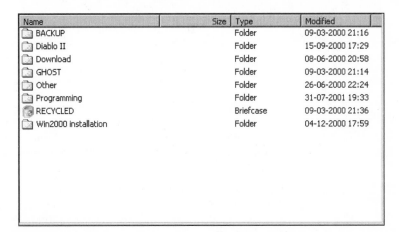

The list view is usually used to present data where the user is allowed some control over the detail and style of the presentation. It is possible to display the data contained in the control as columns and rows much like in a grid, as a single column or with varying icon representations. The most commonly used list view is like the one seen above which is used to navigate the folders on a computer.

The `ListView` control is easily the most complex control we're going to encounter in this chapter, and covering all of it is beyond the scope of this book. What we'll do is provide a solid base for you to work on by writing an example that utilizes many of the most important features of the `ListView` control, and by a thorough description of the numerous properties, events, and methods that can be used. We'll also take a look at the `ImageList` control, which is used to store the images used in a `ListView` control.

ListView Properties

Name	Description
Activation	By using this property, you can control how a user activates an item in the list view. The possible values are: ❑ Standard: This setting is that which the user has chosen for his or her machine. ❑ OneClick: Clicking an item activates it. ❑ TwoClick: Double-clicking an item activates it.
Alignment	This property allows you to control how the items in the list view are aligned. The four possible values are: ❑ Default: If the user drags and drops an item it remains where he or she dropped it. ❑ Left: Items are aligned to the left edge of the ListView control. ❑ Top: Items are aligned to the top edge of the ListView control. ❑ SnapToGrid: The ListView control contains an invisible grid to which the items will snap.
AllowColumnReorder	If you set this property to true, you allow the user to change the order of the columns in a list view. If you do so, you should be sure that the routines that fill the list view are able to insert the items properly, even after the order of the columns is changed.
AutoArrange	If you set this property to true, items will automatically arrange themselves according to the Alignment property. If the user drags an item to the center of the list view, and Alignment is Left, then the item will automatically jump to the left of the list view. This property is only meaningful if the View property is LargeIcon or SmallIcon.
CheckBoxes	If you set this property to true, every item in the list view will have a CheckBox displayed to the left of it. This property is only meaningful if the View property is Details or List.
CheckedIndices CheckedItems	These two properties gives you access to a collection of indices and items respectively, containing the checked items in the list.
Columns	A list view can contain columns. This property gives you access to the collection of columns through which you can add or remove columns.

Name	Description
FocusedItem	This property holds the item that has focus in the list view. If nothing is selected, it is null.
FullRowSelect	When this property is true, and an item is clicked, the entire row in which the item resides will be highlighted. If it is false, only the item itself will be highlighted.
GridLines	Setting this property to true will cause the list view to draw grid lines between rows and columns. This property is only meaningful when the View property is Details.
HeaderStyle	You can control how the column headers are displayed. There are three styles: ❑ Clickable: The column header works like a button. ❑ NonClickable: The column headers do not respond to mouse clicks. ❑ None: The column headers are not displayed.
HoverSelection	When this property is true, the user can select an item in the list view by hovering the mouse pointer over it.
Items	The collection of items in the list view.
LabelEdit	When this property is true, the user can edit the content of the first column in a Details view.
LabelWrap	If this property is true, labels will wrap over as many lines is needed to display all of the text.
LargeImageList	This property holds the ImageList, which holds large images. These images can be used when the View property is LargeIcon.
MultiSelect	Set this property to true to allow the user to select multiple items.
Scrollable	Set this property to true to display scrollbars.
SelectedIndices SelectedItems	These two properties contain the collections that hold the indices and items that are selected, respectively.
SmallImageList	When the View property is SmallIcon this property holds the ImageList that contain the images used.

Table continued on following page

Name	Description
Sorting	You can allow the list view to sort the items it contains. There are three possible modes: ❑ Ascending ❑ Descending ❑ None
StateImageList	The ImageList contains masks for images that are used as overlays on the LargeImageList and SmallImageList images to represent custom states.
TopItem	Returns the item at the top of the list view.
View	A list view can display its items in four different modes: ❑ LargeIcon: All items are displayed with a large icon (32x32) and a label. ❑ SmallIcon: All items are displayed with a small icon (16x16) and a label. ❑ List: Only one column is displayed. That column can contain an icon and a label. ❑ Details: Any number of columns can be displayed. Only the first column can contain an icon.

ListView Methods

For a control as complex as the list view, there are surprisingly few methods specific to it. They are described in the table below.

Name	Description
BeginUpdate()	By calling this method you tell the list view to stop drawing updates until EndUpdate() is called. This is useful when you are inserting many items at once, because it stops the view from flickering and dramatically increases speed.
Clear()	Clears the list view completely. All items and columns are removed.
EndUpdate()	Call this method after calling BeginUpdate. When you call this method, the list view will draw all of its items.
EnsureVisible()	When you call this method, the list view will scroll itself to make the item with the index you specified visible.
GetItemAt()	Returns the ListViewItem at position x, y in the list view.

ListView Events

The `ListView` control events that you might want to handle are:

Name	Description
AfterLabelEdit	This event occurs after a label has been edited.
BeforeLabelEdit	This event occurs before a user begins editing a label.
ColumnClick	This event occurs when a column is clicked.
ItemActivate	This event occurs when an item is activated.

ListViewItem

An item in a list view is always an instance of the `ListViewItem` class. The `ListViewItem` holds information such as text and the index of the icon to display. `ListViewItem` objects have a `SubItems` property that holds instances of another class, `ListViewSubItem`. These sub items are displayed if the `ListView` control is in `Details` mode. Each of the sub items represents a column in the list view. The main difference of the sub items and the main items is that a sub item cannot display an icon.

You add `ListViewItems` to the `ListView` through the `Items` collection and `ListViewSubItems` to a `ListViewItem` through the `SubItems` collection on the `ListViewItem`.

ColumnHeader

To make a list view display column headers you add instances of a class called `ColumnHeader` to the `Columns` collection of the `ListView`. `ColumnHeaders` provide a caption for the columns that can be displayed when the `ListView` is in `Details` mode.

The ImageList Control

The `ImageList` control provides a collection that can be used to store images used in other controls on your form. You can store images of any size in an image list, but within each control every image must be of the same size. In the case of the `ListView`, this means that you need two `ImageList` controls to be able to display both large and small images.

The `ImageList` is the first control we've visited in this chapter that does not display itself at runtime. When you drag it to a form you are developing, it'll not be placed on the form itself, but below it in a tray, which contains all such components. This nice feature is provided to stop controls that are not part of the user interface from clogging up the forms designer. The control is manipulated in exactly the same way as any other control, except that you cannot move it around.

You can add images to the `ImageList` at both design-time and run-time. If you know at design-time what images you want to display, you can add the images by clicking the button at the right-hand side of the `Images` property. This will bring up a dialog on which you can browse to the images you wish to insert. If you choose to add the images at run-time, you add them through the `Images` collection.

Try it Out – ListView Example

The best way of learning about using a `ListView` control and its associated image lists is through an example. We'll create a dialog with a `ListView` and two `ImageLists`. The `ListView` will display files and folders on your hard drive. For the sake of simplicity, we will not be extracting the correct icons from the files and folders, but rather use a standard folder icon for the folders and an information icon for files.

By double-clicking the folders you can browse into the folder tree and a back button is provided to move up the tree. Four radio buttons are used to change the mode of the list view at runtime. If a file is double-clicked we'll attempt to execute it.

As always we'll start by creating the user interface:

1. Create a new Windows application called `ListView` in the `C:\BegVCSharp\Chapter13` directory.

2. Add a `ListView`, a `Button`, a `Label`, and a `GroupBox` to the form. Then, add four radio buttons to the group box to get a form looking like the picture below.

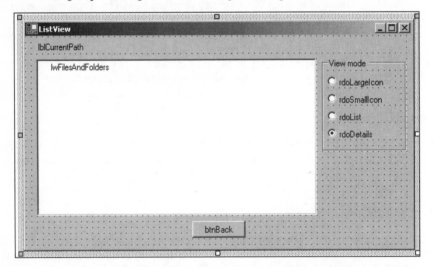

3. Name the controls as shown in the picture above. The `ListView` will not display its name as in the picture above; I've added an extra item just to show the name here – you don't need to add this item.

4. Change the `Text` properties of the radio buttons and button to be the same as the name, except for the first three letters, and set the `Text` property of the form to ListView.

5. Clear the `Text` property of the label.

6. Add two `ImageList` controls to the form by double-clicking the control's icon in the Toolbox. Rename the controls `ilSmall` and `ilLarge`.

7. Change the Size property of the ImageList named ilLarge to 32, 32.

8. Click the button to the right of the Images property of the ilLarge image list to bring up the dialog on which you can browse to the images you want to insert.

9. Click Add and browse to the folder under Visual Studio .NET that contains the images. The files are:

```
<Drive>:\Program Files\Microsoft Visual Studio
.NET\Common7\Graphics\Icons\Win95\clsdfold.ico
    and

<Drive>:\Program Files\Microsoft Visual Studio
.NET\Common7\Graphics\Icons\Computer\msgbox04.ico
```

10. Make sure the folder icon is at the top of the list.

11. Repeat steps 8 and 9 with the other ImageList, ilSmall.

12. Set the Checked property of the radio button rdoDetails to true.

13. Set the following properties on the list view:

Property	Value
MultiSelect	true
LargeImageList	ilLarge
SmallImageList	ilSmall
View	Details

Adding the Event Handlers

That concludes our user interface and we can move on to the code. First of all, we'll need a field to hold the folders we've browsed through in order to be able to return to them when the back button is clicked. We will store the absolute path of the folders, and so we choose a StringCollection for the job:

```
public class Form1 : System.Windows.Forms.Form
{
    // Member field to hold previous folders
    private System.Collections.Specialized.StringCollection folderCol;
```

We didn't create any column headers in the forms designer, so we'll have to do that now. We create them in a method called CreateHeadersAndFillListView():

```
private void CreateHeadersAndFillListView()
{
    ColumnHeader colHead;
```

```
    // First header
    colHead = new ColumnHeader();
    colHead.Text = "Filename";
    this.lwFilesAndFolders.Columns.Add(colHead); // Insert the header

    // Second header
    colHead = new ColumnHeader();
    colHead.Text = "Size";
    this.lwFilesAndFolders.Columns.Add(colHead); // Insert the header

    // Third header
    colHead = new ColumnHeader();
    colHead.Text = "Last accessed";
    this.lwFilesAndFolders.Columns.Add(colHead); // Insert the header
}
```

We start by declaring a single variable, colHead, which we will use to create the three column headers. For each of the three headers we declare the variable as new, and assign the Text to it before adding it to the Columns collection of the ListView.

The final initialization of the form as it is displayed the first time is to fill the list view with files and folders from your hard disk. This is done in another method:

```
private void PaintListView(string root)
{
    try
    {
        // Two local variables that is used to create the items to insert
        ListViewItem lvi;
        ListViewItem.ListViewSubItem lvsi;

        // If there's no root folder, we can't insert anything
        if (root.CompareTo("") == 0)
            return;

        // Get information about the root folder.
        System.IO.DirectoryInfo dir = new System.IO.DirectoryInfo(root);

        // Retrieve the files and folders from the root folder.
        DirectoryInfo[] dirs = dir.GetDirectories(); // Folders
        FileInfo[] files = dir.GetFiles();           // Files

        // Clear the ListView. Note that we call the Clear method on the
        // Items collection rather than on the ListView itself.
        // The Clear method of the ListView remove everything, including column
        // headers, and we only want to remove the items from the view.
        this.lwFilesAndFolders.Items.Clear();

        // Set the label with the current path
        this.lblCurrentPath.Text = root;

        // Lock the ListView for updates
        this.lwFilesAndFolders.BeginUpdate();
```

```csharp
        // Loop through all folders in the root folder and insert them
        foreach (System.IO.DirectoryInfo di in dirs)
        {
            // Create the main ListViewItem
            lvi = new ListViewItem();
            lvi.Text = di.Name; // Folder name
            lvi.ImageIndex = 0; // The folder icon has index 0
            lvi.Tag = di.FullName; // Set the tag to the qualified path of the
                              // folder

            // Create the two ListViewSubItems.
            lvsi = new ListViewItem.ListViewSubItem();
            lvsi.Text = ""; // Size - a folder has no size and so this column
                         // is empty
            lvi.SubItems.Add(lvsi); // Add the sub item to the ListViewItem

            lvsi = new ListViewItem.ListViewSubItem();
            lvsi.Text = di.LastAccessTime.ToString(); // Last accessed column
            lvi.SubItems.Add(lvsi); // Add the sub item to the ListViewItem

            // Add the ListViewItem to the Items collection of the ListView
            this.lwFilesAndFolders.Items.Add(lvi);
        }

        // Loop through all the files in the root folder
        foreach (System.IO.FileInfo fi in files)
        {
            // Create the main ListViewItem
            lvi = new ListViewItem();
            lvi.Text = fi.Name; // Filename
            lvi.ImageIndex = 1; // The icon we use to represent a folder has
            // index 1
            lvi.Tag = fi.FullName; // Set the tag to the qualified path of the
            // file

            // Create the two sub items
            lvsi = new ListViewItem.ListViewSubItem();
            lvsi.Text = fi.Length.ToString(); // Length of the file
            lvi.SubItems.Add(lvsi); // Add to the SubItems collection

            lvsi = new ListViewItem.ListViewSubItem();
            lvsi.Text = fi.LastAccessTime.ToString(); // Last Accessed Column
            lvi.SubItems.Add(lvsi); // Add to the SubItems collection

            // Add the item to the Items collection of the ListView
            this.lwFilesAndFolders.Items.Add(lvi);
        }

        // Unlock the ListView. The items that have been inserted will now
        // be displayed
        this.lwFilesAndFolders.EndUpdate();
    }
    catch (System.Exception err)
    {
        MessageBox.Show("Error: " + err.Message);
    }
}
```

Before the first of the two `foreach` blocks we call `BeginUpdate()` on the `ListView` control. Remember that the `BeginUpdate()` method on the `ListView` signals the `ListView` control to stop updating its visible area until `EndUpdate()` is called. If we did not call this method, filling the list view would be slower and the list may flicker as the items are added. Just after the second `foreach` block we call `EndUpdate()`, which makes the `ListView` control draw the items we've filled it with.

The two `foreach` blocks contain the code we are interested in. We start by creating a new instance of a `ListViewItem` and then setting the `Text` property to the name of the file or folder we are going to insert. The `ImageIndex` of the `ListViewItem` refers to the index of an item in one of the `ImageLists`. Because of that, it is important that the icons have the same indexes in the two `ImageLists`. We use the `Tag` property to save the fully qualified path to both folders and files, for use when the user double-clicks the item.

Then, we create the two sub items. These are simply assigned the text to display and then added to the `SubItems` collection of the `ListViewItem`.

Finally, the `ListViewItem` is added to the `Items` collection of the `ListView`. The `ListView` is smart enough to simply ignore the sub items, if the view mode is anything but `Details`, so we add the sub items no matter what the view mode is now.

Note that there are some aspects of the code we haven't discussed here – namely the lines that actually obtain information about the files:

```
// Get information about the root folder.
System.IO.DirectoryInfo dir = new System.IO.DirectoryInfo(root);

// Retrieve the files and folders from the root folder.
DirectoryInfo[] dirs = dir.GetDirectories(); // Folders
FileInfo[] files = dir.GetFiles();           // Files
```

These lines use classes from the `System.IO` namespace for accessing files, so we need to add the following `using` directive to the top of our code:

```
using System.IO;
```

We'll talk more about file access and `System.IO` in Chapter 20, but to give you an idea of what's going on, the `GetDirectories()` method of the `DirectoryInfo` object returns a collection of objects that represent the folders in the directory we're looking in, and the `GetFiles()` method returns a collection of objects that represent the files in the current directory. We can loop through these collections, as we do in the code above, using the object's `Name` property to return the name of the relevant directory or file, and create a `ListViewItem` to hold this string.

All that remains to be done for the list view to display the root folder is to call the two functions in the constructor of the form. At the same time we instantiate the `folderCol StringCollection` with the root folder:

```
InitializeComponent();

// Init ListView and folder collection
folderCol = new System.Collections.Specialized.StringCollection();
CreateHeadersAndFillListView();
PaintListView(@"C:\");
folderCol.Add(@"C:\");
```

In order to allow the user to double-click an item in the ListView to browse the folders, we need to subscribe to the `ItemActivate` event. We add the subscription to the constructor:

```
this.lwFilesAndFolders.ItemActivate += new
                    System.EventHandler(this.lwFilesAndFolders_ItemActivate);
```

The corresponding event handler looks like this:

```
private void lwFilesAndFolders_ItemActivate(object sender, System.EventArgs e)
{
    // Cast the sender to a ListView and get the tag of the first selected
    // item.
    System.Windows.Forms.ListView lw = (System.Windows.Forms.ListView)sender;
    string filename = lw.SelectedItems[0].Tag.ToString();

    if (lw.SelectedItems[0].ImageIndex != 0)
    {
        try
        {
            // Attempt to run the file
            System.Diagnostics.Process.Start(filename);
        }
        catch
        {
            // If the attempt fails we simply exit the method
            return;
        }
    }
    else
    {
        // Insert the items
        PaintListView(filename);
        folderCol.Add(filename);
    }
}
```

The `Tag` of the selected item contains the fully qualified path to the file or folder that was double-clicked. We know that the image with index 0 is a folder, so we can determine whether the item is a file or a folder by looking at that index. If it is a file, we attempt to load the file.

If it is a folder, we call `PaintListView()` with the new folder and then add the new folder to the `folderCol` collection.

Before we move on to the radio buttons we'll complete the browsing abilities by adding the click event to the **Back** button. Double-click the button and fill the event handle with this code:

```
private void btnBack_Click(object sender, System.EventArgs e)
{
    if (folderCol.Count > 1)
    {
        PaintListView(folderCol[folderCol.Count-2].ToString());
        folderCol.RemoveAt(folderCol.Count-1);
```

```
    }
    else
    {
        PaintListView(folderCol[0].ToString());
    }
}
```

If there is more than one item in the `folderCol` collection then we are not at the root of the browser, and we call `PaintListView()` with the path to the previous folder. The last item in the `folderCol` collection is the current folder, which is why we need to take the second to last item. We then remove the last item in the collection, and make the new last item the current folder. If there is only one item in the collection we simply call `PaintListView()` with that item.

All that remains is to be able to change the view type of the list view. Double-click each of the radio buttons and add the following code:

```
private void rdoLargeIcon_CheckedChanged(object sender, System.EventArgs e)
{
    RadioButton rdb = (RadioButton)sender;
    if (rdb.Checked)
        this.lwFilesAndFolders.View = View.LargeIcon;
}

private void rdoList_CheckedChanged(object sender, System.EventArgs e)
{
    RadioButton rdb = (RadioButton)sender;
    if (rdb.Checked)
        this.lwFilesAndFolders.View = View.List;
}

private void rdoSmallIcon_CheckedChanged(object sender, System.EventArgs e)
{
    RadioButton rdb = (RadioButton)sender;
    if (rdb.Checked)
        this.lwFilesAndFolders.View = View.SmallIcon;
}

private void rdoDetails_CheckedChanged(object sender, System.EventArgs e)
{
    RadioButton rdb = (RadioButton)sender;
    if (rdb.Checked)
        this.lwFilesAndFolders.View = View.Details;
}
```

We check the radio button to see if it has been changed to `Checked` – if it has we set the `View` property of the `ListView` accordingly.

That concludes the `ListView` example. When you run it, you should see something like this:

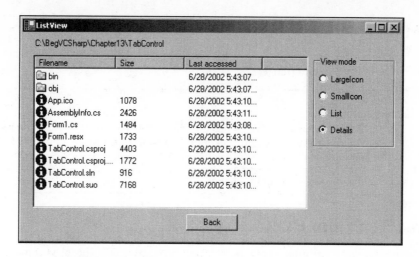

The StatusBar Control

A status bar is commonly used to provide hints for the selected item or information about an action currently being performed on a dialog. Normally the status bar is placed at the bottom of the screen, as it is in Microsoft Office applications, but it can be located anywhere you like. The `StatusBar` control provided with the .NET Framework can be used to simply display text, or you can add panels to it and display text, or create your own routines for drawing the contents of the panel.

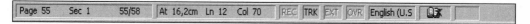

The above picture shows the status bar as it looks in Word. The panels in the status bar can be identified as the sections that appear sunken.

StatusBar Properties

As mentioned above, you can simply assign to the `Text` property of a `StatusBar` control to display simple text to the user, but it is possible to create panels and use them to the same effect.

Name	Description
BackgroundImage	It is possible to assign an image to the status bar that will be drawn in the background.
Panels	This is the collection of panels in the status bar. Use this collection to add and remove panels.
ShowPanels	If you want to display panels, this property must be set to `true`.
Text	When you are not using panels this property holds the text that is displayed in the status bar.

StatusBar Events

There are not a whole lot of new events for the status bar, but if you are drawing a panel manually, the `DrawItem` event is of crucial importance.

Name	Description
DrawItem	Occurs when a panel that has the OwnerDraw style set needs to be redrawn. You must subscribe to this event if you want to draw the contents of a panel yourself.
PanelClick	Occurs when a panel is clicked.

The StatusBarPanel Class

Each panel in a status bar is an instance of the `StatusBarPanel` class. This class contains all the information about the individual panels in the `Panels` collection. The information that can be set ranges from simple text and alignment of text to icons to be displayed and the style of the panel.

If you want to draw the panel yourself, you must set the `Style` property of the panel to `OwnerDraw` and handle the `DrawItem` event of the `StatusBar`.

Try it Out – Working with a Status Bar

We'll change the `ListView` example we created earlier to demonstrate the use of the `StatusBar` control. We'll remove the label used to display the current folder and move that piece of information to a panel on a status bar. We'll also display a second panel, which will display the current view mode of the list view.

1. Remove the label `lblCurrentFolder`.

2. Double-click the `StatusBar` control in the toolbox to add it to the form (again it is near to the bottom of the list). The new control will automatically dock with the bottom edge of the form.

3. Change the name of the `StatusBar` to sbInfo and clear the `Text` property.

4. Find the `Panels` property and double-click the button to the right of it to bring up a dialog to add panels.

5. Click Add to add a panel to the collection. Set the `AutoSize` property to `Spring`. This means that the panel will share the space in the StatusBar with other panels.

6. Click Add again, and change the `AutoSize` property to `Contents`. This means that the panel will resize itself to the size of the text it contains. Set the `MinSize` property to 0.

7. Click OK to close the dialog.

8. Set the `ShowPanels` property on the `StatusBar` to true.

Adding the Event Handlers

That's it for the user interface and we'll move on to the code. We'll start by setting the current path in the `PaintListView` method. Remove the line that set the text in the label and insert the following in its place:

```
this.sbInfo.Panels[0].Text = root;
```

The first panel has index 0, and we simply set its `Text` property just as we set the `Text` property of the label. Finally we change the four radio button `CheckedChanged` events to set the text of the second panel:

```
private void rdoLarge_CheckedChanged(object sender, System.EventArgs e)
{
    RadioButton rdb = (RadioButton)sender;
    if (rdb.Checked)
    {
        this.lwFilesAndFolders.View = View.LargeIcon;
        this.sbInfo.Panels[1].Text = "Large Icon";
    }
}

private void rdoList_CheckedChanged(object sender, System.EventArgs e)
{
    RadioButton rdb = (RadioButton)sender;
    if (rdb.Checked)
    {
        this.lwFilesAndFolders.View = View.List;
        this.sbInfo.Panels[1].Text = "List";
    }
}

private void rdoSmall_CheckedChanged(object sender, System.EventArgs e)
{
    RadioButton rdb = (RadioButton)sender;
    if (rdb.Checked)
    {
        this.lwFilesAndFolders.View = View.SmallIcon;
        this.sbInfo.Panels[1].Text = "Small Icon";
    }
}

private void rdoDetails_CheckedChanged(object sender, System.EventArgs e)
{
    RadioButton rdb = (RadioButton)sender;
    if (rdb.Checked)
    {
        this.lwFilesAndFolders.View = View.Details;
        this.sbInfo.Panels[1].Text = "Details";
    }
}
```

The panel text is set in exactly the same way as in `PaintListView` above.

That concludes the `StatusBar` example. If you run it now, you should see something like this:

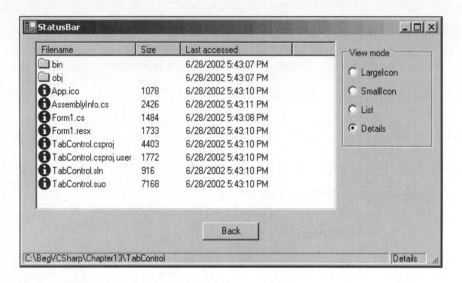

The TabControl Control

The TabControl provides an easy way of organizing a dialog into logical parts that can be accessed through tabs located at the top of the control. A TabControl contains TabPages that essentially work like a GroupBox control, in that they group controls together, although they are somewhat more complex.

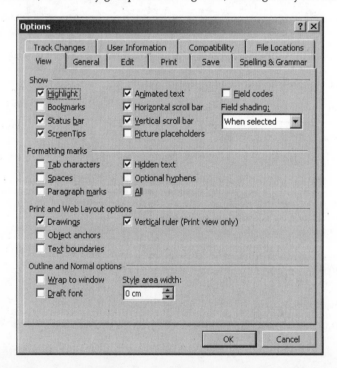

The above screenshot shows the Options dialog in Word 2000 as it is typically configured. Notice the two rows of tabs at the top of the dialog. Clicking each of them will show a different selection of controls in the rest of the dialog. This is a very good example of how to use a tab control to group related information together, making it easier for the user to find the information s/he is looking for.

Using the tab control is easy. You simply add the number of tabs you want to display to the control's collection of TabPage objects and then drag the controls you want to display to the respective pages.

TabControl Properties

The properties of the TabControl are largely used to control the appearance of the container of TabPage objects, in particular the tabs displayed.

Name	Description
Alignment	Controls where on the tab control the tabs are displayed. The default is at the top.
Appearance	Controls how the tabs are displayed. The tabs can be displayed as normal buttons or with flat style.
HotTrack	If this property is set to true the appearance of the tabs on the control change as the mouse pointer passes over them.
Multiline	If this property is set to true, it is possible to have several rows of tabs.
RowCount	Returns the number of rows of tabs that is currently displayed.
SelectedIndex	Returns or sets the index of the selected tab.
TabCount	Returns the total number of tabs.
TabPages	This is the collection of TabPage objects in the control. Use this collection to add and remove TabPage objects.

Working with the TabControl

The TabControl works slightly differently from all other controls we've seen so far. When you drag the control on to a form, you will see a gray rectangle that doesn't look very much like the control in the screenshot as shown above. You will also see, below the Properties window, two buttons that look like links with the captions Add Tab and Remove Tab. Clicking Add Tab will insert a new tab page on the control and the control will start to be recognizable. Obviously, you can remove the tab with the Remove Tab link button.

The above procedure is provided in order for you to get up and running quickly with the control. If, on the other hand, you want to change the behavior or style of the tabs you should use the TabPages dialog – accessed through the button when you select TabPages in the Properties window.

The `TabPages` property is also the collection used to access the individual pages on a tab control. Let's create an example to demonstrate the basics of the control. The example demonstrates how to develop controls located on different pages on the tab control.

Try it Out – Working with Tab Pages

1. Create a new Windows application called `TabControl` in the directory `C:\BegVCSharp\Chapter13`.

2. Drag a `TabControl` control from the Toolbox to the form.

3. Click **Add Tab** from under the Properties window to add a tab page to the control.

4. Find the `TabPages` property and click the button to the right of it after selecting it, to bring up the following dialog:

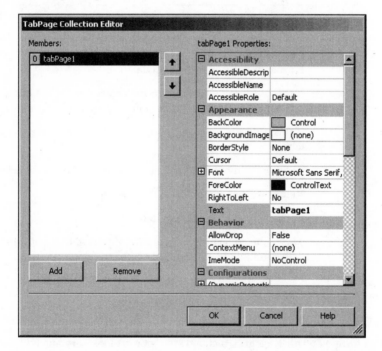

5. Add another tab page to the control by clicking **Add**.

6. Change the `Text` property of the tab pages to **Tab One** and **Tab Two** respectively, and click **OK** to close the dialog.

7. You can select the tab pages to work on by clicking on the tabs at the top of the control. Select the tab with the text **Tab One**. Drag a button on to the control. Be sure to place the button within the frame of the `TabControl`. If you place it outside then the button will be placed on the form rather than on the control.

8. Change the name of the button to `btnShowMessage` and the `Text` of the button to Show Message.

9. Click on the tab with the `Text` property **Tab Two**. Drag a `TextBox` control onto the `TabControl` surface. Name this control `txtMessage` and clear the `Text` property.

10. The two tabs should look like these two screenshots:

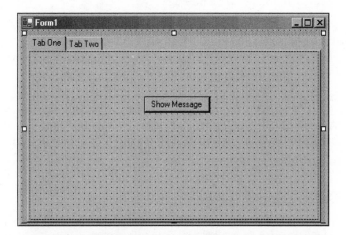

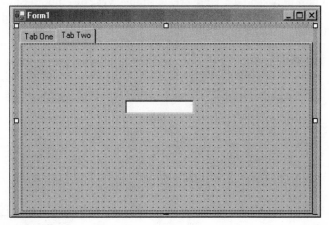

Adding the Event Handler

We are now ready to access the controls. If you run the code as it is, you will see the tab pages displayed properly. All that remains for us to do to demonstrate the use of the tab control is to add some code such that when the user clicks the Show Message button on one tab, the text entered in the other tab will be displayed in a message box. First, we add a handler for the `Click` event by double-clicking the button on the first tab and adding the following code:

```
private void btnShowMessage_Click(object sender, System.EventArgs e)
{
    // Access the TextBox

    MessageBox.Show(this.txtMessage.Text);
}
```

You access a control on a tab just as you would any other control on the form. We get the `Text` property of the `TextBox` and display it in a message box.

Earlier in the chapter, we saw that it is only possible to have one radio button selected at a time on a form (unless you put them in group boxes). The `TabPages` work in precisely the same way as group boxes and it is therefore possible to have multiple sets of radio buttons on different tabs without the need to have group boxes.

The last thing you must know to be able to work with a tab control is how to determine which tab is currently being displayed. There are two properties you can use for this purpose: `SelectedTab` and `SelectedIndex`. As the names imply, `SelectedTab` will return the `TabPage` object to you or `null` if no tab is selected, and `SelectedIndex` will return the index of the tab or -1 if no tab is selected.

Summary

In this chapter we visited some of the most commonly used controls when creating Windows applications and saw how they can be used to create simple, yet powerful user interfaces. We discussed the properties and events of these controls, with examples of their use, and looked at how to add event handlers for the particular events of a control.

The controls discussed in this chapter were:

- ❑ Label
- ❑ Button
- ❑ RadioButton
- ❑ CheckBox
- ❑ ListBox
- ❑ ListView
- ❑ GroupBox
- ❑ RichTextBox
- ❑ StatusBar
- ❑ ImageList
- ❑ TabControl

In the next chapter, we will be looking at more complex controls such as menus and toolbars, and we will use them to develop Multi-Document Interface (MDI) Windows applications. Also, we'll demonstrate how to create a user control which combines the functionality of simple controls into a composite control.

Advanced Windows Forms Features

In the previous chapter we looked at some of the most common controls used in Windows Application development. With controls such as these it is possible to create impressive dialogs, but very few full scale Windows applications have a user interface consisting solely of a single dialog. Rather, these applications use a Single Document Interface (SDI), or a Multiple Document Interface (MDI). Applications of either of these types usually make heavy use of menus and toolbars, neither of which we discussed in the previous chapter, but we'll make amends for that now.

We will start this chapter as we left off the previous one, by looking at controls, starting with the menu control and then moving on to toolbars, where we'll see how to link buttons on toolbars to specific menu items and vice versa. Then we'll move on to creating SDI and MDI applications, with the focus on MDI applications, as SDI applications are basically subsets of MDI applications.

So far we've only consumed controls that ship with the .NET Framework. These controls are, as we've seen, very powerful and provide a wide range of functionality, but there are times where they are not sufficient. To overcome this, it is possible to create custom controls, and we'll look at how this is done towards the end of this chapter.

Menus

How many Windows applications can you think of that do not contain a menu of some kind? The chances are that the number is very close to none. Menus are therefore likely to be an important part of any application you will write for the Windows operating system. To assist us in creating menus for our applications, Visual Studio .NET provides us with a control that lets us create simple menus quickly, and more refined menus with a little more work.

Using the Menu Control

The menu control we'll be using here is called `MainMenu` and it is, like the two other kinds of menus that come with Visual Studio .NET, derived from a base class called `Menu` located in the `System.Windows.Forms` namespace.

There is another kind of menu that we'll discuss briefly after the discussion of the `MainMenu` – the `ContextMenu`. A context menu appears when a user right-clicks on an item, and will typically display information relevant to that item. Technically there is a third menu type, named `MenuItem`, which is also derived from the `Menu` class. A `MenuItem` represents the individual items displayed in a menu. In the picture below, the **Type Here** field represents a `MenuItem`. The `MenuItem` will be discussed in detail shortly. `ContextMenu` and `MenuItem` are also derived from the base class `Menu`.

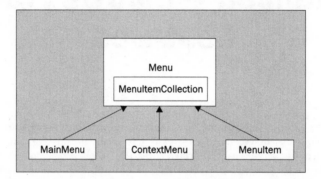

When you drag the `MainMenu` control from the Toolbox to the design surface you will see that this control places itself both on the form itself and in the control tray, but can be edited directly on the form. To create new menu items you simply place the pointer in the box marked **Type Here**:

Type the caption of the menu in the highlighted box, including an ampersand (&) in front of the letter you want to function as the mnemonic character for the menu item – this is the character that appears underlined in the menu item and which can be selected pressing *Alt* and the key together.

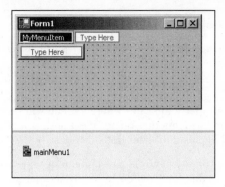

Note that it is quite possible to create several menu items in the same menu with the same mnemonic character. The rule is, that a character can be used only once for each pop-up menu (for example, once in the Files pop-up menu, once in the View menu etc.). If you accidentally assign the same mnemonic character to multiple menu items in the same pop-up menu, you'll find that only the one closest to the top of the control will respond to the character.

To create a separator in the menu, you simply type a single dash (-) as the text. Note that you cannot do this for top-level menu items, only for submenu items, which we will come to very shortly.

When you click in the highlighted box, you will notice that the properties displayed in the Properties window changed. This is because the majority of the properties that can be used with menus are used with respect to the individual menu items.

The MenuItem Control

If you select a `MenuItem` by clicking on it in the `MainMenu` control, you will see several properties that are used to control the appearance and behavior of the item. Each menu item can contain other menu items, which allows you to create submenus for each item in the main menu. A collection is defined in the base `Menu` class to hold all the `MenuItem` objects, `MenuItemCollection`, as shown in the class diagram earlier.

Let's look at the properties provided by `MenuItem`. Some of these properties are inherited from `Menu`. This list is not exhaustive – if you require a complete listing please refer to .NET Framework SDK Documentation.

Name	Description
BarBreak	By setting this value to `true`, you specify that the menu should appear on a new line. Using this property you can create menus with multiple top-level rows. Submenu items with this property set will be placed in a new column. This property is not visible in the Properties window.
Checked	Indicates whether the menu is checked.
DefaultItem	A default item is drawn with boldface. If a user double-clicks a `MenuItem` that contain subitems, and one of these items is a default item, that item is selected.

Table continued on following page

Name	Description
Enabled	An item with Enabled set to false will be grayed and cannot be selected.
MdiList	Indicates whether the menu will be populated with a list of the child windows in an MDI.
MergeOrder	This property indicates where a menu will be positioned when it is merged with another menu. We'll look at menu merging when we discuss MDI applications later in this chapter.
MergeType	This property controls how a menu behaves when it should be merged, but has the same MergeOrder as another menu.
Mnemonic	This property returns the mnemonic character that is associated with the MenuItem. The mnemonic character is the first character following an ampersand (&). This property is not visible in the Properties window.
OwnerDraw	If you set this property to true, you take responsibility for all drawing of the MenuItem. If you want to add images to your menus, you must set this property to true and implement handlers for the item's DrawItem and MeasureItem events.
RadioCheck	If this property is set to true, a check is displayed as a radio button rather than a check mark.
Shortcut	The shortcut is a key combination which access the menu item directly (for example, *Ctrl+S* for **Save**).
ShowShortcut	Setting this property to true means that the shortcut text is displayed in the MenuItem.
Text	The text of the MenuItem. Include an ampersand (&) before a character in the string to assign the mnemonic character.

MenuItem Events

How many events are needed for a MenuItem? One you would think – the Click event. In fact there are five events of interest you can subscribe to, two of which you must use if you are drawing the items yourself. Let's look at the events now, and then move on to an example using the control.

Name	Description
Click()	This event occurs when a user clicks a menu item. You can also raise this event manually by calling the PerformClick() method of the MenuItem.
DrawItem()	Occurs when the MenuItem needs to be drawn. If you set the OwnerDraw property to true, you must handle this event.

Name	Description
MeasureItem()	Occurs before a MenuItem is drawn. If you are drawing the MenuItem yourself, you should calculate and return the width and height for the item in this event.
Popup()	Occurs when the MenuItems list of subitems is displayed. You can use this event to perform validation of the availability of the items and set their state appropriately.
Select()	Occurs when a user places the mouse pointer over the item or when he or she changes the focus using the keyboard.

The ContextMenu Control

A context menu is a menu that is opened when the user right-clicks on an item on the form. The context menu in the screenshot below is the menu I get when I right-click the desktop of my computer:

In Visual Studio .NET, you can create a context menu by dragging it onto the form and adding items to it, in exactly the same way as you would a MainMenu control. The only difference is that you cannot have any top-level items in a context menu. To bind the context menu to a particular control on the form, you select the control and set its ContextMenu property to point to the context menu you've created.

Try it Out – Menu Example

We are now ready to create an example using menus. We'll keep this example basic as we'll see more advanced examples of menus as we discuss MDI applications. We'll create one main menu and a context menu in this example.

1. Begin by creating a new Windows application called MenuExample in the directory C:\BegVCSharp\Chapter14.

2. Add a MainMenu control and a ContextMenu control to the form by double-clicking the controls in the Toolbox. Name the controls MainMenuFiles and ContextMenuFonts respectively.

3. Add the following items to the `MainMenu` control by selecting it and typing the text into the menu items. When you type text in the menu item using the designer, you are setting the `Text` property of the item. After setting the text for an item, use the Properties window to change the default name chosen by Visual Studio .NET. The menu named `menuItemFiles` is known as a top-level menu. Remember that you create a separator by typing a single dash in the menu and create a mnemonic character by adding an ampersand (&) in front of the letter you wish to choose:

Name	Text
menuItemFiles	&Files
menuItemNew	&New
menuItemOpen	&Open
menuItemSave	&Save
menuItemSeperator0	-
menuItemExit	E&xit

4. Now select the context menu, and create the following menu items just as you did above.

Name	Text
menuItemBold	&Bold
menuItemItalic	&Italic
menuItemUnderline	&Underline

5. Now add a single `RichTextBox` control to the form. Name it `rtfText` and set its `Dock` property to Fill to make it fill the entire form, and clear its `Text` property.

6. Select the `RichTextBox` control and select the `ContextMenu` property. From the drop-down list, select ContextMenuFonts to bind the context menu to the rich text box.

You should now have a form that looks something like this:

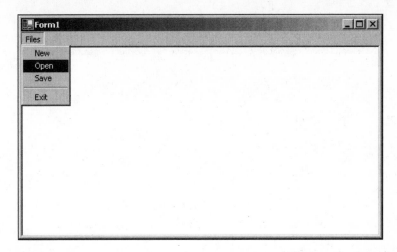

Adding the Event Handlers

We are now ready to add code to our menus. We'll keep the Open, Save, and New methods simple, and we'll use a fixed file for the demonstration – in the next chapter we'll look at using the common dialogs that allow the user to select a file to open or save. To add a handler for the Click event of a menu item, you simply double-click it, as for buttons and other controls. We will add handlers for the New, Open, Save, and Exit menu items. Clicking on a separator is not possible and nothing should be done when the user clicks the files menu, so there's no need to add Click event handlers to this menu item.

Begin by double-clicking the New menu item:

```
private void menuItemNew_Click(object sender, System.EventArgs e)
{
    this.rtfText.Clear();
}
```

We said we'd keep this simple, and we did. The sender parameter is a reference to the menu item that was clicked. In this case we know that it was the New item, but an event handler can be assigned to many items, in which case this identifies the menu to be used.

Repeat the process with the Open, Save, and Exit:

```
private void menuItemOpen_Click(object sender, System.EventArgs e)
{
    // Load the file
    try
    {
        this.rtfText.LoadFile("../../test.rtf");
    }
    catch (System.Exception err)
    {
MessageBox.Show("Error while loading:\n" + err.Message);
    }
```

```
}

private void menuItemSave_Click(object sender, System.EventArgs e)
{
    // Save the file
    try
    {
        this.rtfText.SaveFile("../../test.rtf");
    }
    catch (System.Exception err)
    {
        MessageBox.Show("Error while saving file:\n" + err.Message);
    }
}

private void menuItemExit_Click(object sender, System.EventArgs e)
{
    // Exit the application
    Application.Exit();
}
```

The `LoadFile()` method of the `RichTextBox` class does exactly that – it loads the contents of an RTF (as can be exported from WordPad or Word), or ASCII file into the rich text box. Note that we have put error handling in here to deal with situations where the text file does not exist. However, there is another way of achieving this check, which we will look at now.

The `menuItemFiles` item contains the other items in our main menu. Because of that, every time the menu item is asked to show its members, it dispatches a `Popup` event. If we subscribe to that event, we can check if the file exists and disable the **Open** menu item if it doesn't. We'll subscribe to the event by selecting the `menuItemFiles` control, and double-clicking on the **Popup** event in the Events list in the Properties window.

Then we add the code to the event handler itself:

```
private void menuItemFiles_Popup(object sender, System.EventArgs e)
{
    // Check to see if the file exist by setting the Enabled property to the
    // return value of the File.Exists method.
    this.menuItemOpen.Enabled = System.IO.File.Exists("../../test.rtf");
}
```

The static method `Exists` of the `File` class returns a Boolean which is `true` if the file exists and `false` otherwise – which is exactly what we want the **Open** menu item to reflect, so we simply set the value of the `Enabled` property to the return value of this function.

We are now done with the main menu and can move on to the context menu. We add the `Click` events just as we did in the main menu – by double-clicking the items and adding the following code:

```
private void menuItemBold_Click(object sender, System.EventArgs e)
{
    Font newFont = new Font(rtfText.SelectionFont,
```

```
                              (rtfText.SelectionFont.Bold ?
                      rtfText.SelectionFont.Style & ~FontStyle.Bold :
                      rtfText.SelectionFont.Style | FontStyle.Bold));
   rtfText.SelectionFont = newFont;
}

private void menuItemItalic_Click(object sender, System.EventArgs e)
{
   Font newFont = new Font(rtfText.SelectionFont,
                      (rtfText.SelectionFont.Italic ?
                      rtfText.SelectionFont.Style & ~FontStyle.Italic :
                      rtfText.SelectionFont.Style | FontStyle.Italic));
   rtfText.SelectionFont = newFont;
}

private void menuItemUnderline_Click(object sender, System.EventArgs e)
{
   Font newFont = new Font(rtfText.SelectionFont,
                      (rtfText.SelectionFont.Underline ?
                      rtfText.SelectionFont.Style & ~FontStyle.Underline :
                      rtfText.SelectionFont.Style| FontStyle.Underline));
   rtfText.SelectionFont = newFont;
}
```

In each of the three functions we create a new font from the one that is currently being used by the selection in the rich text box. If the style of the font is already set, we remove it from the new font, otherwise we include the style in the font. We then set the font of the selection to the new font.

The single line that creates the objects can look a bit daunting so we'll explain it here. To create the objects we make use of the ternary operator – we first saw this in Chapter 4. Let's look at the code from the `menuItemBold_Click` method:

```
Font newFont = new Font(rtfText.SelectionFont,
                   (rtfText.SelectionFont.Bold ?
                   rtfText.SelectionFont.Style & ~FontStyle.Bold :
                   rtfText.SelectionFont.Style | FontStyle.Bold));
rtfText.SelectionFont = newFont;
```

On the second line of the first statement, we examine whether the `Bold` property of the selected font is `true`. If it is, then we must create a new style for the font we are creating, which retains all the styles that are currently set except for the bold style, which is the code between the `?` and the `:` on the third line. On the fourth line of the statement, after the colon, this code is run if the value of the `Bold` property is `false`, whereby we add in the bold style rather than remove it. Finally the entire sequence of events just discussed is wrapped in parentheses, often used to separate out the ternary operator logic from other code and aid readability.

This concludes the first example of menus. If you run the code, you should be able to create something like this:

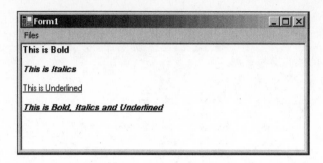

Toolbars

While menus are great for providing access to a multitude of functionality in your application, some items benefit from being placed in a toolbar as well as on the menu. These items are those that are used frequently by the user, such as Open and Save, and a toolbar provides one-click access to such commonly-used functionality.

The screenshot below shows the selection of toolbars that are visible as I'm writing this chapter in Word.

A button on a toolbar usually contains a picture and no text, though it is possible to have buttons with both. Examples of toolbars with no text are those found in Word (see above), and examples of toolbars that include text can be found in Internet Explorer. If you let the mouse pointer rest above a button in a toolbar, it should display a tooltip that provides some clue as to the purpose of the button, especially when only an icon is displayed.

Unlike the menu controls we've just discussed, the ToolBar control is not merely a container for other objects. You can set several properties on the control itself, such as where it is positioned on the screen. All the buttons on the toolbar are, however, objects in their own right. Each button in a ToolBar control is a ToolBarButton object, and they hold information about which image to display, the style of any text displayed along with the icon, and tooltips.

We'll start by describing the properties and events of the ToolBar control and then move on to the ToolBarButton.

ToolBar Properties

The properties of the ToolBar control manage how and where the control is displayed. They also manage some display settings for the buttons of the control, which would be the same for all the buttons contained in the control:

Name	Description
Appearance	This property controls the appearance of all the buttons contained within the control. You can set this property to `Flat` or to `Normal`. The normal setting will draw a 3D border around the button.
AutoSize	Setting this property to `false` allows you to change the size of the control. The default, `true`, allows the control to size itself to make room for images and text.
Buttons	Returns the collection of buttons contained in the control.
ButtonSize	This property controls the size of the buttons. If the `AutoSize` property is `true` this property has no effect.
Divider	If this property is set to `true`, the control will draw a border at the top of the `ToolBar` control.
DropDownArrows	If you have toolbar buttons that provide a drop-down list, this property determines whether an arrow is drawn to the right of the button.
ImageList	The image list from which the images used on the buttons contained in the control are taken.
ShowToolTips	Setting this property to `true` will make the control display tooltips for each button contained in the control.
Wrappable	If this property is `true`, and the toolbar is too long to display all the buttons it contains in one line, it will wrap to the next line.

ToolBar Events

The two events on the `Toolbar` class that are not derived from `Control` are raised when a button or down arrow on a drop-down list is clicked. You could be forgiven for thinking that the buttons themselves would more logically raise these events, but Microsoft has chosen otherwise. The result is that a single event handler must handle clicks on all the buttons in a toolbar, and thus be able to distinguish between the buttons.

Name	Description
ButtonClick	This event occurs whenever a button contained in the toolbar is clicked. To determine which button was clicked you should use the `Button` property of the `ToolBarButtonClickEventArgs` parameter that is sent to the event handler. By examining this property you can determine which action you should take.
ButtonDropDown	This event occurs when a toolbar button with its `Style` property set to `DropDownButton` or its corresponding arrow is clicked. The `ToolBarButtonClickEventArgs` can be used to determine which button was clicked and thus which action to take.

The ToolBarButton Properties

The `ToolBarButton` class manages individual settings for each button in a toolbar, including image, style and text and tool tip. One interesting feature of the `ToolBarButton` is, that if its style is set to `DropDownButton`, it is able to contain a menu – more specifically a `MenuItem` containing the menu items to display.

Name	Description
DropDownMenu	By using this property you can assign a `MenuItem` to the button. If the `Style` property of the button is `DropDownButton` (see below) the `MenuItem` will be displayed when the user clicks the button.
Enabled	By setting this property to `false` you make the button unavailable to the user. If you are using bitmap images on the button, then the button is only able to draw the image in monochrome.
ImageIndex	The index of the image to use. The image list is assigned to the `Toolbar` control.
PartialPush	You can use this property when the style of the toolbar button is set to `ToggleButton`. Setting this property to `true` will make the button appear grayed. Unlike setting the `Enabled` property to `false`, this setting causes the entire button face to become hazed.
Pushed	If the style of the `ToolBarButton` is `ToggleButton` then setting this property to `true` will make the button appear pressed.
Style	There are four different styles that can be used: ❑ PushButton: Appears like a normal button. ❑ ToggleButton: When this style is selected the button can appear to be pressed and will remain in that state until pressed again. An example of such a button is the Bold button on the toolbars used in Word. ❑ Separator: A button with this style is not drawn – which is exactly the point; it creates a small space between buttons. ❑ DropDownButton: A button with this style can be assigned a ContextMenu. This menu will be dropped down when the user clicks the button.
Text	The text to display in the toolbar button.
ToolTipText	The tooltip text of the button.

Try it Out – Toolbar Example

We will extend our first menus example to include a toolbar. The toolbar will contain three buttons, each of which corresponds to one of the three items we placed in the context menu of the previous example – bold, italic, and underline. There will also be a fourth button, a drop-down button from which you can select a font. (Note that the bitmap we've used here for the button that selects the font can be found in the code download.)

So, starting with the MenuExample code from earlier in the chapter make the following changes:

1. Because of the toolbar we are going to add, you should change the Dock property of the RichTextBox to None, and set the Anchor property to Left, Top, Right, Bottom.

2. Add an ImageList and an additional ContextMenu to the form by double-clicking the controls in the toolbox. Name them ImageListToolbar and ContextMenuFontFamilies respectively. The ImageList will contain the images we'll use on the buttons and the ContextMenu will be the menu that we'll use in the drop-down list button.

3. Add three MenuItems to the ContextMenuFontFamilies control and set the properties as follows:

Name	Text
menuItemMS	MS Sans Serif
menuItemTimes	Times New Roman

4. Add four images to the ImageListToolbar control by clicking the button to the right of the Images property on the ImageList. Three of these bitmaps can be found under the Common7 directory where you installed Visual Studio:

```
<VS.NET install directory>\Common7\Graphics\bitmaps\Tlbr_W95
```

The names are: BLD.BMP, ITL.BMP and UNDRLN.BMP

You can use any bitmap you like for the final item, or you can download the source code from Wrox to get the bitmap used in this book (Font.bmp).

5. Double-click the ToolBar control in the Toolbox to add it to the form. Name it toolBarFonts. The toolbar may now be obscuring some of the RichTextBox – to correct that, click the RichTextBox and move it to be below the toolbar. If you haven't already, modify the RichTextBox as presented at Step 1.

6. Set the ImageList property of the ToolBar to ImageListToolbar.

7. Select the Toolbar's Buttons property and click the button at the right of it to add buttons to the Toolbar control.

8. Add five buttons to the tool bar, and set the properties of the five buttons like this:

ToolBarButton	Properties
First button	Name = toolBarButtonBold
	ImageIndex = Index of the bold image (B)
	Style = ToggleButton
Second button	Name = toolBarButtonItalic
	ImageIndex = Index of the italic image (I)
	Style = ToggleButton
Third button	Name = toolBarButtonUnderline
	ImageIndex = Index of the underline image (U)
	Style = ToggleButton
Fourth button	Name = toolBarButtonSeparator
	Style = Separator
Fifth button	Name = toolBarButtonFonts
	ImageIndex = Index of the last remaining image (the font bitmap)
	Style = DropDownButton
	DropDownMenu = ContextMenuFontFamilies

The form should now look something like this:

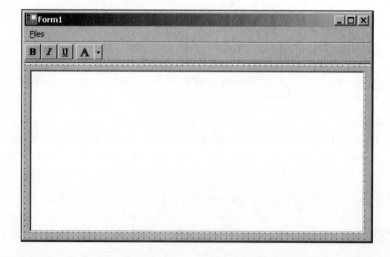

Adding the Event Handlers

Now we are ready to add code to the event handler for the `ButtonClick` event of the `ToolBar`. You can add the event handler by double-clicking on the control:

```
private void toolBarFonts_ButtonClick(object sender,
                          System.Windows.Forms.ToolBarButtonClickEventArgs e)
{
   Font newFont;

   // Switch on the index of the button in the Buttons collection of the
   // ToolBar
   switch (toolBarFonts.Buttons.IndexOf(e.Button))
   {
   case 0: // Bold
       if (e.Button.Pushed)
        // Create a new font with Bold face
          newFont = new Font(rtfText.SelectionFont,
                        rtfText.SelectionFont.Style | FontStyle.Bold);
       else
          // Create a new font without bold face
          newFont = new Font(rtfText.SelectionFont,
rtfText.SelectionFont.Style & ~FontStyle.Bold);
        rtfText.SelectionFont = newFont;
        break;
    case 1: // Italic
       if (e.Button.Pushed)
        // Create a new font with italic
        newFont = new Font(rtfText.SelectionFont,
                        rtfText.SelectionFont.Style | FontStyle.Italic);
       else
        // Create a new font without italic
        newFont = new Font(rtfText.SelectionFont,
                        rtfText.SelectionFont.Style & ~FontStyle.Italic);
      rtfText.SelectionFont = newFont;
      break;
    case 2: // Underline
       if (e.Button.Pushed)
        // Create a new font with underline
        newFont = new Font(rtfText.SelectionFont,
                        rtfText.SelectionFont.Style | FontStyle.Underline);
       else
        // Create a new font without underline
        newFont = new Font(rtfText.SelectionFont,
                        rtfText.SelectionFont.Style & ~FontStyle.Underline);
      rtfText.SelectionFont = newFont;
      break;
   }
}
```

In this function we first check the index of the button that has been clicked – this is necessary because each Button in the Buttons collection of the ToolBar uses this event to signal a click. After we've found the button that was clicked, we test its Pushed property to see if we should set or remove the font style, and we create a new font accordingly, in much the same way as we did earlier. Finally, we set the SelectionFont of the rtfText control to that new font.

One final touch for each ToolBarButton that controls the style of the font is that they should reflect the font used on the current selection. To do this, double-click on the SelectionChanged event of the RichTextBox control in its list of Events in the Properties window, and add the following code to the handler:

```
private void rtfText_SelectionChanged(object sender, System.EventArgs e)
{
    // Set the toolbar buttons to the correct state of pushed or not
    this.toolBarButtonBold.Pushed = rtfText.SelectionFont.Bold;
    this.toolBarButtonItalic.Pushed = rtfText.SelectionFont.Italic;
    this.toolBarButtonUnderline.Pushed = rtfText.SelectionFont.Underline;
}
```

The RichTextBox control can tell us the style of the current font, so we simply assign the appropriate properties to the Enabled property of the toolbar buttons.

All that remains is to handle the Click event of the two menu items in our DropDownButton style fonts button. We do this by adding the Click events to the menu items just like we did in the menu example earlier in this chapter (just double-click the items):

```
private void menuItemMS_Click(object sender, System.EventArgs e)
{
    // Create a new font with the correct font family.
    Font newFont = new Font("MS Sans Serif", rtfText.SelectionFont.Size,
                            rtfText.SelectionFont.Style);
    rtfText.SelectionFont = newFont;
}

private void menuItemTimes_Click(object sender, System.EventArgs e)
{
    // Create a new font with the correct font family.
    Font newFont = new Font("Times New Roman", rtfText.SelectionFont.Size,
                            rtfText.SelectionFont.Style);
    rtfText.SelectionFont = newFont;
}
```

We create a new font from the font family we wish to use, and then set the SelectionFont to the new font.

Now compile and run the application to try it out.

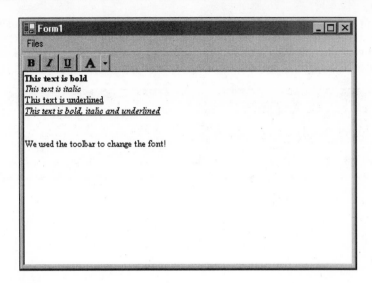

SDI and MDI Applications

Traditionally there are three kinds of application that can be programmed for Windows. These are:

- ❑ Dialog based applications. These present themselves to the user as a single dialog from which all functionality can be reached.

- ❑ Single Document Interfaces (SDI). These present themselves to the user with a menu, one or more toolbars and one window in which the user can perform some task.

- ❑ Multiple Document Interfaces (MDI). These present themselves to the user in the same manner as an SDI does, but have the ability to hold multiple open windows at a time.

Dialog based applications are usually small single purpose applications that aim themselves at a specific task that needs a minimum of data entered by the user, or targets a very specific type of data. An example of such an application is the Calculator, which comes with Windows.

Single Document Interfaces are usually aimed at solving one specific task, as they allow the user to load a single document into the application to be worked on. This task however, usually involves a lot of user interaction, and very often the user will want the ability to save or load the result of his or her work. Good examples of SDI applications are WordPad, and Paint, that both come with Windows:

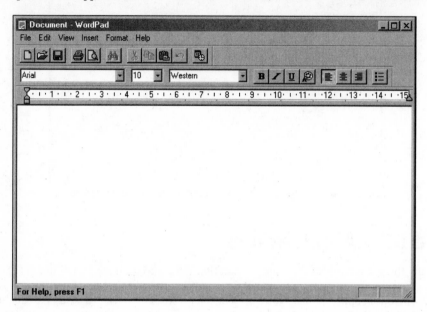

However, only one document can be open at any one time, so if a user wants to open a second document, a fresh instance of the SDI application will be opened which will have no reference to the first instance and so any configuration you do to one instance will not be carried over into the other. Thus in one instance of Paint, you might set the drawing color to red, and if you open a second instance of Paint the drawing color will be the default, which is black.

Multiple Document Interfaces are very much the same as SDI applications, except they are able to hold more than one document open in different windows at any given time. A tell-tale sign of an MDI application is the inclusion of the Window menu at the right-hand side of the menu bar, just before the Help menu. Examples of MDI applications are Adobe Acrobat Reader and Word 97.

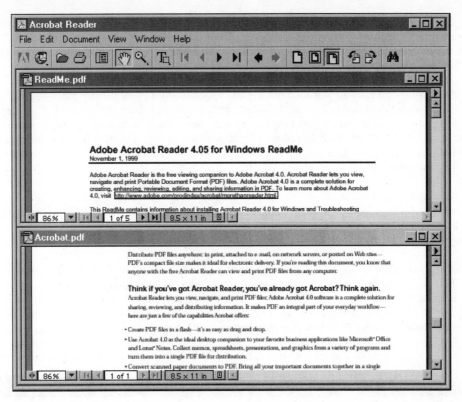

A fourth type of application was introduced with Office 2000. This type of application appears to be a cross between an SDI and MDI in that the windows presented to the user do not occupy the same area and each window shows up in the task bar. Essentially the applications themselves are MDI applications because the main application will not shut down until all the windows are closed, and you can select which open document to view using the Windows menu item, but the user interface itself is presented as an SDI.

In this chapter we will focus on creating an MDI application and the tasks involved in doing so. The reasoning behind this is that any SDI application is basically a subset of an MDI, so if you are able to create an MDI you can also create an SDI. In fact in Chapter 15, we will create a simple SDI application that we will use to demonstrate using the Windows Common Dialogs.

Building MDI Applications

What is involved in creating an MDI? First of all, the task you want the user to be able to accomplish should be one where he or she would want to have multiple documents open at a time. A good example of this is a text editor or, as in the screenshot above, a text viewer. Secondly, you should provide toolbars for the most commonly used tasks in the application, such as setting the font style, and loading and saving documents. Thirdly, you should provide a menu that includes a Window menu item, which allows the user to reposition the open windows in respect of each other (tile and cascade) and presents a list of all open windows. Another feature of MDI applications is that if a window is open and that window contains a menu, that menu should be integrated into the main menu of the application.

An MDI application consists of at least two distinct windows. The first window you create is called an **MDI container**. A window that can be displayed within that container is called an **MDI child**. We will refer to the MDI container as "MDI container" or "main window" interchangeably and to the MDI child as "MDI child" or "child window".

To create an MDI application, you start out in just the same way as you do any other application, by creating a Windows application in Visual Studio .NET. To change the main window of the application from a form to an MDI container you simply set the `IsMdiContainer` property of the form to `true`. The background of the form changes color to indicate that it is now merely a background that you should not place visible controls on, although it is possible to do so, and may even be reasonable under certain circumstances.

To create a child window you add a new form to the project by selecting a Windows Form from the dialog brought up by selecting Project | Add New Item. This form becomes a child window when you set the `MdiParent` property of the child window to a reference to the main window. You cannot set this property through the Properties panel, so you will have to do this using code.

Two things remain before the MDI application is able to display itself in its most basic mode. You must tell the MDI container which windows to display, and then you must then display them. You simply do this by creating a new instance of the form you wish to display, and then calling `Show()` on it. The constructor of the form to display as a child should hook itself up with the parent container. It does so by setting its `MdiParent` property to the instance of the MDI container.

Let's look at a small example that takes us through these steps, before moving on to more complicated tasks.

Try it Out – Creating an MDI Application

1. Create a new Windows application called `MdiBasic` in the directory `C:\BegVCSharp\Chapter14`.

2. Select the form and set the following properties:

Property	Value
Name	frmContainer
IsMdiContainer	True
Text	MDI Basic
WindowState	Maximized

3. Add a new form to the solution by choosing Windows Form from the Project | Add New Item menu. Name the form `frmChild`.

All the code that we need to display a child form is found in the constructors of the forms. First we'll look at the constructor for the child window:

```
public frmChild(MdiBasic.frmContainer parent)
```

```
    {
        InitializeComponent();

        // Set the parent of the form to the container
        this.MdiParent = parent;
    }
```

In order to bind a child form to the MDI container, the child must register itself with the container. This is done by setting the `MdiParent` property of the form as shown in the code above. You will notice that the constructor we are using includes the parameter `parent`.

Because C# does not provide default constructors for a class that defines its own constructor, the above code prevents us from creating an instance of the form that is not bound to the MDI container.

Finally we want to display the form. We do so in the constructor of the MDI container:

```
    public frmContainer()
    {
        InitializeComponent();

        // Create a new instance of the child form
        MdiBasic.frmChild child = new MdiBasic.frmChild(this);

        // Show the form
        child.Show();
    }
```

We create a new instance of the child class and pass `this` to the constructor, where `this` represents the current instance of the MDI container class. Then we call `Show()` on the new instance of the child form and that's it. If you want to show more than one child window, all you have to do is repeat the two highlighted lines in the above code for each window.

If you run the code now, you should see something like this (although the MDI Basic form will initially be maximized, we've resized it here to fit on the page):

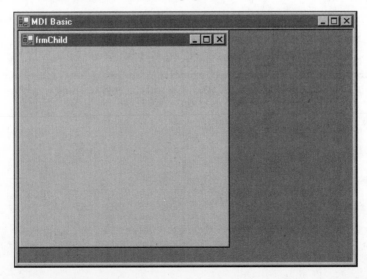

It's not the most intriguing user interface ever designed, but it is clearly a solid start. The next example we'll produce is a simple text editor, based on what we have already achieved in this chapter using menus and toolbars.

Try it Out – Creating an MDI Text Editor

Let's create the basic project first and then discuss what is happening:

1. Create a new Windows application called `SimpleTextEditor` in the `C:\BegVCSharp\Chapter14` directory. Set the following properties on the form:

Properties	Value
Name	frmContainer
IsMdiParent	True
Text	Simple Text Editor
WindowState	Maximized

2. Rename the file that contains the form (the file itself, not the property) to `frmContainer.cs` and change the following code in `Main()`:

```
static void Main()
{
    Application.Run(new frmContainer());
}
```

3. We'll add the code from the previous toolbar example (in the `MenuExample` project) – select **Project | Add Existing Item** and browse to the `MenuExample` folder, and add the file `Form1.cs`.

4. Rename the newly inserted form `frmEditor`, and rename the file that contains it `frmEditor.cs`. Set the `Text` property to `Editor`, and ensure that you change the namespace in the `frmEditor.cs` from `MenuExample` to `SimpleTextEditor`.

   These steps are very similar to those of the MDI Basic application, other than using an existing form rather than creating a new one. However what follows is where things get interesting.

5. Find the `Main` method of the `frmEditor` form and remove it.

6. Change the constructor of the `frmEditor` form to:

```
public frmEditor(SimpleTextEditor.frmContainer parent)
{
    InitializeComponent();

    // Bind to the parent
    this.MdiParent = parent;
}
```

7. Change the constructor of the `frmContainer` form to:

```
public frmContainer()
{
    InitializeComponent();

    SimpleTextEditor.frmEditor newForm = new frmEditor(this);
    newForm.Show();
}
```

If you run the application now, you will see something like this:

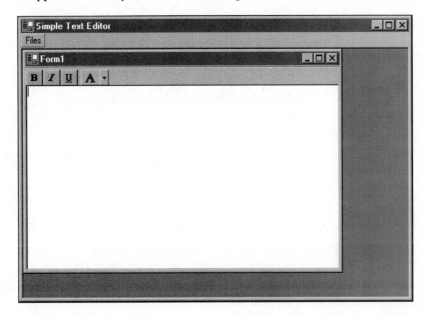

Notice that a bit of magic has happened. We haven't created any menus for the container, yet the menu Files is right there at the top. What has happened? The answer is that we did create a menu for the Editor form, and as that form is now a child of the container, the main menu items have been merged. Since there are no menus in the container yet, we only see one menu item.

The menus that should be contained on child windows are those that are specific to that window. The Files menu should be general for all windows, and shouldn't be contained in the child windows. The reason for this becomes apparent if you close the editor window – the Files menu disappears! To change this behavior we need to go though a few more steps:

8. Remove the menu named `MainMenuFiles` from the `frmEditor` form.

9. Go to the code and remove the event handlers for this menu:

- ❑ menuItemFiles_Popup
- ❑ menuItemSave_Click
- ❑ menuItemNew_Click
- ❑ menuItemOpen_Click
- ❑ menuItemExit_Click

10. Remove the line in the constructor where the menuItemFiles_Popup event is subscribed.

A more appropriate menu for the frmEditor form is an **Edit** menu. Create this by going through the following steps:

11. Add a new MainMenu to the editor form. Name the control MainMenuEdit.

12. Add seven items to it and set the following properties:

Name	Text
menuItemEdit	&Edit
menuItemUndo	&Undo
menuItemRedo	&Redo
menuItemSeperatorEdit0	-
menuItemCut	Cu&t
menuItemCopy	&Copy
menuItemPaste	&Paste

13. Set the Menu property of the frmEditor form to MainMenuEdit. The menu will now be merged with the menu of the container.

It is now time to create the menu that should be displayed no matter which window is selected. Follow the steps below carefully to add the menu to the container:

14. Add a MainMenu to the form frmContainer. Name this menu MainMenuContainer.

15. Add the following items to it. Notice that the MenuItemWindow should be a top-level menu item – that is, it should be placed to the right of the **Files** menu:

Name	Text	Top level
menuItemFiles	&Files	Yes
menuItemNew	&New	No
menuItemOpen	&Open	No

Name	Text	Top level
menuItemClose	&Close	No
menuItemSepFiles0	-	No
menuItemSave	&Save	No
menuItemSaveAll	Save &All	No
menuItemSepFiles1	-	No

Name	Text	Top level
menuItemExit	E&xit	No
menuItemWindow	&Window	Yes
menuItemTile	&Tile	No
menuItemCascade	&Cascade	No
menuItemSepWindow0	-	No
menuItemWindowsOpen	Open Windows	No

Finally, set the MergeOrder property for menuItemWindowsOpen to 1, and its MdiList property to True.

If you run the application now, you will see that the Edit menu has been nicely inserted between the Files menu and the Window menu. The reason this has happened is that we set the MergeOrder property of the Window MenuItem to 1 and the MergeOrder of the Edit menu is 0 (this is the default value and we haven't changed it). Because the MergeType is Add, the Edit menu is added to the right of all top-level menu items that have a MergeOrder less than or equal to its MergeOrder.

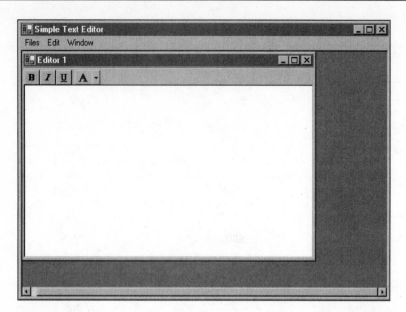

Another thing you will notice is that the **Open Windows** menu item contains a subitem with a check mark. The text of this subitem is the same as the text of the frmEditor form. In this menu all open windows will be listed – without us having to code a single line. This is the result of setting the MdiList property of the MenuItemWindowsOpen menu item to true:

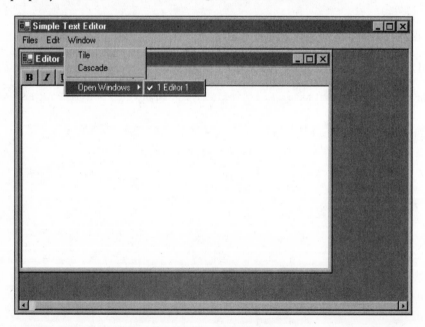

Adding the Event Handlers

Let's move on to the code. First we'll create the menu handlers for the Edit menu. Double-click all the menu items in the menu except for the separator and top-level item, and add the following code:

```
private void menuItemUndo_Click(object sender, System.EventArgs e)
{
    rtfText.Undo();
}

private void menuItemRedo_Click(object sender, System.EventArgs e)
{
    rtfText.Redo();
}

private void menuItemCut_Click(object sender, System.EventArgs e)
{
    rtfText.Cut();
}

private void menuItemCopy_Click(object sender, System.EventArgs e)
{
    rtfText.Copy();
}

private void menuItemPaste_Click(object sender, System.EventArgs e)
{
    rtfText.Paste();
}
```

Happily, the RichTextBox control provides us with methods that correspond exactly to all of our menu items, so we simply call these functions. Just as we did in the MenuExample earlier, we need to check if the menus should be enabled or disabled, and we do this in the Popup event handler. This time we'll subscribe to the event in the constructor of the form frmEditor:

```
public frmEditor(SimpleTextEditor.frmContainer parent)
{
    InitializeComponent();

    // Bind to the parent
    this.MdiParent = parent;

    // Subscribe to the popup event of the Edit menu
    this.menuItemEdit.Popup += new EventHandler(this.menuItemEdit_Popup);
}
```

Then we add the event handler:

```
private void menuItemEdit_Popup(object sender, System.EventArgs e)
{
    // If there is no text selected, we cannot cut it.
    this.menuItemCut.Enabled = rtfText.SelectedText.Length > 0 ? true : false;
```

```
    // If there is no text selected, we cannot copy it.
    this.menuItemCopy.Enabled = rtfText.SelectedText.Length > 0 ? true : false;

    // The CanPaste method of the RichTextBox tells us if there's anything to
    // paste
    this.menuItemPaste.Enabled =
                rtfText.CanPaste(DataFormats.GetFormat(DataFormats.Rtf));

    // The CanUndo property of the RichTextBox tells us if we can undo an
    // action
    this.menuItemUndo.Enabled = rtfText.CanUndo;

    // The CanRedo property of the RichTextBox tells us if we can redo an
    // action
    this.menuItemRedo.Enabled = rtfText.CanRedo;
}
```

Once again, the `RichTextBox` control helps us out. It is possible to check all of the items to see if they should be enabled or not, simply by calling a function or querying a property. The only method that needs further explanation is `CanPaste()`. This method takes the text that you want to paste and returns a Boolean value which is `true` if it is possible to do the paste.

Now let's move on to the menus in the MDI container. We'll start with the **New** menu item on the **Files** menu. When **New** is clicked we want to create an additional window. We've already seen how to do this, as it already happens in the constructor, but there's a problem. At the moment all of our windows have the exact same caption – **Editor** – which makes it impossible to distinguish between them in the `MdiList` we created. To change this, we'll add a new parameter to the constructor of the `frmEditor` form in which we'll send the text that should be displayed in the new windows caption:

```
public frmEditor(SimpleTextEditor.frmContainer parent, string caption)
{
    InitializeComponent();

    // Bind to the parent
    this.MdiParent = parent;
    // Set the caption
    this.Text = caption;

    // Subscribe to the popup event of the Edit menu
    this.menuItemEdit.Popup += new EventHandler(this.menuItemEdit_Popup);
}
```

This change means that we have to change the call to the constructor that is made in the constructor of the container:

```
public frmContainer()
{
    InitializeComponent();

    SimpleTextEditor.frmEditor newForm = new frmEditor(this, "Editor 1");
    newForm.Show();
}
```

Now we are ready to create new windows. Double-click the **New** menu item and add the following code:

```
private void menuItemNew_Click (object sender, System.EventArgs e)
{
    string caption = "Editor " + nextFormNumber++; // The caption

    // Create the new window
    SimpleTextEditor.frmEditor newForm = new SimpleTextEditor.frmEditor(this,
                                                            caption);
    newForm.Show(); // Show the form
}
```

First, we create the new caption. The `nextFormNumber` variable is defined at the top of the class as:

```
private int nextFormNumber = 2;
```

If we chose to use the number of windows currently in the array of forms (`MdiChildren`) we would have a problem if two forms had been opened, and the form with number 1 was subsequently closed. We'll therefore simply add one to this number each time a new form is opened. The reason the next form number is two rather than one when we start is that the constructor used the text `"Editor 1"` to initialize the first window.

After that we create a new instance of the editor form and show it.

If you run the code and add a new window, you will notice that the events in the **Edit** menu target the correct window – which is lucky, because we didn't do anything to achieve this. Because the events handlers are defined for each instance of the form, the events are sent to the correct place every time. Also you will see the two windows showing up in the **Open Windows** list:

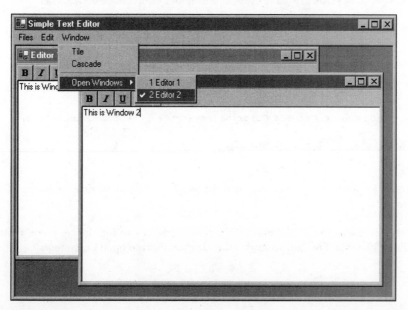

Next, we want to be able to close the window again. The `frmContainer` form has a property called `ActiveMdiChild`, which lets us identify the child window we want to close. Double-click the **Close** menu and add the following code:

```
private void menuItemClose_Click(object sender, System.EventArgs e)
{
    // Get the active MDI child
    SimpleTextEditor.frmEditor frm =
                (SimpleTextEditor.frmEditor)this.ActiveMdiChild;
    if (frm != null) // Make sure the child is valid before using it
    {
        frm.Close(); // Close the window
    }
}
```

First, we cast the form contained in the `ActiveMdiChild` property to a `SimpleTextEditor` class. Then we make sure that the instance is not `null` before doing anything with it, and then call `Close()` on the window.

We are not going to cover implementing the other **Files** menu items, as the **Open**, **Save** and **SaveAll** options use the standard open and save file dialogs which are discussed in full in the next chapter. The **Exit** menu item uses the very same code as we have seen in earlier examples.

Now we move on to the two remaining menus in the Window menu – **Tile** and **Cascade**. There are two possible ways to tile open documents – vertically or horizontally, but in this example we'll just use one, and tile the windows horizontally. There is only one option for cascading multiple document windows. Double-click the **Tile** menu, and add the following code:

```
private void menuItemTile_Click(object sender, System.EventArgs e)
{
    this.LayoutMdi(MdiLayout.TileHorizontal);
}
```

Now double-click the **Cascade** menu and add the following code:

```
private void menuItemCascade_Click(object sender, System.EventArgs e)
{
    this.LayoutMdi(MdiLayout.Cascade);
}
```

The `LayoutMdi()` method on the container window allows you to change the layout of all the MDI children.

This concludes our discussion of SDI and MDI applications. If you run the code you should be able to create something like this (the figure shows a tiled layout of three open documents):

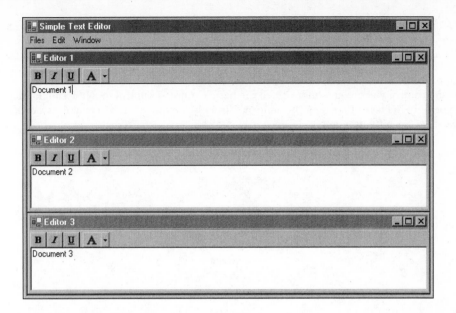

Creating Controls

There are times where the controls that ship with Visual Studio .NET just don't meet your needs. The reasons for this can be many – the controls don't draw themselves in the way you want them to, or the controls are restrictive in some way, or the control you need simply doesn't exist. Recognizing this, Microsoft has provided us with the means to create controls that meet our needs. Visual Studio .NET provides a project type named Windows Control Library, which you use when you want to create a control yourself.

> **The Windows Control Library project is not available from Visual C# Standard Edition.**

Two distinct kinds of home-made controls can be developed, named user controls (or composite controls) and custom controls:

❑   User or composite controls – these controls build on the functionality of existing controls to create a new control. Such controls are generally made to encapsulate functionality with the user interface of the control, or to enhance the interface of a control by combining several other controls into one unit.

❑   Custom controls – these controls can be created when no control fits your needs, that is, you start from scratch. It draws its entire user interface itself and no existing controls are used in the creation of the control. You will normally need to create a control like this when the user interface control you want to create is unlike that of any other available control.

In this chapter we'll focus on user controls as the second option of designing and drawing a custom control from scratch is beyond the scope of this book. Chapter 16 on GDI+ gives you the means to draw items by yourself, and you should then be able to move on to custom controls easily.

ActiveX controls as used in Visual Studio 6 existed in a special kind of file with the extension `ocx`. These files were essentially COM DLLs. In .NET a control exists in exactly the same way as any other assembly, and because of that the `ocx` extension has disappeared and controls exist in DLLs.

User controls inherit from the `System.Windows.Forms.UserControl` class. This base class provides the control you are creating with all the basic features a control in .NET should include – leaving you only the task of creating the control. Virtually anything can be created as a control, ranging from a label with a nifty design to full-blown grid controls.

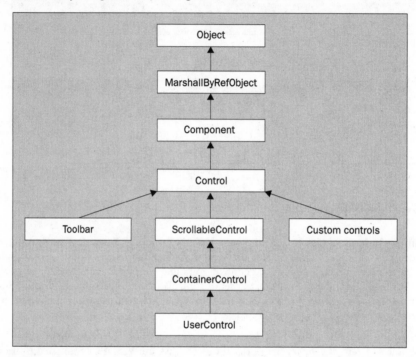

Unlike user controls, custom controls derive from the `System.Windows.Forms.Control` class rather than `UserControl`.

We take a number of things for granted when we are working with controls. If your control doesn't fulfill those expectations, the chances are that people will be discouraged from using it. These criteria are:

❑ The behavior of the design-time control should be very similar to its behavior at run-time. This means that if the control consists of a `Label` and a `TextBox` that have been combined to create a `LabelTextbox`, the `Label` and `TextBox` should both be displayed at design time and the text entered for the `Label` should also be shown at design time. While this is fairly easy in the above example, it can present problems in more complex cases, where you'll need to find an appropriate compromise.

❑ Access to the properties of the control should be possible from the form designer in a logical manner. A good example of this is the `ImageList` control that presents a dialog from which you can browse to the images you want to include, and once the images are imported, they are shown in a list in the dialog.

Over the next few pages we will introduce you to the creation of controls by means of an example. The example creates the `LabelTextbox` and demonstrates the basics of creating a user control project, creating properties and events and debugging controls.

Try it Out – LabelTextbox Example

As the name of the control implies, this is a control that combines two existing controls to create a single one that performs in, one go, a task extremely common in Windows programming: adding a label to a form, then adding a text box to the same form and positioning the text box in relation to the label. Let's look at what a user of this control will expect it to do:

❑   It should be possible for the user to position the text box either to the right of the label or below it. If the text box is positioned to the right of the label, it should be possible to specify a fixed distance from the left edge of the control to the text box in order to align text boxes below each other.

❑   The usual properties and events of the text box and label should be available to the user.

Now that we know what we are up against, it is time to start Visual Studio and create a new project:

1.   Create a new **Windows Control Library** project called `LabelTextbox` in the `C:\BegVCSharp\Chapter14` directory:

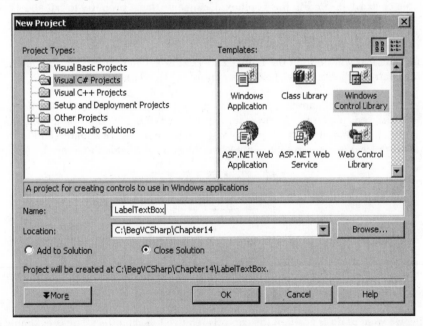

The form designer presents you with a design surface that looks somewhat different from what we're used to. First of all the surface is much smaller than normal, and secondly it doesn't look like a dialog at all. You should not let this new look discourage you in any way – things still work as usual. The main difference is that up until now we have been placing controls on a form, but now we are creating a control to be placed on a form:

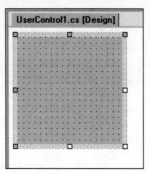

2. Click the design surface and bring up the properties for the control. Change the Name of the control to ctlLabelTextbox.

3. Double-click a Label in the Toolbox to add it to the control, placing it in the top left-hand corner of the surface. Change its Name property to lblTextBox. Set the Text property to Label. Set the AutoSize property to True. This will make the label control size itself to the size of the text.

4. Double-click a TextBox in the Toolbox. Change its Name property to txtLabelText and clear the Text property.

At design time we do not know how the user will want to position these controls. Because of that we are going to write code that will position the Label and TextBox. That same code will determine the position of the controls when a LabelTextbox control is placed on a form.

The design of the control looks anything but encouraging – not only is the TextBox floating freely on the surface, the surface is too large. However this is of no consequence, because unlike what we've been used to up until now, what you see is not what you get! The code we are about to add to the control will change the appearance of the control, but only when the control is added to a form.

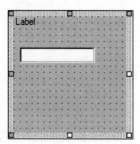

The first thing we want to do is position the controls relative to each other. The user should be able to decide how the controls are positioned and for that we add not one but two properties to the control. One property is called Position and gives the user a choice between two options: Right and Below. If the user chooses Right then the other property comes into play. This property is called TextboxMargin and is an int that represents the number of pixels from the left edge of the control to where the TextBox should be placed. If the user specifies 0 the TextBox is placed with its right edge aligned with the right edge of the control.

Adding Properties

In order to give the user a choice between `Right` and `Below` we start by defining an enumeration with these two values. Return to the control project , go to the code editor and add this code:

```
public class ctlLabelTextbox : System.Windows.Forms.UserControl
{
    // Enumeration of the two possible positions
    public enum PositionEnum
    {
        Right,
        Below
    }
```

This is just a normal enumeration as we saw in Chapter 5. Now for the magic – we want the position to be a property the user can set through code and the designer. We do this by adding a property to the `ctlLabelTextbox` class. First, however, we create two member fields that will hold the values the user selects:

```
// Member field that will hold the choices the user makes
private PositionEnum mPosition = PositionEnum.Right;
private int mTextboxMargin = 0;

public ctlLabelTextbox()
{
    ...
```

Then we add the `Position` property as follows:

```
public PositionEnum Position
{
    get
    {
        return mPosition;
    }
    set
    {
        mPosition = value;
        MoveControls();
    }
}
```

The property is added to the class like any other property. If we are asked to return the property, we return the `mPosition` member field, and if we are asked to change the `Position`, we assign the value to `mPosition` and call the method `MoveControls()`. We'll return to `MoveControls()` in a short while, for now it is enough to know that this method positions the two controls by examining the values of `mPosition` and `mTextboxMargin`.

The `TextboxMargin` property is the same, except it works with an integer:

```
public int TextboxMargin
{
   get
   {
      return mTextboxMargin;
   }
   set
   {
      mTextboxMargin = value;
      MoveControls();
   }
}
```

Adding the Event Handlers

Before we move on to test the two properties, we'll add two event handlers as well. When the control is placed on the form, the Load event is called. You should use this event to initialize the control and any resources the control may use. We handle this event in order to move the controls and to size the control to fit neatly around the two controls it contains. The other event we'll add is the SizeChanged event. This event is called whenever the control is resized, and we should handle the event to allow the control to draw itself correctly. We subscribe to the events in the constructor of the control:

```
// Handle the SizeChanged event
this.SizeChanged += new System.EventHandler(this.OnSizeChanged);

// Handle the Load event
this.Load += new EventHandler(this.OnLoad);
```

Then we add the event handlers:

```
private void OnLoad(object sender, EventArgs e)
{
   lblTextBox.Text = this.Name; // Add a text to the label
   // Set the height of the control
   this.Height = txtLabelText.Height + lblTextBox.Height;
   MoveControls(); // Move the controls
}

private void OnSizeChanged(object sender, System.EventArgs e)
{
   MoveControls();
}
```

Once again, we call MoveControls() to take care of the positioning of the controls. It is time to see this method, before we test the control again:

```
private void MoveControls()
{
   switch (mPosition)
   {
```

```
        case PositionEnum.Below:
            // Place the top of the Textbox just below the label
            this.txtLabelText.Top = this.lblTextBox.Bottom;
            this.txtLabelText.Left = this.lblTextBox.Left;

            // Change the width of the Textbox to equal the width of the control
            this.txtLabelText.Width = this.Width;        this.Height = txtLabelText.Height
  + lblTextBox.Height;
            break;
        case PositionEnum.Right:
            // Set the top of the textbox to equal that of the label
            txtLabelText.Top = lblTextBox.Top;

            // If the margin is zero, we'll place the textbox next to the label
            if (mTextboxMargin == 0)
            {
                int width = this.Width-lblTextBox.Width-3;
                txtLabelText.Left = lblTextBox.Right + 3;
                txtLabelText.Width = width;
            }
            else
            {
                // If the margin isn't zero, we place the textbox where the user
                // has specified
                txtLabelText.Left = mTextboxMargin;
                txtLabelText.Width = this.Right-mTextboxMargin;
            }
            break;
    }
}
```

The value in mPosition is tested in a switch statement to determine whether we should place the text box below or to the right of the label. If the user chooses Below, then we move the top of the text box to the position that is the bottom of the label. We then move the left edge of the text box to the left edge of the control and set the width of it to the width of the control.

If the user chooses Right, then there are two possibilities. If the TextboxMargin is zero, then we start by determining the width that is left in the control for the text box. We then set the left edge of the text box to just a nudge right of the text and set the width to fill the remaining space. If the user did specify a margin, then we place the left edge of the text box at that position and set the width again.

We are now ready to test the control. Before we move on, build the project.

Debugging User Controls

Debugging a user control is quite different from debugging a Windows application. Normally you would just add a breakpoint somewhere, hit *F5* and see what happens. If you are still unfamiliar with debugging you should refer to Chapter 7 for a detailed explanation.

A control needs a container in which to display itself, and we will have to supply it with one. We do this by creating a Windows application project:

Try it Out – Debugging User Controls

1. In Solution Explorer, right click on the `LabelTextbox` solution and select **Add | Add New Project**. In the **Add New Project** dialog, create a new Windows application called `LabelTextboxTest` in the directory `C:\BegVCSharp\Chapter14`.

In Solution Explorer you should now see two projects open. The first project we created, `LabelTextbox`, is written in bold face. This means that if we try to run the solution the debugger will attempt to use the control project as the startup project. This will fail because the control isn't a stand-alone type of project. In order to fix this, right-click the name of the new project – `LabelTextboxTest` and select **Set as Startup Project**. If you run the solution now, the Windows application project will be run and no errors will occur.

2. In order for the Windows application project to know about the control we are creating we need to add a reference to it. Right-click the **References** heading in the **Solution Explorer** under the project `LabelTextboxTest` and select **Add Reference...**

3. Choose the tab named **Projects**. Here you should see the control project listed. Click **Select** and click **OK** to add a reference to the **LabelTextBox** project. You should now be able to find the `LabelTextBox` control in the **Windows Form** section of the Toolbox, along side the standard Windows forms controls.

4. Add the control `ctlLabelTextbox` to the form by double-clicking it. Note: If you get an error when you double-click `ctlLabelTextbox` then try the following: Right-click **LabelTextBox** in the **Solution Explorer** and select **Remove**. Repeat step 3 but instead of selecting the project on the **Projects** tab, click **Browse** and browse to the location of the DLL named `LabelTextbox.dll`. Select it and click **OK**.

5. Go to the code and find the line which you will find in the `InitializeComponent()` method.

```
this.MyControl = new LabelTextbox.ctlLabelTextbox();
```

To get at this line you will probably have to unfold the region marked as "Windows Form Designer generated code".

6. Place a breakpoint on this line.

7. Run the code. As you would expect the code stops at the breakpoint we placed. Now step into the code (if you are using the default keyboard maps, then press *F11* to do so). When you step into the code you are transferred to the constructor of our new control, which is exactly what we want in order to debug the component. You are also able to place breakpoints. Hit *F5* to allow the application to run.

Extending the LabelTextbox Control

Finally, we are ready to test the properties of the control. Go through the steps to create a project in a new instance of Visual Studio .NET that includes the `LabelTextbox` control. Drag the control onto the form. You will see the label displaying the name of the control and the text box occupying the remaining area of the control. Also notice that the controls within the `LabelTextbox` control move to the correct positions when the control is added to the form:

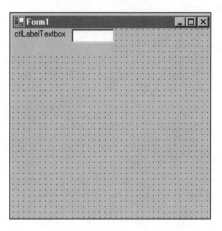

Adding More Properties

We can't do much with the control at the moment, as it is sadly missing the ability to change the text in the label and text box. We'll add two properties to handle this: `LabelText` and `TextboxText`. The properties are added in the same way as we did the two previous properties:

```
public string LabelText
{
    get
    {
        return lblTextBox.Text;
    }
    set
    {
        lblTextBox.Text = value;
        MoveControls();
    }
}

public string TextboxText
{
    get
    {
        return txtLabelText.Text;
    }
    set
    {
        txtLabelText.Text = value;
    }
}
```

We simply assign the text to the Text property of the Label and TextBox controls if we want to insert the text, and return the value of the Text properties. In the case that the label text is changed, we need to call MoveControls(), because the label text may influence where the text box is positioned. Text inserted into the text box on the other hand does not move the controls, and if the text is longer than the text box, it will disappear out of sight.

Adding More Event Handlers

Now it is time for us to begin thinking about which events the control should provide. Because the control is derived from the UserControl class, we have inherited a lot of functionality that we don't need to worry about. There are, however, a number of events that we don't want to hand to the user in the standard way. Examples of this include the KeyDown, KeyPress, and KeyUp events. The reason we need to change these events is that the user will expect them to be sent when he or she presses a key in the text box. As they are now, the events are only sent when the control itself has focus, and the user presses a key.

To change this behavior, we must handle the events sent by the text box, and pass them on to the user. We start by subscribing to the events in the constructor of the form:

```
// Handle the SizeChanged event
this.SizeChanged += new System.EventHandler(this.OnSizeChanged);
```

```
// Textbox Keyboard events
this.txtLabelText.KeyDown += new KeyEventHandler(this.txtLabelText_KeyDown);
this.txtLabelText.KeyUp += new KeyEventHandler(this.txtLabelText_KeyUp);
this.txtLabelText.KeyPress += new
                        KeyPressEventHandler(this.txtLabelText_KeyPress);
```

Then we add the three event handlers:

```
private void txtLabelText_KeyDown(object sender, KeyEventArgs e)
{
    OnKeyDown(e);
}

private void txtLabelText_KeyUp(object sender, KeyEventArgs e)
{
    OnKeyUp(e);
}

private void txtLabelText_KeyPress(object sender, KeyPressEventArgs e)
{
    OnKeyPress(e);
}
```

Calling the OnKeyXXX method invokes a call to any methods that are subscribed to the event.

Adding a Custom Event Handler

When we want to create an event that does not exist in one of the base classes, we need to do a bit more work. We will create an event called PositionChanged that will occur when the Position property changes.

In order to create this event we need three things:

❑ We need an appropriate delegate that can be used to invoke the methods the user assigns to the event.

❑ The user must be able to subscribe to the event by assigning a method to it.

❑ We must invoke the method the user has assigned to the event.

The delegate we will use is the `EventHandler` delegate that is provided by the .NET Framework. As we learned in Chapter 12, this is a special kind of delegate that is declared by its very own keyword, `event`. The following line declares the event, and enables the user to subscribe to it:

```
public event System.EventHandler PositionChanged;

// Constructor
public ctlLabelTextbox()
{
```

Now all that remains for us to do is raise the event. As it should occur when the `Position` property changes, we raise the event in the `set` accessor of the `Position` property:

```
public PositionEnum Position
{
    get
    {
        return mPosition;
    }
    set
    {
        mPosition = value;
        MoveControls();
        if (PositionChanged != null) // Make sure there are subscribers
        {
            // Get the list of methods to call
            System.Delegate[] subscribers = PositionChanged.GetInvocationList();
            // Loop through the methods
            foreach (System.EventHandler target in subscribers)
            {
                target(this, new EventArgs()); // Call the method
            }
        }
    }
}
```

First we make sure that there are some subscribers by checking if `PositionChanged` is `null`. If it isn't we call `GetInvocationList` on it, to retrieve a list of the delegates to call. Then we loop through all the delegates and call them one by one.

Our custom event is subscribed to in the constructor of our `LabelTextboxTest` project:

```
public Form1()
{
    //
    // Required for Windows Form Designer support
    //
    InitializeComponent();

    ctlLabelTextbox1.PositionChanged +=
                    new EventHandler(this.myControl_PositionChanged);
    }
}
```

Our custom event handler doesn't really do anything sparkling – it simply points out that the position has changed!

```
private void myControl_PositionChanged(object sender, EventArgs e)
{
    MessageBox.Show("Changed");
}
```

Now we can compile and run our test application that contains our user control. The application also contains a button, which will toggle to appearance of the control by setting and resetting the Position property and displaying a message box:

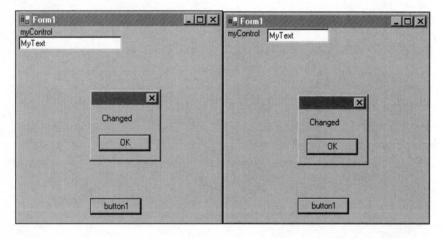

Our example is now finished. It could be refined rather a bit, but we will leave that to you and the exercises.

Summary

In this chapter we started where we left of in the previous chapter, by examining the MainMenu and ToolBar controls. We saw how to create MDI and SDI applications and how menus and toolbars are used in those applications. We then moved on to create a control of our own, designing properties, user interface and events for the control. The next chapter will complete our discussion on Windows Forms by looking at the one special type of form we have only glossed over so far, the Windows common dialogs.

Exercises

1. Using the LabelTextbox example as the base, create a new property called MaxLength that stores the maximum number of characters that can be entered into the textbox. Then create two new events called MaxLengthChanged and MaxLengthReached. The MaxLengthChanged event should be raised when the MaxLength property is changed and MaxLengthReached should be raised when the user enters a character making the length of the text in the text box equal to the value of MaxLength.

Using Common Dialogs

In the last two chapters we have looked at various aspects of programming Windows Forms applications, and seen how to implement such things as menus, toolbars, and SDI and MDI forms. We also know how to display simple message boxes to get information from the user, and how to create more sophisticated custom dialogs to ask the user for specific information. However, for common tasks such as opening and saving files, there are prewritten dialog classes that can be used instead of having to create your own custom dialog.

This not only has the advantage of requiring less code, but also that it uses the familiar Windows dialogs, giving your application a standard look and feel. The .NET Framework has classes which hook up to the Windows dialogs to open and save files, to access printers, and to select colors and fonts. Using these dialogs instead of custom dialogs means that it's not necessary for you to have to learn the complex methodology that would be required to code such functionality from scratch.

In this chapter we will learn how to use these standard dialog classes. In particular, we will:

❑   Use the `OpenFileDialog` and `SaveFileDialog` classes

❑   Learn about the .NET printing class hierarchy and use the `PrintDialog`, `PageSetupDialog`, and `PrintPreviewDialog` classes to implement printing and print preview

❑   Look at how to change fonts and colors with the `FontDialog` and `ColorDialog` classes

Common Dialogs

A dialog is a window that is displayed within the context of another window. With a dialog we can ask the user to enter some data before we continue the flow of our program. A common dialog is a dialog that used to get information from the user that most applications will typically require, such as the name of a file, and is a part of the Windows operating system.

With the .NET Framework we have the following dialog classes:

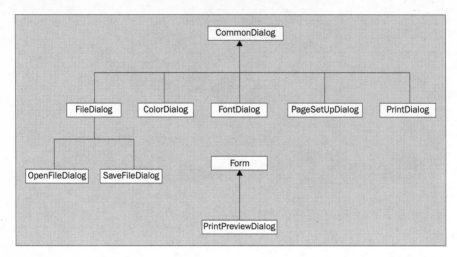

All these dialog classes, except the `PrintPreviewDialog`, derive from the abstract `CommonDialog` base class that has methods to manage a Windows common dialog.

The `CommonDialog` class defines the following methods and events common to all common dialog classes:

Public Instance Methods and Events	Description
ShowDialog()	This method is implemented from the derived class to display a common dialog.
Reset()	Every derived dialog class implements the Reset() method to set all properties of the dialog class to their default values.
HelpRequest	This event is thrown when the user clicks the Help button on a common dialog.

All these dialog classes wrap up a Windows common dialog to make the dialog available for .NET applications. `PrintPreviewDialog` is an exception because it adds its own elements to a Windows Form to control the preview of a print, and hence is not really a dialog at all. The `OpenFileDialog` and `SaveFileDialog` classes derive from the abstract base class `FileDialog` that adds file features that are common to both the opening and closing file dialogs.

Let's get an overview of how the different dialogs can be used:

❑   To let the user select and browse **files to open** the `OpenFileDialog` is used. This dialog can be configured to allow the selection of a single file or multiple files.

❑   With the `SaveFileDialog` the user can specify a filename and browse for a directory to **save files**.

❑ The `PrintDialog` is used to **select a printer** and set the printing options.

❑ To **configure the margins** of a page the `PageSetupDialog` is usually used.

❑ The `PrintPreviewDialog` is one way to preview on the screen what is to be printed on paper, with options such as zoom.

❑ The `FontDialog` lists all installed Windows **fonts** with styles and sizes, and a preview to select the font of choice.

❑ The `ColorDialog` class makes it easy to select a **color**.

I have seen some applications developed (by the same company) where not only were the common dialogs not reused, but also no style guide for building custom dialogs was used. The development of these dialogs resulted in functionality that was not consistent, with some buttons and other controls found in different locations, such as the OK and Cancel buttons being reversed between dialogs.

Sometimes that inconsistency can also be found within one application. That's frustrating for the user and increases the time to do a task.

Be consistent in the dialogs you build and use! Consistency can be easy to attain by using the common dialogs.

How to Use Dialogs

As `CommonDialog` is the base class for the dialog classes, all the dialog classes can be used similarly. Public instance methods are `ShowDialog()` and `Reset()`. `ShowDialog()` invokes the protected `RunDialog()` instance method to display the dialog and finally returns a `DialogResult` instance with the information on how the user interacted with the dialog. `Reset()`, on the other hand, sets properties of the dialog class to their default values.

The following code segment shows an example of how a dialog class can be used. Later, we will take a more detailed look at each of the steps, but first let's introduce the overall concept of how dialogs can be used.

As you can see in the following code segment:

❑ First a new instance of the dialog class is created.

❑ Next, we have to set some properties to enable / disable optional features and set dialog state. In this case we set the `Title` property to "Sample", and the `ShowReadOnly` property to `true`.

❑ By calling the `ShowDialog()` method, the dialog is displayed and waits and reacts to user inputs.

❑ If the user presses the OK button the dialog is closed, and we check for the OK by comparing the result of the dialog with `DialogResult.OK`. After that we can get the values from the user input by querying for the specific property values. In this case we are storing the value of the `FileName` property in the `fileName` variable.

```
OpenFileDialog dlg = new OpenFileDialog();
dlg.Title = "Sample";
dlg.ShowReadOnly = true;

if (dlg.ShowDialog() == DialogResult.OK)
{
    string fileName = dlg.FileName;
}
```

It's really that easy! Of course every dialog has its own configurable options, which we look at in the following sections.

If you use a dialog from within a Windows Forms application in Visual Studio .NET, it's even easier than the few lines of code above. The Windows Forms designer creates the code to instantiate a new instance, and the property values can be set from the Properties window. We just have to call ShowDialog() and get to the changed values, as we shall see.

File Dialogs

With a file dialog the user can select a drive and browse through the file system to select a file. From the file dialog, all we want returned is a file name from the user.

With the OpenFileDialog we can allow the user to select a name for the file that they want to open, whereas using the SaveFileDialog, allows the user to specify a name for a file that they want to save. These dialog classes are very similar since they derive from the same abstract base class, though there are some properties unique to each class. In this section, we will at first have a look at the features of the OpenFileDialog, and then we will look at where the SaveFileDialog differs. We will develop a sample application that uses both of them.

OpenFileDialog

The OpenFileDialog class enables the user to select a file to open. As we have seen in our example above, a new instance of the OpenFileDialog class is created before the ShowDialog() method is called.

```
OpenFileDialog dlg = new OpenFileDialog();
dlg.ShowDialog();
```

Running a Windows application program with these two code lines will result in this dialog:

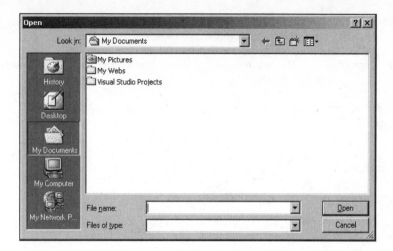

As we have seen already, we can set the properties of this class before calling ShowDialog(), which changes the behavior and appearance of this dialog, or limits the files that can be opened. In the next sections we will look at possible modifications.

Note that if you want to use the OpenFileDialog with console applications, the System.Windows.Forms assembly must be referenced, and the System.Windows.Forms namespace must be included.

Dialog Title

The default title for the OpenFileDialog is **Open**. You can change the title of the dialog by setting the Title property. **Open** is not always the best name if, for example, in the application you want to analyze log files to check some information and to perform calculations on it, or to get file sizes, and after doing whatever processing is required, you close the files straight away afterwards. In this case the files don't stay opened for the user, so a title of **Analyze Files** would be better. Visual Studio .NET itself has different titles for the file open dialogs to differentiate the file types that are opened: **Open Project, Open File, Open Solution,** and **Open File from Web**.

This code segment shows how a different title can be set.

```
OpenFileDialog dlg = new OpenFileDialog();
dlg.Title = "Open File";
dlg.ShowDialog();
```

Specifying Directories

By default, the dialog opens the directory that was opened by the user when they last ran the application, and displays the files in this directory. Setting the InitialDirectory property changes this behavior. The default value of InitialDirectory is an empty string, which represents the My Documents directory of the user, and is shown the first time that the dialog is used in the application. The second time that the dialog is opened, the directory shown will be the same one as for the previously opened file. The Windows common dialog called by the OpenFileDialog uses the Registry to locate the name of the previously opened file.

You should never use a hard-coded directory string in your application as this directory may not exist on the user's system. To get special system folders you can use the static method GetFolderPath() of the System.Environment class. The GetFolderPath() method accepts an Environment.SpecialFolder enumeration member that defines which system directory you want the path for.

In the following code example I'm using the common user directory for templates to set it as InitialDirectory.

```
string dir = Environment.GetFolderPath(Environment.SpecialFolder.Templates);
dlg.InitialDirectory = dir;
```

Setting the File Filter

The file filter defines the file types that the user can select to open. A simple filter string can look like this:

```
Text Documents (*.txt)|*.txt|All Files|*.*
```

The filter is used to display the entries in the **Files of type:** list box. Microsoft WordPad displays these entries:

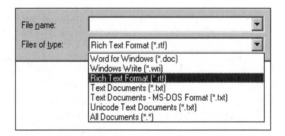

A filter has multiple segments that are separated with the pipe character (|). Two strings are required for each entry, so the number of segments should always be an even number. The first string for each entry defines the text that will be presented in the listbox; the second string is used to specify the extension of the files to display in the dialog. We can set the filter string with the Filter property as in the code below:

```
dlg.Filter = "Text documents (*.txt)|*.txt|All Files|*.*";
```

Setting a wrong Filter value results in a run-time exception, System.ArgumentException, with the error message The provided filter string is invalid. A blank before or after the filter is also not allowed.

The FilterIndex property specifies the number of the default selection in the listbox. With WordPad the default selection is Rich Text Format (*.rtf) as highlighted in the screenshot above. If you have multiple file types to choose from then you can set the FilterIndex to the default file type. It's worth paying attention to the fact that the FilterIndex is one-based!

Validation

The `OpenFileDialog` can do some automatic validation of the file before you attempt to open it. When the `ValidateNames` property is `true`, the filename entered by the user is checked to see if it is a valid Windows filename. Pressing the **OK** button of the dialog with an invalid filename displays the following dialog, and the user must correct the filename or click **Cancel** to leave the `OpenFileDialog`. Invalid characters for a filename include characters such as \ \, /, or :.

With `ValidateNames` set to `true`, you can use `CheckFileExists` and `CheckPathExists` as additional validation. With `CheckPathExists` the path is validated, whereas `CheckFileExists` validates the file. If the file doesn't exist, the following dialog is displayed when the **OK** button is pressed:

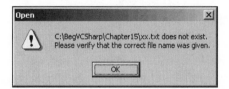

The default for these three properties is `true`, so the validation happens automatically.

Help

The `OpenFileDialog` class supports a help button that is by default invisible. Setting the `ShowHelp` property to `true` makes this button visible, and you can add an event handler to the `HelpRequest` event to display help information to the user.

Results

The `ShowDialog()` method of the `OpenFileDialog` class returns a `DialogResult` enumeration value. The `DialogResult` enumeration defines the members `Abort`, `Cancel`, `Ignore`, `No`, `None`, `OK`, `Retry`, and `Yes`.

`None` is the default value that is set as long as the user hasn't closed the dialog. Depending on the button pressed the corresponding result is returned. With the `OpenFileDialog`, only `DialogResult.OK` and `DialogResult.Cancel` are returned.

If the user pressed the **OK** button the selected file name can be accessed using the `FileName` property. If the user cancelled the dialog the `FileName` is just an empty string. If the `Multiselect` property is set to `true` so that the user can select more than one file you get all the selected filenames by accessing the `FileNames` property, which returns a string array.

Note that the `FileNames` property contains the files in the reverse order to which they were selected – thus the first string in the `FileNames` array is the last file selected. Also, the `FileNames` property always contains the file name of the *last* file that is selected.

This small code extract shows how multiple file names can be retrieved from an OpenFileDialog:

```
OpenFileDialog dlg = new OpenFileDialog();
dlg.Multiselect = true;

if (dlg.ShowDialog() == DialogResult.OK)
{
    foreach (string s in dlg.FileNames)
    {
        // now display the filenames in a list box
        this.listBox1.Items.Add(s);
    }
}
```

The ShowDialog() method opens up the dialog. Because the Multiselect property was set to true, the user can select multiple files. Pressing the **OK** button of the dialog ends the dialog if all goes well, and DialogResult.OK is returned. With the foreach statement, we go through all strings in the string array that is returned from the FileNames property to display every selected file.

OpenFileDialog Properties

In summary, the diagram below shows the OpenFileDialog with its properties – you can easily see what properties influence which user interface elements.

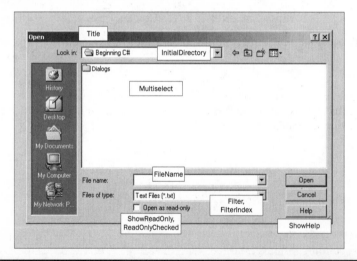

Try it Out – Creating the Simple Text Editor Windows Application

To demonstrate the use of the standard dialogs we will create a simple text editor Windows application called SimpleEditor, that will allow the user to load, save, and edit text files. As we progress further through the chapter, we will also see how to print the text file. First we'll start by seeing how to use the open and save file dialogs.

1. Create a new Windows application called SimpleEditor in the directory C:\BegVCSharp\Chapter15.

2. Rename the generated file `Form1.cs` to `SimpleForm.cs` and the class `Form1` to `SimpleEditorForm`. I'm also changing the namespace to `Wrox.Editor`.

Don't forget that when changing the name of the class you also have to change the implementation of the `Main()` method to reflect the name change, because this isn't changed automatically by setting the `Name` property of the `Form` class:

```
[STAThread]
static void Main()
{
    Application.Run(new SimpleEditorForm());
}
```

3. Set the `Text` property of the form to **Simple Editor**, and change its `Size` to 570,270. A multi-line text box will be the area to read and modify the data of the file, so add a `TextBox` from the toolbox to the Windows Forms designer. The text box should be multi-line and should cover the complete area of the application, so set these properties to the specified values:

Property	Value
(Name)	textBoxEdit
Text	
Multiline	True
Dock	Fill
ScrollBars	Both
AcceptsReturn	True
AcceptsTab	True

4. Next, we add a `MainMenu` to the application. The main menu should have a **File** entry with sub menus **New**, **Open**, **Save**, and **Save As**, as the following graphic demonstrates:

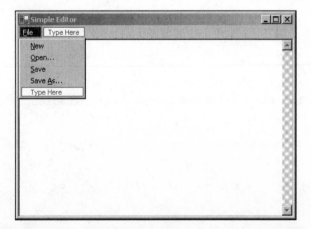

The ... in the Text property of the **Open** and **Save As** menu entries advises the user that they will be asked for some data before the action happens. When choosing the **File**, **New**, and **Save** menus the action happens without additional intervention.

Menu item Name	Text
miFile	&File
miFileNew	&New
miFileOpen	&Open...
miFileSave	&Save
miFileSaveAs	Save &As...

5. The handler for the menu entry **&New** should clear the data of the text box by calling the Clear() method of the TextBox:

```
private void miFileNew_Click(object sender, System.EventArgs e)
{
    fileName = "Untitled";
    textBoxEdit.Clear();
}
```

6. Also, the fileName member variable should be set to "Untitled". We must declare and initialize this member variable in the SimpleEditorForm class:

```
private string fileName = "Untitled";
```

With the SimpleEditor it should be possible to pass a filename as an argument when starting the application. The filename passed should be used to open the file and display it in the text box.

7. Change the implementation of the Main() method so that an argument can be passed.

```
static void Main(string[] args)
{
    string fileName = null;
    if (args.Length != 0)
        fileName = args[0];
    Application.Run(new SimpleEditorForm(fileName));
}
```

8. Now we also have to change the implementation of the SimpleEditorForm constructor to use a string:

```
public SimpleEditorForm(string fileName)
{
    //
    // Required for Windows Form Designer support
    //
    InitializeComponent();
```

```
            if (fileName != null)
            {
               this.fileName = fileName;
               OpenFile();
            }
         }
```

9. And we have to implement the `OpenFile()` method that opens a file and fills the text box with data from the file.

Note that the `OpenFile()` method actually accesses the file in question, and uses methods that we will not discuss at length here. The subject of accessing files is covered in Chapter 20, and we will not talk too much about such things so as not to interrupt our coverage of the dialogs.

```
      protected void OpenFile()
      {
         try
         {
            using (StreamReader reader = File.OpenText(fileName))
            {
               textBoxEdit.Clear();
               textBoxEdit.Text = reader.ReadToEnd();

            }
         }
         catch (IOException ex)
         {
            MessageBox.Show(ex.Message, "Simple Editor",
               MessageBoxButtons.OK, MessageBoxIcon.Exclamation);
         }
      }
```

Here we use the `StreamReader`, and `File` classes to read the file – these classes are in the `System.IO` namespace, so we also need to add the following `using` directive at the start of our program:

```
using System.IO;
```

The `StreamReader` class and the `System.IO` namespace will be explored in Chapter 20 along with other file access classes.

10. As we saw in Chapter 7, it's possible to define command line parameters within Visual Studio .NET for debugging purposes. In the Solution Explorer you just have to select the project, and choose **Project | Properties**. If you select **Configuration Properties | Debugging** in the left tree you can enter the **Command Line Arguments**. For testing purposes here, enter the following:

```
C:\BegVCSharp\Chapter15\SimpleEditor\AssemblyInfo.cs
```

11. Now we can run the application, and the `AssemblyInfo.cs` file of our current project will be opened immediately and displayed, as can be seen in the screenshot below:

```
AssemblyInfo.cs - Simple Editor                                    _ □ ×
File
using System.Reflection;
using System.Runtime.CompilerServices;

//
// General Information about an assembly is controlled through the following
// set of attributes. Change these attribute values to modify the information
// associated with an assembly.
//
[assembly: AssemblyTitle("")]
[assembly: AssemblyDescription("")]
[assembly: AssemblyConfiguration("")]
[assembly: AssemblyCompany("")]
[assembly: AssemblyProduct("")]
[assembly: AssemblyCopyright("")]
[assembly: AssemblyTrademark("")]
[assembly: AssemblyCulture("")]

//
// Version information for an assembly consists of the following four values:
//
```

How It Works

The first six steps simply set up the form – you should be familiar with this process from the previous two chapters, and we will not discuss these steps any further.

Step 7 is where the meat of our application begins. By adding the `string[]` to the parameters of the `Main()` method we can use any command line arguments that the user supplied when starting the application.

```
static void Main(string[] args)
```

In the `Main()` method we check to see if arguments are passed by using the `Length` property. If at least one argument was passed, the first argument is set to the `fileName` variable which is then passed to the constructor of the `SimpleEditorForm`.

```
{
    string fileName = null;
    if (args.Length != 0)
        fileName = args[0];
    Application.Run(new SimpleEditorForm(fileName));
}
```

In the `SimpleEditorForm` constructor we check if the filename variable already has a value set. If it has, we set the member variable `fileName` and call the `OpenFile()` method to open the file. We use a separate `OpenFile()` method, and don't write the calls to open the file and fill the text box directly in the constructor of the class because `OpenFile()` can be used again in other parts of the program.

```
    if (fileName != null)
    {
        this.fileName = fileName;
        OpenFile();
    }
```

In the `OpenFile()` method we read the data from the file. We use the static method `OpenText()` of the `File` class to open a file and get a `StreamReader` returned. The `StreamReader` class is then used to read the file with `ReadToEnd()`, which loads the text as a string that is passed to the `TextBox` object. The `StreamReader` should be closed after use to free managed and unmanaged resources. We do this with the `using` statement. `using` calls `Dispose()` at the end of the block, and the `Dispose()` implementation of the `StreamReader` class calls `Close()` to close the file.

```
using (StreamReader reader = File.OpenText(fileName))
{
    textBoxEdit.Clear();
    textBoxEdit.Text = reader.ReadToEnd();
}
```

Because file operations can easily generate exceptions, caused, for example, by the user not having the right access permissions to the file, the code is wrapped in a `try` block. In the case of an IO exception a message box shows up to inform the user about the problem, but the application keeps running.

```
try
{
    //...
}
catch (IOException ex)
{
    MessageBox.Show(ex.Message, "Simple Editor",
        MessageBoxButtons.OK, MessageBoxIcon.Exclamation);
}
```

If we enter a non-existent filename for the command-line argument when starting the application, this message box is displayed:

Try it Out – Adding and Using an Open File Dialog

Now we can read files with the simple editor by passing a filename when starting the application. Of course, we would prefer to use a common dialog class, which we will add next to our application.

1. In the Windows Forms category of the Toolbox we can find the `OpenFileDialog` component. Drag this component from the Toolbox and drop it onto the form in the Windows Forms designer. Here we'll just change three properties: the name for the instance to `dlgOpenFile`, the `Filter` property will be set to the following string, and the `FilterIndex` property is set to 2 to make `Wrox Documents` the default selection:

```
Text Documents (*.txt)|*.txt|Wrox Documents (*.wroxtext)|*.wroxtext|All Files|*.*
```

2. Add a handler to the click event of the **Open** menu entry in which we display the dialog and read the selected file with this code:

```
private void miFileOpen_Click(object sender, System.EventArgs e)
{
    if (dlgOpenFile.ShowDialog() == DialogResult.OK)
    {
        fileName = dlgOpenFile.FileName;
        OpenFile();
    }
}
```

How it Works

By adding the `OpenFileDialog` component to the Windows Forms designer, a new private member is added to the `SimpleEditorForm` class:

```
public class SimpleEditorForm : System.Windows.Forms.Form
{
    private System.Windows.Forms.TextBox textBoxEdit;
    private System.Windows.Forms.MenuItem miFile;
    private System.Windows.Forms.MenuItem miFileNew;
    private System.Windows.Forms.MenuItem miFileOpen;
    private System.Windows.Forms.MenuItem miFileSave;
    private System.Windows.Forms.MenuItem miFileSaveAs;
    private System.Windows.Forms.MainMenu mainMenu;
    private System.Windows.Forms.OpenFileDialog dlgOpenFile;
```

In the region of designer code by the Windows Forms, in `InitializeComponent()`, a new instance of this `OpenFileDialog` class is created, and the specified properties are set. Click on the + character of the line **Windows Forms Designer generated code** and then on the + character of the line `private void InitializeComponent()` to see the following code.

```
private void InitializeComponent()
{
    this.textBoxEdit = new System.Windows.Forms.TextBox();
    this.mainMenu = new System.Windows.Forms.MainMenu();
    this.miFile = new System.Windows.Forms.MenuItem();
    this.miFileNew = new System.Windows.Forms.MenuItem();
    this.miFileOpen = new System.Windows.Forms.MenuItem();
    this.miFileSave = new System.Windows.Forms.MenuItem();
    this.miFileSaveAs = new System.Windows.Forms.MenuItem();
    this.dlgOpenFile = new System.Windows.Forms.OpenFileDialog();
    // ...
    //
    // dlgOpenFile
    //
    this.dlgOpenFile.Filter =
        "Text Documents (*.txt)|*.txt|Wrox Documents
(*.wroxtext)|*.wroxtext|All Files|*.*";
    this.dlgOpenFile.FilterIndex = 2;
```

Of course all that has happened here is exactly as we would expect if we dragged any another standard control onto our form, but with the support of the Windows Forms designer we have created a new instance of the `OpenFileDialog` and set the properties. Now we have to display the dialog.

The `ShowDialog()` method displays the file open dialog and returns the button that the user pressed. We do nothing if the user presses anything other than the **OK** button. That's the reason why we check for `DialogResult.OK` in the `if` statement. If the user cancels the dialog we just do nothing.

```
if (dlgOpenFile.ShowDialog() == DialogResult.OK)
{
```

Next we get the selected filename by accessing the `FileName` property of the `OpenFileDialog` class and setting the member variable `fileName` to this value. This is the value that's used by the `OpenFile()` method. It would also be possible to open the file directly with the `OpenFileDialog` class by calling `dlgOpenFile.OpenFile()` that already returns a `Stream` object, but as we already have an `OpenFile()` method that opens and reads a file we will use this.

```
fileName = dlgOpenFile.FileName;
OpenFile();
```

Now we can start our simple editor program. Only the **New** and **Open...** menu entries are functional at the moment. **Save** and **Save As...** will be implemented in the next section.

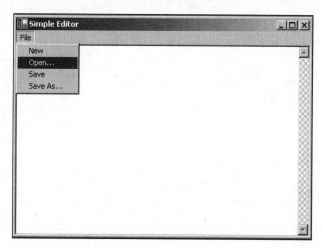

Selecting the menu entry **File | Open...** the `OpenFileDialog` shows up and we can select a file. I assume you currently don't have files with the file extension `.wroxtext`. Up to this time we cannot save files, so you can choose a different file type in the dialog editor to open a file, or you can copy a text file to a file with the extension `.wroxtext`.

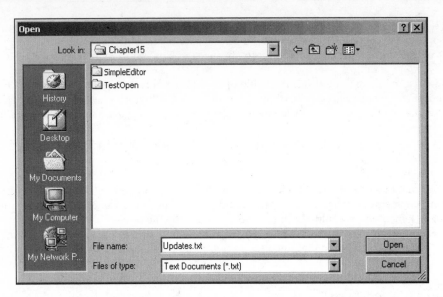

Select a text file, press the **Open** button, and the text shows up in the text box of the dialog. I selected a sample text file, `GlobalKnowledge.txt`, on my local system, as can be seen in the picture below.

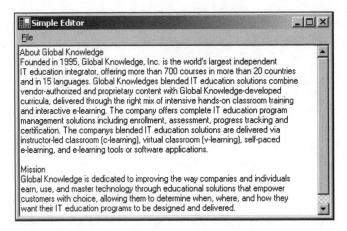

At this point, we can only read existing files. Now it would be great to create new files and modify existing ones. We will use the `SaveFileDialog` to do this now.

SaveFileDialog

The `SaveFileDialog` class is very similar to the `OpenFileDialog` and they have a set of common properties – we will not talk about those properties that operate in the same way as those of the `OpenFileDialog`. Instead, we will focus on the properties specific to the save dialog and where the application of the common properties differs.

Title

With the `Title` property you can set the title of the dialog similar to the `OpenFileDialog`. If nothing is set, the default title is **Save As**.

File Extensions

File extensions are used to associate files with applications. It is best to add a file extension to a file, otherwise Windows won't be able to know which application should be used to open the file, and it's likely that you would also eventually forget this.

`AddExtension` is a Boolean property that defines if the file extension should be automatically added to the file name the user enters – the default value is `true`. If the user enters a file extension, no additional extension will be appended. Thus with `AddExtension` set to `true`, if the filename `test` entered by the user, the filename `test.txt` will be stored. If the filename `test.txt` is entered, the filename will still be `test.txt`, and not `test.txt.txt`.

The `DefaultExt` property sets the file extension that will be used if the user doesn't enter one. If you leave the property blank the file extension that's defined with the currently selected `Filter` will be used instead. If you set both a `Filter` and the `DefaultExt`, the `DefaultExt` will be used regardless of the `Filter`.

Validation

For automatic file name validation we have the properties `ValidateNames`, `CheckFileExists`, and `CheckPathExists`, as with the `OpenFileDialog`. The difference between `OpenFileDialog` and `SaveFileDialog` is that with the `SaveFileDialog` the default value for `CheckFileExists` is `false` which means you can supply the name of a brand new file to save.

Overwriting Existing Files

As we have seen, the validation of file names is similar to that of the `OpenFileDialog`. However, for the `SaveFileDialog` class, there is more checking to do and some more properties to set. First, if the `CreatePrompt` property is set to `true` the user will be asked if a new file is to be created. If the `OverwritePrompt` property is set to `true`, that means that the user is asked if he really wants to overwrite an already existing file. The default setting for `OverwritePrompt` is `true`, and `CreatePrompt` is `false`. With this setting the following dialog is displayed if the user wants to save an already existing file:

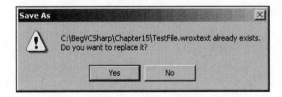

SaveFileDialog Properties

Here is a diagram summarizing the properties of the `SaveFileDialog`:

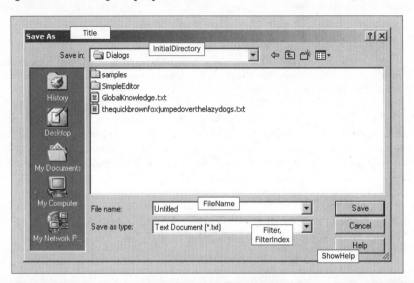

Try it Out – Adding a SaveFileDialog

1. In the same way that we could add an `OpenFileDialog` to our form, so we can add a `SaveFileDialog`: select the `SaveFileDialog` component from the Toolbox and drop it onto the form. Change the name to `dlgSaveFile`, `FileName` to `Untitled`, the `FilterIndex` to 2, and the `Filter` property to the following string as we did with the `OpenFileDialog` earlier. As we only want to allow the file extensions `.txt` and `.wroxtext` to be saved with this editor, `*.*` will now be left out.

```
Text Document (*.txt)|*.txt|Wrox Documents (*.wroxtext)|*.wroxtext
```

2. Double-click on the **Save As** menu entry to add a handler for its `Click`, and then add the following code. In this code we will display the `SaveFileDialog` with the `ShowDialog()` method. As with the `OpenFileDialog`, we are only interested in the results if the user has pressed the **OK** button. We call the `SaveFile()` method that stores the file to the disk. This method will have to be implemented in the next step.

```csharp
private void miFileSaveAs_Click(object sender, System.EventArgs e)
{
    if (dlgSaveFile.ShowDialog() == DialogResult.OK)
    {
        fileName = dlgSaveFile.FileName;
        SaveFile();
    }
}
```

3. Add the `SaveFile()` method as can be seen here to your file:

```
protected void SaveFile()
{
   try
   {
      Stream stream = File.OpenWrite(fileName);
      using (StreamWriter writer = new StreamWriter(stream))
      {
         writer.Write(textBoxEdit.Text);
      }
   }
   catch (IOException ex)
   {
      MessageBox.Show(ex.Message, "Simple Editor",
         MessageBoxButtons.OK, MessageBoxIcon.Exclamation);
   }
}
```

Similar to the `OpenFile()` method we use the `File` class to open the file, but now we open it for write access with `OpenWrite()`. `OpenWrite()` returns a `Stream` object that is passed to the constructor of the `StreamWriter` class. The `Write()` method of the `StreamWriter` writes all the data of the `textBox` to the file. At the end of the `using` block the `StreamWriter` gets closed. Because the `stream` object is associated with the `writer`, the `stream` gets closed too, and no additional `Close()` for the `stream` is needed.

Again, you can read more about the classes used for file access in Chapter 20.

4. After building the project we can start the application using the **Debug | Start** menu of Visual Studio .NET. Write some text to the text box and choose the menu **File | Save As...** as shown in the picture below.

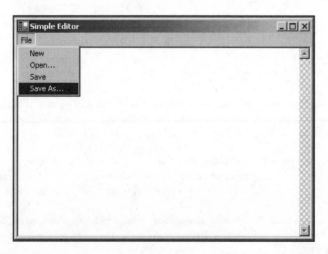

The `SaveFileDialog` as shown below will pop up. Now you can save the file and open it again to make some more changes.

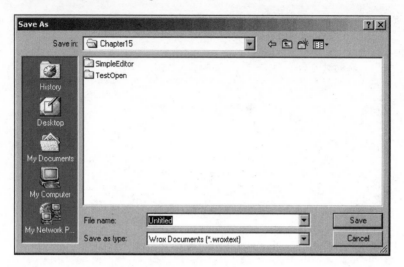

5. We can do a **Save As**, but the simple **Save** isn't available at the moment. Add a handler to the `Click` event of the **Save** menu entry and add this code:

```
private void miFileSave_Click(object sender, System.EventArgs e)
{
    if (fileName == "Untitled")
    {
        miFileSaveAs_Click(sender, e);
    }
    else
    {
        SaveFile();
    }
}
```

How It Works

With the **Save** menu, the file should be saved without opening any dialog. There's one exception to this rule, in that if a new document is created and the user did not supply a filename, then the **Save** handler should work as the **Save As** handler does and display the save file dialog.

With the `fileName` member variable we can easily check if a file is opened or if the file name is still set to the initial value `Untitled` after creating a new document. If the `if` statement returns `true` we call the handler `miFileSaveAs_Click()` that we implemented previously for the **Save As** menu.

In the other case when a file was opened and the user now chooses the Save menu, the thread of execution passes into the else block. We can use the same SaveFile() method that we implemented previously.

Try it Out – Setting the Title of the Form

With Notepad, Word, and other Windows applications the name of the file that's currently edited is displayed in the title of the application. We should add this feature too.

1. Create a new member function `SetFormTitle()` and add this implementation:

```
protected void SetFormTitle()
{
    FileInfo fileinfo = new FileInfo (fileName);
    this.Text = fileinfo.Name + " - Simple Editor";
}
```

The `FileInfo` class is used to get the file name without the preceding path that's stored in the `fileName` variable. The `FileInfo` class and the `StreamWriter` class are covered in Chapter 20.

2. Add a call to this method in the `miFileNew_Click()`, `miFileOpen_Click()`, and `miFileSaveAs_Click()` handler after setting the member variable `fileName` as can be seen in the following code segments:

```
private void miFileNew_Click(object sender, System.EventArgs e)
{
    fileName = "Untitled";
    SetFormTitle();
    textBoxEdit.Clear();
}

private void miFileOpen_Click(object sender, System.EventArgs e)
{
    if (dlgOpenFile.ShowDialog() == DialogResult.OK)
    {
        fileName = dlgOpenFile.FileName;
        SetFormTitle();
        OpenFile();
    }
}

private void miFileSaveAs_Click(object sender, System.EventArgs e)
{
    if (dlgSaveFile.ShowDialog() == DialogResult.OK)
    {
        fileName = dlgSaveFile.FileName;
        SetFormTitle();
        SaveFile();
    }
}
```

How It Works

Every time the file name changes, the `Text` property of the actual form will be changed to the file name appended with the name of the application.

Starting the application now you see the following screen. Here, as I'm editing the file `sample.txt`, this information is displayed in the title of the form.

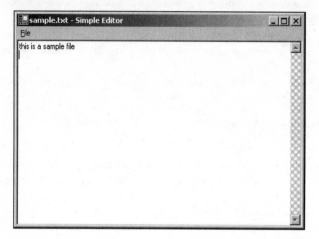

Now we have a simple editor – we can open, create, and save files (and edit them too). So are we finished? Not really! Because the paperless office still doesn't exist, we should add some print functionality!

Printing

With printing there are many things to worry about, such as the selection of a printer, page settings, and how to print multiple pages. By using classes from the `System.Drawing.Printing` namespace, we can get a lot of help to solve these problems, and print documents from our own applications with ease.

Before we look at the `PrintDialog` class that makes it possible to select a printer we must take a quick look at how .NET handles printing. The foundation of printing is the `PrintDocument` class which has a method `Print()` that starts a chain of calls culminating in a call to `OnPrintPage()`, which is responsible for passing the output to the printer. However, before we go deeper into how we implement printing code, let us look in a little bit more detail at the .NET printing classes.

Printing Architecture

The following diagram shows the major parts of the printing architecture in a diagrammatic form, which shows the relations between the classes and some of the properties and methods.

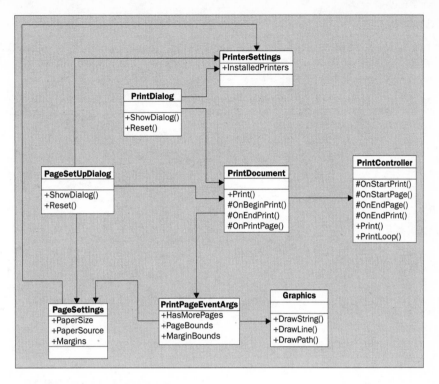

Let's look at the functionality of these classes.

❑ Let's start with the most important class, PrintDocument. In the diagram you can see that nearly all other classes have a relationship with this class. To print a document an instance of PrintDocument is required. In a moment we'll have a look at the printing sequence initiated by this class.

❑ The PrintController class controls the flow of a print job. From starting the print job, the print controller has events for the start of the print, for each page, and for the end of the print. The class is abstract since the implementation of normal printing is different from that of print preview.

❑ With the PrinterSettings class we can get and set the printer configurations such as duplex printing, landscape or portrait, and number of copies.

❑ Which printer to print to and how the PrinterSettings should be configured is a job of the PrintDialog class. This class is derived from CommonDialog like the other dialog classes we have already dealt with.

❑ The PageSettings class specifies the sizes and boundaries of a page, and if the page is in black and white or color. The configuration of this class can be done with the PageSetupDialog class that again is a CommonDialog.

Printing Sequence

Now that we know about the roles of the classes in the printing architecture, let's look at the main printing sequence. The diagram below shows the major players – our application, an instance of the `PrintDocument` class, and a `PrintController` in a timely sequence.

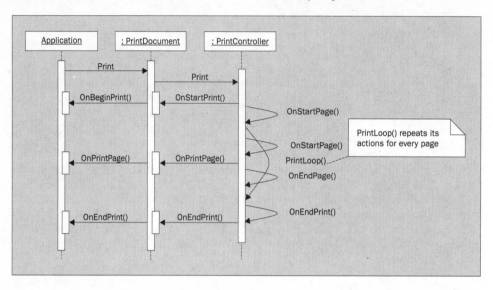

The application has to call the `Print()` method of the `PrintDocument`. This starts the printing sequence. As the `PrintDocument` itself is not responsible for the printing flow, the job is given to the `PrintController` by calling the `Print()` method of this class. The print controller now takes the action and informs the `PrintDocument` that the printing has started by calling `OnBeginPrint()`. If our application should do something at the start of a print job, we have to register an event handler in the `PrintDocument` so that we get informed in our application class. In the diagram above it is assumed that we registered the handler `OnBeginPrint()`, so this handler is called from the `PrintDocument` class.

After the beginning phase has ended, the `PrintController` goes into a `PrintLoop()` to call the method `OnPrintPage()` in the `PrintDocument` class for every page to print. `OnPrintPage()` invokes all `PrintPage` event handlers. We have to implement such a handler in every case otherwise nothing would be printed. In the diagram above you can see the handler is called `OnPrintPage()`.

After the last page is printed the `PrintController` calls `OnEndPrint()` in the `PrintDocument` class. Optionally, we can implement a handler to be invoked here, too.

To summarize, the most important thing for us to know is:

> We can implement the printing code in the **`PrintDocument.PrintPage`** event handler. This will be called for every page that is to be printed. If there's printing code that should be called only once for a print job, we have to implement the **`BeginPrint`** and **`EndPrint`** event handlers.

PrintPage Event

So what we know now is that we have to implement an event handler for the `PrintPage` event. The delegate `PrintPageEventHandler` defines the arguments of the handler:

```
public delegate void PrintPageEventHandler(object sender,
                                           PrintPageEventArgs e);
```

As you can see, we receive an object of type `PrintPageEventArgs`. You can have a look back to the class diagram to see the main properties of this class. This class has associations to the `PageSettings` and `Graphics` classes; the first enables us to set the paper size, the margins, and we can get device information from the printer. The `Graphics` class, on the other hand, makes it possible to access the device context of the printer and send such things as strings, lines, and curves to the printer.

> *GDI stands for Graphics Device Interface and makes it possible to do some graphical output to a device like the screen or a printer. GDI+ is the next generation of GDI that adds features like gradient brushes and alpha blending, and is the drawing technology of the .NET Framework.*
>
> *In the next chapter you can read more about drawing with GDI+ and the* `Graphics` *class.*

If at this point you think that printing is complex, don't be worried! The following example should convince you that adding printing features to an application is quite an easy task.

Before we can add the `PrintDialog` we have to add some menu entries for printing. Add two separators and **Print**, **Print Preview**, **Page Setup**, and **Exit** menu items to our `Simple Editor` application.

Here the `Name` and `Text` properties of the new menu items are listed:

Menu Item Name	Text
miFilePrint	&Print...
miFilePrintPreview	Print Pre&view...
miFilePageSetup	Page Set&up...
miFileExit	E&xit

The menu should look like the following screenshot:

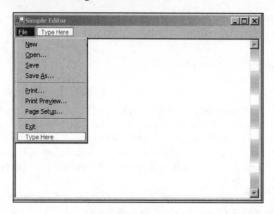

Try it Out – Adding a PrintDocument Component

1. Before we go any further, add the following `using` directive to the start of your code so we can make use of the classes for printing:

```
using System.Drawing.Printing;
```

2. Drag a `PrintDocument` component from the toolbox and drop it on to the form. Change the Name to `printDocument` and add an event handler `OnPrintPage()` to the `PrintPage` event by selecting the **Events** button in the Properties window. Then add the following code to the implementation of the event handler:

```
private void OnPrintPage(object sender,
                         System.Drawing.Printing.PrintPageEventArgs e)
{
    char[] param = {'\n'};
    string[] lines = textBoxEdit.Text.Split(param);

    int i = 0;
    char[] trimParam = {'\r'};
    foreach(string s in lines)
    {
        lines[i++] = s.TrimEnd(trimParam);
    }

    int x = 20;
    int y = 20;
    foreach (string line in lines)
    {
        e.Graphics.DrawString(line, new Font("Arial", 10),
            Brushes.Black, x, y);
        y += 15;
    }
}
```

3. Then add a handler to the `Click` event of the **Print** menu to call the `Print()` method of the `PrintDocument` class.

```
private void menuItemFilePrint_Click(object sender,
                                     System.EventArgs e)
{
    printDocument.Print();
}
```

4. Now you can build and start the application and print a document. Of course, you must have a printer installed for the example to work.

How It Works

The `Print()` method of the `printDocument` object invokes the `PrintPage` event of the `printDocument` with the help of the `PrintController` class.

```
printDocument.Print();
```

In the `OnPrintPage()` handler, we split up the text in the text box line by line using the `String.Split()` method and the newline character `\n`. The resultant strings are written to the string array `lines`.

```
char[] param = {'\n'};
string[] lines = textBoxEdit.Text.Split(param);
```

Depending on how the text file was created, the lines are not only separated with the `\n` (newline) character, but also the `\r` (return) character. With the `TrimEnd()` method of the string class the character `\r` is removed from every string:

```
int i = 0;
char[] trimParam = {'\r'};
foreach(string s in lines)
{
    lines[i++] = s.TrimEnd(trimParam);
}
```

In the second `foreach` statement in the code below, you can see that we go through all lines and send every line to the printer by a call to `e.Graphics.DrawString()`. `e` is a variable of type `PrintPageEventArgs` where the property `Graphics` is connected to the printer context. The printer context makes it possible to draw to a printing device; the `Graphics` class has some methods to draw into this context.

As we cannot yet select a printer, the default printer, whose details are stored in the Windows Registry, is used.

With the `DrawString()` method we use the Arial font with a size of 10 points and a black brush for the print output. The position for the output is defined with the x and y variables. The horizontal position is fixed to 20 pixels; the vertical position is incremented with every line.

```
            int x = 20;
            int y = 20;
            foreach (string line in lines)
            {
                e.Graphics.DrawString(line, new Font("Arial", 10),
                                        Brushes.Black, x, y);
                y += 15;
            }
```

The printing we have done so far has a problem:

❑ Printing **multiple pages** doesn't work. If the document to print spans multiple pages, only the first page gets printed. It would also be nice, if a header (for example, the file name) and footer (for example, the page number) were printed.

❑ **Page boundaries** are fixed to hard-coded values in our program. To let the user set values for other page boundaries we use the `PageSetupDialog` class.

❑ The print output is sent to the **default printer,** as set through the Control Panel by the user. It would be better for our application to allow the user to choose a printer. We will use the `PrintDialog` class for this problem.

❑ The **font is fixed**. To enable the user to choose the font, we can use the `FontDialog` class, which we will look at later in more detail.

So let's continue with the printing process to get these items fixed.

Printing Multiple Pages

The `PrintPage` event gets called for every page to print. We just have to inform the `PrintController` that the current page printed was not the last page by setting the `HasMorePages` property of the `PrintPageEventArgs` class to `true`.

Try it Out – Modifying OnPrintPage() for Multiple Pages

1. You must also declare a member variable `lines` of type `string[]` and a variable `linesPrinted` of type `int` in the class `SimpleEditorForm`:

```
    private string[] lines;
    private int linesPrinted;
```

2. Modify the `OnPrintPage()` handler. In the previous implementation of `OnPrintPage()` we split the text into lines. Because the `OnPrintPage()` method is called with every page, and splitting the text into the lines is just needed once at the beginning of the printing operation, remove all the code from `OnPrintPage()` and replace it with the new implementation:

```
    private void OnPrintPage(object sender,
                        System.Drawing.Printing.PrintPageEventArgs e)
    {
```

```
            int x = 20;
            int y = 20;

            while (linesPrinted < lines.Length)
            {
                e.Graphics.DrawString (lines[linesPrinted++],
                         new Font("Arial", 10), Brushes.Black, x, y);
                y += 15;
                if (y >= e.PageBounds.Height - 80)
                {
                    e.HasMorePages = true;
                    return;
                }
            }

            linesPrinted = 0;
            e.HasMorePages = false;
        }
```

3. Add an event handler to the BeginPrint event of the printDocument object called
OnBeginPrint(). OnBeginPrint() is called just once for each print job and here we
create our lines array:

```
    private void OnBeginPrint(object sender,
                        System.Drawing.Printing.PrintEventArgs e)
    {
        char[] param = {'\n'};
        lines = textBoxEdit.Text.Split(param);

        int i = 0;
        char[] trimParam = {'\r'};
        foreach (string s in lines)
        {
            lines[i++] = s.TrimEnd(trimParam);
        }
    }
```

4. After building the project you can start a print job of a multi-page document.

How It Works

Starting the print job with the Print() method of the PrintDocument in turn calls
OnBeginPrint() once and OnPrintPage() for every page.

In OnBeginPrint() we split up the text of the text box into a string array. Every string in the array
represents a single line because we split it up at the newline (\n) character and removed the carriage
return character (\r), as we've done before.

```
            char[] param = {'\n'};
            lines = textBoxEdit.Text.Split(param);
```

```
int i = 0;
char[] trimParam = {'\r'};
foreach (string s in lines)
{
    lines[i++] = s.TrimEnd(trimParam);
}
```

`OnPrintPage()` is called after `OnBeginPrint()`. We want to continue printing as long as the number of lines printed is less than the total number of lines we have to print. The `lines.Length` property returns the number of strings in the array `lines`. The `linesPrinted` variable gets incremented with every line we send to the printer.

```
while (linesPrinted < lines.Length)
{
    e.Graphics.DrawString(lines[linesPrinted++],
                new Font("Arial", 10), Brushes.Black, x, y);
```

After printing a line, we check if the newly calculated vertical position is outside of the page boundaries. Additionally, we decrement the boundaries by 80 pixels, because we don't really want to print to the very end of the paper, particularly since many printers can't do this anyway. If this position is reached, the `HasMorePages` property of the `PrintPageEventArgs` class is set to `true` in order to inform the controller that the `OnPrintPage()` method must be called once more, and another page needs to be printed – remember that `PrintController` has the `PrintLoop()` method that has a sequence for every page to print, and `PrintLoop()` will stop if `HasMorePages` is `false`. (The default value of the `HasMorePages` property is `false` so that only one page is printed).

```
y += 15;
if (y >= e.PageBounds.Height - 80)
{
    e.HasMorePages = true;
    return;
}
```

Page Setup

The margins of the page so far are hard-coded in the program. Let's modify the application to allow the user to set the margins on a page. To make this possible another dialog class is available: `PageSetupDialog`.

This class makes it possible to configure paper sizes and sources, orientation, paper margins, and because these options depend on a printer, the selection of the printer can be done from this dialog too.

The following picture gives an overview about the properties that enable or disable specific options of this dialog and what properties can be used to access the values. We will discuss these properties in a moment:

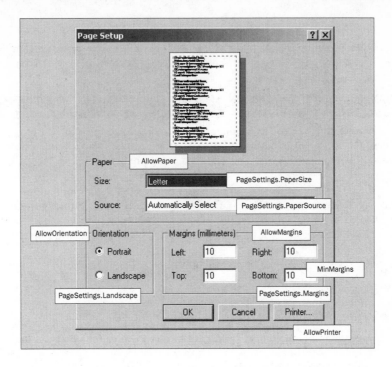

Paper

A value of true for the `AllowPaper` property means that the user can choose paper size and paper source. The `PageSetupDialog.PageSettings.PaperSize` property returns a `PaperSize` instance where we can read the height, width, and name of the paper with the properties `Height`, `Width`, and `PaperName`. `PaperName` specifies names like Letter, and A4. The `Kind` property returns an enumeration where we can get a value of the `PaperKind` enumeration. This can be one of three values representing `European`, `American`, or `Japanese` paper sizes.

The `PageSetupDialog.PageSettings.PaperSource` property returns a `PaperSource` instance where we can read the name of the printer paper source and the type of paper that fits in there (as long as the printer is correctly configured with the printer settings).

Margins

Setting the `AllowMargins` property to `true` allows the user to set the margin value for the printout. We can define minimum values for the user to enter by specifying the `MinMargins` property. To read the margins, we use the `PageSetupDialog.PageSettings.Margins` property. The returned `Margins` object has `Bottom`, `Left`, `Right`, and `Top` properties.

Orientation

The `AllowOrientation` property defines if the user can choose between portrait and landscape printing. The selected value can be read by querying the value of `PageSetupDialog.PageSettings.Landscape` which is a Boolean value specifying landscape mode with `true` and portrait mode with `false`.

Printer

The `AllowPrinter` property defines if the user can choose a printer. Depending on the value of this property the **Printer** button is enabled (`true`) or not (`false`). The handler to this button in turn opens up the `PrintDialog` that we will use next.

1. Drag a `PageSetupDialog` component from the Toolbox and drop it onto the form in the Windows Forms designer. Set its `Name` to `dlgPageSetup`, and the `Document` property to printDocument to associate the dialog with the document to print.

2. Now add a `Click` event handler to the **Page Setup** menu entry and add the code below to display the dialog using the `ShowDialog()` method. It's not necessary to check the return value of `ShowDialog()` here because the implementation of the handler for the **OK** click event already sets the new values in the associated `PrintDocument` object.

```
private void menuItemFilePageSetup_Click(object sender,
                                         System.EventArgs e)
{
    dlgPageSetup.ShowDialog();
}
```

3. Now change the implementation of `OnPrintPage()` to use the margins that are set by the `PageSetupDialog`. In our code, the x and y variables are set to the properties `MarginBounds.Left` and `MarginBounds.Top` of the `PrintPageEventArgs` class. We check the boundary of a page with `MarginBounds.Bottom`.

```
private void OnPrintPage(object sender,
                         System.Drawing.Printing.PrintPageEventArgs e)
{
    int x = e.MarginBounds.Left;
    int y = e.MarginBounds.Top;

    while (linesPrinted < lines.Length)
    {
        e.Graphics.DrawString(lines[linesPrinted++],
            new Font("Arial", 10), Brushes.Black, x, y);

        y += 15;
        if (y >= e.MarginBounds.Bottom)
        {
            e.HasMorePages = true;
            return;
        }
    }

    linesPrinted = 0;
    e.HasMorePages = false;
}
```

4. Now you can build the project and run the application. Selecting File | Page Setup displays the following dialog. You can change the boundaries and print with the configured boundaries.

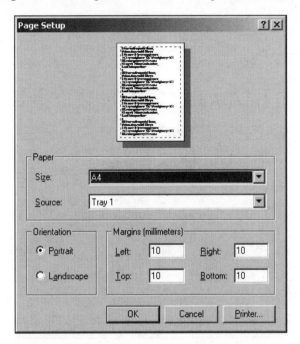

> If the display of the **PageSetupDialog** fails, an exception of type **System.ArgumentException** is thrown; this is probably because you forgot to associate the **PrintDocument** object with the **PageSetupDialog**. The **PageSetupDialog** needs an associated **PrintDocument** to query and set the values that are displayed in the dialog.

Print Dialog

The PrintDialog class allows the user to select a printer from the installed printers, and choose a number of copies, and some printer settings like the layout and paper sources of the printer. Because the PrintDialog is very easy to use, we will start immediately by adding the PrintDialog to our Editor application.

Try it Out – Adding a PrintDialog

1. Add a PrintDialog component from the Toolbox onto the form. Set the Name to dlgPrint and the Document property of this object to printDocument.

Change the implementation of the event handler to the click event of the Print menu to the following code:

```
private void miFilePrint_Click(object sender, System.EventArgs e)
{
    if (dlgPrint.ShowDialog() == DialogResult.OK)
    {
        printDocument.Print();
    }
}
```

2. Build and run the application. Selecting File | Print opens up the `PrintDialog`. Now you can select a printer to print the document.

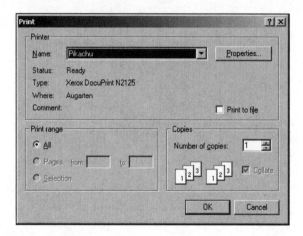

Options for the Print Dialog

In our SimpleEditor program we didn't change any of the properties of the `PrintDialog`. But this dialog has some options, too. In the dialog above you can see three groups: Printer, Print range, and Copies.

❑ In the Printer group not only the printer can be chosen, but there's also a Print to File option. By default this option is enabled, but it is not checked. Selecting this check box enables the user to write the printing output to a file instead of to the printer. You can disable this option by setting the `AllowPrintToFile` property to `false`.

If the user selects this option the following dialog is opened by the `printDocument.Print()` call to ask for a file name where the printout should be written to.

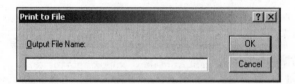

❑ In the Print Range section of the dialog, only All can be selected – Pages and Selection are disabled by default. We will look at how these options can be implemented in the following section.

❑ The Copies group allows the user to select the number of copies to print.

Printing Selected Text

Setting the AllowSelection property to true allows the user to print selected text, but you also have to change the printing code so that only the text selected gets printed.

Try it Out – Adding a Print Selection

1. Add the highlighted code to the click handler of the Print button.

```
private void miFilePrint_Click(object sender, System.EventArgs e)
{
    if (textBoxEdit.SelectedText != "")
    {
        dlgPrint.AllowSelection = true;
    }
    if (dlgPrint.ShowDialog() == DialogResult.OK)
    {
        printDocument.Print();
    }
}
```

2. In our program all the lines that will be printed are setup in the OnBeginPrint() handler. Change the implementation of this method:

```
private void OnBeginPrint(object sender,
                          System.Drawing.Printing.PrintEventArgs e)
{
    char[] param = {'\n'};

    if (dlgPrint.PrinterSettings.PrintRange == PrintRange.Selection)
    {
        lines = textBoxEdit.SelectedText.Split(param);
    }
    else
    {
        lines = textBoxEdit.Text.Split(param);
    }

    int i = 0;
    char[] trimParam = {'\r'};
    foreach (string s in lines)
    {
        lines[i++] = s.TrimEnd(trimParam);
    }
}
```

3. Now you can build and start the program. Open a file, select some text, start the print dialog with the menu File | Print, and select the Selection option button from the Print Range group. With this selected, pressing the Print button will only print the selected text.

How It Works

We set the `AllowSelection` property to `true` only if some text is selected. Before we show the `PrintDialog` we have to check if some text is selected, and this is done by simply checking that the value of the `SelectedText` property of the text box is not `null`. If there is some text selected the property `AllowSelection` is set to `true`.

```
if (textBoxEdit.SelectedText != "")
{
    dlgPrint.AllowSelection = true;
}
```

`OnBeginPrint()` is called at the start of every print job. Accessing the `printDialog.PrinterSettings.PrintRange` property, we get the information on whether the user has chosen the Selection option. The `PrintRange` property takes a value from the `PrintRange` enumeration: `AllPages`, `Selection`, or `SomePages`.

```
if (printDialog.PrinterSettings.PrintRange == PrintRange.Selection)
{
```

If the option is indeed Selection, we get the selected text from the `SelectedText` property of the `TextBox`. This string is split up the same way as the complete text.

```
    lines = textBoxEdit.SelectedText.Split(param);
}
```

Printing Page Ranges

Printing a range of pages can be implemented in similar way to printing a selection. The option button can be enabled by setting the `AllowSomePages` property to `true`. The user can now select the page range to print. However, where are the page boundaries in our Simple Editor? What's the last page? We should set the last page by setting the `PrintDialog.PrinterSettings.ToPage` property. How does the user know the page numbers he wants to print? This is no problem in a document processing application like Microsoft Word where a Print Layout can be selected as a view on the screen. This is not possible with the simple `TextBox` that's used in our Simple Editor application. That's the reason why we will not implement this feature in our application.

Of course, you could do this as an exercise. What must be done? The `AllowSomePages` property must be set to `true`. Before displaying the `PrintDialog`, you can also set the `PrinterSettings.FromPage` to 1 and the `PrinterSettings.ToPage` to the maximum page number.

PrintDialog Properties

Let's summarize the properties influencing the layout of the `PrintDialog` again with a single picture.

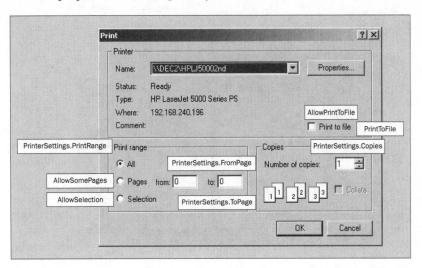

Print Preview

For the user to see what the printout will actually look like, we use a Print Preview. Implementing Print Preview can easily be done in .NET – we can use a `PrintPreviewControl` class that is used to preview the document in a form to show how it will be printed. The `PrintPreviewDialog` is a dialog that wraps the control.

PrintPreviewDialog

If you look at the properties and inheritance list from the MSDN documentation of the `PrintPreviewDialog` class, you can see that it is actually a `Form` and not a wrapped common dialog – the class derives from `System.Windows.Forms.Form`, and you can work with it as with the forms we created in the previous chapter.

We will add a `PrintPreviewDialog` class to our Simple Editor application.

Try it Out – Adding a Print Preview Dialog

1. Add a `PrintPreviewDialog` component from the Toolbox onto the Windows Forms designer. Set the `Name` to dlgPrintPreview and the `Document` property to printDocument.

2. Add and implement a handler for the `Click` event of the Print Preview menu entry.

```
private void miFilePrintPreview_Click(object sender,
                                      System.EventArgs e)
{
    dlgPrintPreview.ShowDialog();
}
```

PrintPreviewControl

The print preview in Microsoft Word and WordPad is different from the PrintPreviewDialog in that the preview in these applications doesn't show up in its own dialog, but in the main window of the application.

To do the same, you can place the PrintPreviewControl class in your form. The Document property must be set to the printDocument object, and the Visible property to false – when you want to display the print preview, you simply set the Visible property to true. Then the PrintPreviewControl is in front of the other control as shown in the following graphic.

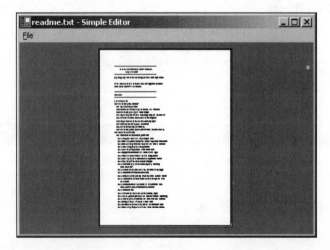

You can see from the title and the single File menu item that it is the main window of the Simple Editor application that is displayed. What still needs to be done is to add some elements to control the `PrintPreviewControl` class to do zooming, printing and display several pages of text at once. A specific toolbar can be used to make these features available. The `PrintPreviewDialog` class already has this implemented as you can see in the following picture with a 4-pages preview.

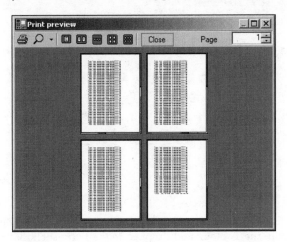

FontDialog and ColorDialog

The last dialogs in this chapter we will look at are the `FontDialog` and the `ColorDialog`.

Here again we will only concentrate on discussing the dialogs to set the font and color, and not the Font *and* Color *classes, as these are covered in the next chapter.*

FontDialog

The `FontDialog` lets the user of the application choose a font. The user can change the font, the style, size, and the color of the font.

The following picture gives you an overview of the properties that change the elements in the dialog.

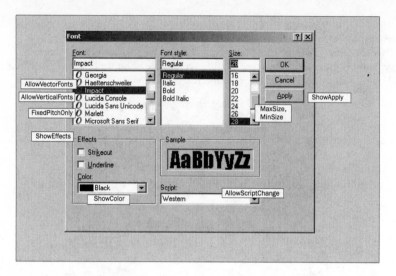

How to Use the FontDialog

The dialog can be used in the same way as the previous dialogs. In the Windows Forms Designer the dialog can be dragged from the Toolbox and dropped to the Form such that an instance of the `FontDialog` gets created.

The code to use the `FontDialog` can look like this:

```
if (dlgFont.ShowDialog() == DialogResult.OK)
{
    textBoxEdit.Font = dlgFont.Font;
}
```

The `FontDialog` is displayed by calling the `ShowDialog()` method. If the user presses the **OK** button, `DialogResult.OK` is returned from the method. The selected font can be read by using the `Font` property of the `FontDialog` class; this font is then passed to the `Font` property of the `TextBox`.

Properties of the FontDialog

We have already seen a picture with properties of the `FontDialog` class; but now let's see what these properties are used for:

Property	Description
AllowVectorFonts	Boolean value that defines if vector fonts can be selected in the font list. The default is `true`.
AllowVerticalFonts	Boolean value that defines if vertical fonts can be selected in the font list. Vertical texts are used in far eastern countries. There probably isn't a vertical font installed on your system. The default is `true`.

Property	Description
FixedPitchOnly	Setting the property FixedPitchOnly displays only fixed pitch fonts in the font list. With a fixed pitch font every character has the same size. The default is false.
MaxSize	Specifying a value for the MaxSize property defines the maximum font size the user can select.
MinSize	Similar to MaxSize you can set the minimum font size the user can select with MinSize.
ShowApply	If the Apply button should be displayed you have to set the ShowApply property to true. By pressing the Apply button the user can see an updated font in the application without leaving the font dialog.
ShowColor	By default the Color selection is not shown in the dialog. If you want the user to select the font color in the font dialog you just have to set the ShowColor property to true.
ShowEffects	By default the user can select the Strikeout and Underline check boxes to manipulate the font. If you don't want these options to be displayed you have to set the ShowEffects property to false.
AllowScriptChange	Setting the AllowScriptChange property to false prevents the user from changing the script of a font. The available scripts depend on the selected font, for example, the font Arial supports Western, Hebrew, Arabic, Greek, Turkish, Baltic, Central European, Cyrillic, Vietnamese scripts.

Enabling the Apply Button

An interesting difference from the other dialogs presented so far is that the FontDialog supports an Apply button, which is not displayed by default. If the user presses the Apply button the dialog stays opened, but the font should be applied.

By selecting the FontDialog in the Windows Forms designer you can set the ShowApply property in the Properties window to True. But how are we informed if the user now presses the Apply button? The dialog is still opened, so the ShowDialog() method will not return. Instead, we can add an event handler to the Apply event of the FontDialog class. You can do this by pressing the Events button in the Properties window, and by writing a handler name to the Apply event.

As you can see in the following code, I have entered the name OnApplyFontDialog. In this handler you can access the selected font of the FontDialog using the member variable of the FontDialog class:

```
private void OnApplyFontDialog(object sender, System.EventArgs e)
{
    textBoxEdit.Font = dlgFont.Font;
}
```

ColorDialog

There isn't as much to configure in the ColorDialog as for the FontDialog. With the ColorDialog it is possible for the user to configure custom colors, if he doesn't want any of the basic colors on offer; this is done by setting the AllowFullOpen property. The custom color configuration part of the dialog can also be automatically expanded with the FullOpen property. If AllowFullOpen is false, then the value of FullOpen will be ignored. The SolidColorOnly property specifies that only solid colors may be selected. The CustomColors property can be used to get and set the configured custom color values.

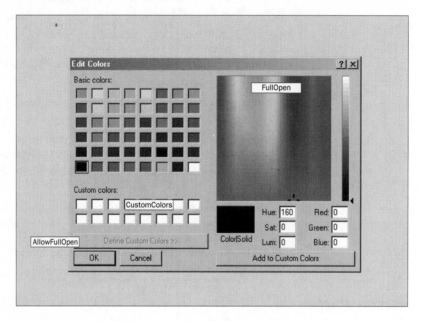

How to Use the Color Dialog

The ColorDialog can be dragged from the Toolbox and dropped onto the form in the Windows Forms designer, as we have done with the other dialogs. ShowDialog() displays the dialog until the user presses the OK or Cancel button. You can read the selected color by accessing the Color property of the dialog as can be seen in the following code example:

```
if (dlgColor.ShowDialog() == DialogResult.OK)
{
    textBoxEdit.ForeColor = dlgColor.Color;
}
```

Properties of the Color Dialog

The properties to influence the look of the dialog are summarized in this table:

Properties	Description
AllowFullOpen	Setting this property to `false` disables the **Define Custom Colors** button, thus preventing the user from defining custom colors. The default value of this property is `true`.
FullOpen	Setting the `FullOpen` property to `true` before the dialog is displayed opens up the dialog with the custom color selection automatically displayed.
AnyColor	Setting this property to `true` shows all available colors in the list of basic colors.
CustomColors	With the `CustomColors` property you can preset an array of custom colors, and you can read the custom colors defined by the user.
SolidColorOnly	By setting the `SolidColorOnly` property to true the user can only select solid colors.

Summary

In this chapter we have seen how to use the dialog classes in applications. We looked at how to open and to save files, and after reviewing the .NET framework printing classes, we showed you how to add printing capabilities to your applications. To summarize, in our Simple Editor application we've used the following dialog classes:

- ❑ `FileOpenDialog` to ask the user for a file to open
- ❑ `FileSaveDialog` to ask for a file name to save the data
- ❑ `PrintDialog` to get the printer to print to and the printing configurations
- ❑ `PageSetupDialog` to modify the margins of the page where we do the print
- ❑ `PrintPreviewDialog` to view a preview of the print so that the user knows in advance what the print will look like
- ❑ We've also shown you the basics of the `FontDialog` and `ColorDialog` classes; adding these classes to the Simple Editor application is part of your exercises

Exercises

Because the FontDialog and the ColorDialog work in a similar way to the other dialogs we went through in this chapter, it's an easy job to add these dialogs to our Simple Editor application.

1. Let the user change the font of the text box. To make this possible add a new menu entry to the main menu: **F&ormat**, and a sub menu for **Format: &Font...** Add a handler to this menu item. Add a FontDialog to the application with the help of the Windows Forms Designer. Display this dialog in the menu handler, and set the Font property of the text box to the selected font.

You also have to change the implementation of the OnPrintPage() method to use the selected font for a printout. In the previous implementation we created a new Font object in the DrawString() method of the Graphics object. Now use the font of the textBoxEdit object by accessing the Font property instead. We also have to be aware of a font location problem if the user chooses a big font. To avoid one line partly overwriting the one above/below, change the fixed value we used to change the vertical position of the lines. A better way to do this would be to use the size of the font to change the vertical increment: use the Height property of the Font class.

2. Another great extension to the Simple Editor application would be to change the font color. Add a second submenu to the **Format** menu entry: **Color...** Add a handler to this menu entry where you open up a ColorDialog. If the user presses the **OK** button, set the selected color of the ColorDialog to the ForeColor property of the text box.

In the OnPrintPage() method make sure that the chosen color is used only if the printer supports colors. You can check the color support of the printer with the PageSettings.Color property of the PrintPageEventArgs argument. You can create a brush object with the color of the text box with this code:

```
Brush brush = new SolidBrush(textBoxEdit.ForeColor);
```

This brush can then be used as an argument in the DrawString() method instead of the black brush we used in the example before.

Introduction to GDI+

In the previous chapter, the term GDI+ was briefly introduced when we looked at printing in the .NET Framework. In this chapter, we will have a real introduction to programming using the Graphics Device Interface classes (GDI+), the drawing technology of the .NET Framework. Mapping applications, games, Computer Aided Design / Computer Aided Manufacture (CAD/CAM), drawing programs, charting programs, and many other types of applications require developers to write graphics code for their Windows Forms applications. Writing custom controls can also require graphics code. With this latest class library, Microsoft has made writing graphics code easier than it ever has been before.

Writing graphics code is one of the most enjoyable programming tasks. It is very rewarding to change your code and see the results in a visible form immediately. Whether you are writing a custom graphics window that presents something in your application in a new and different way, or writing a custom control that makes your application more stylish and more usable, your application will be well received by the general public.

First, we will explain the mechanics of drawing using GDI+, and write a few simple graphical example programs. Then we will take a high-level look at some of the extensive capabilities of GDI+ such as clipping.

After the overview on each of the above topics, we'll look at what classes we can use to implement the features. Knowing what we can do and understanding the class hierarchy is half the battle.

Overview of Graphical Drawing

The first idea to learn about writing graphics code is that Windows does not remember what every open window looks like if that window is obscured by other windows. Instead, if a covered-up window comes to the forefront so that it becomes visible, Windows will tell our application, "Your window (or some portion of it) has now become visible. Will you please draw it?" We only need to draw the contents of our window. Windows itself takes care of the border of the window, the title bar, and all of the other window features.

In programming terms, when we create a window into which we want to draw, we will typically declare a class that derives from System.Windows.Forms.Form. If we are writing a custom control, we will declare a class that derives from System.Windows.Forms.UserControl. In either of these cases, we override the virtual function OnPaint(). Windows will call this function whenever any portion of our window needs to be repainted.

With this event, a PaintEventArgs class is passed as an argument. There are two pertinent pieces of information in PaintEventArgs: a Graphics object, and a ClipRectangle. We'll explore the Graphics class first. We'll touch on clipping near the end of the chapter.

The Graphics Class

The Graphics class encapsulates a GDI+ drawing surface. There are three basic types of drawing surfaces:

- ❑ Windows and controls on the screen
- ❑ Pages being sent to a printer
- ❑ Bitmaps and images in memory

The Graphics class provides us with functions so that we can draw on any of these drawing surfaces. Among other capabilities, we can use it to draw arcs, curves, Bezier curves, ellipses, images, lines, rectangles, and text.

We can get a Graphics object for the window in two different ways. The first is to override the OnPaint() method. The Form class inherits the OnPaint() method from Control, and this method is the event handler for the Paint event that is raised whenever the control is redrawn. We can get the Graphics object from the PaintEventArgs that is passed in with the event:

```
protected override void OnPaint(PaintEventArgs e)
{
    Graphics g = e.Graphics;

    // do our drawing here

}
```

At other times, we may want to draw directly into our window without waiting for the Paint event to be raised. This would be the case if we are writing code for selecting some graphical object on the window (similar to selecting icons in Windows Explorer), or dragging some object with the mouse. We can get a Graphics object by calling the CreateGraphics() method on the form, which is another method that Form inherits from Control:

```
protected void Form1_Click (object sender, System.EventArgs e)
{
    Graphics g = this.CreateGraphics();

    // do our drawing here

    g.Dispose();    // this is important
}
```

Building an application that handles dragging and dropping is a somewhat involved affair, and is beyond the scope of this chapter. In any case, this is a less common technique. Primarily, we will do almost all of our drawing in response to an `OnPaint()` method.

There are other ways to get a `Graphics` object, which we'll examine later.

Disposing of Objects

Everybody is familiar with the behavior of Windows when it runs out of resources. It starts to run very slowly and sometimes applications will not be drawn correctly. Well-behaved applications free up their resources after they are done with them. When developing using the .NET Framework, there are several data types on which it is important to call the `Dispose()` method, or else some resources will not be freed. These classes implement the `IDisposable` interface, and `Graphics` is one of these classes.

> However, it is important that if we get a **Graphics** object by calling
> **CreateGraphics()**, then we should call **Dispose()**.

When we get a `Graphics` object from the `OnPaint()` method, this was not created by us, so it is not our responsibility to call `Dispose()`, but in the example just above, it is our responsibility.

The `Dispose()` method is automatically called in the destructor for the various classes that implement `IDisposable`. You might think that this removes our responsibility to call `Dispose()`, but it does not. The reason is that only the garbage collector (GC) ever calls the destructor, and you cannot guarantee when the GC will run. In particular, on a Windows 9X operating system with lots of memory, the GC may run very infrequently, and all resources may very well be used up before the GC runs. Whereas running out of memory will trigger the GC to run, running out of resources does not. However, Windows 2000 is much less sensitive to running out of resources. According to the specifications, Windows 2000 does not have any finite limits on these types of resources; however, I have seen this operating system misbehave when too many applications are open, and closing some applications quickly restores correct behavior. In any case, it is better coding practice to manually dispose of any resource-hungry objects correctly, and in a timely fashion.

A `using` construct automatically calls `Dispose()` when an object goes out of scope. The following code shows the correct use of the `using` keyword in this context:

```
using (Graphics g = this.CreateGraphics())
{
    g.DrawLine(Pens.Black, new Point(0, 0), new Point(3, 5));
}
```

According to the documentation the above code is precisely equivalent to:

```
Graphics g = this.CreateGraphics();
try
{
    g.DrawLine(Pens.Black, new Point(0, 0), new Point(3, 5));
}
```

```
finally
{
    if (g != null)
        ((IDisposable)g).Dispose();
}
```

Don't confuse this use of the `using` keyword with the `using` directive that creates an alias for a namespace, or that permits the use of types in a namespace such that we do not need to fully qualify the use of the type. This is an entirely separate use of the `using` keyword – if you like, the block of code enclosed by the `using` keyword can be referred to as a `using` block.

Examples in this chapter will handle calls to `Dispose()` using both styles. Sometimes we will call `Dispose()` directly, and other times we will use the `using` block. The latter is a much cleaner solution, as you can see from the above code snippets, but there is no recommendation as to which is the preferred method.

Before we jump into our first example, there are two other aspects of drawing graphics that we should examine – the coordinate system and colors.

Coordinate System

When designing a program that will draw a complicated, intricate graphic, it is very important that our code draws exactly what we intend, and nothing but what we intend. It is possible for a single misplaced pixel to have a negative influence on the visual impact of a graphic, so it is important to understand exactly what pixels are drawn when invoking drawing operations. This is most important when creating custom controls, where we would draw lots of rectangles, horizontal lines, and vertical lines. Having a line run one pixel too long, or fall one pixel short is very noticeable. However, this is somewhat less important with curves, diagonal lines, and other graphical operations.

GDI+ has a coordinate system based on imaginary mathematical lines that run through the center of the pixels. These lines are numbered starting at zero – the intersection of these mathematical lines in the upper left pixel in any coordinate space is point X=0, Y=0. As a shorter notation, we can say point 1, 2, which is shorthand for saying X=1, Y=2. Each window into which we will draw has its own coordinate space. If we would create a custom control that can be used in other windows, this custom control itself has its own coordinate space. In other words, the upper-left pixel of the custom control is point 0, 0 when drawing in that custom control. We don't need to worry about where the custom control is placed on its containing window.

When drawing lines, GDI+ centers the pixels drawn on the mathematical line that we specify. When drawing a horizontal with integer coordinates, it can be thought of that half of each pixel falls above the imaginary mathematical line, and half of each pixel falls below it. When we draw a horizontal line that is one pixel wide from point 1, 1 to point 5, 1, the following pixels will be drawn:

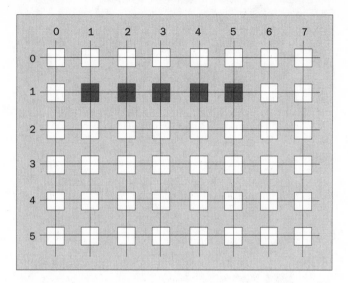

When we draw a vertical line that is one pixel wide and four pixels long, from point 2, 1 to point 2, 4, the following pixels will be colored in:

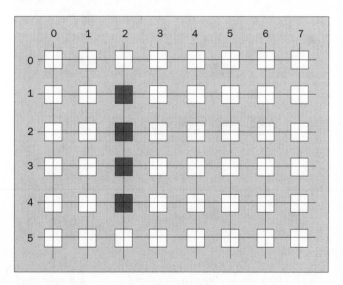

When we draw a diagonal line from point 1, 0 to point 4, 3, the following pixels will be drawn:

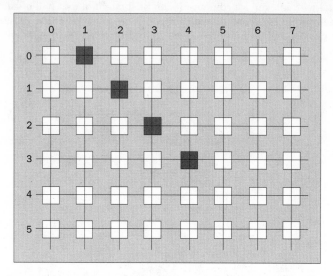

When we draw a rectangle with the upper left corner at 1, 0 and a size of 5, 4, the rectangle drawn is:

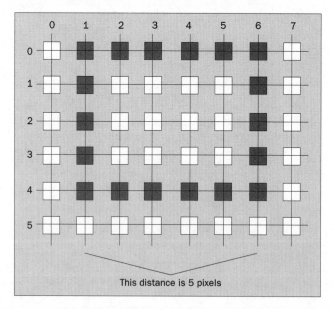

This distance is 5 pixels

There is something interesting to note here. We specified a width of 5, and there are 6 pixels drawn in the horizontal direction. However, if you consider the mathematical lines running through the pixels, this rectangle is only five pixels wide, and the line drawn falls half a pixel outside and half a pixel inside of the mathematical line that we specified.

There is more to the story than this. If we draw with anti-aliasing, other pixels will be "half" colored in, creating an appearance of a smooth line, and partially avoiding a "stair step" appearance to diagonal lines.

Here is a line drawn without anti-aliasing:

The same line drawn with anti-aliasing appears as follows:

When viewed at a high resolution, this line will appear much smoother, without a stair step effect.

Understanding the relationship between the coordinates passed to drawing functions, and the resulting effect on the drawing surface makes it easy to visualize exactly which pixels will get affected by a given call to a drawing function.

There are three structs that we will use often to specify coordinates when drawing: `Point`, `Size`, and `Rectangle`.

Point

GDI+ uses `Point` to represent a single point with integer coordinates. This is a point in a two dimensional plane – a specification of a single pixel. Many GDI+ functions, such as `DrawLine()`, take a `Point` as an argument. We declare and construct a `Point` struct as follows:

```
Point p = new Point(1, 1);
```

There are public properties, `X` and `Y`, to get and set the X and Y coordinates of a `Point`.

Size

GDI+ uses `Size` to represent a size in pixels. A `Size` struct contains both width and height. We declare and construct a `Size` as follows:

```
Size s = new Size(5, 5);
```

There are public properties, `Height` and `Width`, to get and set the height and width of a `Size`.

Rectangle

GDI+ uses this structure in many different places to specify the coordinates of a rectangle. A `Point` structure defines the upper left corner of the rectangle and a `Size` structure defines its size. There are two constructors for `Rectangle`. One takes as arguments the X position, the Y position, the width, and the height. The other takes a `Point` and a `Size` structure. Two examples of declaring and constructing a `Rectangle` are as follows:

```
Rectangle r1 = new Rectangle(1, 2, 5, 6);

Point p = new Point(1, 2);
Size s = new Size(5, 6);
Rectangle r2 = new Rectangle(p, s);
```

There are public properties to get and set all aspects of the location and size of a `Rectangle`. In addition, there are other useful properties and methods to do such activities as determining if the rectangle intersects with another rectangle, taking the intersection of two rectangles, and taking the union of two rectangles.

GraphicsPaths

There are two more important data types that we can use as arguments to various drawing functions in GDI+. The `GraphicsPath` class represents a series of connected lines and curves. When constructing a path, we can add lines, Bezier curves, arcs, pie shapes, polygons, rectangles, and more. After constructing a complex path, we can draw the path with one operation: a call to `DrawPath()`. You can fill the path with a call to `FillPath()`.

We construct a `GraphicsPath` using an array of points and `PathTypes`. `PathTypes` is a byte array, where each element in the array corresponds to an element in the array of points, and gives additional information about how the path is to be constructed through each particular point. The information about the path through a point can be gleaned by using the `PathPointType` enumeration. For instance, if the point is the beginning of the path, the path type for that point is `PathPointType.Start`. If the point is a junction between two lines, the path type for that point is `PathPointType.Line`. If the point is used to construct a Bezier curve from the point before and after, the path type is `PathPointType.Bezier`.

Try it Out – Creating a Graphics Path

1. Create a new Windows application called `DrawingPaths` in the directory `C:\BegVCSharp\Chapter16`.

2. Add the following `using` directive for `System.Drawing.Drawing2D` to the top of the code:

```
using System;
using System.Drawing;
using System.Collections;
using System.ComponentModel;
using System.Windows.Forms;
using System.Data;

using System.Drawing.Drawing2D;
```

3. Enter the following code into the body of `Form1`.

```
protected override void OnPaint (PaintEventArgs e)
{
    GraphicsPath path;
    path = new GraphicsPath(new Point[]{ new Point(10, 10),
                                         new Point(150, 10),
                                         new Point(200, 150),
                                         new Point(10, 150),
                                         new Point(200, 160)},
                         new byte[] {(byte)PathPointType.Start,
                                     (byte)PathPointType.Line,
```

```
                                              (byte)PathPointType.Line,
                                              (byte)PathPointType.Line,
                                              (byte)PathPointType.Line });
        e.Graphics.DrawPath(Pens.Black, path);
}
```

4. Run the application, and you should see the following path drawn:

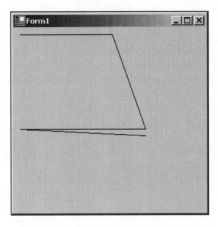

How it Works

The code to construct this path is a quite complex. The constructor for `GraphicsPath` takes two arguments. The first argument is a `Point` array; here we use the C# syntax for declaring and initializing the array in the same place, and create each new `Point` object as we go:

```
new Point[]{
    new Point(10, 10),
    new Point(150, 10),
    new Point(200, 150),
    new Point(10, 150),
    new Point(200, 160)
}
```

The second argument is an array of bytes that we also construct right in place:

```
new byte[] {
    (byte)PathPointType.Start,
    (byte)PathPointType.Line,
    (byte)PathPointType.Line,
    (byte)PathPointType.Line,
    (byte)PathPointType.Line
}
```

Finally, we call the `DrawPath()` method:

```
e.Graphics.DrawPath(Pens.Black, path);
```

Regions

The Region class is a complex graphical shape that is comprised of rectangles and paths. After constructing a Region, we can draw that region using the method FillRegion().

Try it Out – Creating a Region

The following code creates a region, adds a Rectangle to it, adds a GraphicsPath to it, and then fills that region with the color blue:

1. Create a new Windows application called DrawingRegions in the directory C:\BegVCSharp\Chapter16.

2. Add a using directive for System.Drawing.Drawing2D to the top of the code:

```
using System;
using System.Drawing;
using System.Collections;
using System.ComponentModel;
using System.Windows.Forms;
using System.Data;

using System.Drawing.Drawing2D;
```

3. Enter the following code into the body of Form1.

```
protected override void OnPaint ( PaintEventArgs e)
{
    Rectangle r1 = new Rectangle(10, 10, 50, 50);
    Rectangle r2 = new Rectangle(40, 40, 50, 50);
    Region r = new Region(r1);
    r.Union(r2);

    GraphicsPath path = new GraphicsPath(new Point[] {
                            new Point(45, 45),
                            new Point(145, 55),
                            new Point(200, 150),
                            new Point(75, 150),
                            new Point(45, 45)
                        }, new byte[] {
                            (byte)PathPointType.Start,
                            (byte)PathPointType.Bezier,
                            (byte)PathPointType.Bezier,
                            (byte)PathPointType.Bezier,
                            (byte)PathPointType.Line
                        });
    r.Union(path);
    e.Graphics.FillRegion(Brushes.Blue, r);
}
```

4. When you run this code, it will display the following:

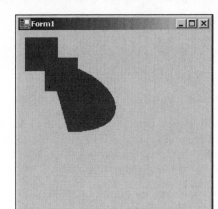

How It Works

The code to construct a region is also quite complex, though the most complex part of our example is constructing any paths that will go into the region, and you have already seen how to construct these from the previous example.

Constructing regions consists of constructing rectangles and paths, before calling the `Union()` method. If we desired the intersection of a rectangle and a path, we could have used the `Intersection()` method instead of the `Union()` method.

Further information on paths and regions is not particularly needed for an introduction to GDI+, so we will not explore them in any more depth in this chapter.

Colors

Many of the drawing operations in GDI+ involve a color. When drawing a line or rectangle, we will need to specify what color it should be.

In GDI+, colors are encapsulated in the `Color` structure. We can create a color by passing red, green, and blue values to a function of the `Color` structure, but this is almost never necessary. The `Color` structure contains approximately 150 properties that get a large variety of preset colors. Forget about red, green, blue, yellow and black – if we need to do some drawing in the color of `LightGoldenrodYellow` or `LavenderBlush`, there is a predefined color made just for us! We declare a variable of type `Color` and initialize it with a color from the `Color` structure as follows:

```
Color redColor = Color.Red;
Color anotherColor = Color.LightGoldenrodYellow;
```

We're almost ready to do some drawing, but a couple of notes before we go on.

Another way to represent a color is to break it down into three components: Hue, Saturation, and Brightness. The `Color` structure contains utility methods to do this, namely: `GetBrightness()`, `GetHue()`, and `GetSaturation()`.

You can use the `ColorDialog` that we met in the previous chapter to experiment with colors. In a new Windows application, drag a `ColorDialog` control onto your form, and add the following line to the `Form1` constructor, after the `InitializeComponent()` call:

```
this.colorDialog1.ShowDialog();
```

Run the application, and click the **Define Custom Colors** button. You will see a dialog box that allows you to pick a color using the mouse and see the RGB values for the color. You can also get the Hue, Saturation, and Luminosity values for the color (where Luminosity corresponds to Brightness). You can also directly enter the RGB values and see the resulting color.

Colors in GDI+ have a fourth component, the Alpha component. Using this component, we can set the opacity of the color, and this allows us to create fade in / fade out effects, such as the menu effects in Windows 2000 and Windows XP. Using the Alpha component is beyond the scope of this chapter.

Drawing Lines Using the Pen Class

Our first example here draws lines. We draw lines using the `Pen` class, which allows us to define the color, width, and pattern of the line that our code is drawing. The color and width properties are obvious. However, the pattern of a line indicates whether the line is a solid line, or is comprised of dashes and dots. The `Pen` class is in the `System.Drawing` namespace.

Try it Out – Pen Example

1. Create a new Windows application called `DrawingLines` in the directory `C:\BegVCSharp\Chapter16`.

2. Enter the following code into the body of `Form1`.

```
protected override void OnPaint(PaintEventArgs e)
{
    Graphics g = e.Graphics;

    using (Pen blackPen = new Pen(Color.Black, 1))
    {
        if (ClientRectangle.Height/10>0)
        {
            for (int y = 0; y < ClientRectangle.Height;
                y += ClientRectangle.Height / 10)
            {
                g.DrawLine(blackPen, new Point(0, 0),
                        new Point(ClientRectangle.Width, y));
            }
        }
    }
}
```

3. Now press *F5* to compile and run the code. When you run it, it will create this window:

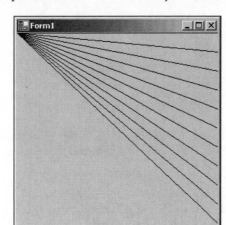

How it Works

Earlier in the chapter, we introduced the `Graphics` class. The first thing that we do in the `OnPaint()` method is to get the `Graphics` object from the `PaintEventArgs` parameter:

```
Graphics g = e.Graphics;
```

Note that because we are passed the reference to the `Graphics` object, and we did not create it, we do not need to (and should not) manually call `Dispose()` on it. However, since we are using a potentially resource-hungry `Pen` object for this example we have wrapped the rest of the code in a `using` block, as described earlier, which will ensure that the object is destroyed as soon as possible.

When we construct the pen, we pass as parameters to the constructor a color and a width of the pen. In this example, the color is black, and the width is one. This is the line of code to construct the pen:

```
using (Pen blackPen = new Pen(Color.Black, 1))
```

Every window into which we can draw has a client area, which is a rectangle that exists within the border and defines the exact area into which we can draw. We can get the client area from `ClientRectangle`, which is a public, read-only property of the form (inherited from `Control`). It contains the size (that is the width and height) of the client area of the window into which we are drawing. The following code starts a loop that goes from zero up to the height of the client area (given by `ClientRectangle.Height`) in steps of 10. Note that we first check that `ClientRectangle.Height/10` is bigger than zero – without this, the loop will run indefinitely if the form is resized below a certain height, since `ClientRectangle.Height/10` is the loop increment, and if this is zero we'll loop forever.

```
if (ClientRectangle.Height/10>0)
{
   for (int y = 0; y < ClientRectangle.Height;
        y += ClientRectangle.Height / 10)
```

Now we can draw the lines – when we draw each line, we pass the `Pen` that we just created, along with the starting point and ending point of the line:

```
g.DrawLine(blackPen, new Point(0, 0),
                new Point(ClientRectangle.Width, y));
```

> **Always call** `Dispose()` **on** `Pen` **objects.**

Just as for `Graphics` objects, it is important to either call `Dispose()` on `Pen` objects when we are finished with them, or use the `using` block, otherwise our application may deplete the Windows resources.

In this example, we constructed a `Pen`. However, there is an easier way to get a `Pen`. The `Pens` class contains properties for getting approximately 150 pens, one for each of the pre-defined colors that we learned about previously. The following version of the example works identically to the previous one, but instead of constructing a `Pen`, we get it from the `Pens` class:

```
protected override void OnPaint(PaintEventArgs e)
{
    if (ClientRectangle.Height/10>0)
    {
        for (int y = 0; y < ClientRectangle.Height;
            y += ClientRectangle.Height / 10)
        {
            e.Graphics.DrawLine(Pens.Black, new Point(0, 0),
                        new Point(ClientRectangle.Width, y));
        }
    }
}
```

In this case, we did not create the `Pen`, so it is not necessary to call `Dispose()`.

There are many more features of the `Pen` class. We could create a pen to draw a dashed line, or we could create a pen with a width thicker than one pixel. There is an `Alignment` property of the `Pen` class that allows us to define whether the pen is drawn to the left or right (or above/below) of the line that we specify. By setting the `StartCap` and `EndCap` properties, we can specify that our lines are ended with an arrow, a diamond, a square, or rounded off. We can even program a custom start cap and end cap using the `CustomStartCap` and `CustomEndCap` properties. After learning about images, we will see how to specify a `Brush` with a `Pen`, so that we can draw the line using a bitmap instead of a solid color.

Drawing Shapes using the Brush Class

Our next example uses the `Brush` class to draw shapes, such as rectangles, ellipses, pie charts, and polygons. The `Brush` class is an abstract base class. To instantiate a `Brush` object, we use classes derived from `Brush`, such as `SolidBrush`, `TextureBrush`, and `LinearGradientBrush`.

The `Brush` and `SolidBrush` classes are in the `System.Drawing` namespace. However, the `TextureBrush` and `LinearGradientBrush` are in the `System.Drawing.Drawing2D` namespace. This is what each brush class achieves:

- ❑ `SolidBrush` – fills a shape with a solid color.

- ❑ `TextureBrush` – fills a shape with a bitmap. When constructing this brush, we also specify a bounding rectangle, and a wrap mode. The bounding rectangle specifies what portion of the bitmap to use for the brush – we don't need to use the entire bitmap if we don't want to. The wrap mode has a number of options, including `Tile`, which tiles the texture, `TileFlipX`, `TileFlipY`, and `TileFlipXY`, which tile while flipping the image for successive tiles. We can create very interesting and imaginative effects using the `TextureBrush`.

- ❑ `LinearGradientBrush` – encapsulates a brush that draws a gradient of two colors, where the first color transitions to the second color at a specified angle. We specify angles in terms of degrees. An angle of zero specifies that the colors will transition from left to right. An angle of 90 degrees means that the colors will transition from top to bottom.

One more brush that we will mention is the `PathGradientBrush`, which creates an elaborate shading effect, where the shading runs from the center of the path to the edge of the path. This brush reminds me of when I was a child, and I would shade maps with colored pencils, making the color darker at the boundary between different states or countries.

> **Always call** `Dispose()` **on Brush objects.**

Just as for `Graphics` objects and `Pen` objects, it is important to call `Dispose()` on `Brush` objects that we create, or use the `using` block, otherwise our application may deplete the Windows resources.

Try it Out – Brush Example

1. Create a new Windows application called `UsingBrushes` in the directory `C:\BegVCSharp\Chapter16`.

2. Add a using directive for `System.Drawing.Drawing2D` for the `LinearGradientBrush` to the top of the code:

```
using System;
using System.Drawing;
using System.Collections;
using System.ComponentModel;
using System.Windows.Forms;
using System.Data;

using System.Drawing.Drawing2D;
```

3. In the constructor of the `Form1` class, add a call to `SetStyle()` after the call to `InitializeComponent()`.

```
public Form1()
{
    //
    // Required for Windows Form Designer support
    //
    InitializeComponent();
    SetStyle(ControlStyles.Opaque, true);

    //
    // TODO: Add any constructor code after InitializeComponent call
    //
}
```

4. Now, add an `OnPaint()` method to our class:

```
protected override void OnPaint(PaintEventArgs e)
{
    Graphics g = e.Graphics;
    g.FillRectangle(Brushes.White, ClientRectangle);
    g.FillRectangle(Brushes.Red, new Rectangle(10, 10, 50, 50));

    Brush linearGradientBrush = new LinearGradientBrush(
            new Rectangle(10, 60, 50, 50), Color.Blue, Color.White, 45);
    g.FillRectangle(linearGradientBrush, new Rectangle(10, 60, 50, 50));

    // Manually call Dispose()
    linearGradientBrush.Dispose();

    g.FillEllipse(Brushes.Aquamarine, new Rectangle(60, 20, 50, 30));
    g.FillPie(Brushes.Chartreuse, new Rectangle(60, 60, 50, 50), 90, 210);
    g.FillPolygon(Brushes.BlueViolet, new Point[] {
                          new Point(110, 10),
                          new Point(150, 10),
                          new Point(160, 40),
                          new Point(120, 20),
                          new Point(120, 60),
                          });
}
```

5. When you compile and run this program, it will display the following:

How It Works

The first thing to remark about is the call to `SetStyle()` in the form's constructor. `SetStyle()` is a method of the `Form` class:

```
SetStyle(ControlStyles.Opaque, true);
```

This method changes the behavior of the `Form` class, so that it will not automatically draw the background of the window. If we include this line, but we don't draw the background of the window ourselves, then anything underneath the window at the time of creation would show through, which is not what we want. Thus our next activity is to draw our own background onto the client area of our window.

Just as with the `Pens` class, there is a `Brushes` class that contains properties for getting approximately 150 brushes, one for each pre-defined color. We use this class to get most of the brushes in this example, with the exception of the `LinearGradientBrush` which we create ourselves.

The first call to `FillRectangle()` draws the background of the client area of our window:

```
g.FillRectangle(Brushes.White, ClientRectangle);
```

The creation of the `LinearGradientBrush` takes a rectangle specifying the size of the rectangle, the two colors to be used for the gradient, and the angle, in this case 45:

```
Brush linearGradientBrush = new LinearGradientBrush(
        new Rectangle(10, 60, 50, 50), Color.Blue, Color.White, 45);
g.FillRectangle(linearGradientBrush, new Rectangle(10, 60, 50, 50));
linearGradientBrush.Dispose();
```

When we specified the rectangle for the brush, we used a rectangle of width 50, and height 50, which is the same size as the rectangle used when we defined the brush. The result of this is that the brush area just fits the rectangle that we want filling in. Try changing the rectangle defined in the creation of the brush so that the width and height are 10 and see what happens. Also, try changing the angle to different values to see the change in effect.

Drawing Text using the Font Class

Our next example uses the Font class to draw text. The Font class encapsulates the three main characteristics of a font, which are the font family, the font size, and the font style. The Font class is in the System.Drawing namespace.

According to the .NET documentation, a font family "abstracts a group of type faces having a similar basic design". This is a fancy way of saying that font families are things like Courier, Arial, or Times New Roman.

The font Size property represents the size of the font type. However, in the .NET Framework, this size is not strictly the point size. It can be the point size, but we can change a property called the GraphicsUnit via the Unit property, which defines the unit of measure for the font. To refresh your memory, one point is equal to 1/72 of an inch, so a 10-point font is 10/72 of an inch high. Based on the GraphicsUnit enumeration, we can specify the unit for the font as one of the following:

❑ point (1/72 of an inch)

❑ display (1/75 of an inch)

❑ document (1/300 of an inch)

❑ inch

❑ millimeter

❑ pixel

This means that we have an unprecedented flexibility in specifying the desired size of our font. One possible use for this might be if we are writing a text drawing routine that needs to work in an acceptable way on very high-resolution displays, low-resolution displays, and printers.

When drawing text, given a specific font, and given a specific drawing surface, we often need to know the width in pixels of a specified string of text. It is pretty clear why different fonts will have an effect on the width in pixels of a string – a smaller font will result in a width of fewer pixels. However, it is equally as important to know the drawing surface, because the pixel resolutions of different drawing surfaces are different. Typically, the screen has 72 pixels per inch. Printers can be 300 pixels per inch, 600 pixels per inch, and sometimes even more. We use the MeasureString() method of the Graphics object to calculate the width of a string for a given font.

The font Style property refers to whether the type is italicized, emboldened, struck-through, or underlined.

> **Always call** Dispose() **on** Font **objects.**

It is important to call Dispose() on Font objects that we create, or use the using block, otherwise our application may deplete Windows resources.

When drawing text, we use a Rectangle to specify the bounding coordinates of the text to be drawn. Typically, the height of this rectangle should be the height of the font or a multiple of the height of the font. This would only be different when drawing some special effect using clipped text.

The `StringFormat` class encapsulates text layout information, including alignment and line spacing. The following example shows right and centered text justification using the `StringFormat` class.

Try it Out – Font Example

1. Create a new Windows application called `DrawText` in the directory `C:\BegVCSharp\Chapter16`.

2. In the constructor of the `Form1` class, add a call to `SetStyle()` after the call to `InitializeComponent()`. We also change the bounds of the window to give us enough room to display the text that we want to display. The modified constructor is as follows:

```
public Form1()
{
    //
    // Required for Windows Form Designer support
    //
    InitializeComponent();
    SetStyle(ControlStyles.Opaque, true);
    Bounds = new Rectangle(0, 0, 500, 300);

    //
    // TODO: Add any constructor code after InitializeComponent call
    //
}
```

3. Now, add an `OnPaint()` method to our class:

```
protected override void OnPaint(PaintEventArgs e)
{
    Graphics g = e.Graphics;
    int y = 0;

    g.FillRectangle(Brushes.White, ClientRectangle);

    // Draw left justified text
    Rectangle rect = new Rectangle(0, y, 400, Font.Height);
    g.DrawRectangle(Pens.Blue, rect);
    g.DrawString("This text is left justified.", Font,
                 Brushes.Black, rect);
    y += Font.Height + 20;

    // Draw right justified text
    Font aFont = new Font("Arial", 16, FontStyle.Bold | FontStyle.Italic);
    rect = new Rectangle(0, y, 400, aFont.Height);
    g.DrawRectangle(Pens.Blue, rect);

    StringFormat sf = new StringFormat();
    sf.Alignment = StringAlignment.Far;
    g.DrawString("This text is right justified.", aFont, Brushes.Blue,
                 rect, sf);
    y += aFont.Height + 20;
```

```
    // Manually call Dispose()
    aFont.Dispose();

    // draw centered text
    Font cFont = new Font("Courier New", 12, FontStyle.Underline);
    rect = new Rectangle(0, y, 400, cFont.Height);
    g.DrawRectangle(Pens.Blue, rect);
    sf = new StringFormat();
    sf.Alignment = StringAlignment.Center;
    g.DrawString("This text is centered  and underlined.", cFont,
                Brushes.Red, rect, sf);
    y += cFont.Height + 20;

    // Manually call Dispose()
    cFont.Dispose();

    // Draw multiline text
    Font trFont = new Font("Times New Roman", 12);
    rect = new Rectangle(0, y, 400, trFont.Height * 3);
    g.DrawRectangle(Pens.Blue, rect);
    String longString = "This text is much longer, and drawn ";
    longString += "into a rectangle that is higher than ";
    longString += "one line, so that it will wrap.  It is ";
    longString += "very easy to wrap text using GDI+.";
    g.DrawString(longString, trFont, Brushes.Black, rect);

    // Manually call Dispose()
    trFont.Dispose();
}
```

4. When you compile and run the code, it will create this window:

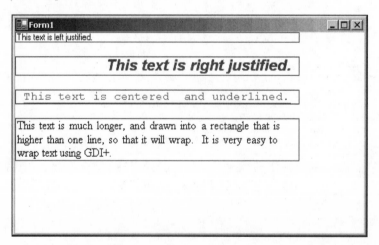

How It Works

This example contains a few of the most common text drawing operations.

As usual, we assign a reference to the `Graphics` object to a local variable, for our convenience. We also paint the background of the window white.

When drawing the text, we calculate the bounding rectangle for our text. We get the height of the font using the `Height` property. For illustrative purposes, we draw this rectangle in blue, so that the bounding rectangle of our text is very clear. When we draw the text, we pass the text, the font, a brush, and a bounding rectangle:

```
// Draw left justified text
Rectangle rect = new Rectangle(0, y, 400, Font.Height);
g.DrawRectangle(Pens.Blue, rect);
g.DrawString("This text is left justified.", Font,
             Brushes.Black, rect);
```

We only specify the rectangle in which the text will go. The baseline of a font is the imaginary line that most of the characters of the font "sit" on. GDI+ and the font itself determine where the actual baseline will go – we have no control over that.

When we draw the text, we pass a brush to the `DrawString()` function. In this example, we only pass brushes that have a solid color. We could just as easily have passed other types of brushes, such as a gradient brush. After we have introduced images in the next section, we will demonstrate drawing text using a `TextureBrush`.

The first time that we draw text in this example, we use the default font for the form. This font is referenced in the `Font` property, which is inherited from `Control`.

```
g.DrawString("This is a left justified string.", Font,
             Brushes.Black, rect);
```

The next time that we draw text in this example, we create a new instance of a `Font`:

```
Font aFont = new Font("Arial", 16, FontStyle.Bold | FontStyle.Italic);
```

This example shows not only how to create a new instance of a font, but how to give it a style. In this case, the style is bold and italic.

The example also shows creating a `StringFormat` object, so that we can draw right-justified and centered text. In GDI+, right-justified text alignment is referred to as `Far` alignment. Left-justified text is `Near` alignment.

```
StringFormat sf = new StringFormat();
sf.Alignment = StringAlignment.Far;
```

Finally, we draw some multi-line text. Using GDI+, it could not be easier. All we need to do is to specify a rectangle where the width is less than the length of the string (in pixels), and the height is sufficient to draw multiple lines. In this case, we made the height equal to three times the font height.

Drawing Using Images

Images have many uses in GDI+. Of course, we can draw images into our windows, but we can also create a brush (TextureBrush) with an image, and draw shapes that are then filled in with the image. We can create a pen from the TextureBrush, and draw lines using the image. We can supply a TextureBrush when drawing text, and the text will then be drawn using the image. The Image class is in the System.Drawing namespace.

Another very important use of images is the graphics programming technique of **double buffering**. Sometimes the drawing that we wish to create is very elaborate and intricate, and takes quite a bit of time to draw, even with today's fast machines. It is not a pleasing effect to see the graphic "creep" onto the screen as it is being drawn. Examples of these types of applications are mapping applications, and complex CAD/CAM applications. In this technique, instead of drawing into a window, we draw into an image, and after our drawing into the image is completed, we draw the image to the window. This is the technique known as double buffering. Certain other graphics techniques involve drawing in layers, where first we draw the background, then we draw objects on top of the background, and finally we draw some text on top of the objects. If this drawing is done directly to the screen, the user will see a flickering effect. Double buffering eliminates this flickering effect. We'll take a look at a double buffering example a bit later.

Image itself is an abstract class. There are two descendants of Image: Bitmap, and Metafile.

The Bitmap class is a general-purpose image, with height and width properties. Our examples in this section will use the Bitmap class. We will load a Bitmap image from a file and draw it. We will also create a brush from it and use that brush to create a pen to draw lines, and also use that brush to draw some text.

We'll take a look at the Metafile class near the end of this chapter, when we are taking an overview of the advanced capabilities of GDI+.

> **Always call** Dispose() **on** Image **objects.**

It is important to call Dispose() on Image objects that we create, or use the using blocks, otherwise our application may deplete the Windows resources.

There are several possible sources for a bitmap. We can load the bitmap from a file, or create the bitmap from another existing image, or it can be created as an empty image, onto which we can draw. When we read the image from a file, it can be in the JPEG, GIF, or BMP format.

Try it Out – Image Example

The following is a very simple example to read an image from a file and draw it in a window.

1. Create a new Windows application called DrawImage in the directory
   C:\BegVCSharp\Chapter15.

2. First, we need to declare a private variable in our `Form1` class to hold the image after we read it from a file. After the declaration of the components variable, add the declaration of `theImage` as follows:

```
public class Form1 : System.Windows.Forms.Form
{
    /// <summary>
    ///    Required designer variable.
    /// </summary>
    private System.ComponentModel.Container components;
    private Image theImage;
```

3. Modify the constructor so that it appears as follows:

```
public Form1()
{
    //
    // Required for Windows Form Designer support
    //
    InitializeComponent();
    SetStyle(ControlStyles.Opaque, true);
    theImage = new Bitmap("Person.bmp");
    //
    // TODO: Add any constructor code after InitializeComponent call
    //
}
```

4. Now, add an `OnPaintEvent()` method to our class:

```
protected override void OnPaint(PaintEventArgs e)
{
    Graphics g = e.Graphics;

    g.DrawImage(theImage, ClientRectangle);
}
```

5. Finally, we need to dispose of the `Image` that is stored in a member variable of our class. Modify the `Dispose()` method of the form class as follows:

```
protected override void Dispose( bool disposing )
{
    if( disposing )
    {
        theImage.Dispose();
        if (components != null)
        {
            components.Dispose();
        }
    }
    base.Dispose( disposing );
}
```

Before building this class, you must get the BMP file called `Person.bmp` and place it in the `DrawBitmap\bin\Debug` directory. The `Person.bmp` file can be found in the code download, or else you can use another bitmap you have, but remember to change the line

```
theImage = new Bitmap("Person.bmp");
```

that you added in step 3 above to hold the filename of your own bitmap.

When you compile and run this code, you should see the following display:

How It Works

In the constructor, we instantiate a `Bitmap` object and assign it to our `Image` variable that we declared.

Then, in the `OnPaint()` method, we draw the image. When we draw the image, we pass a `Rectangle` as one of the arguments to the `DrawImage()` method. If the image is not the same size as the rectangle that we pass to `DrawImage()`, GDI+ automatically resizes the image to fit in the specified rectangle. One way to enforce that GDI+ will not resize the image is to pass the size of the image, retrieved from the `Width` and `Height` properties, to the `DrawImage()` method.

Drawing with a Texture Brush

We will now create a `TextureBrush` from the image we have just used, and look at the following three different examples of its use:

❑   Drawing an ellipse

❑   Creating a `Pen`

❑   Drawing text

We will start with the last code example and make a few modifications to it.

Try it Out – Drawing an Ellipse with an Image

1. Starting with the code in the previous `DrawImage` example, add another `Image` variable declaration to the `Form1` class:

```
public class Form1 : System.Windows.Forms.Form
{
    /// <summary>
    ///    Required designer variable.
    /// </summary>
    private System.ComponentModel.Container components;
    private Image theImage;
    private Image smallImage;
```

2. In the form's constructor, we will create `smallImage` from `theImage`. When we create it, we specify a rectangle that is half the height and half the width of `theImage`. This creates a smaller version of the original image:

```
public Form1()
{
    //
    // Required for Windows Form Designer support
    //
    InitializeComponent();
    SetStyle(ControlStyles.Opaque, true);
    theImage = new Bitmap("Person.bmp");
    smallImage = new Bitmap(theImage,
            new Size(theImage.Width / 2, theImage.Height / 2));

    //
    // TODO: Add any constructor code after InitializeComponent call
    //
}
```

3. Replace the `OnPaint()` method with this one:

```
protected override void OnPaint(PaintEventArgs e)
{
    Graphics g = e.Graphics;

    g.FillRectangle(Brushes.White, ClientRectangle);

    Brush tBrush = new TextureBrush(smallImage, new Rectangle(0, 0,
            smallImage.Width, smallImage.Height));
    g.FillEllipse(tBrush, ClientRectangle);
    tBrush.Dispose();
}
```

4. Finally, we need to dispose of the two images that are stored in member variables of our class. Modify the `Dispose()` method of the class as follows:

```
protected override void Dispose( bool disposing )
{
    if( disposing )
    {
        theImage.Dispose();
        smallImage.Dispose();

        if (components != null)
        {
            components.Dispose();
        }
    }
    base.Dispose( disposing );
}
```

5. When we run this application, the window looks like this:

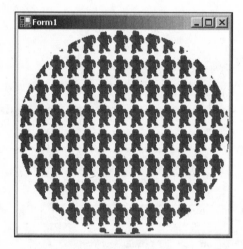

How It Works

When we create the `TextureBrush`, we pass a rectangle to the constructor to specify what part of the image will be used for the brush. In this case, we specify that we will use the entire image. Whatever is drawn using the `TextureBrush` uses the bitmap instead of a solid color.

Most of the code for this example has already been explained in this chapter. The difference is that we call the `FillEllipse()` method of the `Graphics` class, passing our newly created texture brush, and the `ClientRectangle` draws the ellipse in the window:

```
g.FillEllipse(tBrush, ClientRectangle);
```

Try it Out – Creating a Pen from an Image

Now that we have created a `TextureBrush`, we can create a pen using that brush.

1. Starting with the code in the `DrawImage` example that we modified in the previous *Try it Out*, change the `OnPaint()` method so that it looks like this:

```
protected override void OnPaint(PaintEventArgs e)
{
    Graphics g = e.Graphics;

    g.FillRectangle(Brushes.White, ClientRectangle);

    Brush tBrush = new TextureBrush(smallImage, new Rectangle(0, 0,
                    smallImage.Width, smallImage.Height));
    Pen tPen = new Pen(tBrush, 40);
    g.DrawRectangle(tPen, 0, 0,
                    ClientRectangle.Width, ClientRectangle.Height);
    tPen.Dispose();
    tBrush.Dispose();
}
```

2. When we run this code, it looks like the following:

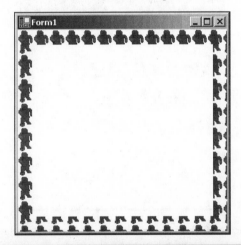

Try it Out – Drawing Text with an Image

We can draw text using our `TextureBrush` also.

1. Continuing with the code from the previous *Try it Out*, modify the `OnPaint` method as follows:

```
protected override void OnPaint(PaintEventArgs e)
{
    Graphics g = e.Graphics;
```

```
        g.FillRectangle(Brushes.White, ClientRectangle);

        Brush tBrush = new TextureBrush(smallImage, new Rectangle(0, 0,
                        smallImage.Width, smallImage.Height));
        Font trFont = new Font("Times New Roman", 32,
                        FontStyle.Bold | FontStyle.Italic);
        g.DrawString("Hello from Beginning Visual C#",
                    trFont, tBrush, ClientRectangle);
        tBrush.Dispose();
        trFont.Dispose();
    }
```

2. For this example, we'll actually use a different bitmap – change the line in the form constructor that sets the source for the Image to:

```
        theImage = new Bitmap("Tile.bmp");
```

The Tile.bmp file can also be found in the download code.

3. When we run this code, it appears as follows:

The call to the DrawString() method is similar to previous uses of that method. It takes as arguments the text, the font, our texture brush, and a bounding rectangle:

```
        g.DrawString("Hello from Beginning Visual C#",
                    trFont, tBrush, ClientRectangle);
```

Double Buffering

We previously touched on the problems when drawing takes too long, and the user has to wait a long time to see the graphics drawn. As we explained before, the solution is to draw into an image, and when we have completed all drawing operations, draw the complete image to the window.

Try it Out – Double Buffering Example

1. Create a new Windows application called `DoubleBuffer`, and add the following
`OnPaint()` method, which a draws a large number of lines in random colors.

```
protected override void OnPaint(PaintEventArgs e)
{
    Graphics g = e.Graphics;
    Random r = new Random();

    g.FillRectangle(Brushes.White, ClientRectangle);

    for (int x = 0; x < ClientRectangle.Width; x++)
    {
        for (int y = 0; y < ClientRectangle.Height; y += 10)
        {
            Color c = Color.FromArgb(r.Next(255), r.Next(255), r.Next(255));
            using (Pen p = new Pen(c, 1))
            {
                g.DrawLine(p, new Point(0, 0), new Point(x, y));
            }
        }
    }
}
```

2. When you run this, you can see the drawing take place before your eyes (that is, if your
machine is not *too* fast). After all the drawing is completed, the window looks like this:

3. Now we'll add the double buffering – if you replace the `OnPaint()` method with this version,
the graphics are drawn all at once, after a second or two:

```
protected override void OnPaint(PaintEventArgs e)
{
    Graphics displayGraphics = e.Graphics;
```

```
        Random r = new Random();
        Image i = new Bitmap(ClientRectangle.Width, ClientRectangle.Height);
        Graphics g = Graphics.FromImage(i);

        g.FillRectangle(Brushes.White, ClientRectangle);

        for (int x = 0; x < ClientRectangle.Width; x++)
        {
            for (int y = 0; y < ClientRectangle.Height; y += 10)
            {
                Color c = Color.FromArgb (r.Next(255), r.Next(255), r.Next(255));
                Pen p = new Pen(c, 1);
                g.DrawLine(p, new Point(0, 0), new Point(x, y));
                p.Dispose();
            }
        }
        displayGraphics.DrawImage(i, ClientRectangle);
        i.Dispose();
    }
```

How it Works

The part of the code responsible for drawing the lines is straightforward – we've seen the DrawLine() method earlier in the chapter. The only real thing of note in this part of the code is the FromArgb() static Color method, which creates a Color struct from the three supplied integer values, corresponding to the red, green and blue parts of the color.

In the double buffering code, (step 3 above), we create a new image that has the same height and width of the ClientRectangle with the following line:

```
    Image i = new Bitmap(ClientRectangle.Width, ClientRectangle.Height);
```

We then get a Graphics object from the image using the following line:

```
    Graphics g = Graphics.FromImage(i);
```

All of the drawing operations are the same as the previous code, except that they now draw into the image instead of directly onto the window.

Finally, at the end of the function, we draw the image to the window:

```
    displayGraphics.DrawImage(i, ClientRectangle);
```

Because the lines are drawn first to an invisible image, you do have to wait a short while before you see anything.

Advanced Capabilities of GDI+

We have only just touched on the many capabilities of GDI+. There is much more that you can do with it – far more than can be achieved in a single chapter. However, to round off this chapter, we will introduce several areas of these advanced capabilities.

Clipping

There are three contexts where clipping is important.

First, when the OnPaint() method gets called, in addition to the Graphics object, the event is passed a clipping rectangle. For simple drawing routines, we don't need to pay much attention to this clipping rectangle, but if we have a very elaborate drawing routine that takes a lot of time, we can reduce this drawing time by testing against this clipping rectangle before we draw. We know the bounding rectangle of whatever graphic or figure that we need to draw. If this bounding rectangle does not intersect with the clipping rectangle, then we can skip the drawing operation.

The following screenshot shows one window containing a bar chart that is partially obscured by another window:

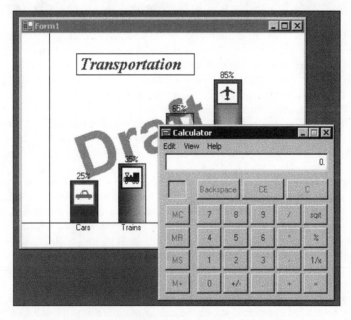

After the calculator has been closed, and after the Windows operating system has drawn the border of the window, the bar chart window would look like this:

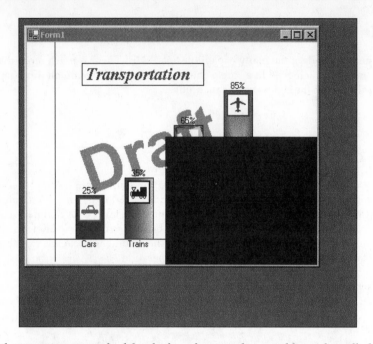

At this point, the OnPaint() method for the bar chart window would now be called, with the clipping rectangle set to the area exposed by the closed window, shown above in black. The bar chart would now need to draw the portions of its window that were previously underneath the overlying window. It would not need to redraw the car or trains bars, and in fact, even if the OnPaint() method tried to draw into the window in an area other than the exposed area, it could not. Any drawing that it did would be ignored. The bar chart window knows the bounding rectangle for the cars bar, and can determine if this rectangle intersects with the exposed portion of the window. Having determined that it does not intersect, the drawing routine will not redraw the part of the display covering the cars bar.

Sometimes when drawing, if we need to draw only part of a figure or graphic, it is more convenient to draw the entire figure, and clip the drawing to just what we want to see. We may have an image, and want to draw just a portion of that image. Rather than create a new image that is just a portion of the original image, we can set the clipping rectangle, and then draw the image such that just the portion that we want to see "shows through" the clipping area. When creating a marquee, this is the technique that we would use. By successively changing where we draw the text, and at the same time setting a clipping region, we can create the effect of horizontally moving text.

Finally, there is a technique where we can create a "view port" into a larger graphic. The user can move this view port around, perhaps by dragging the mouse on the graphic, or manipulating scroll bars. The view port also may be moved programmatically based on other actions that the user takes. In this case, setting a clipping region and drawing such that only what we want to see shows through is a good technique.

See the Clip property of the Graphics class for more information.

System.Drawing.Drawing2D

The classes in this namespace provide advanced two-dimensional and vector graphics functionality. We could use these classes to build a sophisticated drawing and image processing application.

Vector graphics is a technique where the programmer doesn't address pixels at all. Rather, the programmer records multiple "vectors", indicating such operations as "draw from one point to another", draw a rectangle at a certain location, etc. Then the developer can apply scaling, rotation, and other transformations. Having applied the transformations, all the operations are rendered at once to the window.

This namespace includes advanced brushes. We have already seen the `LinearGradientBrush` and we touched on the `PathGradientBrush`. There is also a `HatchBrush`, which draws using a hatch style, a foreground color, and a background color.

This namespace also includes the `Matrix` class, which defines geometric transforms. Using this class, we can do transforms on the drawing operations. For instance, using the `Matrix` class, we can draw an oval that is at a slant.

Also included in this namespace is the `GraphicsPath` class, which we have already touched on. Using this class, we can define a complex path and draw the entire path at once.

System.Drawing.Imaging

The classes in this namespace provide advanced imaging support, such as support for metafiles. A metafile describes a sequence of graphics operations that can be recorded and later played back, and there are classes within the `System.Drawing.Imaging` namespace that allow us to extend GDI+ to support other image formats.

Summary

In this chapter, we covered some of the classes in the `System.Drawing` namespace. We saw how the `Graphics` class encapsulates a drawing surface. We reviewed the mechanics of drawing, where the `OnPaint` event is called whenever our window needs to be redrawn.

We explored colors and coordinate systems. We covered the `Point`, `Size`, and `Rectangle` structures that we use to specify positions and sizes on our drawing surface. Next, we saw some examples of drawing lines, shapes, text, and images.

Overall, the topics that we covered were:

- ❑ The `Graphics` class
- ❑ The `Color` structure
- ❑ Drawing lines using the `Pen` class
- ❑ Drawing shapes using the `Brush` class

Chapter 16

- ❑ Drawing text using the Font class
- ❑ Drawing images using the Bitmap class
- ❑ Drawing into images (double-buffering)

We learned that it is very important to call Dispose() on certain classes when we are done with them. Those classes are:

- ❑ Graphics
- ❑ Pen
- ❑ Brush
- ❑ Font
- ❑ Image

Finally, we had an overview of additional graphical capabilities in the .NET Framework.

Deploying Windows Applications

One of the big features of .NET is that installation can often be done using a simple xcopy. In .NET, assemblies simply consist of a number of files, and the Registry is no longer needed to store assembly configurations, so copying files can often be enough to install an application.

However, you will soon come to find some good reasons not to use xcopy for installing Windows applications – for the deployment of Windows applications xcopy should be used only for the simplest applications. With small applications that are only installed on a few systems, xcopy can do a good job, but for bigger applications or applications that are installed to a lot of systems we have to think about a better installation mechanism. xcopy does not register or verify assembly locations and it cannot take advantage of Windows Installer Zero Administration Windows (ZAW) features, which means that files can be overwritten unintentionally, and there's no built-in uninstall.

> Microsoft's Zero Administrative Initiative facilitates the job of system administrators to update and to install applications automatically on client systems, and to do central administration of applications.

In this chapter we will look at:

- ❑ Microsoft Windows Installer and its advantages for deploying applications
- ❑ Deployment Project Types in Visual Studio .NET
- ❑ Features of the Windows Installer
- ❑ Creating Windows Installer Packages using Visual Studio .NET

What is Deployment?

Deployment is the process of installing applications to the target systems.

The Process Model of the Microsoft Solutions Framework
(http://www.microsoft.com/business/services/mcsmsf.asp) defines the process model
with four phases in a development lifecycle: **Envisioning**, here the idea of the solution gets articulated.
The **Planning** phase is mainly used to analyze and design the solution. In the **Developing** phase most of
the development takes place, and **Stabilizing** is where no more new features are introduced, but instead
bugs are fixed, and beta and finally release versions of the product are sent to the customer's site.

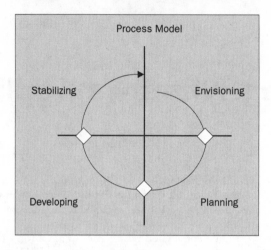

Between these four phases you can see three major milestones – but these major milestones don't finalize a
sequence as with today's application development, the customer's goals can often change, and in a later
process phase you can detect that some parts don't work as expected. Thus developing can also happen in
the planning phase to get some prototypes to work, and design can still change in the developing phase.

> It is good practice to think about deployment of projects early in the process cycle, as
> deployment strategies can influence the design of applications.

Deployment Project Types

Starting the Visual Studio .NET Add New Project dialog, we get this screen after selecting Setup and
Deployment Projects:

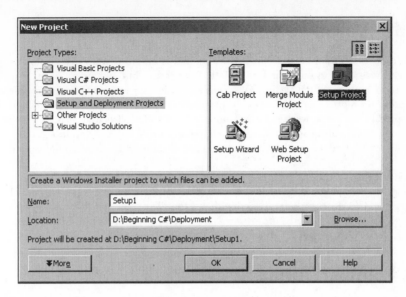

These are the project types and what can be done with them:

❑ With the **Cab Project** template, cabinet files can be created. Cabinet files can be used to merge multiple assemblies into a single file and compress it. Since the cabinet files can be compressed, a Web client can download a smaller file from the server.

Creating components is not in the scope of this book, so we will not look at the creation of cabinet projects. You can read Professional C# 2nd Edition *(Wrox Press, ISBN 1-86100-704-3) for information on how to create .NET components for download from a Web Server.*

❑ The **Merge Module Project** template is used to create Windows Installer merge modules. A merge module is an installer file that can be included in multiple Microsoft Installer installation packages. For components that should be installed with more than one installation program a merge module can be created to include this module in the installation packages. One example of a merge module is the .NET runtime itself: it is delivered in a merge module, and as such the .NET runtime can be included with the installer package of an application. We will use a merge module in our sample application.

❑ The **Setup Project** template is the one we will use. This template is used to create Windows Installer Packages, and so it is the best way for deploying of Windows Applications.

❑ The **Setup Wizard** is a step-by-step way to choose the other templates. The first question to ask yourself is this: do you want to create a setup program to install an application or a redistributable package? Depending on your choice a Windows Installer Package, a Merge Module, or a CAB File will be created.

The last template in this list is the **Web Setup Project**. We will not be using this template in this chapter because the main focus of this book is on developing Windows desktop applications.

Microsoft Windows Installer Architecture

Before the Windows Installer existed, programmers had to create custom installation programs. It was not only much more work to build such installation programs, but also many of these programs didn't follow the Windows rules. Often system-DLLs were overwritten with older versions because the installation program didn't check the version. In addition to this, the directory where the application files were copied to was often wrong; for example, a hard-coded directory string C:\Program Files was used. If the system administrator changed the default drive letter, or an international version of the operating system was used where this directory is named differently, the installation failed.

The first version of the Windows Installer was released as part of Microsoft Office 97, and as a distributable package that could be included with other application packages. Version 1.1 added support to register COM+ components, and with 1.2 the file protection mechanism of Windows ME was supported. Version 1.5 added support for .NET assemblies and for the 64-bit release of Windows. With Visual Studio .NET we get a new version: 2.0.

Windows Installer Terms

Working with the Windows Installer requires us to be familiar with some terms that are used with the Windows Installer technology: Packages, Features, and Components.

Be aware of one important note about the term **component**, used for installer programs:

> In the context of the Windows Installer, a component is not the same as a *component* in the .NET Framework. A Windows Installer component is just a single file (or multiple files that logically belong together). Such a file can be an executable, a DLL, or even a simple text file.

As you can see in the following picture, a **package** consists of one or more features. A package is a single Microsoft Installer (MSI) database. A **feature** is the user's view of the capabilities of a product and can consist of features and components. A **component** is the developer's view of the installation; it is the smallest unit of installation and consists of one or more files. The differentiation of features and components is used because a single component can be included in multiple features (as shown in the diagram below by Component 2). A single feature cannot be included within multiple features.

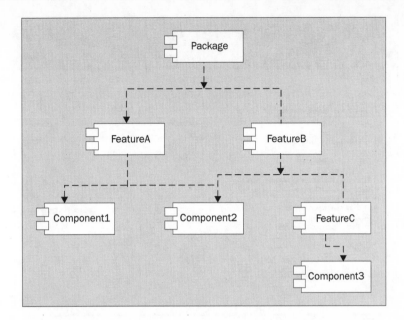

Let's look at the features of a real world example that you should already have: Visual Studio .NET. Using the Add/Remove Programs option from the Control Panel, we can change the installed features of Visual Studio .NET after installation by pressing the Change/Remove button:

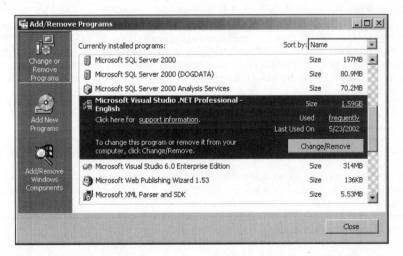

By pressing the Change/Remove button, you can visit the Visual Studio .NET Maintenance wizard. This is a good way to see features in action. As you can see in the picture below, the Visual Studio .NET package includes the features Language Tools, .NET Framework SDK, Crystal Reports for Visual Studio .NET, Tools for Redistributing Apps, and Server Components. The Language Tools feature has the sub-features Visual Basic .NET, Visual C++ .NET, and Visual C# .NET:

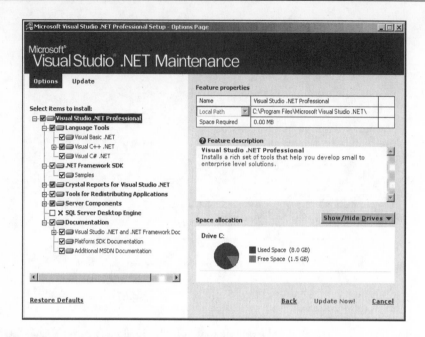

Advantages of the Windows Installer

The advantages of the Windows installer are as follows:

❑   Features can be installed, not installed, or advertised. With **advertisement**, a feature of the package will be installed at first time use. Maybe you have already seen the Windows Installer starting during your work with Microsoft Word. If you use an advertised feature of Word that was not installed, it will be installed automatically as soon as you use this feature.

❑   If an application gets corrupted, the applications can **self-repair** by using the repair feature of Windows Installer packages.

❑   An automatic **rollback** will be done if the installation fails. After the installation fails everything is left as before: no additional Registry keys, no files, etc. are left on the system.

❑   With an **uninstall,** all the relevant files, Registry keys, etc. are removed – the application can be completely uninstalled. No temporary files are left out, and the Registry is also reinstated.

By reading the tables of the MSI database file it's possible to get the information about such things as what files are copied, and what registry keys are written.

Creating an Installation Package for the Simple Editor

We will use the Simple Editor solution from Chapter 15 to create a Windows Installer Package using Visual Studio .NET. Of course, you can use any other Windows Forms application you have developed while you follow the steps; you just have to change some of the names used accordingly.

Planning the Installation

Before we can start building the installation program, we have to plan what we are going to put in it. There are some questions to be considered first:

❑   **What files are needed for the application?** Of course the executable and probably some component assemblies. It won't be necessary for you to identify all dependencies of these items because the dependencies will automatically be included. Maybe some other files are needed, too. What about a documentation file, a readme.txt, a license file, a document template, pictures, configuration files, among others. We have to know all required files.

   For our Simple Editor we need the executable, and we will also include the files readme.rtf, license.rtf, and a bitmap from Wrox Press to show in the installation dialogs.

❑   **What directories should be used?** Application files should be installed in Program Files\Application name. The Program Files directory is named differently for each language variant of the operating system. Also, the administrator can choose different paths for this application. It is not necessary to know where this directory really is because there's an API function call to get this directory. With the installer, we can use a special predefined folder to put files in the Program Files directory.

> It's worth making this point again – under no circumstances should the directories be hard-coded. With international versions these directories are named differently! Even if your application just supports English versions of Windows (which you really shouldn't do), the System Administrator could have moved these directories to different drives.

   The Simple Editor will have the executable in the default application directory unless the installing user selects a different path.

❑   **How should the user access the application?** We can put a shortcut to the executable in the Start menu, or place an icon on the desktop, for example. If you want to place an icon on the desktop, you should check whether the user is happy with that. With Windows XP, the guideline is to have the desktop as clean as possible.

   The Simple Editor should be accessible from the Start menu.

❑   **What is the distribution media?** Do we want to put the installation packages on a CD, floppy disks, or a network share?

❑   **What will we ask the user?** Should he or she accept license information, display a ReadMe file, ask for the path to install? Are some other options required for the installation?

   The default dialogs that are supplied with the Visual Studio .NET Installer will be ample for this example. We will ask for the directory where the program should be installed (the user may choose a path that is different from the default), show a ReadMe file, and ask the user to accept the license agreement.

Create the Project

After knowing what should be in the installation package we can use the Visual Studio .NET installer to create an installer project and add all files that should be installed. In the first steps we will use the Project wizard and configure the project.

Try it Out – Creating a Windows Installer Project

1. Open the solution file of the Simple Editor project we created in Chapter 15. We will add the installation project to the existing solution. If you didn't create the solution in Chapter 15 yourself (shame on you!), you'll find it in the download code.

2. Add a Setup Project called SetupSimpleEditor to the solution with the File | Add Project | New Project menu.

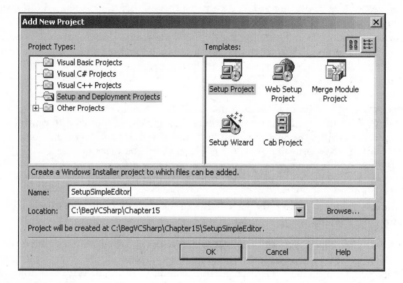

Project Properties

Up to this point we only have a project file for the setup solution. The files to be installed must be defined. But we also have to configure the project properties. To do this we have to know what the **Packaging** and **Bootstrapper** options mean.

Packaging

MSI is where the installation is started, but we can define how the files that are to be installed are packaged with three options in the dialog shown. This dialog is opened if you right-click on the SetupSimpleEditor project, and select Properties:

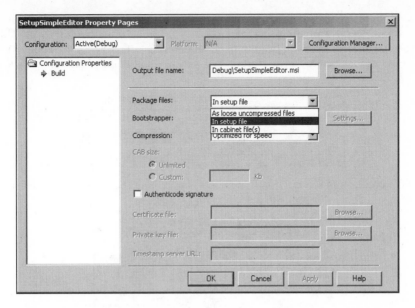

Let's look at options in the **Package files** drop-down list:

❑ With **As loose uncompressed files** all program and data files are stored as they are. No compressing takes place.

❑ With **In setup file** means that all the files are merged and compressed into the MSI file. This option can be overridden for single components in the package. If you put all your files into a single MSI file you have to pay attention that the size of the installation program fits in the target you want to use, for example, CDs or floppy disks. If you have so many files to install that they exceed the capacity of a single floppy, you can try to change the compression rate by selecting the **Optimized for size** option from the **Compression** drop-down list. If the size still doesn't fit you can choose the next option for packaging.

❑ The third way to package files is **In cabinet file(s)**. With this method the MSI file is just used to load and install the CAB files. With CAB files it is possible to set file sizes that enable installations on CDs or floppy disks (we can set sizes of 1440 KB for installations from floppy disks).

Bootstrapper

Another option we can configure in the same dialog is the **bootstrapper**. A bootstrapper is a program that must be executed before the actual application can run.

On the target system where your application should be installed, version 1.5 of the Windows Installer is required for installer packages created with Visual Studio .NET. Version 1.5 of the Windows Installer was first delivered with Windows XP, and if your program needs to be deployed to earlier systems you will need a **bootstrapper** that installs the new version of the Windows Installer. Selecting the **Windows Installer Bootstrapper** includes the bootstrapper in the installation program, and on installation it installs version 1.5 of the Windows Installer before starting the installation of the target program. The space that's needed for this option is around 3 MB.

If we use the **Web Bootstrapper** we have to place the bootstrapper program on a web site. When selecting this option in the Property pages we are asked for the URL of the download. This URL will then allow the user installing the application to download and install the bootstrapper. With this option you don't need additional space in your installation package, but the user installing the application must have access to the Internet.

If you select the option **None** to not install the bootstrapper, and the target system doesn't have the Windows Installer 1.5 installed you will get this error message at installation time:

Try it Out – Configuring the Project

1. Change the **Bootstrapper** option in the Property page that we've just been looking at to **Windows Installer Bootstrapper** so that the application can be installed on systems where the Windows Installer 1.5 is not available. Also change the output file name to `WroxSimpleEditor.msi`.

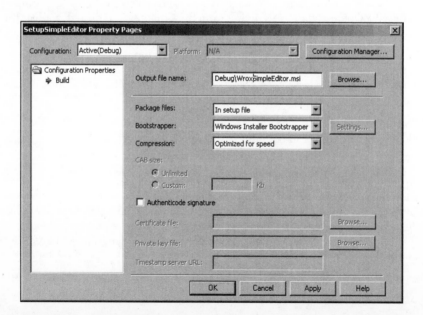

2. Set the project properties to the values in the following table:

Property	Value
Author	Christian Nagel
Description	Simple Editor to print and edit text files.
Keywords	Installer, Wrox Press, Simple Editor
Manufacturer	Wrox Press
ManufacturerUrl	http://www.wrox.com
Product Name	Simple Editor
SupportUrl	http://p2p.wrox.com
Title	Installation Database for Simple Editor
Version	1.0.0

Setup Editors

With a Visual Studio .NET Setup Project we have six editors available. You can select the editor by opening a deployment project, and selecting the menu View | Editor as you see in the picture below:

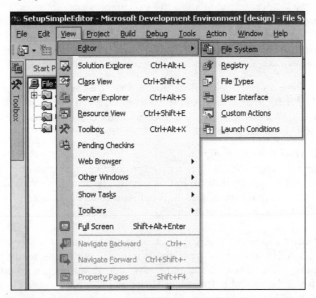

❑ The **File System** editor is used to add files to the installation package.

❑ With the **Registry** editor, Registry keys can be created for the application.

❑ The **File Types** editor allows registration of specific file extensions for an application

❑ With the **User Interface** editor we can add and configure dialogs that are shown during installation of the product

❑ The **Custom Actions** editor allows it to start custom programs during installation and uninstallation

❑ With the **Launch Conditions** editor we can specify requirements for our application, for example, that the .NET runtime already has to be in place

File System Editor

With the **File System Editor** we can add files to the installation package and configure the locations where they should be installed. This editor is opened with View | Editor | File System menu. Some of the predefined special folders are automatically opened as shown in the following picture:

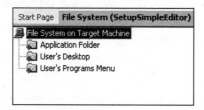

❑ The **Application Folder** is used to store the executables and libraries. The location is defined as [ProgramFilesFolder][Manufacturer][ProductName]. On English language systems the [ProgramFilesFolder] is resolved to C:\Program Files. The directories for [Manufacturer] and [ProductName] are defined with the Manufacturer and ProductName project properties.

❑ If we want to place an icon on the desktop the **User Desktop** option can be used. The default path to this folder is C:\Documents and Settings\[username]\Desktop or C:\Documents and Settings\All Users\Desktop depending if the installation is done for a single user or for all users.

❑ The user will usually start a program by starting it from the **User Programs Menu**. The default path is C:\Documents and Settings\[username]\Start Menu\[Programs]. You can put a shortcut to the application in this menu. The shortcut should have a name that includes the company and the application name, so that the user can easily identify the application, for example, Microsoft Excel.

Some applications create a sub menu where more than one application can be started, for example, Microsoft Visual Studio.NET 7.0. According to the Windows Guidelines, many programs do this for the wrong reason, listing programs which are not necessary: you shouldn't put an uninstall program in these menus, because this feature is available from Add/Remove Programs in the Control Panel, and should be used from there. A help file should also not be placed in this menu because this should be available directly from the application. Thus for many applications it will be enough to place a shortcut to the application directly in the User's Programs Menu. The goal of these restrictions is that the Start menu doesn't get too cluttered with too many items in it.

A great reference to this information can be found in "Application Specification for Microsoft Windows 2000". You can download this paper at `http://msdn.microsoft.com`, by following the **Partners & Certification | Windows Logo Program** links.

There are other folders that you can add by right-clicking and selecting **Add Special Folder**. Some of these folders include:

❑ In the **Global Assembly Cache Folder** we can install shared assemblies. The Global Assembly Cache is used for assemblies that should be shared between multiple applications. You can read more about sharing assemblies in Chapter 21.

❑ The **User Personal Data Folder** is the default folder of a user where documents should be stored. `C:\Documents and Settings\[username]\My Documents` is the default path. This path is the default directory used by Visual Studio .NET to store projects.

❑ Adding a shortcut to **User Send To Menu** extends the Send To context menu when a file is selected. With this context menu the user can typically send a file to the target program like the floppy drive, a mail recipient, or the My Documents folder.

Adding Items to Special Folders

Selecting a folder and choosing the menu **Action | Add**, we can choose from a list to add items to a special folder as you can see in the picture:

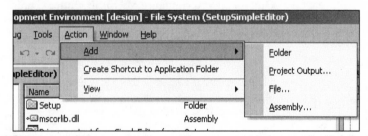

We can select **project output**, **folders**, **files**, or **assemblies**. Selecting the output of a project to a folder automatically adds the generated output files, a .DLL or .EXE depending if the added project is a component library or an application. Selecting one of the menus Project Output or Assembly automatically adds all dependencies (all referenced assemblies) to the folder.

File Properties

Selecting the properties of a file in a folder we can set the following properties. Depending on the file types some of these properties don't apply, and there are additional properties not listed below.

Property	Description
Condition	With this property a condition can be defined to determine if the selected file should be installed. This can be useful if you want to add this file only for specific operating system versions, or something the user has to choose in a dialog.

Table continued on following page

Property	Description
Exclude	Can be set to `True` if this file should not be installed. This way the file can stay in the project but doesn't install. You can exclude a file if you are sure that it's not a dependency or that it already exists on every system where the application gets deployed.
PackageAs	With `PackageAs` we can override the default how the file should be added to the installer package; for example, if the project configuration says In Setup File we can change the package configuration with this option for a specific file to `Loose`, so that this file will not be added to the MSI database file. This is specifically useful if we want to add a `Readme` file that the user should read before starting the installation. Obviously we would not compress this file even if all the others were.
Permanent	Setting this property to `True` means that the file will stay on the target computer after uninstallation of the product. This can be used for configuration files. One example where you may have already seen this, is when installing a new version of Microsoft Outlook: if you configure Microsoft Outlook, uninstall the product and install it again, it's not necessary to configure it again as the configuration of the last install is not deleted.
ReadOnly	This property sets the read only file attribute at installation.
Vital	This property means that this file is essential for the installation of this product. If installation of this file fails, the complete installation is aborted and a rollback occurs.

Try it Out – Add Files to the Installer Package

1. Add the primary output of the Simple Editor project to the installer project using the Project | Add | Project Output menu. In the Add Project Output Group dialog, select the Primary Output as follows:

Pressing the **OK** button adds the primary output of the `SimpleEditor` project to the Application Folder in the automatically opened File System Editor. In our case the primary output is `SimpleEditor.exe`. As you can see in the Solution Explorer, the dependencies are automatically detected; the merge module `dotnetfxredist_x86_enu.msm` is added to the project, but is by default excluded from the project. This merge module includes all files of the .NET runtime. If the .NET runtime is not already installed on the target system, it will be installed along with our application.

Our installation program will require the runtime to be already installed. The runtime needs around 15 MB, thus not including it makes our installation file about 15 MB smaller. With the runtime excluded from our solution, the installation will be successful even if the .NET runtime is not installed on the target system, but `SimpleEditor.exe` will not start. A better way would be if we get an error message during installation if the runtime is not installed. We can do this by defining a .NET Framework Launch Condition. We will do this later.

2. Additional files we want to add are a logo, a license, and a ReadMe file. In the File System Editor create a subdirectory named `Setup` in the **Application Folder**. You can do this by selecting the **Application Folder**, and choosing the menu **Action | Add | Folder**.

> **The Action menu in Visual Studio .NET is only available if you select items in the Setup Editors. If an item in the Solution Explorer or Class View is selected, the Action menu is not available.**

3. Add the files `wroxlogo.bmp`, `wroxsetuplogo.bmp`, `readme.rtf` and `license.rtf` to the folder `Setup` by right-clicking on the `Setup` folder and selecting **Add | File**. These files are available with the code download for this chapter, but you can easily create these files yourself. You can fill the text files with license and ReadMe information. It is not necessary to change the properties of these files. These files will be used in the dialogs of the installation program.

4. Drag and drop the file `readme.txt` to the application folder. We want this file to be available for the user to read before the installation is started. Set the property `PackageAs` to **vsdpaLoose**, so that this file will not be compressed into the Installer package. Also set the `ReadOnly` property to `True` so that this file cannot be changed.

5. Drag and drop the file `demo.wroxtext` to the **User's Desktop** folder. This file should only be installed after asking the user whether he or she really wants to install it. Therefore set the `Condition` property of this file to **CHECKBOXDEMO**. The value must be written in uppercase. The file will only be installed if the `CHECKBOXDEMO` condition is set to `true`. Later we will define a dialog where this property will be set.

We want to make the program available from the Start | Programs menu – we need a shortcut to the `SimpleEditor` program.

6. Select the **Primary output from SimpleEditor** item in the **Application Folder** and open the menu **Action | Create Shortcut to Primary output from SimpleEditor**. Set the `Name` property of the generated shortcut to **Wrox Simple Editor**, and drag and drop this shortcut to the **User's Programs Menu**.

File Types Editor

If your application uses **custom file types**, and you want to register file extensions that should start up your application when the user double-clicks on the file, you can use the File Types Editor. This editor can be started with **View | Editor | File Types**.

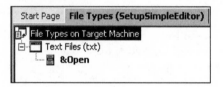

With the File Types Editor you can configure a file extension that should be handled from your application. The file extension has these properties:

Property	Description
Name	Here you should add a useful name describing the file type. This name is displayed in the File Types Editor and is also written to the Registry. The name should be unique. An example for `.doc` file types is `Word.Document.8`. It's not necessary to use a ProgID as in the Word example; a simple text like `wordhtmlfile` as used for the `.dochtml` file extension can also be used.
Command	With the `Command` property you can specify the executable that should be started when the user opens a file with this type.
Description	Here you can add a description.

Property	Description
Extensions	The file extension where your application should be registered.
	The file extension will be registered in a section of the registry.
Icon	Specify an icon to display it for the file extension.

Create Actions

After creating the file types in the File Types Editor you can add **actions**. The default action that is automatically added is Open. You can add additional actions like New and Print or whatever actions your program can do with files. With the actions the Arguments and Verb properties must be defined. The Arguments property specifies the argument that is passed to the program, which is registered for the file extension; for example "%1" means that the file name is passed to the application. The Verb property specifies the action that should occur. With a print action a /print can be added if supported by the application.

Let's add an action to our Simple Editor installation program. We want to register a file extension, so that the Simple Editor application can be used from Windows Explorer to open files with the extension .wroxtext. After this registration we can double-click on these files to open them, and the Simple Editor application will be started automatically.

Try it Out – Set the File Extension

1. Start the File Types Editor with View | Editor | File Types. Add a new file type using the menu Action | Add File Type with the following properties set. Because we don't want to change the ownership for Notepad of the .txt file extension, we are using the .wroxtext file extension.

Property	Value
(Name)	Wrox.SimpleEditor.Text
Command	Primary output from SimpleEditor
Description	Wrox Text Documents
Extensions	wroxtext

You can also set the Icon property to define an icon for the opening of files.

Leave the properties of the Open action with the default values, so that the file name is passed as an application argument.

Launch Condition Editor

With the **Launch Condition Editor** we can specify some requirements of the target system before the installation can take place. The Launch Condition Editor can be started by selecting the menu View | Editor | Launch Conditions.

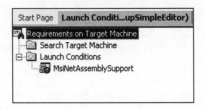

The editor has two sections to specify the requirements: Search Target Machine and Launch Conditions. With the first section we specify what specific file, or Registry key to search for, and the second section defines the error message if the search was not successful.

Let's look into some of the launch conditions that we can define using the Action

- ❑ With the **File Launch Condition** we can search for installed files on the target system.

- ❑ The **Registry Launch Condition** allows it to look for registry keys before the installation starts.

- ❑ The **Windows Installer Launch Condition** makes it possible to search for Windows Installer files.

- ❑ The **.NET Framework Launch Condition** checks if the .NET Framework is already installed on the target system.

- ❑ The **Internet Information Services Launch Condition** checks for an installed Internet Information Server. Of course you can also check for the version of this server.

By default, a .NET Framework Launch Condition is included, and its properties have been set to predefined values: `Condition` is set to MsiNetAssemblySupport and `Message` is set to [VSDNETMSG]. The property `MsiNetAssemblySupport` is set at installation time to `true` by Windows Installer 1.5 if the Common Language Runtime is installed on the system. The message [VSDNETMSG] displays the following error message to the user at installation time if the .NET runtime is not installed.

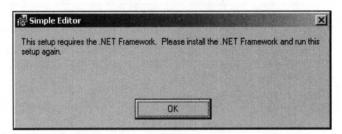

User Interface Editor

With the User Interface Editor we can define the dialogs that the user will see to configure the installation. Here we can inform the user about license agreements, ask for installation paths and other information to configure the application.

Try it Out – Start the User Interface Editor

1. Start the User Interface Editor by selecting View | Editor | User Interface. We use the User Interface Editor to set properties for predefined dialog boxes. You should see the following view with automatic generated dialogs and two installation modes:

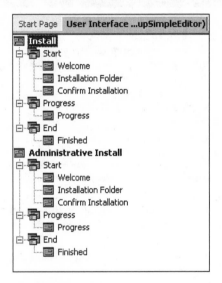

Install and Administrative Install

As can be seen in the above picture, we have two installation modes: Install and Administrative Install. The **Install** mode is the typical installation that is used to install the application on a target system. With an **Administrative Install** we can install an image of the application on a network share. A user can then install the application from the network.

Default Dialogs

In both installation modes we have three sequences where dialogs can be shown: Start, Progress, and End. Let's look at the default dialogs:

❑ The **Welcome** dialog displays a welcome message to the user. You can replace the default welcome text with your own message. The user can just cancel the installation or press the next button.

❑ With the second dialog, **Installation Folder**, the user can choose the folder where the application should be installed. If you add custom dialogs (we'll look at this in a moment) you have to add the dialogs before this one.

547

❑ The **Confirm Installation** dialog is the last dialog before the installation starts.

❑ The **Progress** dialog displays a progress control so that the user can see the progress of the installation.

❑ When installation is finished the **Finished** dialog shows up.

The default dialogs that we looked at will show up automatically at installation time, even if you never opened the User Interface Editor in the solution. But we should configure these dialogs so that useful messages for our application are displayed.

Try it Out – Configuring the Default Dialogs

1. Select the **Welcome** dialog. In the Properties window you can see three properties that can be changed for this dialog: `BannerBitmap`, `CopyrightWarning`, and `WelcomeText`. Select the `BannerBitmap` property by pressing (**Browse...**) in the combo box, and select the file `wroxsetuplogo.bmp` that we have placed in the folder `Application Folder\Setup`. This bitmap will show up on top of this dialog.

The default text for the property `CopyrightWarning` says:

```
WARNING: This computer program is protected by copyright law and international
treaties. Unauthorized duplication or distribution of this program, or any portion
of it, may result in severe civil or criminal penalties, and will be prosecuted to
the maximum extent possible under the law.
```

This text will show up in the Welcome dialog, too. Change this text if you want a stronger warning. The `WelcomeText` property defines more text that is displayed in the dialog – its default value is:

```
The installer will guide you through the steps required to install [ProductName]
on your computer.
```

You can change this text, too. The string `[ProductName]` will automatically be replaced with the property `ProductName` that we defined with the properties of the project.

2. Select the **Installation Folder** dialog. This dialog just has a single property: `BannerBitmap`. We will change the value of this property to the `wroxsetuplogo.bmp` file as we did with the `Welcome` dialog. Since each dialog can display a bitmap with this property, change this property in all the other dialogs too.

Additional Dialogs

With the Visual Studio .NET installer we cannot design a custom dialog and add it to the installation sequence. A more sophisticated tool like InstallShield or Wise for Windows is required to do this – but with the Visual Studio .NET installer we can add and customize many of the predefined dialogs in the Add Dialog screen.

By selecting the Start sequence in the User Interface Editor and by choosing the menu Action | Add Dialog, the Add Dialog is displayed as can be seen in the picture below. All these dialogs are configurable.

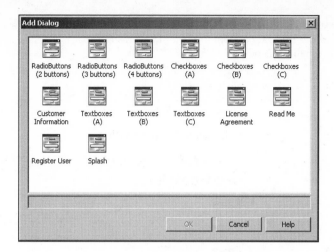

There are dialogs in which two, three, or four radio buttons show up, check box dialogs that show up to four check boxes, and text box dialogs that show up to four text boxes. We can configure these dialogs by setting their properties.

Let's have a quick discussion of some of the dialogs: the Customer Information dialog will ask the user for the name, company, and serial number. If you don't have a serial number with the product, you can hide the serial number by setting the ShowSerialNumber property to False. With the License Agreement dialog the user can accept a license before the installation starts. A license file is defined with the LicenseFile property. With the Register User dialog the user can press a Register Now button where a program defined with the Executable property will be started. The custom program can send the data to an FTP server, or do the data transfer by e-mail. The Splash dialog just displays a splash screen before the installation starts with a bitmap specified by the SplashBitmap property.

Try it Out – Adding Other Dialogs

1. Add a Read Me, a License Agreement, and a Checkboxes (A) dialog to the Start sequence with the menu Action | Add Dialog. Define the order in the start sequence by dragging and dropping in this way:

Welcome – Read Me – License Agreement – Checkboxes (A) - Installation Folder – Confirm Installation.

> **All customizable dialogs must be put before the Installation Folder dialog; otherwise you will get a warning when building the installation package.**

2. We have to configure the BannerBitmap property for all these dialogs as we did earlier. For the Read Me dialog, set the ReadmeFile property to readme.rtf, the file we have added earlier to Application Folder\Setup.

3. For the License Agreement dialog set the LicenseFile property to license.rtf.

4. The Checkboxes (A) dialog should be used to ask the user if the file demo.wroxtext (that we have put into the User's Desktop) should be installed or not. Change the properties of this dialog according to this table:

Property	Values
BannerText	Optional Files
BodyText	Installation of optional files
Checkbox1Label	Do you want a demo file put on to the desktop?
Checkbox1Property	CHECKBOXDEMO
Checkbox2Visible	False
Checkbox3Visible	False
Checkbox4Visible	False

The Checkbox1Property property is set to the same value as the Condition property of the file demo.wroxtext – we set this Condition value earlier when we added the file to package using the File System Editor. If the user checks this check box, the value of CHECKBOXDEMO will be true, and the file will be installed; if the check box is not checked, the value will be false, and the file will not be installed.

The CheckboxXVisible property of the other check boxes is set to False, because we only need a single check box.

Building the Project

Now you can start the build of the installer project.

Try it out – Build the Project

1. To create the Microsoft Installer Package, right-click on the SetupSimpleEditor project and select Build. With a successful build you will find the following files in the Debug or Release directory (depending on your build settings):

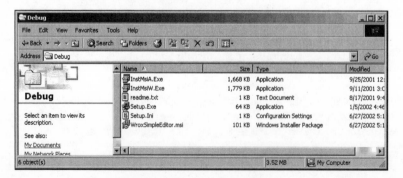

Setup.exe will start the installation of the MSI database file WroxSimpleEditor.msi. All files that we have added to the installer project (with one exception) are merged and compressed into the MSI file because we have set the project properties to **Package Files in Setup File**. The exception to this is the file readme.txt. With this file we changed the PackageAs property so that it can be read immediately before installation of the application. The Windows Installer itself is represented in the files InstMsiA.exe and InstMsiW.exe; an ASCII version for Windows 98/ME and a Unicode version for Windows NT4/2000/XP.

Installation

We can now start the installation of our Simple Editor application. You can double-click on the Setup.exe file, or select the file WroxSimpleEditor.msi and right-click to open the context menu and choose the **Install** option. You can also start the installation from within Visual Studio .NET by right-clicking on the opened installation project in the Solution Explorer and selecting **Install**:

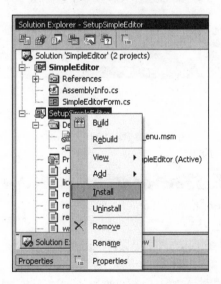

As you can see in the following screenshots, all the dialogs have the Wrox logo, and the inserted ReadMe and License Agreement dialogs show up with the configured files.

Let's walk through the installation sequence.

Welcome

The first dialog to be seen is the Welcome dialog. Here in this dialog we can see the Wrox logo that was inserted by setting the value of the BannerBitmap property. The text that can be seen is defined with the WelcomeText and CopyrightWarning properties. The title of this dialog results in the ProductName property that we have set with the project properties.

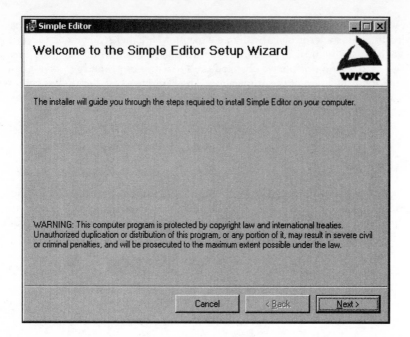

Read Me

After pressing the Next button we can see the Read Me dialog that we configured. It shows the rich text file readme.rtf that was configured by setting the ReadmeFile property.

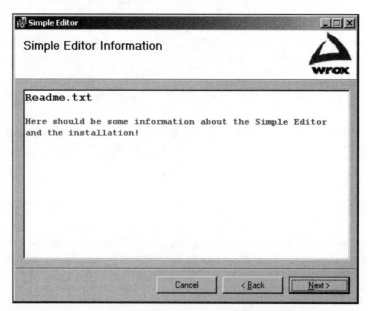

License Agreement

The third dialog to show up is the license agreement. Here we have only configured the `BannerBitmap` and the `LicenseFile` properties. The radio buttons to agree to the license are added automatically. As you can see in the picture below, the **Next** button stays disabled until the **I agree** button is pressed. This functionality is automatic with this dialog.

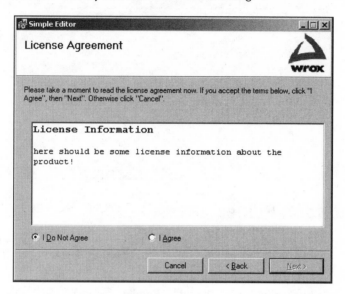

Optional Files

Agreeing to the license information and pressing the **Next** button displays the **Checkboxes (A)** dialog. With this dialog, we should have not only the bitmap, but also the text for the `BannerText`, `BodyText`, and `Checkbox1Label` properties. All the other check boxes are not visible because the specific `CheckboxVisible` property was set to `False`.

Selecting the check box will install the file `demo.wroxtext` to the desktop.

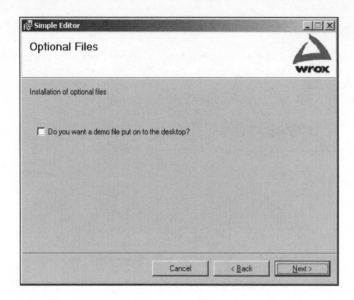

Select Installation Folder

With this dialog the user can select the path where the application should be installed. This dialog just allowed us to set the property BannerBitmap. The default path shown is [Program Files]\[Manufacturer]\[Product Name].

The user can also select if the application should be installed for everyone or just for the currently logged on user. Depending on this option the shortcut to the program file will be put in the user specific or in the All Users directory.

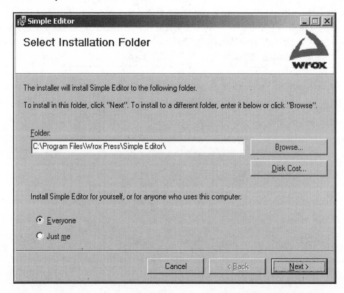

Disk Cost

Pressing the Disk Cost button opens up a dialog that is shown below where the disk space of all disks is displayed, and the required space for every disk is calculated. This helps the user to choose a disk where the application should be installed.

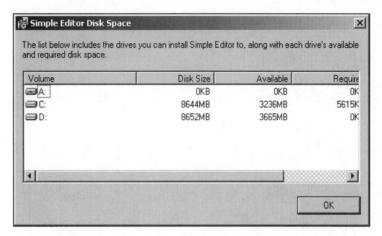

Confirm Installation

The next dialog is the last one before the installation finally starts. No more questions are asked, this is just the last place where we can cancel the installation before it really starts.

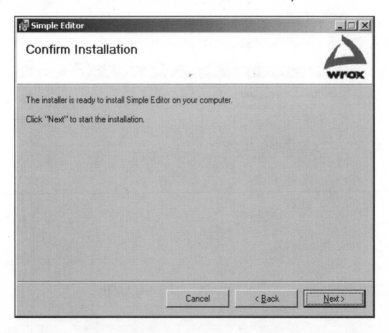

Progress

The Progress dialog shows a progress control during installation to keep the user informed that the installation is going on and to give a rough idea of how long the installation will last. Because our editor is a small program, this dialog finishes very fast.

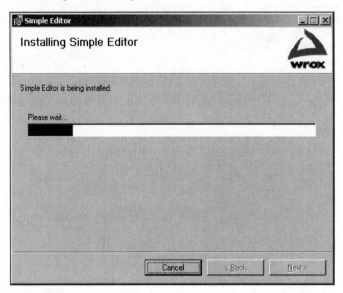

Installation Complete

With a successful installation we see the last dialog: Installation Complete.

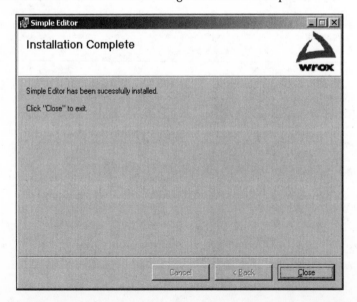

Running the Application

The Editor can be started from the menu entry Start | Programs | Wrox Simple Editor as can be seen in the following picture.

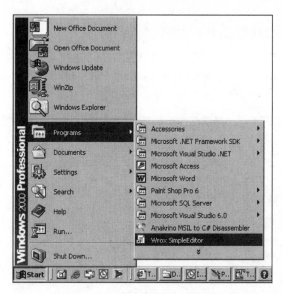

Because we registered a file extension there's another way to start the application: double-click on a file with the file extension `.wroxtext`. If you selected the check box with the Optional Files dialog you can find `demo.wroxtext` on your desktop, otherwise you can create such a file with the now installed Wrox Simple Editor tool.

Self-Repair

So the Simple Editor is installed. Now let's assume a file gets corrupted. In order to do this exercise I'm deleting the file `C:\Program Files\Wrox Press\Simple Editor\SimpleEditor.exe`. Now we could select the context menu of the `msi` file and select the Repair menu. You can try a much cooler way instead: double-click on a `.wroxtext` file, or start the editor with Start | Programs | Wrox Simple Editor. The repair is automatically started, because a mandatory file is missing! You will just see the dialog below when the repair takes place if the setup files can be found at the same place where the installation was done.

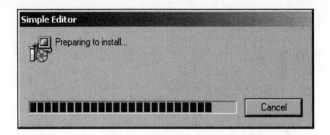

If you installed the files from a CD, or the installation directory is not available anymore, another dialog pops up to ask for the installation file:

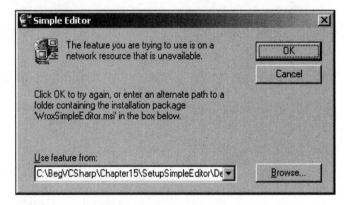

Uninstall

If you really want to get rid of the Wrox Simple Editor you can use Add / Remove Programs from the Control Panel and press the Remove button for the Simple Editor.

Summary

In this chapter we have covered the functionality of the Windows Installer and how to create Installer packages using Visual Studio .NET. The Windows Installer makes it easy to do standardized installations, uninstalls, and repairs.

The Visual Studio .NET Installer is restricted in functionality and doesn't propose all functionality of the Windows Installer, but for many applications the features of the Visual Studio .NET Installer are more than enough. We have a lot of Editors where the generated Windows Installer file can be configured. With the File System Editor we specify all files and shortcuts, the Launch Conditions Editor can define some mandatory prerequisites, the File Types Editor is used to register file extensions for applications, and the User Interface Editor makes it easy to adapt the dialogs used for the installation.

When developing Windows Applications, the best way is to build a Windows Installer package, and with Visual Studio .NET this can easily be done.

Getting At Your Data

Despite the title of this chapter, we've actually been manipulating data in C# since Chapter 3, when we introduced variables and literals. After all, what is a string or a number other than a piece of data? However, so far we've just been using data that's been hard-coded into our programs. If this data changes, we have to change the program itself. What we're going to look at in this chapter is how we can access data held outside your program, such as the data held in a database.

The heart of any business application is data. Think of all the data any company holds describing employee details, such as salary and job descriptions, customer details, and so on. Most of the programs you write will access external data like this in some way, whether it's a simple data-entry application that allows personnel staff to enter and edit employee details in their database, or a full-blown e-commerce web site that reads the product catalog and customer details such as credit card numbers and shipping addresses from a back-end database.

The .NET Framework provides a special set of objects within the System.Data namespace that provides us with relatively easy access to all of this data. Collectively these objects are known as ADO.NET (the name derives from an earlier data access technology called ActiveX Data Objects). We will look at ADO.NET in detail in the next chapter, but in this chapter we'll look at how we can get Visual Studio.NET to do almost all of the hard work for us. We'll use VS's powerful features to write a simple data-driven application. This will allow us to look at the most important concepts for working with databases, without having to worry too much about the code. For those of you that love to write pages upon pages of code to get even the simplest task done, this chapter is not for you! For those of you that enjoy getting your job done well but quickly in order to have a life, welcome!

Data Access in VS

ADO.NET is a large enough topic to fill a book on its own, and while we will look at it in more detail in the next chapter, we will cover enough of the basics here to get you up and running very quickly. ADO.NET builds on and can make use of earlier data access technologies, so we'll start off by reviewing the situation before the arrival of .NET.

A (Very) Brief History of Data Access

When the first database systems, such as Oracle and IBM's DB2, were written, any developers who wanted their programs to access the data in them needed to use sets of functions that were specific to that database system. Each system had its own library of functions, such as the Oracle Call Interface (OCI) for Oracle, or DBLib for Sybase's SQL Server (later bought by Microsoft). This allowed the programs to have fast access to the data, because their programs communicated directly with the database. However, it meant that programmers had to be familiar with a different library for every database they worked with, so the task of writing data-driven applications was very complicated. It also meant that if a company changed the database system they used, their applications had to be completely rewritten.

This problem was solved by **Open Database Connectivity** (ODBC). ODBC was developed by Microsoft, in collaboration with other companies, in the early 1990s. ODBC provided a common set of functions that developers could use against any database system. These functions were translated into database-specific function calls by drivers for that specific database system.

This solved the main problems of the proprietary database libraries – developers only needed to know how to use one set of functions (the ODBC functions), and if a company changed their database system, all they needed to change in their applications was the code to connect to the database. However, there was still one problem. While the "paperless office" is still largely a myth, companies do have a vast amount of electronic data stored in a whole variety of places – e-mails, web pages, Project 2000 files, and so on. ODBC was fine for accessing data in traditional databases, but couldn't access other types of data, which aren't stored in nice neat columns and rows, and don't necessarily have a coherent structure at all.

The answer to this problem was provided by **OLE DB**. OLE DB works in a similar way to ODBC, providing a layer of abstraction between the database and applications that need access to the data. Client applications communicate with the data source, which can be a traditional database or any other place where data is held, through an OLE DB provider for that data source. Data from any source is exposed to the application in table format – just as if it came from a database. And because OLE DB allowed access to data exposed by the existing ODBC drivers, it could be used to access all the databases supported by ODBC. As we'll see shortly, ADO.NET supports both OLE DB and ODBC in a very similar way.

The last "legacy" data access technology we'll mention is ActiveX Data Objects (ADO). ADO is simply a thin layer, which sits on top of OLE DB, and allows programs written in high-level languages such as Visual Basic to access OLE DB data.

An Introduction to ADO.NET

Although it derives its name from ADO, ADO.NET is actually a very different beast. In terms of its architecture, it's actually more similar to OLE DB. ADO.NET consists of a set of objects in the `System.Data` namespace which communicate with the database via **.NET data providers**. The ADO.NET objects allow us to connect to the database, to retrieve, edit, delete and insert data in the database, and to manipulate the data within our program.

.NET Data Providers

There are two fundamental parts to ADO.NET – the `DataSet` and the .NET data provider. The `DataSet` is used to hold a set of data within our program in table format; it doesn't care where that data actually comes from. The data provider consists of a number of data source-specific components that allow us to connect to and communicate with individual data sources. Each data provider resides in its own namespace within the `System.Data` namespace. At the time of writing, there are three data providers available:

❑   The data provider for SQL Server. This resides in the `System.Data.SqlClient` namespace, and is used to connect to SQL Server 7.0 or greater and MSDE databases (MSDE is a cut-down version of SQL Server). The SQL Server provider is shipped as part of the .NET Framework. If you need to connect to a SQL Server 6.5 or earlier database, you will need to use the OLE DB provider.

❑   The data provider for OLE DB. This is used to connect to data sources through OLE DB and resides in the `System.Data.OleDb` namespace. Like the SQL Server provider, it also ships with the .NET Framework. The OLE DB provider cannot be used to connect to databases through ODBC drivers.

❑   The data provider for ODBC. The ODBC provider can be used to connect to databases which have ODBC drivers. The ODBC data provider namespace is `Microsoft.Data.Odbc`. It can be downloaded from Microsoft's web site, at:

```
http://msdn.microsoft.com/downloads/default.asp?URL=/downloads/sample.asp?url=/MSD
N-FILES/027/001/668/msdncompositedoc.xml
```

Although at the moment we can only connect directly to SQL Server and MSDE databases, the number of data providers available is expected to rise as more people move to .NET. In particular, a data provider for Oracle can't be too far away. For the moment, though, if you want to connect to any other data source, you will need to go through either OLE DB or ODBC.

The data providers consist of four main components:

Component Name	Description
Connection	Used to connect to a database or other data source.
Command	Used to retrieve, edit, delete, or insert data in the database.
DataReader	Provides a stream of data from the data source. This data can only be read (it can't be modified), and we can only move forwards through the data.
DataAdapter	Used to fill a `DataSet` with data from the data source, and to update the data source with any changes made in the `DataSet`.

However, when we use these objects, we don't actually refer to them by these names. Each of the providers has its own implementation of these classes. The provider-specific classes implement the same interfaces, so they all have the same methods and properties (although there's nothing to stop a specific class adding other methods and properties of its own). For example, if we want to create a connection to a SQL Server database, then we use a `SqlConnection` object, or if we want a connection to an ODBC data source, we use an `OdbcConnection`. Both of these objects implement `IDbConnection`, so they both have the same set of methods and properties.

The DataSet

Once we've created a connection to the database and retrieved data from it, we can manipulate that data within our program using a `DataSet` object. The `DataSet` contains a collection of `DataTable` objects, and any relations between them. A `DataTable` – as its name suggests – stores data in a tabular format; that is, in columns and rows. Because the `DataSet` doesn't form part of the data provider (there's only one type of `DataSet` object, regardless of whether the data comes from SQL Server, or an OLE DB data source), the `DataSet` doesn't maintain a connection to the data source. This means that when we manipulate data in a `DataSet`, we're just working with a copy of the data in memory on the local machine. This eases the strain on the database server and on the network, because we only connect to the data source when we first get the data, and when we've finished editing it and want to upload our changes back to the database.

However, with the advantages of a disconnected architecture there also come problems. When in a completely disconnected environment, the user is not notified of data changes made by other users. Therefore, if we use the data we see on the screen to make decisions, we may have out-of-date information if other users are editing the same data.

But for now, that's enough theory – we'll talk more about ADO.NET and the `DataSet` and its parts in the next chapter.

Fire up Visual Studio .NET, create a new Windows application in the `C:\BegVCSharp\Chapter18` directory, name it `GettingData`, and let's connect to a database!

Viewing Data in VS

First of all, though, we'll need a database to connect to! For this example, we'll connect to the SQL Server `Northwind` database. However, don't worry if you haven't got SQL Server! The Microsoft Data Engine (MSDE), which is shipped with both Visual Studio .NET and Visual C# Standard Edition, is nothing other than a cut-down version of the SQL Server engine, and you can access that exactly as if you had the full version of SQL Server installed. MSDE isn't installed by default, but if you haven't already got it on your system, there's a step-by-step guide to installing it and importing the `Northwind` database in Appendix B.

> If you are using Visual C# Standard Edition, then you will find that its Server Explorer allows access only to MSDE or Access databases – you are not able to connect to a SQL Server database.

Connecting to the Database

Once VS.NET is open, open up Server Explorer by hovering the mouse pointer over the tab on the right-hand side of the screen (by default, the **Server Explorer** tab is just above the **Toolbox** tab). If Server Explorer isn't visible, you can select it from **View | Server Explorer**. This window shows the services available on the local machine, and also those on any other accessible machines. What interests us, though, is the top node in the Server Explorer treeview, because this allows us to add data connections to our project:

Right-click on this **Data Connections** node, and select **Add Connection...** This will bring up the **Data Link Properties** window:

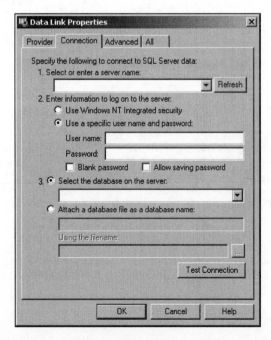

By default, the connection provider assumes that we will be accessing a SQL Server database, so all the settings displayed are for the OLE DB Provider for SQL Server. For this example, we will be accessing the Northwind sample database in MSDE or SQL Server, so we want to leave these settings. However, if you want to use another database system, you will need to move back to the Provider tab, and select the appropriate provider for your database:

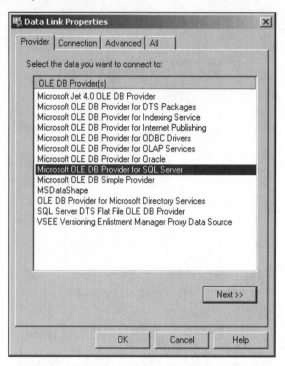

Clicking on the Provider tab will bring up a list of the providers installed on your system. However, we want to use the default SQL Server provider, so just click on Next >>.

> **In this chapter, we are using SQL Server/MSDE and the Northwind sample database. However, if you want to use another database, simply select the appropriate OLE DB provider for your database system (for example, the Microsoft Jet provider to connect to an Access database). Do not, however, confuse this with the .NET data providers. Data Link doesn't let us choose a .NET data provider, so we have to use the data provider for OLE DB, even with SQL Server. However, VS will recognize that it is connecting to a SQL Server database, and create a SqlConnection object for us.**

Clicking on the Next >> button brings us back to the Connection tab. Here we need to fill out all the information VS needs to connect to our database. First of all, in the top text box, either type the name of the server where SQL Server or MSDE is installed, or select the server name from the drop-down list.

Next, you need to specify the user account you want to use to connect to the database. If you select **Use Windows NT Integrated Security**, VS will attempt to connect to the database with the same user account that you used to log onto Windows. If you use a different username and password to connect to your SQL Server, select the next option (**Use a specific username and password**), and enter them in the appropriate boxes. The default user account installed with both MSDE and SQL Server has the username sa, and a blank password.

Finally, select the Northwind database from the **Select the database on the server** drop-down list. If you're using MSDE and Northwind doesn't appear in the list, please see Appendix B for details on how to import the database.

When you've finished entering this information, click on the **Test Connection** button. Hopefully, you will now see a dialog box saying that the connection succeeded:

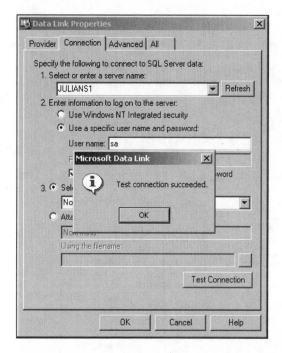

Congratulations, you have just successfully added your first ADO.NET database connection! You can now see it nested under the **Data Connections** section of the **Server Explorer**:

The Database Diagrams feature is only available in the Visual Studio .NET Enterprise Architect edition

We now have access to the database and all the data in it, without even leaving VS! Let's have a look at this data, so we can see how it's structured. This will help us once we come to write code to access the data in the next chapter.

Database Tables and Relationships

In Server Explorer, open up the Tables node underneath the connection we've just added. You should now see a list of the tables in the database:

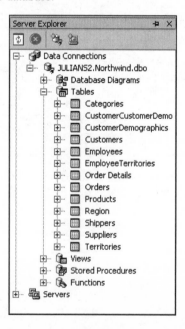

Relational databases such as SQL Server and Oracle store data within a series of related tables. These tables consist of rows and columns; each row represents a record within the database, and the columns represent the individual fields for each record. To see a visual representation of this, right-click on the Customers node in Server Explorer, and select Retrieve Data from Table. VS will now load and display the data from the Customers table in the Northwind database:

CustomerID	CompanyName	ContactName	ContactTitle	Address
ALFKI	Alfreds Futterkiste	Maria Anders	Sales Representative	Obere Str. 57
ANATR	Ana Trujillo Emparedados y helados	Ana Trujillo	Owner	Avda. de la Cor
ANTON	Antonio Moreno Taquería	Antonio Moreno	Owner	Mataderos 231
AROUT	Around the Horn	Thomas Hardy	Sales Representative	120 Hanover Sc
BERGS	Berglunds snabbköp	Christina Berglund	Order Administrator	Berguvsvägen
BLAUS	Blauer See Delikatessen	Hanna Moos	Sales Representative	Forsterstr. 57
BLONP	Blondel père et fils	Frédérique Citeaux	Marketing Manager	24, place Klébe
BOLID	Bólido Comidas preparadas	Martín Sommer	Owner	C/ Araquil, 67
BONAP	Bon app'	Laurence Lebihan	Owner	12, rue des Bou
BOTTM	Bottom-Dollar Markets	Elizabeth Lincoln	Accounting Manager	23 Tsawassen E
BSBEV	B's Beverages	Victoria Ashworth	Sales Representative	Fauntleroy Circ
CACTU	Cactus Comidas para llevar	Patricio Simpson	Sales Agent	Cerrito 333
CENTC	Centro comercial Moctezuma	Francisco Chang	Marketing Manager	Sierras de Gran
CHOPS	Chop-suey Chinese	Yang Wang	Owner	Hauptstr. 29
COMMI	Comércio Mineiro	Pedro Afonso	Sales Associate	Av. dos Lusíada
CONSH	Consolidated Holdings	Elizabeth Brown	Sales Representative	Berkeley Garde
DRACD	Drachenblut Delikatessen	Sven Ottlieb	Order Administrator	Walserweg 21

The Northwind sample database contains the data for a fictional food wholesaler that supplies various restaurants and food shops. The Customers table contains the details of each of these customers. Each row in this table represents a specific company that Northwind supplies, and each column contains a specific piece of data about the company, such as the company's name, its address, and the name of Northwind's contact in the company.

Each row in the table is distinguished by a unique five-character ID code, which is stored in the CustomerID field. This distinguishing field is known as the **primary key**, and is vital for relating the Customers table to the other tables in the database. To see how this works, right-click on the Orders node, and again select Retrieve Data from Table:

OrderID	CustomerID	EmployeeID	OrderDate	RequiredDate	ShippedDate
10330	LILAS	3	16/11/1994	14/12/1994	28/11/1994
10331	BONAP	9	16/11/1994	28/12/1994	21/11/1994
10332	MEREP	3	17/11/1994	29/12/1994	21/11/1994
10333	WARTH	5	18/11/1994	16/12/1994	25/11/1994
10334	VICTE	8	21/11/1994	19/12/1994	28/11/1994
10335	HUNGO	7	22/11/1994	20/12/1994	24/11/1994
10336	PRINI	7	23/11/1994	21/12/1994	25/11/1994
10337	FRANK	4	24/11/1994	22/12/1994	29/11/1994
10338	OLDWO	4	25/11/1994	23/12/1994	29/11/1994
10339	MEREP	2	28/11/1994	26/12/1994	05/12/1994
10340	BONAP	1	29/11/1994	27/12/1994	09/12/1994
10341	SIMOB	7	29/11/1994	27/12/1994	06/12/1994
10342	FRANK	4	30/11/1994	14/12/1994	05/12/1994
10343	LEHMS	4	01/12/1994	29/12/1994	07/12/1994
10344	WHITC	4	02/12/1994	30/12/1994	06/12/1994
10345	QUICK	2	05/12/1994	02/01/1995	12/12/1994
10346	RATTC	3	06/12/1994	17/01/1995	09/12/1994

569

This table represents the orders received by the Northwind company. Again, each row represents one order. Notice that this table also has a `CustomerID` field with the same five-character ID codes as in the `Customers` table. The values in this column serve as a pointer to the row in the `Customers` table where more information about the customer can be found. This type of column is known as a **foreign key**.

Visual Studio .NET (*not* the Visual C# Standard Edition) provides us with a tool for creating diagrammatic representations of these relationships between the primary and foreign keys in a database. To see this in action, right-click on the **Database Diagrams** node for our `Northwind` connection in **Server Explorer**, and select **New Diagram**. VS will now ask us which tables we want to add to the diagram:

Select all the tables in the list box, and click on **Add**. Then click on **Close** to get rid of the **Add Table** dialog.

VS will now create a diagram showing the tables and the relationships between them:

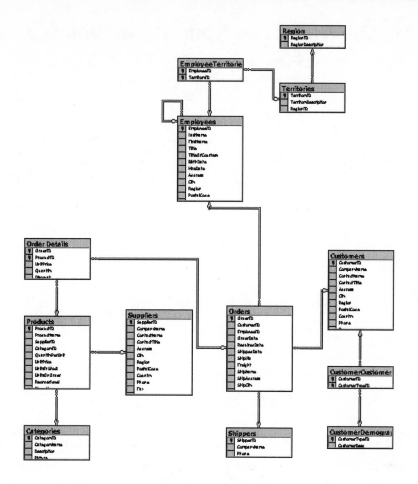

If you are using MSDE and imported the `Northwind` *database using the **Import and Export Data** wizard, the relationships won't show up in the diagram, as the wizard doesn't import primary and foreign key information.*

To view the entire diagram in one go, right-click on some blank space in the diagram and select **Zoom | To Fit** from the pop-up menu. However, you might not be able to read all the column names! The relationships are represented by lines between the tables, with symbols at both ends. A key symbol next to a table indicates that a primary key in that table relates to a foreign key in the table at the other end of the line. Conversely, an infinity sign indicates a foreign key that points to a primary key in the related table.

However, you didn't buy VS to use it as a front-end for your database, so let's see how we can use our connection from our C# programs!

Accessing the Database from an Application

Go back to the design view for the form in the `GettingData` project, add a `TextBox` and a `Label`, and change the properties of these objects as follows:

Control	Property	Value
Form	Text	GettingData
TextBox	Name	txtCustID
	Text	(blank)
Label	Name	lblCustID
	Text	Customer ID

The finished result should look something like this:

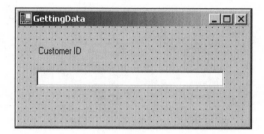

Now let's add a database connection to the project. Open the **Toolbox** window, and select the **Data** section. In this menu, we can see all the data-related controls that are available to us:

As you can see, there are separate `DataAdapter`, `Connection`, and `Command` objects for the SQL Server and OLE DB data providers. The SQL Server objects are prefixed with `Sql`, while the OLE DB objects begin with `OleDb`. In our case, as we are accessing a SQL Server database, we will be working with the SQL Server provider. Double-click on the `SqlDataAdapter`; this will open the **Data Adapter Configuration** wizard.

The Data Adapter Configuration Wizard

After a splash screen, the wizard will first ask which connection we would like to use:

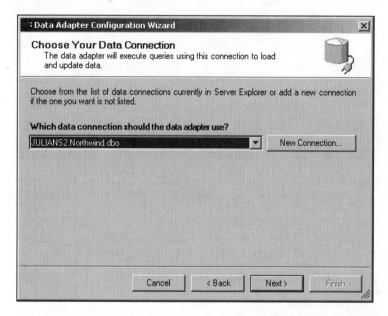

Since we only have one connection configured (the one we set up earlier to access the `Northwind` database), this is the only one available in our list. If we had not built one yet, we could also select **New Connection...** and add it here.

Click **Next >** to move on to the next screen, where the wizard asks us to choose how we want to select the data to retrieve:

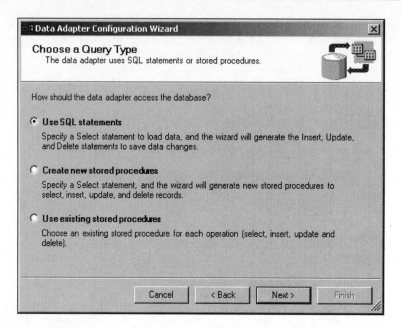

Select the Use SQL statements option for this example. This option allows us to use Structured Query Language (SQL) commands to choose the data we want to retrieve. SQL (not to be confused with SQL Server) is a special language used to communicate with relational databases, and we will look at this shortly.

Click on Next >; this takes us to a screen where we can type in the SQL statement we want to use to retrieve the data. However, we don't have to write the SQL statement ourselves – we'll get VS to do it for us!

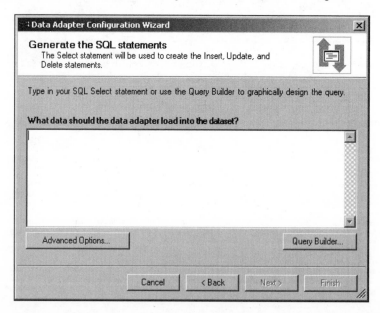

To get VS to build the SQL statement, click on the **Query Builder...** button:

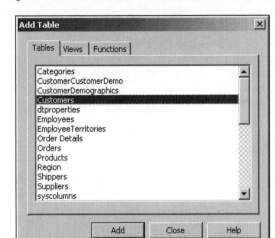

We're now presented with a list of the tables in the `Northwind` database. In the **Add Table** window, select **Customers**. Click on the **Add** button to add the `Customers` table to the Query Builder, and then click on **Close**. We now have the chance to select individual columns from the `Customers` table:

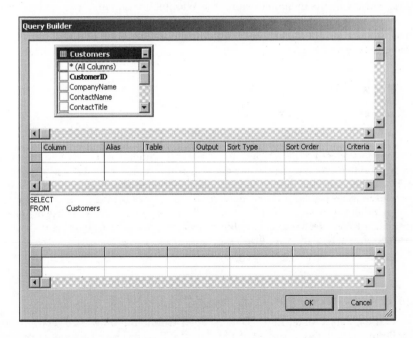

Structured Query Language

At this point, we need to say a little bit about SQL. As we've said, SQL (variously pronounced either "Sequel" or "ess-queue-ell", according to taste) is a language used for communicating with databases. SQL provides commands for retrieving data from the database, for inserting and deleting data, and for changing data. We'll have a look at the SQL language in more detail in the next chapter, but for now we'll look at the commands we use to retrieve data from the database.

SELECT statements take the form SELECT *column1, column2, ... columnx* FROM *table*; for example:

```
SELECT CompanyName, ContactName FROM Customers
```

This command will retrieve the value of the CompanyName and ContactName columns for every row in the Customers table.

We can also limit the number of rows to be retrieved by adding a WHERE clause to the SELECT statement. The WHERE clause allows us to specify a value for a specific column, and only rows with that value for that column will be retrieved from the database. For example:

```
SELECT CompanyName FROM Customers WHERE Region = 'WA'
```

This query retrieves the company names within the Washington region.

We can also use an asterisk instead of a list of column names. This will select all the columns in the table. For example:

```
SELECT * FROM Customers
```

This will select the entire Customers table.

> Be careful when selecting the "*" option. While this option is available and tempting, almost any database administrator or database programmer will advise against this. If you use *, all columns in the table at the time of execution are retrieved, not just the ones available when you built the project. If someone were to add fields to the table, your application would select them as well as the ones you intended for use in your application. All this additional data being transferred can have a significant performance impact on your application.

Generating the SQL Statement

Let's get back to the Query Builder in the Data Adapter Configuration wizard. For our example, we will select three columns – CompanyName, ContactName, and CustomerID. Select these columns in the **Customers** box in the Query Builder, and click on **OK**. The Query Builder will now create the SQL statement shown below for us:

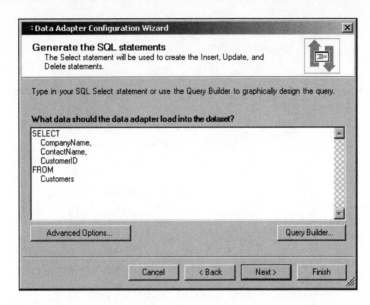

Click Next >, and the data adapter will now verify all settings and configure itself for further use within your application. When complete, click Finish. You will now see two objects added below your form, a `SqlDataAdapter` and a `SqlConnection`:

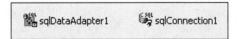

The data adapter contains the basic information for the data that we can expect to return from the database. Think of the data adapter as the bridge between the `DataSet` and the database. The data adapter, which is one of the components of the .NET data provider, is used to fill a `DataSet` with data from the database, and to send changes made in the `DataSet` back to the database. The `SqlConnection` object contains all the information that ADO.NET needs to connect to our database.

Now that we have a data adapter and a connection to the database, we will want to add a `DataSet`, so that we can work with the data in our application. Right-click on the `sqlDataAdapter1` we have just created and select Generate Dataset... In the resulting dialog, we can specify whether we want to associate our data adapter with an existing `DataSet`, or to create a new one:

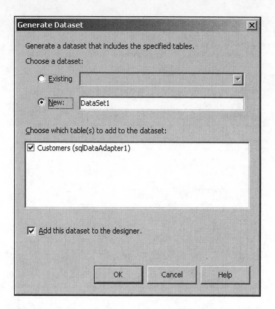

In our case, we will create a new DataSet. As we do not have an existing DataSet in our project, **New** will be selected by default. Change the name of the DataSet to be created to dsCustomers and click **OK**.

There is now a new DataSet object next to the connection and data adapter – notice that VS has rather sneakily appended a 1 to the name of the DataSet – this is because dsCustomers1 is the first instance of the dsCustomers DataSet. (VS also changes the first letter of the name to lower case if it isn't already, so watch out for these changes!)

What you may not have noticed is the addition to the **Solution Explorer**. If you look, a new file has been added to our project, named dsCustomers.xsd:

This file is the schema for our DataSet. The XSD (XML Schema Definition) schema is a document by which we can verify the structure of an XML document. XML is a text format used to represent data, which has become particularly important with the growth of the Internet. We will look at XML and at XSD schemas in the last section of this chapter. The schema is an important tool for ADO.NET because a DataSet object uses XML under the covers to organize and structure data. Automatically generated by Visual Studio, the schema file specifies the structure of the DataSet, each table, and all relationships between tables.

With our `DataSet` created, we can now bind the `TextBox` on the form to the data from the database. Click on the `txtCustID` `TextBox`, and scroll down the properties for the text box until you come to the **DataBindings** subsection. If you click on the **Text** section under **DataBindings**, you will notice a combo box containing `dsCustomers1` – clicking on this will reveal the tables it contains, and clicking on one of these tables will reveal its columns. By selecting any column within that combo box, you will be binding that column to the text box. This simply means that, as the `DataSet` is scrolled through, the value of that column will be visible in the text box. Any changes made by the user in the text box will also be made in the `DataSet`. However, because the `DataSet` doesn't maintain a permanent connection to the data source, the data source itself won't be updated until we specifically request this.

In this case, we want to bind the text box to the `CustomerID` column, so select `CustomerID` from the combo box:

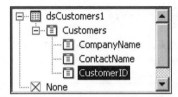

If you now save and run your project, you will see a blank text box. Why is that? Shouldn't the data we have labored over for the last few pages be ready at our disposal? The short answer is no. Bear in mind that so far we have only been defining the structure we can expect for the data coming from the table. At no point did we request any actual data. To retrieve some data, we will need to add some code to the example. (In fact, this will be one of only a handful of lines of code that we use in this chapter.)

We need to tell the data adapter to fill the `DataSet`. Double-click on the background of the form to go to the handler for the `Load` event of the form, and add the following code:

```
private void frmMain_Load(object sender, System.EventArgs e)
{
    // Fill the dataset with the data in the Northwind database,
    // Customers table
    this.sqlDataAdapter1.Fill(this.dsCustomers1,0,0,"Customers");
}
```

This line executes the `Fill()` method of the data adapter. The `Fill()` method fills a `DataTable` within the `DataSet` with data from the data source. The method used here takes four parameters (but note that the `Fill()` method has many overloads).

❑ The first parameter specifies the `DataSet` we want to fill, in this case our `dsCustomers1` `DataSet`.

❑ The second parameter specifies that it should start at the first record. (This parameter is zero-based.)

❑ The third parameter indicates how many records we want to be returned. If we place a zero here, all records will be returned.

❑ The fourth parameter specifies the name of the table the data originates from.

Now, save and run the application again. You should now see the first record's `CustomerID` value:

Seeing the Whole Picture

Seeing the first value is all well and good, but not very useful. I'm sure users would like to see the customer and contact names that correspond to the IDs as well, so let's add some more text boxes to this form:

Control	Property	Value
Label	Name	lblCustName
	Text	Customer Name
TextBox	Name	txtCustName
	Text	(blank)
	DataBindings/Text	dsCustomers1 – Customers.CompanyName
Label	Name	lblContactName
	Text	Contact Name
TextBox	Name	txtContactName
	Text	(blank)
	DataBindings/Text	dsCustomers1 – Customers.ContactName

The DataBindings properties for the two new text boxes are set in exactly the same way as our original `txtCustID` *TextBox – just select the appropriate column from the combo box next to the Text subsection underneath the DataBindings property of the* `TextBox`.

Your form should now look something like this:

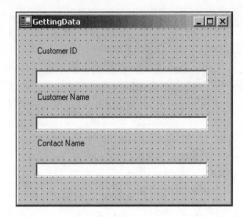

If you now run the application, you should see the additional information from the database. At this point you can add as many, or as few, fields as you want. In our case, we only included three columns from the table in our data adapter. If we wanted to display more, we could do so by right-clicking on the data adapter, and selecting the **Configure Data Adapter...** option. This brings up the same **Configure Data Adapter** wizard that we used earlier, and allows us to modify the number of columns we want to retrieve from the data source.

Navigating through the DataSet

So now we have the first record displayed, but the user wants to see the next record. I bet once they see that second they'll want to see the third. I swear, there's no appeasing them!

All joking aside, navigating through a DataSet is very important. Because every aspect of .NET is object-based, the DataSet is also an object with tables, columns, and rows as collections. As such, navigating through these objects is much like navigating through any collection – you increment a counter representing the current position in the collection.

Add the following objects to the form:

Control	Property	Value
Button	Name	cmdBack
	Text	Back
Button	Name	cmdNext
	Text	Next

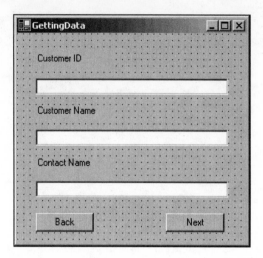

Double-click on the cmdNext button and add the following code to the Click event handler:

```
private void cmdNext_Click(object sender, System.EventArgs e)
{
    // Move to the next record in the DataSet, Customers table
    this.BindingContext[this.dsCustomers1,"Customers"].Position++;
}
```

This code uses the BindingContext of the form to change the current position. All Windows forms can have a BindingContext object, which manages the data-bound controls on the form. By incrementing the Position property returned from the BindingContext for the Customers table of our DataSet, we move to the next record in the table, and display new data in all the text boxes.

We can move backwards through the data in the same way. Type the following in the cmdBack click event:

```
private void cmdBack_Click(object sender, System.EventArgs e)
{
    // Move to the previous record in the dataset, customer table
    this.BindingContext[this.dsCustomers1,"Customers"].Position--;
}
```

Now when you execute the application, you are able to move backwards and forwards through the DataSet by clicking on the **Back** and **Next** buttons, and the text boxes are updated accordingly.

Adding Lists

It is just as easy to bind a ListBox to a DataSet as it is to bind a TextBox. Add the following object to the form:

Control	Property	Value
ListBox	Name	lstCustID
	DataSource	dsCustomers1.Customers
	DisplayMember	CustomerID

Seeing as how we will be using this list box for the CustomerIDs, go ahead and remove the Customer ID text box. Your form should look something like this:

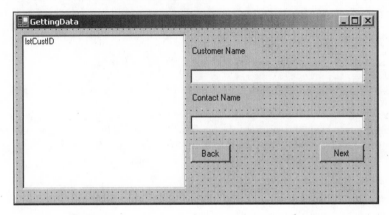

Now save and run the application.

You now have a list box that lists all the CustomerIDs in the DataSet. However, did you notice that selecting the items in the list box did not move the pointer in the BindingContext and therefore did not change the data in the text boxes? Working around this problem may sound daunting at first, but it is a good exercise in object-oriented problem solving.

Let's start with what we know. We know that the user can only select one item from the list box. We also know that object collections have indexes – numeric indexes. Each item in the list box is represented by an object, with the list box as a container, and each object has a corresponding index number. If the list box is populated in the same order as the records in the DataSet table, then we know that the index number for each record will match the index numbers for the list box items. We also know that to move the pointer in a DataSet, we need to specify the new position. Therefore, if we can pass the index for the selected list box item to the DataSet, we will be able to move the pointer and have that record displayed in the text boxes.

Happily, this does work, and (conveniently) the first event handler we get access to when we double-click on the list box while in design mode is for the SelectedIndexChanged event. This is the event that is raised when an item is selected. Double-click on the list box and add this code to the event handler:

```
private void lstCustID_SelectedIndexChanged(object sender,System.EventArgs e)
{
    // Pass the new index number to the bindingcontext
    this.BindingContext[this.dsCustomers1,"Customers"].Position =
        this.lstCustID.SelectedIndex;
}
```

Again, we set the `Position` property using the `BindingContext` object. This time, however, rather than specifying that we are incrementing or decrementing the current index number, we simply pass the index of the item selected in the list box.

This still leaves us with two more changes to make. The command buttons don't change the item selected in the list box. Although the pointer in the `DataSet` is moved, the list box does not reflect this move. In the same way that we moved the position in the `DataSet`, we can change the index of the selected item in the list box. Modify the click event of the `cmdNext` button as follows:

```
private void cmdNext_Click(object sender, System.EventArgs e)
{
    // Move to the next record in the DataSet, Customers table
    this.BindingContext[this.dsCustomers1,"Customers"].Position++;

    // Synchronize the pointers of the ListBox and DataSet
    this.lstCustID.SelectedIndex =
        this.BindingContext[this.dsCustomers1,"Customers"].Position;
}
```

The line we've just added sets the index of the selected item in the list box to the new position in the `DataSet`. In other words, we select the list box item that corresponds to the current record in the `DataSet`. We can make exactly the same change for the `cmdBack` button:

```
private void cmdBack_Click(object sender, System.EventArgs e)
{
    // Move to the previous record in the dataset, Customers table
    this.BindingContext[this.dsCustomers1,"Customers"].Position--;

    // Synchronize the pointers of the listbox and DataSet
    this.lstCustID.SelectedIndex =
        this.BindingContext[this.dsCustomers1,"Customers"].Position;
}
```

Now that we have fixed the user interface, run the project and give it a shot:

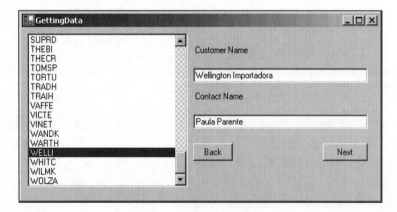

Adding a DataGrid

There is, however, one last thing we can add. Although not typically added to a form that is as complete as ours, the DataGrid is a fast and convenient object that can be added to Windows forms to display data and even provide a user interface for changes.

Add the following DataGrid to the form:

Control	Property	Value
DataGrid	Name	dgCustomers
	DataSource	dsCustomers1.Customers

Your form should now look something like this:

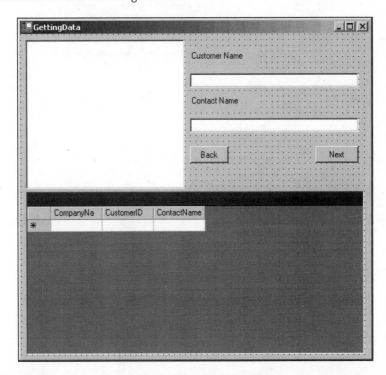

The only additional change we need to make to implement data binding with a DataGrid is to set its DataSource property – in this case to point to dsCustomers1.Customers. For this example, no other properties need to be modified. Of course, if you're using a DataGrid without any other bound controls, you'll still need to configure the connection and DataSet as we did earlier in the chapter, and you'll also need to populate the DataSet by calling the Fill() method of the relevant data adapter.

Save and run the application. Your DataGrid should be populated with the entire table contents.

Formatting the DataGrid

You can even change the appearance of the DataGrid to make your application look more polished. The easiest way to do this is simply to apply one of the many templates built into the object. For example, if you do not like the basic blue and gray, you can modify the template; begin by right-clicking on the DataGrid and selecting Auto Format:

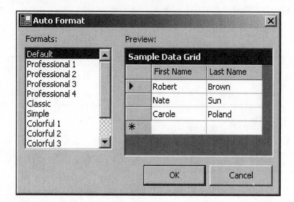

Within the Auto Format dialog, you can select any of the predefined templates to spruce up your DataGrid. However, if you'd prefer to alter the look manually, for example if you have a corporate color scheme you would like to match, you can adjust all the properties for the background colors or font styles.

For example, let's change the caption background color from blue to red. Scroll through the properties for the DataGrid until you find CaptionBackColor. If you click on the current value, you will see a list with three tabs: Custom, Web, and System:

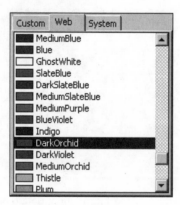

The System has predefined colors, supplied by Windows. For example, if you select the color Desktop from System, this color will change if the user alters the color of his desktop. This can sometimes cause unexpected side effects, such as poor legibility. Therefore, be careful when you alter these values. For now, we'll select the DarkOrchid color on the Web tab. The color across the top of the grid will turn to this interesting shade of purple.

Updating the Database

So far, we can read the data from the database, and we can change it in the text boxes and the DataGrid, but that's not much use if we can't save the changes we make to the database itself. Therefore, we will quickly see how to update the data in the database with the data in our DataSet. For this portion, we will use a little bit of code, instead of using the wizards. Add a button to the form named cmdUpdate, and set its Text to **Update**, so your form looks something like this:

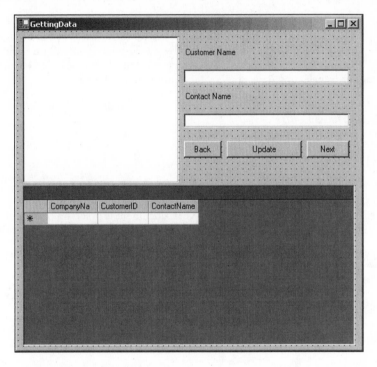

Now add the following code to the cmdUpdate_Click event:

```
private void cmdUpdate_Click(object sender, System.EventArgs e)
{
    // Pass the DataSet back to the database
    int rowsUpdated = this.sqlDataAdapter1.Update(this.dsCustomers1.Customers);
    MessageBox.Show(rowsUpdated.ToString() +
                    ((rowsUpdated==1) ? " row" : " rows") + " updated.");
}
```

Any changes made to the DataSet will be passed back to the database when our button is pressed with the Update() method. This method and its use for updating databases will be covered more in depth in the next chapter, but here we will mention that the Update() method returns an int which represents the number of rows updated, and in our code above we display this number in a message box, making use of the ternary operator that we first saw in Chapter 4 to ensure that our report is grammatically correct – if only one row is returned, (rowsUpdated==1) " row" is displayed, otherwise " rows" is displayed.

XML

So far we've been concentrating solely on relational databases, but before we leave this chapter, we must say something about one other data format – **Extensible Markup Language** (**XML**). XML is a way of storing data in a simple text format, which means that it can be read by pretty well any computer. As we shall see in some of the later chapters about web programming, this makes it a perfect format for transferring data over the Internet. It's even not too difficult for humans to read!

The ins and outs of XML can be very complicated, so we won't look at every single detail here. However, the basic format is very simple, and most of the time you won't require a detailed knowledge of XML, as VS will normally take care of most of the work for you – you will rarely have to write an XML document by hand. Having said that, XML is hugely important in the .NET world, as it's used as the default format for transferring data, so it's vital to understand the basics.

> *If you need a fuller understanding of XML, please check out "Beginning XML 2nd Edition", (Wrox Press, ISBN 1-86100-559-8).*

XML Documents

A complete set of data in XML is known as an **XML document**. An XML document could be a physical file on your computer, or just a string in memory. However, it has to be complete in itself, and must obey certain rules (we'll see what these are shortly). An XML document is made up of a number of different parts. The most important of these are **XML elements**, which contain the actual data of the document.

XML Elements

XML elements consist of an opening tag (the name of the element enclosed in angled brackets, such as `<myElement>`), the data within the element, and a closing tag (the same as the opening tag, but with a forward slash after the opening bracket: `</myElement>`).

For example, we might define an element to hold the title of a book like this:

```
<book>Tristram Shandy</book>
```

If you already know some HTML, you might be thinking that this looks very similar – and you'd be right! In fact, HTML and XML share much of the same syntax. The big difference is that XML doesn't have any predefined elements – we choose the names of our own elements, so there's no limit to the number of elements we can have. The most important point to remember is that XML – despite its name – isn't actually a language at all. Rather, it's a standard for defining languages (known as **XML applications**). Each of these languages has its own distinct vocabulary – a specific set of elements that can be used in the document and the structure these elements are allowed to take. As we'll see shortly, we can explicitly limit the elements allowed in our XML document. Alternatively, we can allow any elements, and allow the program using the document to work out for itself what the structure is.

Element names are case-sensitive, so `<book>` and `<Book>` are counted as different elements. This means that if you attempt to close a `<book>` element using a closing tag that doesn't have identical casing (for example, `</BOOK>`), your XML document won't be legal. Programs that read XML documents and analyze them into their individual elements are known as **XML parsers**, and they will reject any document which contains illegal XML.

Elements can also contain other elements, so we could modify this `<book>` element to include the author as well as the title by adding two sub-elements:

```
<book>
    <title>Tristram Shandy</title>
    <author>Lawrence Sterne</author>
</book>
```

However, overlapping elements aren't allowed, so we *must* close all sub-elements before the closing tag of the parent element. This means, for example, that we can't do this:

```
<book>
    <title>Tristram Shandy
    <author>Lawrence Sterne
    </title></author>
</book>
```

This is illegal, because the `<author>` element is opened within the `<title>` element, but the closing `</title>` tag comes before the closing `</author>` tag.

There's one exception to the rule that all elements must have a closing element. It's possible to have "empty" elements, with no nested data or text. In this case, we can simply add the closing tag straight after the opening element, as above, or we can use a shorthand syntax, adding the slash of the closing element to the end of the opening element:

```
<book />
```

This is identical to the full syntax:

```
<book></book>
```

Attributes

As well as storing data within the body of the element, we can also store data within attributes, which are added within the opening tag of an element. Attributes are in the form:

```
name="value"
```

where the value of the attribute *must* be enclosed in either single or double quotes. For example:

```
<book title="Tristram Shandy"></book>
```

or:

```
<book title='Tristram Shandy'></book>
```

These are both legal, but this is not:

```
<book title=Tristram Shandy></book>
```

At this point, you may be wondering why we need both these ways of storing data in XML. What's the difference between:

```
<book>
   <title>Tristram Shandy</title>
</book>
```

And:

```
<book title="Tristram Shandy"></book>
```

The honest answer is that there isn't any earth-shatteringly fundamental difference between the two. There isn't really any big advantage in using either. Elements are a better choice if there's a possibility that you'll need to add more information about that piece of data later – you can always add a sub-element or an attribute to an element, but you can't do that for attributes. Arguably, elements are more readable and more elegant (but that's really a matter of personal taste). On the other hand, attributes consume less bandwidth if the document is sent over a network without compression (with compression there's not much difference), and are convenient for holding information which isn't essential to every user of the document. Probably the best advice is to use both, using whichever you're most comfortable with storing a particular item of data in. But there really are no hard and fast rules.

The XML Declaration

Besides elements and attributes, XML documents can contain a number of constituent parts (the individual parts of an XML document are known as **nodes** – so elements, the text within elements, and attributes are all nodes of the XML document). Many of these are only important if you really want to delve deeply into XML. However, there's one type of node that occurs in almost every XML document. This is the **XML Declaration**, and, if we include it, it *must* occur as the first node of the document.

The XML declaration is similar in format to an element, but has question marks inside the angled brackets. It always has the name xml, and it always has an attribute named version; currently, the only possible value for this is "1.0". The simplest possible form of the XML declaration is therefore like this:

```
<?xml version="1.0"?>
```

Optionally, it can also contain the attributes encoding (with a value indicating the character set that should be used to read the document, such as "UTF-16" to indicate that the document uses the 16-bit Unicode character set) and standalone (with the value "yes" or "no" to indicate whether or not the XML document depends on any other files). However, these attributes are not required, and you will probably normally include only the version attribute in your own XML files.

Structure of an XML Document

One of the most important things about XML is that it offers a way of structuring data that is very different to relational databases. As we've seen, most modern database systems store data in tables that are related to each other through values in individual columns. Each table stores data in rows and columns – each row represents a single record, and each column a particular item of data about that record. In contrast, XML data is structured hierarchically, a little like the folders and files in Windows Explorer. Each document *must* have a single **root element**, within which all elements and text data is contained. If there is more than one element at the top level of the document, the document will not be legal XML. However, we *can* include other XML nodes at the top level – notably the XML declaration. So this is a legal XML document:

```
<?xml version="1.0"?>
<books>
    <book>Tristram Shandy</book>
    <book>Moby Dick</book>
    <book>Ulysses</book>
</books>
```

But this isn't:

```
<?xml version="1.0"?>
<book>Tristram Shandy</book>
<book>Moby Dick</book>
<book>Ulysses</book>
```

Under this root element, we have a great deal of flexibility about how we structure the data. Unlike relational data, in which every row has the same number of columns, there's no restriction on the number of sub-elements an element can have. And, although XML documents are often structured in a similar way to relational data, with an element for each record, XML documents don't actually have to have any predefined structure at all. This makes XML far better suited than relational databases to store irregular data. For example, XML can be used to mark up a text document. The web markup language, HTML, although not strictly an XML application, is very closely related.

XML Namespaces

Just as everyone can define their own C# classes, everyone can define their own XML elements; and this gives rise to exactly the same problem – how do we know which elements belong to which vocabulary? If you noticed the title of this section, you will already have realized that this question is answered in a similar way. Just as we define namespaces to organize our C# types, we use XML namespaces to define our XML vocabularies. This allows us to include elements from a number of different vocabularies within a single XML document, without the risk of misinterpreting elements because (for example) two different vocabularies define a `<customer>` element.

XML namespaces can be quite complex, so we won't go into great detail here, but the basic syntax is simple. We associate specific elements or attributes with a specific namespace using a prefix, followed by a colon. For example, `<wrox:book>` represents a `<book>` element that resides in the `wrox` namespace. But how do we know what namespace `wrox` represents? For this approach to work, we need to be able to guarantee that every namespace is unique. The easiest way to do this is to map the prefixes to something that's already known to be unique. And this is exactly what happens: somewhere in our XML document we need to associate any namespace prefixes we use with a **Uniform Resource Identifier** (URI). URIs come in several flavors, but the most common type is simply a web address, such as "`http://www.wrox.com`".

To identify a prefix with a specific namespace, we use the `xmlns:<prefix>` attribute within an element, setting its value to the unique URI which identifies that namespace. The prefix can then be used anywhere within that element, including any nested child elements. For example:

```
<?xml version="1.0"?>
<books>
    <book xmlns:wrox="http://www.wrox.com">
        <wrox:title>Beginning C#</wrox:title>
        <wrox:author>Karli Watson</wrox:author>
    </book>
</books>
```

Here we can use the `wrox:` prefix with the `<title>` and `<author>` elements, because they are within the `<book>` element, where the prefix is defined. However, if we tried to add this prefix to the `<books>` element, the XML would be illegal, as the prefix isn't defined for this element.

We can also define a default namespace for an element using the `xmlns` attribute:

```
<?xml version="1.0"?>
<books>
    <book xmlns="http://www.wrox.com">
        <title>Beginning Visual C#</title>
        <author>Karli Watson</author>
        <html:img src="begvcsharp.gif"
                  xmlns:html="http://www.w3.org/1999/xhtml" />
    </book>
</books>
```

Here, we define the default namespace for our `<book>` element as "`http://www.wrox.com`". Everything within this element will therefore belong to this namespace, unless we explicitly request otherwise by adding a different namespace prefix, as we do for the `<img>` element (we set it to the namespace used by XML-compatible HTML documents).

Well-formed and Valid XML

We've been talking up till now about "legal" XML. In fact, XML distinguishes between two forms of "legality". Documents that obey all the rules required by the XML standard itself are said to be **well-formed**. If an XML document is not well-formed, parsers will be unable to interpret it correctly, and will reject the document. In order to be well-formed, a document must:

❑   Have one and only one root element

❑   Have closing tags for every element (except for the shorthand syntax mentioned above)

❑   Not have any overlapping elements – all child elements must be fully nested within the parent

❑   Have all attributes enclosed in quotes

This isn't a complete list, by any means, but it does highlight the most common pitfalls made by programmers who are new to XML.

However, XML documents can obey all these rules, and still not be **valid**. Remember that we said earlier that XML is not itself a language, but a standard for defining XML applications. Well-formed XML documents simply comply with the XML standard; in order to be valid, they also need to conform to any rules specified for the XML application. Not all parsers check whether documents are valid; those that do are said to be **validating parsers**. But in order to check whether a document adheres to the rules of the application, we first need a way of specifying what those are.

Validating XML Documents

XML supports two ways of defining which elements and attributes can be placed in a document and in what order – **Document Type Definitions** and **Schemas**. DTDs use a non-XML syntax inherited from the parent of XML, and are gradually being replaced by schemas. DTDs don't allow us to specify the data types of our elements and attributes, and so are relatively inflexible and not used that much in the context of the .NET Framework. Schemas, on the other hand, are – they do allow us to specify data types, and are written in an XML-compatible syntax. However, unfortunately schemas are very complex, and there are different formats for defining them – even within the .NET world!

Schemas

There are two separate formats for schemas supported by .NET – XML Schema Definition language (XSD), and XML-Data Reduced schemas (XDR). Schemas can be either included within our XML document, or kept in a separate file. These formats are mutually incompatible, and you really need to be very familiar with XML before you attempt to write one, so we won't go into great detail here. It is, however, useful to be able to recognize the main elements in a schema, so we will explain the basic principles. To do this, we'll look at sample XSD and XDR schemas for this simple XML document, which contains basic details about a couple of Wrox's C# books:

```
<?xml version="1.0"?>
<books>
    <book>
        <title>Beginning Visual C#</title>
        <author>Karli Watson</author>
        <code>7582</code>
    </book>
    <book>
        <title>Professional C# 2nd Edition</title>
        <author>Simon Robinson</author>
        <code>7043</code>
    </book>
</books>
```

XSD Schemas

Elements in XSD schemas must belong to the namespace
`"http://www.w3.org/2001/XMLSchema"`. If this namespace isn't included, the schema elements won't be recognized.

In order to associate our XML document with an XSD schema in another file, we need to add a
`schemalocation` element to the root element:

```
<?xml version="1.0"?>
<books schemalocation="file://C:\BegVCSharp\XML\books.xsd">
    ...
</books>
```

Let's have a quick look at an example XSD schema:

```
<schema xmlns="http://www.w3.org/2001/XMLSchema">
    <element name="books">
        <complexType>
            <choice maxOccurs="unbounded">
                <element name="book">
                    <complexType>
                        <sequence>
                            <element name="title" />
                            <element name="author" />
                            <element name="code" />
                        </sequence>
                    </complexType>
                </element>
            </choice>
            <attribute name="schemalocation" />
        </complexType>
    </element>
</schema>
```

The first thing to notice here is that we set the default namespace to the XSD namespace. This tells the parser that all the elements in the document belong to the schema. If we don't specify this namespace, the parser will think that the elements are just normal XML elements, and won't realize it needs to use them for validation.

The entire schema is contained within an element called <schema> (with a lower-case "s" – remember that case is important!). Each element which can occur within the document must be represented by an <element> element. This element has a name attribute which indicates the name of the element. If the element is to contain nested child elements, we must include the <element> tags for these within a <complexType> element. Inside this, we specify how the child elements must occur. For example, we use a <choice> element to specify that any selection of the child elements can occur, or <sequence> to specify that the child elements must appear in the same order as they are listed in the schema. If an element may appear more than once (as our <book> element does), we need to include a maxOccurs attribute within its parent element. Setting this to "unbounded" means that the element can occur as often as we like. Finally, any attributes must be represented by <attribute> elements, including our schemalocation attribute that tells the parser where to find the schema. We place this after the end of the list of child elements.

XDR Schemas

To attach an external XDR schema to an XML document, we specify a namespace for the document with the value `"x-schema:<schema_filename>"`:

```
<?xml version="1.0"?>
<books xmlns="x-schema:books.xdr">
   ...
</books>
```

The schema below is the XDR equivalent of the XSD schema we've just looked at. As you can see, it is very different:

```
<Schema xmlns="urn:schemas-microsoft-com:xml-data">
    <ElementType name="title" content="textOnly" />
    <ElementType name="author" content="textOnly" />
    <ElementType name="code" content="textOnly" />
    <ElementType name="book" content="eltOnly">
        <group order="seq">
            <element type="title" />
            <element type="author" />
            <element type="code" />
        </group>
    </ElementType>
    <ElementType name="books" content="eltOnly">
        <element type="book" />
    </ElementType>
</Schema>
```

Again we set the default namespace to tell the parser that all the elements in the document belong to the schema definition, this time to `"urn:schemas-microsoft-com:xml-data"`. Notice that (unlike XSD schemas) this is a proprietary format, so won't work at all with non-Microsoft products. In fact, XDR schemas are particularly useful when working with SQL Server, Microsoft's database server, as this has in-built support for XDR.

This time our root element is `<Schema>` with a *capital* "S". This root element again contains the entire schema definition (remember that XML documents must have a single root element). After this, though, there's a big difference – the elements that will appear in our document are defined *in reverse order*! The reason for this is that each element in the document is represented in the schema by an `<ElementType>` element, and this contains an `<element>` element (note the lower-case "e" here) for each child element. Within the `<element>` tags, we set the `type` attribute to point to an `<ElementType>` element – and this must already have been defined. If we want to restrict how child elements can appear, we can use a `<group>` element within the `<ElementType>`, and set its `order` attribute. In the case, we set it to `"seq"`, to specify that the elements occur in the same sequence as in the schema – just like the `<sequence>` tag in the XSD schema!

Try it Out – Creating an XML Document in VS

Now we've covered the basic theory behind XML, we can have a go at creating XML documents. Fortunately, VS does a lot of the hard work for us, and will even create an XSD schema based on our XML document, without us having to write a single line of code!

1. Open up VS and select File | New | File... from the menu (you don't need to have a project already open):

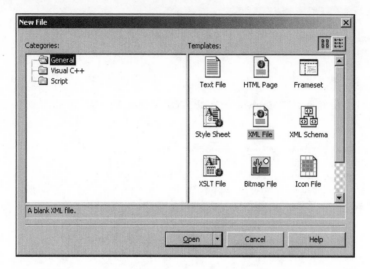

2. In the New File menu, select XML File and click on Open. VS will create a new XML document for us. Notice how VS adds the XML declaration, complete with an `encoding` attribute (it also colors the attributes and elements, but this won't show up well in black and white print):

```
<?xml version="1.0" encoding="utf-8" ?>
```

3. Save the file by pressing *Ctrl + S* or by selecting File | Save XMLFile1 from the menu. VS will ask you where to save the file and what to call the file; save it in the BegCSharp\Chapter18 folder as `GhostStories.xml`.

4. Move the cursor to the line underneath the XML declaration and type the text <stories>. Notice how VS automatically puts the end tag in as soon as we type the greater than sign to close the opening tag:

```
<?xml version="1.0" encoding="utf-8" ?>
<stories></stories>
```

5. Type in this XML file:

```
<?xml version="1.0" encoding="utf-8" ?>
<stories>
```

```
    <story>
       <title>A House in Aungier Street</title>
       <author>
          <name>Sheridan Le Fanu</name>
          <nationality>Irish</nationality>
       </author>
       <rating>eerie</rating>
    </story>
    <story>
       <title>The Signalman</title>
       <author>
          <name>Charles Dickens</name>
          <nationality>English</nationality>
       </author>
       <rating>atmospheric</rating>
    </story>
    <story>
       <title>The Turn of the Screw</title>
       <author>
          <name>Henry James</name>
          <nationality>American</nationality>
       </author>
       <rating>a bit dull</rating>
    </story>
</stories>
```

6. Right-click on the XML in the code window and select **View Data** from the pop-up menu. This gets VS to display the data from the XML file in a tabular format, as though it came from a relational database:

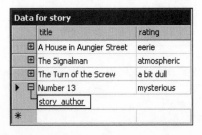

7. We can actually edit the data in this table, so we can modify our XML document here without even having to type the tags. Click on the box for the **title** column in the empty row at the bottom of the grid, and type **Number 13**. Now move to the rating box beside it, and type **mysterious**. This enters a new story, but we still need to enter the author. To do this, click on the plus sign next to the new row. This will bring up a link for the `<author>` element:

8. Click on this link, and another table will be displayed, where we can enter the name and nationality of the author. Enter MR James and English in the two columns (make sure you press *Enter* after typing the nationality, or the data will be lost):

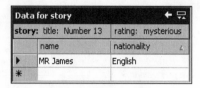

story:	title: Number 13	rating: mysterious
	name	nationality
▶	MR James	English
✳		

9. Now right-click on the table and select XML Source. A new `<story>` element should have been added just before the closing `</stories>` tag:

```
<story>
    <title>Number 13</title>
    <rating>mysterious</rating>
    <author>
        <name>MR James</name>
        <nationality>English</nationality>
    </author>
</story>
```

10. As its final party trick, we'll get VS to create an XSD schema for this XML document. Right-click in the code window and select Create Schema. VS will create an XSD schema, but it also creates a diagram to represent the schema visually:

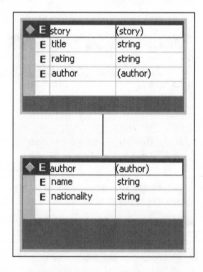

◆ E	story	(story)
E	title	string
E	rating	string
E	author	(author)

◆ E	author	(author)
E	name	string
E	nationality	string

11. To view the actual schema, right-click on the diagram and select View XML Source.

XML Auto-documentation in C#

So far, we've really only been looking at XML in a very abstract way, and you might be wondering, "But what's that got to do with C#? What can XML do for me?" We'll see a few more practical uses of XML throughout the remaining chapters of this book, but there's one use of XML that's very specifically to do with C#, and that we hinted at way back in Chapter 3. VS allows us to create special comments in our C# program files that we can extract and compile into a separate file. This file is – as you've probably guessed already – an XML document. This means that XML parsers (such as the one built into VS.NET) can easily extract data from this file. VS will format this data for display as web pages – so we get snazzy-looking documentation from just a few comments in the code!

VS automatically puts a few of these special comments in our code, so you've probably noticed them already. They start with three forward slashes (///), rather than the usual two. For example, VS adds these lines before the definition for the Class1 class that VS automatically adds to our project when we create a Windows or console application:

```
/// <summary>
/// Summary description for Class1.
/// </summary>
```

Hopefully, you'll instantly recognize <summary> and </summary> as the start and end tags of an XML element by now. To see how we go from this simple element to automatic documentation, let's add some comments to the Mandelbrot application from Chapter 4.

Try it Out – Documenting a Class

1. Open up the Ch04Ex06 project from Chapter 4.

2. Let's start by adding something a bit more useful to the <summary> element that VS has created for us for Class1. Change the text between the tags as follows (making sure you don't delete the three slashes at the start of the line):

```
/// <summary>
/// This class generates Mandelbrot sets in the console window!
/// </summary>
```

3. Next, let's add some documentation for the Main() method. Add a blank line before the start of the method definition, and type three slashes on it. See what happens next!

```
class Class1
{
    /// <summary>
    /// |
    /// </summary>
    /// <param name="args"></param>
    static void Main(string[] args)
    {
```

VS adds the XML tags for a `<summary>` element (the same as for `Class1`), but it also looks at the following line, realizes it's a method definition, and examines its parameters. It then creates a `<param>` element for each one (there's just the one parameter here – a string array called `args`, which we can use to read in data from the command line when a console application is executed). The name of the parameter is stored in a `name` attribute.

4. Add some descriptive text to the `<summary>` and `<param>` elements:

```
/// <summary>
/// This is the Main() method for Class1 -
/// this is where we call the Mandelbrot generator!
/// </summary>
/// <param name="args">
/// The args parameter is used to read in
/// arguments passed from the console window
/// </param>
```

(Incidentally, notice how VS knows you're in the middle of an autodoc comment, and when you reach the edge of the screen and press *Enter*, it automatically adds the three slashes on the new line!)

5. Now let's turn these comments into documentation! From the menu, select Tools | Build Comment Web Pages...:

If our VS solution contains more than one project, we can choose here whether to build the documentation for the entire solution, or just for particular projects. We only have one project in our solution, so leave Build for entire Solution selected. We can also select the directory where we want to save the generated web pages.

6. Click on OK to get VS to generate the web pages. Internet Explorer is integrated into VS, so when we click OK, VS will automatically display the main page for the solution documentation:

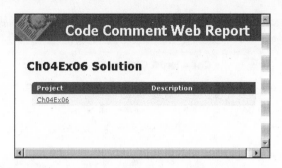

7. Click on the Ch04Ex06 link to open up the documentation for our project (the only one in the solution):

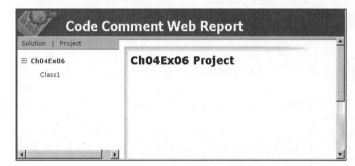

8. Open up the documentation for the Class1 class by clicking on the plus sign next to the Ch04Ex06 link, and then clicking on the Class1 link that appears underneath it:

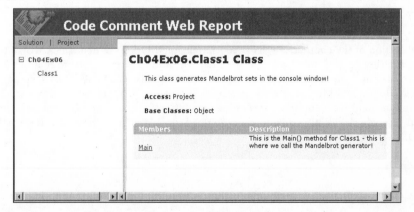

This is where we get to see the actual pages generated from our comments! The page for our documented class has the summary description we typed in and a list of the members of the class, together with their summaries. It also gives some information that VS worked out for itself – the full name of the class, including the namespace, the access level of the class, and the class from which it is derived.

9. Finally, click on the Main link to view the documentation for the Main() method. This page shows our description of the method and its parameter, and the full signature for the method:

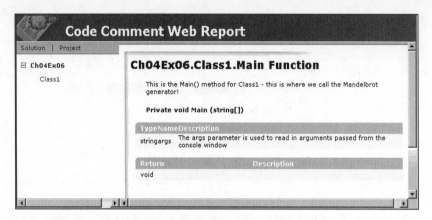

Unfortunately this isn't quite as nicely formatted, as the table for the `args` parameter is a bit scrunched up!

Summary

Visual Studio.NET provides us with a whole range of tools for quickly creating applications that connect to databases, requiring only a small amount of code to be written by hand. Throughout this chapter, we have looked at several mechanisms for displaying data. From the basic `TextBox`, to the more advanced `DataGrid`, they all rely on the power and flexibility of ADO.NET and the `BindingContext` object inherent to all Windows forms.

In this chapter, we looked at how we could use these tools to connect to a data source, and to create a data-driven application with only a handful of lines of code. However, automatically generated code is never quite as efficient as hand-written code, so in the next chapter we'll see how we can build on what we've learned here, and go on to write our own ADO.NET code.

In the last section of the chapter, we discussed Extensible Markup Language (XML), a text format for storing and retrieving data. We looked at the rules we need to obey to ensure that our XML documents are well-formed, and we saw how we can validate them against XSD and XDR schemas. Here, too, we saw how VS does a lot of the hard work for us, even creating XSD schemas from our XML documents. Finally, we looked at C#'s ability to create documentation for our code from special comments in XML format. In case you're still not convinced of the need for XML, in the next chapter, we'll see how XML and ADO.NET are inextricably linked.

Exercises

1. Modify our first example by adding the column `ContactTitle` to `sqlDataAdapter1`.

2. Add a text box to the form that will display the `ContactTitle` information.

3. Create a new application that displays data from the `Products` table of the `Northwind` database.

4. Modify the code for the *Navigating through the DataSet* example to scroll back to the beginning of the `DataSet` when the `Next` button is pressed on the last record, and to scroll to the end of the `DataSet` when the `Back` button is pressed on the first record.

5. Create a set of XML auto-documentation web pages for the final version of the `GettingData` application.

Data Access with ADO.NET

In the previous chapter we learned how to use the wizards and code generation tools within Visual C# to make user interfaces that access relational data.

In this chapter we'll look at how you accomplish this same data access with C# code written directly by the programmer, as opposed to the wizard-generated code used in the previous chapter. We will use the ADO.NET data access classes to accomplish this. In particular, we will look at:

- ❑ An overview of ADO.NET, and the structure of its main classes
- ❑ Reading data with a data reader and with a `DataSet`
- ❑ Updating the database, adding records and deleting records
- ❑ Working with relationships in ADO.NET
- ❑ Reading and writing XML documents in ADO.NET
- ❑ Direct execution of SQL commands from ADO.NET

First, let's look at an overview of ADO.NET.

What is ADO.NET?

ADO.NET is the name for the set of classes you use with C# and the .NET Framework to access data in a relational, table-oriented format. This includes relational databases such as Microsoft Access and SQL Server, as well as other databases and even non-relational data sources. ADO.NET is integrated into the .NET Framework and is designed to be used with any .NET language, especially C#.

ADO.NET is located in the `System.Data.dll` assembly. In a sense ADO.NET **is** the `System.Data.dll` assembly; because any class contained in this assembly is by definition part of ADO.NET. This includes all of the `System.Data` namespace and its nested namespaces such as `System.Data.SqlClient` and `System.Data.OleDb`, plus the odd class from the `System.Xml` namespace. We looked at XML in the previous chapter; we will follow on in this chapter to see ADO.NET's support for XML.

Why is it Called ADO.NET?

You might ask, why does this part of the .NET Framework get its own weird moniker, ADO.NET? Why not just call it `System.Data` and be done with it? ADO.NET takes its name from ADO (ActiveX Data Objects), a widely used set of classes used for data access in the previous generation of Microsoft technologies. The ADO.NET name is used because Microsoft wants to make it clear that this is the preferred data access interface in the .NET programming environment.

ADO.NET serves the same purpose as ADO, providing an easy-to-use set of classes for data access, updated and enhanced for the .NET programming environment. While it fulfills the same role as ADO, the classes, properties, and methods in ADO.NET are quite different from ADO.

Design Goals of ADO.NET

Let's quickly look at the design goals of ADO.NET. These include:

❑ Simple access to relational and non-relational data

❑ Extensibility to support even more data sources than its predecessor technologies

❑ Support for multi-tier applications across the Internet

❑ Unification of XML and relational data access

Simple Access to Relational Data

The primary goal of ADO.NET is to provide simple access to relational data. Straightforward, easy-to-use classes represent the tables, columns, and rows within relational databases. Additionally, ADO.NET introduces the `DataSet` class, which represents a set of data from related tables encapsulated as a single unit, preserving the integrity of the relationships between them. This is a new concept in ADO.NET that significantly extends the capabilities of the data access interface.

Extensibility

ADO.NET is extensible – it provides a framework for plug-in .NET data providers (also called **managed providers**) that can be built to read and write data from any data source. ADO.NET comes with two built-in .NET data providers, one for OLE DB data sources and another for Microsoft SQL Server. Data formats such as Microsoft Access, third-party databases, and non-relational data can be accessed via OLE DB. In addition, an ODBC .NET data provider is available for ADO.NET that allows .NET access to even more legacy data formats and third-party databases.

Support for Multi-Tier Applications

ADO.NET is designed for multi-tier applications. This is the most common architecture today for business and e-commerce applications. In multi-tier architecture, different parts of the application logic are separated into layers, or tiers, and communicate only with the layer around them.

One of the most common approaches is the 3-tier model, which consists of the following:

❑　Data tier – contains the database, and data access code.

❑　Business tier – contains the business logic, which defines the unique functionality of this application, and abstracts this away from other tiers. This tier is sometimes referred to as the "middle tier".

❑　Presentation tier – provides the user interface and control of process flow to the application, as well as such things as validating of user input.

ADO.NET uses the open Internet-standard XML format for communications between the tiers, allowing data to pass through Internet firewalls and allowing the possibility of a non-Microsoft implementation of one or more tiers.

Unification of XML and Relational Data Access

Another important goal of ADO.NET is to provide a bridge between relational data in rows and columns, and XML documents which have a hierarchical data structure. The .NET technology is built around XML and ADO.NET makes extensive use of it.

Now that we've seen what ADO.NET's goals are, let's look at the actual ADO.NET classes themselves.

Overview of ADO.NET Classes and Objects

This diagram shows the basic classes in ADO.NET. Note that this is not an inheritance diagram, but rather shows the relationships between the most commonly used classes:

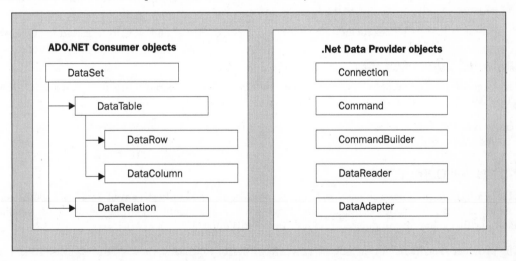

Here we divide the classes into .NET data provider objects and consumer objects.

❑　Provider objects are specific to each type of data source – the actual reading and writing to and from the data source is done with the provider-specific objects

❑　Consumer objects are what you use to access and manipulate the data once you have read it into memory

The provider objects require an active connection; you use these first to read the data, then depending on your needs, you may work with the data in memory using the consumer objects and/or update the data in the data source using the provider objects to write the changes back to the data source. Thus the consumer objects operate in a disconnected fashion; you can work with the data in memory even if the database connection is down.

Provider Objects

These are the objects defined in each .NET data provider. The names are prefaced with a name unique to the provider; so for example the actual connection object for the OLE DB provider is OleDbConnection; the class for the SQL Server .NET provider is SqlConnection.

Connection Object

The connection object is the first object that you will typically use, before using most of the other ADO.NET objects – it provides the basic connection to your data source. If you are using a database that requires a user and password, or one on a remote network server, the connection object takes care of the details of establishing the connection and logging in.

> *If you are familiar with classic ADO, you'll note that* Connection *and other objects that serve a similar function in classic ADO have similar names in ADO.NET.*

Command Object

You use this object to give a command such as a SQL query to a data source, such as "SELECT * FROM Customers" to query the data in the Customers table.

The provider-specific names include SqlCommand for SQL Server and OleDbCommand for OLE DB.

CommandBuilder Object

This object is used to build SQL commands for data modification from objects based on a single-table query. We'll look at this object in more detail when we study how to update data.

The provider-specific names include SqlCommandBuilder for SQL Server and OleDbCommandBuilder for OLE DB.

DataReader Object

This is a fast, simple-to-use object that reads a forward-only read-only stream of data (such as the set of customers found) from a data source. This object gives the maximum performance for simply reading data; our first example will demonstrate how to use this object.

The provider-specific names include SqlDataReader for SQL Server and OleDbDataReader for OLE DB.

DataAdapter Object

This is a general-purpose class that performs various operations specific to the data source, including updating changed data, filling DataSet objects (see below) and other operations, which we'll see in the following examples.

The provider-specific names include `SqlDataAdapter` for SQL Server and `OleDbAdapter` for OLE DB.

Consumer Objects

These are the objects defined for the disconnected, consumer side of ADO.NET. These aren't related to any specific .NET data provider, and live within the `System.Data` namespace:

DataSet Object

The `DataSet` is the king of consumer objects – we had an introduction to it in the previous chapter. The `DataSet` represents a set of related tables referenced as one unit in your application. For example, `Customers`, `Orders`, and `Products` might all be tables in one `DataSet` representing each customer and the products he or she ordered from your company. With this object you can get all the data you need from each table quickly, examine and change it while disconnected from the server, and then update the server with the changes in one efficient operation.

The `DataSet` has features that let you access lower-level objects that represent individual tables and relationships. These objects are:

DataTable Object

This object represents one of the tables in the `DataSet`, such as `Customers`, `Orders`, or `Products`.

The `DataTable` object has features that allow you to access its rows and columns:

❑   `DataColumn` object – this represents one column in the table, for example `OrderID` or `CustomerName`

❑   `DataRow` object – this represents one row of related data from a table; for example a particular customer's `CustomerID`, name, address, and so on

DataRelation Object

This object represents the relationship between two tables via a shared column; for example the `Orders` table might have a `CustomerID` column identifying the customer who placed the order. A `DataRelation` object might be created representing the relationship between `Customers` and `Orders` via the shared column `CustomerID`.

You now have an idea of the overall structure of the objects in ADO.NET. There are more objects than the ones just listed, but let's skip the details for now and get into some examples that show how this all works.

Using the System.Data Namespace

The first step in using ADO.NET within your C# code is to reference the `System.Data` namespace, in which all the ADO.NET classes are located. Put the following `using` directive at the beginning of any program using ADO.NET:

```
using System.Data;
```

Next, you'll need to reference the .NET data provider for the specific data source you'll be using.

SQL Server .NET Data Provider

If you are using SQL Server (version 7 or greater) or MSDE, the best performance and most direct access to the underlying features is available with the SQL Server-specific .NET data provider, referenced with this `using` directive:

```
using System.Data.SqlClient;
```

OLE DB .NET Data Provider

For most data sources other than SQL Server (such as Microsoft Access, Oracle, versions of SQL Server earlier than version 7, and others) you'll use the OLE DB .NET data provider, referenced with this `using` directive:

```
using System.Data.OleDb;
```

If there is a .NET data provider available specifically for your database then you may want to use that .NET data provider instead, which will have its own specific `using` directive. The SQL Server .NET data provider is an example of a product-specific .NET data provider.

ODBC .NET Data Provider

If you have a data source for which no native or OLE DB provider is available (such as PostgreSQL or some other third-party databases), the ODBC .NET data provider is a good alternative. As we mentioned in the previous chapter, it is a separate download from Visual Studio .NET, and after installation of the download, it is located in the `Microsoft.Data.Odbc.dll` assembly – you will need to add a specific reference to this assembly from Visual Studio .NET's **Add Reference** dialog before compiling an application that uses the ODBC .NET provider. The ODBC .NET provider namespace is imported with this `using` directive:

```
using Microsoft.Data.Odbc;
```

The `Microsoft.Data.Odbc` namespace follows the `vendor.Data.xxx` convention recommended for third-party supplied data providers.

Reading Data with the Data Reader

In our first example we'll just get some data from one table, the `Customers` table in the SQL Server/MSDE `Northwind` sample database – the same database that we looked at in the previous chapter. The `Customers` table contains rows and columns with data about the customers of Northwind traders; we spent some time looking at this table in the previous chapter. Our first example here will use a data reader to retrieve the `CustomerID` and `CompanyName` columns from this table.

Try it Out – Reading Data with the Data Reader

    1. Create a new console application called `DataReading` in the directory `C:\BegVCSharp\Chapter19`.

2. We begin by adding the `using` directives for the ADO.NET classes we will be using:

```
using System;
using System.Data;           // Use ADO.NET namespace
using System.Data.SqlClient; // Use SQL Server data provider namespace
```

3. Now add the following code to the Main() method:

```
public static void Main()
{
    // Specify SQL Server-specific connection string
    SqlConnection thisConnection = new SqlConnection(
        @"Data Source=(local);Integrated Security=SSPI;" +
        "Initial Catalog=northwind");

    // Open connection
    thisConnection.Open();

    // Create command for this connection
    SqlCommand thisCommand = thisConnection.CreateCommand();

    // Specify SQL query for this command
    thisCommand.CommandText =
        "SELECT CustomerID, CompanyName from Customers";

    // Execute DataReader for specified command
    SqlDataReader thisReader = thisCommand.ExecuteReader();

    // While there are rows to read
    while (thisReader.Read())
    {
        // Output ID and name columns
        Console.WriteLine("\t{0}\t{1}",
        thisReader["CustomerID"], thisReader["CompanyName"]);
    }

    // Close reader
    thisReader.Close();

    // Close connection
    thisConnection.Close ();
}
```

4. Compile and execute this program. You will see the list of customer IDs and company names, as follows. If you don't see the output below, don't worry, we'll come to the possible problems in a moment:

```
C:\BegVCSharp\Chapter19\DataReading\bin\Debug\DataReading.exe            _ □ ×
        TRADH    Tradiçao Hipermercados                                   ▲
        TRAIH    Trail's Head Gourmet Provisioners
        VAFFE    Vaffeljernet
        VICTE    Victuailles en stock
        VINET    Vins et alcools Chevalier
        WARTH    Wartian Herkku
        WELLI    Wellington Importadora
        WHITC    White Clover Markets
        WILMK    Wilman Kala
        WOLZA    Wolski  Zajazd
Press any key to continue                                                ▼
  ◄                                                              ►      
```

How it Works

The first step is to reference the System.Data namespace and our provider as described before. We're going to use the SQL Server .NET provider in these examples, so we need the following lines at the start of our program:

```
using System.Data;
using System.Data.SqlClient;
```

There are five steps to retrieving the data from our program:

1. Connect to the data source

2. Open the connection

3. Issue a SQL query

4. Read and display the data with the data reader

5. Close the data reader and the connection

We'll look at each of these steps in turn.

First, we need to connect to our data source. This is done by creating a connection object using a connection string. The connection string is just a character string containing the name of the provider for the database you want to connect to, the login information (database user, password, and so on), and the name of the particular database you want to use. Let's look at the specific elements of this connection string; however, keep in mind that these strings differ significantly between data providers so you'll need to look up the specific connection information for your data provider if it is different from this example (the connection information for Access is shown a little later in the chapter).

The line where we create the connection object looks like this:

```
SqlConnection thisConnection = new SqlConnection(
    @"Data Source=(local);Integrated Security=SSPI;" +
    "Initial Catalog=northwind");
```

`SqlConnection` is the name of the connection object for the SQL .NET data provider; if we were using OLE DB we would create an `OleDbConnection`, but we'll see this in our next example. The connection string consists of named entries separated by semicolons; let's look at each one. The first is:

```
Data Source=(local);
```

This is just the name of the SQL Server you are accessing. `(local)` is a handy SQL Server shorthand name that refers to the server instance running on the current machine. If you already have SQL Server running on your machine, this name should work as is.

The .NET Framework SDK Samples will optionally install a SQL Server desktop engine (also called MSDE) for executing the samples. The default name of this instance is `(local)\NetSDK`. Therefore an alternative server name to try is:

```
Data Source=(local)\NetSDK;
```

Note that the @ sign prefacing the connection string indicates a string literal, making the backslash in this name work; otherwise double backslashes (\\) are necessary to escape the backslash character inside a C# string. I could have also specified my actual machine name:

```
Data Source=ROADRUNNER\NetSDK;
```

If you installed the SQL Server you are working with, you'll know the name of the SQL Server instance. Otherwise, you'll have to check with your SQL Server or network administrator to find out what name to use.

The next part of the connection string specifies how to log in to the database; here we use the integrated security of the Windows login so no separate user and password needs to be specified:

```
Integrated Security=SSPI;
```

SSPI stands for **Security Support Provider Interface**; this just specifies the standard built-in security for SQL Server and Windows. Finally the particular database you want to use is specified, in our case the `Northwind` sample:

```
Initial Catalog=northwind
```

The `Northwind` sample is always present in a default SQL Server installation, though many database administrators choose to omit it for space reasons.

Anyway, we now have a connection object that is configured for our machine and database (but the connection is not yet active; to do this we must open it).

Once we have a connection object, we can move on to our second step. The first thing you want to do with the connection object is open it, which establishes the connection to the database:

```
thisConnection.Open();
```

613

If the `Open()` method fails, for example if the SQL Server cannot be found, a `SqlException` exception will be thrown and you will see a message such as:

```
Unhandled Exception: System.Data.SqlClient.SqlException: SQL Server does not exist
or access denied.
   at System.Data.SqlClient.SqlConnection.Open()
   at DataReading.Class1.Main(String[] args) in
c:\begvcsharp\chapter19\datareading\class1.cs:line 25
Press any key to continue
```

This particular message indicates that the program couldn't find the SQL Server specified. Check that the server name in the connection string is correct.

Our third step is to create a command object and give it a SQL command to perform a database operation (such as retrieving some data). The code to do this is as follows:

```
SqlCommand thisCommand = thisConnection.CreateCommand();
thisCommand.CommandText = "SELECT CustomerID, CompanyName from Customers";
```

The connection object has a method called `CreateCommand()` to create a command associated with this connection, so we will use this to get our command object. The command itself is assigned to the `CommandText` property of the command object. We're going to get a list of the customer IDs and the company names from the `Northwind` database, so that is the basis for our SQL query command:

```
SELECT CustomerID, CompanyName from Customers
```

The `SELECT` command is the SQL command to get the data from one or more tables. A common error is to mistype the name of one of the tables, resulting in another exception:

```
thisCommand.CommandText = "SELECT CustomerID, CompanyName from Customer";
```

Whoops! I forgot the "s" in "`Customers`" – I get this exception:

```
Unhandled Exception: System.Data.SqlClient.SqlException: Invalid object name
'Customer'.
   at System.Data.SqlClient.SqlCommand.ExecuteReader(....)
   at System.Data.SqlClient.SqlCommand.ExecuteReader()
   at DataReading.Class1.Main(String[] args) in
c:\begvcsharp\chapter19\datareading\class1.cs:line 35
Press any key to continue
```

Our fourth step is to read and display the data. First, we have to read the data – we do this with a data reader. The data reader is a lightweight, fast object for quickly getting the results of a query. It is read-only, so you can't use it to update data – we'll get to that after we finish this example. As we saw in the previous section, you use a method from the last object you created, the command object, to create an associated instance of the object you need next – in this case, the data reader:

```
SqlDataReader thisReader = thisCommand.ExecuteReader();
```

`ExecuteReader()` executes the SQL command at the database, so any database errors are generated here; it also creates the reader object for reading the generated results – here we assign it to `thisReader`.

There are several methods for getting the results out of the reader, but the following is the usual process. The `Read()` method of `DataReader` reads a single row of the data resulting from the query, and returns `true` while there is more data to read, `false` if there is not. So, we set up a `while` loop to read data with the `Read()` method and print out the results as we get them on each iteration:

```
while (thisReader.Read())
{
    Console.WriteLine("\t{0}\t{1}",
                      thisReader["CustomerID"], thisReader["CompanyName"]);
}
```

So, while `Read()` returns true, `Console.WriteLine("\t{0}\t{1}"`writes out a line with two pieces of data separated by tab characters (`\t`). The data reader object provides an **indexer** property (see Chapter 11 for a discussion of indexers). The indexer is overloaded, and allows you to reference the columns as an array reference by column name: `thisReader["CustomerID"]`, `thisReader["CompanyName"]`, or by an integer: `thisReader[0]`, `thisReader[1]`.

When `Read()` returns `false` at the end of the results, the `while` loop ends.

The fifth and final step is to close the objects we opened, which include the reader object and the connection object. Each of these objects has a `Close()` method, which we call before exiting the program:

```
thisReader.Close();
thisConnection.Close();
```

That's all there is to accessing a single table!

The same program can be written with just a few simple changes to use the Microsoft Access version of this database (`nwind.mdb`). This can be found in the `C:\Program Files\Microsoft Office\Office\Samples` directory, but don't use that directly; make a copy of the file (in a temporary directory such as `C:\tmp\nwind.mdb`), so you can always go back to the original.

Try it Out – Reading from an Access Database

Except for the details of the connection string, these changes will work for any other OLE DB data source.

1. Create a new console application called `ReadingAccessData` in the directory `C:\BegVCSharp\Chapter19`.

2. We begin by adding the `using` directives for the OLE DB provider classes we will be using:

```
using System;
using System.Data;            // Use ADO.NET namespace
using System.Data.OleDb;      // Use namespace for OLE DB .NET Data Provider
```

3. Now add the following code to the Main() method:

```
public static void Main ()
{
    // Create connection object for Microsoft Access OLE DB Provider;
    // note @ sign prefacing string literal so backslashes in path name;
    // work
    OleDbConnection thisConnection = new OleDbConnection(
        @"Provider=Microsoft.Jet.OLEDB.4.0;Data Source=C:\tmp\nwind.mdb");

    // Open connection object
    thisConnection.Open();

    // Create SQL command object on this connection
    OleDbCommand thisCommand = thisConnection.CreateCommand();

    // Initialize SQL SELECT command to retrieve desired data
    thisCommand.CommandText =
        "SELECT CustomerID, CompanyName FROM Customers";

    // Create a DataReader object based on previously defined command object
    OleDbDataReader thisReader = thisCommand.ExecuteReader();

    while (thisReader.Read())
    {
        Console.WriteLine("\t{0}\t{1}",
        thisReader["CustomerID"], thisReader["CompanyName"]);
    }
    thisReader.Close();
    thisConnection.Close();
    }
}
```

How It Works

Instead of the `SqlConnection`, `SqlCommand`, and `SqlDataReader` objects, we create `OleDbConnection`, `OleDbCommand`, and `OleDbDataReader` objects. These objects work essentially the same as their SQL Server counterparts.

Accordingly, we change the `using` directive that specifies the data provider from:

```
using System.Data.SqlClient;
```

to:

```
using System.Data.OleDb;
```

The only other difference is in the connection string, which we need to change completely. The first part of an OLE DB connection string, the `Provider` clause, specifies the name of the OLE DB provider for this type of database. For Microsoft Access databases, this is always the following name (`"Jet"` is the name of the database engine included in Access):

```
Provider=Microsoft.Jet.OLEDB.4.0;
```

If you are using a different OLE DB provider for a different database or data format, then specify the name of that provider in the `Provider` clause.

The second part of the connection string is the `Data Source` clause, and in the OLE DB/Microsoft Access case, this simply specifies the name of the Microsoft Access database file (`.mdb` file) we are going to open:

```
Data Source=C:\tmp\nwind.mdb
```

Once again we have the @ sign preceding the connection string to specify a string literal, so that the backslashes in the path name work; otherwise, double backslashes (\\) would be necessary to escape the file name in C#.

Reading Data with the DataSet

We've just seen how to read data with a data reader, so now let's look at how to accomplish the same task with the `DataSet`. First, let's take a detailed look at the structure of the `DataSet`.

The `DataSet` is the central object in ADO.NET; all operations of any complexity use it.

A `DataSet` contains a set of `DataTable` objects representing the database tables that you are working with. Each `DataTable` object has children `DataRow` and `DataColumn` objects representing the rows and columns of the database table. You can get to all the individual elements of the tables, rows, and columns through these objects, as we will see in a moment.

Filling the DataSet with Data

Our favorite activity with the `DataSet` will probably be to fill it with data – we saw how to do this in the previous chapter, using the `Fill()` method of a data adapter object.

Why is `Fill()` a method of the data adapter and not the `DataSet`? This is because the `DataSet` is an abstract representation of data in memory, while the data adapter is the object that ties the `DataSet` to a particular database. `Fill()` has many overloads, but the one we will be using in this chapter takes two parameters – the first specifies the `DataSet` we want filled, and the second is the name of the `DataTable` within the `DataSet` that will contain the data we want loaded:

Accessing Tables, Rows, and Columns in the DataSet

The `DataSet` object has a property named `Tables` that is a collection of all the `DataTable` objects within the `DataSet`. `Tables` is of type `DataTableCollection`, and has an overloaded indexer, which means that you can access each individual `DataTable` in one of two possible ways:

❑   By table name – `thisDataSet.Tables["Customers"]` specifies the `DataTable` called `Customers`

❑ By index (the index is zero-based) – `thisDataSet.Tables[0]` specifies the first `DataTable` in the `DataSet`

Within each `DataTable`, there is a `Rows` property that is a collection of the individual `DataRow` objects. `Rows` is of type `DataRowCollection`, and is an ordered list, indexed by row number. Thus:

```
myDataSet.Tables["Customers"].Rows[n]
```

specifies row number n – 1 (remember the index is zero-based) in the `Customers` `DataTable` of `thisDataSet`. (Of course we could have used the alternative index syntax to specify the `DataTable` as well.)

You might expect `DataRow` to have a property of type `DataColumnCollection`, but it's not as simple as that, because we want to take advantage of the data type of the individual columns in each row, so that a column containing character data becomes a string, a column containing an integer becomes an integer object, and so on.

The `DataRow` object itself has an indexer property that is overloaded, allowing you to access individual columns by name, and also by number. Thus:

```
thisDataSet.Tables["Customers"].Rows[n]["CompanyName"]
```

specifies the `CompanyName` column of row number n – 1 in the `Customers` `DataTable` of `thisDataSet` – the `DataRow` object here is `thisDataSet.Tables["Customers"].Rows[n]`.

If the structure we just discussed is a little confusing, let's try a picture:

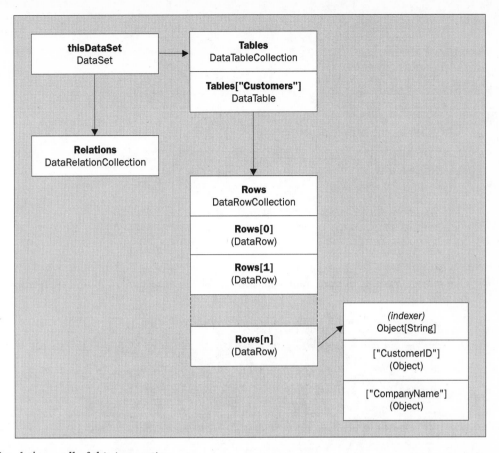

Now let's see all of this in practice.

Try it Out – Reading Data with the DataSet

1. Create a new console application called `DataSetRead` in the directory
`C:\BegVCSharp\Chapter19`.

2. We begin by adding the `using` directives for the ADO.NET classes we will be using:

```
using System;
using System.Data;             // Use ADO.NET namespace
using System.Data.SqlClient;   // Use SQL Server data provider namespace
```

3. Now add the following code to the `Main()` method:

```
public static void Main()
{
    // Specify SQL Server-specific connection string
    SqlConnection thisConnection = new SqlConnection(
```

```
        @"Data Source=(local);Integrated Security=SSPI;" +
        "Initial Catalog=northwind");

    // Create DataAdapter object
    SqlDataAdapter thisAdapter = new SqlDataAdapter(
        "SELECT CustomerID, ContactName FROM Customers", thisConnection);

    // Create DataSet to contain related data tables, rows, and columns
    DataSet thisDataSet = new DataSet();

    // Fill DataSet using query defined previously for DataAdapter
    thisAdapter.Fill(thisDataSet, "Customers");
    foreach (DataRow theRow in thisDataSet.Tables["Customers"].Rows)
    {
        Console.WriteLine(theRow["CustomerID"] + "\t" +
                                        theRow["ContactName"]);
    }
}
```

4. Compile and execute this program. You will see the list of customer IDs and company names, as follows

How It Works

First, we create a connection, and then use this connection to create a `SqlDataAdapter` object:

```
SqlConnection thisConnection = new SqlConnection(
    @"Data Source=(local);Integrated Security=SSPI;" +
    "Initial Catalog=northwind");

SqlDataAdapter thisAdapter = new SqlDataAdapter(
    "SELECT CustomerID, ContactName FROM Customers", thisConnection);
```

The next step is to create the `DataSet` that we want filled with data:

```
DataSet thisDataSet = new DataSet();
```

Now we have our `DataSet` and our data adapter object in place (`SqlDataAdapter` here since we are using the SQL Server provider), we can proceed to fill a `DataTable` in the `DataSet`:

```
thisAdapter.Fill(thisDataSet, "Customers");
```

A `DataTable` named `Customers` will be created in this `DataSet`. Note that this occurence of the word `Customers` does not refer to the `Customers` table in the `Northwind` database – it specifies the name of the `DataTable` in the `DataSet` to be created, and then filled with data.

Now that the `DataSet` has been filled, we can access the individual rows and columns. The process for this is straightforward – we loop through all the `DataRow` objects in the `Rows` collection of the `Customers DataTable`. For each `DataRow`, we retrieve the values in the `CustomerID` and `ContactName` column:

```
foreach (DataRow theRow in thisDataSet.Tables["Customers"].Rows)
{
    Console.WriteLine(theRow["CustomerID"] + "\t" +
                                  theRow["ContactName"]);
}
```

We mentioned earlier that the `DataRow` object has an indexer property that lets you access its individual columns by name, and also by number. Thus `theRow["CustomerID"]` specifies the `CustomerID` column of `theRow DataRow`, and `theRow["ContactName"]` specifies the `ContactName` column of `theRow DataRow`. Alternatively, we could have referred to the columns by number – `CustomerID` would be `theRow[0]` (it is the first column retrieved from the database), and `ContactName` as `theRow[1]`.

You may have noticed that we have not explicitly opened or closed a connection in this example – the data adapter takes care of this for us. The data adapter object will open a connection as needed, and close it again once finished its work. The data adapter will leave the state of the connection unchanged – so if the connection was open before the data adapter started its work, it will be still be open after the data adapter has finished.

OK – we've seen how to read in data from a database. We've used a data reader, which requires a connection to the database to be maintained while it is doing its work. We've also just used the data adapter to fill a `DataSet` – with this method the data adapter deals with the connection for us, opening it and closing it as needed. The data reader also reads in a forward-only manner – it can navigate through records or jump to a given record. The data reader only (its name suggests) *reads* data – the `DataSet` offers tremendous flexibility for *reading* and *writing* data, and working with data from different sources. We will see the power of the `DataSet` unfold as we move through the chapter.

Reading data is only ever going to be half of what you want – you will usually want to modify data, add new data, or delete data. So let's get on with that – our next step is to look at updating a database.

Updating the Database

Now that we can read data from databases, how do we change it? We'll show a very simple example again using just one table, and at the same time introduce a few new objects we will use later in the chapter.

All the actions that we typically wish to perform on the database (updating, inserting and deleting records) can be accomplished with the same pattern:

1. Fill a `DataSet` with the data from the database we wish to work with

2. Modify the data held in the `DataSet` (update, insert, or delete records for example)

3. Once all the modifications are made, persist the `DataSet` changes back to the database

You will see this theme recurring as we move through the examples – there is no need for us to worry about the exact SQL syntax for updating the database, say, and all the modifications to the data in the database can be performed at one time.

Let's begin by looking at how to update data in a database, before moving on to add and delete records.

Try it Out – Updating the Database

Let's imagine that one of our customers, Bottom-Dollar Markets, has changed its name to Acme, Inc. We need to change the company name in our databases. Again, we'll use the SQL Server/MSDE version of the `Northwind` database.

1. Create a new console application called `UpdatingData` in the directory `C:\BegVCSharp\Chapter19`.

2. We begin by adding the `using` directives for the ADO.NET classes we will be using:

```
using System;
using System.Data;              // Use ADO.NET namespace
using System.Data.SqlClient;    // Use SQL Server data provider namespace
```

3. Now add the following code to the `Main()` method:

```
public static void Main()
{
    // Specify SQL Server-specific connection string
    SqlConnection thisConnection = new SqlConnection(
        @"Data Source=(local);Integrated Security=SSPI;" +
        "Initial Catalog=northwind");
    // Create DataAdapter object for update and other operations
    SqlDataAdapter thisAdapter = new SqlDataAdapter(
        "SELECT CustomerID, CompanyName FROM Customers", thisConnection);

    // Create CommandBuilder object to build SQL commands
    SqlCommandBuilder thisBuilder = new SqlCommandBuilder(thisAdapter);
```

```
        // Create DataSet to contain related data tables, rows, and columns
        DataSet thisDataSet = new DataSet();

        // Fill DataSet using query defined previously for DataAdapter
        thisAdapter.Fill(thisDataSet, "Customers");

        // Show data before change
        Console.WriteLine("name before change: {0}",
            thisDataSet.Tables["Customers"].Rows[9]["CompanyName"]);

        // Change data in Customers table, row 9, CompanyName column
        thisDataSet.Tables["Customers"].Rows[9]["CompanyName"] = "Acme, Inc.";

        // Call Update command to mark change in table
        thisAdapter.Update(thisDataSet, "Customers");

        Console.WriteLine("name after change: {0}",
            thisDataSet.Tables["Customers"].Rows[9]["CompanyName"]);

}
```

4. Running the program produces the following output:

How it Works

The first part of the program is similar to the previous SQL Server example; we create a connection object using a connection string:

```
SqlConnection thisConnection = new SqlConnection(
    @"Data Source=(local);Integrated Security=SSPI;" +
    "Initial Catalog=northwind");
```

Then we create a SqlDataAdapter object, with the next statement:

```
SqlDataAdapter thisAdapter = new SqlDataAdapter(
    "SELECT CustomerID, CompanyName FROM Customers", thisConnection);
```

Next, we want to create the correct SQL statements to update the database – we don't have to do this ourselves, the SqlCommandBuilder will take care of this for us:

```
SqlCommandBuilder thisBuilder = new SqlCommandBuilder(thisAdapter);
```

Note that we pass `thisAdapter` to the `SqlCommandBuilder` constructor as an argument. The correct SQL commands are generated and associated with the passed data adapter by the constructor when the `SqlCommandBuilder` object is created. A bit later in the chapter we'll look at different SQL statements; but for now the SQL has been taken care of for us.

Now we create our illustrious `DataSet` object, and fill it with data:

```
DataSet thisDataSet = new DataSet();
thisAdapter.Fill(thisDataSet, "Customers");
```

In our case it is the `Customers` table we want, so we will call the associated `DataTable` in the `DataSet` by the same name. Now that the `DataSet` has been filled, we can access the individual rows and columns.

Before we change the data, we output a "before" picture of the data we want to change:

```
Console.WriteLine("name before change: {0}",
    thisDataSet.Tables["Customers"].Rows[9]["CompanyName"]);
```

What are we doing here? We are printing the value in the `CompanyName` column in the row with index number nine in the `Customers` table. This whole line outputs the following:

```
name before change: Bottom-Dollar Markets
```

We're cheating a little bit here; we just happen to know that we are interested in the row with index number nine (which is actually the tenth row since the indexer is zero-based – the first row is `Rows[0]`). In a real program, rather than an example, we would have probably put a qualifier in our SQL query to select just the rows we were interested in, rather than having to know to go to the row with an index number of nine. In the next example, we'll discuss how to find only the rows we are interested in.

Another way to understand what is going on with all of this is to look at an equivalent example that breaks out each separate object in the expression:

```
// Example using multiple objects
DataTable customerTable = thisDataSet.Tables["Customers"];
DataRow rowTen = customerTable.Rows[9];
object companyName = rowTen["CompanyName"];
Console.WriteLine("name before change: {0}", companyName);
```

In this example, we declare `customerTable` as a `DataTable` and assign the `Customers` table from the `Tables` property of `thisDataSet`. We declare `rowTen` as a `DataRow` and to it we assign the tenth element of the `Rows` property of `customerTable`. Finally, we declare `companyName` as an `object` and use the indexer property of `rowTen` to assign the `CompanyName` field to it.

This example helps us follow the process as we follow the chain of related objects, but it is often simpler to use the one-line expression which gives the same result:

```
Console.WriteLine("name before change: {0}",
            thisDataSet.Tables["Customers"].Rows[9]["CompanyName"]);
```

If the code using multiple objects is more understandable to you, by all means use this method. For a one-time reference like this one it is potentially inefficient to create variables for each object and assign to them every time; however, if the objects are going to be reused the multiple-object method may be more efficient. The compiler's optimizer may compensate for any inefficiency in one way of coding over another; therefore it's often best to code in the most readable manner.

Back to the example – we've displayed the value of the column before we make a change, so now let's make a change to the column. To change the value of a `DataColumn`, simply assign to it, as in the next line of the example:

```
thisDataSet.Tables["Customers"].Rows[9]["CompanyName"] = "Acme, Inc.";
```

This line changes the value of the `CompanyName` column in the row with index number nine of `Customers` to "Acme, Inc.".

However, this change only changes the value of the column in the `DataSet` in memory, not in the database itself.

The `DataSet`, `DataTable`, `DataRow`, and `DataColumn` are in-memory representations of the data in the table. In order to update the database, we need to call the `Update()` method.

`Update()` is a method of the data adapter object. To call it, specify the `DataSet` you want the update to be based on, and the name of the `DataTable` in the `DataSet` to update. It's important that the `DataTable` name ("Customers") match the one we used when calling the `Fill()` method previously:

```
thisAdapter.Update(thisDataSet, "Customers");
```

The `Update()` method automatically goes through the rows in the `DataTable` to check for changes that need to be made to the database. Each `DataRow` object in the `Rows` collection has a property, `RowState`, that tracks whether this row is deleted, added, modified, or is unchanged. Any changes made are reflected in the database.

Now we confirm the change by printing out the "after" state of the data:

```
Console.WriteLine("name after change: {0}",
    thisDataSet.Tables["Customers"].Rows[9]["CompanyName"]);
```

That's all there is to it!

Before we move on, let's have a quick reminder of the new characters we met here:

❑ `SqlCommandBuilder` – the `SqlCommandBuilder` object takes care of the correct SQL statements for updating the database – we don't have to craft these statements ourselves.

❑ `SqlDataAdapter.Update()` – this method goes through the rows in a `DataTable` to check for changes that need to be made to the database. Each `DataRow` object in the `Rows` collection has a property, `RowState`, tracking whether this row is deleted, added, modified, or is unchanged. Any changes made are reflected in the database.

These, of course, are the SQL Server provider versions – there are corresponding OLE DB provider versions that work in the same way.

Adding Rows to the Database

In the previous example we updated values in existing rows, and our next step is to add an entirely new row. We'll see that our procedure to add a new record to the database involves, exactly like the update example earlier, adding a new row to an existing `DataSet` (this is where most of the work is required), and then persisting this change back to the database.

The process for adding a new row to the database is straightforward:

1. Create a new `DataRow`

2. Populate it with some data

3. Add it to the `Rows` collection of the `DataSet`

4. Persist this change back to the database by calling the `Update()` method of the data adapter

Sounds like a perfectly sensible scheme – let's see exactly how it's done.

Try it Out – Adding Rows

1. Create a new console application called `AddingData` in the directory `C:\BegVCSharp\Chapter19`.

We begin by adding our usual `using` directives for the ADO.NET classes we will be using:

```
using System;
using System.Data;              // Use ADO.NET namespace
using System.Data.SqlClient;    // Use SQL Server data provider namespace
```

Now add the following code to the `Main()` method:

```
public static void Main()
{
    // Specify SQL Server-specific connection string
    SqlConnection thisConnection = new SqlConnection(
        @"Data Source=(local);Integrated Security=SSPI;" +
        "Initial Catalog=northwind");

    // Create DataAdapter object for update and other operations
    SqlDataAdapter thisAdapter = new SqlDataAdapter(
        "SELECT CustomerID, CompanyName FROM Customers", thisConnection);

    // Create CommandBuilder object to build SQL commands
    SqlCommandBuilder thisBuilder = new SqlCommandBuilder(thisAdapter);

    // Create DataSet to contain related data tables, rows, and columns
    DataSet thisDataSet = new DataSet();
```

```
        // Fill DataSet using query defined previously for DataAdapter
        thisAdapter.Fill(thisDataSet, "Customers");

        Console.WriteLine("# rows before change: {0}",
                          thisDataSet.Tables["Customers"].Rows.Count);

        DataRow thisRow = thisDataSet.Tables["Customers"].NewRow();
        thisRow["CustomerID"] = "ZACZI";
        thisRow["CompanyName"] = "Zachary Zithers Ltd.";
        thisDataSet.Tables["Customers"].Rows.Add(thisRow);

        Console.WriteLine("# rows after change: {0}",
                          thisDataSet.Tables["Customers"].Rows.Count);

        // Call Update command to mark change in table
        thisAdapter.Update(thisDataSet, "Customers");
    }
```

2. On executing, the output of this example is:

How It Works

The lines of interest here are the lines between the `thisAdapter.Fill()` and `thisAdapter.Update()` method calls.

First, to see the "before" picture we introduce a new property of the `Rows` collection – `Count`. This gives us a count of how many rows are in this table:

```
Console.WriteLine("# rows before change: {0}",
    thisDataSet.Tables["Customers"].Rows.Count);
```

Next, we create the new row object, using the `NewRow()` method of the `DataTable` object:

```
DataRow thisRow = thisDataSet.Tables["Customers"].NewRow();
```

Note that this creates a new row object using the same columns as the `Customers` table, but does not actually add it to the `DataSet`; we need to assign some values to the columns before that can be done:

```
thisRow["CustomerID"] = "ZACZI";
thisRow["CompanyName"] = "Zachary Zithers Ltd.";
```

Now we can actually add the row using the `Add()` method of the `Rows` collection:

```
thisDataSet.Tables["Customers"].Rows.Add(thisRow);
```

If we check the Count property again after calling Add(), we see that we have indeed added one row:

```
Console.WriteLine("# rows after change: {0}",
                  thisDataSet.Tables["Customers"].Rows.Count);
```

The output shows 92 rows, one more than the "before change" output. As with the previous example, the call to Update() is needed to actually add the new row to the database on disk:

```
thisAdapter.Update (thisDataSet, "Customers");
```

Remember, the DataSet is an in-memory, disconnected copy of the data; it is the DataAdapter which is actually connected to the database on disk and therefore its Update() method needs to be called to synchronize the in-memory data in the DataSet with the database on disk.

If we look at the table in Visual Studio .NET after executing this program, we can see that we have indeed successfully added a row by scrolling to the bottom of the table display:

CustomerID	CompanyName	ContactName	ContactTitle	Address	City
WANDK	Die Wandernde Kuh	Rita Müller	Sales Representative	Adenauerallee 900	Stuttgart
WARTH	Wartian Herkku	Pirkko Koskitalo	Accounting Manager	Torikatu 38	Oulu
WELLI	Wellington Importadora	Paula Parente	Sales Manager	Rua do Mercado, 1	Resende
WHITC	White Clover Markets	Karl Jablonski	Owner	305 - 14th Ave. S.	Seattle
WILMK	Wilman Kala	Matti Karttunen	Owner/Marketing Assistant	Keskuskatu 45	Helsinki
WOLZA	Wolski Zajazd	Zbyszek Piestrzeniewicz	Owner	ul. Filtrowa 68	Warszawa
ZACZI	Zachary Zithers Ltd.	<NULL>	<NULL>	<NULL>	<NULL>

Notice that only the Customer ID and Company Name columns are filled, since that's all we used in our program. The remaining columns are blank (actually, they contain the value NULL in SQL terms). You might think filling in, say, Contact Name is simply a matter of adding the line to the code:

```
thisRow["ContactName"] = "Zylla Zithers";
```

However, this not all you do. Recall that when we made the original query, we built the DataSet specifying just two columns CustomerID and CompanyName:

```
SqlDataAdapter thisAdapter = new SqlDataAdapter(
    "SELECT CustomerID, CompanyName FROM Customers", thisConnection);
```

The reference to ContactName would cause an error, as there is no such column in the DataSet that we built. We could rectify this by adding the ContactName column to the original SQL query:

```
SqlDataAdapter thisAdapter = new SqlDataAdapter(
    "SELECT CustomerID, ContactName, CompanyName FROM Customers",
    thisConnection);
```

Or we could select all the columns from `Customers` using this command:

```
SqlDataAdapter thisAdapter = new SqlDataAdapter("SELECT * FROM Customers",
                                                thisConnection);
```

As we saw in the previous chapter, the asterisk (*) in a SQL SELECT command is a shorthand for all the columns in the table; with this change you can add values for any of the columns in the database. However, getting all the columns when you are only working with two or three is inefficient; this is something you should generally avoid.

Finding Rows

If you tried to run the previous example more than once, you would have seen a message like this:

```
Unhandled Exception: System.Data.SqlClient.SqlException:
Violation of PRIMARY KEY constraint 'PK_Customers'.
Cannot insert duplicate key in object 'Customers'.
```

This indicates that the `Add()` failed because it would have created a duplicate row. The definition of the `Customers` table requires that the `CustomerID` field contain unique values, which is required when a column is designated the primary key. The value `"ZACZI"` was already present when we tried to run the code for the second time, as it was placed in the table the first time that we ran the sample.

Let's change the logic so that we search for the row first before we try to add it. The `DataTable Rows` collection provides a method called `Find()` that is very useful for this purpose; let's rewrite the logic surrounding our row addition to use `Find()` instead of counting rows.

Try it Out – Finding Rows

1. Create a new console application called `FindingData` in the directory `C:\BegVCSharp\Chapter19`.

We begin by adding our usual `using` directives for the ADO.NET classes we will be using:

```
using System;
using System.Data;          // Use ADO.NET namespace
using System.Data.SqlClient; // Use SQL Server data provider namespace
```

Now add the following code to the `Main()` method:

```
public static void Main()
{
    // Specify SQL Server-specific connection string
    SqlConnection thisConnection = new SqlConnection(
        @"Data Source=(local);Integrated Security=SSPI;" +
        "Initial Catalog=northwind");

    // Create DataAdapter object for update and other operations
    SqlDataAdapter thisAdapter = new SqlDataAdapter(
        "SELECT CustomerID, CompanyName FROM Customers", thisConnection);
```

```
        // Create CommandBuilder object to build SQL commands
        SqlCommandBuilder thisBuilder = new SqlCommandBuilder(thisAdapter);

        // Create DataSet to contain related data tables, rows, and columns
        DataSet thisDataSet = new DataSet();

        // Fill DataSet using query defined previously for DataAdapter
         thisAdapter.Fill(thisDataSet, "Customers");

        Console.WriteLine("# rows before change: {0}",
            thisDataSet.Tables["Customers"].Rows.Count);

        // Set up keys object for defining primary key
        DataColumn[] keys = new DataColumn[1];
        keys[0] = thisDataSet.Tables["Customers"].Columns["CustomerID"];
        thisDataSet.Tables["Customers"].PrimaryKey = keys;

        DataRow findRow = thisDataSet.Tables["Customers"].Rows.Find("ZACZI");

        if (findRow == null)
        {
            Console.WriteLine("ZACZI not found, will add to Customers table");

            DataRow thisRow = thisDataSet.Tables["Customers"].NewRow();
            thisRow["CustomerID"] = "ZACZI";
            thisRow["CompanyName"] = "Zachary Zithers Ltd.";
            thisDataSet.Tables["Customers"].Rows.Add(thisRow);
            if ((findRow =
                thisDataSet.Tables["Customers"].Rows.Find("ZACZI")) != null)
            {
                Console.WriteLine("ZACZI successfully added to Customers table");
            }
        }
        else
        {
            Console.WriteLine("ZACZI already present in database");
        }

        thisAdapter.Update(thisDataSet, "Customers");

        Console.WriteLine("# rows after change: {0}",
        thisDataSet.Tables["Customers"].Rows.Count);
    }
```

How It Works

The beginning of the program up to the Fill() method call is the same as previous examples. We use the Count property to output the number of rows currently existing, then proceed to use Find() to check that the row we want to add is already present.

Before we can use Find() we need to set up a primary key. The primary key is what you will use when searching; it is made of one or more of the columns of the table and contains a value or set of values that uniquely identifies this particular row in the table, so that when we search by the key we will find one and only one row. The Customers table in the Northwind database uses the CustomerID column as its primary key:

```
DataColumn[] keys = new DataColumn[1];
keys[0] = thisDataSet.Tables["Customers"].Columns["CustomerID"];
thisDataSet.Tables["Customers"].PrimaryKey = keys;
```

First we create a `DataColumn` array – since the key can consist of one or more columns, an array is the natural structure to use; we call our `DataColumn` array keys. Next, we assign the first element of the keys array, `keys[0]`, to the `CustomerID` column in our `Customers` table. Finally, we assign keys to the `PrimaryKey` property of the `Customers DataTable` object.

Alternatively, it is possible to load primary key information directly from the database, which is not done by default. You can explicitly tell ADO.NET to load the primary key information by setting the `DataAdapter MissingSchemaAction` property before filling the `DataSet`, as follows:

```
thisAdapter.MissingSchemaAction = MissingSchemaAction.AddWithKey;
thisAdapter.Fill(thisDataSet, "Customers");
```

This accomplishes the same primary key setup by initializing the `PrimaryKey` property of the `DataTable` implicitly.

In any case, now we're ready to find a row!

```
DataRow findRow = thisDataSet.Tables["Customers"].Rows.Find("ZACZI");
```

`Find()` returns a `DataRow`, so we set up a `DataRow` object named `findRow` to get the result. `Find()` takes a parameter which is the value to look up; this can be an array of objects for a multi-column primary key, but in our case with only one primary key column, we need just one value which we pass as a string containing the value "ZACZI" – this is the `CustomerID` we want to look up.

If `Find()` locates a matching row, it returns the `DataRow` matching that row; if it does not find a match, it returns a `null` reference, which we can check for:

```
if (findRow == null)
{
    Console.WriteLine("ZACZI not found, will add to Customers table");

    DataRow thisRow = thisDataSet.Tables["Customers"].NewRow();
    thisRow["CustomerID"] = "ZACZI";
    thisRow["CompanyName"] = "Zachary Zithers Ltd.";
    thisDataSet.Tables["Customers"].Rows.Add(thisRow);
    if ((findRow = thisDataSet.Tables["Customers"].Rows.Find("ZACZI")) != null)
    {
        Console.WriteLine("ZACZI successfully added to Customers table");
    }
}
else
{
    Console.WriteLine("ZACZI already present in database");
}
```

If findRow is null, we go ahead and add the row as in the previous example. Just to make sure that the Add() was successful, we do a Find() again immediately after the add operation to prove to ourselves that it worked.

As we mentioned at the start of this section, this version using Find() is repeatable; you can run it multiple times without errors. However, it never executes the Add() code once the "ZACZI" row is in the database. Let's learn how to make it repeat that part of the program also.

Deleting Rows

Once we can add rows to the DataSet and to the database, it is logical to follow with the opposite action, removing rows.

The DataRow object has a Delete() method that deletes the current row. Our next example changes the sense of the if statement on findRow so that we test for findRow **not** equal to null (in other words, the row we were searching for was found). Then we remove the row by calling Delete() on findRow.

Try it Out – Deleting Rows

1. Create a new console application called DeletingData in the directory C:\BegVCSharp\Chapter19.

As usual, we begin by adding the using directives for the ADO.NET classes we will be using:

```
using System;
using System.Data;          // Use ADO.NET namespace
using System.Data.SqlClient; // Use SQL Server data provider namespace
```

Now add the following code to the Main() method:

```
public static void Main()
{
    // Specify SQL Server-specific connection string
    SqlConnection thisConnection = new SqlConnection(
        @"Data Source=(local);Integrated Security=SSPI;" +
        "Initial Catalog=northwind");

    // Create DataAdapter object for update and other operations
    SqlDataAdapter thisAdapter = new SqlDataAdapter(
        "SELECT CustomerID, CompanyName FROM Customers", thisConnection);

    // Create CommandBuilder object to build SQL commands
    SqlCommandBuilder thisBuilder = new SqlCommandBuilder(thisAdapter);

    // Create DataSet to contain related data tables, rows, and columns
    DataSet thisDataSet = new DataSet();

    // Fill DataSet using query defined previously for DataAdapter
    thisAdapter.Fill(thisDataSet, "Customers");

    Console.WriteLine("# rows before change: {0}",
        thisDataSet.Tables["Customers"].Rows.Count);
```

```
    // Set up keys object for defining primary key
    DataColumn[] keys = new DataColumn[1];
    keys[0] = thisDataSet.Tables["Customers"].Columns["CustomerID"];
    thisDataSet.Tables["Customers"].PrimaryKey = keys;

    DataRow findRow = thisDataSet.Tables["Customers"].Rows.Find("ZACZI");

    if (findRow != null)
    {
        Console.WriteLine("ZACZI already in Customers table");
        Console.WriteLine("Removing ZACZI  . . .");

        findRow.Delete();

        thisAdapter.Update(thisDataSet, "Customers");
    }

    Console.WriteLine("# rows after change: {0}",
        thisDataSet.Tables["Customers"].Rows.Count);
}
```

How it Works

The code to create the `DataSet` and the data adapter objects is standard – we've seen it before several times in this chapter and we won't go through it again.

The difference between this code and the previous example is that if the row is found, it is deleted! Note that when `Delete()` is called it doesn't remove the row in the database until `Update` is called to commit the change.

> *The `Delete()` method doesn't actually delete a row, it just marks it for deletion.*

Each `DataRow` object in the `Rows` collection has a property, `RowState`, that tracks whether this row is deleted, added, modified, or is unchanged. The `Delete()` method sets the `RowState` of the row to `Deleted`, and then `Update()` deletes any rows it finds in the `Rows` collection marked as `Deleted` from the database.

A word of caution about calling the `AcceptChanges()` method of the `DataSet` after `Delete()` – doing so will remove the row from the `DataSet`, which means that there will be no effect on the row in the actual database, because `Update()` acts only on the rows it finds in the `Rows` collection, and a missing row is simply ignored.

> **Do not call `AcceptChanges()` before `Update()` if you want to delete the row in the database itself.**

This same issue applies to the `Remove()` method; call this only if you want to remove rows from the `Rows` collection of the `DataSet`, but not from the database itself.

Accessing Multiple Tables in a DataSet

One of the big advantages of the ADO.NET model over previous data access models lies in the fact that the DataSet object tracks multiple tables and the relationships between them all within itself. This means that you can pass an entire set of related data between parts of your program in one operation, and the architecture inherently maintains the integrity of the relationships between the data.

Relationships in ADO.NET

The DataRelation object is used to describe the relationships between multiple DataTable objects in a DataSet. Each DataSet has a Relations collection of DataRelations that enables you to find and manipulate related tables.

Let's start with just the Customers and Orders tables. Each customer may place several orders; how can we see the orders placed by each customer? Each row of the Orders table contains the CustomerID of the customer placing the order; you match all the order rows containing a particular CustomerID with that customer's row in the Customers table, as shown here:

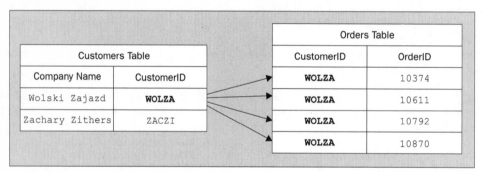

The matching CustomerID fields in the two tables define a **one-to-many relationship** between Customers table and the Orders table. We can use that relationship in ADO.NET by creating a DataRelation object to represent it.

Creating a DataRelation Object

The DataSet has a Relations property that is a collection of all the DataRelation objects representing relationships between tables in this DataSet.

To create a new DataRelation we use the Add() method of Relations which accepts a string name for the relationship and two DataColumns – the parent column, followed by the child column. Thus to create the relationship described above between the CustomerID column of the Customers table and the CustomerID table of the Orders table, we would use the following syntax, giving the relationship the name CustOrders:

```
DataRelation custOrderRel = thisDataSet.Relations.Add("CustOrders",
    thisDataSet.Tables["Customers"].Columns["CustomerID"],
    thisDataSet.Tables["Orders"].Columns["CustomerID"]);
```

We'll see this syntax again in our next example.

Navigating with Relationships

To use the relationship, we need to go from a row of one of our tables to the related rows in the other table. This is called **navigating** the relationship. Often navigations consist of traveling from a parent row in the first table to the related children in the other table. In the diagram shown earlier, the row in the `Customers` table can be considered the parent row and each of the related rows in the `Orders` table can be considered children. Navigations can also go in the opposite direction.

Fetching the Child Rows

Given a row in the parent table, how do we obtain all the rows in the child table that correspond to this row? We can retrieve this set of rows with the `GetChildRows()` method of the `DataRow` object. The `DataRelation` object that we have created between the parent and child tables is passed to the method, and a `DataRowCollection` object is returned, which is a collection of the related `DataRow` objects in the child `DataTable`.

For example, with our `DataRelation` that we created above, if the given `DataRow` in the parent `DataTable` (`Customers`) is `customerRow`, then:

```
customerRow.GetChildRows(custOrderRel);
```

returns the collection of corresponding `DataRow` objects from the `Orders` table. We'll see how to handle this set of objects in our next example.

Try it Out – Getting the Related Rows

1. Create a new console application called `DataRelationExample` in the directory `C:\BegVCSharp\Chapter19`.

2. We begin by adding the `using` directives for the ADO.NET classes we will be using:

```
using System;
using System.Data;              // Use ADO.NET namespace
using System.Data.SqlClient;    // Use SQL Server data provider namespace
```

3. Now add the following code to the `Main()` method:

```
public static void Main()
{
    // Specify SQL Server-specific connection string
    SqlConnection thisConnection = new SqlConnection(
        @"Data Source=(local);Integrated Security=SSPI;" +
        "Initial Catalog=northwind");


    // Create DataAdapter object for update and other operations
    SqlDataAdapter thisAdapter = new SqlDataAdapter(
        "SELECT CustomerID, CompanyName FROM Customers", thisConnection);
```

```
    // Create CommandBuilder object to build SQL commands
    SqlCommandBuilder thisBuilder = new SqlCommandBuilder(thisAdapter);

    // Create DataSet to contain related data tables, rows, and columns
    DataSet thisDataSet = new DataSet();

    // Set up DataAdapter objects for each table and fill
    SqlDataAdapter custAdapter = new SqlDataAdapter(
        "SELECT * FROM Customers", thisConnection);
    SqlDataAdapter orderAdapter = new SqlDataAdapter(
        "SELECT * FROM Orders", thisConnection);
    custAdapter.Fill(thisDataSet, "Customers");
    orderAdapter.Fill(thisDataSet, "Orders");

    // Set up DataRelation between customers and orders
    DataRelation custOrderRel = thisDataSet.Relations.Add("CustOrders",
        thisDataSet.Tables["Customers"].Columns["CustomerID"],
        thisDataSet.Tables["Orders"].Columns["CustomerID"]);

    // Print out nested customers and their order ids
    foreach (DataRow custRow in thisDataSet.Tables["Customers"].Rows)
    {
        Console.WriteLine("Customer ID: " + custRow["CustomerID"] +
                        " Name: " + custRow["CompanyName"]);
        foreach (DataRow orderRow in custRow.GetChildRows(custOrderRel))
        {
            Console.WriteLine("  Order ID: " + orderRow["OrderID"]);
        }
    }
}
```

4. Execute the application, and you will see the following output:

How It Works

Before we construct the `DataRelation` we need to create our `DataSet` object and link the database tables we are going to use with it, as shown here:

```
DataSet thisDataSet = new DataSet();
SqlDataAdapter custAdapter = new SqlDataAdapter(
    "SELECT * FROM Customers", thisConnection);
SqlDataAdapter orderAdapter = new SqlDataAdapter(
    "SELECT * FROM Orders", thisConnection);
custAdapter.Fill(thisDataSet, "Customers");
orderAdapter.Fill(thisDataSet, "Orders");
```

We create a `DataAdapter` object for each table we will reference. We then fill the `DataSet` with data from the columns we're going to work with; in this case we're not worried about efficiency so we'll just use all of the available columns (SELECT * FROM <table>).

Next, we make the `DataRelation` object and link it to the `DataSet`:

```
DataRelation custOrderRel = thisDataSet.Relations.Add("CustOrders",
    thisDataSet.Tables["Customers"].Columns["CustomerID"],
    thisDataSet.Tables["Orders"].Columns["CustomerID"]);
```

Now we're ready to find the customers and orders. First, let's set up a `foreach` loop to display the customer information for each customer:

```
foreach (DataRow custRow in thisDataSet.Tables["Customers"].Rows)
{
    Console.WriteLine("Customer ID: " + custRow["CustomerID"] +
                    " Name: " + custRow["CompanyName"]);
```

We're just looping through the `Rows` collection of the `Customers` table, printing the `CustomerID` and `CompanyName` for each customer. Once we've displayed the customer, we'd like to display the related orders for that customer.

To do that, we add a nested `foreach` loop, initialized by calling the `GetChildRows()` method of `DataRow`. We pass our `DataRelation` object to `GetChildRows()`, and it returns a `DataRowCollection` containing just the related rows in the `Orders` table for this customer. To display these related rows we simply loop through each `DataRow` in this collection with our `foreach` loop:

```
    foreach (DataRow orderRow in custRow.GetChildRows(custOrderRel))
    {
        Console.WriteLine("  Order ID: " + orderRow["OrderID"]);
    }
}
```

Now we repeat the process for each customer. We added some leading spaces to the display of the `OrderID`, so the orders for each customer are displayed indented underneath the customer information. With the indented display you can see the parent-child relationship between each customer and its orders more clearly. Customer ID "**Zachary Zithers Ltd.**" has no `Orders` as we just added it to the table in the previous examples.

That's one relation between two tables – let's go further, and look at relations between more tables. Let's extend this program to see what specific items each customer is placing in each order, and what the names of the products are. This information is available through the other tables in the `Northwind` database. Let's review these relationships; an easy way to see these is to create a database diagram for the `Northwind` database in VS containing all the tables, as we saw in the previous chapter:

637

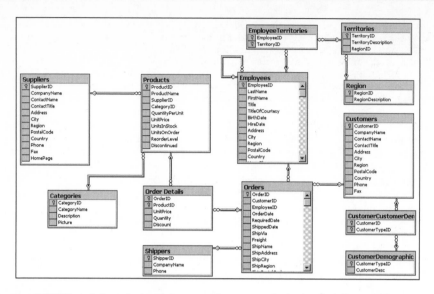

If you're using MSDE and the relationships weren't imported, that's all right – just refer to the diagram shown here. The lines between the tables represent the relationships, with the line on each side going to the column that identifies the relationship. A primary key-foreign key relationship is shown with a key symbol by the parent column and an infinity symbol by the child column.

We're going to display the details of each customer order including the product names, by following the relationships between four tables in the diagram above: `Customers`, `Orders`, `Order Details`, and `Products` tables.

Try It Out – Working with Multiple Relations

1. Create a new console application called `ManyRelations` in the directory `C:\BegVCSharp\Chapter19`.

2. We begin by adding the `using` directives for the ADO.NET classes we will be using:

```
using System;
using System.Data;            // Use ADO.NET namespace
using System.Data.SqlClient;  // Use SQL Server data provider namespace
```

3. Now add the following code to the `Main()` method:

```
public static void Main()
{
    // Specify SQL Server-specific connection string

    SqlConnection thisConnection = new SqlConnection(
        @"Data Source=(local);Integrated Security=SSPI;" +
        "Initial Catalog=northwind");

    DataSet thisDataSet = new DataSet();
```

```
          SqlDataAdapter custAdapter = new SqlDataAdapter(
              "SELECT * FROM Customers", thisConnection);
          custAdapter.Fill(thisDataSet, "Customers");

          SqlDataAdapter orderAdapter = new SqlDataAdapter(
              "SELECT * FROM Orders", thisConnection);
          orderAdapter.Fill(thisDataSet, "Orders");

          SqlDataAdapter detailAdapter = new SqlDataAdapter(
              "SELECT * FROM [Order Details]", thisConnection);
          detailAdapter.Fill(thisDataSet, "Order Details");

          SqlDataAdapter prodAdapter = new SqlDataAdapter(
              "SELECT * FROM Products", thisConnection);
          prodAdapter.Fill(thisDataSet, "Products");

          DataRelation custOrderRel = thisDataSet.Relations.Add("CustOrders",
                  thisDataSet.Tables["Customers"].Columns["CustomerID"],
                  thisDataSet.Tables["Orders"].Columns["CustomerID"]);

          DataRelation orderDetailRel = thisDataSet.Relations.Add("OrderDetail",
                  thisDataSet.Tables["Orders"].Columns["OrderID"],
                  thisDataSet.Tables["Order Details"].Columns["OrderID"]);

          DataRelation orderProductRel = thisDataSet.Relations.Add(
            "OrderProducts",thisDataSet.Tables["Products"].Columns["ProductID"],
            thisDataSet.Tables["Order Details"].Columns["ProductID"]);

          foreach (DataRow custRow in thisDataSet.Tables["Customers"].Rows)
          {
             Console.WriteLine("Customer ID: " + custRow["CustomerID"]);

             foreach (DataRow orderRow in custRow.GetChildRows(custOrderRel))
             {
                Console.WriteLine("\tOrder ID: " + orderRow["OrderID"]);
                Console.WriteLine("\t\tOrder Date: " + orderRow["OrderDate"]);

                foreach (DataRow detailRow in
                        orderRow.GetChildRows(orderDetailRel))
                {
                   Console.WriteLine("\t\tProduct: " +
                   detailRow.GetParentRow(orderProductRel)["ProductName"]);
                   Console.WriteLine("\t\tQuantity: " + detailRow["Quantity"]);
                }
             }
          }
       }
```

4. Execute the application, and you will see output like the following (we've shown an abbreviated version here, with only the last part of the output):

```
Customer ID: WOLZA
        ...
        Order ID: 10998
                Order Date: 4/3/1998 12:00:00 AM
                Product: Guaraná Fantástica
                Quantity: 12
                Product: Sirop d'érable
                Quantity: 7
                Product: Longlife Tofu
                Quantity: 20
                Product: Rhönbräu Klosterbier
                Quantity: 30
        Order ID: 11044
                Order Date: 4/23/1998 12:00:00 AM
                Product: Tarte au sucre
                Quantity: 12
Customer ID: ZACZI
```

How it Works

As usual, we begin by initializing a connection, and then creating a new `DataSet`. Next, we create a data adapter for each of the four tables that will be used:

```
SqlDataAdapter custAdapter = new SqlDataAdapter(
    "SELECT * FROM Customers", thisConnection);
custAdapter.Fill(thisDataSet, "Customers");

SqlDataAdapter orderAdapter = new SqlDataAdapter(
    "SELECT * FROM Orders", thisConnection);
orderAdapter.Fill(thisDataSet, "Orders");

SqlDataAdapter detailAdapter = new SqlDataAdapter(
    "SELECT * FROM [Order Details]", thisConnection);
detailAdapter.Fill(thisDataSet, "Order Details");

SqlDataAdapter prodAdapter = new SqlDataAdapter(
    "SELECT * FROM Products", thisConnection);
prodAdapter.Fill(thisDataSet, "Products");
```

Next, we build `DataRelation` objects for each of the relationships between the four tables:

```
DataRelation custOrderRel = thisDataSet.Relations.Add("CustOrders",
        thisDataSet.Tables["Customers"].Columns["CustomerID"],
        thisDataSet.Tables["Orders"].Columns["CustomerID"]);

DataRelation orderDetailRel = thisDataSet.Relations.Add("OrderDetail",
        thisDataSet.Tables["Orders"].Columns["OrderID"],
        thisDataSet.Tables["Order Details"].Columns["OrderID"]);

DataRelation orderProductRel = thisDataSet.Relations.Add(
    "OrderProducts",thisDataSet.Tables["Products"].Columns["ProductID"],
    thisDataSet.Tables["Order Details"].Columns["ProductID"]);
```

The first relationship is exactly the same as in the previous example. The next one adds the relationship between `Orders` and `Order Details`, using the `OrderID` as the linking column. The last relationship is the one between `Order Details` and `Products`, using `ProductID` as the linking column. Notice that in this relationship, `Products` is actually the parent table (second of the three parameters). This is because it is the "one" side of the one-to-many relation (one `Product` may appear in many `Orders`).

Now that we've set up the relationships we can do processing with them. Again the basic structure is a nested `foreach` loop, this time with three nested levels:

```
foreach (DataRow custRow in thisDataSet.Tables["Customers"].Rows)
{
    Console.WriteLine("Customer ID: " + custRow["CustomerID"]);

    foreach (DataRow orderRow in custRow.GetChildRows(custOrderRel))
    {
        Console.WriteLine("\tOrder ID: " + orderRow["OrderID"]);
        Console.WriteLine("\t\tOrder Date: " + orderRow["OrderDate"]);

        foreach (DataRow detailRow in
                orderRow.GetChildRows(orderDetailRel))
        {
            Console.WriteLine("\t\tProduct: " +
            detailRow.GetParentRow(orderProductRel)["ProductName"]);
            Console.WriteLine("\t\tQuantity: " + detailRow["Quantity"]);
        }
    }
}
```

Just as before, we output the data for the parent row, then use `GetChildRows()` to obtain the child rows related to this parent. The outer loop is the same as the previous example. Next, we print out the additional detail of the `OrderDate` to the `OrderID`, and then get the `OrderDetails` for this `OrderID`.

The innermost loop is different; to get the `Product` row we call `GetParentRow()` which gets the parent object, going from the "many" side to the "one" side of the relationship. Sometimes this navigation from child to parent is called navigating "upstream" as opposed to the normal parent-to-child "downstream" navigation. Upstream navigation requires the `GetParentRow()` call.

The output of the program shows all the details of the orders processed for each customer, indented to show the parent and child hierarchy. Again, the Customer ID "ZACZI" has no orders as we just added it to the table in the previous examples.

XML and ADO.NET

As we said in the introduction, XML support is one of the major design goals of ADO.NET and is also central to ADO.NET's internal implementation. Therefore, it makes sense that ADO.NET would have lots of support for XML built into its object model. XML was introduced in the previous chapter, and we are now going to talk about the support for it in ADO.NET.

XML Support in ADO.NET DataSets

The XML support in ADO.NET is centered around the `DataSet` object, as XML is all about relationships and hierarchically structured data. The `DataSet` has several methods that process XML, and one of the easiest to use is `WriteXml()`, which writes out the contents of the `DataSet` as an XML document.

To use `WriteXml()`, simply construct a `DataSet` from existing data using the same code as in our previous examples; use the `Fill()` method of a data adapter to load the data, define `DataRelation` objects for the relationships, and so on. Then, simply call `WriteXml()` on the `DataSet` you have constructed:

```
thisDataSet.WriteXml("nwinddata.xml");
```

`WriteXml()` can write to various targets; this version of the method simply writes the XML to a file. An external program that accepts XML as an input format can easily read and process the XML.

A `ReadXml()` method is available also to read the contents of an XML file into a `DataSet`.

Try it Out – Writing XML from a DataSet

This example takes the code from the `DataRelationExample`, and simply writes out the data in the `DataSet` to an XML file – the nested `foreach` loops are simply replaced by the single call to `WriteXml()`. You will need to ensure that you have a directory named `C:\tmp` before running this program.

1. Open the `DataRelationExample` project, and replace the `foreach` loop:

```
// Print out nested customers and their order ids
foreach (DataRow custRow in thisDataSet.Tables["Customers"].Rows)
{
    ...
}
```

with the following code:

```
custOrderRel.Nested = true;

thisDataSet.WriteXml(@"c:\tmp\nwinddata.xml");
Console.WriteLine(
    @"Successfully wrote XML output to file c:\tmp\nwinddata.xml");
```

2. Open Internet Explorer, and browse the `C:\tmp\nwinddata.xml` file:

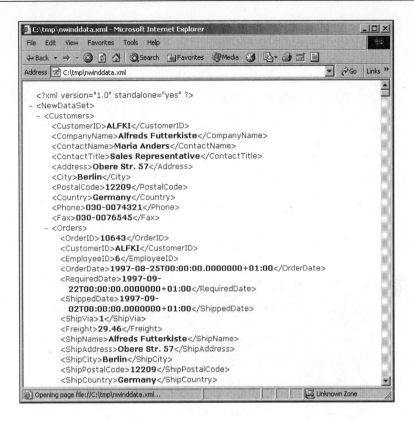

How It Works

The Nested property of the DataRelation objects tells the WriteXml() method to nest the order details and orders underneath each parent customer in the XML output. The file nwinddata.xml contains all the data in our tables (including all the columns since we specified SELECT * FROM when filling the DataSet). It is in human-readable, easy-to-parse XML format, and the file can be browsed directly in Microsoft Internet Explorer.

So the DataSet has a WriteXml() – guess what, it also has a ReadXml() method! The ReadXml() method creates and populates a DataTable in a DataSet with the data from an XML file. Furthermore, the DataTable created is given the name of the root element in the XML document.

Try it Out – Reading XML into a DataSet

Having just created an XML file in our previous example, let's now read it back in and display it!

1. Create a new console application called ReadingXML in the directory C:\BegVCSharp\Chapter19, and add a using directive for the System.Data namespace to the top of the code.

2. Add the following code to the Main() method:

```
static void Main(string[] args)
{
    DataSet thisDataSet = new DataSet();
    thisDataSet.ReadXml(@"c:\tmp\nwinddata.xml");

    foreach (DataRow custRow in thisDataSet.Tables["Customers"].Rows)
    {
        Console.WriteLine("Customer ID: " + custRow["CustomerID"] +
                            " Name: " + custRow["CompanyName"]);
    }

    Console.WriteLine("Table created by ReadXml is called {0}",
                        thisDataSet.Tables[0].TableName);
}
```

3. Execute the application, and you should see output like the following, provided you ran the previous example to create the `C:\tmp\nwinddata.xml` file:

How it Works

Note that we are only using one data namespace here – `System.Data`. We aren't using any database access so we don't have any need for the `System.Data.SqlClient` or `System.Data.OleDb`. All we do is create a new `DataSet`, and then use the `ReadXml()` method to load the data from the `C:\tmp\nwinddata.xml` file. The overload of `ReadXml()` that we use here simply requires us to specify the name of the XML file:

```
DataSet thisDataSet = new DataSet();
thisDataSet.ReadXml(@"c:\tmp\nwinddata.xml");
```

Next we output the contents of the `Customers` table – this code should be familiar from the `DataRelationExample` code – we loop through each `DataRow` in the `Rows` collection of the `Customers` table, and display the value of the `CustomerID` and `CompanyName` columns:

```
foreach (DataRow custRow in thisDataSet.Tables["Customers"].Rows)
{
    Console.WriteLine("Customer ID: " + custRow["CustomerID"] +
                        " Name: " + custRow["CompanyName"]);
}
```

How did we know the table was called Customers? As we mentioned above, the DataTable is named from the root node of the XML document that is read in – if you look back at the screenshot for the WriteXml() method, you will see that the root node of the XML document produced is indeed Customers. Just to prove the point, we write out the name of the first DataTable in the Tables collection of the DataSet, using the TableName property of the DataTable:

```
Console.WriteLine("Table created by ReadXml is called {0}",
                  thisDataSet.Tables[0].TableName);
```

SQL Support in ADO.NET

In this chapter we have covered the basic ADO.NET operations without having to know anything about the SQL database query language. All ADO.NET commands that read and write from the data source are translated to SQL commands that execute the raw database operations.

Practical use of ADO.NET in real-life working situations will require some knowledge of SQL; for a much more complete introduction to SQL than we have space for here, refer to a good book on SQL such as *Beginning SQL Programming* (ISBN 1-7100-180-0) or *Beginning SQL Server 2000 Programming* (ISBN 1-71000-523-7), both from Wrox Press.

That said, there are a few basics we will cover here.

SQL Commands in Data Adapters

In the examples given earlier, we've used SQL SELECT commands that return all the rows of a table, such as:

```
SqlDataAdapter thisAdapter = new SqlDataAdapter(
    "SELECT * FROM Customers", thisConnection);
```

This SELECT command returns all the rows and columns of the customer table when the Fill() method is called, and loads them into the memory of your program. This is fine for a small table like the Customers table of Northwind, which has only 11 columns and less than 100 rows of data; however, it is not likely to work well for a large table typical of those encountered in many business applications with 100,000 or even 1,000,000 rows.

You need to construct the SELECT command so that it only brings in the data you actually need to process. One way is to limit the number of columns used if your program really only interacts with some of the columns, with a SELECT statement specifying only the desired columns, such as:

```
SELECT CustomerID, CompanyName FROM Customers
```

However, you typically don't want to do this when adding rows, as you will want to specify values for all columns.

Use of WHERE with SELECT

Another technique for minimizing the amount of data loaded into memory is to always specify a WHERE clause on the SQL SELECT statement, which limits the number of rows selected. For example, the statement:

```
SELECT * FROM Customers WHERE CustomerID = "ZACZI"
```

will load only the one row containing Zachary Zithers into memory, using a fraction of the memory required to load the entire table. A range can be specified with WHERE clauses as well, so a statement like:

```
SELECT * FROM Orders WHERE OrderID BETWEEN 10900 AND 10999
```

will only load the rows with OrderID in the range shown.

If you can limit the number of rows being loaded from a large table with a WHERE clause, always do so. Never load all the rows of a table into your DataSet and then search them with a foreach loop; use the SELECT statement with WHERE to do this kind of search instead.

Your goal is to find the most effective balance between processing data locally on the client where your ADO.NET program is executing, and processing on the server where the SQL is executed. The ADO.NET object model and C# are better suited than SQL for complex calculations or navigational logic. Fill your DataSet with the data from the tables you want to process and execute this kind of logic on the client. However, limiting the number of rows selected from each table with appropriate conditions will greatly increase the performance, especially if the data is being transferred across a network, and decrease the memory usage.

Viewing SQL SELECT, UPDATE, INSERT, and DELETE Commands

SQL uses four basic commands for querying, updating, adding, and deleting rows from a table. These are, respectively, the SELECT, UPDATE, INSERT, and DELETE commands. In our earlier examples we have used the CommandBuilder object to create the SQL commands used to update the database:

```
SqlDataAdapter thisAdapter =
    new SqlDataAdapter("SELECT CustomerID from Customers", thisConnection);

SqlCommandBuilder thisBuilder = new SqlCommandBuilder(thisAdapter);
```

The command builder generates the SQL commands for modifying the data (UPDATE, INSERT, and DELETE) based on the SELECT command.

In the program which we create here, we can see the generated commands with the GetUpdateCommand(), GetInsertCommand(), and GetDeleteCommand() methods of the CommandBuilder object:

Try it Out – Show SQL Example

1. Create a new console application called ShowSQL in the C:\BegVCSharp\Chapter19 directory, and add our usual using directives to the top of the code:

```
using System;
using System.Data;           // Use ADO.NET namespace
using System.Data.SqlClient; // Use SQL Server data provider namespace
```

2. Now add the following code to the Main() method:

```
public static void Main()
{
    // Specify SQL Server-specific connection string
    SqlConnection thisConnection = new SqlConnection(
        @"Data Source=(local);Integrated Security=SSPI;" +
        "Initial Catalog=northwind");

    thisConnection.Open();

    SqlDataAdapter thisAdapter = new
      SqlDataAdapter("SELECT CustomerID from Customers", thisConnection);

    SqlCommandBuilder thisBuilder = new SqlCommandBuilder(thisAdapter);

    Console.WriteLine("SQL SELECT Command is:\n{0}\n",
                      thisAdapter.SelectCommand.CommandText);

    SqlCommand updateCommand = thisBuilder.GetUpdateCommand();
    Console.WriteLine("SQL UPDATE Command is:\n{0}\n",
                      updateCommand.CommandText);

    SqlCommand insertCommand = thisBuilder.GetInsertCommand();
    Console.WriteLine("SQL INSERT Command is:\n{0}\n",
                      insertCommand.CommandText);

    SqlCommand deleteCommand = thisBuilder.GetDeleteCommand();
    Console.WriteLine("SQL DELETE Command is:\n{0}",
                      deleteCommand.CommandText);

    thisConnection.Close();
}
```

The output of this example is:

```
C:\BegVCSharp\Chapter19\ShowSQL\bin\Debug\ShowSQL.exe
SQL SELECT Command is:
SELECT CustomerID from Customers

SQL UPDATE Command is:
UPDATE Customers SET CustomerID = @p1 WHERE ( (CustomerID = @p2) )

SQL INSERT Command is:
INSERT INTO Customers( CustomerID ) VALUES ( @p1 )

SQL DELETE Command is:
DELETE FROM  Customers WHERE ( (CustomerID = @p1) )
Press any key to continue
```

How It Works

Note that the UPDATE and DELETE commands use a WHERE clause that was generated by the CommandBuilder object.

The question marks (?) are markers for parameters, where the ADO.NET runtime will substitute an actual value into the command; for example when we used the Delete() method to delete the row containing CustomerID "ZACZI", at the time Update() was called the command:

```
DELETE FROM  Customers WHERE ( CustomerID = 'ZACZI' )
```

was executed to remove the ZACZI row.

Notice that to output the SELECT command we used the SelectCommand property to get the command directly from the DataAdapter. The DataAdapter also has the UpdateCommand, InsertCommand, and DeleteCommand properties to get or set the SQL commands used at update time directly. A developer familiar with SQL can optimize these commands to perform better than the commands automatically generated by CommandBuilder, especially when all columns are included in the SQL SELECT statement.

Direct Execution of SQL Commands

If your program needs to perform a set-oriented operation such as deleting or updating all rows meeting a certain condition, it is much more efficient, especially for large tables, to do this as a single SQL command than to do extended processing in C# code.

ADO.NET provides the SqlCommand or OleDbCommand objects for executing SQL commands. These objects provide methods for executing SQL commands directly. We used the ExecuteReader() method at the beginning of the chapter when we looked at the data reader object. Here we'll look at the other methods for executing SQL statements – ExecuteScalar() and ExecuteNonQuery().

Retrieving Single Values

On many occasions it is necessary to return a single result from a SQL query, such as the number of records in a given table. The ExecuteScalar() method allows you to achieve this – this method is used to execute SQL commands that return only a scalar (a single value), as opposed to returning multiple rows, as with ExecuteReader().

This example uses the ExecuteScalar() method of SqlCommand to execute the query.

Try it Out – Retrieving Single Values with ExecuteScalar()

As a first example, let's consider a program that gets a count of the rows in the Customers table; this is similar to the data reader example at the start of the chapter, but uses a different SQL statement and method of execution.

```
using System;
using System.Data;
using System.Data.SqlClient;

class ExecuteScalarExample
{
    public static void Main()
    {
        SqlConnection thisConnection = new
        SqlConnection("Data Source=(local);" +
                    "Integrated Security=SSPI;Initial Catalog=northwind");
        thisConnection.Open();
```

```
            SqlCommand thisCommand = thisConnection.CreateCommand();
            thisCommand.CommandText = "SELECT COUNT(*) FROM Customers";
            Object countResult = thisCommand.ExecuteScalar();
            Console.WriteLine("Count of Customers = {0}", countResult);
            thisConnection.Close();
        }
    }
```

How it Works

This program uses the SQL Server .NET data provider. The core of the program is the same as the first example in this chapter, opening a connection to SQL Server on the local machine with SSPI security and the Northwind database.

We create a SqlCommand object and assign the SELECT COUNT(*) command to its CommandText property. COUNT() is a SQL function that returns the count of rows that match the WHERE condition. Then, we call the ExecuteScalar() method of SqlCommand to execute the query to retrieve the count. We display the count and exit. When executed against the Northwind database, the program displays:

```
Count of Customers = 91
```

(Provided you've deleted Zachary Zithers Ltd!) This is equivalent to loading the Customers table into the DataTable object and using the Count property of the Rows object as in our earlier examples; why would you want to do the job this way? It depends on the structure of your data and what else you are doing in your program. If you have a small amount of data, or are loading all the rows into your DataSet for any other reason, it makes sense to just use DataTable.Rows.Count. However, if you wanted to count the exact number of rows in a very large table with 1,000,000 rows, it is much more efficient to issue a SELECT COUNT(*) query with the ExecuteScalar() method rather than trying to load 1,000,000 rows into memory.

Retrieving No Data

A rather strange heading, but bear in mind that data modification operations such as SQL INSERT, UPDATE, and DELETE do not return data; what is interesting for these commands is the number of rows affected. This number is returned by the ExecuteNonQuery() method.

Try it Out – Data Modification with ExecuteNonQuery

Let's assume one of our suppliers has increased all prices by 5% for all of its products. The program below shows how to use the SqlCommand object to execute a SQL UPDATE command to increase all the prices by 5% for products supplied by that supplier:

```
using System;
using System.Data;
using System.Data.SqlClient;

class ExecuteNonQueryExample
{
    public static void Main()
    {
        SqlConnection thisConnection = new SqlConnection(
```

```
            "Data Source=(local);" +
            "Integrated Security=SSPI;Initial Catalog=northwind");
        thisConnection.Open();

        SqlCommand thisCommand = thisConnection.CreateCommand();
        thisCommand.CommandText = "UPDATE Products SET " +
            "UnitPrice=UnitPrice*1.05 WHERE SupplierId=12";
        int rowsAffected = thisCommand.ExecuteNonQuery();
        Console.WriteLine("Rows Updated = {0}", rowsAffected);
        thisConnection.Close();
    }
}
```

How it Works

This program opens the connection just as in the previous example. We create a `SqlCommand` object and assign the UPDATE command shown as the text of the command. Then we call the `ExecuteNonQuery()` method of `SqlCommand` to execute the query, returning the number of rows affected in the database. We display the number of rows and exit. When executed against the `Northwind` database, the program displays:

```
Rows Updated = 5
```

Indicating that the prices were adjusted for 5 products.

Summary

We have learned that ADO.NET is the part of the .NET Framework that enables access to relational databases and other data sources. ADO.NET is designed to provide a simple, flexible framework for data access; it is designed for multi-tier application architectures and integrates relational data with XML.

The ADO.NET classes are contained in the `System.Data` namespace. We reviewed the object model of ADO.NET and learned the roles of its major objects, including the connection, command, data reader, data adapter, `DataSet`, `DataTable`, `DataRow`, and `DataColumn` objects.

We learned that .NET data providers give access to specific data sources, and that ADO.NET can be extended to new data sources by writing .NET data providers for the new data source. We examined the .NET data providers included with ADO.NET for Microsoft SQL Server and OLE DB data sources, and learned that these are contained in the `System.Data.SqlClient` and `System.Data.OleDb` namespaces, respectively.

We saw how to implement quick read-only access to data via the data reader object, and how to write an equivalent program for both the `SqlClient` and `OleDb` .NET data providers. We learned how to update data and add rows via the `DataSet`, data adapter, and `CommandBuilder` objects. We saw how to find rows using the primary key, and also how to delete rows.

We learned how to access multiple tables in a `DataSet` via the `DataRelation` object, and how to generate an XML view of that data. Finally we looked briefly at how to take advantage of the SQL database language support within ADO.NET, including display of automatically generated SQL commands, and direction execution of SQL.

Exercises

1. Modify the program given in the first sample to use the `Employees` table in the `Northwind` database. Retrieve the `EmployeeID` and `LastName` columns.

2. Modify the first program showing the `Update()` method to change the company name back to Bottom-Dollar Markets.

3. Write a program that asks the user for a Customer ID.

4. Write a program to create some orders for the customer "Zachary Zithers"; use the sample programs to view the orders.

5. Write a program to display a different part of the relationship hierarchies in the `Northwind` database than the one used in this chapter; for example, `Products`, `Suppliers`, and `Categories`.

6. Write out the data generated in the previous exercise as an XML document.

7. Change the program used to print all customer order details and products to use a `WHERE` clause in the `SELECT` statement for `Customers` limiting the customers processed.

8. Modify the program shown to print out `UPDATE`, `INSERT`, and `DELETE` statements to use `"SELECT * FROM Customers"` as the SQL `SELECT` command. Note the complexity of the generated statements.

Working With Files

In this chapter you will learn how to read and write text files, an essential aspect of many .NET applications. We will discuss the major classes used to create files, read from and write to them, and the supporting classes used to manipulate the file system from C# code. Although we won't be able to cover all of the classes in detail, we will go into enough depth to give you a good idea of the concepts and fundamentals.

Files can be a great way to store data between instances of your application, or they can be used to transfer data between applications. User and application configuration settings can be stored to be retrieved the next time your application is run. Delimited files, such as comma-separated files, are used by many legacy systems, and to interoperate with such systems you will need to know how to work with delimited data. As we will see, the .NET Framework provides us with the tools to use files effectively in our applications.

By the end of this chapter, you will have learned:

- ❑   What a stream is and how .NET uses stream classes to access files
- ❑   How to use the `File` object to manipulate the file structure
- ❑   How to write to a file
- ❑   How to read from a file
- ❑   How to read and write formatted data from and to files
- ❑   How to populate a `DataSet` from a delimited file
- ❑   How to monitor files and directories for changes

Streams

All input and output in the .NET Framework involves the use of streams. A stream is an abstract representation of a serial device. A serial device is something that stores data in a linear manner, and is accessed the same way: one byte at a time. This device can be a disk file, a network channel, a memory location, or any other object that supports reading and writing to it in a linear manner. By keeping the device abstract, the underlying destination/source of the stream can be hidden. This level of abstraction enables code reuse and allows us to write more generic routines. Therefore, similar code can be transferred and reused when the application is reading from either a file input stream or a network input stream. Also, by using a stream we can ignore the physical mechanics of each device. Thus to read from a file stream we don't need to worry about hard disk heads or memory allocation.

An output stream is used when data is written to some external destination. This can point to a physical disk file, a network location, a printer, or another program. Understanding stream programming opens many advanced possibilities. For this chapter we will limit our discussion to writing to disk files.

An input stream is used to read data into memory or variables that our program can access. The most common form of input stream we have worked with so far is the keyboard. An input stream can come from almost any source but we will concentrate on reading disk files. The concepts applied to reading/writing of disk files will apply to most devices, so we will gain a basic understanding of streams and see a proven approach that can be applied to many situations.

The Classes for Input and Output

The System.IO namespace contains all of the classes that we will be covering in this chapter. System.IO contains the classes for reading and writing data to files, and you must reference this namespace in your C# application to gain access to these classes. There are quite a few classes contained in System.IO, as you can see in the following diagram, but we will be covering only the primary classes needed for file input and output:

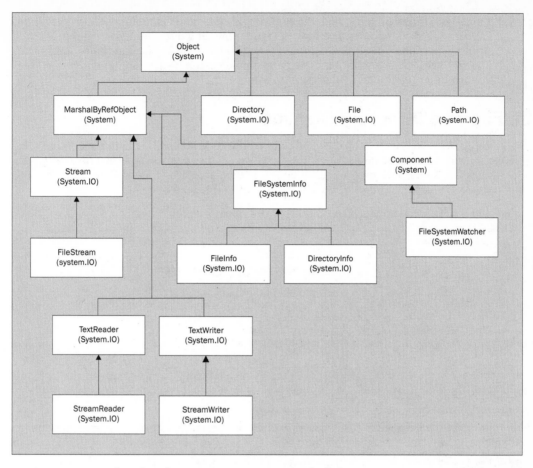

- ❑   `File` – a utility class that exposes many static methods for moving, copying, and deleting files.

- ❑   `Directory` – a utility class that exposes many static methods for moving, copying, and deleting directories.

- ❑   `Path` – a utility class used to manipulate path names.

- ❑   `FileInfo` – represents a physical file on disk, and has methods to manipulate this file. For any reading and writing to the file, a `Stream` object must be created.

- ❑   `DirectoryInfo` – represents a physical directory on disk, and has methods to manipulate this directory.

- ❑   `FileStream` – represents a file that can be written to or read from, or both. This file can be written to and read from asynchronously or synchronously.

- ❑   `StreamReader` – reads character data from a stream and can be created by using a `FileStream` as a base.

- ❑   `StreamWriter` – writes character data to a stream and can be created by using a `FileStream` as a base.

❑   FileSystemWatcher – the FileSystemWatcher is the most advanced class we will be examining in this chapter. It is used to monitor files and directories, and exposes events that your application can catch when changes occur in these locations. This functionality has always been missing from Windows programming, but now the .NET Framework makes it much easier to respond to file system events.

The File and Directory Classes

As utility classes, both the File and Directory classes expose many methods for manipulating the file system and the files and directories within it. These are the static methods that involve moving files, querying and updating attributes, and creating FileStream objects. As we learned in Chapter 8, static methods can be called on classes without having to create instances of them.

Some of the most useful static methods of the File class are:

Method	Description
Copy()	Copies a file to the specified location.
Create()	Creates a file in the specified path.
Delete()	Deletes a file.
Open()	Returns a FileStream object at the specified path.
Move()	Moves a specified file to a new location. We can specify a different name for the file in the new location.

Some useful static methods of the Directory class are:

Method	Description
CreateDirectory()	Creates a directory with the specified path.
Delete()	Deletes the specified directory and all the files within it.
GetDirectories()	Returns an array of Directory objects that represent the directories below the current directory.
GetFiles()	Returns an array of File objects in the current directory.
Move()	Moves the specified directory to a new location. We can specify a new name for the folder in the new location.

The FileInfo Class

Unlike the File class, the FileInfo class does not have static methods, and can only be used on instantiated objects. The FileInfo object represents a file on a disk or network location, but note that it is not a stream. To read or write to a file, a Stream object has to be created. The FileInfo object aids you in doing this by exposing several methods that return instantiated Stream objects. But first, to create a FileInfo object you must supply a path to a file or directory.

```
FileInfo aFile = new FileInfo(@"C:\Log.txt");
```

Since we will be working with strings representing the path of a file throughout this chapter, which will mean a lot of \ characters in our strings, it's worth reminding yourself that the @ that prefixes the string above means that this string will be interpreted literally. Thus \ will be interpreted as \, and not as an escape character. Without the @ prefix, we would need to use \ \ instead of \ to avoid this character being interpreted as an escape character. In this chapter we will stick to the @ prefix for our strings.

Many of the methods exposed by the `FileInfo` class are similar to those of the `File` class but because `File` is a static class, it requires a string parameter specifying the file location for every method call. Therefore, the following calls do the same thing:

```
FileInfo aFile = new FileInfo("Data.txt");
if (aFile.Exists)
   Console.WriteLine("File Exists");

if (File.Exists("Data.txt"))
   Console.WriteLine("File Exists");
```

Most of the `FileInfo` methods mirror the `File` methods in this manner. The question is when should you use the instance methods, and when should you use the static methods?

❏   It makes sense to use the static `File` class if you are only making a single method call on the object – the single call will be faster because the .NET Framework will not have to go through the process of instantiating a new object and then calling the method.

❏   However, if your application is performing several operations on a file it makes more sense to instantiate the `FileInfo` object and use its methods – this will save time because the object will already be referencing the correct file on the file system, whereas the static class will have to find it every time.

The `FileInfo` class also exposes the following properties about the underlying file, which can be manipulated to update the file:

Property	Description
Attributes	Gets or sets the attributes of the current file.
CreationTime	Gets the creation date and time of the current file.
DirectoryName	Returns the path to the file's directory.
Exists	Determines whether a file exists.
FullName	Retrieves the full path of the file.
Length	Gets the size of the file.
Name	Returns just the name of the file, not the full file location path.

The DirectoryInfo Class

The DirectoryInfo class works exactly like the FileInfo class. It is an instantiated object that represents a single directory on a machine. Like the FileInfo class, many of the method calls are duplicated across Directory and DirectoryInfo. The same guideline applies as to when to use each: if you are making a single call use the static Directory class. If you are making a series of calls, use an instantiated DirectoryInfo object.

The DirectoryInfo class shares almost all of the same properties as the FileInfo class, except that they operate on directories not files.

Pathnames and Relative Paths

When specifying a path name in .NET code you can use either absolute or relative path names. An absolute path name explicitly specifies where a file or directory is from a known location – like the C: drive. An example of this would be C:\Work\LogFile.txt. Note that it is defined exactly where it is, with no ambiguity.

Relative pathnames are relative to where the application is running on the file system. By using relative pathnames, no drive or known location needs to be specified; the current directory is the starting point. For example, if the application is running in the C:\Development\FileDemo directory, and uses a relative path "LogFile.txt," that file would be C:\Development\FileDemo\LogFile.txt. To move "up" a directory the .. character is used. Thus, in the same application, the path ..\Log.txt points to a file in C:\Development called Log.txt.

The tricky part about using relative pathnames in the development process is that it is relative to where the **application** is running. When you are developing with the Visual Studio .NET this means the application is several directories beneath the project folder you created. It is usually located in ProjectName\bin\Debug. This means to access a file in the project's root folder, you will have to move up *two* directories with ..\..\ – you will see this happen often in the chapter.

The FileStream Object

The FileStream object represents a stream pointing to a file on a disk or a network path. While the class does expose methods for reading and writing bytes from and to the files, most often you will use a StreamReader or StreamWriter to perform these functions. This is because the FileStream class operates on bytes and byte arrays, while the Stream classes operate on character data. Character data is easier to work with, but we will see that there are certain operations, such as random file access, that can only be performed by a FileStream object, which we will examine later.

There are several ways to create a FileStream object. The constructor has many different overloads/versions but the simplest takes just two arguments, the filename and a FileMode enumeration.

```
FileStream aFile = new FileStream("Log.txt", FileMode.OpenOrCreate);
```

The FileMode enumeration has several members that specify how the file is opened or created. These can be combined to work together.

FileMode Enumeration Members	Description
`Append`	Opens the file if it exists and moves the file position to the end of the file, or creates a new file. `FileMode.Append` can only be used in conjunction with the enum `FileAccess.Write`.
`Create`	A new file is created; if one already exists it is destroyed.
`CreateNew`	A new file is created, but if one already exists an exception will be thrown.
`Open`	Opens an existing file. If the file specified does not exist, an exception is thrown.
`OpenOrCreate`	Specifies that the file should be opened if it exists, otherwise a new file is created. If it exists, the data in the file is retained.
`Truncate`	An existing file is opened and its contents erased. We can then write completely new data to the file, but the original creation date will be retained. The file must exist or an exception is thrown.

The previous constructor opens the file in read-write mode by default. An additional parameter is required to specify a different level of access, the `FileAccess` parameter.

```
FileStream aFile = new FileStream("Log.txt", FileMode.OpenOrCreate,
FileAccess.Write)
```

This line of code would open the file with write access to the file. Any attempt to read from the file would result in an exception being thrown. The `FileAccess` enumeration has three values: `Read`, `Write`, and `ReadWrite`. Therefore, you can open a file for reading only, writing only, or both. This property is often used as a way of varying user access to the file based on the authorization level of the user.

Both the `File` and `FileInfo` classes expose `OpenRead()` and `OpenWrite()` methods that make it easier to create `FileStream` objects. The first opens the file for read-only access, and the second allows you to write to the file as well. These provide shortcuts, so you do not have to provide all of the previous information. For example, the following line opens the `Data.txt` file for read-only access:

```
FileStream aFile = File.OpenRead("Data.txt");
```

Note that the following code performs the same function:

```
FileInfo aFileInfo = new FileInfo("Data.txt");
FileStream aFile = aFileInfo.OpenRead();
```

File Position

The `FileStream` class maintains an internal file pointer. This points to the location within the file where the next read or write operation will occur. In most cases, when a file is opened it points to the beginning of the file, but this pointer can be modified. This allows an application to read or write anywhere within the file. This allows for random-access to a file, or the ability to seek directly to a specific location in the file. This can be very time saving when dealing with very large files, because you can instantly seek to the correct location.

The method that implements this functionality is the `Seek()` method. Seek takes two parameters, the first parameter specifying how far to move the file pointer, in bytes. The second parameter specifies where to start counting from, and this parameter takes values from the `SeekOrigin` enumeration – this enumeration contains three values: `Begin`, `Current`, and `End`.

For example, the following line would move the file pointer to the eighth byte in the file, starting from the very first byte in the file:

```
aFile.Seek(8,SeekOrigin.Begin);
```

The following line would move the file pointer two bytes forward, starting from the current position. If this were executed directly after the previous line, the file pointer would now point to the tenth byte in the file:

```
aFile.Seek(2,SeekOrigin.Current);
```

Note that when you read from or write to a file the file pointer changes as well. After you have read ten bytes, the file pointer now points to the byte after the tenth byte read.

You can specify negative seek positions as well, which could be combined with the `SeekOrigin.End` enumeration value to seek near the end of the file. The following line will seek to the fifth byte from the end of the file:

```
aFile.Seek(-5, SeekOrigin.End);
```

Files accessed in this manner are sometimes referred to as random access files, because an application can access any position within the file. The `Stream` classes we will look at later access files sequentially, and do not allow the manipulation of the file pointer.

Reading Data

Reading data using the `FileStream` class is not as easy as the `StreamReader` class that we will look at later in this chapter. This is because the `FileStream` class deals exclusively with raw bytes. Working in raw bytes makes the `FileStream` class useful for any kind of data file, not just text files. By reading byte data, the `FileStream` object can be used to read files such as images, or sound files. The cost of this flexibility is that you cannot use the `FileStream` to read data directly into a string as you can with the `StreamReader` class. However, there are several conversion classes that make it fairly easy to convert byte arrays into character arrays and vice versa.

The `FileStream.Read()` method is the primary means to access data from a file that a `FileStream` object points to. This method *reads* the data from a file, and then *writes* this data into a `byte` array. There are three parameters, the first parameter being a `byte` array passed in to accept data from the `FileStream` object. The second parameter is the position in the `byte` array to begin writing data to – this will normally be zero to begin writing data from the file at the beginning of the array. The last parameter specifies how many bytes to read from the file.

The following example will demonstrate reading data from a random access file. The file we will read from will actually be the class file we create for the example.

Try it Out – Reading Data from Random Access Files

1. Create a new console application called `ReadFile` in the directory `C:\BegVCSharp\Chapter20`.

2. Add the following two using directives to the top of the `Class1.cs` file. `System.IO` is needed for our `FileStream` class, and `System.Text` is required for the conversion we must do on the bytes read from the file.

```
using System;
using System.IO;
using System.Text;
```

3. Add the following code to the `Main()` method:

```
static void Main(string[] args)
{
    byte[] byData = new byte[100];
    char[] charData = new Char[100];

    try
    {
        FileStream aFile = new FileStream("../../Class1.cs",FileMode.Open);
        aFile.Seek(55,SeekOrigin.Begin);
        aFile.Read(byData,0,100);
    }
    catch(IOException e)
    {
        Console.WriteLine("An IO exception has been thrown!");
        Console.WriteLine(e.ToString());
        Console.ReadLine();
        return;
    }

    Decoder d = Encoding.UTF8.GetDecoder();
    d.GetChars(byData, 0, byData.Length, charData, 0);

    Console.WriteLine(charData);
    Console.ReadLine();

    return;
```

4. Run the application. You should see output similar to the following:

```
C:\BegVCSharp\Chapter21\ReadFile\bin\Debug\ReadFile.exe
namespace ReadFile
{
        /// <summary>
        /// Summary description for Class1.
        /// </summary>
        class
```

How It Works

This application opens its own `.cs` file to read from. It does this by navigating two directories up the file structure with the `..` symbol in the following line:

```
FileStream aFile = new FileStream("../../Class1.cs",FileMode.Open);
```

The two lines that implement the actual seeking and reading from a specific point in the file are:

```
aFile.Seek(55,SeekOrigin.Begin);
aFile.Read(byData,0,100);
```

The first line moves the file pointer to byte number 55 in the file. This is the "n" of namespace in the `Class1.cs` file; the 54 characters preceding it are the three lines of using directives. The second line reads the next 100 bytes into the `byte` array `byData`.

Note that these two lines were enclosed in `try...catch` blocks to handle any exceptions that may be thrown:

```
try
{
    aFile.Seek(55,SeekOrigin.Begin);
    aFile.Read(byData,0,100);
}
catch(IOException e)
{
    Console.WriteLine("An IO exception has been thrown!");
    Console.WriteLine(e.ToString());
    Console.ReadLine();
    return;
}
```

Almost all operations involving file IO can throw an exception of type `IOException`. All production code must contain error handling, especially when dealing with the file system. The examples in this chapter will all have a basic form of error handling.

Once we have the `byte` array from the file, then we need to convert it into a character array so that we can display it to the console. To do this we will use the `Decoder` class from the `System.Text` namespace. This class is designed to convert raw bytes into more useful items, such as characters:

```
Decoder d = Encoding.UTF8.GetDecoder();
d.GetChars(byData, 0, byData.Length, charData, 0);
```

These lines create a `Decoder` object based on the UTF8 encoding schema. This is the Unicode encoding schema. Then the `GetChars()` method is called, which takes an array of bytes and converts it to an array of characters. Once this has been done, the character array can be printed to the console.

Writing Data

The process for writing data to a random access file is very similar. A byte array must be created; the easiest way to do this is to first build the character array we wish to write to the file. Then use the `Encoder` object to convert it to a byte array, very much like we used the `Decoder` object. Lastly, call the `Write()` method to send the array to the file.

Let's build a simple example to demonstrate how this is done.

Try it Out – Writing Data to Random Access Files

1. Create a new console application called `WriteFile` in the directory `C:\BegVCSharp\Chapter20`.

2. Just like before, add the following two using directives to the top of the `Class1.cs` file:

```
using System;
using System.IO;
using System.Text;
```

3. Add the following code to the `Main()` method:

```
static void Main(string[] args)
{
    byte[] byData = new byte[100];
    char[] charData = new Char[100];

    try
    {
        FileStream aFile = new FileStream("Temp.txt",FileMode.OpenOrCreate);
        charData = "Hello World".ToCharArray();
        Encoder e = Encoding.UTF8.GetEncoder();
        e.GetBytes(charData,0,charData.Length, byData,0,true);

        //Move file pointer to beginning of file
        aFile.Seek(0,SeekOrigin.Begin);
        aFile.Write(byData,0,byData.Length);
    }
    catch(IOException ex)
```

```
        {
            Console.WriteLine("An IO exception has been thrown!");
            Console.WriteLine(ex.ToString());
            Console.ReadLine();
            return;
        }

        return;
    }
```

4. Run the application. It should run briefly then close.

5. Navigate to the application directory – the file will have been saved there because we used a relative path. This is located in the `WriteFile\bin\Debug` folder. Open the `Temp.txt` file. You should see the following text in the file:

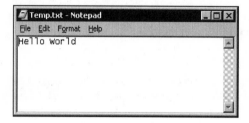

How It Works

This application opens up a file in its own directory and writes a simple string to it. In structure, this example is very similar to the previous example, except we use `Write()` instead of `Read()`, and `Encoder` instead of `Decoder`!

The following line creates a character array by using the `ToCharArray()` static method of the `String` class. Because everything in C# is an object, and the text "`Hello World`" is actually a `string` object, these static methods can be called even on a string of characters.

```
CharData = "Hello World".ToCharArray();
```

The following lines show how to convert the character array to the correct byte array needed by the `FileStream` object.

```
Encoder e = Endoding.UTF8.GetEncoder();
e.GetBytes(charData,0,charData.Length, byData,0,true);
```

This time, an `Encoder` object is created based on the UTF8 encoding. We used Unicode for the decoding as well, and this time we need to encode the character data into the correct byte format before we can write to the stream. The `GetBytes()` method is where the magic happens. This converts the character array to the byte array. It accepts a character array as the first parameter (`charData` in our example), and the index to start in that array as the second parameter (0 for the start of the array). The third parameter is the number of characters to convert (`charData.Length` – the number of elements in the `charData` array). The fourth parameter is the byte array to place the data into (`byData`), and the fifth parameter is the index to start writing in the byte array (0 for the start of the `byData` array).

The sixth and final parameter determines if the `Encoder` object should flush its state after completion. This refers to the fact that the `Encoder` object retains an in memory record of where it was in the byte array. This aids in subsequent calls to the `Encoder` object, but is meaningless when only a single call is made. The final call to the `Encoder` must set this parameter to `true` to clear its memory and free the object for garbage collection.

After this it is a simple matter of writing the byte array to the `FileStream` using the `Write()` method:

```
aFile.Seek(0,SeekOrigin.Begin);
aFile.Write(byData,0,byData.Length);
```

Like the `Read()` method, the `Write()` method has three parameters; the array to write from, the index in the array to start writing from, and the number of bytes to write.

The StreamWriter Object

Working with arrays of bytes is not most people's idea of fun – having worked with the `FileStream` object you may be wondering if there is an easier way. Fear not, for once you have a `FileStream` object you will usually wrap it in a `StreamWriter` or `StreamReader` and use their methods to manipulate the file. If you do not need the ability to change the file pointer to any arbitrary position, then these classes make working with the file much easier.

The `StreamWriter` class allows us to write characters and strings to the file, handling the underlying conversions and writing to the `FileStream` object.

There are many ways to create a `StreamWriter` object. If you already have a `FileStream` object then you can use this to create a `StreamWriter`:

```
FileStream aFile = new FileStream("Log.txt",FileMode.CreateNew);
StreamWriter sw = new StreamWriter(aFile);
```

A `StreamWriter` object can also be created directly from a file:

```
StreamWriter sw = new StreamWriter("Log.txt",true);
```

This constructor takes the file name, and a Boolean value that specifies whether to append to the file or create a new one:

❑   If this is set to `false` then a new file is created, or the existing file is truncated and then opened.

❑   If it is set to `true` then the file is opened, and the data is retained. If there is no file, a new one is created.

Unlike when creating a `FileStream` object, creating a `StreamWriter` does not provide you with a similar range of options – other than the Boolean value to append or create a new file, you have no option for specifying the `FileMode` property as we did with the `FileStream` class. Also, you do not have an option of setting the `FileAccess` property, so you will always have read/write privileges to the file. To use any of the advanced parameters you must first specify them in the `FileStream` constructor, and then create a `StreamWriter` from the `FileStream` object.

Try it Out – Output Stream

1. Create a new console application called `StreamWrite` in the directory
`C:\BegVCSharp\Chapter20`.

2. We will be using the `System.IO` namespace again, so add the following using directive near
the top of the `Class1.cs` file.

```
using System;
using System.IO;
```

3. Add the following code to the `Main()` method:

```
static void Main(string[] args)
{
    try
    {
        FileStream aFile = new FileStream("Log.txt",FileMode.OpenOrCreate);
        StreamWriter sw = new StreamWriter(aFile);

        bool truth = true;
        //Write data to file
        sw.WriteLine("Hello to you.");
        sw.WriteLine("It is now {0} and things are looking good.",
DateTime.Now.ToShortDateString());
        sw.Write("More than that,");
        sw.Write(" it's {0} that C# is fun.",truth);
        sw.Close();
    }
    catch(IOException e)
    {
        Console.WriteLine("An IO exception has been thrown!");
        Console.WriteLine(e.ToString());
        Console.ReadLine();
        return;
    }
    return;
}
```

4. Build and run the project. If no errors are found it should quickly run and close. Since we are
not displaying anything on the console, it is not a very exciting program to watch.

5. Go to the application directory and find the `Log.txt` file. This is located in the
`StreamWrite\bin\Debug` folder because we used a relative path.

6. Open up the file and you should see the following characters:

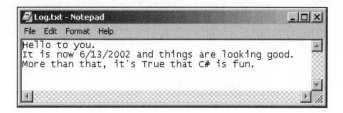

How It Works

This simple application demonstrates the two most important methods of the `StreamWriter` class, `Write()` and `WriteLine()`. Both of them have many overloaded versions for doing more advanced file output, but we use basic string output in this example.

The `WriteLine()` method will write the string passed to it, followed immediately by a newline character. We can see in the example that this causes the next write operation to begin on a new line.

Just as you can write formatted data to the console, so you can also do this to files. For example, we can write out the value of variables to the file using standard format parameters:

```
        sw.WriteLine("It is now {0} and things are looking good.",

    DateTime.Now.ToShortDateString());
```

`DateTime.Now` holds the current date, the `ToShortDateString()` method is used to convert this date into the shorter, easier to read form.

The `Write()` method simply writes the string passed to it to the file, without a newline character appended, allowing us to write a complete sentence or paragraph using more than one `Write()` statement.

```
        sw.Write("More than that,");
        sw.Write(" it's {0} that C# is fun.",truth);
```

Here again we use format parameters, this time with `Write()` to display the Boolean value `truth` – we set this variable to true earlier, and its value is automatically converted into `True` for the formatting.

We can use `Write()` and format parameters to write comma-separated files:

```
    Write("{0},{1},{2}",100,"A nice product",10.50);
```

In a more sophisticated example this data could come from a `DataSet` or other data source. In fact, you'll find an exercise at the end of the chapter to write comma-separated files from a `DataSet`.

The StreamReader Object

Input streams are used to read data from an external source. Many times this will be a file on a disk or network location. But remember that this source could be almost anything that can send data, such as a network application, web service, or even the console.

The StreamReader class is the one that we will be using to read data from files. Like the StreamWriter class, this is a generic class that can be used with any stream. We will again be constructing it around a FileStream object so it points to the correct file.

StreamReader objects are created in much the same way as StreamWriter objects. The most common way to create one is to use a previously created FileStream object:

```
FileStream aFile = new FileStream("Log.txt",FileMode.Open);
StreamReader sr = new StreamReader(aFile);
```

Like the StreamWriter, the StreamReader class can be created directly from a string containing the path to a particular file:

```
StreamReader sr = new StreamReader("Log.txt");
```

Try it Out – Stream Input

1. Create a new console application called StreamRead in the directory
    C:\BegVCSharp\Chapter20.

2. Again we must import the System.IO namespace, so place the following line of code near the top of Class1.cs:

```
using System;
using System.IO;
```

3. Add the following code to the Main() method:

```
static void Main(string[] args)
{
    string strLine;

    try
    {
        FileStream aFile = new FileStream("Log.txt",FileMode.Open);
        StreamReader sr = new StreamReader(aFile);
        strLine = sr.ReadLine();
//Read data in line by line
        while(strLine != null)
        {
            Console.WriteLine(strLine);
            strLine = sr.ReadLine();
        }
        sr.Close();
    }
    catch(IOException e)
    {
        Console.WriteLine("An IO exception has been thrown!");
        Console.WriteLine(e.ToString());
        return;
    }

    return;
}
```

4. Copy the `Log.txt` file, created in the previous example, into the `StreamRead\bin\Debug` directory. If you don't have a file named `Log.txt`, the `FileStream` constructor will throw an exception when it doesn't find the file.

5. Run the application – you should see the text of the file written to the console:

```
C:\BegVCSharp\Chapter20\StreamRead\bin\Debug\StreamRead.exe
Hello to you.
It is now 6/13/2002 and things are looking good.
More than that, it's True that C# is fun.
Press any key to continue
```

How it Works

This application is very similar to the previous one, with the obvious difference being that it is reading a file rather than writing one. As before you must import the `System.IO` namespace to be able to access the necessary classes.

We use the `ReadLine()` method to read text from the file. This method reads text until a carriage return is found, and returns the resulting text as a string. The method returns a `null` when the end of the file has been reached, which we use to test for the end of the file. Note that we use a `while` loop, which checks the line read isn't null *before* any code in the body of the loop is executed – this way only the genuine contents of the file are displayed:

```
strLine = sr.ReadLine();
while(strLine != null)
{
    Console.WriteLine(strLine);
    strLine = sr.ReadLine();
}
```

Reading Data

The `ReadLine()` method is not the only way we have of accessing data in a file. The `StreamReader` class has many methods for reading data.

The simplest of the reading methods is `Read()`. This method returns the next character from the stream as a positive integer value or a `-1` if it has reached the end. This value can be converted into a character by using the `Convert` utility class. In the example above the main parts of the program could be rewritten as such:

```
int nChar;
nChar = sr.Read();
while(nChar != -1)
{
    Console.Write(Convert.ToChar(nChar));
    nChar = sr.Read();
}
```

A very convenient method to use with smaller files is the `ReadToEnd()` method. This method reads the entire file and returns it as a string. In this case the earlier application could be simplified to this:

```
strLine = sr.ReadToEnd();
Console.WriteLine(strLine);
```

While this may seem very easy and convenient, care must be taken. By reading all the data into a string object you are forcing the data in the file to exist in memory. Depending on the size of the data file, this can be prohibitive. If the data file is extremely large, it is better to leave the data in the file and access it with the methods of the `StreamReader`.

Delimited Files

Delimited files are a common form of data storage, and are used by many legacy systems – if your application must interoperate with such a system then you will encounter the delimited data format quite often. A particularly common form of delimiter is a comma – for example, the data in an Excel spreadsheet, an Access database, or a SQL Server database can be exported as a comma-separated value (CSV) file.

We've seen how to use the `StreamWriter` class to write such files using this approach – it is also easy to read comma-separated files. If you cast your mind back to Chapter 5, you may remember that we saw the `Split()` method of the `String` class, that is used to convert a string into an array based on a supplied separator character. If we specify a comma as the separator, it will create a correctly dimensioned string array containing all of the data in the original comma-separated string. Let's see how useful this can be.

Our example for dealing with comma-separated values will make use of the `DataSet` object that you met in the previous chapter, and will read data from a comma-delimited file and populate a `DataSet` object with this data.

This way our example will become more useful, since you can then use it from within your own applications if you need to work with comma-separated values.

Try it Out– Comma-Separated Values

1. Create a new console application called `CommaValues` in the directory `C:\BegVCSharp\Chapter20`.

2. Place the following line of code near the top of `Class1.cs`. We need to import the `System.IO` namespace for our file-handling, and also the `System.Data` namespace for our data-handling:

```
using System;
using System.IO;
using System.Data;
```

3. Now add the following `GetData()` method into the body of `Class1`, before the `Main()` method:

```
    private static DataSet GetData()
    {
        string strLine;
        string[] strArray;
        char[] charArray = new char[] {','};

        DataSet ds = new DataSet();
        DataTabel dt = ds.Tables.Add("TheData");
        try
        {
            FileStream aFile = new FileStream("../../../SomeData.txt",FileMode.Open);
            StreamReader sr = new StreamReader(aFile);

            strLine = sr.ReadLine();

            // Obtain the columns from the first line

            //Split row of data into string array
            strArray = strLine.Split(charArray);

            for(int x=0;x<=strArray.GetUpperBound(0);x++)
            {
                dt.Columns.Add(strArray[x]);
            }

            strLine = sr.ReadLine();
            while(strLine != null)
            {
                //Split row of data into string array
                strArray = strLine.Split(charArray);

                DataRow dr = dt.NewRow();
                for(int x=0;x<=strArray.GetUpperBound(0);x++)
                {
                    dr[x] = strArray[x];
                }
                dt.Rows.Add(dr);
                strLine = sr.ReadLine();
            }

            sr.Close();
            return ds;

        }
        catch(IOException ex)
        {
            Console.WriteLine("An IO exception has been thrown!");
            Console.WriteLine(ex.ToString());
            Console.ReadLine();
            return ds;
        }
    }
}
```

4. Now add the following code to the Main() method:

```
static void Main(string[] args)
{
    DataSet myDataSet = GetData();
    foreach (DataColumn c in myDataSet.Tables["TheData"].Columns)
    {
        Console.Write("{0,-20}",c.ColumnName);
    }
    Console.WriteLine();

    foreach (DataRow r in myDataSet.Tables["TheData"].Rows)
    {
        foreach (DataColumn c in myDataSet.Tables["TheData"].Columns)
        {
            Console.Write("{0,-20}",r[c]);
        }
        Console.WriteLine();
    }
}
```

5. In VS, create a new text file by choosing **Text File** from the **File | New File** dialog:

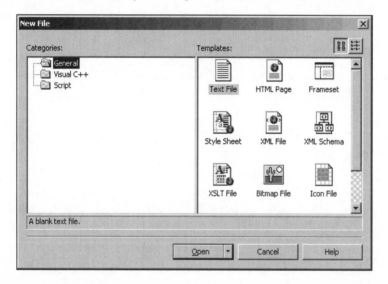

6. Enter the following text into this new text file:

```
ProductID,Name,Price
1,Spiky Pung,1000
2,Gloop Galloop Soup,25
4,Hat Sauce,12
```

7. Save the file as `SomeData.txt` in the `CommaValues` project directory.

8. Run the application– you should see the text of the file written to the console:

How it Works

Like the previous example, this application reads the file line by line into a string. However, since we know this is a file containing comma-separated text values, we are going to handle it differently. Not only that, but we will actually store the values we read in a `DataSet`.

First, let's look at the some of the comma-separated data itself:

```
ProductID,Name,Price
1,Spiky Pung,1000
```

Note that the first line holds the names of the columns of data, and subsequent lines hold the data. Thus our procedure will be to obtain the column names from the first line of the file, and then proceed to retrieve the data in the remaining lines.

Now let's look at the `GetData()` method – this method is declared as `static` so we can call this method without creating an instance of our class. This method returns a `DataSet` object that we will create and then populate with data from the comma-separated text file. The following lines create the `DataSet`, add a new `DataTable` called `TheData` to the `DataSet` object's `Tables` collection:

```
DataSet ds = new DataSet();
DataTable dt = ds.Tables.Add("TheData");
```

This `DataTable` will hold all the values that we read in from the comma-separated text file, and each row in the file will correspond to a `DataRow` in the `DataTable`. The first row of the file actually holds the names of the columns for the `DataTable`, and it is these that we must retrieve first.

We create our `FileStream` object, and then construct our `StreamReader` around that as we did in our earlier examples. Now we can read the first line of the file, and create an array of strings from that one string:

```
strLine = sr.ReadLine();
strArray = strLine.Split(charArray);
```

We saw the `Split()` method in Chapter 5 – it accepts a character array, in this case consisting of just `','`, so that `strArray` will hold the array of strings formed from splitting `strLine` at each instance of `,`. Since we are currently reading from the first line of the file, and this line holds the names of the columns of data, we wish to loop through each string in `strArray` and add a new `DataColumn` to our `DataTable`, with the name of the column taken from `strArray`:

673

```
for(int x=0;x<=strArray.GetUpperBound(0);x++)
{
    dt.Columns.Add(strArray[x]);
}
```

Now that we have the names of the columns for our data, we can read in the data. The code for this is essentially the same as for the earlier `StreamRead` example, except for the presence of the `DataRow` code:

```
strLine = sr.ReadLine();
while(strLine != null)
{
    //Split row of data into string array
    strArray = strLine.Split(charArray);

    DataRow dr = dt.NewRow();
    for(int x=0;x<=strArray.GetUpperBound(0);x++)
    {
        dr[x] = strArray[x];
    }
    dt.Rows.Add(dr);
    strLine = sr.ReadLine();
}
```

For each line in the file, we create a new `DataRow` with the `NewRow()` method. We fill that row with data by setting column x of that row to the value of `strArray[x]` – thus the x-th piece of data in the line is placed into the x-th `DataColumn` of the `DataRow`. Once we have looped through all the pieces of data in the line, we add the `DataRow` to the `DataTable` object's `DataRow` collection.

Once we've read all the data in from the file, we close the `StreamReader` and return our populated `DataSet`.

The code in the `Main()` method obtains the `DataSet` from the `GetData()` method, and displays this information to the console. First, the name of each column is displayed:

```
foreach (DataColumn c in myDataSet.Tables["TheData"].Columns)
{
    Console.Write("{0,-20},c.ColumnName);
}
Console.WriteLine();
```

The `-20` part of the formatting string `{0,-20}` ensures that the name we display is left-aligned in a column of 20 characters – this will help to format the display. Finally, we loop through each `DataRow` in the `Rows` collection and display the values in that row, once again using the formatting string to format our output. This process of looping through the `Rows` collection should be familiar from the last chapter.

```
foreach (DataRow r in myDataSet.Tables["TheData"].Rows)
{
    foreach (DataColumn c in myDataSet.Tables["TheData"].Columns)
    {
        Console.Write("{0,-20},r[c]);
    }
```

```
            Console.WriteLine();
        }
```

As you can see, it is very simple to extract meaningful data from comma-separated value (CSV) files using the .NET Framework, and combined with the data access techniques we learned from the last chapter, we have been able to put this data into a form that means it can be used like data from any other data source, thanks to the `DataSet`. However, there is currently no information about the data types of the data in our `DataSet` – for an enterprise level business application we will to go this extra step and add type information to the `DataSet`, then our comma-separated data from a text file is as good as data from most other sources, once again thanks to the `DataSet`.

Even though XML is a much superior method of storing and transporting data, you will find that CSV files are still very common, and will be for quite some time. Delimited files such as comma-separated files also have the advantage of being very terse and therefore smaller than their XML counterparts.

Monitoring the File Structure

Sometimes an application must do more than just read and write files to the file system. Sometimes it is important to know when files or directories are being modified. The .NET Framework has made it easy to create custom applications that do just that.

The class that helps us to do this is the `FileSystemWatcher` class. This class exposes several events that our application can catch. This enables our application to respond to file system events.

The basic procedure for using the `FileSystemWatcher` is simple. First we must set a handful of properties, which specify where to monitor, what to monitor, and when it should raise the event that our application will handle. Then we give it the addresses of our custom event handlers, so that it can call these when significant events occur. Then we turn it on and wait for the events.

The properties that must be set before a `FileSystemWatcher` object is enabled are:

Property	Description
Path	This must be set to the file location or directory to monitor.
NotifyFilter	This is a combination of `NotifyFilters` enumeration values that specify what to watch for within the monitored files. These represent properties of the file or folders being monitored. If any of the specified properties change, an event is raised. The possible enumeration values are: `Attributes`, `CreationTime`, `DirectoryName`, `FileName`, `LastAccess`, `LastWrite`, `Security`, `Size`. Note that these can be combined using the binary OR operator.
Filter	A filter on which files to monitor, for example `*.txt`.

Once these settings have been set, you must write event handlers for the four events, `Changed`, `Created`, `Deleted`, and `Renamed`. As we saw in Chapter 12, this is simply a matter of creating your own method and assigning it to the object's event. By assigning your own event handler to these methods, your method will be called when the event is fired. Each event will fire when a file or directory matching the `Path`, `NotifyFilter`, and `Filter` property is modified.

Once you have set the properties and the events, set the `EnableRaisingEvents` property to true to begin the monitoring.

Try it Out – Monitoring the File System

Let's build a more sophisticated example utilizing most of what we have learned in this chapter.

1. Create a new Windows application called `FileWatch` in the directory `C:\BegVCSharp\Chapter20`.

2. Set the various form properties using the table below:

Property	Setting
FormBorderStyle	FixedDialog
MaximizeBox	False
MinimizeBox	False
Size	302, 160
StartPosition	CenterScreen
Text	FileMonitor

3. Using the list below, add the required controls to the form and set the appropriate properties:

Control	Name	Location	Size	Text
TextBox	txtLocation	8, 24	184,20	
Button	cmdBrowse	208, 24	64, 24	Browse...
Button	cmdWatch	88, 56	80, 32	Watch!
Label	lblWatch	8, 104	264, 32	

Ensure that you see the `Enabled` property of the `cmdWatch` Button to **False**, since we can't watch a file before one has been specified. Also add an `OpenFileDialog` control to the form, set its `Name` to **FileDialog**, and its `Filter` to **All Files|*.***. When you are finished your form should look like the following picture. The expanse of gray at the bottom is the `Label` control that will display the current status of the application:

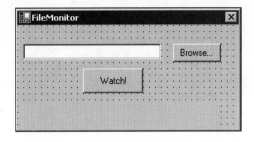

4. Now that our form looks good, let's add some code to make it do some work. The first thing we need to do is add our usual `using` directive for the `System.IO` namespace to the existing list of `using` directives:

```
using System;
using System.Drawing;
using System.Collections;
using System.ComponentModel;
using System.Windows.Forms;
using System.Data;
using System.IO;
```

5. Now we must add the `FileSystemWatcher` class to the `Form1` class. Below the private declarations for the Windows Forms objects write the following line of code:

```
private System.Windows.Forms.TextBox txtLocation;
private System.Windows.Forms.Button cmdBrowse;
private System.Windows.Forms.Button cmdWatch;
private System.Windows.Forms.Label lblWatch;
private System.Windows.Forms.OpenFileDialog FileDialog;
//File System Watcher object
private FileSystemWatcher watcher;
```

6. We need to add some code to the `InitializeComponent()` method. First, expand the region marked **Windows Form Designer generated code** to view the `InitializeComponent()` method. At the end of the `InitializeComponent()` method add the following code. This code is needed to initialize the `FileSystemWatcher` object and associates the events to methods that we are going to create next:

```
this.watcher = new System.IO.FileSystemWatcher ();
this.watcher.Deleted += new System.IO.FileSystemEventHandler(this.OnDelete);
this.watcher.Renamed += new System.IO.RenamedEventHandler(this.OnRenamed);
this.watcher.Changed += new System.IO.FileSystemEventHandler(this.OnChanged);
this.watcher.Created += new System.IO.FileSystemEventHandler(this.OnCreate);
```

7. Add the following four methods after the `InitializeComponent()` method. These are our methods that will handle the events that the `FileSystemWatcher` raises:

```csharp
// Define the event handlers.
public void OnChanged(object source, FileSystemEventArgs e)
{
   try
   {
      StreamWriter sw = new StreamWriter("C:/FileLogs/Log.txt",true);
      sw.WriteLine("File: {0} {1}", e.FullPath, e.ChangeType.ToString());
      sw.Close();
      lblWatch.Text = "Wrote change event to log";
   }
   catch(IOException ex)
   {
      lblWatch.Text = "Error Writing to log";
   }
}

public void OnRenamed(object source, RenamedEventArgs e)
{
   try
   {
      StreamWriter sw =new StreamWriter("C:/FileLogs/Log.txt",true);
      sw.WriteLine("File renamed from {0} to {1}", e.OldName, e.FullPath);
      sw.Close();
      lblWatch.Text = "Wrote renamed event to log";
   }
   catch(IOException ex)
   {
      lblWatch.Text = "Error Writing to log";
   }
}

public void OnDelete(object source, FileSystemEventArgs e)
{
   try
   {
      StreamWriter sw = new StreamWriter("C:/FileLogs/Log.txt",true);
      sw.WriteLine("File: {0} Deleted", e.FullPath);
      sw.Close();
      lblWatch.Text = "Wrote delete event to log";
   }
   catch(IOException ex)
   {
      lblWatch.Text = "Error Writing to log";
   }
}

public void OnCreate(object source, FileSystemEventArgs e)
{
   try
   {
      StreamWriter sw = new StreamWriter("C:/FileLogs/Log.txt",true);
```

```
        sw.WriteLine("File: {0} Created", e.FullPath);
        sw.Close();
        lblWatch.Text = "Wrote create event to log";
    }
    catch(IOException ex)
    {
        lblWatch.Text = "Error Writing to log";
    }
}
```

8. We will now add the `Click` event handler for the **Browse...** button. The code in this event handler will open the Open File dialog, allowing the user to select a file to monitor. Double-click on the **Browse...** button and enter the following code:

```
private void cmdBrowse_Click(object sender, System.EventArgs e)
{
    if (FileDialog.ShowDialog() != DialogResult.Cancel )
    {
        txtLocation.Text = FileDialog.FileName;
        cmdWatch.Enabled = true;
    }
}
```

The `ShowDialog()` method returns a `DialogResult` enumeration value representing how the user exited the File Open dialog. The user could have clicked **OK** or hit the **Cancel** button. We need to check that the user did not click the **Cancel** button, so we compare the result from the method call to the `DialogResult.Cancel` enumeration value before saving the user's file selection to the `TextBox`. Finally we set the `Enabled` property of the **Watch** button to true so that we can watch the file.

9. Now for the last bit of code. Follow the same procedure as above with the **Watch** button. Add the following code to launch the `FileSystemWatcher`:

```
private void cmdWatch_Click(object sender, System.EventArgs e)
{
    watcher.Path =Path.GetDirectoryName(txtLocation.Text);
    watcher.Filter = Path.GetFileName(txtLocation.Text);
    watcher.NotifyFilter = NotifyFilters.LastWrite | NotifyFilters.FileName |
NotifyFilters.Size;
    lblWatch.Text = "Watching " + txtLocation.Text;
    // Begin watching.
    watcher.EnableRaisingEvents = true;
}
```

10. We need to make sure the `FileLogs` directory exists for us to write data to. Add the following code to the `Form1` constructor that will check to see if the directory exists, and create the directory if it does not already exist.

```
public Form1()
{
    //
```

```
// Required for Windows Form Designer support
//
InitializeComponent();

DirectoryInfo aDir = new DirectoryInfo("C:/FileLogs");
if(!aDir.Exists)
    aDir.Create();
}
```

11. Build the project. If everything builds successfully click the **Browse** button and select a text file somewhere on your computer.

12. Click the **Watch** button to begin monitoring the file. The only change you will see in your application is the label control showing the file is being watched.

13. Using Windows Explorer navigate to the same file you are currently watching. Open it in Notepad and add some text to the file. Save the file.

14. We can now check the log file to see the changes. Navigate to the C:\FileLogs\Log.txt file and open it in Notepad. You should see a description of the changes to the file you selected to watch.

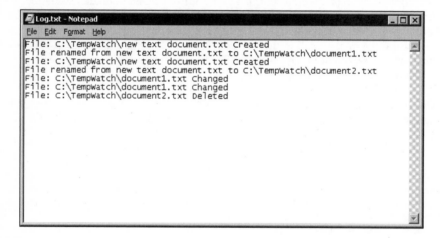

How It Works

This application is fairly simple, but it demonstrates how the `FileSystemWatcher` works. Try playing with the string you put into the monitor text box. If you specify `*.*` in a directory it will monitor all changes in the directory.

Most of the code in the application is based around setting up the `FileSystemWatcher` object to watch the correct location:

```
watcher.Path = Path.GetDirectoryName(txtLocation.Text);
watcher.Filter = Path.GetFileName(txtLocation.Text);
watcher.NotifyFilter = NotifyFilters.LastWrite | NotifyFilters.FileName |
NotifyFilters.Size;

lblWatch.Text = "Watching " + txtLocation.Text;
// Begin watching.
watcher.EnableRaisingEvents = true;
```

The code first sets the path to the directory to monitor. This uses a new object we have not looked at yet: the System.IO.Path object. This is a static class, very much like the static File object. It exposes many static methods to manipulate and extract information out of file location strings. We first use it to extract the directory name the user typed in from the text box, using the GetDirectoryName() method.

The next line sets the filter for the object. This can be an actual file, in which case it would only monitor the file, or it could be something like *.txt, in which case it would monitor all the .txt files in the directory specified. Again we use the Path static object to extract the information from the supplied file location.

The NotifyFilter is a combination of NotifyFilters enumeration values that specify what constitutes a change. In this example we have said that if the last write timestamp, the filename, or the size of the file changes then it will notify our application of the change. After updating the UI we set the EnableRaisingEvents property to true to begin monitoring.

But before this we have to create the object and set the event handlers.

```
this.watcher = new System.IO.FileSystemWatcher();
this.watcher.Deleted += new System.IO.FileSystemEventHandler(this.OnDelete);
this.watcher.Renamed += new System.IO.RenamedEventHandler(this.OnRenamed);
this.watcher.Changed += new System.IO.FileSystemEventHandler(this.OnChanged);
this.watcher.Created += new System.IO.FileSystemEventHandler(this.OnCreate);
```

This is how we hook up the event handlers for the watcher object with the private methods we have created. Here we will have event handlers for the event raised by the watcher object when a file is deleted, renamed, changed or created. In our own methods we decide how to handle the actual event. Note that we are notified *after* the event takes place.

In the actual event handler methods we simply write the event to a log file. Obviously this could be a more sophisticated response depending on our application. When a file is added to a directory we could move it somewhere else or read the contents and fire off a new process using the information. The possibilities are endless!

Summary

In this chapter, we have learned about streams and why they are used in the .NET Framework to access files and other serial devices. We looked at the basic classes in the System.IO namespace, including:

- ❏ `File`
- ❏ `FileInfo`
- ❏ `FileStream`

We saw that the `File` class exposes many static methods for moving, copying, and deleting files, `FileInfo` represents a physical file on disk, and has methods to manipulate this file. A `FileStream` object represents a file that can be written to, or read from, or both.

We also explored `StreamReader` and `StreamWriter` classes and saw how useful they were for writing to streams. We saw how to read and write to random files using the `FileStream` class. Finally, we built an entire application to monitor files and directories using the `FileSystemWatcher` class.

In summary, we have covered:

- ❏ Opening a file
- ❏ Reading from a file
- ❏ Writing to a file
- ❏ The difference between the `StreamWriter` and `StreamReader` classes and the `FileStream` class
- ❏ Working with delimited files to populate a `DataSet`
- ❏ Monitoring the file system with the `FileSystemWatcher` class

Exercises

1. What is the namespace that must be imported to allow an application to work with files?

2. When would you use a `FileStream` object to write to a file instead of using a `StreamWriter` object?

3. What methods of the `StreamReader` class allow you to read data from files and what does each one do?

4. What events does the `FileSystemWatcher` class expose and what are they for?

5. Modify the FileWatch application we built in this chapter. Add the ability to turn the file system monitoring on and off without exiting the application.

6. Modify the *"Reading Data with the DataSet"* example from the previous chapter so that instead of displaying the data read in, the data is written to a comma separated value file.

.NET Assemblies

An **assembly** is a .NET executable program (or part of an executable program) delivered as a single unit. Assemblies are the means used to package C# programs for execution and delivery. When you build a C# program, the .exe file produced is an assembly. If you build a class library, the DLL (Dynamic Link Library) file produced is also an assembly.

All the code in an assembly is built, delivered, and assigned a version number as a single unit. The assembly makes the public classes, properties, and methods visible to other programs. Everything private to your program is kept inside the assembly.

In this chapter we will explore assemblies. In particular, we will look at:

- ❑ A brief review of components
- ❑ Features of an assembly, including its self-description ability
- ❑ The structure of an assembly, and how to view its contents
- ❑ Assembly versioning
- ❑ Private and shared assemblies
- ❑ Signing assemblies and the Global Assembly Cache

While every C# program is packaged as an assembly, many of the features of assemblies are designed to make it easy to deliver a special class of programs called **components**. Understanding components is essential to understanding the benefits of assemblies, so let's review what a component is.

Components

A component is a subprogram or part of a program designed to be used by other programs. In addition, a component is a **binary** unit (executable code as opposed to source code) that can be used by other programs without having to recompile either the source code of the component itself or the program using the component. This means that third-party suppliers don't have to provide the source code for their components.

In the loosest sense, a component includes any binary subprogram; thus any DLL is by definition a component since it is a subprogram containing executable code.

A stricter definition of a component requires it to provide a means of advertising its contents to other programs. Assemblies provide this advertising ability within .NET.

The strictest definition of a component requires it to provide known interfaces to release no-longer-used system resources and to support integration with design tools. In the .NET Framework, a component in this strictest sense is required to implement the `System.ComponentModel.IComponent` interface, which provides these features.

For understanding the benefits of assemblies, we're using the less strict definition, including the requirement of advertising the contents of the component.

Benefits of Components

Components provide improved reusability, flexibility, and delivery of subprograms. In addition, binary reuse saves time and increases reliability.

For example, consider a class named `Shapes` that contains objects for representing circles, triangles, or other shapes. It might contain methods for calculating the area of a shape or performing other operations with shapes. Many kinds of programs might use a `Shapes` class: painting/drawing programs, engineering, architecture/building design, computer-aided design, games, and others.

Wouldn't it be great if the routines for drawing and manipulating shapes could be defined just once and reused by all these programs? This is the reusability benefit.

What if this reuse could be accomplished without having to recompile and link the `Shapes` class library for every program that uses it? This saves time and helps reliability, since it removes the possibility of introducing problems each time you compile and link.

Even better, maybe some other person or company has already written a shapes component that does what you want; then you can use the component (by downloading and/or purchasing it) without having to write it yourself. If you could share components at the binary level, you wouldn't have to worry about what programming language was used to develop the component. The .NET Framework and assemblies provide all of these benefits.

A Brief History of Components

In order for different programs to reuse components at the binary level, there must be some standard for implementing the way classes and objects are named and used at the binary level. The standard for doing this in Microsoft-based products has evolved over time.

Microsoft Windows introduced the DLL (Dynamic-Link Library) where one or more programs could use a chunk of code stored in a separate file. This worked at a very basic level if the programs were written in the same language (typically C). However, programs needed to know a lot in advance about the DLLs they used, and DLLs did not enable programs to use one another's data.

To exchange data, DDE (Dynamic Data Exchange) was developed. This defined a format and mechanism for piping data from one program to another, but was not flexible. OLE 1.0 (Object Linking and Embedding) followed, which enabled a document such as a Word document to actually contain a document from another program (such as Excel). This was something like components, but OLE 1.0 was not truly a general-purpose component standard.

Microsoft defined its first true component standard with the COM (Component Object Model) standard implemented in Windows in the mid-1990s. OLE version 2 and many successor technologies were built on COM. DCOM (Distributed COM) introduced the ability for COM components to interact over a network, and COM+ added services that components could call on to ensure high performance in multi-tier environments.

COM works well but is difficult to learn (especially when used from C++) and to use. COM requires information about components to be inserted into the Windows system registry, making installation more complex and component removal more difficult.

COM was originally designed for use with C/C++; it was enhanced so that Visual Basic could use it ("Automation") and indeed this works well, but it became even harder for the C/C++ programmer to make components compatible with Visual Basic (you still could not inherit from a class defined in another language, for example).

Additionally, as users installed multiple versions of DLLs and COM components from Microsoft and other companies over time, problems arose with programs using different versions of the same shared DLL. It was very easy for one program to install a different version of a DLL already used by another program, and this would cause the original program to break (this phenomenon was the infamous "DLL Hell"). The burden of tracking all the information about the different DLLs installed on a system made it very hard to upgrade and maintain components.

The .NET programming model brings a new standard that addresses these problems, the .NET assembly.

.NET Assembly Features

Before we look at the structure of an assembly, let's first discuss some of the features of .NET assemblies.

Self-Description

The most important aspect of .NET assemblies that distinguishes them from their predecessors is that they are fully **self-describing**; the description is contained within the assembly so the system or calling program does not have to look up information in the Registry or elsewhere about the objects contained within the assembly.

The self-description of .NET assemblies goes beyond names of objects and methods, and the data types of parameters; it also contains information about what version the objects are (think of Shapes 1.0 followed by Shapes 1.1 or Shapes 2.0), and controls the security for the contained objects. All of this information is contained within the assembly itself – there is no need to look up information elsewhere. This makes installation of a .NET component much easier and more straightforward than with the existing Windows technologies. In fact, it can be literally as easy as copying the assemblies onto the disk of the target system.

.NET Assemblies and the .NET Framework Class Library

Every .NET program, including all C# programs, makes extensive use of the .NET Framework Class Library. You are using these classes whenever you call a method from the System namespace with the using System directive – all the System namespaces (System.Data, System.Drawing, and so on) belong to the .NET Framework Class Library.

Each class within this library is part of a self-describing assembly. The drawing classes, for example, are contained in the System.Drawing.dll assembly. If you add a reference to this assembly in Visual Studio .NET, the compiler will include a reference to that assembly when it builds the assembly for your program. At run-time, the CLR reads the metadata in your program's assembly to see what other assemblies it needs, then locates and loads those assemblies for your program to use. Assemblies referenced by your program may reference other assemblies, so that even a simple program with a single using directive may actually be referencing several different assemblies. The self-description in each assembly keeps track of all these references, without you having to even be aware of it.

I should clarify something here so as to not cause confusion later on.

> **The correspondence between namespaces and assemblies is not necessarily one-to-one. In other words, an assembly may contain information from more than one namespace, and conversely, a single namespace may be spread across several assemblies.**

For example, the System.Data.dll assembly actually contains some functionality from both the System.Data and System.Xml namespaces, while other functionality in the System.Xml namespace is implemented in the System.Xml.dll assembly. Within your program you are referring to a namespace when specifying the using directive; the references in your Visual Studio .NET project specify the actual assemblies used.

Cross-Language Programming

One additional benefit of assemblies and .NET is that they enable cross-language programming, since components can be called from any .NET language, regardless of the language they were originally written in.

.NET provides a number of features which enable cross-language programming:

❑   The Common Language Runtime (CLR), which manages the execution of all .NET assemblies.

❑   MSIL (Microsoft Intermediate Language), generated by all the .NET language compilers. This is a common standard for the binary code generated by the compilers and is what is executed by the CLR. The CLR also defines the format for storing an assembly's metadata, and this means that all assemblies, whatever language they were written in, share a common format for storing their metadata.

❑ The Common Language Specification (CLS), provided so that programs written in C#, Visual Basic .NET, Visual C++.NET, or any other .NET language that is CLS-compliant can share components with full inheritance across language boundaries. The CLS defines the features that languages must support in order to support interoperability with other .NET languages. It is possible to use features that are not in the CLS, but there is no guarantee that these will be supported by other languages.

❑ The Common Type System (CTS), which defines the basic types used by all .NET languages and rules for defining our own classes. This prevents languages implementing, say, the String type in incompatible ways.

By following the CLS specification, you can write a component in C# and the assembly containing the component can be used by a program written in another .NET language, such as Visual Basic .NET, because both the C# and Visual Basic .NET components will be executed by the CLR. Similarly, C# programs can use components written in Visual Basic .NET, Visual C++.NET, and so on. At the assembly level, all classes, objects, and data types used by .NET languages are shared, so you can inherit classes and make full use of components no matter what language they are written in.

Interoperation with COM and Other Legacy Code

The .NET Framework also allows components or libraries written using COM and other "legacy" technologies to be used with C# and other .NET languages.

This mechanism also works via self-describing assemblies; what happens is that a **wrapper** assembly is created for the legacy code that allows it to describe itself to the .NET runtime and convert the COM data types to .NET data types and allow calls back and forth from the .NET languages to the legacy code and vice-versa. Visual Studio .NET automatically creates a wrapper assembly when you add a reference to a COM component (using the **COM** tab in the **Add Reference** dialog).

This diagram shows such a wrapper (also called a Runtime Callable Wrapper) in use; calls made by the .NET client assembly go through the wrapper to get to the COM component; from the .NET assembly's point of view, the wrapper *is* the component:

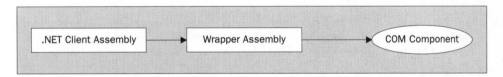

There are difficulties to interoperating with legacy technologies such as COM, and such a subject is beyond the scope of this book.

Structure of Assemblies

The parts of an assembly provide the means for .NET programs to find out about one another and resolve the references between programs and components.

An assembly contains the executable code for a program or class library, along with **metadata** (data describing other data), which enables other programs to look up classes, methods, and properties of the objects defined within the assembly. The metadata acts in two ways: as a table of contents, describing what is contained inside the assembly; and as a bibliography describing references to data outside the assembly. Let's look at this in more detail.

Single-file .NET assemblies have the following general format:

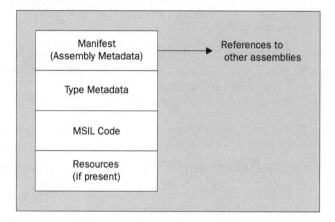

Each assembly contains a **manifest**, which describes the contents of the assembly (like a manifest for a shipment of goods). The manifest is also called the **assembly metadata**, as it describes the assembly itself – what modules it contains, what other assemblies it references, and so on. We'll examine this in more detail later on in this chapter when we view the contents of an assembly we've created. Previous component technologies such as COM have no in-built concept like the manifest; the manifest is the heart of the self-description built into .NET assemblies.

The .NET runtime uses the manifest in the program's assembly when executing the program for resolving references to other assemblies, such as `System`, that contains the `Console.WriteLine()` method for printing out "Hello, World!".

The manifest is followed by the **type metadata** – the description of the classes, properties, methods, and so on contained within the assembly along with the data types for their parameters and return values. This is followed by the actual binary code for each of the types, stored as machine-independent Microsoft Intermediate Language (MSIL) code. Finally, there are any **resources** that form part of the assembly. Resources are non-executable parts of your program (specified in `.Resources` files) such as images, icons, or message files.

Although an assembly often consists of only one file, it can also be composed of several files, as shown here:

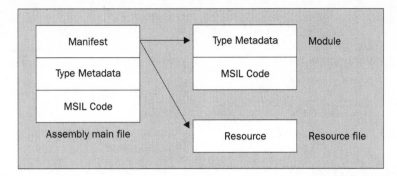

From the .NET runtime's point of view, a multiple-file assembly is a single logical DLL or EXE that just happens to consist of multiple files. Only one file contains the manifest. The manifest points to the other files that make up the multiple-file assembly. The files that contain executable code are called **modules**; these contain type metadata and MSIL code. There may also be resource files containing no executable code.

Multiple-file assemblies are usually needed only in certain advanced applications. A module or resource is loaded only when it is actually executed or brought into use, so you can save download time and memory when modules and resources that are rarely used are stored in separate files. For example, an application delivered internationally may have modules or resources written in different languages; you would separate these so only the module for the language actually in use is loaded into memory.

Now we've seen what assemblies are, let's create one and look at its properties. First, we need to create a simple class library in C# that we'll refer to in the rest of this chapter. Let's make a simple version of the `Shapes` component we imagined in the first part of the chapter.

Try it Out – Creating the Shapes Component

1. Create a new class library project called `Shapes` in the directory
`C:\BegVCSharp\Chapter21`. Rename the default `Class1.cs` file created by default to
`Shapes.cs` and type in the source code shown below. The binary file built from `Shapes.cs`
will be `Shapes.dll`, and we will be using that as our example of an assembly.

2. Enter the following code for into the `Shapes` namespace as follows:

```
namespace Shapes
{
    public class Circle
    {
        double Radius;

        public Circle()
        {
            Radius = 0;
        }

        public Circle(double givenRadius)
        {
            Radius = givenRadius;
        }
```

```
        public double Area()
        {
            // area = pi r squared
            return System.Math.PI * (Radius * Radius);
        }
    }

public class Triangle
{
    double Base;
    double Height;

    public Triangle()
    {
        Base = 0;
        Height = 0;
    }

    public Triangle(double givenBase, double givenHeight)
      {
         Base = givenBase;
         Height = givenHeight;
      }

    public double Area()
    {
        return 0.5F * Base * Height;  // area = 1/2 base * height
    }
    }
    }
```

The code is very simple and obviously not a complete implementation of everything you might want to do with a set of shapes, but it will do for our purposes. The one bit of complexity is that the `Circle` and `Triangle` classes each have two constructors, one that takes no parameters and another that takes parameters to initialize the instance variables. We will see this again later on, when we examine the contents of the assembly that is produced.

3. Before we move on, build the **Shapes** project with **Build | Build** (*Ctrl-Shift-B*).

Viewing the Contents of an Assembly

Let's view the contents of the assembly we just created using the self-description in the `shapes.dll` assembly. The tool we can use to view the contents of an assembly is `Ildasm`, the .NET Framework Intermediate Language DisASseMbler tool. This is a handy tool for viewing and understanding the internal structure of assemblies, and can also be used by the curious to view the contents of the `System` assemblies. However, it is not something you will need to use in day-to-day development of C# programs; don't feel that you have to memorize the details of using it.

Adding Ildasm as an External Tool to VS

Ildasm is an external tool that can be added to the Visual Studio .NET environment. To do this, go to the Tools | External Tools... menu in Visual Studio .NET. Click on the Add button in this dialog. You will see [New Tool 1] in the Menu Contents list and the Title entry box; type in Ildasm in the Title entry box, then click on the browse button (...) to the right of the Command entry box. In the Open dialog that appears, navigate to this path:

```
C:\Program Files\Microsoft Visual Studio .NET\FrameworkSDK\Bin
```

Click on Ildasm.exe in the Bin directory, and then click Open. Ildasm will now appear in the Menu Contents list:

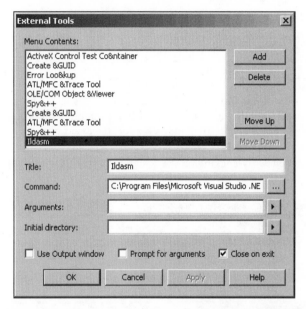

Now click on OK, and Ildasm will appear as a choice in the Tools menu of Visual Studio .NET.

Try it Out – Viewing the Contents of an Assembly with Ildasm

1. Now that Ildasm has been added to Visual Studio .NET, open it by selecting Tools | Ildasm. Ildasm will appear in a separate window:

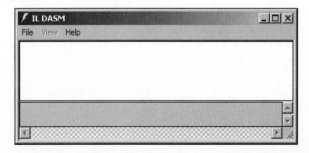

2. Use the File | Open menu to find the directory containing Shapes.dll and open it. Shapes.dll will be located in the bin subdirectory of your project, probably in the Debug subdirectory if you built the default configuration.

Once you have located Shapes.dll, click on the **Open** button. The view of the assembly then appears in the Ildasm main window, as shown in the following screenshot:

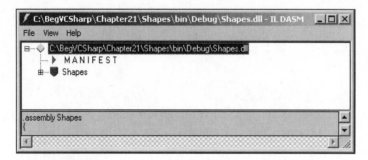

We can see the manifest and the Shapes class in the display. The manifest is the assembly information; we'll look at that in a bit. The **Shapes** shield icon represents the Shapes namespace; it comes from the type metadata for this assembly.

3. Expand the tree view by clicking on the + sign in front of the **Shapes** shield icon. We now see the two classes defined in our source file, Circle and Triangle:

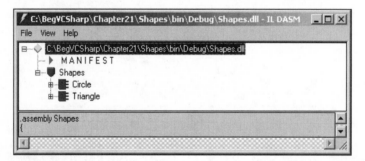

4. Expand the view of each class by clicking on the + signs in front of Circle and Triangle respectively:

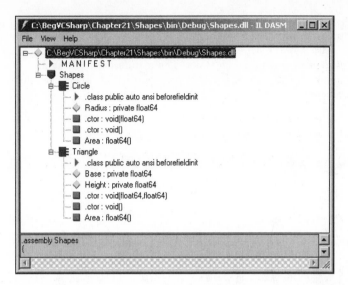

Now we begin to see something that corresponds to the source code we created. We can see the class instance variables radius for the Circle class and Base and Height for the Triangle class, as well as the Area method for both. Since private is the default access modifier for class instance variables such as radius and Base, this explains why we can see these variables marked with private in the screenshot above. We can also see some funny-looking lines of text that seem to be additional to our source code, such as the lines beginning with .ctor and .class.

If we look closely, we notice that the .ctor lines actually correspond to the constructors we defined for Circle and Triangle. There are two constructors for each, one that takes no parameters and another that takes parameters to initialize the instance variables. In Circle's case, the constructor with parameters takes one float value, which corresponds to the line:

```
.ctor void(float64)
```

in the Ildasm display of the assembly. For the Triangle class, the parameterized constructor takes two float parameters. This corresponds to the line:

```
.ctor(float64, float64)
```

The lines beginning with the period are directives in MSIL, which is the language C# code is compiled into for execution in the .NET environment. The .ctor directive is the MSIL instruction to make a class constructor. We don't need to understand MSIL completely in order to examine the contents of assemblies; we'll just point out interesting aspects of it as we come across them.

We also see the line at the top that is labeled MANIFEST; let's talk a little bit about that now.

Manifests

We talked about the manifest of an assembly earlier – it describes each file or module within the assembly (remember we said an assembly could consist of multiple files though typically it is just one file).

More importantly, it also describes the *external* assemblies that are referenced by this assembly. For example, if your program uses System.Data.dll, that fact is reflected in the manifest. This makes it much easier to keep track of the dependencies between assemblies, making deployment and verification of correct installation of a program much easier. The manifest also tracks the version number of the assembly, making upgrading to new versions of programs easier. Let's take a look at the manifest of the assembly we just created.

Double-click on the line labeled MANIFEST at the top of the Ildasm listing for shapes.dll. This opens a new window with the manifest details:

```
 MANIFEST                                                                        _|□|x|
.assembly extern mscorlib
{
    .publickeytoken = (B7 7A 5C 56 19 34 E0 89 )                   // .z\U.4..
    .ver 1:0:3300:0
}
.assembly Shapes
{
    .custom instance void [mscorlib]System.Reflection.AssemblyKeyNameAttribute::.ctor(string) =
    .custom instance void [mscorlib]System.Reflection.AssemblyKeyFileAttribute::.ctor(string) =
    .custom instance void [mscorlib]System.Reflection.AssemblyDelaySignAttribute::.ctor(bool) =
    .custom instance void [mscorlib]System.Reflection.AssemblyTrademarkAttribute::.ctor(string) =
    .custom instance void [mscorlib]System.Reflection.AssemblyCopyrightAttribute::.ctor(string)
    .custom instance void [mscorlib]System.Reflection.AssemblyProductAttribute::.ctor(string) =
    .custom instance void [mscorlib]System.Reflection.AssemblyCompanyAttribute::.ctor(string) =
    .custom instance void [mscorlib]System.Reflection.AssemblyConfigurationAttribute::.ctor(str
    .custom instance void [mscorlib]System.Reflection.AssemblyDescriptionAttribute::.ctor(strin
    .custom instance void [mscorlib]System.Reflection.AssemblyTitleAttribute::.ctor(string) = (
    // --- The following custom attribute is added automatically, do not uncomment -------
    //   .custom instance void [mscorlib]System.Diagnostics.DebuggableAttribute::.ctor(bool,
    //                                                                               bool) = (
    .hash algorithm 0x00008004
    .ver 1:0:899:28398
}
.module Shapes.dll
// MVID: {211989B5-2732-4E63-BF5D-65F85A517DA1}
```

The manifest for Shapes.dll contains two .assembly directives and a .module directive. Don't worry about the contents of the .assembly blocks; that is, ignore everything inside the curly braces {} for now. The first line we can see is:

```
.assembly extern mscorlib
```

This is an external assembly reference to mscorlib.dll, which is where most of the base System classes in the .NET Framework are defined. This external reference is needed for every C# and .NET program that uses the classes in the System namespace. The .assembly Shapes line is the declaration of the Shapes assembly itself. This is followed by a .module declaration for the shapes.dll file. Our assembly has just one file, so there is a single .module declaration for that file.

Let's see what happens when an additional reference is added to the source file. Suppose we wanted to draw a shape using some of the methods from the System.Drawing namespace. Close Ildasm and go back to the Shapes project in Visual Studio .NET. Modify Shapes.cs as follows. First, add a using directive referencing the System.Drawing namespace:

```
namespace Shapes
{
    using System.Drawing;

    public class Circle
    {
```

Then, add a `Draw()` method for `Circle` following the `Area()` method:

```
public void Draw()
{
    Pen p = new Pen(Color.Red);
}
```

This isn't enough code to actually draw anything, but you see where we're going!

Now we need to add a reference to the `System.Drawing.dll` assembly to the project. If we don't add this reference, we will see the following error:

```
error CS0234: The type or namespace name 'Drawing' does not exist in the class or
namespace 'System' (are you missing an assembly reference?)
```

To add a reference in VS, select **Project | Add Reference...** from the menu. The **Add Reference** dialog will appear as shown below. The **.NET** tab shows the .NET system assemblies that are available; scroll down the list, select the `System.Drawing.dll` assembly, and then click the **Select** button:

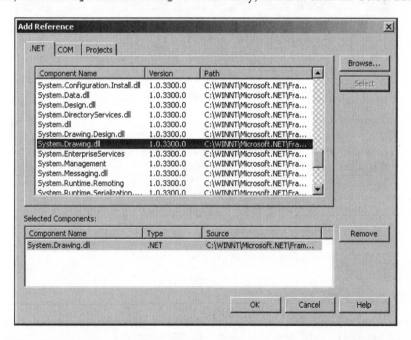

Now press **OK** to add the reference. This adds the `System.Drawing.dll` reference to the `Shapes.dll` file. Save your source file changes, close `Ildasm` (otherwise you get a compiler error because `Ildasm` has `Shapes.dll` open), and then recompile `Shapes.cs` with the above changes.

Now, start `Ildasm` again and open `Shapes.dll`. You'll notice the `Draw()` method under the `Circles` object now:

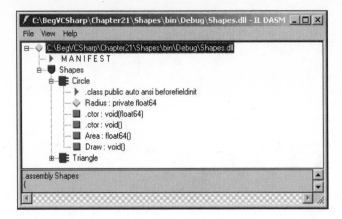

Now, double-click on MANIFEST again to see the changes we have made to it. Now there is an external assembly reference to the System.Drawing assembly:

The Shapes assembly will now inform the system that it requires the System.Drawing assembly whenever Shapes itself is referenced. We'll look at how another program makes use of the Shapes assembly in just a bit, but after looking at the screen above your curiosity about the stuff inside the .assembly directives (that we told you to ignore earlier) is probably getting too much. Let's put you out of your misery, and discuss that information now.

Assembly Attributes

Besides the external assembly references, the manifest of an assembly contains other information that pertains to the assembly itself. These are called **assembly attributes**.

AssemblyInfo.cs

When building your class library project in Visual Studio .NET, you have probably noticed that it creates a second C# source file as part of your project. This file is called AssemblyInfo.cs, and is used to set properties of the assembly in the manifest such as the assembly version number, name, and so on. Let's have a look at the contents of this file (some comments have been removed to save space):

```
using System.Reflection;
using System.Runtime.CompilerServices;

//
// General Information about an assembly is controlled through the following
// set of attributes. Change these attribute values to modify the information
// associated with an assembly.
//
[assembly: AssemblyTitle("")]
[assembly: AssemblyDescription("")]
[assembly: AssemblyConfiguration("")]
[assembly: AssemblyCompany("")]
[assembly: AssemblyProduct("")]
[assembly: AssemblyCopyright("")]
[assembly: AssemblyTrademark("")]
[assembly: AssemblyCulture("")]


//
// Version information for an assembly consists of the following four values:
//
//        Major Version
//        Minor Version
//        Build Number
//        Revision
//
// You can specify all the values or you can default the Revision and
// Build Numbers by using the '*' as shown below:

[assembly: AssemblyVersion("1.0.*")]

[assembly: AssemblyDelaySign(false)]
[assembly: AssemblyKeyFile("")]
[assembly: AssemblyKeyName("")]
```

Each of the statements in square brackets that look like [assembly: Assembly...] is an *attribute*, a special syntax in C# that is covered in more depth in the next chapter. For our purposes here, it's enough to know that each of these statements sets a particular property of the assembly. The word assembly: at the beginning of each attribute tells the system that the directive following is targeted at the assembly itself, not a class, method, or other part of the program.

Visual Studio .NET supplies this file containing the assembly attributes as a template for you to fill in with the properties you want your assembly to have. You could use these attributes in a source file compiled with csc as well (we'll look at compiling with csc at the end of the chapter). Most of the attributes such as title, company, and so on, are purely informational, and can be filled in with any descriptive value you want associated with your component, such as:

```
[assembly: AssemblyTitle("MyCompany Shapes Class Library")]
[assembly: AssemblyDescription("Classes for Manipulation of Shapes")]
[assembly: AssemblyConfiguration("Enterprise Version")]
[assembly: AssemblyCompany("MyCompany, Inc.")]
[assembly: AssemblyProduct("Shapes")]
[assembly: AssemblyCopyright("Copyright 2001, MyCompany, Inc.")]
[assembly: AssemblyTrademark("Shapes is a trademark of MyCompany, Inc.")]
```

699

The `AssemblyCulture` attribute refers to the national language used for this assembly and if it is specified, it is a special abbreviation following an international standard. For more information, see the `System.Globalization` namespace and culture topics in the .NET Framework online documentation. You don't need to set the culture unless you're distributing different language versions of a component; if you are doing this then the .NET runtime will automatically search for the version of your assembly that matches the current culture, so that, for example, in France you display the French messages (using your French message resources and/or code) and in Britain you display English messages (using your English message resources and/or code). You mark the appropriate assembly with the correct culture attribute for this to happen.

Because they appear in the `AssemblyInfo.cs` file, they are also included in the assembly's manifest. For example, if you look again at the manifest for `Shapes.dll`, you'll see this line within the `.assembly Shapes` section:

```
.custom instance void [mscorlib]System.Reflection.AssemblyTitleAttribute::
.ctor(string) =
   ( 01 00 1E 4D 79 43 6F 6D 70 61 6E 79 20 53 68 61    // ...MyCompany Sha
     70 65 73 20 43 6C 61 73 73 20 4C 69 62 72 61 72    // pes Class Librar
     79 00 00 )                                          // y..
```

This line indicates that the assembly contains an `AssemblyTitle` attribute, and the value of this attribute.

Version Numbers

The version for a .NET assembly has four parts, as shown here:

Major version	Minor version	Build Number	Revision

The first two parts are probably familiar to you if you are a user of consumer software – they are a major version number and a minor version number, as in Shapes version 1.0 (where 1 is the major version and 0 the minor version).

The next two parts take the versioning to a finer level of detail. The build number indicates which build of the assembly this is; the build number would typically change every time the assembly is rebuilt.

The revision number goes one level deeper, and is designed to be used for a patch or a "hot fix" to an assembly that is exactly the same as its predecessor, except for this one bug fix.

Version Attributes

You can see an assembly's version attributes in `Ildasm`. Look in the manifest of the `shapes.dll` file, and you will see that each referenced assembly has a `.ver` directive inside the `.assembly` block for that assembly.

You may also notice that the version information for the external assembly references, such as the references to the `mscorlib` and `System` assemblies, are all the same. This is because the .NET runtime uses assembly version numbers for compatibility checking. We'll talk more about this when we discuss version compatibility.

If you were to use the command-line C# compiler (csc), then the `.ver` directive for the shapes assembly has all zeros in it, like this:

```
.ver 0:0:0:0
```

This is because we haven't assigned a version number to the shapes assembly yet. However, when using VS, it adds some version information automatically, and the version number you will see probably looks something like:

```
.ver 1:0:486:7484
```

AssemblyVersion attribute

Within the `AssemblyInfo.cs` file created by Visual Studio .NET, the version number is set with the `AssemblyVersion` attribute:

```
[assembly: AssemblyVersion("1.0.*")]
```

The `AssemblyVersion` attribute allows an asterisk (*) to be specified for the last two parts of the version number. This directs VS to set the build and revision numbers automatically. You can also specify the asterisk just for the revision number (as in `1.1.1.*`) but not the major and minor version numbers (`1.*` is not allowed). If you look at the assembly version number with `Ildasm`, you'll see that the actual version number VS sets will be something like:

```
.ver 1:0:585:24784
```

If you change some code in your classes and build again; you'll see the number change automatically to something like:

```
.ver 1:0:585:25005
```

You can directly set all the parts of the version by specifying a specific number instead of the asterisk:

```
[assembly: AssemblyVersion("1.0.1.2")]
```

This will force VS to produce an assembly with this specific major, minor, build, and revision number.

If you are just developing a program for your own use, you won't need to set or care about version numbers. However, if you are releasing software to other end users, you will want to change major and minor version numbers as you add significant new functionality to your releases: 1.0 for the first production release, 1.1 for a release introducing minor enhancements, 2.0 for major changes, and so on. It's OK to let VS set the build/revision numbers automatically, and you won't even need to be aware of them most of the time.

It is handy to be able to use `Ildasm` to check the full version number. For example, if an end user reports a bug, you can compare the version of the assembly on your computer and the one installed on the end-user's computer. You can tell exactly which version that user has; with the revision and build numbers you can even distinguish between the build made this morning and the one made just before noon.

Version Compatibility

The .NET runtime checks version numbers when loading assemblies to determine version compatibility. This is done only for **shared assemblies**, which we'll look at later in this chapter. However, the way version checking works with version numbers can be described here.

You'll recall that the manifest of an assembly contains the version number of the current assembly as well as the version numbers of referenced external assemblies. When the .NET runtime loads a referenced assembly, it checks the version in that assembly's manifest and compares it to the version stored in the reference to make sure the versions are compatible.

If the assemblies have different major or minor version numbers they are assumed to be incompatible and the referenced assembly will not load – for example, Shapes version 1.1 is not compatible with a program referencing Shapes version 1.0, 1.2, or 2.0.

What if you have program A that uses Shapes 1.0 and program B that uses Shapes 1.1 on the same system? This is actually taken care of in the .NET runtime; there is a feature called side-by-side execution, which enables Shapes 1.0 and Shapes 1.1 to both be installed on the same computer and both be available to the programs that need each version.

The next two parts of the version number take the versioning to a finer level of detail. The build number indicates which build of the assembly this is; this typically changes every time the assembly is rebuilt. Two assemblies with the same major/minor version number and a differing build number may or may not be compatible; the runtime assumes that they are compatible so that they are allowed to load; it is up to the developer to make sure to change the major or minor version if incompatible changes are introduced.

You'll notice in our earlier examples that the version number of the `mscorlib` assembly and the `System.Drawing` assembly were both version 1.0 with a build number of 3300; that is the build number of the .NET System assemblies currently on my system as I write this. If one of these libraries were updated to build number 3302 or even 9999 the .NET runtime would try to use the new build; however, the build number is not guaranteed to be compatible.

The revision number goes one more level, enabling you to specify a very specific patch or fix to a particular build number. 1.0.3300.0 and 1.0.3300.1 are assumed to be totally compatible. In the side-by-side scenario, if the major and minor versions of two co-existing assemblies match and differ only by build number and/or revision, the system will execute the newer assembly (namely, the one with a higher build/revision number).

Calling Assemblies

Now let's look at what happens when `Shapes` is referenced by a program. We'll make a simple client for `Shapes` named `ShapeUser`, and take a look at this client in `Ildasm` before we execute it.

Try it Out – Creating a Shapes Client

1. Create a new console application project named `ShapeUser` in the directory `C:\BegVCSharp\Chapter21`, rename the `Class1.cs` source file to `ShapeUser.cs`, and enter the following code:

```
using System;
using Shapes;

namespace ShapeUser
{

   public class ShapeUser
   {
      public static void Main()
      {
         Circle c = new Circle(1.0F);

         Console.WriteLine("Area of Circle(1.0) is {0}", c.Area());
      }
   }
}
```

2. This project will need a reference to the Shapes project to compile, so choose **Add Reference...** from the **P**roject menu (or right-click on **References** in the Solution Explorer and select **Add Reference...**), and the **Add Reference** dialog will appear. From the **.NET** tab, press the **Browse** button (at the top right), navigate to the Shapes.dll file in your Shapes\bin\Debug project directory, and click the **Open** button. The Shapes.dll file will appear in the list of **Selected Components**:

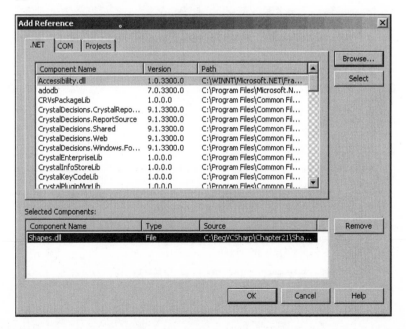

Press **OK** and Shapes is added to the list of references for the ShapesUser project:

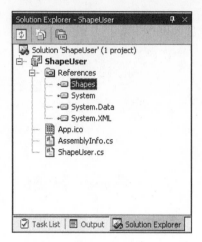

A private copy of Shapes.dll has been added to the ShapeUser bin\Debug directory – we'll discuss this more in the next section.

3. Build the ShapeUser application.

4. Now that ShapeUser.exe has been built, open up Ildasm to examine its contents:

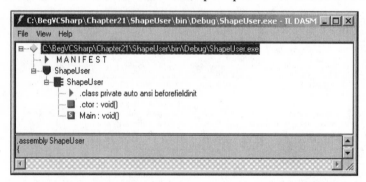

5. Note that even though this is a stand-alone program, it has metadata just like a class library does. Double-click on MANIFEST to see the external reference to the Shapes component:

```
.assembly extern mscorlib
{
  .publickeytoken = (B7 7A 5C 56 19 34 E0 89 )
  .ver 1:0:3300:0
}
.assembly extern Shapes
{
  .ver 1:0:901:23852
}
.assembly ShapeUser
{
```

6. Finally, execute `ShapeUser.exe`:

Private and Shared Assemblies

Up to now we have been dealing only with **private assemblies** – assemblies that are deployed as part of a single application. However, the .NET Framework also has special facilities to provide for **shared assemblies** that are used by multiple programs simultaneously.

Private Assemblies

By default, an assembly is private to your project. Private assemblies *must* be in the same directory as the application.

Our `Shapes.dll` assembly is private; in order to refer to it from our `ShapeUser` project we had to browse into the `Shapes` development directory from the `ShapeUser` project when adding the reference in Visual Studio .NET – in which case Visual Studio .NET makes a private copy of `Shapes.dll` and places it in the `ShapeUser` directory.

Copying the `Shapes.dll` assembly ensures that `ShapeUser` can execute even if the original `Shapes.dll` is unavailable because of ongoing development. However, making copies of every referenced DLL is not very efficient for widely used components, so the .NET Framework provides for shared assemblies.

Shared Assemblies

Shared assemblies are available for use by all the programs on the system. A program does not need to know the location of a shared assembly because all shared assemblies are stored in a special .NET system directory called the **Global Assembly Cache** (GAC). Because they are available system-wide, the .NET runtime imposes several extra checks on shared assemblies to ensure that they are valid for the program requesting them, such as security and version compatibility.

Security and Strong Names

A shared assembly must provide proof that it has not been replaced by another assembly using the same name and version, and that it has not been altered in any way, for example by a virus. This is done by requiring that a shared assembly be **signed** with a cryptographic key before it is loaded into the Global Assembly Cache. The key helps protect not only against a security breach but also against a simple name/version collision due to two components having the same name and version number.

If the keys are different, the components are considered to be different even if they have the same name.

The unique combination of the assembly name, version, and key is called a **strong name**.

Global Assembly Cache

The Global Assembly Cache is a special directory, located in the `WINNT\assembly` directory. All shared assemblies, including the .NET Framework `System` assemblies supplied by Microsoft, are located and loaded from here. If you browse this directory with the Windows Explorer, a special Windows shell extension displays the properties of the assemblies, including the key incorporated into the strong name of each.

The Windows shell extension (called `shfusion.dll`) plugs into Windows Explorer and extends its capabilities beyond a normal file listing. This screenshot shows the GAC viewed in Windows Explorer. The name, version, key, and other properties of the assemblies are listed:

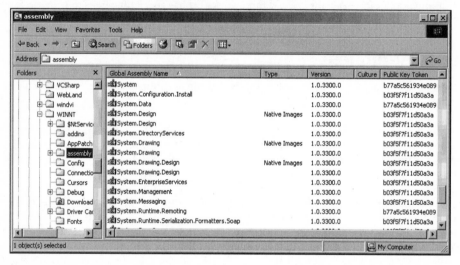

The Windows shell extension enforces the security policy for the Global Assembly Cache, enabling assemblies to be copied into this directory via drag and drop, but only if the rules are adhered to. Let's look at the rules we have to follow to allow us to place an assembly into the Global Assembly Cache.

Creating a Shared Assembly

In order to create a shared assembly with a strong name, you must generate a public/private key pair that is used to **sign** an assembly. Public/private key cryptographic systems use a private key known only to the originator of the information to be encrypted, and a public key published to the world. The .NET environment uses this same mechanism to ensure that a referenced shared assembly is really the assembly wanted (assemblies from different companies could have the same name and version number, for example, or a hacker could try to "spoof" a program by creating an assembly with the same name/version, or try to tamper with an existing assembly). The keys in the reference to the assembly and the key in the (signed) shared assembly itself are checked to make sure they match; if they do not, the shared assembly will not load.

The combination of the assembly name, version, and public key are guaranteed to be unique; this combination is called a **strong name**.

The .NET Framework provides a tool for generating the strong name called sn.exe (sn stands for Strong Name). Unfortunately, this can only be used from the command prompt, and you may need to set the PATH environment variable before using it (please see Appendix A for instructions on how to do this).

Try it Out – Signing the Shapes Assembly

1. From the command-line, change the directory to C:\BegVCSharp\Chapter21\Shapes. Use the following command to generate a key file, giving a filename (usually with the .snk extension) that you will reference from your assembly:

```
>sn -k Shapes.snk
```

2. This creates the key file Shapes.snk in the current directory. To sign the assembly with this key, modify the AssemblyKeyFile attribute in the last part of the AssemblyInfo.cs file for your project:

```
[assembly: AssemblyKeyFile("Shapes.snk")]
```

In Visual Studio .NET, the key file location is relative to the obj\Debug or obj\Release directory in your project; if you place the file in another directory, such as the project root directory, include a path relative to this file, such as [assembly: AssemblyKeyFile(@"..\..\Shapes.snk")] – you may recall the .. notation from Chapter 20, which is used to signify moving back up a directory level.

3. Now recompile the Shapes.dll assembly. If Visual Studio .NET can't find the Shapes.snk file, the project won't compile, and you will get an error such as:

```
Cryptographic failure while signing assembly
'C:\BegVCSharp\Chapter21\Shapes\obj\Debug\Shapes.dll' --
'Error reading key file 'Shapes.snk' -- The system cannot find the file
specified.'
```

This tells you exactly where Visual Studio .NET is looking for the key file, and you can either move the file to that directory, or specify a directory relative to it.

4. Once you have successfully rebuilt the project, the assembly is now signed.

5. Open up Ildasm, and examine the manifest of the Shapes.dll assembly – we can see that a public key has been generated and embedded within:

```
MANIFEST                                                           _|□|x|
.assembly Shapes                                                        ▲
{
   .custom instance void [mscorlib]System.Reflection.AssemblyKeyNameAttribute:
   .custom instance void [mscorlib]System.Reflection.AssemblyKeyFileAttribute:

   .custom instance void [mscorlib]System.Reflection.AssemblyDelaySignAttribut
   // --- The following custom attribute is added automatically, do not uncomm
   //   .custom instance void [mscorlib]System.Diagnostics.DebuggableAttribute:
   //
   .publickey = (00 24 00 00 04 80 00 00 94 00 00 00 06 02 00 00    // .$......
                 00 24 00 00 52 53 41 31 00 04 00 00 01 00 01 00    // .$..RSA1
                 5F 16 7B F0 EB 59 1E 21 D9 4A 2D 87 96 68 CA FD    // _.{..Y.!
                 BF BA F6 3E 30 69 47 EA 1E C7 F5 67 0E A1 1A EC    // ...>0iG.
                 45 51 D6 25 77 5D A6 94 85 90 7D A9 F2 A4 74 3A    // EQ.%w]..
                 BB AB 0D 95 AA 2B 16 BD C3 D6 45 EC 79 6C 3C 04    // .....+..
                 23 27 76 0A 9F 7E BD D0 23 31 55 AF A6 30 C4 22    // #'v..~..
                 90 B9 3B C4 E1 D1 BF FA 6D BF 4B 76 C4 8F 1E 47    // ..;.....
                 40 FA 14 F3 19 8E 0A 6A 8A C0 99 46 47 B0 CD 09    // @......j
                 BF 9F D9 D7 5A 25 D2 3A AD 89 E8 DD D2 68 60 BF )  // ....Z%.:
   .hash algorithm 0x00008004
   .ver 1:0:899:30056
}                                                                      ▼
◄|                                                                  |►|
```

6. We need to recompile `ShapeUser.cs` to update the external assembly reference inside `ShapeUser.exe` with the signed version of `Shapes.dll`. Once recompiled, it works just as before, still using the local copy of `Shapes.dll`.

Now that our assembly is signed, we are able to install it into the Global Assembly Cache. This can be done simply by dragging and dropping the `.dll` file into the GAC folder (`WINNT\assembly`), or alternatively, we can use a .NET command-line tool called `Gacutil` (Global Assembly Cache Utility). To install `Shapes.dll` into the Global Assembly Cache, use the `Gacutil` with the `/i` option from a command-line prompt:

```
>Gacutil /i Shapes.dll
```

The message "Assembly successfully added to the cache" will indicate successful installation of the assembly.

> *Note that for deployment of a commercial application, the preferred way to add a shared assembly to the Global Assembly Cache is to use the Windows Installer.*

To prove that `Shapes.dll` is in the cache, delete the copy of `Shapes.dll` in the current directory. Now, from the command-line, go to the directory containing the `ShapeUser` executable, which is:

```
C:\BegVCSharp\Chapter21\ShapeUser\bin\Debug
```

and run `ShapeUser.exe`. You should see the output:

```
Area of Circle(1.0) is 3.14159265358979
```

It still runs, even with `Shapes.dll` absent, because it is loading the `Shapes` assembly from the GAC. To test this further, use `Gacutil` with the `/u` option to uninstall shapes:

```
>Gacutil /u shapes
```

Note that the `.dll` extension is omitted for the uninstall option.

Note that you must have local administrator privileges on a computer to uninstall assemblies from the Global Assembly Cache for that machine.

Now try to run `ShapeUser` as above, and you will see the following message:

```
Unhandled Exception: System.IO.FileNotFoundException: File or assembly name
Shapes, or one of its dependencies, was not found.
```

This shows that `Shapes.dll` was indeed being loaded from the GAC.

Assembly Searching

The .NET runtime follows a predefined set of rules in order to locate an external assembly when it is referenced. We have just seen how the local directory is searched first for shared assemblies, followed by the GAC.

For private assemblies, the local directory is searched first, and then the system looks for a subdirectory with the same name as the assembly. The runtime also looks for either a DLL or EXE file with the same name as the requested assembly. For our `Shapes` class the combination of these results in the following set of searches:

```
./Shapes.DLL.
./Shapes/Shapes.dll
./Shapes/Shapes.exe
./Shapes.exe
```

Additional search paths or even URLs for downloading an assembly from a remote location via the Internet may be specified with a **configuration file**. Configuration files for an assembly are XML-format files that specify rules for the .NET runtime to apply when searching for an assembly. Configuration files can also override the default behavior for version checking. The details of configuration files and XML are quite complex and beyond the scope of this book.

Compiling C# Code from the Command-Line

So far in the book, we've been working exclusively with Visual Studio .NET to construct and compile our applications. The C# compiler that compiles all of our code is in fact independent of Visual Studio .NET, and can be used from a command-line prompt with the following command:

```
>csc <filename.cs>
```

Often you may find that you don't want to create an entire project in Visual Studio .NET if you wish to test a very simple piece of code – in this case you may prefer to use a simple text editor (such as the one we created in Chapter 15!) and compile and run your program from the command-line. By doing this you are of course sacrificing the benefits of Visual Studio .NET's IDE.

Let's take the opportunity to have a quick look at compiling our `Shapes.cs` and `ShapeUser.cs` files from the command-line, and also adding references to external assemblies as we do. Before you start this *Try it Out*, ensure that your PATH environment variable is set properly, otherwise the C# compiler won't be found. Please see Appendix A for instructions on how to set this variable correctly.

Try it Out – Compiling and Linking from the Command-Line

1. Copy the files `Shapes.cs` and `ShapeUser.cs` into the directory `C:\BegVCSharp\Chapter21`.

2. Start a command-line prompt, and change to the directory `C:\BegVCSharp\Chapter21` (see Appendix A for a quick tip on how to start the command-line prompt in any directory).

3. Compile `Shapes.cs` with the following command:

```
>csc /target:library Shapes.cs
```

This will create `Shapes.dll` in the current directory. The `/target:library` option directs the compiler to create the result assembly as a DLL instead of an executable (`.exe`) file.

4. Compile `ShapeUser.cs` with this command:

```
>csc /reference:Shapes.dll ShapeUser.cs
```

This will create `ShapeUser.exe` in the current directory. The `/reference:Shapes.dll` option specifies a reference to the `Shapes.dll` assembly.

5. Execute `ShapeUser`, and it will run happily.

Now we'll look at signing the `Shapes` assembly, and compiling `Shapes.cs` and its `AssemblyInfo.cs` file together.

6. Copy `AssemblyInfo.cs` from the `Shapes` directory into `C:\BegVCSharp\Chapter21`, and modify the line that specifies the key file to the following:

```
[assembly: AssemblyKeyFile(@"NewShapesKey.snk")]
```

7. Now, we'll create a new key file in the `Chapter21` directory in the same way as we did earlier:

```
>sn -k NewShapesKey.snk
```

8. To recompile `Shapes.cs` along with its `AssemblyInfo.cs` file, use the following command:

```
>csc /target:library Shapes.cs AssemblyInfo.cs
```

If we try to execute `ShapeUser.exe` now, without recompiling, we get the following error because the `Shapes.dll` assembly no longer matches:

```
Unhandled Exception: System.IO.FileLoadException: The located assembly's manifest
definition with name 'Shapes' does not match the assembly reference. File name:
"Shapes"
    at ShapeUser.ShapeUser.Main()
```

This is because `Shapes.dll` has now been signed, and as such, is a different assembly to the one originally specified when `ShapeUser.cs` was compiled. Note this error didn't occur earlier when we created and compiled `ShapeUser` with VS, as VS creates a private copy of the assembly in the project directory, and obviously this copy hasn't changed.

9. To finish, recompile `ShapeUser.cs` as we did earlier, and it will work properly now.

This whole process has been reasonably straightforward, but then we were only compiling (at most) two files at once, and only referencing one external assembly. We also made things easier for ourselves by copying all the required files into the same directory!

The C# compiler has many options to control its output – you can find a full list of these in the .NET Framework documentation. For example, we've already used the `/reference` and `/target` options – the `/target` option tells the C# compiler what kind of project it needs to build:

- ❑ The `/target:exe` argument tells the C# compiler to produce a console application.

- ❑ The `/target:winexe` argument tells the C# compiler to produce a Windows Form application.

- ❑ The `/target:library` argument tells the C# compiler to produce a stand-alone assembly containing a manifest.

- ❑ The `/target:module` argument also tells the C# compiler to produce an assembly file, but without a manifest. Manifest-less assemblies produced with the `/target:module` argument can be subsumed into other assembly components that do contain manifests.

The `/reference` option can be shortened to `/r`, and the `/target` option to `/t`. Another useful option is `/recurse` – this searches subdirectories for source files to compile. For example,

```
>csc /recurse:*.cs
```

will compile all the `.cs` source files in the current directory.

Summary

C# programs and class libraries are delivered as assemblies, which have many features that ease the delivery of components in the Microsoft .NET Framework. Components provide for binary reuse of objects. The essential feature of .NET components is self-description; this distinguishes them from their historical ancestors (such as COM components).

Self-description has a number of benefits, including ease of installation and integration with the Common Language Runtime (CLR) to provide cross-language and legacy support, as well as C# development.

We created a C# class library component and compiled it into an assembly. We then created a C# application that used this component, and learned how to view the contents of assemblies using Ildasm. This helped us to understand the structure of assemblies.

We examined the various parts of an assembly, including the manifest, version number, and other assembly attributes. Besides helping us to understand the structure, this enables us to compare version numbers in external references for debugging purposes.

Assemblies can be either private assemblies local to an application, or shared assemblies, which are available system-wide. We learned how to create shared assemblies by creating a key file and signing the assembly to create a strong name for the assembly. We learned about version checking for shared assemblies, and looked at the Global Assembly Cache where shared assemblies are stored.

Finally, we examined briefly how references to assemblies are searched and resolved in the .NET runtime.

These features of assemblies all help to make development in the .NET environment much easier.

Exercises

1. Change the version number and other assembly attributes in AssemblyInfo.cs or Shapes.cs, and view the resulting changes in Shapes.dll using Ildasm.

2. Make a new MoreShapes assembly with a Square class in addition to Circle and Triangle, and then examine its properties with Ildasm.

3. Change the assembly reference in ShapeUser.exe to use MoreShapes.dll, and then view the changed properties in Ildasm.

4. Make your own client for MoreShapes that uses the Square and Triangle objects as well as Circle. Examine the assembly for this client with Ildasm.

5. Display the command options for Gacutil with the /? flag, then use its options to list the properties of all the global assemblies on your system.

6. Create a strong name for MoreShapes and sign the assembly. View the results with Ildasm. Try executing your client program, then recompile to reference the signed assembly.

7. Install MoreShapes.dll into the Global Assembly Cache using Gacutil, and experiment with ShapeUser and your own client by running with and without the MoreShapes assembly present in the local directory and/or GAC.

Attributes

This chapter introduces the subject of attributes. It will describe what they are and what they can be used for, and will give examples of several of the attributes available with the .NET Framework.

We'll also discuss custom attributes – attributes that you can write yourself to extend the system – and provide several worked examples. We'll also show how the Intermediate Language Disassembler (Ildasm) can be used to discover the attributes of existing assemblies.

Attributes are one of the most useful features of the .NET Framework, used frequently by Microsoft. To use them effectively, we need to make a significant time investment, but it is worth the effort. In the following sections we'll see how they can be applied to areas such as:

- ❑ Debugging
- ❑ Providing information about an assembly
- ❑ Marking methods and classes as obsolete
- ❑ Conditional compilation
- ❑ Database access

We'll also describe in detail how to write your own attributes that extend the system, and show several worked examples of custom attributes. By the end of the chapter you should have enough knowledge of what attributes are and how to use them to apply to your own projects.

What is an Attribute?

It's difficult to define an attribute in a single sentence – it's best to learn by examining how they are used. For now we'll define an attribute as extra information that can be applied to chunks of code within an assembly – such as a class, method, or property. This information is accessible to any other class that uses the assembly.

In the previous chapter we discussed assemblies, and mentioned the AssemblyInfo.cs file. Let's have a look at this file – create a new Windows application called AttributePeek in the C:\BegVCSharp\Chapter22 folder, and open Solution Explorer.

You will see something like the following:

If you double-click on this file, you'll see some code created by VS. Part of this code is shown below:

```
using System.Reflection;
using System.Runtime.CompilerServices;

//
// General Information about an assembly is controlled through the following
// set of attributes. Change these attribute values to modify
// the information associated with an assembly.
//
[assembly: AssemblyTitle("")]
[assembly: AssemblyDescription("")]
[assembly: AssemblyConfiguration("")]
[assembly: AssemblyCompany("")]
[assembly: AssemblyProduct("")]
[assembly: AssemblyCopyright("")]
[assembly: AssemblyTrademark("")]
[assembly: AssemblyCulture("")]
```

For brevity only part of the file is shown here. Within this file there are a number of lines beginning
"[assembly:" – these are attribute definitions. When the file is compiled, any attributes defined are saved
into the resulting assembly – this process is known as "pickling". To see this in action, modify one of the
attributes above – say the AssemblyTitle attribute, and compile your assembly:

```
[assembly: AssemblyTitle("Wrox rocks")]
```

Once compiled, right-click on the assembly (which you can find in the project \bin\Debug directory) in
Windows Explorer and select Properties. The image below shows the Version information tab in
Windows 2000 Professional. The Description field contains the description contained in the
AssemblyTitle attribute:

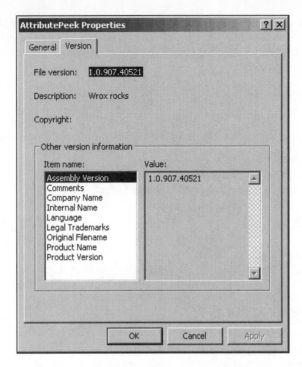

The assembly attributes and their corresponding names on the Version information tab are listed below:

Attribute	Version Information
AssemblyTitle	Description
AssemblyDescription	Comments
AssemblyCompany	Company Name
AssemblyTrademark	Legal Trademarks
AssemblyVersion	Assembly Version and Product Version
AssemblyCopyright	Copyright
AssemblyProduct	Product Name

You may have noticed that the list of attributes available through the assembly's Properties sheet is fewer than the list of attributes defined within the assembly. Microsoft has mapped some of the most common attributes onto the Properties sheet but to get at the other attributes you'll either have to write code (shown in the upcoming section on *Reflection*), or you can use Ildasm.

In order to find all attributes on a given assembly, you can use Ildasm to inspect the assembly and look for the attribute(s) defined. We were introduced to Ildasm in the previous chapter, and saw how to add it as an external tool to Visual Studio .NET – if you haven't done so, now is a good opportunity to go back and see how to do this.

Open `Ildasm` and select the assembly using **File | Open**. Double-clicking on the highlighted MANIFEST section will open a secondary window that contains the assembly manifest as described in the previous chapter. Scrolling down the file a little will reveal some lines of strange looking code – this code is the IL produced from the C# compiler:

```
.assembly AttributePeek
{
   .custom instance void
   [mscorlib]System.Reflection.AssemblyCopyrightAttribute::.ctor(string)
      = (01 00 00 00 00)

   .custom instance void
   [mscorlib]System.Reflection.AssemblyKeyNameAttribute::.ctor(string)
      = (01 00 00 00 00)

   ...

   .custom instance void
   [mscorlib]System.Reflection.AssemblyTitleAttribute::.ctor(string)
      = (01 00 0A 57 72 6F 78 20 72 6F 63 6B 73 00 00) // ...Wrox rocks..

.  hash algorithm 0x00008004
   .ver 1:0:907:40521
}
```

Looking down through the file, you'll notice a number of declarations that look something like type declarations:

```
[mscorlib]System.Reflection.AssemblyTitleAttribute::.ctor(string)
   = (01 00 0A 57 72 6F 78 20 72 6F 63 6B 73 00 00)   // ...Wrox rocks..
```

The `AssemblyTitle` that we typed in has been persisted into the assembly manifest – if you get your hex/ASCII conversion tables out you'll see that the set of characters after `01 00 0A` are the ASCII codes for "Wrox rocks". Just in case you are curious, the prolog bytes `01 00` are a two-byte ID, and `0A` is the length of the string (ten characters). This process of storing the attribute within the assembly is known as "pickling", which you may come across if you look at some of the background .NET material available on the Web.

You may have noticed that in the code snippet from `AssemblyInfo.cs`, the term `AssemblyTitle` was used; however, in the IL code that we have just looked at, this is shown as `AssemblyTitleAttribute`. The C# compiler will look up an attribute class called `AssemblyTitle` first, and if it is not found it will then append the word `Attribute` and search again. So whether you type the whole class name, or omit the final `Attribute`, both versions generate the same code. Throughout the chapter the `Attribute` suffix has been dropped.

The attribute declaration persisted (pickled) into the manifest looks suspiciously like an object and its constructor. The bytes in brackets are the parameters passed to the constructor.

Having examined the background, we can define what an attribute is:

> **An attribute is a class that can include additional data within an assembly, concerning the assembly or any type within that assembly.**

Given that an attribute is a class, and in the manifest the attribute is stored in the format shown above, let's revisit the attribute definition from earlier in the chapter:

```
[assembly: AssemblyTitle("Wrox rocks")]
```

The syntax is a little different to normal C#, as the square brackets are there to enclose the attribute. The `assembly:` tag defines the scope of the attribute (which is covered later in the chapter), and the rest of the code declares the attribute. The `AssemblyTitle` attribute has a constructor that takes only one argument – a string value. The compiler includes this value in the assembly. This value can be accessed by the standard Windows Explorer **Properties** sheet, by viewing the assembly within `Ildasm`, or programmatically by **reflection** – which we will discuss next.

In addition to the simple attributes dealing with assembly information, the .NET Framework defines nearly two hundred attributes used for things as diverse as debugging, design-time control behavior, serialization, and much more. We'll see some standard attributes after the *Reflection* section, and then continue by showing how to extend .NET with our own custom attributes.

Reflection

Unless you have a grounding in Java, reflection is probably a new topic so we will spend a couple of pages defining it and showing how it can be used.

Reflection allows you to programmatically inspect an assembly, and get information about the assembly, including all object types contained within. This information includes the attributes you have added to those types. The reflection objects reside within the `System.Reflection` namespace.

In addition to reading the types defined within a given assembly, we can also generate (emit) our own assemblies and types using the services of `System.Reflection.Emit`. This topic is a little too hectic for a beginning book on C#, but if you are interested, then MSDN contains some information on emitting dynamic assemblies.

The first example in this section will inspect an assembly and display a list of all attributes defined on the assembly – this should produce a list similar to that shown above.

In this chapter we're going to be a bit more relaxed about the format of our code examples, since if you've got to this point in the book you must be pretty confident with what you're doing! All of the code can be found in the `Chapter22` folder of the code download – for some examples we may only show you the most important parts of the code, so don't forget to look through the download code to see the whole picture.

Our first example can be found in the `Chapter22\FindAttributes` directory. The entire source file is reproduced here:

```
// FindAttributes.cs
// Import types from System and System.Reflection
using System;
using System.Reflection;

/// <summary>
/// Corresponds to section titled 'Reflection' in Chapter 22
/// </summary>
```

```
public class FindAttributes
{
    /// <summary>
    /// Main .exe entry point
    /// </summary>
    /// <param name="args">Command line args - should be an assembly</param>
    static void Main(string[] args)
    {
        // Output usage information if necessary
        if (args.Length == 0)
            Usage ();
        else if ((args.Length == 1) && (args[0] ==  "/?"))
            Usage ();
        else
        {
            // Load the assembly
            string assemblyName = null;

            foreach (string arg in args)
            {
                if (assemblyName == null)
                    assemblyName = arg;
                else
                    assemblyName = string.Format("{0} {1}" , assemblyName , arg);
            }

            try
            {
                // Attempt to load the named assembly
                Assembly a = Assembly.LoadFrom(assemblyName);

                // Now find the attributes on the assembly
                object[] attributes = a.GetCustomAttributes(true);

                // If there were any attributes defined...
                if (attributes.Length > 0)
                {
                    Console.WriteLine("Assembly attributes for '{0}'...",
                        assemblyName);

                    // Dump them out...
                    foreach (object o in attributes)
                        Console.WriteLine("  {0}" , o.ToString ());
                }
                else
                    Console.WriteLine("Assembly {0} contains no Attributes.",
                        assemblyName);
            }
            catch (Exception ex)
            {
                Console.WriteLine("Exception thrown loading assembly {0}...",
                    assemblyName);
                Console.WriteLine ();
```

```
                Console.WriteLine(ex.ToString ());
            }
        }
    }

    /// <summary>
    /// Display usage information for the .exe
    /// </summary>
    static void Usage()
    {
        Console.WriteLine("Usage:");
        Console.WriteLine("  FindAttributes <Assembly>");
    }
}
```

Now build the executable in Visual Studio .NET, or if you prefer use the command line compiler:

>**csc FindAttributes.cs**

This will compile the file and produce a console executable, which you can then call.

To run the FindAttributes application, you need to supply the name of an assembly to inspect. For now, we can use the FindAttributes.exe assembly itself:

The example code first checks the parameters passed to the command-line – if none are supplied, or if the user types FindAttributes /? then the Usage() method will be called, which will display a simple command usage summary:

```
if (args.Length == 0)
    Usage ();
else if ((args.Length == 1) && (args[0] == "/?"))
    Usage ();
```

Next we reconstitute the command-line arguments into a single string. The reason for this is that it's common to have spaces in directory names, such as "Program Files", and this would be considered as two arguments by virtue of there being a space. So, we iterate through all the arguments stitching them back into a single string, and use this as the name of the assembly to load:

```
foreach (string arg in args)
{
    if (assemblyName == null)
        assemblyName = arg;
    else
        assemblyName = string.Format ("{0} {1}" , assemblyName , arg);
}
```

We then attempt to load the assembly, and retrieve all custom attributes defined on that assembly with the `GetCustomAttributes()` method:

```
Assembly a = Assembly.LoadFrom (assemblyName);

// Now find the attributes on the assembly
object[] attributes = a.GetCustomAttributes(true);
```

Any attributes that are found are output to the console. When we tested the program against the FindAttributes.exe file, an attribute called `DebuggableAttribute` was displayed. Although we have not specified the `DebuggableAttribute`, it has been added by the C# compiler, and you will find that most of your executables have this attribute.

We can alter the code as appropriate to add on as many assembly attributes as you wish. As an example, try updating the source code for `FindAttributes` as follows:

```
using System;
using System.Reflection;

[assembly: AssemblyTitle("Wrox rocks")]

public class FindAttributes
```

Then when you recompile and run the code you will see output similar to that shown below:

We'll return to reflection later in the chapter, to show how to retrieve attributes on classes and methods defined within an assembly.

Built In Attributes

We saw in previous sections that the .NET Framework includes a number of attributes, such as the `DebuggableAttribute` and `AssemblyTitleAttribute` attributes. This section will discuss some of the more common attributes defined in the .NET Framework, and discuss when you might want to use them.

The attributes covered in this section are:

❑ `System.Diagnostics.ConditionalAttribute`

❑ `System.ObsoleteAttribute`

❑ `System.SerializableAttribute`

❑ `System.Reflection.AssemblyDelaySignAttribute`

There is more information about the other attributes that ship with the .NET Framework in the .NET Framework SDK documentation.

Another extremely useful tool when working with .NET is a program called "Reflector" which is downloadable from http://www.aisto.com/roeder/dotnet/. This uses reflection to inspect assemblies. We can use it to find all classes that derive from System.Attribute with a few mouse clicks. It's one tool you shouldn't be without.

System.Diagnostics.ConditionalAttribute

This is one of the most useful attributes of all, as it permits sections of code to be included or excluded based on the definition of a symbol at compilation time. This attribute is contained within the System.Diagnostics namespace, which includes classes for debug and trace output, event logging, performance counters, and process information. The following code shows an example of using this attribute:

```
using System;
using System.Diagnostics;

class TestConditional
{
    static void Main(string[] args)
    {
        // Construct a new TestConditional object
        TestConditional tc = new TestConditional ();

        // Call a method only available if DEBUG is defined...
        tc.DebugOnly ();
    }

    // Class constructor
    public TestConditional ()
    {
    }

    // This method is attributed, and will ONLY be included in
    // the emitted code if the DEBUG symbol is defined when
    // the program is compiled
    [Conditional("DEBUG")]
    public void DebugOnly ()
    {
        // This line will only be displayed in debug builds...
        Console.WriteLine ("This string only displays in Debug");
    }
}
```

The source code for this example is available in the Chapter22/Conditional directory. The code constructs an instance of the TestConditional class within the static Main() function. It then calls the DebugOnly() method, which is attributed with the Conditional attribute. This function just displays a line of text on the console.

When a C# source file is compiled, you can define symbols on the command line. The Conditional attribute will prevent calls to a method that is conditional on a symbol that is not present.

The DEBUG symbol will be set automatically for you if you compile a Debug build within Visual Studio .NET. If you want to define or refine the symbols for a particular project then display the project Properties dialog and navigate to the Build option of Configuration Properties as shown below:

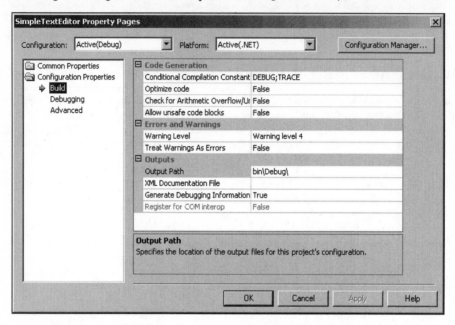

Notice that the defaults for a Debug build are to define DEBUG and TRACE.

To define a symbol on the command line you use the /d: switch (the short form for /define: – you can type the entire string if you wish):

```
>csc /d:DEBUG conditional.cs
```

If you compile and run the file with the command-line shown, you'll see the output string This string only displays in Debug. If you compile without defining the DEBUG symbol on the command line then the program will display nothing. Note that the options for csc are case-sensitive.

To get a clearer picture of what is happening within the generated code, use Ildasm to view the generated code:

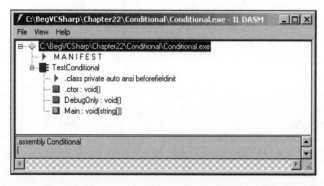

When the DEBUG symbol is **not** defined, the IL generated for the Main() method is as follows:

```
.method private hidebysig static void Main(string[] args) cil managed
{
    .entrypoint
    // Code size   7 (0x7)
    .maxstack  1
    .locals init (class TestConditional V_0)
    IL_0000:    newobj  instance void TestConditional::.ctor()
    IL_0005:    stloc.0
    IL_0006:    ret
} // end of method TestConditional::Main
```

This code simply creates an instance of the TestConditional() object (IL_0000), stores this in a local variable, and returns.

If, however, you compile the file with the /d:DEBUG switch, you'll see code produced as shown below:

```
.method private hidebysig static void Main(string[] args) cil managed
{
    .entrypoint
    // Code size   13 (0xd)
    .maxstack  1
    .locals init (class TestConditional V_0)
    IL_0000:    newobj  instance void TestConditional::.ctor()
    IL_0005:    stloc.0
    IL_0006:    ldloc.0
    IL_0007:    callvirt instance void TestConditional::DebugOnly()
    IL_000c:    ret
} // end of method TestConditional::Main
```

The two lines highlighted are added to call the conditional method. Use of Conditional() will remove calls to a method, but not the method itself.

> The Conditional attribute can only be used on methods that return void – otherwise removing the call would mean that no value was returned; however, you can attribute a method that has out or ref parameters – the variables will retain their original value.

System.ObsoleteAttribute

It may seem strange to include such an attribute in something as new the .NET Framework, but it shows the attention to detail that the Microsoft engineers have put into the .NET Framework. The Obsolete attribute can be used to mark a class, method, or any other entry in an assembly as being no longer used.

This attribute would be useful, for example, when publishing a library of classes. It is inevitable that through the course of developing a set of classes, some of those classes/methods/properties will be superseded. This attribute can be used to prepare the users of your code for the eventual withdrawal of a particular feature.

Suppose in version one of your application, you have a class like this:

```
public class Developer
{
   public Developer ()
   {
   }

   public void OriginalMethod ()
   {
   }
}
```

You compile and use this class for several years, but then something new comes along to replace the old functionality:

```
public void NewMethod ()
{
}
```

Naturally you want to allow the users of your library to use OriginalMethod() for some time, but you would also like to alert them to the fact that there is a newer method by displaying a warning message at compile time, informing your users of the existence of NewMethod(). To do this, all you need to add is the Obsolete attribute as shown below:

```
[Obsolete("Use NewMethod instead.")]
public void OriginalMethod ()
{
}
```

When you compile again, for Debug or Release, you'll receive a warning from the C# compiler that you are using an obsolete (or soon to be obsolete) method:

```
Obsolete.cs(20,1): warning CS0618: 'Developer.OriginalMethod()' is obsolete:
        'Use NewMethod instead.'
```

Over the course of time, everyone will become tired of seeing this warning message each time the code is compiled, so eventually everyone (well, almost everyone) will utilize NewMethod(). Eventually you'll want to entirely drop support for OriginalMethod(), so you add an extra parameter to the Obsolete attribute:

```
[Obsolete("You must use NewMethod instead.", true)]
public void OriginalMethod()
{
}
```

When a user attempts to compile this method, the compiler will generate an error and halt the compilation with the following message:

```
Obsolete.cs(20,1): error CS0619: 'Developer.OriginalMethod()' is obsolete:
        'You must use NewMethod instead.'
```

Using this attribute provides users of your class with help in modifying applications that use your class, as the class evolves.

For binary classes, such as components that you purchase without source code, this isn't a good way to do versioning – the .NET Framework has excellent built-in versioning capabilities that we looked at in the previous chapter. But the `Obsolete` attribute does provide a useful way for us to hint that a particular feature of our classes should no longer be used.

System.SerializableAttribute

Serialization is the name for storing and retrieving an object, either in a disk file, memory, or anywhere else you can think of. When serialized, all instance data is persisted to the storage medium, and when deserialized, the object is reconstructed and is indistinguishable from its original instance.

For any of you who have programmed in MFC, ATL, or VB before, and had to worry about storing and retrieving instance data, this attribute will save you a great deal of typing. Suppose you have a C# object instance that you would like to store in a file, such as:

```
public class Person
{
    public Person ()
    {
    }

    public int Age;
    public int WeightInPounds;
}
```

In C# (and indeed any of the languages built on the .NET Framework) you can serialize an instance's members without writing any code – well almost. All you need to do is add the `Serializable` attribute to the class, and the .NET runtime will do the rest for you.

When the runtime receives a request to serialize an object, it checks if the object's class implements the `ISerializable` interface, and if not checks if the class is attributed with the `Serializable` attribute. We will not discuss `ISerializable` any further here – it is an advanced topic.

If the `Serializable` attribute is found on the class, then .NET uses Reflection to get all instance data – whether public, protected, or private – and store this as the representation of the object. Deserialization is the opposite of the process – data is read from the storage medium and this data is assigned to instance variables of the class.

The following shows a class marked with the `Serializable` attribute:

```
[Serializable]
public class Person
{
    public Person ()
    {
    }

    public int Age;
    public int WeightInPounds;
}
```

727

The entire code for this example is available in the `Chapter22/Serialize` subdirectory. To store an instance of this `Person` class, we use a `Formatter` object – which converts the data stored within your class into a stream of bytes. The system comes with two default formatters, `BinaryFormatter` and `SoapFormatter` (these have their own namespaces below `System.Runtime.Serialization.Formatters`). The code below shows how to use the `BinaryFormatter` to store a person object:

```
using System;
using System.Runtime.Serialization.Formatters.Binary;
using System.IO;

  public static void Serialize ()
  {
    // Construct a person object
    Person  me = new Person ();

    // Set the data that is to be serialized
    me.Age = 34;
    me.WeightInPounds = 200;

    // Create a disk file to store the object to...
    Stream  s = File.Open ("Me.dat" , FileMode.Create);

    // And use a BinaryFormatted to write the object to the stream...
    BinaryFormatter bf = new BinaryFormatter ();

    // Serialize the object
    bf.Serialize (s , me);

    // And close the stream
    s.Close ();
  }
```

The code first creates the person object and sets the `Age` and `WeightInPounds` data, and then it constructs a stream on a file called `Me.dat`. The binary formatter utilizes the stream to store the instance of the person class into `Me.dat`, and the stream is closed.

The default serialization code will store all the public contents of the object, which in most cases is what you would want. But under some circumstances you may wish to define one or more fields that should not be serialized. That's easy too:

```
[Serializable]
public class Person
{
    public Person ()
    {
    }

    public int Age;
    [NonSerialized]
    public int WeightInPounds;
}
```

When this class is serialized, only the `Age` member would be stored – the `WeightInPounds` member would not be persisted and so would also not be retrieved on deserialization.

Deserialization is basically the opposite of the above serialization code. The example below opens a stream on the `Me.dat` file created earlier, constructs a `BinaryFormatter` to read the object, and calls its `Deserialize` method to retrieve the object. It then casts this into a `Person`, and writes the age and weight to the console:

```
public static void DeSerialize ()
{
  // Open the file this time
  Stream  s = File.Open ("Me.dat" , FileMode.Open);

  // And use a BinaryFormatted to read object(s) from the stream
  BinaryFormatter bf = new BinaryFormatter ();

  // Deserialize the object
  object  o = bf.Deserialize (s);

  // Ensure it is of the correct type...
  Person  p = o as Person;

  if (p != null)
    Console.WriteLine ("DeSerialized Person aged: {0} weight: {1}" ,
                        p.Age , p.WeightInPounds);

  // And close the stream
  s.Close ();
}
```

You can use the `NonSerialized` attribute to mark data that does not need to be serialized, such as data that can be recomputed or calculated when necessary. An example would be where you have a class which computes prime numbers – you may well cache primes to speed up response times whilst using the class; however, serializing and deserializing a list of primes would be unnecessary as they can simply be recomputed on request. At other times the member may only be relevant to that specific use of the object. For example in an object representing a word processor document, we would want to serialize the content of the document but usually not the position of the insertion point – when the document next loads we simply place the insertion point at the start of the document.

If you want yet more control over how an object is serialized, you can implement the `ISerializable` interface. This is an advanced topic and we won't take this discussion any further in this book.

System.Reflection.AssemblyDelaySignAttribute

The `System.Reflection` namespace provides a number of attributes, some of which have been shown earlier in the chapter. One of the more complex to use is `AssemblyDelaySign`. From the previous chapter you'll have learned about building assemblies, creating shared assemblies and registering them in the Global Assembly Cache (GAC). The .NET Framework also permits you to delay sign an assembly, which basically means that you can register it in the GAC for testing purposes without a private key.

One scenario where you might use delayed signing is when developing commercial software. Each assembly that is developed in-house needs to be signed with your company's private key before being shipped to your customers. So when you compile your assembly you reference the key file before you can register the assembly in the GAC.

However, many organizations would not want their private key to be on every developer's machine. For this reason the runtime enables us to partially sign the assembly, and tweak a few settings so that your assembly can be registered within the GAC. When fully tested it can be signed by whoever holds the private key file. This may be your QA department, one or more trusted individuals, or the marketing department.

In the following example we'll show how you can delay sign a typical assembly, register it in the GAC for testing, and finally complete the signing by adding in the private key.

Extracting the Public Key

Firstly we need to create a key file with the sn.exe utility – we saw how to do this in the previous chapter. The key file will contain the public and private keys, so we'll call it Company.Key:

```
>sn -k Company.Key
```

Then we need to extract the public key portion for use by developers with the -p option:

```
>sn -p Company.Key Company.Public
```

This command will produce a key file Company.Public with only the public part of the key. This public key file can be copied onto all machines and doesn't need to be kept safe – it's the private key file that needs to be secure. Store the Company.Key file somewhere safe, as it only needs to be used when you wish to finally sign your assemblies.

In order to delay-sign an assembly and register that assembly within the GAC, you also need to obtain the public key token – this is basically a shorter version of the public key, used when registering assemblies. You can obtain the token in one of two ways:

❑ From the public key file itself:

```
>sn -t Company.Public
```

❑ From any assembly signed with the key:

```
>sn -T <assembly>
```

Both of these will display a hashed version of the public key, and are case-sensitive. We'll explain this more when we register the assembly.

Delay Signing the Assembly

The following code shows how to attribute an assembly for delayed signing. It is available in the Chapter22/DelaySign directory:

```
using System;
using System.Reflection;

// Define the file which contains the public key
[assembly: AssemblyKeyFile ("Company.Public") ]
// And that this assembly is to be delay signed
[assembly: AssemblyDelaySign (true) ]

public class DelayedSigning
{
  public DelayedSigning ()
  {
  }
}
```

The `AssemblyKeyFile` attribute defines which file the key is to be found in. This can be either the public key file, or for more trusted individuals the file containing both public and private keys. The `AssemblyDelaySign` attribute defines whether the assembly will be fully signed (`false`) or delay-signed (`true`).

The `AssemblyInfo.cs` file created for a project by Visual Studio .NET contains various attributes, such as the versioning and file information shown earlier in the chapter. It's also the place to define the `AssemblyDelaySign` attributes, and default values are created with every new project.

When compiled, the assembly will contain an entry in the manifest for the public key. In fact, the manifest will also contain enough room for the private key too, so re-signing the assembly will not change it in any way (other than writing a few extra bytes into the manifest).

Registering in the GAC

Attempting to use the `Gacutil` tool (which we met in the previous chapter) to register a delay-signed assembly in the GAC will generate the following error message (or something very similar):

```
Microsoft (R) .NET Global Assembly Cache Utility.  Version 1.0.3705.0
Copyright (C) Microsoft Corporation 1998-2001. All rights reserved.

Failure adding assembly to the cache: Strong name signature could not be verified.
Was the assembly built delay-signed?
```

The assembly is only partially signed at the moment, and by default the GAC will only accept assemblies with a complete strong name. We can however instruct the GAC to skip verification of the strong name on a delay signed assembly by using the `sn` utility. Remember the public key token from earlier? This is where it comes into play.

```
>sn -Vr *,34AAA4146EE01E4A
```

This instructs the GAC to permit any assemblies with a public key token of `34AAA4146EE01E4A4A` to be registered. Typing this at the command prompt will generate the following message:

```
Microsoft (R) .NET Framework Strong Name Utility  Version 1.0.3705.0
Copyright (C) Microsoft Corporation 1998-2001. All rights reserved.

Verification entry added for assembly '*,34AAA4146EE01E4A4A'
```

Attempting to install the assembly into the GAC with `Gacutil` will now succeed. We don't need to use the public key value when adding a verification entry for your assembly – we can specify that all assemblies can be registered by using:

```
>sn -Vr *
```

Or we can specify the assembly by typing its full name like so:

```
>sn -Vr DelaySign.dll
```

This data is permanently held in what is called the "Verification Skip Table", which is a file stored on disk. To obtain a list of the entries in the verification skip table, type the following (these commands are case-sensitive):

```
>sn -Vl
```

This is the output on my machine:

```
Microsoft (R) .NET Framework Strong Name Utility   Version 1.0.3705.0
Copyright (C) Microsoft Corp. 1998-2001. All rights reserved.

Assembly/Strong Name                 Users
===========================================
*,03689116d3a4ae33                   All users
*,33aea4d316916803                   All users

*,34AAA4146EE01E4A                   All users
*,631223CD18E5C371                   All users
*,b03f5f7f11d50a3a                   All users
*,b77a5c561934e089                   All users
```

Notice the `Users` column – we can define that a given assembly can be loaded into the GAC by a subset of all users. Check out the `sn.exe` documentation for further details of this and other assembly naming options.

Completing the Strong Name

The last stage in the process is to compile the public and private keys into the assembly – an assembly with both entries is said to be strong named, and can be registered in the GAC without a skip verification entry.

Once again we use the `sn.exe` utility, this time with the `-R` switch. The `-R` switch means that we want to re-sign the assembly and add in the private key portion:

```
>sn -R delaysign.dll Company.Key
```

This will display the following:

```
Microsoft (R) .NET Framework Strong Name Utility   Version 1.0.3705.0
Copyright (C) Microsoft Corp. 1998-2001. All rights reserved.

Assembly 'delaysign.dll' successfully re-signed
```

The other parameters along with the –R switch are the name of the assembly to be re-signed and the key file that contains the public and private keys.

Custom Attributes

The first half of this chapter has concentrated on some of the attributes that are contained within the .NET Framework. That's not the whole story though – we can also create our own attributes.

In this chapter we will only scratch the surface of what can be done with custom attributes. In this section we will look at the following – invented – attributes:

❑ **TestCaseAttribute** – links the code used to test a class to the class itself

❑ **BugFixAttribute** – records who altered what and when within the source code

❑ **DatabaseTableAttribute** and **DatabaseColumnAttribute** – shows how to produce database schemas from .NET classes

A custom attribute is simply a special class that must comply with these two specifications:

❑ A custom attribute must derive from `System.Attribute`

❑ The constructor(s) for an attribute may only contain types that can be resolved at compile time – such as strings and integers

The restriction on the types of parameters allowable on the attribute constructor(s) is due to the way that attributes are persisted into the assembly metadata. When you use an attribute within code, you are using the attribute's constructor inline. For example:

```
[assembly: AssemblyKeyFile ("Company.Public") ]
```

This attribute is persisted into the assembly metadata as an instruction to call a constructor of `AssemblyKeyFileAttribute`, which accepts a string. In the above example that string is `"Company.Public"`. If we define a custom attribute, users of the attribute are basically writing parameters to the constructor of the class.

The first example, `TestCaseAttribute`, shows how test classes can be coupled with the code that they test.

TestCaseAttribute

When unit testing software it is common to define a set of test classes that exercise your classes to ensure that they perform as expected. This is especially true in regression testing, where you want to ensure that by fixing a bug or adding extra functionality, you have not broken something else.

When working with regulated customers (such as producing software for Pharmaceutical companies who work under strict controls from government agencies), it is necessary to provide cross-references between code and tests. The `TestCaseAttribute` presented here can help to trace between a class and its test class.

The full source code is available in the `Chapter22/TestCase` directory.

In order to create a custom attribute class, we must:

❑ Create a class derived from `System.Attribute`

❑ Create the constructor(s) and public properties as required

❑ Attribute the class to define where it is valid to use your custom attribute

We will discuss each of these steps in turn.

Creating the Custom Attribute Class

This is the simplest step. All you need to do here is create a class derived from `System.Attribute`:

```
public class TestCaseAttribute : Attribute
{
}
```

Creating Constructors and Properties

As mentioned earlier, when the user uses an attribute they are effectively calling the attribute's constructor. For the test case attribute, we want to define the type of object used to test a given class, so we'll use a `System.Type` value:

```
using System;
public class TestCaseAttribute : Attribute
{
  /// <summary>
  /// Constructor for the class
  /// </summary>
  /// <param name="testCase">The object which contains
  /// the test case code</param>
  public TestCaseAttribute (System.Type testCase)
  {
     TestCase = testCase;
  }

  /// <summary>
  /// The test case object
  /// </summary>
  public readonly System.Type TestCase;

  /// <summary>
  /// Perform the test
  /// </summary>
  public void Test ()
  {
    // Create an instance of the class under test
    // The test case object created is assumed to
    // test the object in its' constructor
```

```
        object o = Activator.CreateInstance (TestCase);
   }
}
```

This defines a single constructor, and a read only member variable `TestCase`. The `Test` method is used to instantiate the test case, as this simple example will perform the tests within the constructor of the test case class.

Attributing the Class for Usage

The last thing we need to do is attribute your attribute class to indicate where your attribute class can be used. For the test case attribute we want to say "this attribute is only valid on classes". We can decide where an attribute that we create is valid. This will be explained in more detail later in the chapter:

```
[AttributeUsage(AttributeTargets.Class,
               AllowMultiple=false,
               Inherited=true)]
public class TestCaseAttribute : Attribute
...
```

The `AttributeUsage` attribute has a single constructor, which takes a value from the `AttributeTargets` enum (described in full later in this section). Here we have stated that the only valid place to put a `TestCase` attribute is on a class. We can specify several values in this enum using the | symbol for a logical OR – so other attributes might be valid on classes, or constructors, or properties.

In the definition of the attribute here we have also utilized two properties of that attribute – `AllowMultiple` and `Inherited`. We will discuss these properties more fully later in the section.

Now we need an object to test with a test case. There's nothing particularly magic about this class:

```
[TestCase (typeof(TestAnObject))]
public class SomeCodeOrOther
{
    public SomeCodeOrOther ()
    {
    }

    public int Do ()
    {
        return 999;
    }
}
```

The class is prefixed with the `TestCase` attribute, and uses `typeof()` to define the class used to test the code in question. To complete this example we need to write the test class. This object is used to exercise an instance of the code under test, and is presented below:

```
public class TestAnObject
{
    public TestAnObject ()
    {
        // Exercise the class under test
```

```
        SomeCodeOrOther scooby = new SomeCodeOrOther ();

     if (scooby.Do () != 999)
        throw new Exception ("Pesky Kids");
  }
}
```

This class simply instantiates the class under test, calls a method, and throws an exception if the returned value is not what was expected. A more complete test case would exercise the object under test completely, by calling all methods on that class, passing in values out of range to check for error conditions, and possibly setting up some other classes used for contextual information – if testing a class that accesses a database, you might pass in a connection object.

Now for the main code. This class will loop through all types in the assembly, looking for those that have the `TestCaseAttribute` defined. When found, the attribute is retrieved and the `Test()` method called:

```
using System;
using System.Reflection;

[AttributeUsage(AttributeTargets.Class,AllowMultiple=false,Inherited=true)]
public class TestCaseAttribute : Attribute
{
    // Code removed for brevity
}

/// <summary>
/// A class that uses the TestCase attribute
/// </summary>
[TestCaseAttribute(typeof(TestAnObject))]
public class SomeCodeOrOther
{
    // Code removed for brevity
}

// Main program class
public class UnitTesting
{
  public static void Main ()
  {
    // Find any classes with test cases in the current assembly
    Assembly a = Assembly.GetExecutingAssembly ();

    // Loop through the types in the assembly and test them if necessary
    System.Type[] types = a.GetExportedTypes ();

    foreach (System.Type t in types)
    {
      // Output the name of the type...
      Console.WriteLine ("Checking type {0}", t.ToString ());

      // Does the type include the TestCaseAttribute custom attribute?
      object[] atts = t.GetCustomAttributes (typeof(TestCaseAttribute),
                                             false);
```

```
            if (1 == atts.Length)
            {
               Console.WriteLine ("  Found TestCaseAttribute: Running Tests");

               // OK, this class has a test case. Run it...
               TestCaseAttribute tca = atts[0] as TestCaseAttribute;

               try
               {
                  // Perform the test...
                  tca.Test ();
                  Console.WriteLine ("  PASSED!");
               }
               catch (Exception ex)
               {
                  Console.WriteLine ("  FAILED!");
                  Console.WriteLine (ex.ToString ());
               }
            }
         }
      }
   }
}
```

The new section of code is highlighted. When run, the program gets the executing assembly via the static `GetExecutingAssembly()` method of the `Assembly` class. It then calls `GetExportedTypes()` on that assembly to find a list of all object types publicly accessible in the assembly.

For each exported type in the assembly, it then checks to see if it includes the `TestCase` attribute. It retrieves the attribute if it exists (which internally constructs the attribute instance, passing the parameters used within the code to the constructor of the object) and calls the `Test` method, which tests the code.

When run, the output from the program is as follows:

```
Checking type TestCaseAttribute
Checking type SomeCodeOrOther
   Found TestCaseAttribute: Running Tests
   PASSED!
Checking type TestAnObject
Checking type UnitTesting
```

System.AttributeUsageAttribute

When defining a custom attribute class, it is necessary to define the type or types that the attribute may be used on. In the preceding example, the `TestCase` attribute is valid only for use on classes. In order to define where an attribute can be placed, you add another attribute – `AttributeUsage`.

In its simplest form, this can be used as shown below:

```
[AttributeUsage(AttributeTargets.Class)]
```

The single parameter is an enumeration of where your attribute is valid. If you attempt to attribute a method with the `TestCase` attribute, you'll receive an error message from the compiler. An invalid usage could be:

```
public class TestAnObject
{
    [TestCase (typeof(System.String))]   // Invalid here
    public TestAnObject ()
    {
        etc...
    }
}
```

The error reported is:

```
TestCase.cs(54,4): error CS0592: Attribute 'TestCase' is not valid on this
        declaration type. It is valid on 'class' declarations only.
```

The `AttributeTargets` enum defines the following members, which can be combined together using the or operator (|) to define a set of elements that this attribute is valid on:

AttributeTargets value	Description
All	The attribute is valid on anything within the assembly.
Assembly	The attribute is valid on the assembly – an example is the `AssemblyKeyFile` attribute shown earlier in the chapter.
Class	The attribute is valid on a class definition. Our `TestCase` attribute used this value. Another example is the `Serializable` attribute.
Constructor	The attribute is valid only on class constructors.
Delegate	The attribute is valid only on a delegate.
Enum	The attribute can be added to enumerated values. One example of this attribute is the `System.FlagsAttribute`, which when applied to an enum defines that the user can use the bitwise or operator to combine values from the enumeration. The `AttributeTargets` enum uses this attribute.
Event	The attribute is valid on event definitions.
Field	The attribute can be placed on a field, such as an internal member variable. An example of this is the `NonSerialized` attribute, which was used earlier to define that a particular value should not be stored when the class was serialized.
Interface	The attribute is valid on an interface. One example of this is the `GuidAttribute` defined within `System.Runtime.InteropServices`, which permits you to explicitly define the GUID for an interface.
Method	The attribute is valid on a method. The `OneWay` attribute from `System.Runtime.Remoting.Messaging` uses this value.

AttributeTargets value	Description
Module	The attribute is valid on a module. An assembly may be created from a number of code modules, so you can use this to place the attribute on an individual module and not the whole assembly.
Parameter	The attribute can be applied to a parameter within a method definition.
Property	The attribute can be applied to a property.
ReturnValue	The attribute is associated with the return value of a function.
Struct	The attribute is valid on a structure.

Attribute Scope

In the first examples in the chapter we saw the `Assembly*` attributes, which all included syntax similar to that below:

```
[assembly: AssemblyTitle("Wrox rocks")]
```

The `assembly:` string defines the scope of the attribute, which in this case tells the compiler that the `AssemblyTitle` attribute should be applied to the assembly itself. You only need to use the scope modifier when the compiler cannot work out the scope itself. For example, if you wish to add an attribute to the return value of a function:

```
[MyAttribute ()]
public long DoSomething ()
{
    ...
}
```

When the compiler reaches this attribute, it takes an educated guess that you are applying the attribute to the method itself, which is not what we want here, so you can add a modifier to indicate exactly what the attribute is attached to:

```
[return:MyAttribute ()]
public long DoSomething ()
{
    ...
}
```

If you wish to define the scope of the attribute, choose one of the following values.

- ❑ `assembly` – attribute applies to the assembly
- ❑ `field` – attribute applies to a field of an `enum` or class
- ❑ `event` –attribute applies to an event
- ❑ `method` – attribute applies to the method it precedes
- ❑ `module` – attribute is stored in the module

❑   `param` – attribute applies to a parameter

❑   `property` – attribute is stored against the property

❑   `return` – apply the attribute to the return value of a function

❑   `type` – the attribute applies to a class, interface, or struct

Many of these are rarely used as the scope is not normally ambiguous. However for `assembly`, `module`, and `return` values you will have to use the scope flag. If there is some ambiguity as to where the attribute is defined, the compiler will choose which object the attribute will be assigned to. This is most common when attributing the return value of a function as shown below.

```
[SomeAttribute]
public string DoSomething ();
```

Here the compiler guesses that the attribute applies to the method, and not the return value. You need to define the scope in the following way to get the desired effect.

```
[return:SomeAttribute]
public string DoSomething ();
```

AttributeUsage.AllowMultiple

We define whether the user can add one or more of the same attributes to the element. For example you could create an attribute that lists all of the bug fixes applied to a section of code. As the assembly evolves, you may want to supply details of several bug fixes on a method.

BugFixAttribute

The code below defines a simple `BugFixAttribute`, and uses the `AllowMultiple` flag so that the attribute can be used more than once on any given chunk of code:

```
[AttributeUsage (AttributeTargets.Class | AttributeTargets.Property |
                 AttributeTargets.Method | AttributeTargets.Constructor ,
                 AllowMultiple=true)]
public class BugFixAttribute : Attribute
{
   public BugFixAttribute (string bugNumber , string comments)
   {
      BugNumber = bugNumber;
      Comments = comments;
   }

   public readonly string BugNumber;
   public readonly string Comments;
}
```

The `BugFix` attribute constructor takes a bug number and a comment string, and is marked with `AllowMultiple=true` to indicate that it can be used as follows:

```
[BugFix("101","Created some methods")]
public class MyBuggyCode
{
    [BugFix("90125","Removed call to base()")]
    public MyBuggyCode ()
    {
    }

    [BugFix("2112","Returned a non null string")]
    [BugFix("38382","Returned OK")]
    public string DoSomething ()
    {
        return "OK";
    }
}
```

The syntax for setting the AllowMultiple flag is a little strange. The constructor for AttributeUsage only takes a single parameter – the list of flags where the attribute can be used. AllowMultiple is a property on the AttributeUsage attribute, and so the syntax below means "construct the attribute, and then set the value of the AllowMultiple property to true":

```
[AttributeUsage (AttributeTargets.Class | AttributeTargets.Property |
                 AttributeTargets.Method | AttributeTargets.Constructor ,
                 AllowMultiple=true)]
public class BugFixAttribute : Attribute
{
    ...
}
```

A similar method is used for the Inherited property shown later in the chapter. If a custom attribute has properties, you can set these in the same manner. One example might be to add on the name of the person who fixed the bug:

```
public readonly string BugNumber;
public readonly string Comments;
public string Author = null;

public override string ToString ()
{
    if (null == Author)
        return string.Format ("BugFix {0} : {1}" ,
                               BugNumber , Comments);
    else
        return string.Format ("BugFix {0} by {1} : {2}" ,
                               BugNumber , Author , Comments);
}
```

This adds the Author property, and an overridden ToString() implementation which will display the full details if the Author property is set or else just show the bug number and comments. The ToString() method would be used to display a list of bug fixes for a given section of code – perhaps to print and file away somewhere.

Once you have written the `BugFix` attribute, you need some way to report the fixes made on a class and the members of that class.

The method of reporting bug fixes for a class is to pass the class type (again a `System.Type`) to the `DisplayFixes` function shown below. This also uses reflection to find any bug fixes applied to the class, and then iterates through all methods of that class looking for bug fix attributes.

This example can be found in the `Chapter22\BugFix` directory:

```
public static void DisplayFixes (System.Type t)
{
  // Get all bug fixes for the given type,
  // which is assumed to be a class
  object[] fixes = t.GetCustomAttributes (typeof (BugFixAttribute) , false);

  Console.WriteLine ("Displaying fixes for {0}" , t);

  // Display the big fix information
  foreach (BugFixAttribute bugFix in fixes)
    Console.WriteLine (" {0}" , bugFix);

  // Now get all members (i.e. functions) of the class
  foreach (MemberInfo member in t.GetMembers (BindingFlags.Instance |
                                              BindingFlags.Public |
                                              BindingFlags.NonPublic |
                                              BindingFlags.Static))
  {
    // And find any big fixes applied to these too
    object[] memberFixes = member.GetCustomAttributes(typeof(BugFixAttribute)
                                                      , false);

    if (memberFixes.Length > 0)
    {
      Console.WriteLine (" {0}" , member.Name);

      // Loop through and display these
      foreach (BugFixAttribute memberFix in memberFixes)
        Console.WriteLine ("   {0}" , memberFix);
    }
  }
}
```

The first thing the code does is to retrieve all `BugFix` attributes from the type itself:

```
object[] fixes = t.GetCustomAttributes (typeof (BugFixAttribute) ,
                                        false);
```

These are enumerated and displayed. The code then loops through all members defined on the class, by using the `GetMembers()` method:

```
foreach (MemberInfo member in t.GetMembers (
         BindingFlags.Instance | BindingFlags.Public |
         BindingFlags.NonPublic | BindingFlags.Static))
```

`GetMembers` retrieves properties, methods and fields from a given type. To limit the list of members that are returned, the `BindingFlags` enum is used (which is defined within `System.Reflection`).

The binding flags passed to this method indicate which members we are interested in – in this case we'd like all instance and static members, regardless of visibility, so we specify `Instance` and `Static`, together with `Public` and `NonPublic` members.

After getting all members, we then loop through these finding any `BugFix` attributes associated with the particular member, and output these to the console. To output a list of bug fixes for a given class, all you do is call the static `DisplayFixes()` method, passing in the class type:

```
BugFixAttribute.DisplayFixes (typeof (MyBuggyCode));
```

For the `MyBuggyCode` class presented earlier, this results in the following output:

```
Displaying fixes for MyBuggyCode
   BugFix 101 : Created some methods
   DoSomething
      BugFix 2112 : Returned a non null string
      BugFix 38382 : Returned OK
   .ctor
      BugFix 90125 : Removed call to base()
```

If you wanted to display fixes for all classes in a given assembly, you could use reflection to get all the types from the assembly, and pass each one to the static `BugFixAttribute.DisplayFixes` method.

AttributeUsage.Inherited

An attribute may be defined as inheritable by setting this flag when defining the custom attribute:

```
[AttributeUsage (AttributeTargets.Class,
                 Inherited = true)]
public class BugFixAttribute { ... }
```

This indicates that the `BugFix` attribute will be inherited by any subclasses of the class using the attribute, which may or may not be desirable. In the case of the `BugFix` attribute, this behavior would probably not be desirable, as a bug fix normally applies to a single class and not the derived classes.

Say you have the following abstract class with a bug fix applied:

```
[BugFix("38383","Fixed that abstract bug")]
public abstract class GenericRow : DataRow
{
   public GenericRow (System.Data.DataRowBuilder builder) : base (builder)
   {
   }
}
```

If we create a subclass from this class, we wouldn't want the same `BugFix` attribute to be reflected in the subclass – the subclass has not had that fix done on it. However, if we were defining a set of attributes that linked members of a class to fields in a database table, then we probably would want to inherit these attributes.

It's fairly common when defining database schema to come up with a set of standard columns that most tables include, such as `Name` and `Description`. You could code up a base class with these fields, and include a custom attribute that links a property in the class with a database column. Further subclasses could add more fields in as appropriate.

In the following example, we'll create `DatabaseTable` and `DatabaseColumn` attributes that can be applied to a class so that a database table suitable for persisting that class can be generated automatically.

Generating Database Tables using Attributes

This final example will show how attributes can be used from .NET classes to generate the database schema – a database design including tables, columns, and data types – so that .NET objects can create their own database tables to be persisted into. We will see how to extract this schema information to generate the SQL to create the tables in a database, and to construct in-memory `DataTable` objects.

As we saw in Chapter 19, we use `DataSet`, `DataTable`, `DataRow` and `DataAdapter` objects to access data in ADO.NET. It is important to keep our use of these objects in synch with the underlying database structure. If a database structure changes over time then we need to ensure that updates to tables, such as adding in new columns, are reflected in the classes that access the database.

In this example we will create subclasses of `DataRow` that are designed specifically for storing data from a particular database table. In cases where the underlying database schema will not change often, this can provide a very effective way to access databases. If your schema is likely to change frequently, or if you permit users to modify the database structure, it might be better to generate the `DataTable` objects dynamically by requesting schema information from the database and building the data tables on the fly.

The following diagram shows the relationship between the ADO.NET classes and the underlying database table:

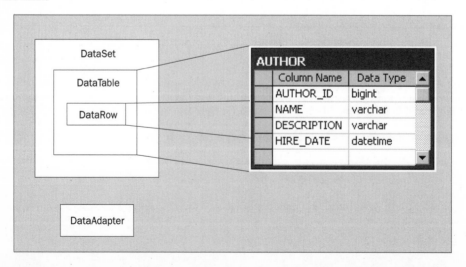

The DataSet consists of one or more DataTable objects, each one having DataRow objects that map to a single row within the database table. The data adapter is used to retrieve data from the database into the DataTable, and to write data from the DataTable back to the database.

The DataTable consists largely of boilerplate code, so we will define a base class DataTable object that can serve as a generic container for DataRow objects. The DataRow, however, needs to provide type-safe access to columns within the database, so we will subclass it. The relationship between this object and the underlying table is shown below:

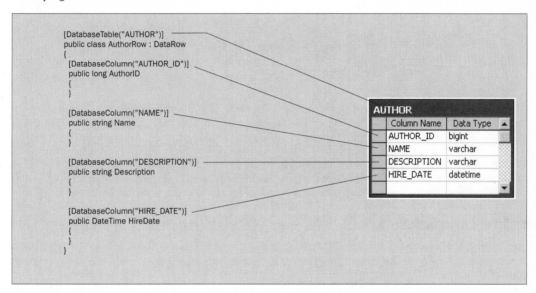

For this example we are concentrating on Books and Authors. The example consists of just these two tables, which are shown over the course of the next few pages. Although the example is designed to work with SQL Server, you could alter the code to work with Oracle or any other database engine.

The AuthorRow class derives from DataRow, and includes properties for each of the columns within the underlying Author table. A DatabaseTable attribute has been added to the row class, and for each property that links to a column in the table there is now a DatabaseColumn attribute. Some of the parameters to these attributes have been removed so that the image will fit on screen. The full details will appear in the following sections.

DatabaseTable Attribute

The first attribute in this example is used to mark a class, in this instance a DataRow, with the name of the database table where the DataRow will be saved. The example code is available in the Chapter22/DatabaseAttributes directory:

```
// Excerpt from DatabaseAttributes.cs
/// <summary>
/// Attribute to be used on a class to define which database table is used
/// </summary>
[AttributeUsage (AttributeTargets.Class , Inherited = false ,
                 AllowMultiple=false)]
```

```
  public class DatabaseTableAttribute : Attribute
  {
    /// <summary>
    /// Construct the attribute
    /// </summary>
    /// <param name="tableName">The name of the database table</param>
    public DatabaseTableAttribute (string tableName)
    {
      TableName = tableName;
    }

    /// <summary>
    /// Return the name of the database table
    /// </summary>
    public readonly string TableName;
  }
```

The attribute consists of a constructor that accepts the name of the table as a string, and is marked with the `Inherited=false` and `AllowMultiple=false` modifiers. It's unlikely that you would want to inherit this attribute by any subclasses, and it is marked as single use as a class will only link to a single table.

Within the attribute class we store the name of the table as a field rather than a property. This is a matter of personal choice. In this instance there is no method to alter the value of the table name so a read only field will suffice. If you prefer using properties then feel free to alter the example code.

DatabaseColumn Attribute

This attribute is designed to be placed on public properties of the `DataRow` class, and is used to define the name of the column that the property will link to, together with such things as whether the column can contain a null value:

```
// Excerpt from DatabaseAttributes.cs
/// <summary>
/// Attribute to be used on all properties exposed as database columns
/// </summary>
[AttributeUsage (AttributeTargets.Property , Inherited=true ,
                AllowMultiple=false) ]
public class DatabaseColumnAttribute : Attribute
{
  /// <summary>
  /// Construct a database column attribute
  /// </summary>
  /// <param name="column">The name of the column</param>
  /// <param name="dataType">The datatype of the column</param>
  public DatabaseColumnAttribute (string column , ColumnDomain dataType)
  {
    ColumnName = column;
    DataType = dataType;
    Order = GenerateOrderNumber ();
  }

  /// <summary>
  /// Return the column name
```

```csharp
        /// </summary>
        public readonly string ColumnName;
        /// <summary>
        /// Return the column domain
        /// </summary>
        public readonly ColumnDomain DataType;
        /// <summary>
        /// Get/Set the nullable flag. A property might be better
        /// </summary>
        public bool Nullable = false;
        /// <summary>
        /// Get/Set the Order number. Again a property might be better.
        /// </summary>
        public int Order;
        /// <summary>
        /// Get/Set the Size of the column (useful for text columns).
        /// </summary>
        public int Size;

        /// <summary>
        /// Generate an ascending order number for columns
        /// </summary>
        /// <returns></returns>
        public static int GenerateOrderNumber ()
        {
          return nextOrder++;
        }

        /// <summary>
        /// Private value used whilst generating the order number
        /// </summary>
        private static int nextOrder = 100;
}

/// <summary>
/// Enumerated list of column data types
/// </summary>
public enum ColumnDomain
{
        /// <summary>
        /// 32 bit
        /// </summary>
        Integer,
        /// <summary>
        /// 64 bit
        /// </summary>
        Long,
        /// <summary>
        /// A string column
        /// </summary>
        String,
        /// <summary>
        /// A date time column
```

```
    /// </summary>
    DateTime
}
```

This class is again marked with `AllowMultiple=false`, as there is always a one to one correspondence between a property of a `DataRow` and the column to which it is linked.

We have marked this attribute as inheritable so that we can create a class hierarchy for database rows, as it is likely that we will have some similar columns throughout each table within the schema.

The constructor accepts two arguments. The first is the name of the column that is to be defined within the database. The second argument is an enumerated value from the `ColumnDomain` enumeration, which consists of four values for this example, but which would be insufficient for production code.

The attribute also has three other properties, which are summarized below:

❑   `Nullable` – Defaulting to `false`, this property is used when the column is generated to define whether the database value can be set to NULL.

❑   `Order` – Defines the order number of the column within the table. When the table is generated, the columns will be output in ascending order. The default is to generate an incrementing value, which is done within the constructor. You can naturally override this value as necessary.

❑   `Size` – Defines the maximum number of characters allowed in a string type.

To define a `Name` column we might use the following code:

```
[DatabaseColumn("NAME",ColumnDomain.String,Order=10,Size=64)]
public string Name
{
    get { return (string) this ["NAME"]; }
    set { this["NAME"] = value; }
}
```

This defines a field called NAME, and it will be generated as a VARCHAR(64) because the column domain is set to `String` and the size parameter has been set to 64. It sets the order number to 10 – we will see why later in the chapter. The column will also not allow `null` values, as the default for the `Nullable` property is `false` (thus the column will be generated as NON NULL).

The `DataRow` class has an indexer that takes the name of a field (or ordinal) as the parameter. This returns an object, which is cast to a string before returning it in the get accessor shown above.

Creating Database Rows

The point of this example is to produce a set of strongly typed `DataRow` objects. In this example we'll create two classes, `Author` and `Book`, which both derive from a common base class as each shares some common fields.

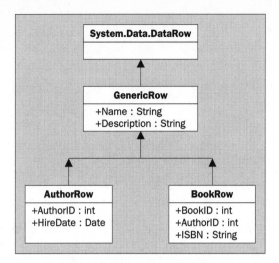

The GenericRow class defines the Name and Description properties, and the code for this is included below. It is derived from DataRow, the base class for all database rows in the framework.

For the example, two classes derive from GenericRow – one to represent an Author (AuthorRow) and another representing a Book (BookRow). These both contain additional properties, which are linked to fields within the database:

```
// Excerpt from DatabaseTables.cs
/// <summary>
/// Base class row - defines Name and Description columns
/// </summary>
public abstract class GenericRow : DataRow
{
  /// <summary>
  /// Construct the object
  /// </summary>
  /// <param name="builder">Passed in from System.Data</param>
  public GenericRow (System.Data.DataRowBuilder builder)
    : base (builder)
  {
  }

  /// <summary>
  /// A column for the record name
  /// </summary>
  [DatabaseColumn("NAME",ColumnDomain.String,Order=10,Size=64)]
  public string Name
  {
    get { return (string) this["NAME"]; }
    set { this["NAME"] = value; }
  }

  /// <summary>
  /// A column for the description, which may be null
```

```
    /// </summary>
    [DatabaseColumn("DESCRIPTION",ColumnDomain.String,Nullable=true,Order=11,
                    Size=1000)]
    public string Description
    {
      get { return (string) this["DESCRIPTION"]; }
      set { this["DESCRIPTION"] = value; }
    }
  }
```

Deriving from `DataRow` requires that you create a constructor that accepts a single parameter, a `DataRowBuilder`. This class is internal to the `System.Data` assembly.

Two properties are then defined, `Name` and `Description`, and each of these is attributed accordingly. The name field is attributed as follows:

```
[DatabaseColumn("NAME",ColumnDomain.String,Order=10,Size=64)]
```

This defines the column name as `NAME`, defines its domain as a string of size 64 characters, and sets its order number to 10. I've done this because when creating database tables I always prefer the primary key fields to be emitted before any other fields within the table. Setting this value to ten gives me space for numerous identity fields. Any more than ten fields in a primary key will require a redesign!

The description column is also given a name, domain, and size. The `Nullable` property is set to `true` so that we are not forced to define a description column. The other option would be to define a "default" property and set this to an empty string, which would avoid the use of `NULL` in the database. The order number is set to eleven, so that the name and description columns are always kept together in the generated schema:

```
[DatabaseColumn("DESCRIPTION",ColumnDomain.String,Nullable=true,
                                        Order=11,Size=1000)]
```

Each property accessor defines a get and set method for the value of the property, and these are strongly typed so that in the case of a string column, a `string` value is returned to the caller:

```
        get { return (string) this["NAME"]; }
        set { this["NAME"] = value; }
```

There is some duplication of code here, as the attribute defines the name of the column, so you could use reflection within these methods to retrieve the value of the appropriate column. However, reflection is not the most efficient of API's – as these classes are used to access the underlying columns we want them to be as fast as possible. To squeeze every last ounce of performance from these accessors we could use numeric indexes for the columns, as using strings involves a look up for the numeric index value. Be careful when using numeric indexers as they are slightly more difficult to maintain, especially in the instance where a subclass is defined.

The `Author` row is constructed as follows:

```
// Excerpt from DatabaseTables.cs
/// <summary>
/// Author table, derived from GenericRow
/// </summary>
```

```
[DatabaseTable("AUTHOR")]
public class AuthorRow : GenericRow
{
  public AuthorRow (DataRowBuilder builder)
    : base (builder)
  {
  }

  /// <summary>
  /// Primary key field
  /// </summary>
  [DatabaseColumn("AUTHOR_ID",ColumnDomain.Long,Order=1)]
  public long AuthorID
  {
    get { return (long) this["AUTHOR_ID"]; }
    set { this["AUTHOR_ID"] = value; }
  }

  /// <summary>
  /// Date the author was hired
  /// </summary>
  [DatabaseColumn("HIRE_DATE",ColumnDomain.DateTime,Nullable=true)]
  public DateTime HireDate
  {
    get { return (DateTime) this["HIRE_DATE"]; }
    set { this["HIRE_DATE"] = value; }
  }
}
```

Here we have subclassed the GenericRow class, and added in AuthorID and HireDate properties. Note the order number chosen for the AUTHOR_ID column – it is set to one so that it appears as the first column within the emitted table. The HireDate property has no such order number, so its value is generated by the attribute, and these generated values all start from 100, so the table will be laid out as AUTHOR_ID, NAME, DESCRIPTION, and finally HIRE_DATE.

The BookRow class again derives from GenericRow, so as to include the name and description properties. It adds BookID, PublishDate and ISBN properties:

```
// Excerpt from DatabaseTables.cs
/// <summary>
/// Table for holding books
/// </summary>
[DatabaseTable("BOOK")]
public class BookRow : GenericRow
{
  public BookRow (DataRowBuilder builder)
    : base (builder)
  {
  }

  /// <summary>
  /// Primary key column
```

```
/// </summary>
[DatabaseColumn("BOOK_ID",ColumnDomain.Long,Order=1)]
public long BookID
{
  get { return (long) this["BOOK_ID"]; }
  set { this["BOOK_ID"] = value; }
}

/// <summary>
/// Author who wrote the book
/// </summary>
[DatabaseColumn("AUTHOR_ID",ColumnDomain.Long,Order=2)]
public long AuthorID
{
  get { return (long) this["AUTHOR_ID"]; }
  set { this["AUTHOR_ID"] = value; }
}

/// <summary>
/// Date the book was published
/// </summary>
[DatabaseColumn("PUBLISH_DATE",ColumnDomain.DateTime,Nullable=true)]
public DateTime PublishDate
{
  get { return (DateTime) this["PUBLISH_DATE"]; }
  set { this["PUBLISH_DATE"] = value; }
}

/// <summary>
/// ISBN for the book
/// </summary>
[DatabaseColumn("ISBN",ColumnDomain.String,Nullable=true,Size=10)]
public string ISBN
{
  get { return (string) this["ISBN"]; }
  set { this["ISBN"] = value; }
}
}
```

Generating the SQL

Now that the database rows have been defined, it's time for the code that will generate a database schema from these classes. The example dumps its output to the console, so we could for example pipe the output to a text file by running the .exe from a command prompt.

The following class calls `OutputTable` for each type that we wish to create a database table for:

```
public class DatabaseTest
{
  public static void Main ()
  {
    OutputTable (typeof (AuthorRow));
```

```
        OutputTable (typeof (BookRow));
    }
    public static void OutputTable (System.Type t)
    {
        // Code in full below
    }
}
```

We could utilize reflection to loop through each class in the assembly, check if it is derived from `GenericRow`, and output the classes automatically. For simplicity's sake we have hard-coded the name of the tables that are to be generated: `AuthorRow` and `BookRow`.

The `OutputTable` method is shown below:

```
// Excerpt from Database.cs
/// <summary>
/// Produce SQL Server style SQL for the passed type
/// </summary>
/// <param name="t"></param>
public static void OutputTable (System.Type t)
{
  // Get the DatabaseTable attribute from the type
  object[]  tableAttributes = t.GetCustomAttributes
              (typeof (DatabaseTableAttribute) , true) ;

  // Check there is one...
  if (tableAttributes.Length == 1)
  {
    // If so output some SQL
    Console.WriteLine ("CREATE TABLE {0}" ,
      ((DatabaseTableAttribute)tableAttributes[0]).TableName);
    Console.WriteLine ("(");
    SortedList columns = new SortedList ();

    // Roll through each property
    foreach (PropertyInfo prop in t.GetProperties ())
    {
      // And get any DatabaseColumnAttribute that is defined
      object[]  columnAttributes = prop.GetCustomAttributes
        (typeof (DatabaseColumnAttribute) , true);

      // If there is a DatabaseColumnAttribute
      if (columnAttributes.Length == 1)
      {
        DatabaseColumnAttribute dca = columnAttributes[0]
                                  as DatabaseColumnAttribute;

        // Convert the ColumnDomain into a SQL Server data type
        string  dataType = ConvertDataType (dca);

        // And add this column SQL into the sorted list - I want the
        // columns to come out in ascending order of order number
```

```
            columns.Add (dca.Order, string.Format ("  {0,-31}{1,-20}{2,8},",
                dca.ColumnName ,
                dataType ,
                dca.Nullable ? "NULL" : "NOT NULL"));
        }
    }
    // Now loop through the SortedList of columns
    foreach (DictionaryEntry e in columns)
        // And output the string...
        Console.WriteLine (e.Value);

    // Then terminate the SQL
    Console.WriteLine (")");
    Console.WriteLine ("GO");
    Console.WriteLine ();
    }
}
```

This code reflects over the type passed in, and looks for the `DatabaseTable` attribute. If the `DatabaseTable` attribute is found, it writes a `CREATE TABLE` clause to the console, including the name of the table from the attribute.

We then loop through all properties of the type to find any `DatabaseColumn` attributes. Any property that has this attribute will become a column in the generated table:

```
foreach (PropertyInfo prop in t.GetProperties ())
{
    object[] columnAttributes = prop.GetCustomAttributes (
                    typeof (DatabaseColumnAttribute) , true);
```

The string representation of the column is constructed by calling the `ConvertDataType()` method, shown in a moment. This is stored within a sorted collection so that the columns are generated based on the value of the `Order` property of the attribute.

After looping through all attributes and creating entries within the sorted list, we then loop through the sorted list and write each value to the console:

```
foreach (DictionaryEntry e in columns)
    Console.WriteLine(e.Value);
```

Finally we add the closing bracket and a `GO` command, which will instruct SQL Server to execute the batch of statements and thereby create the table.

The last function in this assembly, `ConvertDataType()`, converts values from the `ColumnDomain` enumeration into a database specific data type. In addition, for string columns, we create the column representation to include the size of the column, so for instance the `Name` property from the generic base class is constructed as `VARCHAR(64)`. This column type represents a varying array of characters up to 64 characters in length.

```
// Excerpt from Database.cs
/// <summary>
/// Convert a ColumnDomain to a SQL Server data type
/// </summary>
/// <param name="dca">The column attribute</param>
/// <returns>A string representing the data type</returns>
private static string ConvertDataType (DatabaseColumnAttribute dca)
{
  string dataType = null;

  switch (dca.DataType)
  {
    case ColumnDomain.DateTime:
    {
      dataType = "DATETIME";
      break;
    }
    case ColumnDomain.Integer:
    {
      dataType = "INT";
      break;
    }
    case ColumnDomain.Long:
    {
      dataType = "BIGINT";
      break;
    }
    case ColumnDomain.String:
    {
      // Include the size of the string...
      dataType = string.Format ("VARCHAR({0})" , dca.Size);
      break;
    }
  }

  return dataType;
}
```

For each member of the enumeration, we create a column string appropriate for SQL Server. The SQL emitted for the Author and Book classes from this example is shown below:

```
CREATE TABLE AUTHOR
(
    AUTHOR_ID              BIGINT             NOT NULL,
    NAME                   VARCHAR(64)        NOT NULL,
    DESCRIPTION            VARCHAR(1000)      NULL,
    HIRE_DATE              DATETIME           NULL,
)
GO

CREATE TABLE BOOK
(
```

```
        BOOK_ID                 BIGINT                  NOT NULL,
        AUTHOR_ID               BIGINT                  NOT NULL,
        NAME                    VARCHAR(64)             NOT NULL,
        DESCRIPTION             VARCHAR(1000)           NULL,
        PUBLISH_DATE            DATETIME                NULL,
        ISBN                    VARCHAR(10)             NULL,
    )
    GO
```

This SQL can be run against an empty or pre-existing SQL Server database to create the tables. The `DataRow` classes created can be used to provide type safe access to the data within these tables.

To utilize the derived `DataRow` classes, we need to provide some code such as the following. This class overrides the minimum set of functions from `DataTable`, and is passed the type of the row in the constructor:

```csharp
// Excerpt from DatabaseTables.cs
/// <summary>
/// Boilerplate data table class
/// </summary>
public class MyDataTable : DataTable
{
  /// <summary>
  /// Construct this object based on a DataRow
  /// </summary>
  /// <param name="rowType">A class derived from DataRow</param>
  public MyDataTable (System.Type rowType)
  {
    m_rowType = rowType;
    ConstructColumns ();
  }


  /// <summary>
  /// Construct the DataColumns for this table
  /// </summary>
  private void ConstructColumns ()
  {
    SortedList columns = new SortedList ();

    // Loop through all properties
    foreach (PropertyInfo prop in m_rowType.GetProperties ())
    {
      object[]  columnAttributes = prop.GetCustomAttributes
          (typeof (DatabaseColumnAttribute) , true);

      // If it has a DatabaseColumnAttribute
      if (columnAttributes.Length == 1)
      {
        DatabaseColumnAttribute dca = columnAttributes[0]
                                  as DatabaseColumnAttribute;

        // Create a DataColumn
        DataColumn  dc = new DataColumn (dca.ColumnName ,
                                  prop.PropertyType);
```

```
        // Set its nullable flag
        dc.AllowDBNull = dca.Nullable;
        // And add it to a temporary column collection
        columns.Add (dca.Order , dc);
     }
   }

   // Add the columns in ascending order
   foreach (DictionaryEntry e in columns)
     this.Columns.Add (e.Value as DataColumn);
 }

/// <summary>
/// Called from within System.Data
/// </summary>
/// <returns>The type of the rows that this table holds</returns>
protected override System.Type GetRowType ()
{
   return m_rowType;
}

/// <summary>
/// Construct a new DataRow
/// </summary>
/// <param name="builder">Passed in from System.Data</param>
/// <returns>A type safe DataRow</returns>
protected override DataRow NewRowFromBuilder (DataRowBuilder builder)
{
   // Construct a new instance of my row type class
   return (DataRow) Activator.CreateInstance (GetRowType() ,
                                        new object[1] { builder });
 }

/// <summary>
/// Store the row type
/// </summary>
private System.Type m_rowType;
}
```

The `ConstructColumns()` function, called from the constructor, will generate a `DataColumn` array for the `DataTable` – these are again retrieved using reflection. The other methods, `GetRowType()` and `NewRowFromBuilder()`, override methods in the base `DataTable` class.

Once you have this derived `MyDataTable` class, you can easily use it in your own code. The following shows an example of adding a couple of author records into the `Author` table, then outputting these rows to an XML file:

```
    DataSet      ds = new DataSet ();
    MyDataTable t = new MyDataTable (typeof (AuthorRow));

    ds.Tables.Add (t);
    AuthorRow    author = (AuthorRow)t.NewRow ();
```

```
            author.AuthorID = 1;
            author.Name = "Me";
            author.HireDate = new System.DateTime (2000,12,9,3,30,0);

            t.Rows.Add (author);

            author = (AuthorRow) t.NewRow ();
            author.AuthorID = 2;
            author.Name = "Paul";
            author.HireDate = new System.DateTime (2001,06,06,23,56,33);

            t.Rows.Add (author);

            t.DataSet.WriteXml (@"c:\BegVCSharp\Chapter22\authors.xml");
```

When run, this code produces the following output:

```
<?xml version="1.0" standalone="yes"?>
<NewDataSet>
  <Table1>
    <AUTHOR_ID>1</AUTHOR_ID>
    <NAME>Me</NAME>
    <HIRE_DATE>2000-12-09T03:30:00.0000000-00:00</HIRE_DATE>
  </Table1>
  <Table1>
    <AUTHOR_ID>2</AUTHOR_ID>
    <NAME>Paul</NAME>
    <HIRE_DATE>2001-06-06T23:56:33.0000000+01:00</HIRE_DATE>
  </Table1>
</NewDataSet>
```

This example has shown a practical example of using custom attributes in your code. If you don't mind coupling the database structure into the classes that access the database then this is a good starting point. Tying database tables to classes is acceptable if your schema doesn't change very often, but for more dynamic back ends it may be better to work in a way that keeps data access classes in step with the database tables they access.

In a full implementation, we might also include attributes to define some or all of the following:

❑ Primary key columns

❑ Constraints – foreign key and check

❑ Versions – a version number on each column attribute and table attribute would simplify generation of upgrade scripts – you could in fact generate the whole upgrade based on attributes

❑ Default values for columns

Summary

This chapter described what attributes are, and discussed some of the attributes defined within the framework. There are many more attribute classes within the framework, and the best way to find out what they are used for is to take a look through the .NET Framework SDK documentation.

We discussed the attributes that could be placed within an assembly, to provide the end user with details that show up on the file properties dialog, and used Ildasm to explore how attributes are stored within an assembly. We touched on the subject of **reflection** to show how to read attributes from within code, and then described some of the inbuilt attributes such as Conditional, Obsolete and Serializable.

We then saw how to create custom attributes, which included a discussion of the AttributeUsage attribute. We created a BugFix attribute using many of the tactics demonstrated earlier. Finally we explored a lengthy example on generating database schema information from classes.

ASP.NET Applications

ASP.NET is .NET's way of letting us build dynamic web sites. As with ADO.NET, ASP.NET takes its name from a previous technology, Active Server Pages or ASP, but again, the similarities don't extend much beyond the name. Whereas ASP pages were interpreted and written in functionally limited scripting languages (such as VBScript and JScript), ASP.NET applications are compiled into MSIL, just like other .NET applications. This means that we can write them in the powerful languages available to other .NET projects. What matters to us, of course (since this is a book about C#), is that we can write our ASP.NET applications in C#.

The second big advantage to ASP.NET is the introduction of **server-side controls**. In ASP, we could add HTML controls (such as buttons and other form elements) to our pages – but we had to do this by hand, and we had to react to any user input to these (such as the user clicking on a button) either in client-side JavaScript or by resubmitting the page to the server. The problem with the first of these is that different browsers implement JavaScript in different ways, so it's almost impossible to write sophisticated routines that will work on both Netscape and IE, and in any case some older browsers don't support JavaScript at all. If we resubmit to the server, the stateless nature of the Internet means that we will lose any information held in variables on the page, unless we set up complex code to store them in HTML elements or a URL query string.

ASP.NET solves these problems through server-side controls. These controls generate the HTML code that is sent to the browser to display the control, but they also generate JavaScript functions and hidden HTML elements that store their current state. When the page is submitted, this information is passed back to the server, and the control will automatically process this information and alter the HTML to display the control. At its simplest, this means that we can have text boxes that "remember" the values entered by the user, but taking the technique further, it allows ASP.NET to have far more complicated controls (a calendar control, for example) than ASP could ever cope with.

Finally, and perhaps most importantly, ASP.NET provides us with an easy way of creating **web services**. Think of these as components for the web for now, but web services are a complex topic, and we'll devote the whole of the next chapter to them.

To see some server-side code in action, visit Amazon.com and look up your favorite novel. The page that you see detailing the novel doesn't exist on the server. What does exist is a template describing the general look of the page, and when you request the page, code on the server executes and extracts information about the book from a database and inserts it into the template. What gets passed back to you is HTML – and we talk about this later.

What's important is that throughout this chapter we're concentrating on code that is run on the server-side. Your web browser has to do relatively little to display the page.

> **From here on, whenever we refer to "active pages" we're talking about pages that can be built with classic ASP and ASP.NET. Both technologies use the same basic approach for building pages – it's just that ASP.NET is far more powerful and you'll find putting together dynamic web sites far easier with ASP.NET.**

Here's an example. This looks like an ordinary web page:

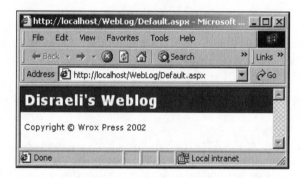

However, notice at the bottom of the page the copyright message. Imagine that this message appears on each page of our web site. Currently, this is set to 2002, and this means that when the year changes to 2003, we'll have to go through our site and update every page from 2002 to 2002-2003.

With "active pages" we can configure the page in such a way that it determines the year for itself and makes the change automatically. This means that this simple yet frustrating administration task goes away, year on year.

OK, so this is a fairly trite example. Active page technology really comes into its own when you connect the web site to some database or some other form of functionality, like an e-commerce shopping cart. In this chapter, we're going to take a look at how to build a "Weblog". A Weblog is the web equivalent of a diary, which instead of being written down on paper and locked away in a drawer, is available on the web for everyone to see. The principle is the same – you have a date and under the date is a list of thoughts and events of the day. They are sometimes known as "blogs" and you can find a cool list of them here: www.bloghop.com.

Building our Weblog

To illustrate the power and functionality of ASP.NET, we shall develop a Weblog application from first principles – starting with a single blank web page and adding features bit by bit explaining everything as we go along. We will first show how to display Weblog entries, either one at a time or multiple entries. Then we'll move onto sorting, adding, and editing entries before looking briefly at security issues, such as restricting access to the site and authenticating users using a login page. As you progress through this worked example, you will learn about the following things:

❑ Adding dynamic (active) content to your web pages using Web Form controls

❑ Implementing event handlers for each control using C# code

❑ Creating a visually appealing user interface

❑ Extending the user interface to support additional features

The Application Basics

We can build applications in Visual Studio .NET using the **ASP.NET Web Application** template. This will create a new project for us and automatically configure IIS so that we can debug our project as we build it.

The first thing we'll do is to build a simple static page (in other words, one that has no dynamic elements) on the web site so that we can make sure everything works as intended. We're going to create this as an ASP.NET page (with the `.aspx` extension) because although initially this page will have no dynamic elements, it will eventually have some.

> **In order to build ASP.NET projects you will need to have the local web server IIS installed. To install IIS open Add/Remove Programs from the Control Panel, switch to the Add/Remove Windows Components screen, and check the Internet Information Services (IIS) option. Click Next and follow the installation instructions to install.**

Try it Out – Creating the Weblog Page

1. Open Visual Studio .NET and select File | New | Project from the menu. From the Project Types list, select Visual C# Projects and from the Templates list select ASP.NET Web Application. In the Location box, enter http://localhost/WebLog.

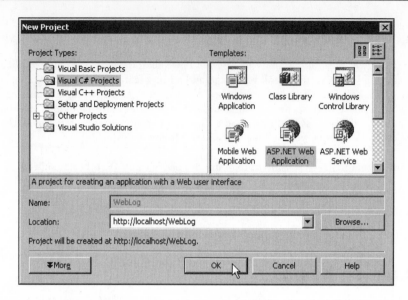

2. Notice that in the **Location** box we are specifying the URL http://localhost/WebLog. This tells you where your new web site will be created, and when we're talking about the Internet, localhost always refers to your own computer.

3. Click **OK** to create the new project.

4. Using Solution Explorer, right-click on the WebLog project and select **Add | Add Web Form**. Enter the name as Default.aspx and click **Open**.

The new page should open in Designer mode; however, there is a chance that it won't if you've previously experimented with ASP.NET. If the page is in design mode, you'll see this:

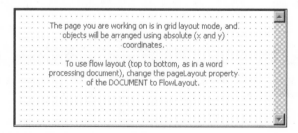

If you see what appears to be a ton of HTML, select View | Design from the menu. You should see the grid layout that we see above.

5. With the Designer, you can build pages in two ways – in GridLayout mode or in FlowLayout mode. In my opinion, it's better to use FlowLayout mode. From the **Properties** window, change the pageLayout property to FlowLayout. The dots will disappear from the Designer.

The Designer also offers you a bunch of tools to make building a web site easier. In effect, this means that you can build web pages as if you were using Microsoft Word to write a letter. However, the tools offered to you by the Designer are quite restrictive as they are aimed at people who are only interested in designing web interfaces and not in programming. I think I can be confident in saying that as you have progressed this far in the book you enjoy writing computer software, so we're going to go "old school" and build our pages in HTML.

6. From the menu, select **View | HTML Source**. The HTML editor will appear. (Alternatively, at the bottom of the code editor you'll see small buttons marked **Design** and **HTML**. You can use these two to swap between views if you prefer.)

7. To the skeleton HTML code add the lines shown in gray:

```
<%@ Page language="c#" Codebehind="Default.aspx.cs" AutoEventWireup="false"
        Inherits="webLog._Default" %>
<!DOCTYPE HTML PUBLIC "-//W3C//DTD HTML 4.0 Transitional//EN" >
<HTML>
    <HEAD>
        <meta name="GENERATOR" Content="Microsoft Visual Studio 7.0">
        <meta name="CODE_LANGUAGE" Content="C#">
        <meta name="vs_defaultClientScript" content="JavaScript">
        <meta name="vs_targetSchema"
              content="http://schemas.microsoft.com/intellisense/ie5">
    </HEAD>
    <body>
        <form id="Default" method="post" runat="server">
            <div>
                Disraeli's Weblog
            </div>
            <br>
            <div>
                Copyright &copy; Wrox Press 2002
            </div>
        </form>
    </body>
</HTML>
```

8. Before we run the project, we have to tell Visual Studio that our new `Default.aspx` page is the page we want to debug. Using Solution Explorer, right-click `Default.aspx` and select **Set as Start Page**.

Compile and run the project as normal. You should see this output:

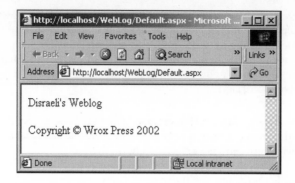

How it Works

All we've done is create a new project and add a page to it. Visual Studio .NET has dealt with most of the magic behind the scenes.

However, there's nothing active about that page – it's just static text that we've typed in. Now let's take a look at how we can add active elements to the page.

Adding Active Elements

If you've ever built ASP pages before, or built dynamic web pages using a competing technology, it's time to throw away everything you thought you knew about building active pages. ASP.NET uses a totally different approach to anything you've seen before.

For Microsoft, taking on board the fact that Visual Basic was so phenomenally successful now means that you use a similar paradigm for building web applications as you do with Windows Forms applications. Everything is control-centric and event-driven.

For example, imagine you have a Windows application, either one written in VB.NET or C#. If you want to add a button to the form and make it do something you use the Toolbox to draw one onto the form, double-click on it to create an event handler and add some code. This is both a "control-centric" and "event-driven" way of programming.

Previously on the web, there was no concept of controls. Everything was flat HTML. If I wanted to draw a button, my server-side script had to send the HTML to get the browser to display the button. When the button was pressed, the browser would request the page again, but add some extra information to the page indicating that the button was pressed. My server-side script could then react to the presence of this extra information and send new or different information back to the browser.

With .NET, a lot of this happens under the hood. I draw a button on the Designer, and ASP.NET deals with turning that control into HTML and sending it to the browser, whereupon the browser draws it. If the button is pressed, a request is sent back to the server, but we "feel" that button press as an event that we can react to. In this section we'll see this in action.

Try it Out – Adding a Copyright Element

1. If the project is running, close the Internet Explorer window.

2. From the menu, select View | Design. Whenever we add active elements to the page, we have to be in Design View.

3. To help you lay out the controls, select View | Details from the menu. You'll see something like this:

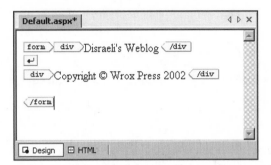

4. Select and delete the copyright message, but not the `div` tags.

5. Using the Toolbox, drag a `Label` control and drop it between the two `div` tags that once delineated the copyright message. You'll see this:

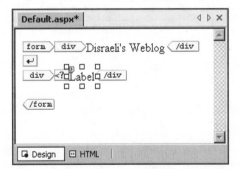

The small <?> box you can see is telling you that the tag created is not an HTML tag per se. This is actually a tag that only ASP.NET understands, so it chooses to show it as a <?>. (You would imagine that Microsoft would want to draw a small icon here indicating what it is – perhaps they will in a later release!)

6. The important thing to realize here is that *conceptually*, the Web Forms label control is no different to the Windows Forms label control that you already know how to use. In fact, if you look at the Properties window with the control selected you can change its properties, which is what we will do:

❑ Set the ID property to labelCopyright

❑ Set the Text property to (copyright)

7. Double-click on the background of the page. This is conceptually similar to double-clicking on the background of a Windows Forms form and does exactly the same thing! It creates an event handler that will be called when the page loads.

8. Enter this code into the Page_Load() method:

```
private void Page_Load(object sender, System.EventArgs e)
{
    // what year is this?
    int year = DateTime.Now.Year;
    if(year == 2002)
        labelCopyright.Text = "Copyright &copy; Disraeli " + year;
    else
        labelCopyright.Text = "Copyright &copy; Disraeli 2002-" + year;
}
```

Compile and run the project. (You can't right-click the code editor and select View in Browser. You have to run the code as you did before.) You'll see what you saw before:

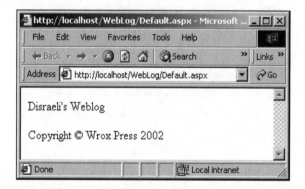

VERY IMPORTANT! If you're running Outlook or another program that supports scheduling CLOSE IT! We're about to set the system clock forward and unless you want twelve months of schedule reminders appearing in an instant, you will want to close it. This may also happen with other applications that are sensitive for date changes – if you're unsure of what will happen if you change the date, don't. It's not that exciting anyway!

Now, set your system clock one year in the future. Refresh the page. You'll see this.

How it Works

What we've done is proved that the copyright message is dynamic. When the page is built, it uses `DateTime.Now()` to get the current date and alter the copyright message.

But how did the active element get onto the page? To find out, open the HTML editor for the page. Some way down, you'll find this tag:

```
<%@ Page language="c#" Codebehind="Default.aspx.cs" AutoEventWireup="false"
        Inherits="WebLog._Default" %>
<!DOCTYPE HTML PUBLIC "-//W3C//DTD HTML 4.0 Transitional//EN" >
<HTML>
    <HEAD>
        <meta name="GENERATOR" Content="Microsoft Visual Studio 7.0">
        <meta name="CODE_LANGUAGE" Content="C#">
        <meta name="vs_defaultClientScript" content="JavaScript">
        <meta name="vs_targetSchema"
            content="http://schemas.microsoft.com/intellisense/ie5">
    </HEAD>
    <body>
        <form id="Default" method="post" runat="server">
            <div>
                Disraeli's Weblog
            </div>
            <br>
            <div>
                <asp:Label id="labelCopyright"
                        runat="server">(copyright)</asp:Label>
            </div>
        </form>
    </body>
</HTML>
```

When a request for an `.aspx` page is received, ASP.NET examines the entire page before it does anything with it. What it's trying to do is discover which parts of the page are static and which parts of the page are active. In the above code sample, I've highlighted the `<asp:Label>` tag. ASP.NET knows that this tag is an active part of the page. By a process of elimination, it determines that the rest of the page is static.

Ultimately, though, ASP.NET needs the entire page to be static, so in a way you can look at the primary role of ASP.NET as turning the dynamic elements of the page into static HTML. Most web browsers today are very limited on what they can do. ASP.NET's approach is to keep the vast majority of the processing happening on the server and sending back HTML that the browser can display. In some cases, ASP.NET can send code to the browser that the browser should execute, and it's likely that over the next few years more and more work will be done on the browser, but today we want everything to happen on the server. That's actually exactly what's happened here. Here's the ASP.NET code again:

```
<div>
    <asp:Label id="labelCopyright" runat="server">(copyright)</asp:Label>
</div>
```

And here's the code that IE actually receives:

```
<div>
    <span id="labelCopyright">Copyright &copy; Disraeli 2002-2003</span>
</div>
```

By writing ASP.NET pages using Visual Studio .NET, we default to the model whereby a page is actually coded in two halves. The first part is an `.aspx` file that contains the template of the page and defines where the active elements actually appear. The second part is a `.cs` or `.vb` file that contains the event handling code. Microsoft calls this second part the **code-behind**. When we double-clicked on the background of the page to access the `Load` event handler, we actually opened a new file.

This C# source file, the code-behind file, shares the same base name as the `.aspx` file and is intrinsically linked to the `.aspx` file. If you look at this file, you'll notice that it contains a class definition. You'll also notice that this class is derived from `System.Web.UI.Page`.

```
/// <summary>
/// Summary description for _Default.
/// </summary>
public class _Default : System.Web.UI.Page
```

This class exposes a `Load` event that gets fired when, unsurprisingly, the page is loaded. This happens after ASP.NET has loaded the `.aspx` file and examined it to learn what dynamic elements exist on the page.

But, there's more. Each dynamic element we define on the page also exists as a protected member of the class. We changed the `ID` property of our label control to `labelCopyright`, and here is that member defined on the form:

```
/// <summary>
/// Summary description for _Default.
/// </summary>
public class _Default : System.Web.UI.Page
{
    protected System.Web.UI.WebControls.Label labelCopyright;
```

Again, this is another classic illustration of how similar Web Forms and Windows Forms actually are. When we paint a control onto a Windows Form, we also get the same kind of member added. With the member in place, we can access it through code:

```
private void Page_Load(object sender, System.EventArgs e)
{
    // what year is this?
    int year = DateTime.Now.Year;
    if(year == 2002)
        labelCopyright.Text = "Copyright &copy; Disraeli " + year;
    else
        labelCopyright.Text = "Copyright &copy; Disraeli 2002-" + year;
}
```

Let's look at what's happening here. At this point, ASP.NET has loaded the .aspx file and looked for the dynamic elements. Effectively, ASP.NET has an HTML code image of the page stored in memory, but has inserted placeholders in the HTML code wherever it found an active element. ASP.NET now gives the page and the controls on the page as much opportunity as possible to put their own HTML code into those placeholders. By setting the Text property on the label control, we're telling the control that when ASP.NET finally asks for the HTML code to put into the placeholder in the HTML code image that ASP.NET has reserved for it, the label control will supply some HTML that looks like this:

```
<span id="labelCopyright">Copyright &copy; Disraeli 2002-2003</span>
```

In other words, it takes the value stored in Text and wraps <span> and </span> tags around it.

Eventually, ASP.NET decides that all of the controls have supplied the HTML that makes up the part of the page that they are responsible for, and sends the entire HTML image down to the browser where it can be rendered.

Weblog Entries

Now you understand the principle of building ASP.NET pages using the control/event paradigm, let's take a look at how we can use that principle to build something that's useful. What we'll do now is build a separate page that lists an entire Weblog entry, a list of events and thoughts for a given day.

One of the advantages of building an active web site is that each time you want to add or change the content you don't have to resort to writing HTML code. This means that firstly, people who don't understand HTML can add content to the site and secondly, experienced HTML coders can add content quickly and simply.

The traditional method to add content to the site is to present a form that the user can enter his or her content into. When the Save Changes button is clicked, the new content appears on the site. This content is usually stored in a database of some kind.

In this example, we're going to store the content in separate XML files on the web server, rather than in a database, as it is a more flexible format. Each file will contain one Weblog "entry", or something that happened at a specific time. We'll look at how to create these entries first and then how to store them on the page.

Storing Weblog Entries

As we said, we're going to store the XML files containing the Weblog entries on the server. However, we have to go through a few hoops before we can do this.

You might have noticed that although we've created the new project, we don't actually know where the files are being stored. That's because Visual Studio communicates with the web server through something called "FrontPage Extensions" to store the files.

FrontPage Extensions have had a chequered history. The principle behind them is that it's supposed to make updating a remote web site on the Internet as simple as copying files from one folder on your computer to another. In reality FrontPage Extensions have historically been hard for systems administrators to configure, have problems with web site security, and have generally been a little flaky. We can only hope that the version included in .NET sorts these problems out.

This causes us our first problem because ideally we need to know where these files are so that we can back them up. Luckily, ASP.NET is able to tell us where they are.

Try it Out – Finding Where the Web Site is Stored

1. Open the HTML editor for `Default.aspx` and add the code shown in gray. (I've omitted some of the code that already exists for brevity.)

```
<form id="Default" method="post" runat="server">
   <div>
      Disraeli's Weblog
   </div>
   <br>
   <div>
      <asp:Label id="labelCopyright"
                 runat="server">(copyright)</asp:Label>
   </div>
   <br>
   <div>
   </div>
</form>
```

2. Select View | Design from the menu to show the Designer.

3. Using the toolbox, drag a new Label control and drop it between the two new div tags. Set the ID property of the control to labelServerPath and the Text property to (serverpath).

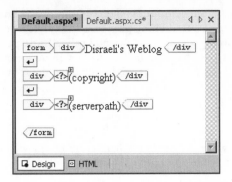

4. Double-click on the page background to open the Load handler again. Add this code:

```
private void Page_Load(object sender, System.EventArgs e)
{
    // what year is this?
    int year = DateTime.Now.Year;
    if(year == 2002)
        labelCopyright.Text = "Copyright &copy; Disraeli " + year;
    else
        labelCopyright.Text = "Copyright &copy; Disraeli 2002-" + year;

    // set the server path...
    labelServerPath.Text = Server.MapPath("");
}
```

Run the project. You should see this:

How it Works

In the first instance, we added a new control to the form. We want to use this control to report the path that the web site is stored in.

`System.Web.UI.Page`, which our `_Default` class is derived from, has a number of properties that help us understand what has been asked of the page and lets us access some information about the environment. The `Server` property contains a method called `MapPath` that can transform a virtual path on the web site into a physical path on the web server. In our instance, we've asked it to transform a blank string, which tells it that we want the folder containing the root of the web site.

```
// set the server path...
labelServerPath.Text = Server.MapPath("");
```

If we use Windows Explorer and navigate to the path given on the web page, we can indeed see the files. I've highlighted the `.aspx` file and the `.cs` "code behind" file.

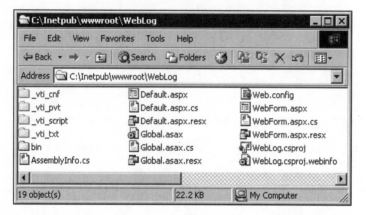

Let's now create an XML file that can be used to hold an entry in the Weblog.

Try it Out – Creating an Entry XML File

1. Create a new folder called `Entries` in the folder containing the web site. For example, on my computer, this new folder would be here:

`c:\Inetpub\wwwroot\webLog\Entries`

Throughout the rest of this chapter, we'll call this file the "entries folder".

2. Open Notepad. Create this file:

```
<?xml version="1.0" ?>
<Entry xmlns:xsi="http://www.w3.org/2002/XMLSchema-instance"
       xmlns:xsd="http://www.w3.org/2002/XMLSchema">
  <Title>Hello!</Title>
  <Details>These are the details of the Weblog entry</Details>
</Entry>
```

XML is case-sensitive, so make sure you enter the file exactly as you see here, so where it says "`<Title>`" make sure you enter "`<Title>`" and not "`<title>`", "`<TItLe>`", etc.

3. Save the file as `Entry.xml` and place it into the entries folder you created a moment ago.

Displaying Weblog Entries

Now that we have an XML file that contains a single entry, we can go ahead and create more files for each of the entries that we want our Weblog to display. We can also build a class that can load up those files and present the data contained within as properties.

Let's look now at how we can load in the files.

Try it Out – Loading Weblog Files

1. To load the XML files, we're going to add a static method to a class already created by Visual Studio .NET called `Global`. This class is a neat place to put shared methods and properties that need to be available to all of the pages in a web application and you'll find it by looking inside the `Global.asax` page.

2. To find `Global`, using Solution Explorer right-click on the `Global.asax` file and select **View Code**.

3. You'll notice that the `Global` class is derived from `System.Web.HttpApplication`. This class provides some events that we can respond to when certain application-scope events happen. (In ASP.NET, "application scope" can be considered to be "web site scope".)

4. Add this member to `Global`:

```
/// <summary>
/// Summary description for Global.
/// </summary>
public class Global : System.Web.HttpApplication
{
    // members...
    public static String EntryFilePath;
```

Note that we have used the class name `String` (capital 's') rather than the C# keyword `string` (smalls 's').

5. Next, add this code to the `Application_Start()` method:

```
protected void Application_Start(Object sender, EventArgs e)
{
    // set the shared entry path member...
    EntryFilePath = Server.MapPath("Entries");
}
```

6. Using Solution Explorer, create a new class called `Entry`. First, add these `using` statements to the top of the new file:

```
using System;
using System.IO;
using System.Xml.Serialization;
```

7. Then, add these members and corresponding properties:

```
/// <summary>
/// Summary description for Entry.
/// </summary>
public class Entry
{
    // members...

    private DateTime _timestamp;
    private String _title;
    private String _details;

    public Entry()
    {
        //
        // TODO: Add constructor logic here
        //
    }

    [XmlIgnore()] public DateTime Timestamp
    {
        get
        {
            return _timestamp;
        }
        set
        {
            _timestamp = value;
        }
    }

    public String Title
    {
        get
```

```
        {
            return _title;
        }
        set
        {
            _title = value;
        }
    }

    public String Details
    {
        get
        {
            return _details;
        }
        set
        {
            _details = value;
        }
    }
}
```

You'll notice that the names of these properties match the names of the entries in the XML file that we created. That's quite deliberate!

8. Now, flip back to the code editor for `Global.asax.cs`. Add the same namespace references to the top of the file:

```
using System;
using System.Collections;
using System.ComponentModel;
using System.Web;
using System.Web.SessionState;
using System.IO;
using System.Xml.Serialization;
```

9. Next, add this static method to the `Global` class:

```
// LoadEntry - load an entry from disk...
public static Entry LoadEntry(String filename)
{
    // we have the name, but we need the path...
    String filepath = EntryFilePath + "\\" + filename;

    // open the file...
    FileStream file = new FileStream(filepath, FileMode.Open);

    // create a serializer...
    XmlSerializer serializer = new XmlSerializer(typeof(Entry));
    Entry newEntry = (Entry)serializer.Deserialize(file);
```

```
        // close the file...
        file.Close();

        // return the entry...
        return newEntry;
    }
```

10. Technically, we can now create new `Entry` objects and populate their `Title` and `Details` properties from the data stored in the XML file. We now need to create some controls on the `Default.aspx` page so that we can see the results.

11. Open the HTML editor for `Default.aspx`. Add this code:

```
<form id="Default" method="post" runat="server">
    <div>
        Disraeli's Weblog
    </div>
    <br>
    <div>
    </div>
    <div>
    </div>
    <br>
    <div>
        <asp:label id="labelCopyright" runat="server">(copyright)</asp:label>
    </div>
...
</form>
```

12. Now flip over to design view for `Default.aspx`. Into the two new `div` elements that have appeared, drop a new Label control into each.

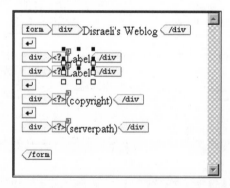

- ❏ On the first new control, set the `ID` property to `labelEntryTitle`. Set the `Text` property to (entryTitle).

- ❏ On the second new control, set the `ID` property to `labelEntryDetails`. Set the `Text` property to (entryDetails).

13. Double-click on the background of the page to open the Load event handler. First of all, change the last line to use the Global.EntryFilePath shared property:

```
private void Page_Load(object sender, System.EventArgs e)
{
    // what year is this?
    int year = DateTime.Now.Year;
    if(year == 2002)
        labelCopyright.Text = "Copyright &copy; Disraeli " + year;
    else
        labelCopyright.Text = "Copyright &copy; Disraeli 2002-" + year;

    // set the server path...
    labelServerPath.Text = Global.EntryFilePath;
}
```

14. Then, add this code to use the shared method on Global to create a new Entry object based on the data stored in Entry.xml and then populate the two new controls we just added: labelEntryTitle and labelEntryDetails.

```
private void Page_Load(object sender, System.EventArgs e)
{
...

    // set the server path...
    labelServerPath.Text = Global.EntryFilePath;

    // load the entry from disk...
    Entry entry = Global.LoadEntry("Entry.xml");
    labelEntryTitle.Text = entry.Title;
    labelEntryDetails.Text = entry.Details;
}
```

> In order for the ASP.NET process to be able to see the XML file, you will need to give it permissions to read and write the file. This is very easy to do. Simply right-click the **Entries** folder in Windows Explorer, choose **Properties** from the context menu, and switch to the **Security** tab. Click the **Add** button, then click on the **ASPNET** user in the top pane. Choose **Add**, then **OK**, then check the **Full Control** box in the **Allow** column, then click **OK** again. The ASP.NET worker process now has permission to read and write to this folder.

Run the project. You should see this:

15. To convince yourself that the changes are being loaded from disk, use Notepad to edit the `Entry.xml` file once more. Change the data so that it looks like this:

```xml
<?xml version="1.0"?>
<Entry xmlns:xsi="http://www.w3.org/2001/XMLSchema-instance"
xmlns:xsd="http://www.w3.org/2001/XMLSchema">
    <Title>Hello, again!</Title>
    <Details>I have changed the details in the XML file...</Details>
</Entry>
```

16. Save the file and refresh the Internet Explorer page. You should see the changes.

How It Works

In `Global.asax`, the first thing we did was use `Server.MapPath` again to resolve the virtual `Entries` directory into a physical path that we can use from code. `Application_Start()` is called the instant the first request for an `.aspx` page is received. It gives you the opportunity to set up application global (or "web site global") data. In this case, we're storing the physical path in the shared `EntryFilePath` member.

```
protected void Application_Start(Object sender, EventArgs e)
{
    // set the shared entry path member...
    EntryFilePath = Server.MapPath("Entries");
}
```

Now we come to the static `LoadEntry()` method which loads the XML data files from the entries folder and places the contents into the `Entry` class we defined. To do this, we use a class in the `System.Xml.Serialization` namespace called `XmlSerializer`, and call its `Deserialize()` method which takes the XML string from the file and converts (deserializes) its data to a set of object properties which are stored in the `Entry` class instance.

```
// LoadEntry - load an entry from disk...
public static Entry LoadEntry(String filename)
{
    // we have the name, but we need the path...
    String filepath = EntryFilePath + "\\" + filename;

    // open the file...
    FileStream file = new FileStream(filepath, FileMode.Open);

    // create a serializer and use it to populate the properties of the
    // a newly created Entry object...
    XmlSerializer serializer = new XmlSerializer(typeof(Entry));
    Entry newEntry = (Entry)serializer.Deserialize(file);

    // close the file...
    file.Close();

    // return the entry...
    return newEntry;
}
```

From `Default.aspx.cs`, we again customize the `Load` event handler. This time, we always assume our XML file is called `Entry.xml` and then set the `Text` property on each of the label controls, like this:

```
private void Page_Load(object sender, System.EventArgs e)
{
    // what year is this?
    int year = DateTime.Now.Year;
    if(year == 2002)
        labelCopyright.Text = "Copyright &copy; Disraeli " + year;
    else
        labelCopyright.Text = "Copyright &copy; Disraeli 2002-" + year;

    // set the server path...
    labelServerPath.Text = Global.EntryFilePath;

    // load the entry from disk...
    Entry entry = Global.LoadEntry("Entry.xml");
    labelEntryTitle.Text = entry.Title;
    labelEntryDetails.Text = entry.Details;
}
```

Displaying the Time

What we haven't done is displayed the time next to the entry. To do this, we're going to take the time that file was last saved and store the date in the `Timestamp` property of the entry. We can then tweak our code to display the time and date before we render the details.

Try it Out – Displaying the Time

1. To get the time, we're going to use the date that the entry was last modified. In most cases, this will be the time the entry was last saved to disk.

2. Using Solution Explorer, right-click on `Global.asax` and select **View Code**. Find the `LoadEntry` method and add this code:

```
// LoadEntry - load an entry from disk...
public static Entry LoadEntry(String filename)
{
    ...

    // close the file...
    file.Close();

    // update timestamp...
    newEntry.Timestamp = new FileInfo(filepath).LastWriteTime;

    // return the entry...
    return newEntry;
}
```

3. Now, open the code editor for `Default.aspx.cs`. Make this change:

```
private void Page_Load(object sender, System.EventArgs e)
{
    ...

    // set the server path...
    labelServerPath.Text = Global.EntryFilePath;

    // load the entry from disk...
    Entry entry = Global.LoadEntry("Entry.xml");
    labelEntryTitle.Text = entry.Title;
    labelEntryDetails.Text = entry.Timestamp.ToString("dddd") + ", " +
        entry.Timestamp.ToLongDateString() + " - " + entry.Details;
}
```

Run the project. You should now see that the time is displayed.

How It Works

The `Entry` object already contained a member for holding the timestamp. We used the `XmlIgnore` attribute to tell the `XmlSerializer` not to worry about it, which is why we didn't have to include it in our XML file. Anything marked with this attribute will not be saved to an XML file, nor will it be loaded from an XML file.

```
/// <summary>
/// Summary description for Entry.
/// </summary>
public class Entry
{
    // members...
    [XmlIgnore()] public DateTime Timestamp;
    public String Title;
    public String Details;
```

When we created the `Entry` object, we used a `System.IO.FileInfo` object to tell us the date that the file was last changed.

```
// LoadEntry - load an entry from disk...
public static Entry LoadEntry(String filename)
{
    ...

    // close the file...
    file.Close();

    // update timestamp...
    newEntry.Timestamp = new FileInfo(filepath).LastWriteTime;

    // return the entry...
    return newEntry;
}
```

When we actually came to render the page, we used two methods to transform the date into strings. The first call, `ToString()`, was configured to render the name of the day. The second call, `ToLongDateString()`, renders the rest of the long date using the locale settings of the computer. If you're in the US, the month will be written before the day. If you're in the UK, the day will be written before the month and so on. It's a good idea to use the localization-aware versions of date functions in this way, otherwise you could confuse your users.

```
private void Page_Load(object sender, System.EventArgs e)
{
    ...

    // set the server path...
    labelServerPath.Text = Global.EntryFilePath;

    // load the entry from disk...
    Entry entry = Global.LoadEntry("Entry.xml");
    labelEntryTitle.Text = entry.Title;
    labelEntryDetails.Text = entry.Timestamp.ToString("dddd") + ", " +
        entry.Timestamp.ToLongDateString()+ " - " + entry.Details;
}
```

Improving the Look

It won't have escaped your attention that the look of our page is very ugly indeed! HTML is (in today's terms) an old technology that was primarily designed for sharing drab, scientific documents. It's primarily the consumer adoption of the web that's driven it to look fresh and contemporary. If we want a fresh, contemporary look, we have to do it ourselves.

There are a number of technologies we can use to improve the design of the page, but the easiest one for us to use here is going to be **Cascading Style Sheets** or **CSS**. CSS is a huge topic, so we won't be going into it in much detail here. Suffice to say that a CSS is a specially formatted text file that contains all the fonts, colors and styles that the browser needs to render the HTML to a more visually pleasing format.

Try it Out – Improving the Look

1. The first thing we need to do is build a style sheet that all of the pages on the site will share. To do this, from Solution Explorer, right-click on the `WebLog` project and select **Add | Add New Item**. Search through the **Templates** list until you find **Style Sheet**. Select it and set the name to `Style.css`.

2. Add this code to the new style sheet:

```
body
{
    padding-right: 0px;
    padding-left: 0px;
    font-size: 8pt;
    padding-bottom: 0px;
    margin: 0px;
```

```
      padding-top: 0px;
      font-family: Verdana, Arial;
}
.header
{
      padding-right: 5px;
      padding-left: 5px;
      padding-bottom: 10px;
      padding-top: 10px;
      background-color: #000099;
      font-weight: bold;
      font-size: 14pt;
      color: white;
}
.normal
{
      padding-right: 5px;
      padding-left: 5px;
      font-size:8pt;
}
.normalHeading
{
      padding-right: 5px;
      padding-left: 5px;
      font-size:12pt;
      font-weight: bold;
}
.entryTitle
{
      padding-right: 5px;
      padding-left: 5px;
      padding-bottom: 1px;
      padding-top: 1px;
      font-weight: bold;
      font-size: 10pt;
      color: white;
      background-color: #66cc99;
}
.entryDate
{
      font-weight: bold;
      color: #333399;
      font-size: 8pt;
}
.entry
{
      padding-right: 5px;
      padding-left: 5px;
      padding-top: 2px;
      font-size: 8pt;
}
}
```

If you don't want to type this all out, then you can add the Styles.css file from the code download; if it is not already included in your project, right-click on the WebLog project node in the Solution Explorer, select Add | Add Existing Item and browse to the CSS file.

3. To use a style sheet, we have to associate it with a page. Open the HTML editor for Default.aspx and add this line to the top:

```
<HTML>
    <HEAD>
        <title>Default</title>
        <meta name="GENERATOR" content="Microsoft Visual Studio 7.0">
        <meta name="CODE_LANGUAGE" content="C#">
        <meta name="vs_defaultClientScript" content="JavaScript" >
        <meta name="vs_targetSchema"
            content="http://schemas.microsoft.com/intellisense/ie5" >
        <link rel="stylesheet" href="Style.css">
    </HEAD>
```

4. Now, change the highlighted lines and add code where necessary:

```
<%@ Page language="c#" Codebehind="Default.aspx.cs" AutoEventWireup="false"
        Inherits="webLog.CDefault" %>
<!DOCTYPE HTML PUBLIC "-//W3C//DTD HTML 4.0 Transitional//EN" >
<HTML>
    <HEAD>
        <title>Default</title>
        <meta name="GENERATOR" content="Microsoft Visual Studio 7.0">
        <meta name="CODE_LANGUAGE" content="C#">
        <meta name="vs_defaultClientScript" content="JavaScript" >
        <meta name="vs_targetSchema"
            content="http://schemas.microsoft.com/intellisense/ie5" >
        <link rel="stylesheet" href="Style.css">
    </HEAD>
    <body>
        <form id="Default" method="post" runat="server">
            <div class="header">
                Disraeli's Weblog
            </div>
            <br>
            <div class="entryTitle">
                <asp:label id="labelEntryTitle" runat="server">
                    (entryTitle)</asp:label>
            </div>
            <div class="entry">
                <asp:label id="labelEntryDetails" runat="server">
                    (entryDetails)</asp:label>
            </div>
            <br>
            <hr color="#000000">
            <div class="normal">
```

```
            <asp:label id="labelCopyright" runat="server">
                (copyright)</asp:label>
        </div>
        <br>
        <div class="normal">
            <asp:Label id="labelServerPath" runat="server">
                (serverpath)</asp:Label>
        </div>
    </form>
  </body>
</HTML>
```

5. The last code change we need to make is in `Default.aspx.cs`. View the code editor for this file and make this change to `Page_Load()`:

```
private void Page_Load(object sender, System.EventArgs e)
{
    ...

    // set the server path...
    labelServerPath.Text = Global.EntryFilePath;

    // load the entry from disk...
    Entry entry = Global.LoadEntry("Entry.xml");
    labelEntryTitle.Text = entry.Title;
    labelEntryDetails.Text = "<font class=entryDate>" +
        entry.Timestamp.ToString("dddd") + ", " +
        entry.Timestamp.ToLongDateString() + "</font> - " +
        entry.Details;
}
```

Compile and run the project and you should see this:

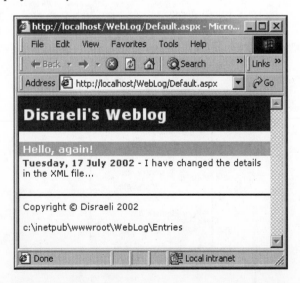

How it Works

Cascading Style Sheets allow you to define styles that can then be applied to any element on the page. We build those styles in .css files, like the Style.css file that we created.

A discussion of CSS is beyond the scope of this book, but the general gist is this: you can either change the style of standard HTML elements, like <body> and <ul> or you can define new classes, which is the CSS term for the grouping of styles into one unit. To modify an existing element, you just enter the name of the element and then add CSS codes. This is how we redefined how the <body> tag is displayed:

```
body
{
    padding-right: 0px;
    padding-left: 0px;
    font-size: 8pt;
    padding-bottom: 0px;
    margin: 0px;
    padding-top: 0px;
    font-family: Verdana, Arial;
}
```

New classes can be given any arbitrary name you like, but must be prefixed with a period. This is how we built the header class:

```
.header
{
    padding-right: 5px;
    padding-left: 5px;
    padding-bottom: 10px;
    padding-top: 10px;
    background-color: #000099;
    font-weight: bold;
    font-size: 14pt;
    color: white;
}
```

Technically, you don't have to understand CSS in order to edit it with Visual Studio .NET. Make sure you're looking at the code for the style sheet. If the style sheet is the currently selected document, select View | Other Windows | Document Outline from the menu, and you'll see the CSS editor.

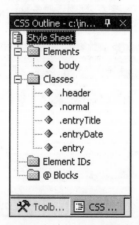

If you right-click on any of the elements or classes and select **Build Style**, you'll be shown a dialog that you can use to adjust the various CSS codes in a reasonably intuitive manner.

Once you have the style sheet built, you need to associate it with the page. This will prompt the browser to download the styles and apply them to the document. This is done with a `link` element, like this:

```
<HTML>
   <HEAD>
      <title>Default</title>
      <meta name="GENERATOR" content="Microsoft Visual Studio 7.0">
      <meta name="CODE_LANGUAGE" content="C#">
      <meta name="vs_defaultClientScript" content="JavaScript" >
      <meta name="vs_targetSchema"
            content="http://schemas.microsoft.com/intellisense/ie5" >
      <link rel="stylesheet" href="Style.css">
   </HEAD>
```

Finally, to set the class that should be used with an element on the page, you use the `class` attribute. This tells the browser which style to apply to the element. Here's how we told the `div` element containing the **Disraeli's Weblog** to use the `header` class:

```
<div class="header">
   Disraeli's Weblog
</div>
```

We'll be using this style sheet as we work through the rest of the chapter but, just a reminder here, we won't be going into style sheets in any more detail.

Displaying Lists of Entries

We're able to display a single Weblog entry, but how do we display many entries on the same page?

Displaying lists is a common activity for active web sites to undertake, whether it's displaying a list of products for sale on an e-commerce site, or displaying customer records from a database. ASP.NET has a number of ways to make displaying lists easier, and we'll be examining some of them here.

Try it Out – Displaying Lists of Weblog Entries

1. Before we can view a list of Weblog entries, we need more than one to be stored in the `Entries` folder! Using Explorer and Notepad, create some entries. You can use any name you like.

789

2. In the `Global` class, we need a new static method that can return a list of *all* of the entries. Open the code editor for `Global.asax.cs` and add this code:

```
// LoadAllEntries - load all entries from disk...
public static Entry[] LoadAllEntries()
{
    // get the path containing the entries...
    DirectoryInfo entryFolder = new DirectoryInfo(EntryFilePath);

    // get a list of files...
    FileInfo[] files = entryFolder.GetFiles();

    // create an array of entries...
    Entry[] entries = new Entry[files.Length];

    // loop through and load each file...
    int index = 0;
    foreach(FileInfo file in files)
    {
        entries[index] = LoadEntry(file.Name);
        index++;
    }

    // return the list...
    return entries;
}
```

3. Now we need to remove the code from `Default.aspx` that uses the two label controls. Open the designer and delete the top two Label controls. You should see this:

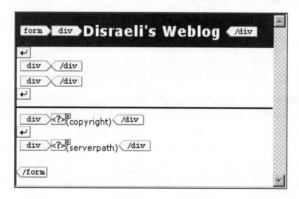

4. Now, delete the two `div` tags:

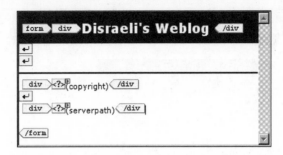

5. Next, using the toolbox drop a `DataList` control in between the two carriage return characters. This is what you should get:

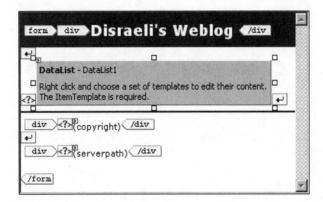

6. I would describe the `DataList` control as being "fiddly". It requires a great deal of tweaking and UI manipulation, but it is a pretty powerful control. It uses data binding in a big way, which means that in `Page_Load()`, we have to give the control the array of `Entry` objects. It will iterate through the whole list and per iteration renders a set of controls that we define. Each of those controls is data bound to a property on the `Entry` class. So, we might add a `Label` control to the `DataList` and bind the `Text` property of the `Label` control to the `Title` property, and so on.

7. Before we do anything, change the `ID` property of the `DataList` control to datalistEntries.

8. Right-click on the `DataList` control and select **Edit Template | Item Templates**. This puts the control into a separate mode where we can manipulate what happens per iteration of the array of `Entry` objects.

9. Using the toolbox, drag a `Label` control and drop it into the white area directly beneath `ItemTemplate`.

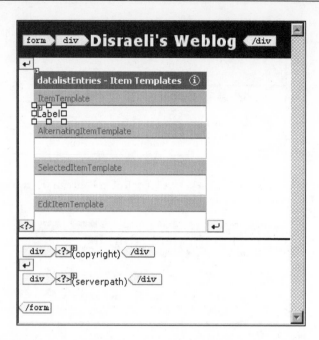

Any controls that appear within the ItemTemplate entry will be rendered once per iteration of the array. So, if we have three Entry objects in our array, we'll end up with three label controls.

10. With the Label control selected, using the Properties window, change the CssClass property to entryTitle. The look of the control should change to reflect the style you just selected.

11. Now, find the (DataBindings) property and select it. Click the ellipsis (...) next to it to bring up the data bindings window.

The left-hand list shows all of the properties on the Label control that can be data-bound. The Text property should be selected. With this selected, anything we do to the controls on the right-hand side of the window will configure the data binding for the Text property.

12. Select the Custom binding expression radio button and enter this code into the text box beneath the radio button.

```
DataBinder.Eval(Container, "DataItem.Title")
```

You should end up with this:

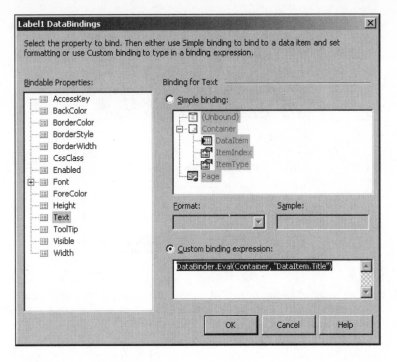

13. Click OK to save the data bindings.

14. What we'll do is prove this part works and then move on to rendering the date and other details. Double-click on the background of the page to open the Load event handler. Remove the previous code which added the entry from the XML file and replace it with this:

```
private void Page_Load(object sender, System.EventArgs e)
{
    ...

    // set the server path...
    labelServerPath.Text = Global.EntryFilePath;

    // load all of the entries from disk...
    Entry[] entries = Global.LoadAllEntries();
    datalistEntries.DataSource = entries;
    datalistEntries.DataBind();
}
```

Now compile and run the project. You should see this:

How it Works

The code to create an array of all the `Entry` objects on disk is pretty straightforward. All we do is ask the `System.IO.DirectoryInfo` object to return a list of `System.IO.FileInfo` objects for the `Entries` folder and iterate through the list calling `LoadEntry`.

```
// LoadAllEntries - load all entries from disk...
public static Entry[] LoadAllEntries()
{
    // get the path containing the entries...
    DirectoryInfo entryFolder = new DirectoryInfo(EntryFilePath);

    // get a list of files...
    FileInfo[] files = entryFolder.GetFiles();

    // create an array of entries...
    Entry[] entries = new Entry[files.Length];

    // loop through and load each file...
    int index = 0;
    foreach(FileInfo file in files)
    {
        entries[index] = LoadEntry(file.Name);
        index++;
    }

    // return the list...
    return entries;
}
```

Once we have the list, on `Page_Load()`, we pass it over the `DataList` control and call `DataBind()`.

```
    private void Page_Load(object sender, System.EventArgs e)
    {
...

        // set the server path...
        labelServerPath.Text = Global.EntryFilePath;

        // load all of the entries from disk...
        Entry[] entries = Global.LoadAllEntries();
        datalistEntries.DataSource = entries;
        datalistEntries.DataBind();
    }
```

This has the effect of asking the DataList to go through each of the Entry objects in turn following the rules defined in the template. The only template rule we defined was that once per iteration, we have to render a Label control – and that the Text property of this Label control should be set to the current value of the Title property of the Entry object that's currently being looked at.

Rendering Details

So, we can render the title, but what about the rest of the information? In this section, we'll look at how we can render the details and the date.

Try it Out – Rendering the Remainder of the Weblog Entry

1. If you recall, the way we rendered the date of the Weblog entry previously was quite complex. As DataList is designed to work with public properties, we'll build a property on Entry that can return the date as a string. Open the code editor for Entry and add this code:

```
public String TimestampAsString
{
    get
    {
        return Timestamp.ToString("dddd") + ", " +
                    Timestamp.ToLongDateString();
    }
}
```

2. Open the Designer for Default.aspx. The DataList control may have dropped into a state where it's not directly editable, which will look like this:

3. If the DataList isn't editable, right-click on it and select **Edit Template | Item Templates** again. Position the cursor after the green Label control, hold down *Shift* and press *Return*. This will add a line break rather than a carriage return. If you add a carriage return, there will be too much space between the title and the entry.

4. Add a Label control beneath the existing, green Label control. After the control add a space, a dash and another space and then add one last Label control.

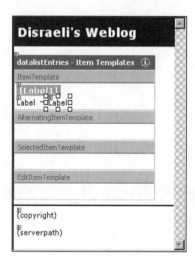

In case you're wondering, the small green arrows in the top-left hand corner of each control denotes a control.

5. Select the first new Label control. Set its CssClass property to **entryDate**.

6. Find and select the (DataBindings) property. Click the ellipsis to open the DataBindings window. Make sure Text is selected in the left-hand list and click the **Custom binding expression** radio button. Add this code:

```
DataBinder.Eval(Container, "DataItem.TimestampAsString")
```

7. Click OK to save the binding.

8. Select the other new Label control. Set its CssClass property to entry.

9. Find and select the (DataBindings) property. Click the ellipsis to open the DataBindings window. Make sure Text is selected in the left-hand list and click the Custom binding expression radio button. Add this code:

```
DataBinder.Eval(Container, "DataItem.Details")
```

Now compile and run the project. You'll see something like this:

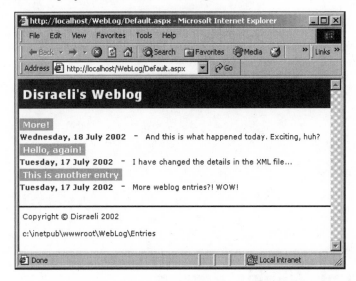

How It Works

As the DataList control works best with properties, we created a read-only property called TimestampAsString that would return a formatted version of the Timestamp property. We didn't bother adding a set clause to this property, as this would imply that the object consumer could ask us to build a System.DateTime value out of a string. Although achievable, that's well outside the scope of what we want this object to do.

```
public String TimestampAsString
{
    get
    {
        return Timestamp.ToString("dddd") + ", " +
                    Timestamp.ToLongDateString();
    }
}
```

Once we added that property, adding more label controls to the item template was simply an issue of repeating what we had done before.

797

Important Note about the DataList and Public Members

The expression that we enter into Custom binding expression field for the `DataList` control will *only* work with properties. It will not work with public members. If you had this:

```
public class Entry
{
    // members...
    Public String Title;
```

And tried to bind to `Title` with this expression:

```
DataBinder.Eval(Container, "DataItem.Title")
```

You'd see an error claiming that the property could not be found. Your only option at this point would be to convert the member into a property, like this:

```
public String Title
{
    get
    {
        return _title;
    }
    set
    {
        _title = value;
    }
}
```

Creating New Weblog Entries

At this point, all the functionality we need to get and display a list of entries to appear on the site is in place. However, we can't at this point create new entries without using Notepad! Ideally, we'd like to add a form to the site that we can use to create new entries.

Try it Out – Creating Weblog Entries

1. Using Solution Explorer, right-click on the `Weblog` project and select **Add | Add Web Form**. Enter the name as `Edit.aspx`.

2. Open the Designer for the page. Click once on the background and using the Properties window change the `pageLayout` property to **FlowLayout**.

3. Select **View | HTML Source** from the menu. Add this code:

```
<%@ Page language="c#" Codebehind="Edit.aspx.cs" AutoEventWireup="false"
         Inherits="webLog.Edit" %>
```

```
<!DOCTYPE HTML PUBLIC "-//W3C//DTD HTML 4.0 Transitional//EN" >
<HTML>
    <HEAD>
        <meta name="GENERATOR" Content="Microsoft Visual Studio 7.0">
        <meta name="CODE_LANGUAGE" Content="C#">
        <meta name="vs_defaultClientScript" content="JavaScript">
        <meta name="vs_targetSchema"
              content="http://schemas.microsoft.com/intellisense/ie5">
        <link rel="stylesheet" href="Style.css">
    </HEAD>
    <body>
        <form id="Edit" method="post" runat="server">
            <div class="header">
                Disraeli's Weblog
            </div>
            <br>
            <div class="normalHeading">
                Create a New Entry
            </div>
            <br>
            <div class="normal">
                <table cellspacing="0" cellpadding="3">
                    <tr>
                        <td class="normal">
                            Title:
                        </td>
                        <td>
                        </td>
                    </tr>
                    <tr>
                        <td class="normal">
                            Details:
                        </td>
                        <td>
                        </td>
                    </tr>
                    <tr>
                        <td colspan="2" align="right">
                        </td>
                    </tr>
                </table>
            </div>
        </form>
    </body>
</HTML>
```

4. Select View | Design from the menu and you should see this:

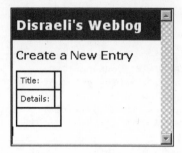

5. Using the Toolbox, drag and drop a TextBox control into the small box to the right of Title. Repeat this action but this time drop the control into the small box to the right of Details.

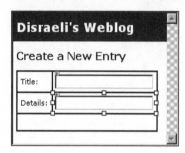

❑ Change the ID property of the top TextBox control to textTitle.

❑ Change the ID property of the bottom TextBox control to textDetails. Also, change the TextMode property to Multiline.

6. Using the Toolbox, drop a button control into the long, empty box at the bottom. Change its ID property to buttonOk and its Text property to Save Changes.

7. Make the two text box controls slightly bigger, like this:

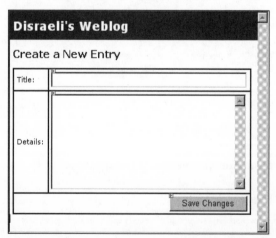

8. When the Save Changes button is pressed, we don't want to create the new entry unless the user has filled in both text boxes. We can use ASP.NET's validation functionality to automatically make sure that the details have been entered and display a message if they have not been.

9. Drag a `RequiredFieldValidator` control from the toolbox and drop it to the right of the `Title` text box. Change its `ErrorMessage` property to Required and set its `ControlToValidate` property to textTitle.

10. Do this again but this time drop the new control to the right of the `Details` box. Change its `ErrorMessage` property to Required and set its `ControlToValidate` property to textDetails.

11. Using Solution Explorer, view the code editor for `Entry.cs`. Add this member:

```
/// <summary>
/// Summary description for Entry.
/// </summary>
public class Entry
{
    // members...
    private String _filename;
    private DateTime _timestamp;
    private String _title;
    private String _details;
```

12. Next, add this property:

```
[XmlIgnore()] public String Filename
{
   get
   {
      return _filename;
   }
   set
   {
      _filename = value;
   }
}
```

13. Now, add this method to the `Entry` class:

```
public void Save()
{
    // do we have a filename?
    if(Filename == null)
    {
        // get a filename based on the date...
        Timestamp = DateTime.Now;
```

```
        Filename =
            String.Format("{0:d4}{1:d2}{2:d2}_{3:d2}{4:d2}.xml",
                (int)Timestamp.Year, (int)Timestamp.Month,
                (int)Timestamp.Day, (int)Timestamp.Hour,
                (int)Timestamp.Minute);
    }

    // get the whole filename...
    String filepath = Global.EntryFilePath + "\\" + Filename;

    // create a serializer and save...
    FileInfo fileInfo = new FileInfo(filepath);
    if(fileInfo.Exists == true)
        fileInfo.Delete();
    FileStream stream =
            new FileStream(fileInfo.FullName, FileMode.Create);
    XmlSerializer serializer = new XmlSerializer(this.GetType());
    serializer.Serialize(stream, this);
    stream.Close();
}
```

14. Open the code editor for Edit.aspx.cs. Find the Page_Load() method and add this code:

```
private void Page_Load(object sender, System.EventArgs e)
{
    // is the page being saved?
    if(IsPostBack == true)
    {
        // create a new entry object...
        Entry newEntry = new Entry();

        // set the values...
        newEntry.Title = textTitle.Text;
        newEntry.Details = textDetails.Text;

        // save it...
        newEntry.Save();

        // show the list...
        Response.Redirect("default.aspx");
    }
}
```

15. Next, open the HTML editor for Default.aspx. Add this code to the page – I've omitted some of the code we've already added to the page for brevity:

```
<asp:DataList id="datalistEntries" runat="server">
...
</asp:DataList>
<br>
<div class="normal">
    <a href="edit.aspx">Create a new entry</a>
```

```
      </div>
      <br>
      <hr color="#000000">
      <div class="normal">
         <asp:label id="labelCopyright" runat="server">(copyright)</asp:label>
      </div>
```

Run the project. Click the **Create a new entry** link. The form will appear. Fill it out and click **Save Changes**. The page will reload and the new entry will be visible.

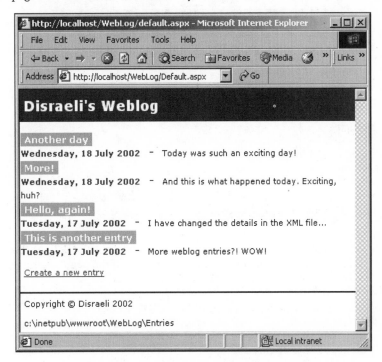

If you look in the `Entries` folder, you notice that a new file has been created:

How it Works

Building the form in `Edit.aspx` itself is not really any different to building the `Default.aspx` page. We used a combination of HTML code and the editor in both cases.

When the button on the form is pressed, two things happen. First, the validation code executes in line with the validation controls that we added to the page. Each of these was assigned to a single text box control. When the button is pressed, code runs that checks to make sure the controls are populated and, if not, a message will appear:

If, however, the validation is successful, the page is posted back to ASP.NET. At this point, the Page_Load() method is called again, but we can check to see if the page has indeed been posted back by using the IsPostBack property.

```
private void Page_Load(object sender, System.EventArgs e)
{
    // is the page being saved?
    if(IsPostBack == true)
    {
```

If the page is posted back, we create a new Entry object.

```
        // create a new entry object...
        Entry newEntry = new Entry();
```

When the page is posted back, the Text property of the text box controls becomes automatically populated with whatever the user filled in. This means that we can do this:

```
        // set the values...
        newEntry.Title = textTitle.Text;
        newEntry.Details = textDetails.Text;
```

Then, we tell the Entry object to save itself. (We'll see this in detail in a moment.)

```
        // save it...
        newEntry.Save();
```

After the entry has been saved, we tell ASP.NET to ask the browser to navigate to default.aspx so that we can see the new entry.

```
            // show the list...
            Response.Redirect("default.aspx");
        }
    }
```

When we come to save an entry, we need a filename. This filename has to be unique (otherwise we'd erase other entries), and so we decide to base the filename on the date and time that the entry was saved.

```
public void Save()
{
    // do we have a filename?
    if(Filename == null)
    {
        // get a filename based on the date...
        Timestamp = DateTime.Now;
        Filename =
        String.Format("{0:d4}{1:d2}{2:d2}_{3:d2}{4:d2}.xml",
                (int)Timestamp.Year, (int)Timestamp.Month,
                (int)Timestamp.Day, (int)Timestamp.Hour,
                (int)Timestamp.Minute);
    }
```

We store the filename as a property – the reason why we do this will become apparent later – and in order for us to save it we need to transform the filename into a full, physical path.

```
        // get the whole filename...
        String filepath = Global.EntryFilePath + "\\" + Filename;
```

Once we have that, we use an XmlSerializer object to save the object to disk. The Serialize() method takes a stream object representing the file to be written to and the Entry object and converts the latter's properties to an XML string; exactly the opposite of what the Deserialize() function did earlier on:

```
        // create a serializer and save...
        FileInfo fileInfo = new FileInfo(filepath);
        if(fileInfo.Exists == true)
            fileInfo.Delete();
        FileStream stream =
                new FileStream(fileInfo.FullName, FileMode.Create);
        XmlSerializer serializer = new XmlSerializer(this.GetType());
        serializer.Serialize(stream, this);
        stream.Close();
    }
```

805

Once `Default.aspx` has been reloaded, `GetAllEntries()` will return a complete list of files, including the new one that we've just created.

Editing Weblog Entries

So, we have a form that we can use to create new entries. Can we use it to edit existing entries stored as XML files on disk?

In this section, we'll see how we can tweak our application so that we can edit an entry once it is in place.

Try it Out – Editing Weblog Entries

1. Open the Designer for `Default.aspx`.

2. Right-click on the `DataList` control select **Edit Template | Item Templates**.

3. Using the Toolbox, drag a new `Hyperlink` control and drop it next to the green `Label` control.

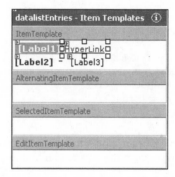

4. Using the Properties window, select the `(DataBindings)` property for the hyperlink control, and click the ellipsis. From the left-hand list, select `NavigateUrl`.

5. Click the **Custom binding expression** radio button and enter this expression:

```
"edit.aspx?filename=" + DataBinder.Eval(Container, "DataItem.Filename")
```

6. Click **OK** to save changes to the binding.

7. Again using the Properties window, change the `Text` property of the link control to **Edit**. Change the `CssClass` property to **entry**.

8. Open the code editor for `Global.asax`. Find the `LoadEntry` method and make this change:

```
// LoadEntry - load an entry from disk...
public static Entry LoadEntry(String filename)
{
```

```
// we have the name, but we need the path...
String filepath = EntryFilePath + "\\" + filename;

// open the file...
FileStream file = new FileStream(filepath, FileMode.Open);

// create a serializer...
XmlSerializer serializer = new XmlSerializer(typeof(Entry));
Entry newEntry = (Entry)serializer.Deserialize(file);

// close the file...
file.Close();

// update timestamp and filename...
newEntry.Timestamp = new FileInfo(filepath).LastWriteTime;
newEntry.Filename = filename;

// return the entry...
return newEntry;
}
```

Run the project. Click one of the **Edit** links and you'll notice that the **Create New Entry** form appears. However, what's really interesting is the **Address** bar. If you look at this you'll notice that the filename of the XML file containing the data for the entry has been "embedded" into the URL:

How it Works

OK, so we can't edit the page yet, but the next stage is to alter `Edit.aspx` and `Edit.aspx.cs` so that we look for the filename entry in the URL and load the entry.

The interesting thing here was the data binding. On the new hyperlink control, we bound the `NavigateUrl` property to this expression:

```
"edit.aspx?filename=" + DataBinder.Eval(Container, "DataItem.Filename")
```

You can see how, per iteration of the array of `Entry` objects, the `Filename` property of the object is extracted and tacked onto the end of the `edit.aspx?filename=` string. This gives us the complete URL.

Loading the Chosen Entry

To load the chosen entry when we view `Edit.aspx`, all we have to do is look for the `filename` "parameter" that may or may not be included in the URL.

Try it Out – Loading the Chosen Entry

1. Open the code editor for `Edit.aspx.cs`. Find the `Page_Load()` method and add this code:

```csharp
private void Page_Load(object sender, System.EventArgs e)
{
    // is the page being saved?
    if(IsPostBack == true)
    {
        // create a new entry object...
        Entry newEntry = new Entry();

        // do we have a filename to use?
        if(Request.Params["filename"] != null)
            newEntry.Filename = Request.Params["filename"];

        // set the values...
        newEntry.Title = textTitle.Text;
        newEntry.Details = textDetails.Text;

        // save it...
        newEntry.Save();

        // show the list...
        Response.Redirect("default.aspx");
    }
    else
    {
        // did we get a filename?
        String filename = Request.Params["filename"];
        if(filename != null)
        {
            // load the entry object...
            Entry entry = Global.LoadEntry(filename);

            // populate the fields...
            textTitle.Text = entry.Title;
            textDetails.Text = entry.Details;
        }
    }
}
```

Run the project. If you click on an **Edit** link, the entry should load into the new page. Any changes you make to the data on the form will be saved to the XML file when you click **Save Changes**.

How it Works

With .NET, parameters can come into the page in two ways: through form variables or through "the query string". By and large, ASP.NET does such a good job of abstracting away the way that forms work on the web, the only ones we need to worry about are query string variables.

These kinds of variables are ones that appear after a question mark in the URL. In our case, we have a single variable called `filename` whose value is `20020718_1419.xml`:

```
http://localhost/WebLog/edit.aspx?filename=20020718_1419.xml
```

The URL below, by contrast, has two variables: a and b; a is set to `Jack` and b is set to `Coffee`. The variables are separated with an ampersand character (`&`):

```
http://anotherserver/page.aspx?a=Jack&b=Coffee
```

In `Page_Load()`, if `IsPostBack` returns `false`, we know that the page is being loaded for the first time. We can take this opportunity to set the initial `Text` properties to whatever is stored in the file. (I've omitted some code here for brevity.)

```
private void Page_Load(object sender, System.EventArgs e)
  {
      // is the page being saved?
      if(IsPostBack == true)
      {
                        ...
      }
      else
      {
          // did we get a filename?
          String filename = Request.Params["filename"];
          if(filename != null)
          {
```

The `Request.Params` property, shown highlighted above, can be used to access the parameters that have been passed into the page. In this instance, we try and get hold of the `filename` parameter. Of course, if we've clicked the **Create a new entry** link, this parameter will be blank. If we have a parameter, we load the entry from disk and update the `Text` property on each of the controls.

```
          // load the entry object...
          Entry entry = Global.LoadEntry(filename);

          // populate the fields...
          textTitle.Text = entry.Title;
          textDetails.Text = entry.Details;
          }
      }
  }
```

The other half of this problem comes when we post the page back to the server. We again need to look in `Request.Params` to see if we already have a filename. If we do, we want to use that, in which case `Save()` will replace the existing file with a new file containing the changes that we made. If we do not, `Save()` will use the current date and time to create a new filename for us. (Again, I've omitted some code here.)

```
private void Page_Load(object sender, System.EventArgs e)
  {
      // is the page being saved?
      if(IsPostBack == true)
      {
          // create a new entry object...
          Entry newEntry = new Entry();
```

```
        // do we have a filename to use?
        if(Request.Params["filename"] != null)
            newEntry.Filename = Request.Params["filename"];

        // set the values...
        newEntry.Title = textTitle.Text;
        newEntry.Details = textDetails.Text;

        // save it...
        newEntry.Save();

        // show the list...
        Response.Redirect("default.aspx");
    }
```

So, now we can display lists of entries and we can use the web site itself to create new entries and make changes to existing ones.

Sorting Entries

You'll notice that as we add more entries, the last one we create does not appear at the top of the page. However, this is traditionally how Weblogs work – the first entry is the latest entry.

What we need to do is sort the entries into date order as we read them from the directory. Luckily for us, .NET returns the files in alphabetical order, which is why we've used the filename format that we have done. Consider these three filenames:

```
20020718_1318.xml
20020719_1003.xml
20020720_1823.xml
```

The format we've gone for is: yyyymmdd_hhmm. This has the drawback that only one file per minute can be created for use with the site. This isn't really a problem in our case as we should usually only have one new file being created per day. Files in this format, when sorted alphabetically, automatically sort from the earliest to the latest. All we have to do is reverse the order that the files were stored on disk.

Try it Out – Sorting Entries

1. First of all, create at least two entries using the tool we've just made. Delete the existing XML files that don't follow the date format we just spoke about. In my case, I have three files:

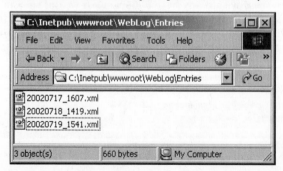

You can see that the files are listed in alphabetical order: an order totally opposite to the way we want it.

2. Open the code editor for `Global.asax`. Find the `LoadAllEntries()` method and make these two changes to the method:

```
// LoadAllEntries - load all entries from disk...
public static Entry[] LoadAllEntries()
{
    // get the path containing the entries...
    DirectoryInfo entryFolder = new DirectoryInfo(EntryFilePath);

    // get a list of files...
    FileInfo[] files = entryFolder.GetFiles();

    // create an array of entries...
    Entry[] entries = new Entry[files.Length];

    // loop through and load each file...
    int index = files.Length - 1;
    foreach(FileInfo file in files)
    {
        entries[index] = LoadEntry(file.Name);
        index--;
    }

    // return the list...
    return entries;
}
```

Compile and run the project. The files will be displayed in the correct order.

How It Works

The trick with this is to fill the array in the *reverse* order to the way the files are presented on disk. When we create the array, we know how big it's supposed to be by virtue of the fact it's supposed to be exactly the same size as the array of `FileInfo` objects returned by `GetFiles()`.

```
// LoadAllEntries - load all entries from disk...
public static Entry[] LoadAllEntries()
{
    // get the path containing the entries...
    DirectoryInfo entryFolder = new DirectoryInfo(EntryFilePath);

    // get a list of files...
    FileInfo[] files = entryFolder.GetFiles();

    // create an array of entries...
    Entry[] entries = new Entry[files.Length];
```

As we loop through each `FileInfo` object, we ask `Global.LoadEntry()` to create a new `Entry` object. We store this new object in the array at the position indicated by `index`, which starts off as the last position in the array and, per iteration, is decremented by one until the `files` array has been complete iterated.

```
    // loop through and load each file...
    int index = files.Length - 1;
    foreach(FileInfo file in files)
    {
        entries[index] = LoadEntry(file.Name);
        index--;
    }

    // return the list...
    return entries;
}
```

User Sessions and Cookies

It can't have escaped your attention that we appear to have built a web site that allows anyone to come along and create new Weblog entries and edit old ones. This is a little silly – ideally only the web site owner should be allowed to make changes.

What we need to do now is provide a way that the owner of the site can authenticate him or herself. Once that's done, whenever we offer the web site user the opportunity to make changes to the site, we can check the user's identity and allow or disallow this as appropriate.

Sessions work by allowing the web server to associate a set of data with a specific web browser. In this scenario, the browser is somehow "tagged" on its first page request from a given site. This tag is unique and on subsequent requests, this tag is used as a key to "unlock" data associated with it.

The web server tags the user's browser by using a cookie. (For those of you who do not know, a cookie is a small piece of information that a web server sends to your client machine which is read whenever you subsequently visit the web site.) On the first page request that you make to a site, that cookie will not exist, so the web server creates a new user session and places the ID of that session in a cookie before sending it to the browser. In ASP.NET code, you set various properties, which we'll introduce in a moment, to add information to the session.

You can store pretty much anything you want in a session, although as they take up memory on the server, try to store as little as possible in them. For example, do you need to store all the details of a customer in a session when you can store just the relatively small ID of the customer in a session and look up the finer details when you need them?

Restricting Access to the Web Site

In this particular example we're going to store a Boolean value in the session that tells us whether or not the user is allowed to edit the information on the site.

Try it Out – Preventing Editing

1. First of all, open the code editor for `Global.asax`. Find the `Session_Start()` method and add this code:

```
protected void Session_Start(Object sender, EventArgs e)
{
    // configure the session...
    Session["canedit"] = false;
}
```

2. Next, open the code editor for `Edit.aspx`. Find the `Page_Load()` method and add this code to the top:

```
private void Page_Load(object sender, System.EventArgs e)
{
    // are we allowed to edit...
    if((bool)Session["canedit"] == false)
        Response.Redirect("CannotEdit.aspx");

    ...
```

3. Next, using Solution Explorer, right-click on the `WebLog` project and select **Add | Add Web Form**. Call the new form `CannotEdit.aspx`. Open the HTML editor for the new page and add this code:

```
<%@ Page language="c#" Codebehind="CannotEdit.aspx.cs" AutoEventWireup="false"
         Inherits="webLog.CannotEdit" %>
<!DOCTYPE HTML PUBLIC "-//W3C//DTD HTML 4.0 Transitional//EN" >
<HTML>
    <HEAD>
```

```
        <meta name="GENERATOR" Content="Microsoft Visual Studio 7.0">
        <meta name="CODE_LANGUAGE" Content="C#">
        <meta name="vs_defaultClientScript" content="JavaScript">
        <meta name="vs_targetSchema"
              content="http://schemas.microsoft.com/intellisense/ie5">
    </HEAD>
    <body MS_POSITIONING="GridLayout">
        <form id="CannotEdit" method="post" runat="server">
            Sorry, you're not allowed to make changes to the site.
            <br>
            <br>
            <a href="default.aspx">Continue...</a>
        </form>
    </body>
</HTML>
```

Compile and run the project. You should notice straight away that the Edit links and the Create a new
entry link take you to the new error page rather than to the page we were previously able to access.

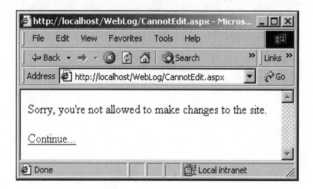

How It Works

The magic here is all done by something called a "session". A session is something ASP.NET gives us
that let's us identify a user. The first time a user requests a page from an ASP or ASP.NET site, you're
allocated a session that's unique to you – no one else can have the same session as you.

Whenever a new session is created, that is, whenever a new user requests the first page from the site,
Session_Start() is called. System.Web.HttpApplication and System.Web.UI.Page each
support a property called Session. This property is a basic collection that we can store values in. In
this case, we've created a value called canedit and stored the value false against it:

```
protected void Session_Start(Object sender, EventArgs e)
{
    // configure the session...
    Session["canedit"] = false;
}
```

These values are called "session variables".

We can retrieve this value from any of the pages on the site. When we do so, we're guaranteed that in accessing the session variables we're getting values back that are *unique* to the user. So, if we have a hundred users all using the site, each one will have his or her own unique session. The canedit variable will be set to an initial value of false when the session is created. However, if we change canedit to true for just one of those users, the change will only have scope for the user that we change it for. Ultimately, we want to change canedit to true for a user that can supply the correct password.

In Edit.aspx.cs, when the page is loaded we check to see if this value is false and, if it is, we redirect the user to another page.

```
private void Page_Load(object sender, System.EventArgs e)
{
    // are we allowed to be edited...
    if((bool)Session["canedit"] == false)
        Response.Redirect("CannotEdit.aspx");
```

Authenticating the User

In this exercise, we're going to create a very simple authentication routine. Basically, we're going to ask the user for a password and if that password matches what we want, we'll set canedit to true and that specific user will be able to edit pages.

Try it Out – Authenticating the User

1. Using Solution Explorer, right-click on the Weblog project and select Add | Add Web Form. Call it Login.aspx.

2. When the Designer for the form appears, click once on the background of the page and using the Properties window change pageLayout to FlowLayout.

3. We won't bother making this page look pretty as this is an administration tool and I'm sure you get the general idea of how to make the pages look appealing. Instead, just drop a new TextBox control and Button control onto the page.

4. Select the TextBox control and change its ID property to textPassword. Change its TextMode property to Password.

5. Select the Button control and change its Text property to Login.

6. Double-click on the background of the form to open the Page_Load() method. Add this code:

```
private void Page_Load(object sender, System.EventArgs e)
{
    // posting back?
    if(IsPostBack == true)
    {
        // do we have the correct password?
        if(textPassword.Text.CompareTo("stringy") == 0)
        {
```

```
                    // update the session...
                    Session["canedit"] = true;

                    // redirect...
                    Response.Redirect("default.aspx");
                }
            }
        }
```

Run the project. Click one of the Edit links and you should, ultimately, be returned to the start page. In the Address bar, change Default.aspx to Login.aspx, and click the Go button.

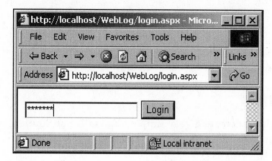

Enter the password as stringy. (Case is important.) Click the Login button and you should be transported to Default.aspx. Now if you click on an Edit link you will be able to make changes.

How It Works

As we know, whenever we load Edit.aspx the code checks to make sure that the canedit session variable is true. If it isn't, we're redirected to an error page.

In Login.aspx, when the Login button is pressed, the Page_Load() method is called. At this point, we look to see if we're being posted back, and then we look at the Text property of textPassword to see if the password has been given as stringy.

```
        private void Page_Load(object sender, System.EventArgs e)
        {
            // posting back?
            if(IsPostBack == true)
            {
                // do we have the correct password?
                if(textPassword.Text.CompareTo("stringy") == 0)
                {
```

If it has, we change the canedit session variable to true and redirect the user back to the home page.

```
                    // update the session...
                    Session["canedit"] = true;

                    // redirect...
                    Response.Redirect("default.aspx");
                }
            }
        }
```

Now, whenever we click on a link and open `Edit.aspx`, the check does indeed discover that `canedit` is set to `true` and therefore the page is displayed as normal. We can then make the desired changes.

Summary

In this chapter we took a look at "Active Server Pages .NET", or ASP.NET. This technology is the next generation technology from Microsoft building on the success of its previous ASP technology that has been available since 1996.

We started off by looking at how the control/event model in ASP.NET works and learned that this is a very similar paradigm to the one employed in Windows Forms. In fact, ASP.NET should be quite easy for newcomers to building active web sites to pick up. However, hardened web developers will find the transition difficult, as the paradigm is completely different.

To illustrate some of the techniques used to develop an ASP.NET application, we created a web site on which we can view entries in a Weblog. These entries are stored as XML files that could be read from and written to using the `XmlSerializer`, an extremely useful .NET Framework class. We created static methods on the `Global` class that are available to all of the pages in the site that could retrieve single `Entry` objects or an array of all of the `Entry` objects from disk. We used the `DataList` control and other built-in ASP.NET controls to display the list of `Entry` objects.

Finally, we looked at how we could create a form that would let the user create and edit new `Entry` objects directly on the web site itself. We also looked at the `Session` collection and learned a little about session state.

Questions

1. What's the general principle behind ASP.NET?

2. With Visual Studio .NET, how many files are associated with an `.aspx` file?

3. What does the `DataList` control allow us to do?

4. What is a style sheet?

5. What was special about the filename format we used for our XML files?

24

Web Services

You may have come across the term *web service* before, though you may not be aware of what they are or how they fit into they way the Web operates, both now and in the future. Suffice to say that web services provide the foundation of the new generation of web applications. Whatever the client application is, whether a Windows application, an ASP.NET Web Forms application, and whatever system the client is running, whether Windows, Pocket Windows, or some other device, they will regularly communicate over the Internet using a web service. Web services are similar to the components we saw in Chapter 21, except that they run over the Internet. They are server-side programs that listen for messages from client applications and pass back specific information. This information may come from the web service itself, from other components in the same domain, or from other web services. Though the whole of the web service concept is evolving as I write, there are several different types of web service which carry out different functions: some provide information specific to a particular industry like manufacturing or healthcare; there are portal services that use services from different providers to offer information on a specific theme; there are services that are specific to single applications, and building block services that can be used by many different applications.

Web services give us the ability to combine, share, exchange or plug in separate services from various vendors and developers to form entirely new services or custom applications created on the fly to meet the requirements of the client.

In this chapter we will look at:

- ❑ Predecessors of web services
- ❑ What is a web service
- ❑ Protocols used for web services
- ❑ Creating an ASP.NET web service
- ❑ Testing the web service
- ❑ Building a client to use web services

We will not go into the inner workings of web services, especially the XML-based SOAP and WSDL formats, but you will get an overview of what all these protocols are used for. After reading this chapter, you can start creating and consuming simple web services with the help of Visual Studio .NET.

Before Web Services

Connecting computers to transfer data was already an important concept in 1969 when just four computers were connected via telephone lines to form the ARPANET. In 1976 the TCP/IP protocol was invented. To make this protocol easy to use the University of Berkeley created the socket model for network programming.

When programming with the **Sockets API,** the client had to initiate a connection to the server, and then send and receive data. To call some operations on the server to get results, additional protocols are needed to describe request and response codes. Examples of such so-called application protocols are FTP, Telnet and HTTP. The FTP protocol is used to get some files from the server and to put the files on the server. The FTP protocol supports request codes like GET and PUT that are sent across the wire from the client to the server. The server analyzes the data stream it receives, and according to the request codes invokes the corresponding method. The HTTP protocol works very similarly to the FTP protocol.

Remote Procedure Call (RPC)

With the Sockets API and the TCP/IP protocol calling custom methods on the server, the programmer would have had to create a means by which the server analyzes the data stream to invoke the corresponding method. To make all this work easier, some companies created an **RPC** (**Remote Procedure Calls**) protocol, an example of which is the still popular **DCE-RPC** protocol (**Distributed Computing Environment – Remote Procedure Calls**) from the Open Software Foundation (OSF), who later became the Open Group (see www.opengroup.org). Using RPC, we define methods in an **IDL** (**Interface Definition Language**) format, which the server has to implement, and which the client can call. We no longer had to deal with the definition of a custom protocol, and to parse the request codes to invoke the methods. This work is done by a special program, called a **stub**, generated by an interface compiler.

RPC is designed to invoke methods, which means that you have to do procedural programming. The RPC technology came in relatively late, when most developers had already started to work with the object-oriented paradigm. In order to bridge the technology gap, several technologies came into being, including CORBA and DCOM.

CORBA

The Object Management Group (OMG, www.omg.org) initiated **CORBA** (**Common Object Request Broker Architecture**) in 1991 to add object-orientation to network programming. Many vendors like Digital Equipment, HP, IBM, and others implemented CORBA servers. Because the OMG didn't define a reference implementation though, only a specification, the servers of these vendors didn't really interoperate. The HP server needed an HP client, the IBM server an IBM client, and so on.

DCOM

With Windows NT 4, Microsoft extended the DCE-RPC protocol with object-oriented features. The DCOM (Distributed COM) protocol made it possible to call COM components across the network and is used in COM+ applications. After some years in which Microsoft operating systems were a requirement to use DCOM, Microsoft opened the protocol for others with The Active Group. DCOM was made available for Unix, VMS, and IBM systems. DCOM was used heavily in the Microsoft environments, but the initiative to bring it to other systems was not really successful. Which IBM mainframe administrator would like to add some Microsoft technology to his system?

RMI

Sun took a different route with its Java technologies. In a pure Java world, the **RMI (Remote Method Invocation)** protocol can be used to call objects remotely. Sun added some bridges to the CORBA and COM world, but the major goal for Sun was to bring the masses to a Java-only solution.

SOAP

All the technologies that we have seen were used for application-to-application communication, but if you have a CORBA, a DCOM, and a RMI solution it is hard to get these different technologies to talk together. Another problem with these technologies is that their architectures are not designed for thousands of clients to achieve the scalability that's required for Internet solutions.

As a result, several companies, including Microsoft, and Userland Software, (www.userland.com) created **SOAP (Simple Object Access Protocol)** in 1999 as a completely new and novel way of invoking objects over the Internet, one that builds upon already accepted standard protocols. SOAP uses an XML based format to describe methods and parameters to make remote calls across the network. A SOAP server in the COM world could translate the SOAP messages to COM calls, whereas a SOAP Server in the CORBA world translates it to CORBA calls. Originally the SOAP definition made use of the HTTP protocol, so that SOAP calls could be done across the Internet.

With SOAP the term **web service** was born.

The W3C spec on SOAP 1.1 can be found at http://www.w3.org/TR/SOAP/.

Nowadays, in a broad sense, *every* application that supplies services through the web *is* a web service. It is not necessary that a web service uses the SOAP protocol as message format and the HTTP protocol to talk between client and server; other protocols may be used instead. With the SOAP specification 1.0 HTTP was a requirement, but version 1.1 was changed so that other transport protocols may be used. To use web services across the Internet though, SOAP and HTTP are the primary protocols. With .NET Remoting, it is possible to create web services that make use of a binary message format and a TCP connection.

In this chapter, the focus will be on web services that can be created with the Visual Studio .NET Project Wizard that itself makes use of .NET Remoting, SOAP, and HTTP behind the scenes.

Where to Use Web Services

To get another view of what web services are, we can distinguish between **user-to-application** communication and **application-to-application** communication.

Let us start with a **user-to-application communication** example, getting some weather information from the web. There are a large number of web sites like http://www.msnbc.com and http://www.weather.com that present the weather information in an easy to digest format for a human reader. So, these pages normally are read directly by a user.

If we wanted to create a rich client application to display the weather (**application-to-application communication**) our application would have to connect to the web site with a URL string containing the city for which we want to know the weather. We would then have to parse the resulting HTML message returned from the web site to get the temperatures and weather conditions, and then we can finally display this information in an appropriate format for the rich client application.

That is a lot of work, considering the fact that we just want to get some temperature readings for a particular city. And, what's more, the process of getting the data from the HTML is not trivial. This is because HTML data is designed to be displayed in the web browser and is not meant to be used by any other client-side business application. Consequently, the data is embedded in the text and is not easily extracted, and you would need to rewrite or adapt the client application to retrieve different data information (such as rainfall) from the same web page. By contrast, using a web browser, users can immediately pick out the data they need and can overlook what is not needed.

To get round the problem of processing HTML data, a web service provides a useful means for returning only the data we requested. Just call a method on the remote server, and get the information that we need, which can be used directly by the client application. At no point do we have to deal with the preformatted text that is meant for the user interface, because the web service presents the information in XML format, and tools already exist to process XML data. All it requires from the client application is to call some methods of the .NET Framework XML classes to get the required information. Better still though, if we are writing a client in C# for a .NET web service, we don't even need to write the code to do that – there are tools which will generate C# code for us!

The weather application we have talked about is one example where web services can be used, but there are a lot of other ones, too.

A Hotel Travel Agency Application Scenario

How do you book your holiday? Going to a travel agency that does all the work for you. Have you already booked your holiday on the Internet? With an airline's web site you can look for possible flights and book them. A web search engine can be used to look for a hotel in the required city. Maybe you are lucky and find a map to get to the hotel. When you find the hotel's home page, you navigate to the booking form page, whereupon you can go ahead and book the room. Next you would search out a car rental firm...

A lot of work you have today is finding the web sites with the help of search engines, and finding ways to navigate on these sites. Instead we could create a **Home Travel Agency Application** that uses web services containing details on hotels, airlines, car rental firms, etc. and present the client with a an easy to use interface to deal with all the holiday issues, including a not-to-be-forgotten early booking of a special musical event. Using your Pocket PC in the location of your holiday you can use the same web services to get a map for some walks, to get actual information about the programs in the cinemas, and so on.

A Book Distributor Application Scenario

Web services can also be useful for two companies that have some partnership. Let's say that a book distributor wants to give information about the books on stock to the bookshops. This could be implemented as a web service. An ASP.NET application using the web service can be created to offer this service directly to users. Another client application of this service is a Windows application for the bookshop, where first the local stock gets checked and then the stock of the distributor. The sales person can immediately answer delivery dates without having to check some different stocks in different applications.

Client Application Types

The client of a web service can be a rich Windows application created using Windows Forms, or an ASP.NET application using Web Forms. A Windows PC, a Unix system, or a Pocket PC can be used to consume (use) the web service. With the .NET Framework, web services can be consumed in every application type: Windows Forms, Web Forms, or console applications.

Application Architecture

What does an application using web services actually look like? Regardless if you develop ASP.NET or Windows applications, or applications for small devices, as you have seen in the presented application scenarios, web services is an important technology in all kind of applications.

The next figure shows a scenario of how web services can be used. Devices and browsers are connected through the Internet to an ASP.NET application developed with Web Forms. This ASP.NET application uses some local web services, and other remote web services that can be reached across the network: portal web services, application-specific web services, and building block web services. The following list should help to elaborate the meaning of these service types:

❑   **Portal web services** offer services from different companies with the same subject matter. This is an easy to use access point for multiple services.

❑   **Application-specific web services** are created just for the use of a single application.

❑   **Building block web services** are services that can easily be used within multiple applications.

The Windows application in this figure can use the web services directly without going through the ASP.NET application:

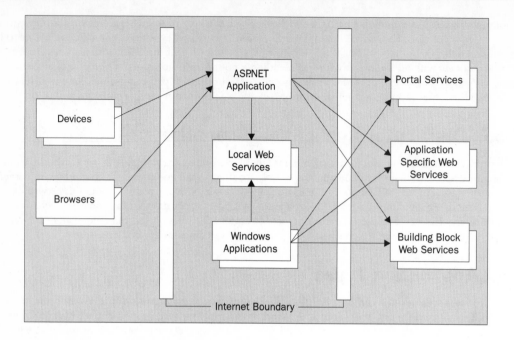

Web Services Architecture

If we want to use existing web services, we have to find one that meets our needs. If we know of a web service that fits, we have to get the information on how we can communicate with it. The following figure shows the important mechanisms for calling web services:

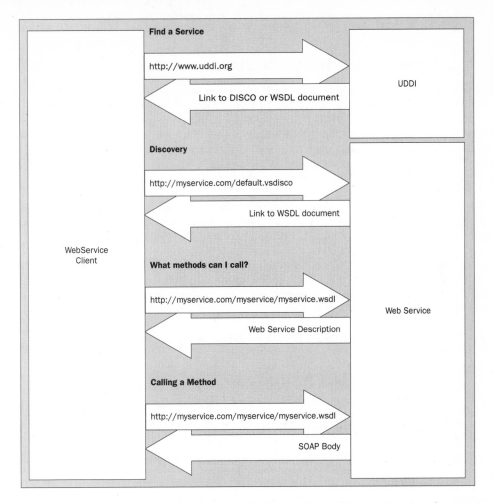

❑ We first find a web service that has already been registered in a registration directory service. This directory service returns binding information for the web service.

❑ The next sequence is called **discovery**. If we know the server which hosts the web services we can ask the server to get a description of the service. For this sequence the **discovery protocol** (**DISCO**) is used.

❑ The **description** of the service is presented in the **Web Services Description Language** (**WSDL**) format. The description describes what methods a service has, and what argument types can be passed. To use a service that doesn't support discovery and isn't registered in the UDDI directory, all we get is a WSDL document.

❑ With the description of the web service we know what methods can be called. The methods will be called using SOAP, so all the method calls including the arguments must be converted to the SOAP protocol.

Both SOAP and WSDL are defined with an XML grammar.

Let's look into the steps of the sequence in more detail.

Search Engine for Web Services

Maybe you can use a web service that is already supported by another company. In order to seek out and find pre-existing web services, Microsoft, IBM, and Ariba got together and initiated the www.uddi.org web site with the **UDDI (Universal Description, Discovery, and Integration)** service. UDDI is a platform-independent, open framework for describing services, discovering businesses, and integrating business services using the web as well as an operational registry. A company that wants to advertise its web service can register it here. With the UDDI business registry and the UDDI API, it is possible to programmatically locate information about web services.

After the initiation of UDDI by three companies, more than 220 companies now support the UDDI project. Among them are Boeing, BT, Compaq, DataChannel, Dell, Fujitsu, HP, Hitachi, KPMG Consulting, Merrill Lynch, Nortel Networks, Oracle, Rational, SAP, Sun Microsystems, VeriSign, and many more.

To find an existing web service, you can search by business name and after a successful search of a service, you get the description of the web service, any information on the classification of the web service, that is the groups it belongs to, and binding information – included in a discovery (DISCO) file and maybe also a WSDL document.

In Visual Studio .NET we can search in Microsoft's UDDI Site by going to Project | Add Web Reference:

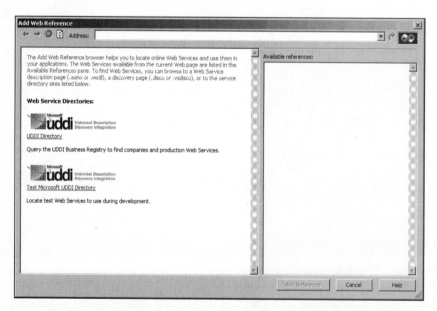

As you can see in the screenshot, beside the Microsoft UDDI Directory there is also a Test Microsoft UDDI Directory. During development-time you can register your service in the test directory, the other directory should only be used for production-stable, active services.

Selecting the Microsoft **UDDI Directory** link, we can specify search strings to find a registered web service. If the result of the search has binding information, a reference to the web service can be added with the **Add Reference** button.

Entering the string **Continental** lists two web services from Continental Airlines as can be seen in the next screenshot:

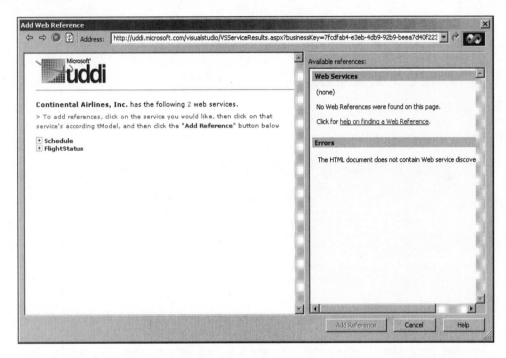

You can find a lot of web services at these pages: www.xmethods.net and www.gotdotnet.com.

Web Services Discovery

As soon as you know the server that supports web services, the **discovery** process can be used to get information about the web services for that server. The web server uses a file with the extension `vsdisco` to return information about web services.

The `vsdisco` file defines the rules that govern how the server finds web services. Such a file defines either that the services should be found dynamically with the exclusion of some directories, or statically in the way that some directories to search are specified.

Requesting the file `default.vsdisco` with the browser, the links to other `vsdisco` files are returned with the `discoveryRef` element. One of the `<discoveryRef>` elements shows the reference to http://localhost/WebServiceSample/WebServiceSample.vsdisco. I am using this link to get more information about this service:

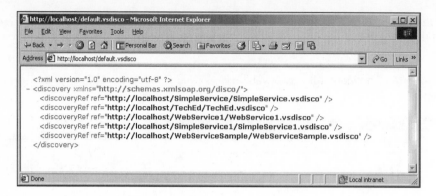

Entering the address http://localhost/WebServiceSample/WebServiceSample.vsdisco in the address box of the browser returns a link to the WSDL information of the service with the `<contractRef>` element: http://localhost/WebServiceSample/Service1.asmx?wsdl:

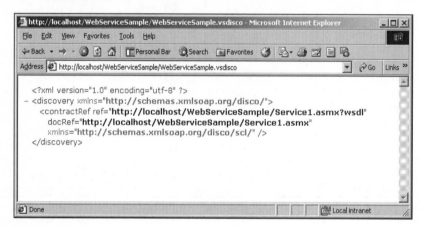

What Methods Can I Call?

A Web Services Description Language (WSDL) document has the information about what methods a web service supports and how they can be called, parameter types passed to the service, and parameter types returned from the service.

Using the link we get from the discovery process with the `<contractRef>` element we can have a look at the WSDL document in the browser:

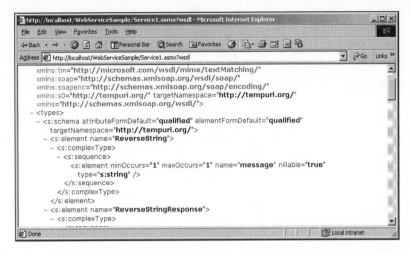

It is not necessary for us to deal with this information directly. The WSDL document will be generated dynamically with the WebMethod attribute; we will have a look at this attribute later on in this chapter. On the client side, adding the web reference using Visual Studio .NET not only gets the discovery information about what web services a server supports, but also requests a WSDL document. This WSDL document in turn is used to create a client proxy with the same methods and arguments. With this proxy, the client application has the advantage that it only needs to call the methods as they are implemented in the server, because the proxy converts them to SOAP calls to make the call across the network.

The WSDL specification is maintained by the World Wide Web Consortium (W3C). You can read the specification at the W3C Web site **www.w3.org/TR/wsdl**.

Calling a Method

To call a method on a web service the call must be converted to the SOAP message as it is defined in the WSDL document. The SOAP specification defines how method names and arguments can be passed.

A SOAP message is the basic unit of communication between a client and a server. The following figure demonstrates the parts of a SOAP message. A SOAP message includes a SOAP envelope, which, as you might guess, wraps all the SOAP information in a single block. The SOAP envelope itself consists of two parts: a SOAP header and a SOAP body. The optional header defines how the client and server should process the body. The mandatory SOAP body includes blocks of the methods that are called. In the SOAP body the client sends, along with the method call itself, the serialized values of all the method arguments. The SOAP server sends back the return values in the SOAP body of the SOAP message that is sent back:

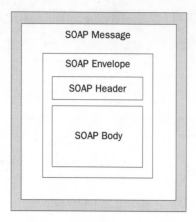

In the following example you see what a SOAP message that is sent from the client to the server looks like. The client calls the web service method `ReverseString()`. The string `Hello World!` is passed as an argument to this method. You can see that the method call is inside the SOAP body, it is within the XML element `<soap:Body>`. The body itself is contained within the envelope `<soap:Envelope>`. Before the start of the SOAP message, you can see the HTTP header, because the SOAP message is sent with a HTTP POST request.

It is not necessary that we have to create such a message, as this is done by the client proxy:

```
POST /WebServiceSample/Service1.asmx HTTP/1.1
Host: localhost
Content-Type: text/xml; charset=utf-8
Content-Length: 508
SOAPAction: "http://www.wrox.com/webservice/ReverseString"

<?xml version="1.0" encoding="utf-8"?>
<soap:Envelope xmlns:xsi="http://www.w3.org/2001/XMLSchema-instance"
xmlns:xsd="http://www.w3.org/2001/XMLSchema"
xmlns:soap="http://schemas.xmlsoap.org/soap/envelope/">
  <soap:Body>
    <ReverseString xmlns="http://www.wrox.com/webservice">
      <message>Hello World!</message>
    </ReverseString>
  </soap:Body>
</soap:Envelope>
```

The server answers with a SOAP message with the result `!dlroW olleH` in the response of the call as can be seen with the `ReverseStringResult` XML element:

```
HTTP/1.1 200 OK
Content-Type: text/xml; charset=utf-8
Content-Length: 446

<?xml version="1.0" encoding="utf-8"?>
<soap:Envelope xmlns:xsi="http://www.w3.org/2001/XMLSchema-instance"
xmlns:xsd="http://www.w3.org/2001/XMLSchema"
xmlns:soap="http://schemas.xmlsoap.org/soap/envelope/">
  <soap:Body>
```

```
    <ReverseStringResponse xmlns="http://www.wrox.com/webservice">
      <ReverseStringResult>!dlroW olleH</ReverseStringResult>
    </ReverseStringResponse>
  </soap:Body>
</soap:Envelope>
```

The SOAP specification is maintained by the XML Protocol Working Group of the W3C (see www.w3.org/TR/soap and www.w3.org/TR/2001/WD-soap12-20010709 for version 1.2).

SOAP and Firewalls

System administrators often ask if the SOAP protocol breaks the security boundaries of the firewalls, or in other words, does SOAP violate the concept of firewalls? In reality there are no more security issues to consider than for normal web servers. With normal web servers the system administrator of the firewall opens the HTTP port 80 to allow the server to communicate with the outside world. Users on the Internet can have direct access to these servers even though they sit behind the firewall. A user can request an HTML file with an HTTP request and the server returns either a static page, or a page created on the fly using ASP or CGI scripts. Web services are just another type of server-side application that communicates using HTTP, though instead of receiving simple HTTP GET or POST requests, it receives an HTTP POST request containing an embedded SOAP message, and instead of returning HTML, it returns an HTTP response containing the SOAP response message. As far as the firewall is concerned, the communication is through HTTP and hence it will allow it through port 80.

However, if this web service does not behave as it should, such as leaking confidential data or breaking the server, then we do have a problem, but such problems are common to all server-side applications whether they be traditional web pages, server-side business objects or web services.

If the system administrator of the firewall is still worried about the security implications of web services, they can use an application filter to not allow SOAP calls with an HTTP request.

Web Services and the .NET Framework

With the .NET Framework, it is easy to create and consume web services. The four major namespaces that deal with web services are listed as follows:

- ❑ The classes in the namespace System.Web.Services are used to create web services

- ❑ With the namespace System.Web.Services.Description, we can describe web services via WSDL

- ❑ To discover web services with the DISCO protocol, classes from the namespace System.Web.Services.Discovery are used

- ❑ With System.Web.Services.Protocols we can create SOAP requests and responses

   In this book we will not cover the use of the System.Web.Services.Description and the System.Web.Services.Discovery namespaces. Indeed, we shall only touch on the other two namespaces in this chapter. More information can be found in the Wrox book ASP.NET Programmer's Reference (ISBN 1-86100-530-X).

Creating a Web Service

For the implementation of a web service, we can derive the web service class from `System.Web.Services.WebService`. The `WebService` class provides access to ASP.NET `Application` and `Session` objects:

WebService Property	Description
Application	Gets an `HttpApplicationState` object for the current request.
Context	Gets an `HttpContext` object that encapsulates HTTP specific information. With this context the HTTP header information can be read.
Server	Gets an `HttpServerUtility` object. This class has some helper methods to do URL encoding and decoding.
Session	Gets an `HttpSessionState` object to store some state for the client.
User	Gets a user object implementing the `IPrincipal` interface. With this interface we can get the name of the user and the authentication type.

WebService Attribute

The sub class of `WebService` should be marked with the `WebService` attribute. The class `WebServiceAttribute` has the following properties:

Property	Description
Description	A description of the service that will be used in the WSDL document.
Name	Gets or sets the name of the web service.
Namespace	Gets or sets the XML namespace for the web service. The default value is http://tempuri.org, which is OK for testing, but before you make the service public you should change the namespace.

We covered attributes in Chapter 22. Here you can see attributes in action once more.

WebMethod Attribute

All methods available from the web service must be marked with the `WebMethod` attribute. Of course the service can have other methods that are not marked using `WebMethod`. Such methods can be called from the `WebMethods`, but they cannot be called from the client. With the attribute class `WebMethodAttribute`, the method will be callable from remote clients, and we can define if the response is buffered, how long the cache should be valid, and if the session state should be stored with named parameters. The following table lists the properties of the `WebMethodAttribute` class:

Property	Description
BufferResponse	Gets or sets a flag if the response should be buffered. The default is true. With a buffered response only the finished package is sent to the client.
CacheDuration	With this property you can set the length of time that the result should be cached. If the same request is done a second time, only the cached value will be returned if the request is made during the period set by this property. The default value is 0; which means that the result will not be cached.
Description	The description is used for the generation of service help pages for prospective consumers.
EnableSession	A Boolean value, indicating if the session state is valid. The default is false, so that the Session property of the WebService class cannot be used for storing session state.
MessageName	By default the name of the message is set to the name of the method.
TransactionOption	This property indicates the transaction support for the method. The default value is Disabled.

Client

To call a method, the client has to create an HTTP connection to the server of the web service, and send an HTTP request to pass a SOAP message. The method call must be converted to a SOAP message. All this is done by the client proxy. The implementation of the client proxy is in the SoapHttpClientProtocol class.

SoapHttpClientProtocol

The class System.Web.Services.Protocols.SoapHttpClientProtocol is the base class for the client proxy. The Invoke() method converts the arguments to build a SOAP message that is sent to the web service. Which web service gets called is defined with the Url property.

The SoapHttpClientProtocol class also supports asynchronous calls with the BeginInvoke() and EndInvoke() methods.

Alternative Client Protocols

Instead of using the SoapHttpClientProtocol class, other proxy classes can be used, too. HttpGetClientProtocol and HttpPostClientProtocol just do a simple HTTP GET or HTTP POST request without the overhead of a SOAP call.

The HttpGetClientProtocol and HttpPostClientProtocol classes can be used if your solution uses .NET on the client and the server. If you want to support different technologies you have to use the SOAP protocol.

833

Compare the HTTP POST request below with the SOAP call we have seen earlier in this chapter:

```
POST /WebServiceSample/Service1.asmx/ReverseString HTTP/1.1
Host: localhost
Content-Type: application/x-www-form-urlencoded
Content-Length: length

message=string
```

The HTTP GET request is even shorter. The disadvantage of the GET request is that the size of the parameters sent is limited. If the size goes beyond 1k you should consider using POST:

```
GET /WebServiceSample/Service1.asmx/ReverseString?message=string HTTP/1.1
Host: localhost
```

With the `HttpGetClientProtocol` and the `HttpPostClientProtocol` the overhead compared to SOAP methods is smaller; the disadvantage here is that there is no support from web services on other platforms.

Creating a Simple ASP.NET Web Service

Let's create a simple web service with Visual Studio .NET.

Try it Out – Creating a Web Service Project

1. Create a new project with File | New | Project..., choose the ASP.NET Web Service template as shown here, name the project WebServiceSample, and hit OK:

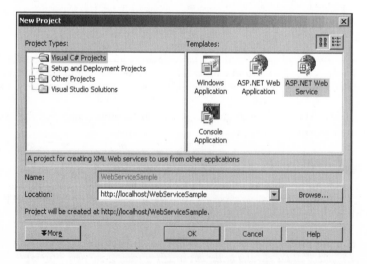

Generated Files

The files generated by the wizard are listed here:

- ❑ AssemblyInfo.cs – Used to supply the assembly attributes, as we know from all other project types.

- ❑ Global.asax – Application and session begin and end requests, the same as in Web Forms applications we have seen in the last chapter.

- ❑ Service1.asmx – Holds our web service class. All ASP.NET web services are identified with the .asmx extension. The file that has the source code is Service1.asmx.cs, as the code-behind feature is used with Visual Studio .NET. However this file is, by default, not visible in Solution Explorer and to get to it, you click the **Show All Files** button in the **Solution Explorer**'s toolbar.

  The wizard generates a class Service1 that derives from System.Web.Services.WebService. In the Service1.asmx.cs file, you can also see some sample code showing how a method for a web service should be coded – it should be public, and marked with the WebMethod attribute:

```
using System;
using System.Collections;
using System.ComponentModel;
using System.Data;
using System.Diagnostics;
using System.Web;
using System.Web.Services;

namespace WebServiceSample
{
  /// <summary>
  /// Summary description for Service1.
  /// </summary>
  public class Service1 : System.Web.Services.WebService
  {
    public Service1()
    {
      //CODEGEN: This call is required by the ASP.NET Web Services Designer
      InitializeComponent();
    }

    #region Component Designer generated code

    //Required by the Web Services Designer
    private IContainer components = null;

    /// <summary>
    /// Required method for Designer support - do not modify
    /// the contents of this method with the code editor.
    /// </summary>
    private void InitializeComponent()
```

```
        {
        }

        /// <summary>
        /// Clean up any resources being used.
        /// </summary>
        protected override void Dispose( bool disposing )
        {
          if(disposing && components != null)
          {
            components.Dispose();
          }
          base.Dispose(disposing);
        }

        #endregion

        // WEB SERVICE EXAMPLE
        // The HelloWorld() example service returns the string Hello World
        // To build, uncomment the following lines then save and build the project
        // To test this web service, press F5

//      [WebMethod]
//      public string HelloWorld()
//      {
//        return "Hello World";
//      }
    }
}
```

❑   Web.config is the configuration file for this application. In this file, we can configure
    tracing, session state, and debug mode.

❑   WebServiceSample.vsdisco is the discovery file for this application. The XML element
    <dynamicDiscovery> means that a search should happen for the web services in all
    directories, except the ones excluded with the <exclude> element:

```
<?xml version="1.0" encoding="utf-8" ?>
<dynamicDiscovery xmlns="urn:schemas-dynamicdiscovery:disco.2000-03-17">
<exclude path="_vti_cnf" />
<exclude path="_vti_pvt" />
<exclude path="_vti_log" />
<exclude path="_vti_script" />
<exclude path="_vti_txt" />
<exclude path="Web References" />
</dynamicDiscovery>
```

Adding a Web Method

The next thing we should do is add a method to our web service. We will add a simple method
ReverseString() that receives a string, and returns the reversed string to the client.

1. Add the following code to the file `Service1.asmx.cs`:

```
[WebMethod]
public string ReverseString(string message)
{
  char[] arr = message.ToCharArray();
  Array.Reverse(arr);
  message = new string(arr);

  return message;
}
```

To uniquely identify the XML elements in the generated description of the web service a namespace should be added. Add the `WebService` attribute with the namespace `http://www.wrox.com/webservices` to the class `Service1`. Of course, you can use any other string that uniquely identifies the XML elements. You can use the URL link to your company's page. It is not necessary that the web link really exists; it is just used for unique identification. If you use a namespace based on your company's web address, you can almost guarantee that no other company is using the very same namespace.

If you don't enter a namespace the default namespace used is `http://tempuri.org`. For learning purposes, this default namespace is good enough, but you shouldn't deploy a production web service using it.

2. So, modify the example code as follows:

```
[WebService(Namespace="http://www.wrox.com/webservices")]
public class Service1 : System.Web.Services.WebService
{
```

3. Now compile the project.

Testing the Web Service

Now we can test our service. Opening the file `Service1.asmx` in the browser (you can start it from within Visual Studio .NET by going to **Debug | Start Without Debugging**) lists all methods of the service as can be seen in the following picture. In our service the only method is `ReverseString()`:

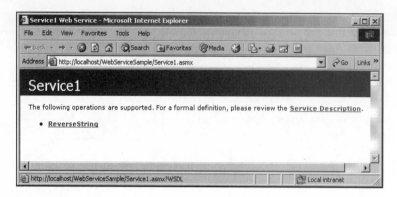

Choosing the link to the ReverseString method, we get a dialog to test the web service. The test dialog has edit fields for every parameter we can pass with this method; in our case it is only a single parameter.

In this page, we also get information on what the SOAP calls from the client and the responses from the server will look like. There is an example with SOAP, HTTP GET and HTTP POST:

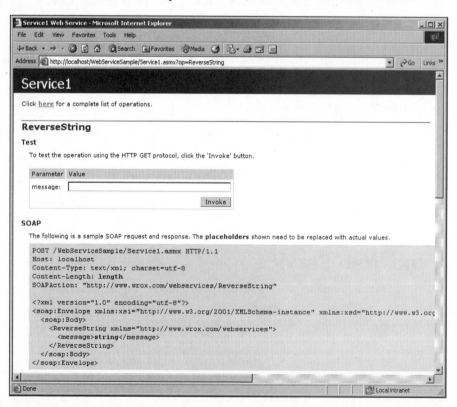

Pressing the Invoke button after entering the string Hello web services! into the text box, we receive this result from the server:

The result is of type `string`, and, as expected, it is the reverse of the entered string.

Implementing a Windows Client

The test is working, but we want to create a Windows client that uses the web service. The client must create a SOAP message that will be sent across an HTTP channel. It is not necessary to make this message ourselves. The `System.Web.Services.Protocols.SoapHttpClientProtocol` class does all the work behind the scenes.

Try it Out – Creating a Client Windows Application

1. Create a new C# Windows Application, call it SimpleClient and on the form, add two text boxes and a button. We will use the button's `Click` handler to invoke the web service:

2. Add a web reference using the **Project | Add Web Reference...** menu and enter the URL of the web service we have just generated, http://localhost/WebServiceSample/Service1.asmx. Then, you can view the contract and documentation, if they exist that is, before pressing the **Add Reference** button:

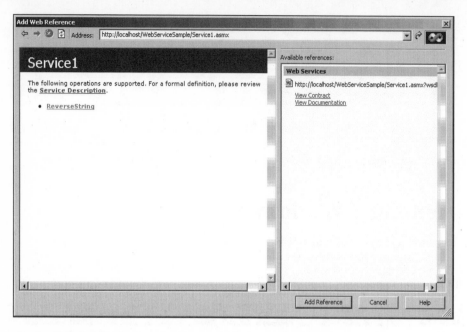

In the Solution Explorer you can now see a new Web Reference to localhost with the corresponding DISCO and WSDL documents that were sent to the client:

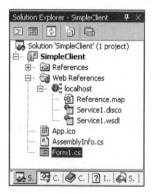

What cannot be seen in the Solution Explorer is that a new class was created which implements the client proxy that converts method calls to the SOAP format. To see this class, we have to switch to the Class View window. A new namespace with the name of the server, in our case `localhost`, was created. The `Service1` class derives from `System.Web.Services.Protocols.SoapHttpClientProtocol`, and implements the method of the web service, `ReverseString()`:

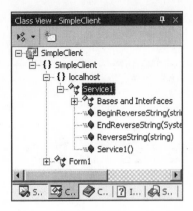

Double-click on the `ReverseString()` method to open the auto-generated `service1.cs` file. Let's look into this wizard-generated code.

The `Service1` class derives from the `SoapHttpClientProtocol` class. This base class creates a SOAP message in the `Invoke()` method. The `WebServiceBindingAttribute` attribute sets binding values to the web service:

```
[System.Web.Services.WebServiceBindingAttribute(Name="Service1Soap",
  Namespace="http://www.wrox.com/webservices")]
public class Service1 :
  System.Web.Services.Protocols.SoapHttpClientProtocol {
```

In the constructor, the `Url` property is set to the web service. This property will be used from the `SoapHttpClientProtocol` class to request a service:

```
public Service1() {
    this.Url = "http://localhost/WebServiceSample/Service1.asmx";
}
```

The most important method is the method that the web service supplies: `ReverseString()`. The method here has the same parameter as we implemented on the server. The implementation of the client-side version of `ReverseString()` calls the `Invoke()` method of the base class `SoapHttpClientProtocol`. `Invoke()` creates a SOAP message using the method name `ReverseString` and the parameter `message`:

```
[System.Web.Services.Protocols.SoapDocumentMethodAttribute(
  "http://www.wrox.com/webservices/ReverseString",
  RequestNamespace="http://www.wrox.com/webservices",
  ResponseNamespace="http://www.wrox.com/webservices",
  Use=System.Web.Services.Description.SoapBindingUse.Literal,
  ParameterStyle
    =System.Web.Services.Protocols.SoapParameterStyle.Wrapped)]
public string ReverseString(string message) {
    object[] results = this.Invoke("ReverseString", new object[]
                        { message});
    return ((string)(results[0]));
}
```

The client may also call the web service asynchronously. The method `BeginReverseString()` only has the parameters that are sent to the server, and `EndReverseString()` returns the result:

```
public System.IAsyncResult BeginReverseString(string message,
   System.AsyncCallback callback, object asyncState) {
      return this.BeginInvoke("ReverseString", new object[] {
                  message}, callback, asyncState);
}

public string EndReverseString(System.IAsyncResult asyncResult) {
      object[] results = this.EndInvoke(asyncResult);
      return ((string)(results[0]));
}
```

Until now we have not written a single line of code ourselves for the client. We have designed a small user interface, and used the **Add Web Reference** menu to create a proxy class. Now we just have to create the link between the two.

3. Add a `Click` event handler to the button and add these two lines of code:

```
private void button1_Click(object sender, System.EventArgs e)
{
   localhost.Service1 ws = new localhost.Service1();
   textBox2.Text = ws.ReverseString(textBox1.Text);
}
```

How It Works

With this line, we create a new instance of the proxy class. As we have seen in the implementation of the constructor the `Url` property is set to the web service:

```
localhost.Service1 ws = new localhost.Service1();
```

By calling the `ReverseString()` method of the proxy class, a SOAP message is sent to the server, and so, the web service gets called:

```
textBox2.Text = ws.ReverseString(textBox1.Text);
```

Running the program gives us output like this:

Implementing an ASP.NET Client

The same service now can be used from an ASP.NET Client application. Referencing the web service can be done the same way as with the Windows application.

Try it Out – Creating an ASP.NET Client Application

1. Create a new C# ASP.NET Web Application, call it ASPNETClient, and add two text boxes and a button to the web form, as seen below:

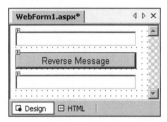

2. Add a web reference to http://localhost/webservicesample/service1.asmx in the same way as we did with the Windows application.

3. With the Web reference added, again, a client proxy class was generated. Add a click handler to the button and write the following lines of code to this handler:

```csharp
private void Button1_Click(object sender, System.EventArgs e)
{
    ASPNETClient.localhost.Service1 ws =
        new ASPNETClient.localhost.Service1();
    TextBox2.Text = ws.ReverseString(TextBox1.Text);
}
```

4. Now build the project and with **Debug | Start**, you can start the browser and enter a test message in the first text box. Pressing the button, the web service gets invoked, and you will get the reversed message returned in the second text box:

As you have just seen, using web services is as easy in web applications as it is in Windows applications!

Summary

In this chapter, we have seen what web services are, and briefly looked at the protocols that are used with them. To locate and run web services, we have to carry out some or all of the following:

- **Directory** – Find a web service by UDDI
- **Discovery** – Discover web services from a well-known server
- **Description** – WSDL describes the methods and arguments
- **Calling** – Platform-independent method calls are done with the SOAP protocol.

We have seen how easy it is to create web services with Visual Studio .NET, where the `WebService` class is used to define some methods with the `WebMethod` attribute. Creating the client that consumes web services is as easy as creating web services – adding a web reference to the client project and using the proxy. The heart of the client is the `SoapHttpClientProtocol` class that converts the method call to a SOAP message.

Setting the PATH Environment Variable

In order to use the C# compiler and other .NET tools from the Windows command line, we need to ensure that the PATH environment variable has been updated. The command prompt looks for files within the current directory; if we want to run a file in another directory, we need to supply information about where Windows can find that file. We do this by setting the PATH environment variable. The PATH variable contains a list of directory names, separated by semi-colons, where Windows will look if it can't find a requested file in the current directory. There are two folders we need to add to this to ensure that Windows can find all the .NET tools: C:\Program Files\Microsoft.Net\FrameworkSDK\Bin, which contains a number of .NET command-line tools, such as Ildasm, Gacutil, and sn. The second is the C:\WINNT\Microsoft.NET\Framework\v1.0.3705 folder (the number in the last sub-directory name may vary, depending on what version of the .NET Framework you have installed). This is where the C# compiler itself (csc), and the System class libraries reside.

Windows 2000/XP

To set the PATH variable on a Windows 2000 or XP machine, open up the **System** applet from the Control Panel, and click on the **Advanced** tab:

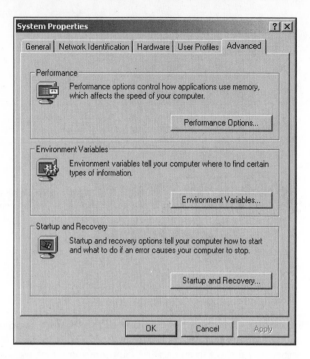

On the **Advanced** tab, click on the **Environment Variables...** button, and scroll down the **System variables** listbox until you find the **Path** variable:

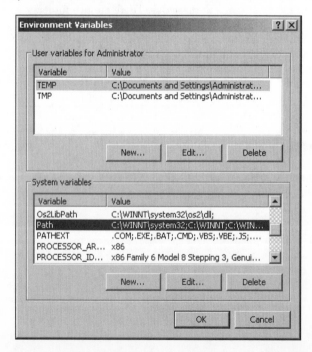

Select this, and click on the Edit... button below the listbox:

In the Variable Value box, add the full paths to the directories you want to include in the PATH variable at the end. The PATH variable is a semicolon-delimited list, so you'll need to add a semi-colon before the first path, and between the two paths. For example, with the current version of the .NET Framework, we need to add the following text to the end of the string:

```
;C:\Program Files\Microsoft.Net\FrameworkSDK\Bin;C:\WINNT\
Microsoft.NET\Framework\v1.0.3705
```

Click on OK to close the Edit System Variable dialog, then twice more to close the Environment Variables and System Properties dialogs. The PATH variable has now been updated. If you already have a command window open, you will need to re-open it, as the new value won't be available to existing windows.

Windows NT

There are a few slight differences in the procedure for setting environment variables under Windows NT4. Open up the System applet from the Control Panel as with Windows 2000, and then click on the Environment tab:

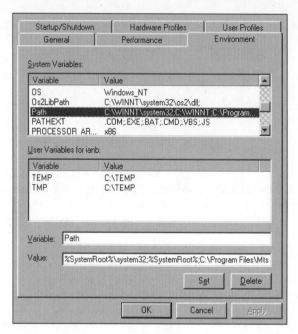

Select the Path variable from the System Variables list box. The current value of this variable will now appear in the Value list box; add the .NET Framework paths to the end of this value as with Windows 2000 (again separated by semi-colons). Click on Set to update the value, and on OK to accept the new value. This value will now be available to any new command windows that you open.

Windows 95/98/ME

If you're running Windows 9x or Windows ME, you need to update the `autoexec.bat` text file to set the PATH variable. This text file contains information used to configure Windows as it starts up, and resides in the root directory of your hard drive (for example, `C:\autoexec.bat`). Open up this file in Notepad or another text editor, and add the line:

```
SET PATH=%PATH%;C:\Windows\Microsoft.NET\Framework\v1.0.3705
```

Again, adjust the path if necessary according to your system and the version of the .NET Framework. This will add the path to the existing PATH variable. Note that not all tools will be installed with the .NET Framework on machines running Windows 9x or ME. Finally, restart Windows for the change to take effect.

Starting the Command Line from any Directory

If you're going to be doing any amount of work from the command-line, continually typing the name of the directory you wish to work from can become quite tiresome. To help you with this, here is a quick tip that allows you to select a folder in Windows Explorer, and then open a command-line prompt starting in that particular folder.

In Windows Explorer, choose Tools | Folder Options, and select the File Types tab. Scroll down to the find the file types with Extensions N/A (pressing *N* will take you there quicker), and select the Folder File Type, as shown in the screenshot below:

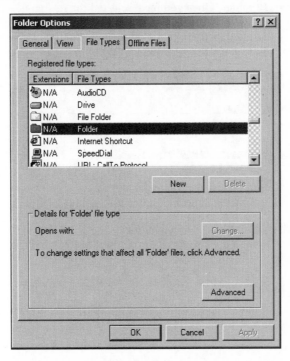

Click on Advanced, and this brings you to the Edit File Type dialog. From here you can set the actions for a particular file type – in this case, we can set the actions that are displayed in the context menu in Windows Explorer when you right-click on a folder:

Click on New..., and you will be brought to the following dialog. Enter a name for our action (I've chosen Command Line), and then select the application that will actually carry out our action by clicking the Browse button and navigating to the command-line program. This is the file CMD.EXE in the <WINDOWS>\System32 folder. Once you have selected the file, enclose the name in double quotes (as seen in the screenshot below), and then add %1 to the end of the line. This specifies that the file you right-click on in Windows Explorer will be passed to the application as a parameter, and this is the little piece of magic that starts the command-line prompt from our chosen folder.

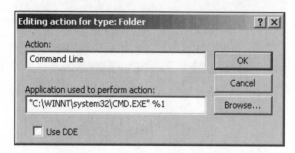

Click OK to close this dialog, then click OK again to close the Edit File Type dialog, and then once you click OK on the File Types tab of the Folder Options dialog you're ready to go!

Installing MSDE

In this appendix, we're going to provide instructions on how to start the MSDE service and set up the sample databases, including the Northwind database that we use extensively in Chapters 18 and 19.

First of all, you should have chosen to install MSDE when you initially installed Visual Studio .NET, or Visual C# Standard Edition.

To setup MSDE, follow these steps:

1. From your Start menu, select Microsoft .NET Framework SDK | Samples and QuickStart Tutorials.

2. Read the instructions on the page that opens, then click Install the .NET Samples Database, and then select Open when prompted from the save or open file dialog.

3. To start the MSDE service, open a command-line prompt (click Start | Run and type cmd). From the command-line type:

```
>net start MSSQL$NetSDK
```

4. The following messages should be displayed:

```
The MSSQL$NetSDK service is starting.
The MSSQL$NetSDK service was started successfully.
```

5. Now the service is started, we can set up the sample databases by returning to the Samples and QuickStart Tutorials page, and clicking the Setup the QuickStarts link. On the dialog that appears, select Open, and the sample SQL Server databases that ship with MSDE (including two extras called IPortal and GrocerToGo) will be created and populated.

Further References

We've covered a lot of ground in this book, but C# and the .NET Framework are topics of monstrous size. There will be times when working with C# and Visual Studio .NET that you will become stuck, and this book has not been able to cover that scenario, or maybe you want to develop your skills further, and learn more about C# and the .NET Framework. Where do you turn to for help? There are many resources around to help you solve your problems when this book can't, and this appendix will point you in the direction of some of those resources, both online and in book form.

.NET Framework SDK Documentation

Available as an option to install with Visual Studio .NET and Visual C# .NET Standard Edition, the .NET Framework SDK documentation contains a vast amount of information, covering almost every aspect of the .NET Framework. Of particular interest and use is the comprehensive class library reference, which has details of almost all the methods, properties, etc. of the classes of the .NET Framework, even including some examples of their use.

Let's take a look at using the documentation – you can find it on your Start menu under Programs | Microsoft .NET Framework SDK | Documentation. You will find a layout similar to that of Visual Studio .NET:

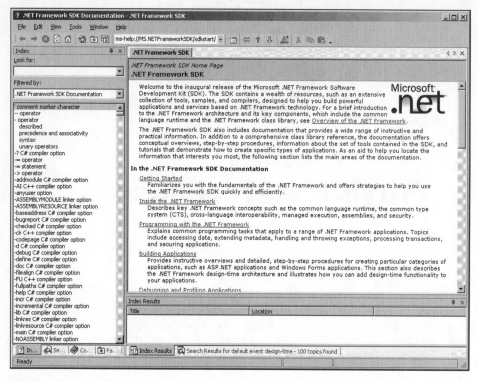

The above screenshot shows the **Index** view – the **Index Results** tab at the bottom right-hand corner shows the results of your searches. Browsing the documentation is quite straightforward, but there is an enormous amount of information available and it is quite easy to get lost, or return more information than you actually are after.

Let's have a look first at the class library reference. From the **View** menu, select **Navigation | Contents** (or press *Alt + Ctrl + F1*), and expand the **.NET Framework SDK** node to see the following pane:

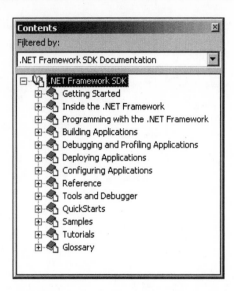

As you can see, there is much available from here, including such things as the **Glossary**, which provides an A-to-Z guide to most of the terms you will encounter when working with the .NET Framework, and their meaning. The **Reference** node is the one of interest to us here, so expand that node, and you will see the following categories:

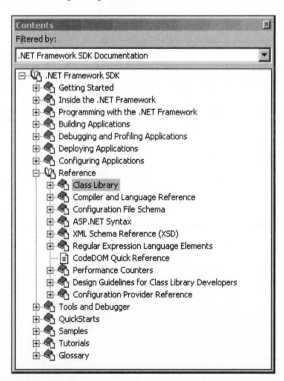

Expand the **Class Library** node, and a list of the namespaces of classes in the .NET Framework class library will appear – the screenshot below shows the **System.Data** namespace expanded, and some classes within that namespace expanded.

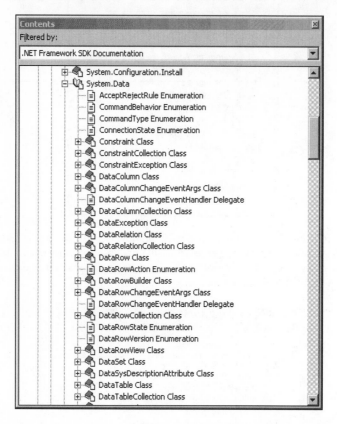

When you select an item from the pane, an overview of that item will appear in the right-hand window. Select **DataSet Class**, and information about the DataSet will appear in the right-hand window, including some remarks about the class, describing its main objects and purpose:

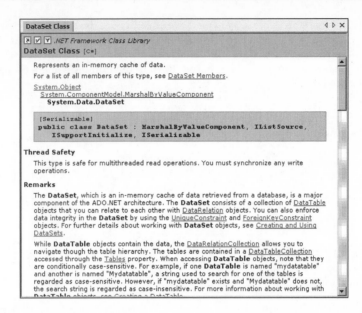

You can see links to other objects pertaining to the DataSet, and at the top of the window is the link to see all the DataSet Members. Click this link, and you will be taken to one of the C# developer's most hallowed areas – the list of the methods, properties, and events of the class:

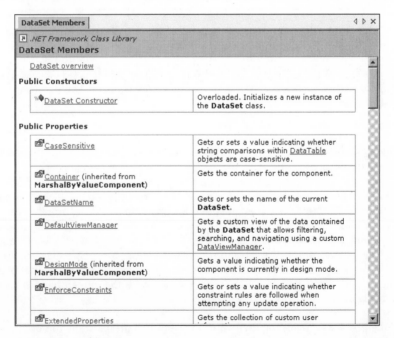

This list contains almost all the information you'd ever need about the specifics of particular objects in the .NET Framework, but this information is sometimes quite limited and occasionally cryptic. The page that displays the members of a class will soon become one of your first stops when you begin working on new C# programming activities. Scroll down to the find the **Tables** property of the **DataSet**, and click the link:

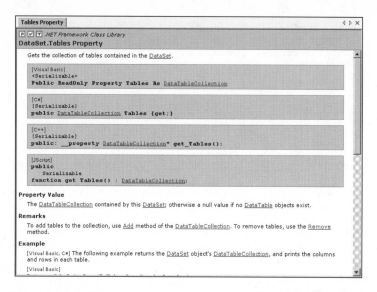

This screenshot shows how the information is structured – you have the name of the object in the header at the top of the window, and then a quick description of it below.

Underneath that you have the definition of the object, in different languages (Visual Basic .NET, C#, Visual C++.NET, and JScript .NET). The C# definition of the **DataSet.Tables** property is:

```
public DataTableCollection Tables {get;}
```

If we were looking at a method, then we would see the method signature(s) here, or if we were looking at a class we'd see the class definition.

Following that is a **Remarks** section, which contains a brief remark about the usage of the object, or some caveat to its use. Underneath that is (possibly) an **Example** of its use, usually in several languages, but often not a particularly detailed example, but useful if you're looking for a basic example to see syntax just to get you started. Below that (not shown on the screenshot above) is a **Requirements** section, which lists the system requirements to support this class, and a **See Also** section, which includes links to related topics or objects. If you start to follow these links to move between topics and find yourself getting lost, then you can always click the back arrow at the top-left hand corner of the application to navigate to your previously viewed page.

If you look at the previous screenshot, then you can see three buttons at the top of the window – clicking the first displays the **See Also** links, the second displays the **Requirements**, and the third button is the **Language Filter**:

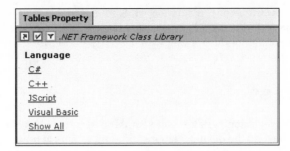

Selecting one of the languages here will ensure that information about an object is displayed only in the language you have chosen – thus you will only see the one class definition or method signature, and the only example shown will be in your chosen language (if one exists at all).

You can also search the documentation index; from the View menu, select Navigation | Index, and the index is displayed in its own pane. The displayed index automatically updates as you start typing in the Look for textbox:

Here I'm looking for some information about default events – you may remember that in Chapter 13 we mentioned that each control has a default event, and when you double-click on that control in Visual Studio .NET the event-handler is automatically generated for that particular event. This leads to the question of how does Visual Studio .NET know which is the default event? Starting to type "defaultevent" into the Index reveals a DefaultEventAttribute, and looking at the about DefaultEventAttribute class page reveals that this attribute (we looked at these in Chapter 22) specifies the default event for that particular class – so that's how Visual Studio .NET knows!

You will also find that items are indexed under a variety of different expressions, so, for example, you can look up the System.Windows.Forms.Control.DataGrid.HitTestInfo class, but you can also find it under HitTestInfo.

Spend some time playing with the documentation – it is something you will be using on a very regular basis when programming with the .NET Framework – there are very few people who do not regard the documentation as an essential tool for working with the .NET Framework.

Online Resources

As you develop your C# programming skills, and your thirst for more C# knowledge increases, you will find that you need to go beyond the documentation, and want to look at other people's already developed applications to learn more about building your own, or you may have a question to which you don't know the answer, and you want to contact other C# programmers to see if they know the answer.

To help with the first situation, *C# Today* is the place for you.

C# Today

C# Today at www.csharptoday.com, is a subscription site that offers you weekly in-depth case studies written by leading professionals, giving you solutions and insight into real-world problems that are relevant to your career. In addition to this, there is an archive of over 170 articles covering a vast range of topics on the C# language and using it to program the .NET Framework.

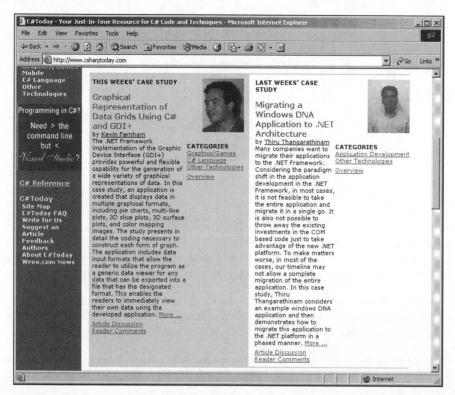

Although a subscription site, you are welcome to visit the site and view an abridged form of the weekly case study for free. These case studies are the ideal way to enhance your knowledge of application development, and see real-world code in action, and clearly explained.

If you have questions that you want answered, then you can post your question to a mailing list, opening it up to a much wider community of developers than you would otherwise have access to. A good place to start is the beginning_csharp list at http://p2p.wrox.com.

P2P Lists

The P2P lists were described in the introduction to the book. Of particular interest is the beginning_csharp list, at http://p2p.wrox.com/list.asp?list=beginning_c_sharp, not just because it is where you register to obtain the answers to the exercises from the book, but also because it is a list dedicated to this book. It contains questions asked (and answered) mainly by readers of this book, so when you post your question, the response isn't likely to be a suggestion to code your method directly in IL, or that your question is too trivial to answer, but a response from someone who's probably been having the same problems that you've had, and has learned the answer and can now help you.

If you're looking for a community of other C# programmers like yourself, this is the place to start.

Other Online Resources

Possibly the most obvious place to look for more information is at Microsoft's own site, including its online library at http://msdn.microsoft.com/library, and it's .NET community site at http://msdn.microsoft.com/vstudio/community/default.asp.

There are many other sites with C# information, such as the following:

- ❑ GotDotNet, the .NET Framework community site, at http://www.gotdotnet.com
- ❑ C# Corner, at http://www.csharp-corner.com
- ❑ C# Help, at http://www.csharphelp.com

When you visit these sites, not only will you find information, articles, and code to help you, you'll also find links to other C# sites and various discussion forums.

BOOKS

There are many books on C# out there to help you take the next step, but if you've enjoyed this one, then the style in which Wrox presents its books will probably suit you best. There are many directions you might take, or supplements to the knowledge you may already have; here a few ideas for books to develop your C# knowledge.

The first book you'll probably want to get your hands on is one about data. Every program, no matter what language or environment it is written in, is concerned with manipulating data. At its simplest, this might just involve variables whose initial values are hard-coded into the application. For more complex programs, though, this is almost certain to mean extracting data from an external data source, displaying it to the user, allowing the user to add, delete, and edit parts of that data, and saving changes back to the original data source. The subject of *Beginning C# Databases* is how to achieve those universal tasks using Microsoft's brand-new C# language – we've already had a hefty introduction to data access with C# in this book, but there's much more to learn.

Beginning C# Databases

ISBN : 1-86100-609-8

> *This book is aimed at anyone who is using, or planning to use, the .NET Framework and the C# language to build Windows applications or ASP.NET web applications that access and manipulate data from a relational database.*

Beginning C# Databases explains clearly, in easy-to-follow language, the concepts behind relational databases, with concise explanations of how to design databases, and how to optimize their performance, for example by using indexes to reduce the look-up time for frequently accessed fields. We also examine SQL – the Structured Query Language – which is used to communicate with database systems and allows us to access and update data in the data store, and we see how we can access the database more efficiently by writing precompiled stored procedures in this language.

However, the core of the book is about accessing databases with C#. C# is dependent on the classes defined in the .NET Framework for most of its functionality, and data access and manipulation is no exception. For this, a set of special classes together known as ADO.NET is provided. ADO.NET provides easy and intuitive classes and methods for connecting to databases, retrieving data (by executing SQL commands or stored procedures), and updating the database. We also see how we can display our data to the user in Windows applications and in ASP.NET web applications, and how we can validate the user's input before saving it to the database.

Once we've got a solid understanding of ADO.NET, we can turn to look in detail at some more advanced database concepts, such as improving the design of your databases, more advanced SQL statements that allow us to join data from multiple tables, creating views and stored procedures and calling them from C# code, optimizing performance with indexes, and assigning permissions for specific database operations to prevent unwanted access to your data.

The later chapters of the book look at some of the more advanced features of ADO.NET, such as using XML documents with ADO.NET, implementing transactions to ensure that if one operation fails, any related operations will also fail, handling exceptions and events raised by ADO.NET, and retrieving and updating irregular data, such as images stored in the database.

Beginning C# Databases *assumes that you have one of the various flavors of Visual Studio .NET installed: either Visual Studio .NET Professional (or higher), or Visual C# .NET Standard Edition. If you have the Standard Edition installed, it is recommended that you also have Access 2000 or later installed for use as a front end to MSDE. Both of these require installation of the .NET Framework. You will also need either MSDE or SQL Server; however, MSDE can be installed free of charge with the .NET Framework, Visual C# Standard Edition, or Visual Studio .NET.*

Developing Windows Software

ISBN : 1-81600-737-X

This book is for developers who want to learn how to create powerful, robust, user-friendly Windows applications based upon Windows Forms.

The power of the C# language, coupled to the simplicity of developing Windows Forms in Visual Studio .NET, makes real-world Windows application development faster and easier than ever before.

Developing C# Windows Software teaches you how to design, implement, and deploy powerful Windows applications based upon Windows Forms and C#. We will show you how to make the most effective use of the Microsoft .NET Framework classes in your applications, and guide you around the Visual Studio .NET IDE – the development tool of choice for Windows applications. In each chapter we will discuss important aspects of Windows application design, and illustrate their use by building up practical, real-world sample applications. In no time at all you will become a skilled Windows application developer.

Professional C# 2nd Edition

ISBN : 1-86100-704-3

You've learned a lot about C# in this book, and worked on some pretty tricky concepts to get a good grounding in C# – congratulations. But if you're serious about programming with C#, the time will come when you need a more detailed reference, code examples, and explanation that take you way beyond the documentation, and a style and level of presentation that is appropriate for your information needs – clear, and fast-paced. That is the time for *Professional C# 2nd Edition*.

Professional C# 2nd Edition begins with a concise and in-depth guide to the C# language, expanding on concepts that we haven't been able to talk about in this book. Wherever we have written "beyond the scope of the book" in this book, the answer is usually to be found in *Professional C# 2nd Edition*.

The span of topics we have met in this book is encompassed by *Professional C# 2nd Edition*, but there the pace is quicker, and the depth of coverage is deeper. It also contains many topics we haven't even been able to touch on this book, but will becoming increasingly important parts of your programming world as you grow:

- ❑ Threading
- ❑ Manipulating XML
- ❑ Working with the Active Directory
- ❑ Accessing the Internet with C#, and network programming
- ❑ Integrating COM and C#
- ❑ Creating Windows Services
- ❑ .NET Remoting
- ❑ Controlling .NET security

When you are ready, *Professional C# 2nd Edition* is there for the next level of your C# development.

Index

A Guide to the Index

The index is arranged hierarchically, in alphabetical order, with symbols preceding the letter A. Most second-level entries and many third-level entries also occur as first-level entries. This is to ensure that users will find the information they require however they choose to search for it.

S

Notes

Notes

Notes

Notes

Notes